ARTTALK

THIRD EDITION

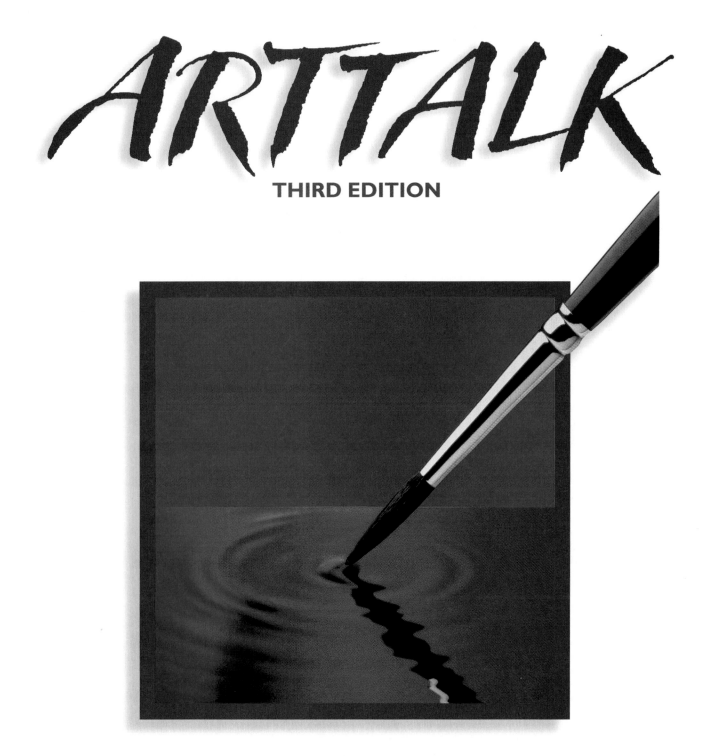

Rosalind Ragans, Ph.D.

Associate Professor Emerita
Georgia Southern University

 **Glencoe McGraw-Hill**

New York, New York   Columbus, Ohio   Woodland Hills, California   Peoria, Illinois

About the Author

Rosalind Ragans

Rosalind Ragans is the author of Glencoe's senior high school art text, *ArtTalk*. She served as senior author on the elementary program *Art Connections* for the SRA division of McGraw-Hill, and was one of the authors of Glencoe's middle school/junior high art series, *Introducing Art, Exploring Art,* and *Understanding Art*. She received a B.F.A. at Hunter College, CUNY, New York, and earned a M.Ed. in Elementary Education at Georgia Southern University and Ph.D. in Art Education at the University of Georgia. Dr. Ragans was named National Art Educator of the Year for 1992.

About Artsource®

A R T
S ● U
R C ▪
ARTSOURCE
The materials provided in the *Performing Arts Handbook* are excerpted from *Artsource®: The Music Center Study Guide to the Performing Arts*, a project of the Music Center Education Division. The Music Center of Los Angeles County, the largest performing arts center in the western United States, established the Music Center Education Division in 1979 to provide opportunities for lifelong learning in the arts, and especially to bring the performing and visual arts into the classroom. The Education Division believes the arts enhance the quality of life for all people, but are crucial to the development of every child.

Cover/Title Page Credit:

Cover Photo by Kazu Okutomi/theStockRep

Glencoe/McGraw-Hill

A Division of The **McGraw·Hill** *Companies*

Printed in the United States of America.

Send all inquiries to:
Glencoe/McGraw-Hill
21600 Oxnard Street, Suite 500
Woodland Hills, California 91367

ISBN 0-02-662434-6 (Student Edition)

4 5 6 7 8 9   004/043   06 05 04 03 02 01

Editorial Consultants

Cris E. Guenter, Ed.D.
Specialist, Portfolio and Assessment
Professer, Fine Arts/Curriculum and Instruction
California State University, Chico
Chico, CA

Holle Humphries
Assistant Professor
The University of Texas at Austin
Austin, TX

Faye Scannell
Specialist, Technology
Bellevue Public Schools
Bellevue, WA

Contributors/Reviewers

Lea Burke
Art Instructor
Bartleville High School
Bartleville, OK

Patricia Carter
Assistant Professor of Art Education
Georgia Southern University
Statesboro, GA

Randy Hayward Jolly
Art Instructor
Warren Central High School
Vicksburg, MS

Audrey Komroy
Art Instructor
Akron High School
Akron, NY

Jack Schriber
Supervisor of Fine Arts
Evansville-Vanderburgh School Corporation
Evansville, IN

Nancy Shake
Art Instructor
Center Grove High School
Indianapolis, IN

Steve Thompson
Visual Art Instructor
Henry County Middle School
McDonough, GA

Performing Arts Handbook Contributors

Joan Boyett
Executive Director
Music Center Education Division
The Music Center of Los Angeles County

Karen Wood
Managing Director

Melinda Williams
Concept Originator and Project Director

Susan Cambigue-Tracey
Project Coordinator

Arts Discipline Writers:
Dance —   Susan Cambigue-Tracey
              Diana Cummins
              Carole Valleskey
Music —   Ed Barguiarena
              Rosemarie Cook-Glover
              Connie Hood
Theatre — Barbara Leonard

Studio Lesson Consultants

Acknowledgements: The author wishes to express her gratitude to the following art coordinators, teachers, and specialists who participated in the field test of the Studio Projects with their students.

Donna Banning
El Modena High School
Orange, CA

Karen Nichols
Reseda High School
Reseda, CA

Barbara Cox
Glencliff Comprehensive High School
Nashville, TN

Roberta Sajda
Klein Forest High School
Houston, TX

Audrey Komroy
Akron High School
Akron, NY

Faye Scannell
Bellevue Public Schools
Bellevue, WA

David Long
Akron High School
Akron, NY

David Sebring
Dobson High School
Mesa, AZ

Student Contributors

The following students contributed exemplary works for Studio Projects and Technology Studio Projects.

Figure 4.25a, Julia Stout, Dobson High School, Mesa, AZ; Figure 4.28a, Xenia Nosov, International School, Bellevue, WA; Figure 5.36a, Victoria Purcell, Glencliff Comprehensive High School, Nashville, TN; Figure 5.38a, Alex Penescu, Reseda High School, Reseda, CA; Figure 6.33a, Mike Nachtrieb, Akron High School, Akron, NY; Figure 7.19a, Binyam Jimma and Jacob Egler, International School, Bellevue, WA; Figure 8.22a, Ruben Garcia, Reseda High School, Reseda, CA; Figure 8.25a, Reed Hague and Myia Bloomfield, International School, Bellevue, WA; Figure 9.23a, Danielle Gupton, Klein Forest High School, Houston, TX; Figure 9.24a, Nena Guin, Glencliff Comprehensive High School, Nashville, TN; Figure 9.26a, Kyoko Kurosawa, International School, Bellevue, WA; Figure 10.29a, Sarah Gushue, Akron High School, Akron, NY; Figure 10.30a, LeaAndrea Glover, Klein Forest High School, Houston, TX; Figure 10.31a, Sarah Rosenfeld, International School, Bellevue, WA; Figure 11.26a, Kristen Bruyere, Akron High School, Akron, NY.

TABLE OF CONTENTS

Credit line on Page 6.

UNIT 1 THE WORLD OF ART

CHAPTER 1 ■ Art in Your World **4**

Lesson 1 What Is Art? 6
Lesson 2 Why Do Artists Create? 10
　　　　　MEET THE ARTIST: GRANT WOOD 12
Lesson 3 The Language of Art 16

Art Criticism in Action *Paris Through the Window* by Marc Chagall 20
Connections: *Social Studies* 22

CHAPTER 1 REVIEW 23

Credit line on Page 26.

CHAPTER 2 ■ Art Criticism and Aesthetic Judgment **24**

Lesson 1 Art Criticism: Learning from a Work of Art 26
　　　　　MEET THE ARTIST: GEORGIA O'KEEFFE 30
Lesson 2 Aesthetics: Thinking about a Work Art 31
Lesson 3 Art History: Learning about a Work of Art 34

Art Criticism in Action
　　　　　Bitter Nest Part II: Harlem Renaissance Party by Faith Ringgold 36
Connections: *Language Arts* 38

CHAPTER 2 REVIEW 39

CHAPTER 3 ■ The Media and
Processes of Art   **40**

Lesson 1   Two-Dimensional Media   42
               MEET THE ARTIST: WINSLOW HOMER   46
Lesson 2   Three-Dimensional Media   50
Lesson 3   Technological Media   57

Art Criticism in Action
               Personal Appearance by Miriam Schapiro   62
Connections: *Science*   64

CHAPTER 3 REVIEW   65

Credit line on Page 51.

UNIT 2 THE ELEMENTS OF ART

CHAPTER 4 ■ Line   **68**

Lesson 1   The Element of Line   70
               LOOKING CLOSELY: *Blessing Rain Chant* by Dan Namingha   75
Lesson 2   The Expressive Qualities of Line   77
               MEET THE ARTIST: JACOB LAWRENCE   80

Studio Projects
               Contour Wire Sculpture   84
               Imagination Landscape   86
               Drawing Expressing Movement   88
               Expressive Line Design   90
Art Criticism in Action
               Abstract (River Mouth Map)
               by David Malangi   92
Connections: *Social Studies*   94

CHAPTER 4 REVIEW   95

Credit line on Page 80.

CHAPTER 5 ■ Shape, Form, and Space   96

Lesson 1   Shapes and Forms   98
Lesson 2   Space   103
                MEET THE ARTIST: M. C. ESCHER   105
Lesson 3   How We Perceive Shape, Form, and Space   108
Lesson 4   How Artists Create Shapes and Forms in Space 111
                LOOKING CLOSELY: *Thanksgiving*
                    by Doris Lee   116
Lesson 5   What Different Spaces, Shapes,
                    and Forms Express   117
Studio Projects
                Drawing an Outdoor Scene   122
                Clay Plaque with High Relief   124
                Landscape Using Surreal Space   126
                One-Point Perspective Drawing   128
Art Criticism in Action   *Wrapped Reichstag*
                    by Christo and Jeanne-Claude   130
Connections: *Math*   132

CHAPTER 5 REVIEW   133

Credit line on Page 107.

CHAPTER 6 ■ Color   134

Lesson 1   The Properties of Color   136
Lesson 2   Color Schemes   144
Lesson 3   Understanding the Nature and Uses of Color   150
                MEET THE ARTIST: ELIZABETH MURRAY   151
                LOOKING CLOSELY: *Hot Still Scape for Six Colors—7th Avenue Style, 1940*
                    by Stuart Davis   156
Studio Projects
                Photo Collage and
                    Mixed Media   158
                Photo Enlargement   160
                Using Color to Create an
                    Expressive Statement   162
                Expressive Portrait   164
Art Criticism in Action
                Family by Romare Bearden   166
Connnections: *Science*   168

CHAPTER 6 REVIEW   169

Credit line on Page 136.

CHAPTER 7 ■ Texture　　　**170**

Lesson 1　Texture in Your Life　　172
　　　　　LOOKING CLOSELY:
　　　　　　Oranges by Janet Fish　　176
Lesson 2　How Artists Use Texture　　177
　　　　　MEET THE ARTIST: EDGAR DEGAS　181
Studio Projects
　　　　　Fantasy Landscape　　184
　　　　　Assemblage　　186
　　　　　Paper Sculpture Creature　　188
　Still-Life Collage　　190
Art Criticism in Action　*Leonardo's Lady*
　　　　　by Audrey Flack　　192
Connections: *History*　　194

CHAPTER 7 REVIEW　　195

Credit line on Page 174.

UNIT 3　THE PRINCIPLES OF ART

Credit line on Page 209.

**CHAPTER 8 ■ Rhythm and
　　　　　　　　　Movement**　　**198**

Lesson 1　Rhythm and Repetition　　200
　　　　　MEET THE ARTIST: ROSA BONHEUR　201
　　　　　LOOKING CLOSELY: *Poor Man's
　　　　　Cotton* by Hale Woodruff　　203
Lesson 2　Types of Rhythm　　205
Lesson 3　How Artists Use Rhythm to
　　　　　Create Movement　　211
Studio Projects
　　　　　Painting with a Rhythmic Activity　214
　　　　　A Pattern Collage　　216
　　　　　Coil Baskets　　218
　Progressive Rhythm　　220
Art Criticism in Action　*Cliff Dwellers*
　　　　　by George Bellows　　222
Connections: *Dance*　　224

CHAPTER 8 REVIEW　　225

CHAPTER 9 ■ Balance   226

Lesson 1	Visual Balance	228
	MEET THE ARTIST: DIEGO RIVERA	229
Lesson 2	Natural Balance	234
Lesson 3	The Expressive Qualities of Balance	239
	LOOKING CLOSELY: *Self Portrait Dedicated to Leon Trotsky* by Frida Kahlo	239

Studio Projects

Formal Portrait	242
Informal Group Portrait	244
Linoleum Print Using Radial Balance	246
Invent an Inside View of a Machine	248

Art Criticism in Action   *Linda Nochlin and Daisy* by Alice Neel   250

Connections: *Language Arts*   252

CHAPTER 9 REVIEW   253

CHAPTER 10 ■ Proportion   254

Lesson 1	The Golden Mean	256
	LOOKING CLOSELY: *Both Members of this Club* by George Bellows	258
Lesson 2	Scale	260
Lesson 3	How Artists Use Proportion and Distortion	267
	MEET THE ARTIST: PABLO PICASSO	270

Studio Projects

Storyteller Figure	274
Papier-Mâché Mask	276
Soft Sculpture	278
Hybrid Creature	280

Art Criticism in Action   *Waiting* by Isabel Bishop   282

Connections: *Math*   284

CHAPTER 10 REVIEW   285

Credit line on Page 292.

CHAPTER 11 ■ Variety, Emphasis, Harmony, and Unity **286**

Lesson 1 Variety, Emphasis, and Harmony 288
LOOKING CLOSELY:
Café Terrace at Night
by Vincent van Gogh 293
Lesson 2 Unity 296
MEET THE ARTIST: ALLAN HOUSER 299

Studio Projects
Assemblage with Handmade Paper 304
Clay Sculpture Unifying Two Ideas 306
Designing a Mural 308
School Web Page Design 310
Art Criticism in Action *Carnival Evening* by Henri Rousseau 312
Connections: *Theatre* 314

CHAPTER 11 REVIEW 315

UNIT 4 ART THROUGH THE AGES

CHAPTER 12 ■ Art Traditions from Around the World **318**

Lesson 1 Art of Earliest Times 320
Lesson 2 Art of Asia and the Middle East 326
MEET THE ARTIST: ANDÖ HIROSHIGE 330
Lesson 3 The Art of Africa 332
Lesson 4 Art of the Americas 339

Art Criticism in Action *Khamseh: Bahram Gur and the Chinese Princess in the Sandalwood Pavilion on Thursday* 346
Connections: *Social Studies* 348

CHAPTER 12 REVIEW 349

Credit line on Page 324.

x

Credit line on Page 358.

CHAPTER 13 ■ Western Traditions in Art 350

Lesson 1	The Beginnings of Western Art Traditions	352
Lesson 2	The Beginnings of Modern Art Traditions	356
	MEET THE ARTIST: MICHELANGELO BUONARROTI	357
Lesson 3	The Nineteenth Century	366
Lesson 4	Early Twentieth Century	374
Lesson 5	Art After 1945	378

Art Criticism in Action *Ginevra de' Benci* by Leonardo da Vinci 384
Connections: *Language Arts* 386

CHAPTER 13 REVIEW 387

CHAPTER 14 ■ Careers in Art 388

Lesson 1	Careers in Business and Industry	390
Lesson 2	Environmental and Education Careers	401
	MEET THE ARTIST: I. M. PEI	402

Art Criticism in Action
The Green House
by Sandy Skoglund 406
Connections: *Technology* 408

CHAPTER 14 REVIEW 409

Credit line on Page 402.

UNIT 5 HANDBOOKS

■ **Artsource® Performing Arts Handbook**   **412**

Chapter 1	*(Theatre)*	Faustwork Mask Theater	413
Chapter 2	*(Dance)*	Martha Graham	414
Chapter 3	*(Dance)*	Merce Cunningham Dance Company	415
Chapter 4	*(Dance/Music)*	Ballet Folklorico de México	416
Chapter 5	*(Dance)*	Lewitzky Dance Company	417
Chapter 6	*(Theatre)*	Joanna Featherstone	418
Chapter 7	*(Music)*	Paul Winter	419
Chapter 8	*(Dance/Music)*	African American Dance Ensemble	420
Chapter 9	*(Theatre)*	Eth-Noh-Tec	421
Chapter 10	*(Music)*	Eugene Friesen	422
Chapter 11	*(Music)*	Vocalworks	423
Chapter 12	*(Music/Dance)*	Korean Classical Music and Dance Company	424
Chapter 13	*(Theatre)*	Kurt Jooss	425
Chapter 14	*(Music)*	John Ramirez	426

■ **Technique Tips Handbook**   **427**

Drawing Tips	1.	Making Contour Drawings	428
	2.	Making Gesture Drawings	428
	3.	Drawing Calligraphic Lines With a Brush	428
	4.	Using Shading Techniques	429
	5.	Using Sighting Techniques	429
	6.	Using a Viewing Frame	430
	7.	Using a Ruler	430
	8.	Making a Grid for Enlarging	431
	9.	Measuring Rectangles	431
Painting Tips	10.	Mixing Paint to Change the Value of Color	431
	11.	Making Natural Earth Pigment Paints	432
	12.	Working with Watercolors	432
	13.	Cleaning a Paint Brush	432
Printmaking Tip	14.	Making a Stamp Print	433
Sculpting Tips	15.	Working with Clay	433
	16.	Joining Clay	433
	17.	Making a Pinch Pot	434
	18.	Using the Coil Technique	434
	19.	Papier Mâché	434
	20.	Making a Paper Sculpture	435

■ **Technique Tips Handbook** (continued)

Other Tips   **21.** Making Paper   435
                        22. Basic Embroidery Stitches   436
                        23. Weaving Techniques   437
                        24. Making a Coil Basket   439
                        25. Making a Tissue Paper Collage   440

Display Tips   **26.** Making a Mat   441
                        27. Mounting a Two-Dimensional Work   442
                        28. Working with Glue   442

SAFETY IN THE ART ROOM   443

ARTISTS AND THEIR WORKS   445

CHRONOLOGY OF ARTWORKS   450

GLOSSARY   456

BIBLIOGRAPHY   464

INDEX   469

PHOTOGRAPHY CREDITS   480

FEATURES

MEET THE
ARTIST

CHAPTER

1	Grant Wood	12
	Marc Chagall	21
2	Georgia O'Keeffe	30
	Faith Ringgold	37
3	Winslow Homer	46
	Miriam Schapiro	63
4	Jacob Lawrence	80
	David Malangi	93
5	M. C. Escher	105
	Christo and Jeanne-Claude	131
6	Elizabeth Murray	151
	Romare Bearden	167
7	Edgar Degas	181
	Audrey Flack	193

CHAPTER

8	Rosa Bonheur	201
	George Bellows	223
9	Diego Rivera	229
	Alice Neel	251
10	Pablo Picasso	270
	Isabel Bishop	283
11	Allan Houser	299
	Henri Rousseau	313
12	Andö Hiroshige	330
	Persian Artists of Islam	347
13	Michelangelo Buonarroti	357
	Leonardo da Vinci	385
14	I. M. Pei	402
	Sandy Skoglund	407

LOOKING CLOSELY

CHAPTER	TITLE OF ART AND ARTIST	
4	*Blessing Rain Chant* by Dan Namingha	75
5	*Thanksgiving* by Doris Lee	116
6	*Hot Still Scape for Six Colors—7th Avenue Style, 1940* by Stuart Davis	156
7	*Oranges* by Janet Fish	176
8	*Poor Man's Cotton* by Hale Woodruff	203
9	*Self Portrait Dedicated to Leon Trotsky* by Frida Kahlo	239
10	*Both Members of This Club* by George Bellows	258
11	*Café Terrace at Night* by Vincent van Gogh	293

Art Criticism in Action

CHAPTER

1	*Paris Through the Window* by Marc Chagall	20
2	*Bitter Nest Part II: Harlem Renaissance Party* by Faith Ringgold	36
3	*Personal Appearance* by Miriam Schapiro	62
4	*Abstract (River Mouth Map)* by David Malangi	92
5	*Wrapped Reichstag* by Christo and Jeanne-Claude	130
6	*Family* by Romare Bearden	166
7	*Leonardo's Lady* by Audrey Flack	192
8	*Cliff Dwellers* by George Bellows	222
9	*Linda Nochlin and Daisy* by Alice Neel	250
10	*Waiting* by Isabel Bishop	282
11	*Carnival Evening* by Henri Rousseau	312
12	*Khamseh: Bahram Gur and the Chinese Princess in the Sandalwood Pavilion on Thursday*	346
13	*Ginevra de'Benci* by Leonardo da Vinci	384
14	*The Green House* by Sandy Skoglund	406

CONNECTIONS

CHAPTER

1	**SOCIAL STUDIES:** The Games Children Play	22
2	**LANGUAGE ARTS:** How Does Imagery Help Us Interpret a Story?	38
3	**SCIENCE:** Pottery and Clay	64
4	**SOCIAL STUDIES:** The History of Ink	94
5	**MATH:** How do Artists Use Geometry?	132
6	**SCIENCE:** Where do Paint Pigments Come From?	168
7	**HISTORY:** The Secret of Silk	194
8	**DANCE:** Rhythm in Design	224
9	**LANGUAGE ARTS:** What Is Symbolism?	252
10	**MATH:** Proportion and Scale	284
11	**THEATRE:** How Does Stage Lighting Create Drama?	314
12	**SOCIAL STUDIES:** The Meaning of Stone Circles	348
13	**LANGUAGE ARTS:** The Harlem Renaissance	386
14	**TECHNOLOGY:** How is 3-D Computer Art Created?	408

Activities

Chapter 1

Learning to Perceive 7
Keeping a Sketchbook 15
Create a Symbol 16
Using Credit Information 19

Chapter 2

Aesthetic Theories 33

Chapter 3

Experimenting with Watercolor 47
Making A Printing Plate 49
Redesigning a Familiar Building 54
Digital Art 60

Chapter 4

Identifying Lines 73
Using Line to Create Value 76
Using Lines Expressively 78
Using Contour Lines 81
Creating Gesture Drawings 82
Calligraphic Lines 83

Chapter 5

Geometric and Free-Form Shapes 100
Creating Forms 102
Using Three Dimensions 107
Shape and Point of View 108
Using Shading 112
Creating Depth 115
Active and Static Shapes 120

Chapter 6

Creating Values 142
Working with Intensity 143
Using Color Schemes 149
Mixing Colors 152
Using Color for Effect 157

Chapter 7

Creating Textures 174
Creating Contrasting Textures 175
Inventing Textures 183

Chapter 8

Motifs and Patterns 204
Using Random Rhythm 205
Alternating Rhythm 208
Progressive Rhythm 210

Chapter 9

Using Symmetry 231
Creating Radial Balance 233
Using Informal Balance 238
Identifying Balance 241

Chapter 10

Experimenting with Scale 261
Human Proportions 264
Drawing the Head 266
Distorting Proportions 273

Chapter 11

Variety and Contrast 289
Using Emphasis 295
Creating Unity 302

Chapter 12

Creating a Writing System 325
Constructing a Mask 338
Sketching an Event 345

Chapter 13

Analyzing Architecture 353
The Gothic Style 355
Analyzing a Work 365
Analyzing a Style 373
Applying the Steps 381

Chapter 14

Critiquing Animation 398
Using Design for Display 403

Listing of Studio Projects by Media

CHALK

Landscape Using Surreal Space 126
Using Color to Create an
Expressive Statement 162
Formal Portrait 242

CLAY

Clay Plaque with High Relief 124
Storyteller Figure 274
Clay Sculpture Unifying Two Ideas 306

FIBERS

Coil Baskets 218

MIXED MEDIA

Photo Collage and Mixed Media 158
Fantasy Landscape 184
Assemblage 186
A Pattern Collage 216
Papier-Mâché Mask 276

OTHER

Contour Wire Sculpture 84
Soft Sculpture 278
Assemblage with Handmade
Paper 304

PAINT

Imagination Landscape 86
Drawing Expressing Movement 88
Landscape Using Surreal Space 126
Photo Enlargement 160
Using Color to Create an
Expressive Statement 162
Painting with a Rhythmic
Activity 214
Formal Portrait 242
Informal Group Picture 244
Designing A Mural 308

PAPER

Paper Sculpture Creature 188
Papier-Mâché Mask 276

**PENCIL, PEN, CHARCOAL,
AND MARKERS**

Drawing Expressing Movement 88
Drawing an Outdoor Scene 122
Formal Portrait 242

PRINTMAKING

Linoleum Print Using
Radial Balance 246

TECHNOLOGY

Expressive Line Design 90
One-Point Perspective Drawing 128
Expressive Portrait 164
Still-Life Collage 190
Progressive Rhythm 220
Invent an Inside View of
a Machine 248
Hybrid Creature 280
School Web Page Design 310

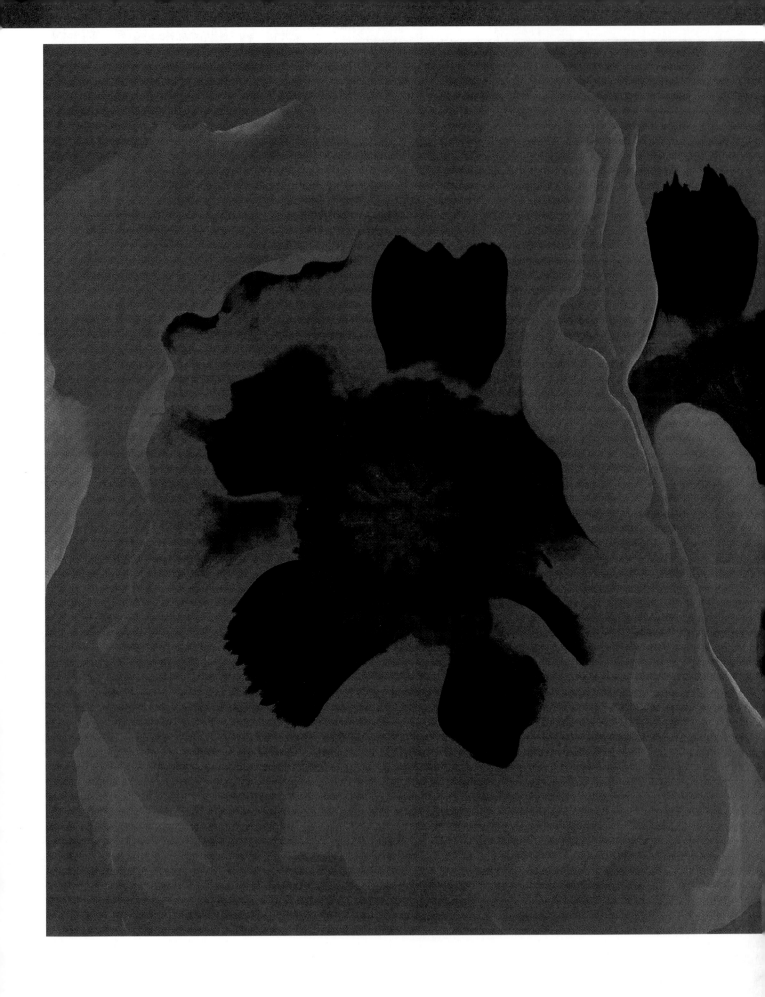

THE
WORLD OF
ART

"So I said to myself—
I'll paint what I see—
what a flower is to me
but I'll paint it big and
they will be surprised
into taking time to look at
it—I will make even
busy New Yorkers take
time to see what I see
of flowers."

*Georgia O'Keeffe
1887–1986*

◄

Georgia O'Keeffe. *Oriental Poppies.* 1927. Oil
on canvas. 76.2 × 101.9 cm (30 × 40⅛").
Collection Frederick R. Weisman Art Museum
at the University of Minnesota, Minneapolis.
Museum Purchase.

▲ **Figure 1.1** Notice how the artist has used color to connect the houses to the environment. See if you can find the same blues in the houses, on the road, and in the sky. The bright colors and strokes of paint indicate that the houses are full of life. The curved strokes of paint connect the person, plants, and clouds.

Vincent van Gogh. *Houses at Auvers.* 1890. Oil on canvas. 75.5 × 61.8 cm (29¾ × 24³/₈″). Courtesy, Museum of Fine Arts, Boston, Massachusetts. Bequest of John T. Spaulding.

Art in Your World

The urge to create art has been with people throughout history. The visual arts satisfy human needs for celebration, personal expression, and communication. We use the visual arts to enhance our environment, to express our deepest feelings about life, and to record events.

Art tells us about places we may never go and people we might never know. Vincent van Gogh painted *Houses at Auvers* **(Figure 1.1)** more than 100 years ago. He painted more than the colors he saw; he selected colors that expressed how he *felt*. He applied paint in short, layered strokes to create a sense of movement. Van Gogh's choices of color and his use of texture in the painting seem to visually echo his intention to replicate his love for the spirit and energy of nature.

The painting tells a story that you can understand if you look closely, even though the landscape and objects in it might be unfamiliar to you. What unusual shapes and colors do you notice? What ideas or feelings do you think the artist was attempting to express by using these colors?

Developing Your
PORTFOLIO
Most people have opinions about what makes an artwork successful and they have reasons why they like certain works of art. List your favorite works of art. Provide the title of the artwork and the name of the artist. Then describe why you like the artwork and what meaning it has for you. Include your list in your portfolio.

OBJECTIVES

After completing this chapter, you will be able to:
- Explain what is meant by *perceive*.
- Understand the purposes of art.
- Name sources of ideas that artists might use for inspiration.
- Identify the elements and principles of art.
- Identify the subject, composition, and content in a work of art.

WORDS TO LEARN

perceive
artists
symbol
elements of art
principles of art
subject
nonobjective art
composition
content
credit line

What Is Art?

A work of art is the visual expression of an idea or experience created with skill. Visual art is more than paintings hanging on a wall. Visual art includes drawing, printmaking, sculpture, architecture, photography, filmmaking, crafts, graphic arts, industrial and commercial design, video, and computer arts.

Art Is Communication

When you talk to someone or write a letter, you communicate. You share your ideas and feelings by using words. You can also communicate through the arts. Art is a language that artists use to express ideas and feelings that everyday words cannot express. Through the arts, artists can convey ideas in ways that go beyond describing and telling. But in order to understand the meaning of a work of art, you must do more than simply look at it with your eyes. In order to experience art fully, you must develop the ability to perceive. To look is to merely notice and label an object with a name such as "chair" or "house." To **perceive** is *to become deeply aware through the senses of the special nature of a visual object.* A perception is a sensation to which you attach a meaning. To understand and receive communication from a work of art you must train yourself to perceive.

The arts cross language barriers. You do not need to be able to speak English to perceive what Meyer Straus is expressing in his painting, *Bayou Teche* **(Figure 1.2).** If you concentrate on his image you can feel the humid atmosphere of the Louisiana swamps and hear

▲ **FIGURE 1.2** Straus painted this bayou scene while working for the Academy of Music in New Orleans painting backdrops for major productions. He captured the feel of the bayou by including details such as the flowers in the foreground and the gray Spanish moss hanging from the limbs of the live oak trees. Look at the figures in the boat. The trees and swamp overwhelm them. What do you think the figures are doing? What atmosphere does the painting capture?

Meyer Straus. *Bayou Teche.* 1870. Oil on canvas. 76.2 × 152.4 cm (30 × 60″). Morris Museum of Art, Augusta, Georgia.

the mosquitoes buzzing. You can understand how it feels to be enclosed by branches dripping with Spanish moss. You can almost hear the water lapping at the boat.

The Purposes of Art

People created art to record ideas and feelings long before they had written words. They used art then as we use it today. The following are some of the most common functions of art.

■ **Personal Functions.** Artists create art to express personal feelings. Edvard Munch had a tragic childhood. His mother died when he was very young, and one of his sisters died when he was 14. His painting, *The Sick Child* (**Figure 1.3**), shocked viewers who were used to seeing happy paintings with bright colors. The work was meant to remind viewers of personal family tragedies. Perhaps the artist wanted to tell them to appreciate what they had. Often people who have suffered a loss remind

others to live each day as if it were their last. That is what Munch is saying with his striking image.

■ **Social Function.** Artists may produce art to reinforce and enhance the shared sense of identity of those in a family, community, or civilization (Figure 12.17, page 332). That is why many families commission or hire an artist or photographer to produce a family portrait. Art produced for this purpose also may be used in celebrations and displayed on festive occasions. Think of the many forms of visual art that might be seen in a parade—costumes, band uniforms, floats, and dances are all forms of visual art that might be included in the public celebration of a parade to commemorate an important holiday or event.

■ **Spiritual Function.** Artists may create art to express spiritual beliefs about the destiny of life controlled by the force of a higher power. Art produced for this purpose may reinforce the shared beliefs of an individual or

▶ **FIGURE 1.3** The child in the painting appears pale and calm. She is not looking at her mother. What is she staring at? Notice the exaggerated drooping of the woman's head. What has the artist done to focus your attention on the sick child?

Edvard Munch. *The Sick Child.* 1907. Oil on canvas. 118.7 × 121 cm (46¾ × 47²/₃″). Tate Gallery, London, England.

a human community. In *Pueblo Scene: Corn Dancers and Church* **(Figure 1.4)**, the artists have created a three-dimensional representation of a religious festival that connects two cultures and two religions. Works of art have been created for religious purposes throughout history. Many experts believe that the prehistoric cave paintings of animals had ceremonial purposes, which means they were more than simple records of events. The Greek Temples were built to honor the ancient gods. During the Middle Ages in Europe, almost all art was created for the Catholic Church.

- **Physical Functions.** Artists and craftspeople constantly invent new ways to create functional art. Industrial designers discover new materials that make cars lighter and stronger. Architects employ new building materials such as steel–reinforced concrete to give buildings more interesting forms. In **Figure 1.5,** notice how the artist has combined a variety of precious and semiprecious materials to create a unique necklace.

- **Educational Function.** In the past, many people could not read and art was often created to provide visual instruction. Artists produced artworks, such as symbols painted on signs, to impart information. Viewers could learn from their artworks. In the Middle Ages, artists created stained-glass windows, sculptures, paintings, and tapestries to illustrate stories from the Bible or about rulers of a kingdom.

▲ **FIGURE 1.4** The figures and buildings for this scene were made by a family of artists. Look closely and you will notice that some of the figures are made of painted clay, while others have hair made from yarn and clothing made of fabric. What do the different figures appear to be doing? What does the procession in the foreground seem to be about?

Vigil Family, Tesuque Pueblo, New Mexico. *Pueblo Scene: Corn Dancers and Church.* c. 1960. Painted earthenware. Girard Foundation Collection at the Museum of International Folk Art, a unit of the Museum of New Mexico, Santa Fe, New Mexico.

◀ **FIGURE 1.5** This necklace is unusual because each unit is different. The repetition of rectangles and the repetition of materials and shapes on the different rectangles create a unified work.

Earl Pardon. Necklace 1057. 1988. 43.1 × 2.8 × 3 cm (17¼ × 1⅛ × ⅛"). Sterling silver, 14k gold, ebony, ivory, enamel, mother of pearl, ruby, garnet, blue topaz, amethyst, spinel, and rhodolite. National Museum of American Art, Smithsonian Institution, Washington, D.C. Renwick collection.

In addition, when we look at art from the past, we learn from it. Art from other places and other times can tell us what people did. Paintings such as *Anne of Cleves* **(Figure 1.6)** show us people from the past, what they wore, and how they looked. Objects such as pottery and arrowheads show us how people worked and survived in the past. Art from other cultures helps us to understand the beliefs and values of those cultures. We know that the ancient Chinese valued nature from the scrolls we have seen.

In this book you will learn to understand and recognize all the visual arts. You will become familiar with a variety of works that range in size from skyscrapers to tiny feather ornaments. The art in this book will take you through time and space to tell you about places and people you might never know.

☑ Check Your Understanding

1. What does it mean to *perceive?*
2. Name the five purposes of art.
3. Describe two of the purposes of art.

▲ **FIGURE 1.6** This portrait of Anne of Cleves, one of the wives of Henry VIII, shows what a royal person in the sixteenth century might have worn for special occasions. The portrait was created before the wedding because King Henry wanted to know what his intended wife looked like. He had never met her. Notice the unusual jewelry on her hat and the rich fabrics of her dress. How many different fabrics can you identify? How does her clothing indicate her social position?

Hans Holbein. *Anne of Cleves.* 1539. Tempera and oil on parchment. 65.5 × 47.5 cm (25⅝ × 18⅞"). The Louvre, Paris, France.

Why Do Artists Create?

The urge to create is universal. Artists are driven by their sense of wonder and curiosity. The creative impulse is often suppressed if one becomes afraid of making mistakes. Artists exhibit the courage to take risks. They are able to see their surroundings in new and unusual ways. They are willing to work intensely for long periods of time to achieve their goals. Some artists are self-taught and have been called folk artists because they are not educated in traditional artistic methods. Most artists learn skills and techniques from other artists. Eventually artists develop their own unique styles.

The impulses that drive artists to create vary. Both Roger Brown and Leo Twiggs created art in response to a devastating natural catastrophe: Hurricane Hugo. Twiggs, who lives in South Carolina and witnessed the hurricane, used strong lines to represent the force of the winds **(Figure 1.7)**. Brown, who lives in Chicago, responded to the same tragedy in a different way. He illustrated only the aftermath of the hurricane. He turned the event into a giant postcard in which he depicted the fury of the storm by showing the trees in neat rows, broken off at exactly the same level **(Figure 1.8)**.

◀ **FIGURE 1.7** Identify the door named in the title. Look at the dark shape near the center of the painting. How many figures are standing in the door? What part of this work tells you about the destructive force of the hurricane?

Leo F. Twiggs. *East Wind Suite: Door.* Hugo Series. 1989. Batik: Dyes and wax resist on cotton. 61 × 51 cm (24 × 20″). Private collection.

Where Do Artists Get Ideas?

Artists are *creative individuals who use imagination and skill to communicate in visual form.* They use the materials of art to solve visual problems. Artists look to many sources for inspiration. Some look outward to their natural and cultural environment for ideas. Others look within themselves for creative motivation.

Nature

Sometimes artists look to their natural surroundings and record them. The first group of landscape artists in the United States was called the Hudson River School because most of them lived near that river in New York. They painted the world around them, paying meticulous attention to realistic detail. One Hudson River School artist, George Inness, lived in Newburgh, New York. His early work depicted the vast American landscape in a romantic manner **(Figure 1.9).**

Grant Wood grew up on a farm and drew with whatever materials could be spared. Often he used charcoal from the wood fire to sketch on a leftover piece of brown paper. He was only ten when his father died, and his mother moved the family to Cedar Rapids, Iowa, where Wood went to school. He studied part-time at the State University of Iowa and attended night classes at the Art Institute of Chicago. When he was 32, he went to Paris to study at the Academie Julian. In 1927, he traveled to Munich, Germany, where some of the most accomplished artists of the period were working. While there, he saw German and Flemish artworks that influenced him greatly, especially the work of Jan van Eyck. After that trip, his style changed to reflect the realism of those painters.

▶ **FIGURE 1.10** This painting has been used and parodied countless times. Because of this, it can be easy to overlook the message Wood intended. Symbols tell a story: the Gothic window represents the couple's European heritage, and the pitchfork stands for their determination. Can you identify other symbols in the painting and tell what they might mean?

Grant Wood. *American Gothic.* 1930. Oil on beaverboard. 74.3 × 62.4 cm (29¼ × 24½″). Friends of American Art Collection. All rights reserved by The Art Institute of Chicago, Chicago, Illinois and VAGA, New York, New York. (1930.934)

People and Real World Events

Another artist, Grant Wood, captured the essence of the Midwestern American spirit during the Great Depression in his work, *American Gothic* **(Figure 1.10).** The stern, small town citizens posed before their house. The couple's determination was meant to reassure those shaken by the stock market crash during the Great Depression.

Myths and Legends

Some artists borrow ideas from famous works of literature. Romare Bearden interpreted one part of an ancient Greek legend, *The Odyssey,* in his painting *Return of Ulysses* **(Figure 1.11).** The Greek legend, written by the poet Homer, describes the adventures that befall a hero returning home from war. Bearden used his unique style to portray an important scene from this story.

FIGURE 1.11 This print is the last in a series of serigraphs illustrating the story of Ulysses, a legendary Greek hero. Bearden has simplified shapes and used unusual colors but you can still recognize people and objects in the work. Describe three things you recognize in this scene.

Romare Bearden. *Return of Ulysses.* 1976. Serigraph on paper. 47 × 57.1 cm (18½ × 22½"). Copyright restricted. National Museum of American Art, Washington, D.C. Gift of the Brandywine Graphic Workshop. © Romare Bearden Foundation/ Licensed by VAGA, New York, NY.

Spiritual and Religious Beliefs

Visual artists in every culture use their skills to create objects and images to be used to express spiritual beliefs. Many non-Western cultures do not even have a word for "art." Those who create objects do the best work they can because it is important. The mask in **Figure 1.12** was made to be worn during ceremonial winter dances by the Yup'ik people who lived in northwestern Alaska.

Creative Techniques

Many artists founded new art movements and developed new techniques to create art. Jackson Pollock was a leader of the Abstract Expressionist movement. He studied painting in the 1930s with Thomas Hart Benton as his teacher. Benton was an American regionalist who painted realistic paintings and

▲ FIGURE 1.12 This bird mask was created for a dance ceremony. Notice how the artist has used natural earth pigments to color the wood, plus natural materials like feathers and sinew to decorate it.

Yup'ik. *Bird Mask.* 1988. Wood, feathers. Height: 65 cm (25½"). Robert H. Lowie Museum, University of California, Berkeley, California.

murals that celebrated American life (Figure 13.29, page 376). Pollock's earliest works were in the realistic style of his teacher. After 1947, he developed the action-painting technique of dripping and splashing paint onto canvases

▶ **FIGURE 1.13** Pollock wanted to express his personal feelings when he created his art. He allowed his feelings to influence his choice of colors and the manner in which he applied them to the canvas.

Jackson Pollock. *Cathedral.* 1947. Enamel and aluminum paint on canvas. 181.6 × 89.1 cm (71½ × 35¹/₁₆″). Dallas Museum of Art, Dallas, Texas. Gift of Mr. and Mrs. Bernard J. Reis.

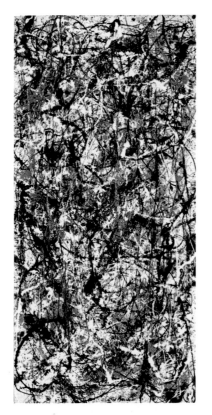

stretched on the floor **(Figure 1.13).** The idea for this style of painting, which influenced many who came after him, came from within himself.

Artists of the Past

Art is not made in a vacuum. Artists of a particular time period often influence each other. Artists also learn from and build on the work of artists who came before them. Pablo Picasso based his 1957 painting, *Las Meninas* (after Velázquez) **(Figure 1.14),** on *Las Meninas (The Maids of Honor)* by Diego Velázquez **(Figure 1.15),** which was painted in 1656. Although Picasso changed the colors and used his own Cubist style, you can recognize some of the figures and objects that are in the realistic Velázquez painting. How many figures and objects can you find that appear in both works?

▲ **FIGURE 1.14** This painting is based on Diego Velázquez's *Las Meninas (The Maids of Honor)* (Figure 1.15). Similar figures and objects are present in both paintings—the artist, the easel with the unfinished painting, the child who appears to be the subject of the artwork in progress, the dog, the figure in the door. Compare these objects with the ones depicted in Velázquez's work. What has Picasso done to make the work uniquely his own? Do you think he was exhibiting a sense of humor?

Pablo Picasso. *Las Meninas* (after Velázquez). 1957. Oil on canvas. 2 × 2.6 m (6′4³/₄″ × 8′ 6³/₈″). Musee Picasso, Barcelona, Spain.

▶ **FIGURE 1.15** This painting was interpreted by Picasso, another Spanish artist, three centuries after Velázquez completed it. Explain what is happening in the painting. The princess, in white, has a regal bearing. She is clearly the center of attention. Do you see the king and queen in the picture? Who is the person in the doorway? Can you describe the roles of the other people in the painting?

Diego Velázquez. *Las Meninas (The Maids of Honor).* 1656. Oil on canvas. 3.18 × 2.8 m (10′5¼″ × 9′¾″). Museo del Prado, Madrid, Spain.

Has Picasso used everything that you see in the Velázquez work?

Ideas Commissioned by Employers

Many artists are hired by individuals or companies to create works of art. Liz Kingslein is a graphic artist who has worked for many years as a commercial artist. **Figure 14.6** on page 392 is an example of images that she designed for an employer, in this case a restaurant. She used a computer draw program to create the art.

Ideas for Your Own Artwork

In the coming chapters, you will need to come up with ideas of your own for original works of art. Like all other artists, you may at times find yourself at a loss for ideas. You can look to the sources listed in this lesson for inspiration. You will also find that keeping a sketchbook can be an enormous help. In addition to recording images in your sketchbook, you may jot down ideas that come to you after participating in other art events such as concerts, movies, and theatre productions. You will also find that a sketchbook can be used to practice skills and techniques you learn in class.

Activity | **Keeping a Sketchbook**

Applying Your Skills. Artists develop perception and artistic skills by constantly sketching the world around them. Begin keeping a sketchbook of your own. Choose a notebook with unlined paper. Make sure it is easy to carry around. Practice drawing anything that catches your eye. The more you draw, the better you will "see" objects. Make written notes about your sketches, such as the quality of light, the colors you notice, or the mood of a scene.

☑ **Check Your Understanding**

1. Define the word *artist*.
2. Identify four different sources for artistic ideas.
3. Why do artists keep sketchbooks?

The Language of Art

People throughout the world speak many different languages. Spanish, Swahili, Japanese, Hindi, French, English, and Apache are just a few of the 3,000 different languages that are spoken. Each language has its own system of words and rules of grammar. To learn a new language, you need to learn new words and a new set of rules for putting those words together.

The language of visual art has its own system. All that you see in a work of art is made up of certain common elements. They are arranged according to basic principles. As you learn these basic elements and principles, you will learn the language of art. Being able to use the language of visual art will help you in many ways. It will increase your ability to understand, appreciate, and enjoy art. It will increase your ability to express yourself clearly when discussing art. It will even help you improve your ability to produce artworks.

The Elements of Art

A **symbol** is *something that stands for, or represents, something else.* In a spoken language, words are symbols. The word chair stands for a piece of furniture that has a seat, a back, legs, and sometimes arms. In the language of art, we use visual symbols to communicate ideas.

The *basic visual symbols in the language of art* are known as the **elements of art.** Just as there are basic kinds of words—such as nouns and verbs— there are basic kinds of art elements. These are *line, shape* and *form, space, color, value,* and *texture.* The elements are the visual building blocks that the artist puts together to create a work of art. No matter how a work is made, it will contain some or all of these elements.

When you look at a visual image, it is difficult to separate one element from another. For example, when you look at **Figure 1.16,** you see a shiny, round bowl outlined with a thin yellow line

---

Activity | **Create a Symbol**

Applying Your Skills. In visual art, symbols can be concrete representations of abstract ideas, such as a heart standing for love. Create a visual symbol that represents something important to you, such as an activity you participate in or an organization you belong to. Share your symbol with your classmates. Can they identify what it represents?

Computer Option. Design a visual symbol using a computer application. Choose from the tools and menus to represent this idea with line, shape, or color. Hold down the Shift key when making straight lines or restricting shapes to circles or squares. Title, save, print, and display your best example. Include a short explanation about your symbol.

◀ **FIGURE 1.16**
Notice how the artist has used color and texture to direct the viewer's eye through this artwork. Look at the number of different surfaces she depicts. How many different textures can you identify? Although the shiny surfaces catch your attention, notice the matte, or dull, surfaces as well.

Janet I. Fish. *Raspberries and Goldfish.* 1981. Oil on canvas. 182.9 × 162.6 cm (72 × 64″). The Metropolitan Museum of Art, New York, New York. Purchase. The Cape Branch Foundation and Lila Acheson Wallace gifts, 1983. (1983.171) © Janet Fish/Licensed by VAGA, New York, NY

filled with bumpy, red raspberries. However, rather than seeing the elements of texture (shiny and bumpy), color (red), shape (round), and line (thin and yellow) separately, you see the bowl of raspberries as a whole. You visually "read" the elements together.

Sometimes the differences between the elements are not clear-cut. A line may be so wide that it looks like a shape, or an artist may manipulate light and dark values to indicate different surface textures. Look at the variety of textures Janet Fish has created in *Raspberries and Goldfish* (Figure 1.16).

When you first learned to read, you did not begin with a full-length novel. You learned by reading one word at a time. That is how you will start to read the language of art: one art element at a time.

The Principles of Art

After you have learned to recognize the elements of art, you will learn the ways in which the elements can be organized for different effects. When you learn a language, you learn the rules of grammar by which words are organized into sentences. Without these rules, people would find it difficult to communicate.

Visual images are also organized according to rules. The *rules that govern how artists organize the elements of art* are called the **principles of art.** They also help artists organize the art elements for specific effects. The principles you will learn about are *rhythm, movement, balance, proportion, variety, emphasis, harmony,* and *unity.*

The Work of Art

In art, it is important to understand the three basic properties, or features, of an artwork. These are *subject, composition,* and *content.*

The Subject

The **subject** is *the image viewers can easily identify in a work of art.* The subject may be one person or many people. It may be a thing, such as a boat. It may be an event, such as a dance. What are the subjects in Gabriele Münter's painting, *Breakfast of the Birds* **(Figure 1.17)**?

Some artists choose to create nonobjective artwork. **Nonobjective art** is *art that has no recognizable subject matter* (Figure 1.13, page 14). In these types of works, the elements of art themselves become the subject matter.

The Composition

The second property of a work of art is the composition of the work. The

▲ **FIGURE 1.17** Gabriele Münter was one of the founders of modern German Abstract Expressionism. In 1911 she joined with other radical artists to form the group known as Der Blaue Reiter ("The Blue Rider") group. She stayed in Germany through World War II but was forced to work in secret during the Nazi era, when German Expressionism was outlawed. Since this was painted in 1934, it is one of her "secret" paintings.

Gabriele Münter. *Breakfast of the Birds.* 1934. Oil on board. 45.7 × 55.2 cm (18 × 21¾"). The National Museum of Women in the Arts, Washington, D.C. Gift of Wallace and Wilhelmina Holladay.

composition is *the way the principles of art are used to organize the elements of art.* Notice how Münter has used the reds to separate indoors from outdoors, yet she ties the woman to the birds by using related colors. The woman is placed with her back toward the viewer, so that the viewer looks in the same direction as the woman, toward the birds. As you learn more about the elements and principles of art, you will discover how to control the composition of your artwork.

The Content

The third property of a work of art is the content. The **content** is *the message the work communicates.* The message may be an idea or a theme, such as patriotism or family togetherness. It may be an emotion, such as pride, love, or loneliness. Sometimes you know what the intention of an artist might have been when he or she created the work, therefore the meaning of the work may be clear. However, at other times, you may not be certain of what the work might mean, and you have to consider all possibilities. Many artists can paint the same subject, a woman looking out a window, but each painting may have a different message. What do you think is the content of Münter's painting?

The Credit Line

Look at Figure 1.17. The credit line appears beneath the caption. A **credit line** is *a list of important facts about a work of art.* Every artwork in this book has a credit line.

Most credit lines contain at list six facts. They are as follows:

- **Name** of the artist.
- **Title** of the work. This always appears in italics.

- **Year** the work was created. Sometimes, in the case of older works, "c." appears before the year. This is an abbreviation for *circa,* a Latin word meaning "about" or "around."
- **Medium** used by the artist. This is *the material used to make art.* If more than one medium is used, the credit line may read "mixed media."
- **Size** of the work. The first number is always the height, the second number is the width, and if the work is three-dimensional, the third number indicates the depth.
- **Location** of the work. The location names the gallery, museum, or collection in which the work is housed and the city, state, and country. The names of the donors may also be included.

Activity | **Using Credit Line Information**

Applying **Your Skills.** Who is the artist of the work in Figure 1.9 on page 11? What is the title of the painting by Vincent van Gogh (Figure 1.1, page 4)? Which work in this chapter was completed most recently? Which is the largest work in this chapter? Which works in this chapter are not housed in the United States?

Check Your Understanding

1. List the elements of art.
2. Name the principles of art.
3. How do subject and composition differ?
4. Name the six facts most credit lines include.

ART CRITICISM IN ACTION

▲ **FIGURE 1.18**

Marc Chagall. *Paris Through the Window.* 1913. Oil on canvas. 135.8 × 141.1 cm (53½ × 55¾"). Solomon R. Guggenheim Museum, New York, New York. Gift, Solomon R. Guggenheim, 1937.

Art criticism is a four-step procedure for helping you use perception to get deeply involved in a work of art. You will learn more about these four steps in Chapter 2.

1 ▶ DESCRIBE What do you see?
During this step you will collect information about the subject of the work. List all of the information found in the credit line and then describe the things you see in the visual image.

- List the objects you see in the painting. Where they are located? Do they seem close to the viewer or in the distance?
- Is this a nonobjective work, or do the shapes in this work represent objects?

2 ▶ ANALYZE How is this work organized?
The second step in art criticism deals with the composition of the work. During this step you will use the knowledge you will learn in each chapter about the elements and principles of art to understand the composition of the work.

- Describe where you find rainbow colors in this work.
- Are the colors in this work bright or dull?
- Does this work look like a realistic painting, such as the George Inness painting in Figure 1.9 on page 11, or does it look like a dream scene with real objects in unusual places?

3 ▶ INTERPRET What is the artist trying to communicate?
The third step in art criticism focuses on the content of the work. This is where you will make guesses about the meaning.

- Why do you think the head has two faces?
- Why does the cat have a human face? What do you think it represents?
- What tells you, besides the title, that this takes place in Paris?

4 ▶ JUDGE What do you think of the work?
The fourth step in art criticism is when you decide if the work of art is successful or not. In Chapter 2 you will learn about theories that will help you to make objective decisions about artworks. When you have studied these theories, return to this painting and make a judgment about the work.

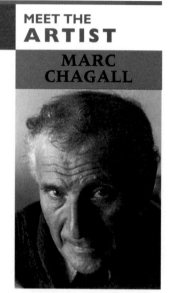

The Games Children Play

◀ **FIGURE 1.19**

Pieter Bruegel, the Elder. *Children's Games.* 1560. Oil on oakwood. 118 × 161 cm (46½ × 63⅓"). Kunsthistorisches Museum, Vienna, Austria.

W hat were some of your favorite games as a young child? Did you like playing hide-and-seek or capture-the-flag or were you more interested in dressing up or having make-believe tea parties? Although games differ from culture to culture, virtually all children play in ways that captivate the imagination and exercise the body.

However, games also have a social dimension. While at play, children often imitate adult behaviors and activities. Games introduce children to social customs and practices. In addition, many games have rules that must be followed or require specific techniques that must be mastered.

By playing games, children also learn important social skills, such as cooperation and competition. At the same time, games may allow us to act out imaginary scenes that are not likely to take place in reality. By stretching our imaginations as children, we learn to be creative and resourceful as adults. So, whether you liked to play with dolls or toy dinosaurs or to pretend you were a parent or a superhero, the games that occupied your childhood helped you to develop into the person you are today.

Making the Connection

1. How many different games can you identify in **Figure 1.19**?
2. Many of these games involve children imitating adult activities. How do children's games prepare us for the activities of adulthood?

Building Vocabulary

On a separate sheet of paper, write the term that best matches each definition given below.

1. To become deeply aware through the senses of the special nature of a visual object.
2. Something that stands for, or represents, something else.
3. The basic visual symbols in the language of art.
4. The rules that govern how artists organize the elements of art.
5. Art that has no recognizable subject matter.
6. The way the principles of art are used to organize the elements of art.
7. A list of important facts about a work of art.
8. A material used to make art.

Reviewing Art Facts

Answer the following questions using complete sentences.

1. Describe the five purposes of art.
2. Name and describe four sources of inspiration for artists.
3. Explain the relationship between the elements of art and the principles of art.
4. Select a work of art in this chapter and name the subject.
5. Read the credit-line information of an artwork from any chapter and list the figure number, the title, the year the work was created, and the medium.

Thinking Critically About Art

1. **Analyze.** Look at the different artworks in this chapter. They represent many different artists and many different time periods. Pick out three or four of your favorites and write a brief paragraph explaining your opinion. Are there similarities among the artworks you selected? What does this tell you about your preferences?

2. **Compare and contrast.** Study Figures 1.14 on page 14 and 1.15 on page 15. List the similarities you find in the two paintings. Then identify the qualities that make each of the paintings unique and different.

3. **Analyze.** Find two artworks in this chapter that were created within a few years of each other. List the similarities and differences. Do you think works of art made in the same time period have more similarities than those created at different times? Find another artwork created at a much earlier or much later time. How is it similar and different from the first two artworks you chose?

Use the Performing Arts Handbook to discover the art of masks and the many ways this art form has been created and worn throughout the world's cultures. Faustwork Mask Theatre presents the message of masks on page 413.

*inter*NET
CONNECTION

Use fun, interactive activities to help you learn the language of art and understand the elements and principles of art. Visit the Glencoe Fine Arts Site at: www.glencoe.com/sec/art

▲ **FIGURE 2.1** Henri Matisse is known for his spectacular use of color. How would you describe this painting? Can you identify the different objects in the painting? What appears to be the subject of the painting?

Henri Matisse. *Purple Robe and Anemones.* 1937. Oil on canvas. 73.1 × 60.3 cm (28¾ × 23⅞″). The Baltimore Museum of Art, Baltimore, Maryland. The Cone Collection, formed by Dr. Claribel Cone and Miss Etta Cone of Baltimore, Maryland.

CHAPTER 2

Art Criticism and Aesthetic Judgment

ave you ever recommended a new music CD to your friends? If you have, you were judging the music and making decisions about why it was a success and not a failure. You were acting as a critic.

Have you ever become so absorbed in watching a wonderful play or movie that you forgot about the passing of time? If you have, you were deeply involved in a work of theatrical or cinematic art and you were having an aesthetic experience. Understanding criticism and aesthetics as they apply to art is the purpose of this chapter.

When you look at Matisse's *Purple Robe and Anemones* **(Figure 2.1),** you may have difficulty understanding what you see because everything looks so flat. Notice that you can see both the top and sides of the table. The artist has used the same effect in painting the woman. Every area of the painting is filled with patterns of lines or shapes. Where do you see patterns in this work? Most of the colors are very bright because Matisse used color to express his emotions and ideas. He was more concerned with visual pleasure through color and pattern than with realism in his paintings.

OBJECTIVES

After completing this chapter, you will be able to:

- Explain the purpose of art criticism.
- Use the steps of art criticism.
- Explain the three aesthetic theories of art.
- Know what to look for when judging functional objects.
- Use the steps of art history operations.

WORDS TO LEARN

criteria
aesthetics
art criticism
aesthetic experience
description
analysis
interpretation
judgment
literal qualities
design qualities
expressive qualities
Imitationalism
Formalism
Emotionalism
individual style

Developing Your
PORTFOLIO The act of creation may be satisfying for an artist. The act of appreciating an artwork—having an aesthetic experience—can be satisfying for a viewer. Select an artwork in the book that attracts your eyes. Study it for several minutes. Read the caption and answer any questions. Give yourself time to perceive the artwork instead of just looking at it. Then write a short paragraph about the experience and what you learned from it. Be sure to list the title of the artwork as well as the artist.

Art Criticism: Learning from a Work of Art

There are professional critics who appear on television or write reviews about new movies, plays, television shows, videos, books, art exhibits, and music. These critics describe their responses to various forms of art, and give you their assessment of the merits of the works. You may not always agree with their opinions because your **criteria,** or *standards of judgment*, may be very different from those of the professional critic. In this chapter you will learn about **aesthetics** (es-**thet**-iks), *the philosophy or study of the nature and value of art.* This will allow you to form your own intelligent opinions about works of art. You will also learn about art criticism. **Art criticism** is *an organized approach for studying a work of art.*

Why Study Art Criticism?

What do you think of when you hear the word *criticism*? Do you think it means saying something negative? This is not true. A criticism can be a positive statement. For example, when you shop for clothes, you try on many things. You act as a critic using personal criteria to determine which pieces of clothing look good on you and which pieces do not suit you. You have developed your own criteria for choosing clothing through personal experience.

When you look at Alma Thomas's painting, *Iris, Tulips, Jonquils, and Crocuses* **(Figure 2.2),** you may experience confusion. You may not have had enough experience to develop a set of criteria to judge a work that has no recognizable subject. If you are like most people who are new to art, you may not know what to say. You may be afraid that you will say the wrong thing.

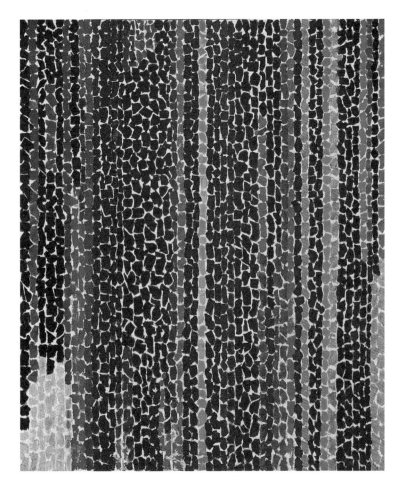

◀ **FIGURE 2.2** At first glance, this painting appears to consist of simple shapes and bright colors. The title of the work, however, should help you understand what the dabs of color represent. Notice how large the painting is. How big does that make each dab of color? Can you imagine the garden these flowers would grow in?

Alma Thomas. *Iris, Tulips, Jonquils, and Crocuses.* 1969. Acrylic on canvas. 152.4 × 127 cm (60 × 50″). The National Museum of Women in the Arts, Washington, D.C. Gift of Wallace and Wilhelmina Holladay.

Art criticism is not difficult. In fact, it can be a lot of fun. At the very least, it can make the study of art less mysterious and more logical. Art criticism is a sequential approach for looking at and talking about art.

Your own life experiences may also help you understand the meaning of each work of art. No one has done or seen exactly the same things you have, so no one will see exactly what you see in a work of art. No one can think exactly the way you think. You may see ideas in a work of art that were never dreamed of by the artist. This does not mean that you are wrong; it simply means that the work of art is so powerful that it has a special meaning for everybody.

Learning art criticism will help you interpret works of art. It will give you the confidence to discuss works of art without worrying about what other people might think. It will help you to organize your thoughts. You will develop the courage to speak your mind and make sound aesthetic judgments.

As you learn the language of art, you will be able to "dig deeper" into the layers of meaning of each art object. The deeper you dig, the more important your feelings for that work of art will become. This will make your **aesthetic experience,** or *your personal interaction with a work of art,* more meaningful and memorable. The work will then become a permanent part of your memory.

The Steps of Art Criticism

When you become involved in the process of art criticism, you learn *from* the work of art. Critiquing an artwork is like playing detective. You must assume the artist has a secret message hidden within the work. Your job is to find the message and solve the mystery.

In this chapter you will learn a special four-step approach that will help you find the hidden meanings in art. The four steps, which must be taken in order, are *Description, Analysis, Interpretation,* and *Judgment.* By following these steps you will be able to answer the following questions:

- What do I see? (*Description*)
- How is the work organized? (*Analysis*)
- What is the artist trying to communicate? (*Interpretation*)
- Is this a successful work of art? (*Judgment*)

As you go through the steps of *description* and *analysis*, you will collect facts and clues. When you get to *interpretation*, you will make guesses about what you think the artist is trying to say. Finally, during *judgment*, you will make your own decisions about the artistic merit of the work.

Step One: Description (What do I see?)

In the first step of art criticism, **description,** you carefully *make a list of all the things you see in the work.* These include the following:

- The size of the work, the medium used, and the process used.
- The subject, object, and details.
- The elements of art used in the work.

During the description step, notice the size of the work and the medium used. You will find these facts in the credit line. This information will help you visualize the real size and look of the work. Notice that Figure 2.1 on page 24 and Figure 3.1 on page 40 are about the same size as reproduced in this book. Read both credit lines and notice the difference in the actual size of each work.

Look at the painting by José Clemente Orozco called *Barricade* **(Figure 2.3)**. Notice that the work is 55 inches tall. How does that compare to your own height? If this artwork were standing on the floor, would the figures be larger or smaller than you? What materials were used to create this work?

During the description step, you must be objective. In describing Orozco's painting, you can say that you see five people. You could not say they are all men. That would be a guess. You can describe the person crouched on the ground as wearing a blue shirt and holding a large knife. You can describe the tense muscles that are bulging on the other four figures, but at this point in the criticism process, you should not try to guess why they are tense.

Look again at Figure 2.3. Line and color are two of the art elements that play an important part in this work. Can you identify the other art elements used?

Look at Figure 2.2 on page 26. This is a nonobjective work. In nonobjective works, the art elements become the subject matter.

Step Two: Analysis (How is the work organized?)

During this step, you are still collecting facts about the elements and principles of art that are used in the artwork. In **analysis** you *discover how the principles of art are used to organize the art elements of line, color, shape, form, space, and texture.* You will learn how the artist has used the elements and principles to create the content of the art, which is known as the theme or the message. Look at *The Blue Wall* by Leo Twiggs **(Figure 2.4)**. Notice the curved lines that outline the two figures. Where do you see the darkest colors? Where are the lightest colors? What textures do you see? Notice how the head of one figure is cut off at the top, and the body of the other is cut off at the waist. As you learn more about the elements and principles you will be able to collect more clues that you can use to interpret each work.

Step Three: Interpretation (What is the artist trying to communicate?)

During Step Three, you will answer the question, "What is the artist trying to communicate?" In **interpretation** you will *explain or tell the meaning or mood of the work.* It is here that you can make guesses about the artwork, as long

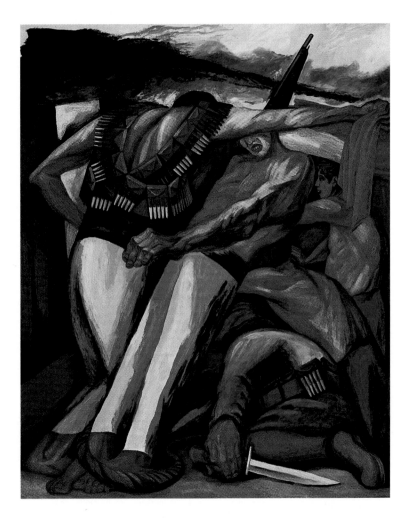

◀ **FIGURE 2.3** Orozco was one of the Mexican muralists who combined the solid forms of ancient Mexican art with the powerful colors of European Expressionism. This work depicts the peasants fighting for freedom during the Mexican Revolution in 1910. What could you do to find out more about the event this painting depicts?

José Clemente Orozco. *Barricade*. 1931. Oil on canvas. 140 × 114.3 cm (55 × 45″). The Museum of Modern Art, New York, New York. Given anonymously. © Estate of José Clemente Orozco/SOMAAP, Mexico/Licensed by VAGA, New York, NY

▶ **FIGURE 2.4** Your interpretation of this work will depend on the clues you have collected during the first two steps of art criticism—description and analysis—plus your personal life experiences. People have different experiences which will produce a variety of interpretations, all of which could be acceptable.

Leo Twiggs. *The Blue Wall.* 1969. Batik painting. 61 × 76.2 cm (24 × 30″). Private collection.

as they appear to be supported by what you see in the work. Interpretation can be the most difficult step in art criticism, because you must dare to be adventurous in stretching the range of your thought processes and imagination. It can also be the most creative and the most rewarding step.

You must use your intelligence, imagination, and courage. You must not be afraid to make an interpretation that is different from someone else's. After all, you are different from other people. Your interpretation will be influenced by what you have experienced and seen in your life.

Your interpretation must be based on the visual facts and clues you collected during your first two steps. Your interpretation can be based on your feelings, but your feelings must be backed up by observation of what you actually see in the artwork.

When you look at the two boys in Figure 2.4, you notice that the boys are frowning and looking away from each other, but you also notice that there is one point in the work where they are touching. What do you think is happening? What is the artist telling you about these two boys?

Step Four: Judgment (Is this a successful work of art?)

In Step Four you will judge whether or not the work is successful. In **judgment** you *determine the degree of artistic merit.* This is the time to make your own decisions. There are two levels of judgment to be made. The first is personal. Do you like the work? No one can ever tell you what to like or dislike. You must make up your own mind. To make a fair judgment, you must be honest with yourself. Only you know why you feel the way you do. Otherwise, you may close yourself off from experiencing different kinds of art. The second level of judgment you must make is also subjective, but it is somewhat different. At this

From the time she was a child, Georgia O'Keeffe knew she was going to be an artist. She studied with several teachers and began creating the flower paintings that made her famous. She painted her flowers big so that they would take viewers by surprise. In 1915, however, she realized that she had ideas for art that were not like anything she had been taught. She decided at age 29 to focus totally on nature and she burned her earlier works in order to start fresh, emphasizing shapes and forms. She continued following her own vision throughout her long life, never being pulled into any of the many movements that have dominated the American art scene during the twentieth century.

O'Keeffe loved to see "connections" in the shapes of ordinary things. After painting a shell and shingle many times, she painted a mountain. It was only later that she realized that she had given the mountain the same shape as the shell and the shingle. She saw beautiful forms everywhere, even in the most unusual places, such as the vast desert spaces and parched bones found near her home in New Mexico.

point, you use aesthetics to help you decide whether the work is successful. A work can be very successful aesthetically, but you might not want to live with it.

To make a judgment, you must take your time. **Figure 2.5** is a painting by Georgia O'Keeffe. To judge this painting, first think about how you would describe the subject of the painting. Then consider how the artist has arranged the art elements according to the art principles in order to create the composition. Notice how she has used shading to make the skull look solid and the drapery look like a hanging banner. However, she has painted the red borders and the black shape behind the skull flat. Then, think about the feeling the painting gives you. By taking time to look at and describe, analyze, and interpret what you think the meaning of the painting might be, you will be able to make an intelligent judgment. Ask yourself, is this a work of artistic merit? Is it successful?

☑ Check Your Understanding

1. What is aesthetics?
2. Name and describe the four steps of art criticism in order.

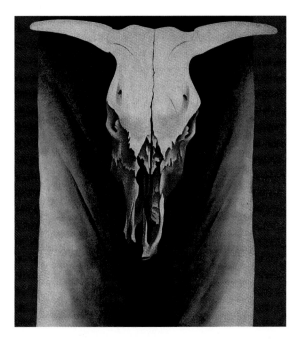

◀ **FIGURE 2.5** Georgia O'Keeffe loved the West. She shocked the public with paintings of objects from her environment that people were not used to seeing hanging on a wall. She painted *Cow's Skull: Red, White, and Blue* because she wanted to create something uniquely American. Do you think she succeeded?

Georgia O'Keeffe. *Cow's Skull: Red, White, and Blue.* 1931. Oil on canvas. 101.3 × 91.1 cm (39⅞ × 35⅞"). The Metropolitan Museum of Art, New York, New York. The Alfred Stieglitz Collection, 1952. (52.203)

Aesthetics: Thinking about a Work of Art

Aesthetics is a branch of philosophy concerned with the nature and value of art. Physical beauty was once the only criterion for judging the quality of art. Today, artwork is judged by a different set of criteria and instead of being called "beautiful," a good work of art is called "successful." Some successful works of art may not look pretty, but they may be well-organized, and/or elicit emotional responses from viewers. If a work of art contains strange, disturbing images, yet makes you think, it may be successful.

Aesthetic Theories and the Quality of Art

The aesthetic qualities that are discussed most often by *aestheticians* (specialists in aesthetics) are the literal qualities, the design qualities, and the expressive qualities. These are directly related to the properties of art discussed in Chapter 1 on pages 18 and 19: subject, composition, and content. The **literal qualities** are *the realistic qualities that appear in the subject of the work.* For instance, if the artist depicts a realistic figure of a man on a horse, the literal qualities of the work are the images of a man on a horse. The **design qualities,** or *how well the work is organized,* are found when you look at the composition of the work. Does it look balanced? Is there a rhythmic quality? Is there variety? Has the artist made a unified work of art? These are the types of questions one must ask to determine how well organized a work is. The **expressive qualities,** or *those qualities that convey ideas and moods,* are those you notice when you study the content of a work. Is there something in the work that makes you feel a certain emotion or conveys an idea to you?

The three aesthetic theories of art criticism are most commonly referred to as Imitationalism, Formalism, and Emotionalism.

Imitationalism and Literal Qualities

Some critics think that the most important thing about a work of art is the realistic presentation of subject matter. It is their opinion that a work is successful if it looks like and reminds the viewer of what he or she sees in the real world. People with this point of view feel that an artwork should imitate life, that it should look lifelike before it can be considered successful. This aesthetic theory, called **Imitationalism,** *focuses on realistic representation.*

Formalism and Design Qualities

Other critics think that composition is the most important factor in a work of art. This aesthetic theory, called **Formalism,** *places emphasis on the design qualities,* the arrangement of the elements of art using the principles of art.

Emotionalism and Expressive Qualities

This theory is concerned with the content of the work of art. Some critics claim that no object can be considered art if it fails to arouse an emotional response in the viewer. The expressive qualities are the most important to them. Their theory, called **Emotionalism,** *requires that a work of art must arouse a response of feelings, moods, or emotions in the viewer.*

Look at *Papiamento* by Julio Larraz **(Figure 2.6).** You may use the theory of Imitationalism to judge this work as successful because the artist has painted everything very accurately. You can recognize the texture of the freshly pressed, white cotton dress, the light flickering on the large, tropical leaves, the texture of the trunk of the palm tree, the palm fronds, the yellow sand of the beach, and the beautiful blue of the Caribbean waters. Someone else may choose the theory of Formalism to judge the work as successful because the artist has arranged the objects so that the foreground is in shadow and the background glows brightly with sunshine. A third person may choose the theory of Emotionalism because of the mysterious mood created by hiding the woman in the shadow of the tree, or because the painting may arouse in the viewer emotional associations with memories of a vacation on a Caribbean island.

You can judge art using just one aesthetic theory or more than one, depending on the type of art and your own purposes. If you limit yourself to using only one theory, however, you may miss some exciting discoveries in a work. Perhaps the best method is to use all three. Then you will be able to discover as much as possible about a particular piece of art.

▲ **FIGURE 2.6** Notice how the artist has blended the woman into the painting. You don't see her until you look carefully. What may have been the artist's reasons for doing this? The title of this work, *Papiamento*, is the name of a language spoken in the Antilles. What else could you find out about the work and its artist that might help you to understand it better?

Julio Larraz. *Papiamento.* 1987. Oil on canvas. 143.5 × 209.5 cm (56½ × 82½″). Courtesy of Nohra Haime Gallery, New York, New York.

Aesthetic Theories

Judging Functional Objects

You can use art criticism to make aesthetic judgments about functional objects such as cars, shoes, or fine china. The objects in **Figure 2.7** are an example. In criticizing functional objects, you follow the first two steps of art criticism—description and analysis—as described earlier. However, during the third step, interpretation, you must consider the purpose of the object as its meaning. Does a silver soup ladle look like it will transfer liquid from one container to another without dripping and splashing? That is, does it look like it will function properly? In the last step, judgment, you must consider if the object works when it is used. A chair may look beautiful, but if it is not comfortable to sit in, then it does not function properly. It is unsuccessful.

Judging Your Own Artwork

Art criticism will help you use critical thinking to analyze your own works of art. The four steps of art criticism will help you be as honest and unbiased as possible. When you apply all four of the steps of art criticism to your work, you should find out why your work either needs improvement or is a success.

☑ Check Your Understanding

1. What are the three aesthetic qualities most often discussed by art critics?
2. What is Imitationalism?
3. How are Formalism and Emotionalism different?
4. How does judging functional objects differ from judging fine art?

▲ **FIGURE 2.7** These chairs are appealing to the eye, but are they successful as functional objects? To find out, you will have to apply the steps of art criticism. Do they appear to be the right height for sitting? Would they provide enough back support? Is the padding thick enough for comfort?

John Dunnigan. *Slipper Chairs.* 1990. Purpleheart wood with silk upholstery. Left: 66.9 × 63 × 57.5 cm (26¼ × 25½ × 23″). Right: 110.5 × 66.7 × 61 cm (43½ × 26¼ × 24″). © John Dunnigan. Renwick Gallery, National Museum of American Art, Smithsonian Institution, Washington, D.C.

Art History: Learning about a Work of Art

You can develop your appreciation for a work of art by gathering information about the artist and the time period in which the work was created. There is a four-step approach for organizing the way you gather information about a work of art. The four steps make up *art history operations*. The names for the four steps of art history operations are the same as the four steps for art criticism: *Description, Analysis, Interpretation*, and *Judgment*. For art history operations, however, there are different definitions for the terms and different questions to be answered.

- **Description.** When, where, and by whom was the work done?
- **Analysis.** What is the style of the work and can the work be associated with an art movement?
- **Interpretation.** How did time and place affect the artist's style, in terms of subject matter, composition, and content?
- **Judgment.** Is the work considered to be significant in the history of art?

Step One: Description

During this step you will look for information *about* the work of art. You want to know who did it, when, and where it was done. If you were looking at an original work of art, you would look for the artist's signature and the date on the work itself. In this book, because the works have been reduced to fit on the page, you will probably not be able to see the artist's signature or the date on the work. You will find that information in the credit line, however. If you look at the credit line for **Figure 2.8,** you will discover that this

▲ **FIGURE 2.8** The objects in this work are easy to recognize—trees, mountains, and night sky—but the colors are not what you might expect. Why do you think the artist used these colors? What does he appear to be saying?

Ernst Ludwig Kirchner. *Winter Landscape in Moonlight.* 1919. Oil on canvas. 120.7 × 120.7 cm (47½ × 47½"). The Detroit Institute of Arts, Detroit, Michigan. Gift of Curt Valentin in memory of the occasion of Dr. William R. Valentiner's 60th birthday.

painting was created by the same artist who painted **Figure 2.9,** Ernst Ludwig Kirchner. Figure 2.9 was painted in 1907. Compare that date to Figure 2.8. Which was painted earlier? To learn more about Kirchner, such as where and when he lived, you would need to do some further research.

Step Two: Analysis

During analysis, you examine the work and look for information about the artist's style. Style is like handwriting. No two people have exactly the same handwriting and no two artists have exactly the same style. **Individual style** is *the artist's personal way of using the elements and principles of art to express feelings and ideas.* To analyze the style of one artist, you will need to see several works by the same artist. When you look at Figure 2.8 and Figure 2.9, you can easily see the unique aspects of the artist's style: his unusual use of color and his exaggeration of shapes for expressive effect.

Step Three: Interpretation

In order to find the answers for this step you will have to do some research. You will discover that the artist was active in a group of young, adventurous artists in Germany who called themselves Die Brücke (The Bridge) and that their work was part of a larger movement known as German Expressionism. In order to interpret his work, you would need to find out what other artists influenced him, details about his life, and information about his surroundings.

Step Four: Judgment

Once again you must research to find out the importance of this work in the history of art. You must discover what different art historians have to say about

▲ **FIGURE 2.9** Spend a few moments describing this work. What is its most unusual feature? What is the subject matter? Then compare it to Figure 2.8, also by the same artist. What are the similarities and differences between the artworks? Can you draw any conclusions about Kirchner's individual style?

Ernst Ludwig Kirchner. *Seated Woman.* 1907. Oil on canvas. 80.6 × 91.1 cm (31¾ × 35⅞″). The Minneapolis Institute of Arts, Minneapolis, Minnesota. The John R. Van Derlip Fund.

Kirchner and use their assessments to help you shape your own. You can also discover if Kirchner influenced other artists, which would help you judge his importance.

As you study the information in this book and learn more about the language of art, you will begin to acquire information from works of art. You will learn more about the artists who created the works. In Chapters 12 and 13, you will find a brief overview of art history. Refer to these chapters to learn more about art movements and time periods as you encounter them throughout the book.

✓ Check Your Understanding

1. What are the art history operations?
2. Describe each of the steps of art history operations.
3. What is individual style?

ART CRITICISM IN ACTION

▲ FIGURE 2.10

Faith Ringgold. *Bitter Nest Part II: Harlem Renaissance Party.* 1988. Acrylic on canvas, printed, tie-dyed, and pieced fabric. 238.8 × 208.3 cm (94 × 82″). National Gallery of Art, Washington, D.C. © 1998 Board of Trustees.

Notice that the work of art in **Figure 2.10** is a quilt. The center of the work is painted with acrylics on canvas. The frame is made of quilted squares.

1 ▶ DESCRIBE What do you see?
During this step you will collect information, or clues, about the subject of the work. Use your perception skills to study what you see in the work. If you are not sure of something, do not guess.

■ List the information found in the credit line.

■ Describe the fabric frame around the painting. List and describe the people you see in the painted center. Explain the setting.

2 ▶ ANALYZE How is this work organized?
The second step in art criticism deals with the composition of the work. This is also a clue-collecting step. Do not make guesses. During this step you will use what you will learn in each chapter about the elements and principles of art.

■ Which person is emphasized? How?

■ What is unusual about the arrangement of objects and people?

■ Where do you see repetition in this work? Describe and locate the objects that are repeated.

3 ▶ INTERPRET What is the artist trying to communicate?
The third step in art criticism is concerned with the content of the work. You are allowed to make guesses about the meaning of the work during this step. Remember that you do not need to know what the artist meant. Instead, decide what this painted quilt says to you.

■ What does the clothing tell you about this scene?

■ What do you think is happening in this scene? What has happened before this moment, and what will happen next?

■ Why do you think the artist has illustrated this scene on a quilt?

4 ▶ JUDGE What do you think of the work?
Now you are ready to make an aesthetic judgment about this work.

■ Do you think this is a successful work of art? Why or why not? Use one or more of the three aesthetic theories explained in this chapter to defend your judgment.

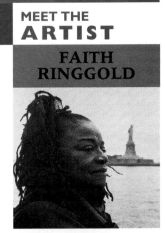

How Does Imagery Help Us Interpret a Story?

▲ FIGURE 2.11

Leo and Diane Dillon. Book cover illustration for *A Wrinkle in Time.* 1979. Watercolor and pastel on paper. 48.4 × 33 cm (19⅟₁₆ × 13"). Private collection.

Writers and painters are both engaged in forms of artistic expression. Writers help us to connect with the characters and "see" their story using vivid imagery. When you look at a painting, you will not always find characters, but you will usually see images that convey visual ideas and moods. In art, imagery refers to the representation of the visible world as well as the mental impressions evoked by such a representation. In literature, imagery refers to the language that a writer uses to convey a visual picture as well as the sensory and emotional experiences of a particular character or situation.

The cover illustration for Madeleine L'Engle's novel *A Wrinkle in Time* **(Figure 2.11)** suggests the story's themes and introduces its main characters using visual imagery. If you have read this novel, then you may already recognize the characters and their predicament as portrayed in the illustration. Even a reader unfamiliar with the text, however, can interpret the imagery in this painting. To interpret literary imagery, we must listen carefully to the writer's words and visualize the images that those words convey.

Making the Connection

1. Describe the composition of this illustration. How does the design of the picture convey the themes of time and time travel?
2. What emotion or mood does this illustration seem to express? How does it compare with the story?
3. Read (or reread) *A Wrinkle in Time.* How does L'Engle use language to paint a mental picture of the characters and their story? Write a short essay explaining your answer.

Building Vocabulary

On a separate sheet of paper, write the term that best matches each definition given below.

1. Standards of judgment.
2. An organized approach for studying a work of art.
3. The art-criticism step in which you make a list of all the things you see in a work of art.
4. The art-criticism step in which you discover how the principles of art are used to organize the art elements of line, color, shape, form, space, and texture.
5. The art-criticism step in which you explain or tell the meaning or mood of the work.
6. The art-criticism step in which you determine the degree of artistic merit of the work.
7. The aesthetic theory that focuses on realistic representation.
8. The aesthetic theory that places emphasis on the design qualities.
9. The aesthetic theory that requires that a work of art must arouse a response of feelings, moods, or emotions in the viewer.

Reviewing Art Facts

Answer the following questions using complete sentences.

1. What will learning the steps of art criticism help you develop?
2. Define the four steps of art criticism.
3. Describe the three aesthetic theories.
4. If the organization of an artwork is most important to an art critic, which aesthetic theory would he or she hold?
5. When criticizing functional objects, what must you consider during interpretation besides beauty?
6. In what ways are the steps of art criticism different from the steps of art history operations? In what ways are they similar?

Thinking Critically About Art

1. **Apply.** Select something from your home that is used solely for aesthetic purposes. Critique it using the four steps of art criticism. When you are finished, ask yourself if the object seems different than it did before. Has your opinion of the object changed?
2. **Analyze.** Find a movie critic's review of a current film in a newspaper or magazine. Read it carefully. Try to find statements that fit each of the four steps of art criticism.
3. **Extend.** Do you think you can appreciate the qualities of a work of art even if you don't like it? Explain your conclusions.

Dance pioneer Martha Graham uses the principles of aesthetics in the development of her modern dances. See how Graham uses literal qualities, design qualities, and expressive qualities through the use of body movement on page 414.

inter NET CONNECTION Challenge yourself and test your knowledge of art history. Visit the Glencoe Fine Arts site (**www.glencoe.com/sec/art**) and discover information about artworks and famous artists.

▲ **FIGURE 3.1**   This is an early example of Murray's transition from traditional painting to paintings that have three dimensions. Although this work is still flat, what has she done with space that makes the artwork different?

Elizabeth Murray. *Painters Progress.* 1981. Oil on canvas in 19 parts. Overall 294.5 × 236.2 cm (9′8″ × 7′9″). The Museum of Modern Art, New York, New York. Acquired through the Bernhill fund and gift of Agnes Gund.

The Media and Processes of Art

Artists use a variety of tools and techniques to create art. These different tools and techniques affect the look of each individual artwork. For example, a watercolor painting and an oil painting of the same outdoor scene will look very different. A photograph of a baby will look very different from a video of the same baby. The watercolor paints, the oil paints, the photograph, and the video tape are art **media,** *the materials used to make art.*

Painters Progress **(Figure 3.1)** was designed using 19 shaped canvases. The artist's selection of media influenced the effect of the artwork. For instance, the art would appear much different if it had been done using a flat, rectangular piece of canvas. The use of many separate shaped canvases changes the impact of the work. The artist could have drawn on the canvas with chalk or charcoal, but instead she chose brightly colored paints. Decisions like these about the tools and techniques of art determine the final impression of a work of art. In this chapter, you will learn about many of these tools and techniques—called *media* and *processes*—and how to use them in your own art.

OBJECTIVES

After completing this chapter, you will be able to:
- Identify four different shading techniques.
- Name the kinds of painting media.
- Follow the basic steps of printmaking.
- Identify the four sculpting techniques.
- Recognize the media of functional crafts.
- Understand how new media influenced the development of architecture.
- Use the media of technology to create artworks.

WORDS TO KNOW

media/medium
shading
printmaking
print
reproduction
edition
sculpture
photography
analog system
digital system
multi-media programs

Developing Your
PORTFOLIO

Select some lines from a favorite poem or song. Make sketches of objects and scenes to go with the words. Look through magazines and cut out interesting shapes, letters, or printed words that illustrate your text. Attach the found objects and cutouts around the sketches that you have created. Use a variety of media to draw and paint the remaining images and words of the poem or song. Write a paragraph about how the different media used affect the art. Place your completed work in your portfolio.

Two-Dimensional Media

Elizabeth Murray applied oil paint onto shaped canvases in Figure 3.1. Leo Twiggs used dyes and wax resist on cotton in Figure 1.7 on page 10. Each of these artists created a two-dimensional work of art using different materials. Any material used to create art is called a medium. The plural form of medium is *media*. A medium can be something as ordinary as a graphite pencil or as exotic as gold leaf gilding. In two-dimensional works, such as drawing and painting, artists use media such as crayons, paints, pastels, and pencils.

Drawing

In baseball, a pitcher throws warm-up pitches before facing a batter. Musicians tune their instruments or warm up their voices before a performance. Artists must also prepare before creating art. By drawing, artists become better at perceiving, or carefully noticing, the lines, shapes, and forms of an object.

Many artists use sketchbooks to record their surroundings and to produce studies of objects. Artists also record ideas for later use. The Renaissance artist Leonardo da Vinci filled more than 100 sketchbooks with his drawings and ideas. His sketchbooks included everything from perceptions of people, to his notations on the movement of water **(Figure 3.2),** to his plans for flying machines.

Drawing is usually the first step in producing artworks. Rough sketches, or studies, are often done before creating a work in another medium such as paint or clay. Fashion designers draw their ideas for new styles long before any fabric is cut. Stage designers, graphic designers, and architects

◀ **FIGURE 3.2** Da Vinci's observations of moving water were confirmed as accurate in this century when fast cameras could photographically freeze the action of the water. Da Vinci filled his notebooks with observational sketches and notes. His writing was backward and could only be read when held up to a mirror.

Leonardo da Vinci. Page from his sketchbook showing movement of water. Royal Library, Windsor Castle, London, England. The Royal Collection 1993, Her Majesty Queen Elizabeth II.

must show presentation drawings for a client's approval. **Figure 3.3** is a costume design for a comic ballet, *The Devil's Holiday.* The designer modeled the costumes and stage designs based on the eighteenth-century paintings of Venice by the artist Canaletto.

Although drawings are often used as guides for other artworks, sometimes an artist's drawing *is* the finished artwork. One example of a drawing as a work of art is Canaletto's *Ascension Day Festival at Venice* **(Figure 3.4).**

Drawing Media

Drawing is the process of moving an instrument over a smooth surface to leave a mark, called a line. In drawing, line is the most important element of art. The characteristics of a line are determined, in part, by the medium used to draw it. The most popular drawing media are graphite pencils, colored pencils, crayons, colored markers, pens, pastels, and chalk. Pen and ink, pen and brush, and brushes with watercolors are also used to make drawings.

▲ **FIGURE 3.3** How does this sketch let you know that this character is in a comedy? What makes him look humorous?

Eugene Berman. *Vendeur de Chapeaux.* 1939. Gouache on paper. 31.7 × 24.1 cm (9³⁄₄ × 12¹⁄₂″). Wadsworth Atheneum, Hartford, Connecticut. Gift of Mr. and Mrs. James T. Soby. 1939.697.

▶ **FIGURE 3.4** Look closely at this meticulous drawing. Can you tell what city is depicted in this work? What helped you decide?

Canaletto. *Ascension Day Festival at Venice.* 1766. Pen and brown ink with gray wash, heightened with white, over graphite on laid paper. 38.6 × 55.7 cm (15³⁄₁₆ × 21¾″). National Gallery of Art, Washington D.C. © 1998 Board of Trustees. Samuel H. Kress Collection.

Each drawing medium has its own qualities. Chalk and crayon, for example, produce rough lines. Pens, by contrast, make smooth lines. **Figure 3.5** shows lines made with different drawing media.

Crayon

Pastel

Hard pencil

Soft pencil

Watercolor pencil

Color pencil

Thin marker

Wide marker

Wet brush

Dry brush

▲ **FIGURE 3.5**   Drawing media.

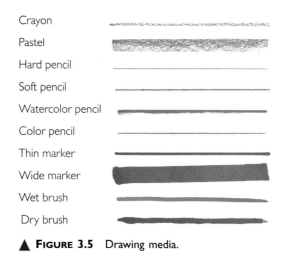

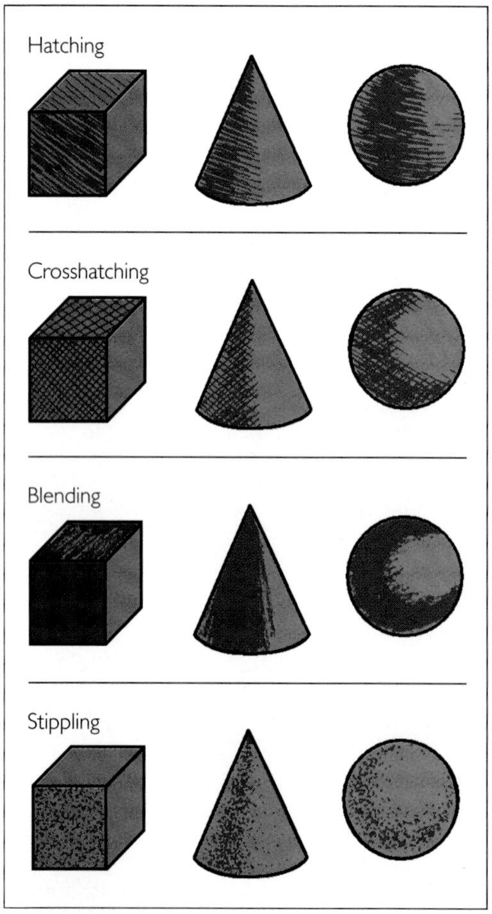

Hatching

Crosshatching

Blending

Stippling

▲ **FIGURE 3.6**   Shading techniques.

Shading Techniques

Shading is *the use of light and dark values to create the illusion of form.* There are four main shading techniques:

- **Hatching.** This technique consists of drawing thin lines that run in the same direction. Find the form in **Figure 3.6** that uses hatching.
- **Crosshatching.** Shading created using crisscrossing lines is called crosshatching. Look at the form in **Figure 3.6** that demonstrates this technique.
- **Blending.** Artists perform blending by changing the color value little by little. Find the form in **Figure 3.6** that is shaded using blending.
- **Stippling.** Shading that creates dark values by means of a dot pattern is referred to as stippling. Locate the form in **Figure 3.6** that shows stippling.

Look at the drawing in **Figure 3.7.** Isabel Bishop used three different drawing media to create a drawing that has the look of three dimensions. The artist accomplished this through shading.

Which shading technique was used in Figure 3.4?

Painting

Painting is the process of applying color to a surface using tools such as a brush, a painting knife, a roller, or even your fingers. The surface is the material to which the paint is applied. Canvas, paper, and wood are frequently used as surface material.

All paints have three basic ingredients:

- **Pigments.** Pigments are finely ground colored powders. Pigments come from natural or synthetic materials. Natural pigments include indigo,

▶ **FIGURE 3.7** Look at this drawing and identify the shading techniques Bishop used.

Isabel Bishop. *Head #5.* No date. Graphite, crayon, and chalk on paper. 29 × 22.6 cm (11¾ × 8¹³/₁₆″). Wadsworth Atheneum, Hartford, Connecticut. Gift of Henry Schnakenberg. 1953.217

a vegetable, and the cochineal beetle, an insect. Natural pigments can also be made from minerals or clay. Synthetic pigments are artificially made from chemicals.

■ **Binder.** A binder is a material that holds together the grains of pigment. The binder allows the pigment to stick to the painting surface. Egg yolks mixed with water have long been used as a strong binder for professional artist's tempera paints.

Other binders are linseed oil and wax.

■ **Solvent.** A solvent is a liquid that controls the thickness or the thinness of the paint. Different painting effects require different thicknesses of paint. Using thin watercolor paint gives a light, washed-out appearance; using thick watercolor paint produces a more intense appearance. Solvents are also used to clean paintbrushes and other applicators.

American, 1836–1910

Winslow Homer is considered one of the artists who has captured the true feelings of the United States in his works. Homer developed an appreciation and love for the outdoors while growing up with his two brothers in Cambridge, Massachusetts. By the age of ten, his interest in art began and his talent for drawing became obvious. When he was 19, Homer was accepted as an apprentice at a large printing firm in Boston, even though he had little formal art training.

When his apprenticeship was over, Homer worked as a draftsman, specializing in woodblock engraving. Soon he began illustrating magazines. By the 1860s he was contributing regularly to *Harper's Weekly* magazine as an illustrator of events occurring in the Civil War. After the Civil War ended, Homer traveled to Europe. There, he was influenced by the works of French artists Édouard Manet and Gustave Courbet.

By the 1880s, Homer had begun painting the subject that was to become his trademark—the sea. He loved nature and spent hours outdoors. He felt at home on the sea although he knew its dangers as well. Because he was able to capture the elemental forces of nature, Homer is considered a Realist. His unique talent enabled him, as few others have done before him, to express the reality of the United States.

The look of a finished painting depends on the combination of media, tools, and the surface the artist chooses. In **Figures 3.8** and **3.9,** you can see how Winslow Homer has created two images that are almost exactly alike. However, he has used different media. Figure 3.8 is made with thin, wet, flowing watercolor on white paper. The white in this painting is the white of the paper showing through. Figure 3.9 is painted with thick, creamy oil paint on canvas. The white in this painting is opaque white paint.

Painting Media

As with drawing media, there are many different kinds of painting media, each with its own unique qualities. The artist chooses the paint based on personal preference and the purpose of the work.

Oil-Based Paint. First used in the 1400s, oil paint remains a popular medium today. True to its name, oil paint uses linseed oil as its binder. Its solvent is turpentine.

One advantage of oil paint is that it dries slowly. This allows the artist to blend colors right on the canvas. The work in Figure 3.9 is an oil painting. Notice how smoothly the colors blend.

Water-Soluble Paint. The most popular of water-based painting media, watercolor takes its name from its solvent, water. The binder is gum arabic. Compare the watercolor in Figure 3.8 with the oil painting in Figure 3.9. What differences do you see?

Tempera is another water-based paint. It dries more quickly than oil paint, and it has a more opaque finish than watercolor.

Acrylic paint, which first appeared in the 1950s, uses an acrylic polymer as a binder. The solvent used for acrylic paint is also water. However, once professional acrylic paint dries, it cannot be dissolved. School acrylics have been developed, however, that can be dissolved with soapy water after they dry.

◀ **FIGURE 3.8**

◀ **FIGURE 3.9**

Activity | Experimenting with Watercolor

Applying Your Skills. Using watercolor paint, choose one bright color and paint several shapes on a dry sheet of watercolor paper. Then thoroughly brush water on both sides of a sheet of watercolor paper and repeat the process. Share and compare your results with those of classmates.

Computer Option. Drawing with color on the computer is like drawing with light. Light as the computer's pigment can vary in opacity from opaque, like tempera paint, to transparent, like watercolors. Find the menu in the application you are using which controls opacity. Explore the settings. Remember, these qualities change as you paint on different surfaces. If available, investigate rough, smooth, or textured papers.

Printmaking

Printmaking is a *process in which an artist repeatedly transfers an original image from one prepared surface to another.* Paper is often the surface to which the printed image is transferred. *The impression created on a surface by the printing plate* is called a **print.** A print is not the same thing as a reproduction, although sometimes people confuse the two. A print is an original work of art. A **reproduction,** such as the artwork shown in this book, is *a copy of a work of art.*

The Basic Steps of Printmaking

While prints may be made using many different media, processes, and surfaces, all require three basic steps.

- **Creating the printing plate.** A printing plate is the surface on which the desired image is created. In producing a printing plate, the artist

makes a mirror image of the final print. Letters and numbers must be made backward on the plate.

- **Inking the plate.** The artist applies ink to the plate. This is done with a *brayer,* a roller with a handle. For a multicolor print, one plate must be made for each color. The ink creates the image on the print.

- **Transferring the image.** The paper or other material is pressed against the inked plate, and the ink is transferred to the new surface. Sometimes this is done by hand. Other times a printing press is used.

Usually, more than one print is made from a single plate. Together, *all the prints made from the same plate, or set of plates,* form an **edition.** Each print in an edition is signed and numbered by the artist. The printmaker signs the work in the bottom margin and writes the title on each print of an edition as well as the number of each print. The number 10/200 indicates the tenth of 200 prints.

Printmaking Techniques

There are four main techniques artists use to make prints: relief, intaglio, lithography, and screen printing.

- **Relief printing.** In this method, the artist cuts away the sections of a surface not meant to hold ink. As a result, the image to be printed is raised from the background. In **Figure 3.10,** Elizabeth Catlett has controlled the light and dark areas of her linoleum-cut relief print by the amount she has cut away. Notice that

◀ **FIGURE 3.10** Catlett has devoted her artistic career to a socially conscious art that represents the struggles of African-Americans.

Elizabeth Catlett. *Sharecropper.* 1970. Linoleum cut on paper. 45.2 × 43 cm (17¹³⁄₁₆ × 16¹⁵⁄₁₆″). National Museum of American Art, Washington, D.C.© Elizabeth Catlett/Licensed by VAGA, New York, NY

the white lines are wider in the very light areas.

- **Intaglio** (in-**tal**-yo or in-**tal**-ee-o). This name comes from the Italian word meaning "to cut into." Intaglio is a process in which ink is forced into lines that have been cut or etched on a hard surface such as metal or wood. Then the plate's surface is wiped clean and the prints are made. You can actually feel the lines of raised ink on an intaglio print.

- **Lithography.** In lithography the image to be printed is drawn on limestone, zinc, or aluminum with a special greasy crayon or pencil. Ink is attracted to this material. When the drawing is completed, the areas that should remain blank are etched with a special solution that repels ink. Then, when the surface is inked, the greasy area alone holds the ink. Because the process is complicated, new materials are being developed to make lithography easier. There are kits for schools that use paper instead of limestone or zinc for the printing plate.

- **Screen Printing.** This is the newest method for making prints. It uses a stencil and screen as the printing plate. The stencil is placed on a fabric screen stretched across a frame. The screen is placed flat on the printing surface. Ink is pressed through the fabric screen where it is not covered by the stencil. If more than one color is used, a separate screen is made for each color. Another term for screen printing is *serigraphy.*

Activity — Making a Printing Plate

Applying Your Skills. You can make your own relief printing plate. Begin by cutting a 4-inch square from a sheet of cardboard. Cut a variety of smaller geometric shapes from the same sheet. Arrange these on the surface of the square. Form an interesting design.

Glue the shapes in place. Let them dry overnight. Apply printing ink to the surface with a brayer. Lay a sheet of paper over your inked plate. Apply pressure evenly. Carefully peel back the print.

Computer Option. Explore the Shape and Line tools in your application. Change line thickness, color menus, gradients, and opacities. Arrange several shapes to make an interesting design. Print onto color transfer paper that is made for your printer. Remember to flip the image before printing if necessary because shapes and letters may be reversed. Follow the instructions on the printing paper package to transfer your design onto paper, cloth, or another surface. (An iron sets some transfer papers while others require more elaborate equipment.)

Check Your Understanding

1. Name four of the most popular media used in drawing.
2. What are the three ingredients found in every type of paint?
3. What are the three basic steps of printmaking?
4. What is an edition?

Three-Dimensional Media

Have you ever taken a lump of clay and formed it into a bowl or an animal? If so, you were working with three-dimensional media. These media make solid forms that have height, width, and depth.

Sculpture

Sculpture is *a three-dimensional work of art.* Sculpture is art that is made to occupy space. This is one way in which sculpture is different from other kinds of art. Although objects in a drawing or painting can look quite real, the work is flat, or two-dimensional. Artists who create sculpture are called sculptors.

The Media of Sculpture

Like other artists, sculptors use a wide variety of media in their work. Sculpting media include clay, glass, plastics, wood, stone, and metal. No matter what medium is used, a sculpture will be one of two types: sculpture in the round or relief sculpture.

- **Sculpture in the round.** This type of sculpture is surrounded *on all sides* by space. Another name for sculpture in the round is *freestanding* sculpture. You can walk around sculpture in the round or turn it over in your hands to see all sides. Sculptures in the round can be realistic representations of people or objects **(Figure 3.11).** Not all freestanding sculptures have recognizable subjects, however. (See Figure 5.7 on page 102).

- **Relief sculpture.** This type of sculpture projects into space from a flat background. Relief sculptures are designed to be viewed only from one side. **Figure 3.12** shows an example of a relief sculpture attached to a smooth, gently–rounded surface. You cannot see the back of the figure. The figure protrudes out into space from the smooth surface of the vase.

Sculpting Techniques

In addition to a wide array of media, sculptors use a variety of processes. The processes include modeling, carving, casting, and assembly.

▶ **FIGURE 3.11** How do the unusual colors and materials affect the expressive quality of this sculpture?

Luis Jimenez. *Vaquero.* Modeled 1980, cast 1990. Fiberglass and epoxy. Height: 5 m (16′6″). National Museum of American Art, Washington, D.C.

▲ **FIGURE 3.12** Al Qoyawayma adds an architectural quality to his pottery by using relief elements that are forced from inside the pottery wall. He then carves details into the raised relief work.

Al Qoyawayma (Hopi). *Blanketed Figure Vase*. c. 1980. Clay pottery. Height: 27.9 cm (11″).

■ **Modeling.** In this process, a soft, pliable material is built up and shaped. Media such as clay, wax, and plaster are used in modeling. Because the sculptor gradually adds more material to build a form, modeling is referred to as an *additive* process.

■ **Carving.** In carving, the sculptor cuts, chips, or drills from a solid mass of material to create a sculpture. Material is removed until the sculpture is completed. Carving is therefore called a *subtractive* process. Wood and stone are the most common carving media.

■ **Casting.** In casting, molten metal or another substance is poured into a mold and allowed to harden. The artist duplicates a form originally molded with clay, wax, or plaster using a more permanent material. Just as in printmaking, an edition of sculptures can be made from the same mold. Once the edition is complete, the mold is destroyed. This prevents the mold from being used again and safeguards the monetary value of the sculptures that were originally cast.

■ **Assembling.** In this process, also called *constructing,* a variety of different materials are gathered and joined together to make a sculpture. One assembly process involves welding metal, but media can be glued, sewn, or otherwise fitted together. Assembling is sometimes used along with other sculpting processes. A combination of casting and assembling was used to create *Zaga* **(Figure 3.13).**

▲ **FIGURE 3.13** Graves collected natural objects and cast them in bronze at a metal foundry. She then selected certain cast objects from her collection of thousands of objects and assembled them to make her sculpture. She adds color in a very unusual manner. She uses chemicals and heat to make pigments adhere to the metal-like skin so that no details are hidden with thick paint.

Nancy Graves. *Zaga*. 1983. Cast bronze with polychrome chemical patination. 182.9 × 124.5 × 81.4 cm (72 × 49 × 32″). Nelson-Atkins Museum of Art, Kansas City, Missouri. © Nancy Graves Foundation/Licensed by VAGA, New York, NY

Crafts

Before machines were invented, people made everything by hand. Today, artists are still creating one-of-a-kind items. Some objects are created for practical use, and others are made purely for decorative purposes. Art made to be experienced visually is called *fine art.* Art made to be functional as well as visually pleasing is called *applied art.* Today the distinction between fine art and applied art is fading.

Artists are currently creating both functional and decorative craft objects. Weavings are made from natural wool, linen, silk, cotton, and manufactured fibers. Quilts are stitched from fine fabrics to be hung on the wall like paintings. Baskets are woven from natural materials such as reeds and wood slats **(Figure 3.14),** as well as manufactured fibers. Pottery is made with clay from the earth. Handmade glass objects are formed by forcing air through a tube to shape globs of melted glass. Jewelry is crafted using expensive materials such as precious stones and gold, but it can also be made using paper. As wonderful as technology has become, we still appreciate having an object that is one-of-a-kind and made by hand.

The Media of Crafts

The most commonly used craft media are clay, glass, wood, fiber, and metal. Clay and glass can be used to make plates and cups, vases, and jars. Wood can be used to make furniture or containers. Fiber is used to weave cloth and to make baskets. Metal is used to make utensils and jewelry.

Each craft contains an almost unlimited number of choices. An artist using clay can choose stoneware, earthenware, or porcelain. A weaver can select natural

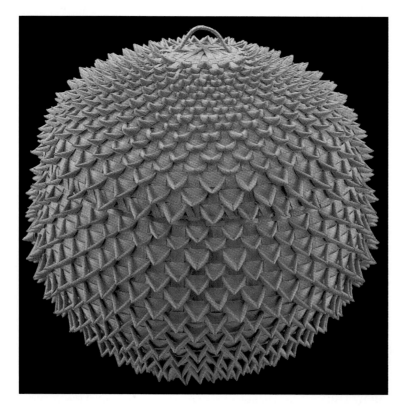

◀ **FIGURE 3.14** Imagine the skill it took to make this basket and lid perfectly round and to make each twist of the warp just the right size to create points in proportion to the shape of the basket. Notice that the points are smaller at the top and bottom and larger near the center.

Edith Bondie. *Porkypine Basket.* ca. 1975. Wood. 20 × 21.6 × 21.6 cm (7⅞ × 8½ × 8½"). National Museum of American Art, Smithsonian Institution, Washington, D.C.

► **FIGURE 3.15** This settee reminds us of an Asante stool from Africa because it incorporates animal totem forms into its structure.

Judy Kensley McKie. *Monkey Settee.* 1995. Walnut and bronze. 90.2 × 182.2 × 61 cm (35½ × 71¾ × 24″). Renwick Gallery, National Museum of American Art, Smithsonian Institution, Washington, D.C.

fibers or synthetic fibers. A woodworker can choose among oak, ash, mahogany, rosewood, ebony, cedar, and pine. What media were used to create **Figure 3.15**?

The Processes of Crafts

The techniques and processes a craft artist uses depends on the media selected. Clay, for example, can be modeled, carved, and assembled. It can also be *thrown* on a potter's wheel. Clay is finished by firing it in a *kiln,* a furnace that reaches high temperatures.

Glass can be mold-made or blown. Blown glass requires a process in which the artist, using special tools, blows air into molten glass in order to shape it.

Wood is worked using techniques such as carving and assembling, turning, and bending. In turning, a piece of wood is rotated on a machine called a lathe. The machine may have a fixed tool that shapes the piece, or the artist may use a special tool. Bending is another shaping process. A piece of wood is soaked in water or another liquid to make it pliable. Then it is slowly manipulated into place.

Fiber can be woven into cloth or baskets. It can be embroidered, sewn, or quilted. Metal can be shaped in molds or it can be cut with special shears. Pliable metals can be hammered or filed into shape. Pieces can be assembled by linking them together or by soldering them together. Soldering is a process using a handheld tool called a soldering iron that melts small areas of the metal. When the metal cools, the pieces are joined. Assembling larger pieces of metal, a process called welding, requires a larger, more powerful tool with an open flame.

Architecture

Of all the arts, architecture has the greatest impact on our daily lives. The quality of the architecture we use for shelter, for gatherings, and for worship affects the quality of our lives. Architecture is the planning and creation of buildings. Because a well-designed building is a shelter as well as a work of art, architecture is considered both an applied art and a fine art. An artist who works in the field of architecture is an architect. To be certified, an architect studies engineering because a structure must be designed to hold its own weight and withstand the physical forces placed on it. An architect also studies the visual arts in order to create buildings that are well-proportioned and pleasing to the eye. Architects

design for individuals as well as for the public. The needs of each group must be considered and met before a building can be called a success.

The Media of Architecture

From the earliest times people have been creating shelters from materials found in their natural environment. Huts constructed from sticks and bark were covered with mud. Nomadic people constructed movable shelters from wood poles and covered them with animal skins. In the north, ice was cut and formed to make shelters. In the tropics, leaves and grasses were woven together. Gradually, people developed skills to make better use of available materials for permanent structures that were used for gathering as well as shelter. People learned to make bricks by firing clay to

---

Activity — Redesigning a Familiar Building

Applying Your Skills. Architects are often hired to renovate an old structure. Look for a building in your community that you would like to see improved. Study it by making sketches from different points of view. Identify and list in your sketchbook the media that were used in the construction of the building you have selected. Think about the media you have just studied. List some that would harmonize with the surrounding buildings and the environment. Using pencil, draw one face of the building. Include the existing doors and windows. Then redesign the look of that side using the media that you believe will improve the look of the building. Use watercolors to indicate the colors of the new construction media.

Computer Option. Use a computer application to redesign the façade of a building in your community. Choose the Grids and Rulers option to guide your drawing so you can maintain scale and proportion. Consider how you can create harmony by repeating the materials, colors, or architectural features of other buildings in your community. Begin by drawing the front view. Hold down the Shift key to draw straight lines or restrict shapes. Use the copy and paste functions to make duplicates of features such as doors and windows. Save and title the line drawing. Then use your choice of brushes, textures, and gradients to simulate natural materials. Use the Save As option to retitle and save. Print and display your work.

---

make it hard. They stacked the bricks to build walls. Stonecutters develop methods for cutting stone so smoothly that one could be stacked on top of the next without anything to hold them in place **(Figure 3.16).** Others learned how to balance one long stone on top of two posts and developed the post-and-lintel method of construction (Figure 12.35, page 348). Today this is called post-and-beam construction because architects use wood or steel beams instead of stone lintels.

Later, architects learned to form an arch with stone. The arch carried the weight of walls and roofs without buckling. Arches led to vaults, or arched roofs that connect walls. Vaulted halls enabled architects to create more open space. A dome is a round roof, as if an arch had been extended into a full circle. Using more advanced construction techniques architects developed a pointed stone arch and supported it with buttresses. This allowed large openings to be made in the walls that were filled with stained-glass windows.

Wood was always a popular material, because it was plentiful. Balloon framing allowed builders to use heavy beams of wood to support thin walls. The truss supported a sloped roof. This technique is still being used today.

Technology has given us steel and reinforced concrete. Steel frames enabled us to cover the outside of skyscrapers with glass. The development of new materials has not eliminated the use of the older materials. New ways of using them are always being developed.

◄ **FIGURE 3.16**
The builders of Machu-Picchu were excellent stone masons. They cut the stones to fit together so perfectly that the buildings have survived to this day without any mortar to hold the stones in place.

David Borsky. Wall of Machu-Picchu. Photograph. Courtesy of the artist.

When Louis Sullivan built the Wainwright Building **(Figure 3.17),** he first created a large frame, or cage, made with steel beams. To cover the frame he used brick which blended in with the surrounding buildings.

An architect is concerned with the environment into which the structure will be placed as well as the purpose of the building. The success of a building is the combination of the right media with good design. The Sydney Opera House (Figure 11.1, page 286), sits on a peninsula in the bay. It looks like a ship sailing into the harbor because the architect was able to design the unusually–shaped walls using steel–reinforced concrete.

Check Your Understanding

1. What are the two main types of sculpture?
2. What are the four basic sculpting methods?
3. Define crafts. Name three categories of functional crafts.
4. Define architecture.

◀ **FIGURE 3.17** This skyscraper echoes its internal steel frame in its exterior design. Sullivan emphasized the height of the skyscraper by stressing the vertical lines that move the viewer's eyes upward, and underplaying the horizontal elements in the window area.

Louis Sullivan. Wainwright Building. St. Louis, Missouri. 1890-91.

Technological Media

Artists try to communicate ideas through their art and as they do so, they constantly seek out new media. In recent times, technological advances have allowed artists to create new and exciting forms of art. In this lesson you will learn about photography, film, video, and computer art.

Photography

Photography is *the technique of capturing optical images on light-sensitive surfaces.* Photographs are all around us. Newspapers, magazines, and books are full of them. Almost everyone has a collection of snapshots that they've taken. It is hard to imagine that photography started out as an expensive, difficult process only 150 years ago.

Although anyone can point a camera and trip the shutter, photography as art requires more than simply recording images. As photographic media and processes have improved, some photographers have begun exploring photography's potential as art. They have gone beyond simply taking pictures of interesting images. Works by Dorothea Lange **(Figure 3.18)** and other photographers are carefully composed, just as a painter composes an artwork. This artistic composition makes photography a fine art, like painting or sculpting.

In recent years some artists have combined painting and photography to create a new kind of visual expression. Look closely at **Figure 3.19.** Notice how the artist has modified a black-and-white photograph of an automobile in front of a house. The finished work combines familiar images from the real world with ideas and feelings originating in the mind of the artist.

The Media of Photography

The idea of capturing an image on film is very old. Attempts to do so date back to the Renaissance, but the first permanent photograph was not made until the nineteenth century. L.J.M.

▶ **FIGURE 3.18** Dorothea Lange did more than take a snapshot of this family. By moving her camera to get just the right image, she tells us all about the family. What does the expression on the mother's face tell you? What emotions do the children convey with their body language?

Dorothea Lange. *Migrant Mother.* 20.3 × 25.4 cm (8 × 10″). Courtesy of the Library of Congress, Washington, D.C.

◄ FIGURE 3.19 This work is based on a black-and-white photo taken by the artist. After printing it, she covered the areas she wished to stay black-and-white with rubber cement to protect them. Then she dipped the photo into an acid bath that changed the unprotected portions into tints and shades of brown. The final step was the addition of color, using paints designed for use on photographs.

Jessica Hines. *Dream Series.* Hand-colored black-and-white photograph. 40.6 × 50.8 cm (16 × 20"). Private collection.

Daguerre invented a process of creating silvery, mirrorlike images on a copper plate. This was called a daguerreotype. Daguerreotype was a time-consuming and very expensive process. In the 1850s, the wet plate method was invented. It used glass coated with chemicals to record the image, which was then transferred to paper or cardboard. As with contemporary photographs, the wet plate photos used *negatives,* the reverse image of the object photographed. Today newer and better methods of making film have been invented. The process is simpler and less expensive. Photographers have many media and processes available to affect the look of a finished photograph.

Film

A movie is like any other work of art; it is created by people for others to appreciate. When you watch a movie, you rarely see all the work that went into it. However, filmmaking is a complicated, expensive process involving many people and considerable technology.

The very first films were silent, and even with all of our technological advances, those films are still appreci-ated today for their aesthetic value. In the 1920s, sound was added. Color came next. Today, many old, faded films have been digitally enhanced by computers to restore color and improve sound. Computers have also aided filmmaking by allowing computer animation and special effects that would have been impossible in the past.

The Media of Film

Filmmaking only became possible about 100 years ago, after photography began to catch on with amateur hobbyists and professional artists. This encouraged the development of different types of film. In 1899, a crude flexible film base called celluloid was introduced. Celluloid could be used to shoot multiple images in a row. When these images were shown in a rapid sequence, they gave the illusion of movement. Early films suffered from jumpy action, flickering light, and other flaws. As cameras, film, film printers, and projectors improved, so did the quality of movies. Cinematographers—artists who use movie cameras—now have the ability to choose from many different film media and production processes to create visually exciting, artistic films.

Video

Videotape records and stores images and sounds as magnetic impulses. Patterns of light beams and wavelengths of sound are translated into electric waves, which are then imprinted magnetically on the videotape. *A system that uses electromagnetic energy to imprint both sound and pictures* is called an **analog system.**

Television studios were the first to record programs on videotape because the method was more efficient and less expensive than traditional cinematography. Gradually, videotape and video cameras made their way into homes, so that anyone could tape television broadcasts, watch movies of their choice, or make and view their own home movies.

The Media of Video

Why is videotape such a remarkable development? Videotape does not require special processing or printing. A person can record an event on videotape and immediately view the results. Video artists record the sights, sounds, and scenes of nature or they create totally new environments with moving and still images and sound. This technology allows an artist to paint a visual story or communicate a message, just like an artist who paints on canvas. Perhaps more importantly, video can be combined with the tools available on computers in order to create artwork never before possible.

Computers

A computer uses a **digital system,** or *a system that processes words and images directly as numbers or digits.* Digital systems are more precise than analog systems. Thanks to digital technology, today's computers are becoming faster and smaller. Tiny computers, called *microprocessors,* can now operate computer programs that once required a computer the size of your classroom!

Using Computers to Create Art

Software programs are computer tools for working, learning, and entertaining. With paint or draw programs, artists can draw, paint, manipulate, and design images. The artwork in **Figure 3.20** was created with a software program. More recent digital technologies, including scanning devices and virtual reality, provide even more exciting ways to stimulate an artist's imagination.

When you use a computer to create art, the art images can be stored as files in the computer's memory. Once saved, they may be opened in a new file and reworked. The advantage is that while the original art is saved, you can try as many variations as you wish, saving

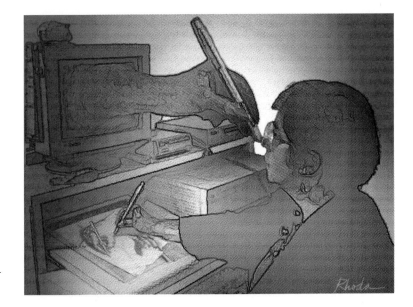

▶ **FIGURE 3.20** This artist has used humor to create a parody of Escher's drawing while making a statement about computer art. What do you think she is saying to you, the viewer?

Rhoda Grossman. *Self-Portrait After Escher.* 1992. Electronic. Salzman International, San Francisco, California.

each as a new file. You never change or lose the original work.

Most computer art applications are one of two main types: paint programs and draw programs.

- **Paint programs.** In paint programs, images are stored as bitmaps, which are a series of tiny dots, or *pixels*. The advantage is the ability to edit pixel by pixel. In general, paint programs are capable of producing more lifelike pictures than draw programs.

- **Draw programs.** In draw programs, images are stored as a series of lines and curves. Each line or curve results from a mathematical formula and is known as an object. An advantage of draw programs over paint programs is that objects can be "resized"—made larger or smaller—without distortion.

Recently, the differences between paint and draw programs have begun to blur. Many paint programs today do jobs that were once performed only by draw programs, and vice versa.

Computer Art Tools

In computer art, the physical tools that the artist actually handles are called hardware. Hardware includes equipment such as the monitor, keyboard, printer, and mouse (the point-and-click device). Along with these pieces of hardware, some other tools used by professional computer artists include the following:

- **Digital Camera.** A digital camera works like a regular camera except that the images are recorded digitally; that is, they are recorded as numbers or digits. The camera usually has a viewer that allows you to see what each picture you have taken looks like. The images a digital camera records are downloaded, or transferred, to a computer. Then they can be printed out, or they can be manipulated with special photography software programs. The digital images can be altered and enhanced in unlimited ways, and each version can be saved as a separate file.

Activity Digital Art

Applying Your Skills. Artists use computers as sketchbooks, design tools, and as painting and collage media because they can store and retrieve artwork quickly. Images can be easily combined and altered which allows the artist to explore many ideas without wasting time or materials. Compare the difference between the media. First, select drawing paper, pencil, pen, brush, and watercolor, tempera, or acrylic paint. Draw a large rectangle or circle on the paper. Explore a mood with a variety of lines made with the pencil, pen, and brush. Change length, thickness, and texture. Arrange a few lines to make a pleasing composition. Choose a color scheme and add color.

Computer Option. Now, repeat the same activity in an art application. Select a Shape tool and draw a large open rectangle or circle on the page. Explore the Pencil and Brush tools. Consider a mood or feeling. Arrange a variety of lines, changing length, thickness, shape, and texture to match this mood. Use the Eraser and Fatbit or Zoom tool, if available, to eliminate unneeded marks. When you are satisfied, title and save with your name or project. Now choose a simple color scheme. Apply color with the Bucket or Brush tools. Select the Save As command to retitle. Add a number behind the original title to indicate a new edition.

Tool	Description	Type of Program
Zoom tool	Magnifies part of painting or drawing.	Paint or Draw
Brush tool	Paints lines of different thicknesses.	Paint
Pencil tool	Draws lines and curves.	Draw
Color eraser	Changes one color to another.	Paint
Fill tool	Adds color to closed objects or shapes.	Paint or Draw
Rectangle tool	Creates rectangles and squares.	Paint or Draw

- **Stylus and graphics tablet.** In simplest terms, a stylus and graphics tablet are electronic answers to the pencil and paper. In recent years, these tools have been improved. The stylus now responds to pressure from the hand to make thick and thin lines, much like a real pencil, pen, or brush.
- **Scanner.** A scanner is a device that "reads" a printed image. It then translates the image into a language the computer can use to make a visual image on the screen or print with a printing device.

On-Screen Tools. Another category of tools that computer artists work with is on-screen tools. These mimic handheld tools used by conventional artists. On-screen tools include pencils, pens, assorted brushes, and erasers.

The set of on-screen tools varies from program to program. The table in **Figure 3.21** shows some common on-screen tools and the type of program in which each is found. It also shows the *icon*, or picture symbol, used to represent each tool.

Multi-media Art

Combining technologies on the computer is made easier by the development of **multi-media programs.** These are *computer software programs that help users design, organize, and combine text, graphics, video, and sound in one document.* With a little imagination, you can make reports, presentations, and art portfolios come alive. Multi-media art combines different media to create a new type of art. For example, an artist might scan a photograph into the computer, then use a paint or draw program to enhance it. The artist might also add sounds to the art that help evoke a feeling or communicate an idea. He or she could add text or quotations to add meaning. The artist might use a special program to make the art appear to move or to take different forms as the viewer watches. Multi-media art expands the boundaries of art by including more sensory experiences.

✓ Check Your Understanding

1. What is photography?
2. Name the kind of film that made movies possible.
3. What advantage does video have over photography?
4. What is the difference between an analog system and a digital system?
5. What is the advantage of a multi-media program?

ART CRITICISM IN ACTION

Miriam Schapiro. *Personal Appearance.* 1985. Acrylic, fabric, and paper on canvas. 215.9 × 195.6 cm (85 × 77").
Courtesy of Steinbaum Krauss Gallery, New York, New York. Collection of Mr. and Mrs. Irvin Arthur.

1 ▸ DESCRIBE What do you see?

List all the information you can find in the credit line, and then list the things that you can describe and recognize in the work. This is a clue-collecting step. If you are not sure of something, do not guess.

- How big is this work? Describe everything you recognize in the work.
- Can you tell which parts of the work were made of cut paper and which parts are painted?
- What is the subject of this work?

2 ▸ ANALYZE How is this work organized?

During this step, you will use the knowledge you learn in each chapter about the elements and principles of art to understand the composition of the work. Even though you have not studied them yet, there are some obvious questions you can answer.

- Where has Schapiro placed the figure? Does it look calm or active?
- How many places can you find squares used in this work?
- Does the background look calm or active? Explain.

3 ▸ INTERPRET What is the artist trying to communicate?

You will make guesses about the meaning of the work during this step. It is not necessary to know what the artist meant. Instead, you will decide what this image says to you.

- What is the figure doing? Why is it within all the squares?
- Who is the figure? Whom does it represent?
- Give the work a new title that sums up your feelings about it.

4 ▸ JUDGE What do you think of the work?

Now you are ready to make an aesthetic judgment about this work.

- Do you like the way the artist has made use of the materials? Can you think of other media that might be used to create a work with the same effect?
- Do you think this work is successful? Why or why not? Use one or more of the theories of art explained in Chapter 2 to defend your decision.

Pottery and Clay

◀ **FIGURE 3.23**

Life-size clay soldiers from the tomb of the first Emperor of a united China, Qin Shihuangdi (c. 246–210 B.C.) discovered in 1974. Terra–cotta. Xian, China.

About 25 years ago, a group of men were digging a well in central China when they uncovered the ancient, enormous tomb of China's first emperor. Imagine the well diggers' astonishment when they found a standing army of life-size clay soldiers, horses, and attendants—at least 7,000 figures in all!

Clay is the perfect medium for such an ambitious artistic project because it can be molded and designed easily. The artist's ability to control and manipulate the density of clay makes possible the creation of large, sturdy pieces. The firing process hardens clay into a permanent, tightly–bonded substance, allowing the sculpture or ceramic work to withstand the test of time, as these figures have.

Clay is produced on the Earth's surface by the weathering and erosion of rocks. The three elements that make up over 80 percent of the Earth also come together in clay: oxygen, silicon, and aluminum. Pottery clay is approximately 40 percent aluminum oxide, 46 percent silicon oxide, and 14 percent water. The presence or absence of particular minerals or impurities in clay makes possible the many variations in pottery, ranging from delicate porcelain Chinese vases to solid Hopi earthenware pots.

Making the Connection

1. Why do you think the people who buried the first emperor of China placed so many life-size statues in his tomb?
2. What allows for the variations in pottery?
3. Using a science textbook, an encyclopedia, or online resources, find out more about oxygen, silicon, and aluminum. Write down your findings.

Building Vocabulary

On a separate sheet of paper, write the term that best matches each definition given below.

1. Any material used to create art.
2. The use of light and dark values to create the illusion of form.
3. A process in which an artist repeatedly transfers an original image from one prepared surface to another.
4. The impression created on a surface by a printing plate.
5. A copy of a work of art.
6. All the prints made from the same plate or set of plates.
7. A three-dimensional work of art.
8. The technique of capturing optical images on light-sensitive surfaces.
9. A system that uses electromagnetic energy to imprint both sound and pictures.
10. A system that processes words and images directly as numbers or digits.
11. Computer software programs that help users design, organize, and combine text, graphics, video, and sound in one document.

Reviewing Art Facts

Answer the following questions using complete sentences.

1. What is the difference between two- and three-dimensional art?
2. Describe the four shading techniques.
3. Name and define the three main ingredients of paint.
4. What are the three basic steps of printmaking?
5. What is the difference between sculpture in the round and relief sculpture?
6. Why are crafts called the applied arts?
7. How is videotape technology an improvement over cinematography?
8. What are the similarities and differences between paint and draw programs?

Thinking Critically About Art

1. **Analyze.** List all the art media you have used. Which media do you prefer? Write a brief paragraph including two or more reasons for your personal preference.
2. **Compare and contrast.** Study Figures 3.13 (page 51), 3.14 (page 52) and 3.15 (page 53). List the similarities you find in all three artworks. Then identify the qualities that makes each work of art different from the others.
3. **Analyze.** Compare Figures 3.3 and 3.4 on page 43. Berman, the costume designer, based his designs on Canaletto's drawings of eighteenth-century Venice. Look at the Berman costume. Can you see this influence? Explain your answer.

Use the Performing Arts Handbook, page 415, to see how choreographer Merce Cunningham uses the computer and other technology to help him create his renowned ballets.

inter NET CONNECTION Take a trip through Glencoe's Fine Arts Site on the World Wide Web. Explore **Glencoe Student Galleria** and see student artworks that were created in two- and three-dimensional media. Then find out how you can submit your own quality works of art for display on the Internet. Visit us at **www.glencoe.com/sec/art**

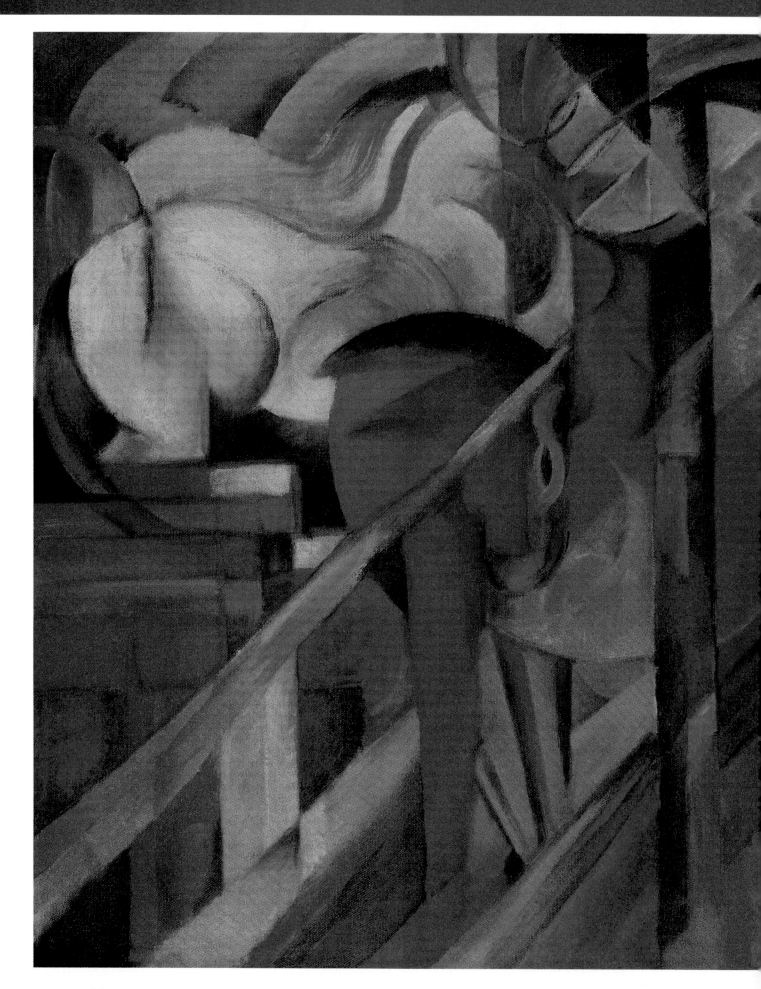

UNIT 2

THE ELEMENTS OF ART

"Is there a more mysterious idea for an artist than to imagine how nature is reflected in the eyes of an animal?**"**

Franz Marc
1880–1916

◄

Franz Marc. Detail from *Stables* (inset). 1913.
Oil on canvas. 73.6 x 157.5 cm (29 x 61").
Solomon R. Guggenheim Museum, New
York, New York.

67

▶ **FIGURE 4.1** This painting of the Brooklyn Bridge was one panel in a series of five paintings that Joseph Stella created as a visual symphony expressing the excitement and energy of New York City. He tried to capture the feeling of steel skyscrapers with straight lines and show light and movement with dynamic, flowing curves.

Joseph Stella. *The Voice of the City of New York Interpreted: The Bridge.* 1920–1922. Oil and tempera on canvas. 224.8 × 137.2 cm (88½ × 54″). Collection of the Newark Museum, Newark, New Jersey.

CHAPTER 4

Line

Lines are everywhere. You use lines to write words, numbers, and symbols. You read lines of printed words. The lines on a map help you find the best route from one place to another. You stand in line to get into a movie theater. When actors are studying a new role, they say they are memorizing their lines. You use lines to draw pictures.

The painting *The Voice of the City of New York Interpreted: The Bridge* **(Figure 4.1)** is by Joseph Stella, an Italian-American artist who came to the United States at the beginning of the twentieth century. He was obsessed by the movement and lights of New York City, and he painted several versions of the Brooklyn Bridge. In this work, you can see how the sweeping lines of the suspension cables dominate the scene. Through the Gothic arches of the great pylons that hold the cables you can see abstractions of skyscrapers. Stella uses many different kinds of line and line variations to capture the excitement of the city. Can you find the lines that represent walkways for pedestrians, roadways for cars, and train tracks for the subway?

OBJECTIVES

After completing this chapter, you will be able to:

- Observe the lines in your environment more closely.
- Name the different kinds of lines.
- Tell the five ways lines can vary in appearance.
- Use lines to change values.
- Understand the expressive qualities or meanings of different lines in works of art.
- Use lines to make contour, gesture, and calligraphic drawings.

WORDS TO KNOW

line
dimension
outline
implied lines
value
crosshatching
contour line
gesture
calligraphy

Developing Your PORTFOLIO

To keep them in order, each entry in your portfolio should be marked clearly for identification. Make sure each piece includes your name and the date you completed the artwork. Any notes about the assignment are valuable and should be kept with your artwork. Make it a point to use the names of the elements of art as you write about your artwork. That way you will demonstrate your growth as an artist and communicate to your readers in the language of art.

The Element of Line

Lines are everywhere. You can see lines in the grain of a piece of wood or in the cracks on a sidewalk. Lines are used to create words, numbers, and symbols. They are also used to create art. In drawing, **line** is *an element of art that is the path of a moving point through space.*

What Is Line?

Artists use line to lead your eyes through a work of art. This is because it takes movement to make a line. When you see a line, your eyes usually follow its movement. Lines can lead your eyes into, around, and out of visual images, as in the painting in **Figure 4.2.** Notice how the artist uses the line of the highway to pull your eyes into the artwork.

A line has width as well as length, but usually the width of a line is very small compared with its length. In fact, a line is thought of as being one-dimensional. Its one dimension is length. **Dimension** means *the amount of space an object takes up in one direction.* Two-dimensional objects have height as well as width. A painting is two-dimensional. Three-dimensional objects have height, width, and depth. A sculpture is three-dimensional. You will learn more about dimensions in the next chapter when you study shape, form, and space.

Artists create lines in many ways. A line can be drawn on paper with a pencil or scratched into wet clay with a stick. Of

▲ **FIGURE 4.2** The artist has used the line of the highway to pull your eyes into and through this artwork. Identify the kinds of line the artist has used in this painting. How do they convey movement and feeling?

Yvonne Jacquette. *Town of Skowhegan, Maine V.* 1988. Oil on canvas. 198.6 × 163 cm (78³⁄₁₆ × 64¹⁄₁₆″). Courtesy DC Moore Gallery, NYC.

course, the world is full of lines that were not drawn with a tool. Some thin, solid objects look like lines. Examples are tree trunks, yarn, spiderwebs, and wires **(Figure 4.3).** These items look like lines because length is their most important dimension.

Some lines that we think we see in nature really do not exist. For instance, when you look at the edges of shapes, you think of lines. In the photo of the dogwood blossom **(Figure 4.4),** notice that there are no black lines around the outside of each petal. However, in a drawing of that same blossom in **Figure 4.5,** lines are used to show the edges of each shape. *A line that shows or creates the outer edges of a shape* is an **outline**.

Implied lines are *a series of points that the viewer's eyes automatically connect.* Implied lines are suggested rather than real lines. A series of dots or dashes, a line of machine stitches, or a trail of wet footprints can create an implied line. A group of shapes arranged in a row can also create an implied line. In **Figure 4.6** on page 72, Abrasha has created a Hanukkah menorah that holds nine cone-shaped candles. The round tops of the cones create an implied line that leads your eyes across the top of the menorah.

▲ **FIGURE 4.3** What lines do you see around you?

▲ **FIGURE 4.4** What edges do you see?

▲ **FIGURE 4.5** Student work. How have the edges on this picture been created?

Abrasha. *Hanukkah Menorah.* 1995. Fabricated stainless steel, silver, and gold. 17.5 × 43.8 × 9.8 cm (6⅞ × 17¼ × 2⅞″). Renwick Gallery, National Museum of American Art, Smithsonian Institution, Washington, D.C.

Kinds of Lines

There are five basic kinds of lines: vertical, horizontal, diagonal, curved, and zigzag.

Vertical lines **(Figure 4.7)** move straight up and down—they do not lean at all. A vertical line drawn on a piece of paper is perpendicular to the bottom edge of the paper. It is also perpendicular to the horizon (the line where earth and sky seem to meet). When you stand up straight, your body forms a vertical line.

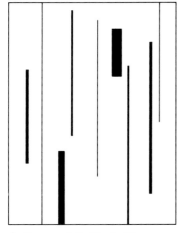

▲ **FIGURE 4.7** Vertical lines move straight up and down.

Horizontal lines **(Figure 4.8)** are parallel to the horizon. They do not slant. When you lie flat on the floor, your body forms a horizontal line.

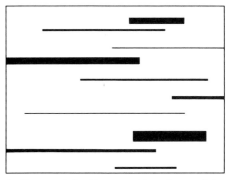

▲ **FIGURE 4.8** Horizontal lines lie parallel to the horizon.

Diagonal lines **(Figure 4.9)** slant. Diagonals are somewhere between a vertical and a horizontal line. Diagonals look as if they are either rising or falling. Imagine you are standing straight up; then, with your body stiff, you fall to the floor. At any point during your fall, your body forms a diagonal line.

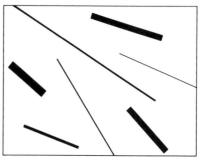

▲ **FIGURE 4.9** Diagonal lines slant.

Zigzag lines **(Figure 4.10)** are made from a combination of diagonal lines. The diagonals form angles and change direction suddenly.

▲ **FIGURE 4.10** Zigzag lines are combinations of diagonals.

Curved lines **(Figure 4.11)** change direction gradually. When you draw wiggly lines, you are putting together a series of curves. Other kinds of curved lines form spirals and circles.

▲ **FIGURE 4.11** Curved lines change direction gradually.

Activity Identifying Lines

Applying Your Skills. Choose one of the following paintings from this chapter: Figure 4.1, 4.12, 4.16, 4.18, or 4.19. Diagram the lines of the painting. Use green for verticals, blue for horizontals, red for diagonals, and violet for curves. Place your diagram on display. Can your classmates identify the painting you represented by looking at the colors?

Computer Option. Use the Line tool to create a series of drawings to illustrate each of the five line types. Vary the widths and lengths of your lines. You may also choose to vary patterns and colors. Label each drawing's line type.

Line Variation

Lines vary in appearance in five major ways:

- **Length.** Lines can be long or short.

- **Width.** Lines can be thick or thin.

- **Texture.** Lines can be rough or smooth.

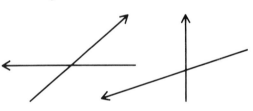

- **Direction.** Lines can move in any direction, such as vertical, horizontal, or diagonal.

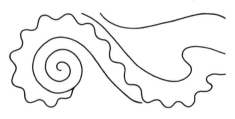

- **Degree of curve.** Lines can curve gradually or not at all, become wavy, or form spirals.

These five variations can be combined in many, many ways. You can make long, wide lines; rough, short lines; and smooth, curved lines.

When Rouault was a boy he was apprenticed to a maker of stained glass. The thick black lines surrounding bright colors in his paintings remind the viewer of stained-glass windows.

Georges Rouault. *Christ and the Apostles.* 1937–38. Oil on canvas. 64.3 × 99.4 cm (25¼ × 39⅛"). The Metropolitan Museum of Art, New York, New York. The Jacques and Natasha Gelman Collection.

▲ **FIGURE 4.13** Although this painting is called a still life, it seems to have movement and activity. This is because of the artist's use of line. How many different line directions and line variations can you find in this painting? Describe them.

Alice Neel. *Still Life, Rose of Sharon.* 1973. Oil on canvas. 101.9 × 76.5 cm (40 × 30"). Collection of Whitney Museum of American Art, New York, New York. Arthur M. Bullowa Bequest.

The media, tools, and surfaces used to make lines affect the way a line looks. As with the combination of various line types, a multitude of possible effects can be created. Some common materials used by artists to make lines are graphite, chalk, crayon, ink, and paint. The material is applied by using a tool. Some tools used for making lines include pencils, markers, pens, brushes, and scissors.

Artists use different tools and materials to create different types of lines. For example, a line drawn with chalk on a chalkboard looks smoother than a line drawn with chalk on a sidewalk. Some artists have discovered very unusual ways of using line, as shown in **Figures 4.12** and **4.13**. In **Figure 4.14**, the artist has used many line types and variations.

Line Types and Variations

In this painting, the artist has used five different kinds of line and many line variations. Can you find other examples of line and line variation combinations?

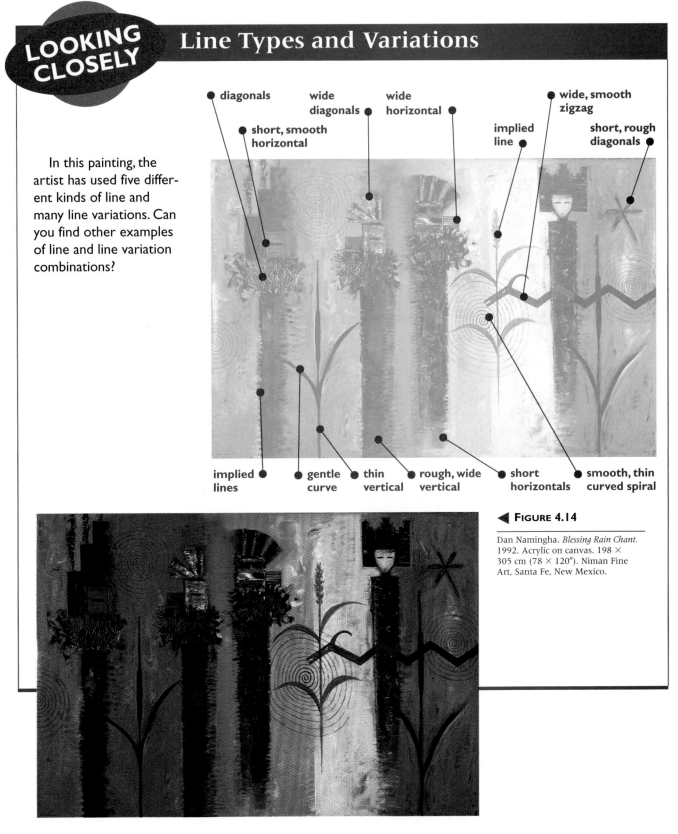

diagonals

short, smooth horizontal

wide diagonals

wide horizontal

implied line

wide, smooth zigzag

short, rough diagonals

implied lines

gentle curve

thin vertical

rough, wide vertical

short horizontals

smooth, thin curved spiral

◀ **FIGURE 4.14**

Dan Namingha. *Blessing Rain Chant.* 1992. Acrylic on canvas. 198 × 305 cm (78 × 120″). Niman Fine Art, Santa Fe, New Mexico.

Line and Value

Value is *the element of art that describes the darkness or lightness of an object.* Value depends on how much light a surface reflects. A surface has a dark value if it reflects little light. It has a light value if it reflects a lot of light. Every time you make a pencil mark on a piece of white paper, you are creating a line with a certain value. The harder you press, the darker the value. A series of closely placed lines can create areas of dark value. The lines may be parallel or they may cross one another. **Crosshatching** is *the technique of using crossed lines for shading.*

The values that line groups create depend on four factors: the number of lines, the size of the spaces between the lines, the media, and the tools. A soft pencil (2B, 4B) makes a wide, dark line. A hard pencil (2H, 4H) makes a thin, gray line. A crayon stroked over a rough surface makes a broken line. A crayon stroked over smooth paper makes a solid line.

Look at the Dürer drawing in **Figure 4.15.** Use a magnifying glass to study the way Dürer has used line combinations to create dark and light values.

▲ **FIGURE 4.15** The artist has used line to create this drawing. Identify the areas where the artist has used crosshatching to indicate shading. What kinds of line variation has Dürer used?

Activity | Using Line to Create Value

Applying Your Skills. Fold a sheet of white drawing paper into nine squares. In each square use a different combination of parallel or crosshatched lines to create a different value. Try a variety of pencils, from hard 2H to soft 4B lead. Try quill pens, ballpoint pens, and felt-tip pens. Think of some other tools and materials to use.

Computer Option. Use the Line tool to draw three diagonal lines (that are not parallel) from screen edge to screen edge. This will divide your screen into six or seven sections. Fill each section with lines. Vary the spacing of the lines by placing them close together in one section and farther apart in another. Lines can be crosshatched. You can choose the Patterns palette and fill the sections by using the Fill Bucket tool, or create your own patterns. Use only black and white. Notice that the value of the area darkens as lines are placed close together and lightens when lines are farther apart.

☑ Check Your Understanding

1. How is line defined in drawing?
2. What are the five basic kinds of lines?
3. In what five ways do lines vary in appearance?
4. Describe the crosshatching technique.

The Expressive Qualities of Line

Depending on its direction, a line can express different ideas or feelings. This is why line is an important element in the language of art. Vertical lines can make certain objects look taller. For example, vertical lines on wallpaper can make low ceilings seem higher. Clothing designers use vertical lines to make short people look taller and heavy people look thinner.

Line Movement

Vertical lines are static, or inactive. They appear to be at rest. For this reason, they express stability. Artists use them to show dignity, poise, stiffness, and formality, as in Figure 4.14 on page 75.

Horizontal lines are also static. They express feelings of peace, rest, quiet, and stability, as in **Figure 4.16.** They give a feeling of permanence or solidarity. Because we stand on solid horizontal ground, horizontal lines make us feel content, relaxed, and calm.

Because curved lines change direction, they express activity. How much activity they express depends on the type and direction of the curve. The less active the curve, the calmer the feeling. Spiral

▲ **FIGURE 4.16**   Strong horizontal lines create a sense of calm on this empty street. As you look at this painting, you get the feeling that everyone is sleeping peacefully. How many real and how many implied horizontal lines can you find in this painting?

Edward Hopper. *Early Sunday Morning.* 1930. Oil on canvas. 89.2 × 152.4 cm (35 × 60″). Collection of Whitney Museum of American Art, New York, New York. Purchase, with funds from Gertrude Vanderbilt Whitney. (31.426)

curves wind around a central point. They are hypnotic and draw the eye to their center. Curved lines are often used in decorative arts to suggest a feeling of luxury, as in **Figure 4.17.**

Diagonal lines express instability, tension, activity, and excitement, as shown in **Figure 4.18.** Since they can appear to be either falling or rising, they sometimes make a viewer feel uncomfortable. Artists use them to add tension or to create an exciting mood. However, when two diagonals meet and seem to support each other, as in the roof of a house, they appear more stable.

Zigzag lines create confusion. They are extremely active and may evoke feelings of excitement **(Figure 4.19,** page 80**)** and nervousness. The degree of intensity is indicated by the direction of the zigzag. Zigzags that move horizontally, such as those across the top of a picket fence, are less active than the irregular zigzags of a streak of lightning.

Activity — Using Lines Expressively

Applying Your Skills. Choose two words from the following list:

swimming	burning	praying
rocking	flowing	jumping
marching	running	growing
dancing	crawling	laughing
wagging	writing	flying

On separate sheets of paper, illustrate the words you have chosen by using line movement only. Do not draw objects.

Choose the medium you think will work best. When you are finished, write the words on the back of each paper. Ask your classmates to look at the lines and guess which words you have illustrated.

Computer Option. Use the Line tool to make two drawings using lines. Let one drawing illustrate quiet, calm piano music, and let the other illustrate loud rock music.

▲ **Figure 4.18** In this print every line that should be static is diagonal. Look at the window, the lamp, the rug, the floor planks, and the fiddler's bench. The diagonal lines fill the work with a sense of excitement. Not only the people but also every corner of the room seems to be alive and dancing to the music of the fiddler.

Thomas Hart Benton. *Country Dance.* 1929. Oil on gessoed canvas. 76.2 × 63.5 cm (30 × 25″). Private collection.
© T.H. Benton and R.P. Benton Testamentary Trusts/Licensed by VAGA, New York, NY

American, 1917–

Jacob Lawrence was born in Atlantic City, New Jersey, in 1917. When he was 12, his family moved to Harlem in New York City. The move would have a great impact on his growth as an artist.

The Harlem Renaissance of the 1920s had attracted many talented minority artists from all over the world, and many still remained in Harlem during the 1930s. These artists served as Lawrence's inspiration.

Lawrence sought every opportunity he could to learn about art. He listened to the Harlem artists as they talked in their studios. The 135th Street Public Library, which he visited often, always had pieces of African sculpture on display. His many trips to the Metropolitan Museum of Art gave him a strong background in art history.

Lawrence became fascinated with black history and its heroic figures. He took as his subjects such important people as Toussaint L'Ouverture, Harriet Tubman, and Frederick Douglass. Lawrence often found he could not express all he wanted to say in just a single picture. Therefore, he often made series of paintings to tell the whole story. In this way, he used his art to convey his ideas about the heritage of African-Americans.

▲ **FIGURE 4.19** The artist has used line to show the movement of the children. Look at their arms, legs, and feet. What kinds of lines do you see? How has Lawrence used line to create a feeling of movement and excitement?

Jacob Lawrence. *Children at Play.* 1947. Tempera on Masonite panel. 50.8 × 60.9 cm (20 × 24″). Georgia Museum of Art, University of Georgia, Athens, Georgia. Eva Underhill Holbrook Memorial Collection of American Art, Gift of Alfred H. Holbrook.

Contour Drawing

A **contour line** *defines the edges and surface ridges of an object.* A contour line also creates a boundary separating one area from another. Learning how to contour draw will add to your drawing skills as well as to your ability to observe and understand objects. See the examples in **Figure 4.20** and **Figure 4.21.**

When drawing contours, let your eyes follow the contour of the object you are drawing. Move your pencil at the same speed as your eyes. Do not lift the pencil from the paper. The line should be continuous. Draw the line slowly and with care. Concentrate in order to draw accurately. See the Technique Tip 1 on page 428 in the Handbook for help in making contour drawings.

◀ **FIGURE 4.20** Andrews indicates that this scholar is concentrating deeply by accenting the head with lines to indicate the wrinkles of thought. He leaves the rest of the scene, except for the book, very simple.

Benny Andrews. *The Scholar.* 1974. Pen and ink on paper. 30 × 23 cm (12 × 9″). Private collection.

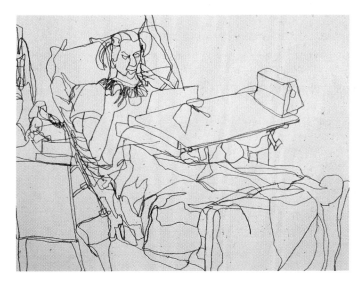

◀ **FIGURE 4.21** Student work. Notice how the line flows through this hospital scene. Look at the difference between the busy zigzag lines that describe the wrinkles in the sheet and the few lines that define the person's face.

Activity — Using Contour Lines

Applying Your Skills. Set up a group of three shoes in an interesting, overlapping composition. Arrange them at different angles so you can view them sideways, head-on, from the top, and from the back. Use a black marker to do a contour line drawing of all the shoes. Use only line. Do not color or shade the drawing. Use line to add details such as laces, stitches, patches, and holes.

Computer Option. Sit at your computer, turn sideways, and look down. Use the Line tool to draw your feet, legs, and free hand. You may start at the feet and work your way up toward your lap, or vice versa. Use the mouse just as you would use a pencil. Be sure to start your drawing near the edge of your screen so you will have room for the entire picture.

Tintoretto describes the gesture and bulk of this figure with just a few rough lines. You can sense the movement of the figure through the looseness of the quickly drawn lines. Why was it unnecessary for the artist to add more detail?

Jacopo Tintoretto. *Standing Youth with His Arm Raised, Seen from Behind*. Black chalk on laid paper. 36.3 × 21.9 cm (14¼ × 8⅝"). National Gallery of Art, Washington, D.C. © 1998 Board of Trustees. Ailsa Mellon Bruce Fund.

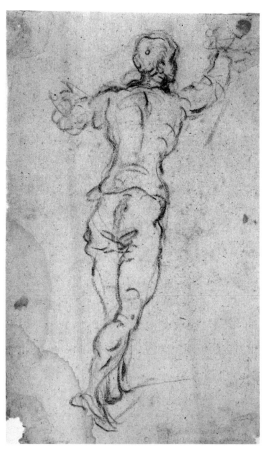

Gesture Drawing

A **gesture** is *an expressive movement.* The purpose of drawing gestures is to capture the feeling of motion. A gesture drawing uses very little detail. (See **Figures 4.22** and **4.23**).

Lines showing gestures are drawn quickly. They should be sketched freely and loosely—even recklessly—in order to capture movement. Unlike contours, they represent the interior of an object. Your gesture drawings may look like scribbles at first, but this is acceptable. Concentrate on showing position and movement.

Activity | **Creating Gesture Drawings**

Applying Your Skills. Make a series of gesture drawings. (See the Technique Tip on page 428 in the Handbook.) Classmates should take turns posing for one another. Start with thirty-second poses. Shorten the time by five seconds for each pose until the pose is held for only ten seconds. Have the model twist, turn, bend, and kick, trying to avoid doing the same thing twice.

Computer Option. Choose a round, medium-size Brush or Pencil tool. Sit at the computer station, turn sideways, and look at other students who are modeling for gesture drawing. They will be changing positions every 20 or 30 seconds. Try to capture the feeling of motion, not detail. Change color each time the model changes positions. Some of your drawings will overlap.

▶ **FIGURE 4.23**
The artist used a brush and paint to create this gesture oil sketch. Compare it to Figure 4.22. Describe the similarities and differences between the two pieces of art. Does this painting have more detail?

Audrey Flack. *Self-Portrait: The Memory*. 1958. Oil on canvas. 127 × 86.4 cm (50 × 34"). Miami University Art Museum, Oxford, Ohio. Gift of the artist.

Calligraphic Drawing

The word **calligraphy** means *beautiful handwriting*. Calligraphy is often associated with Asian writing and art. In China and Japan, calligraphy is used to form *characters* that represent the language. However, characters are more than just a letter of the alphabet. They are like pictures. They can represent an idea, an object, or a verbal sound. The Chinese and Japanese use the same types of calligraphic lines and brushstrokes in their paintings **(Figure 4.24)**. In fact, in the Chinese language, the words *writing* and *painting* are represented by the same character.

Calligraphic lines are usually made with brushstrokes that change from thin to thick in one stroke. To make a very thin line, use the tip of the brush. As you press on the brush and more of it touches the paper, the line becomes wider. (See Technique Tip 3 on page 428 in the Handbook.)

Activity — Calligraphic Lines

Applying Your Skills. Practice making calligraphic lines with ink or watercolor paint. Use round, pointed brushes, both thin and thick. Also, try bamboo brushes. Next, use a watercolor brush and ink or watercolor paint to make a series of five calligraphic studies of one natural object, such as a leaf or a vegetable.

Computer Option. Research either Egyptian hieroglyphics or Southwestern pictographs to gain information about "picture writing." Create your own picture writing by making up symbols. Use any computer tools and options available. Remember that the Cut and Paste options are helpful when you want to repeat a symbol without redrawing it.

☑ Check Your Understanding

1. What do vertical and horizontal lines express?
2. How are contour drawings and gesture drawings different?
3. What type of artwork is often associated with calligraphy?

▲ **FIGURE 4.24** Gu Mei was a famous singer, poet, and painter of landscapes and ink orchids. She created this long handscroll containing three sections depicting orchids and rocks. Notice the long curving lines have been made with one brushstroke. Where else can you find lines that seem to have been painted with one brushstroke?

Gu Mei, *Orchids and Rocks.* 1644. Ming dynasty. Detail of handscroll. Ink on paper. 27 × 170.8 cm (10⅝ × 67¼″). Arthur M. Sackler Gallery, Smithsonian Institution, Washington, D.C. Arthur M. Sackler Collection.

Contour Wire Sculpture

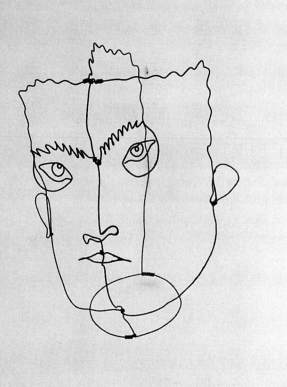

▲ FIGURE 4.25

Alexander Calder. *Varese*. 1931. Wire. 34.2 × 34.9 × 31.1 cm (13½ × 13¾ 12½"). Whitney Museum of American Art, New York, New York. Collection of Whitney Museum of American Art, New York, New York. 50th Anniversary Gift of Mrs. Louise Varèse in honor of Gertrude Vanderbilt Whitney. (80.25)

SUPPLIES

- Sketchbook and pencil
- Needle-nose pliers
- Wire cutter
- Pliable wire

Optional:

- Small block of wood
- Staple gun or staple nail and hammer
- String

Alexander Calder grew up in the studios of his parents, who were both artists. As a child, Calder made spiral-wire jewelry for his sister's dolls. This family atmosphere of creativity sparked his enthusiasm for art and led him to invent mobile sculpture and wire-line sculptures such as *Varese* **(Figure 4.25).**

While attending the Art Students' League in New York City, Calder would go out into the streets and rapidly sketch people as they passed by. He was well known for his skill in capturing a sense of movement with a single, unbroken line. In these simple contour drawings, he captured the essential characteristics of his subjects. He was able to transfer that talent to sculpture.

As Calder experimented with wire sculptures, his figures became three-dimensional forms drawn in space by wire lines. He made animals inspired by his childhood fascination with the circus, and he created portraits of people such as *Varese*. Many of his wire figures were humorous. Each sculpture drew attention from every angle.

Try your hand at wire sculpture and create a lively and interesting three-dimensional figure.

What You Will Learn

You will design and create a three-dimensional sculpture that defines space and shape through the movement of a wire line through space. Make your contour wire sculpture look interesting from every point of view. Base this sculpture on your own series of contour drawings of a single object. Prepare your finished work for display.

Creating

Brainstorm with classmates to identify objects for this project. Some possibilities are a houseplant, a bicycle, an animal, a person, or a head. Choose something that is interesting to you and that you can observe in person. Do not use a photograph. Study the photo of Calder's wire sculpture. Notice how the wire is used.

Step 1 Make a series of three or more contour studies of the object. Make each drawing from a different point of view.

Step 2 Collect your materials and experiment with some scrap wire. Practice using the tools to bend, twist, loop, and cut the wire so that you understand the way the wire behaves.

Step 3 Create your wire sculpture based on the drawings you have made. Work on all sides of the sculpture so that it looks interesting from every point of view.

Step 4 To prepare your work for display, staple or nail it to a small block of wood, hang it with string from a support, or invent a method of display.

EVALUATING YOUR WORK

▶ **DESCRIBE** Name the object you chose as the subject of your wire sculpture. How many contour line drawings of the object did you make? List the contour line variations you used to create the outlines and ridges of your sculpture. How did you prepare your finished work for display?

▶ **ANALYZE** Do the lines of your work follow the contours and ridges of the object you chose? Is the work interesting from every angle?

▶ **INTERPRET** What kind of mood is created by the use of line in three-dimensional space? Describe the difference between the look of the two-dimensional contour line drawings and the three-dimensional wire sculpture. Give your work a title.

▶ **JUDGE** Have you created a three-dimensional contour sculpture that is interesting from all sides and angles? Does your work successfully represent the object you chose? Is there anything you would change to make the work more successful? Which aesthetic theory would be the best to judge your work?

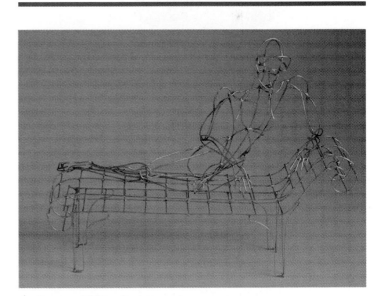

▲ **FIGURE 4.25A** Student work.

Imagination Landscape

L ook at *Amplitude* **(Figure 4.26)** and turn your imagination loose. What might this landscape be? Is it a landscape or a seascape? Can you identify mountains, plains, waves, sky? What does the sphere in the rectangle represent? How has the artist used line to create this landscape?

Carolyn Clive was driving through the Georgia countryside one bleak fall day. "The leaves had fallen and the crops were in. I looked out over the land and told myself, 'I don't know what I'm going to do, but I'm going to capture the spirit of this land.'"

Clive developed her own stenciling technique for working with oil paints and used line and value changes to create her abstract landscape. Notice how she has combined geometric shapes with flowing, overlapping waves of color. Observe how she has brought parts of the design outside the image area to provide added interest.

What You Will Learn

In this project, you will use torn-paper stencils to create an imaginary landscape. Use the stencils to create the land mass edges. Then add objects or figures to the landscape.

Creating

Study the stencil painting by Carolyn Clive. Notice how the edges of the shapes are dark on one side and light on the other. The artist did this by holding a stencil in place and pulling oil color gently from the edge of the stencil into the shape with a stippling brush.

▲ **FIGURE 4.26**

Carolyn Clive. *Amplitude.* 1987. Oil paint used with stencil brush and torn paper stencil on paper. 61 × 46 cm (24 × 18″). Collection of the artist.

SUPPLIES

- **Sketchbook**
- **Oil pastels**
- **Large sheet of white paper**
- **Paper towels**
- **Newspaper for tearing into stencils**
- **Scissors (optional)**

Step 1 First, practice the torn-stencil technique in your sketchbook. Tear a 9 × 6 inch piece of newspaper to create a rough, curving edge that will be your stencil. Draw a heavy line of oil pastel along the rough edge of the stencil. With one hand, hold the stencil firmly on a page of your sketchbook. With the other hand, use a piece of paper towel to pull the color from the stencil onto the paper. Experiment with different techniques until you feel comfortable. Try mixing colors. Compare your results with those of your classmates. Discuss the different effects you have created. For variety, try cutting the edge of your stencil with scissors.

Step 2 Based on your findings from the experiments, make some rough plans in your sketchbook for the final work. Choose your best idea. Now you are ready to create your landscape.

Step 3 Using newspaper or other scratch paper, tear or cut stencils for your finished work. Choose the colors you will use. In order to keep from smudging the pastel lines, work from the top of your page toward the bottom edge. Draw a very heavy line of oil pastel along the edge of your first stencil. Hold the stencil firmly in place and pull the oil pastel color from the stencil onto the large sheet of paper. Repeat this step until you have created the land masses you want.

Step 4 Give your work a title. Mount or mat your finished work for display.

EVALUATING YOUR WORK

▶ **DESCRIBE** Tell what kind of a landscape you have created.

▶ **ANALYZE** How did you create your stencils? What kinds of lines make up the edges of your land masses? How did the stencil technique you used to pull the color from the stencil to the paper affect the look of your work?

▶ **INTERPRET** Describe the mood of your imagination landscape. Did the stencil technique you used contribute to the mood?

▶ **JUDGE** Which aesthetic theory would be best to judge your work? Do you think this work is successful? Is there anything you would change to make it more successful?

▲ **FIGURE 4.26A** Student work.

Drawing Expressing Movement

▲ **FIGURE 4.27**

William H. Johnson. *Jitterbugs IV*. c. 1941. Tempera and ink with pencil on paper. 32.7 × 27.3 cm (12⅞ × 10¾"). National Museum of American Art, Smithsonian Institution, Washington, D.C.

In *Jitterbugs IV* **(Figure 4.27)**, William H. Johnson used diagonal lines to provide energetic movement. Although his dancers are abstract, simple figures, they move. For contrast he used vertical and horizontal lines to show stable, unmoving objects.

Johnson is considered a major African-American artist. He integrated the customs and cultures of New York, Europe, and North Africa into his African-American heritage, finally settling on the abstract forms and limited color palette you see here. In *Jitterbugs IV* Johnson used line and simple shapes to show the expressive movements of the jitterbug dance craze of the 1940s.

What You Will Learn

You will create a drawing that expresses the linear movement of people involved in energetic action. Emphasize the lines that express movement. Base the figures on gesture drawings you make while observing real people in action. If you wish, you may create contrast between the active figures and the background by using static lines for the background objects.

SUPPLIES

- Sketchbook, pencil, and eraser
- Large sheet of white paper
- Colored pencils or crayons
- Watercolor paints
- Variety of watercolor brushes

Creating

Study the painting by William H. Johnson. Notice how he has represented two dancing people with a few geometric shapes and many diagonal lines. Can you find the floor, the drum, and the drumsticks? Observe how the lines of the floor under the dancers are diagonal, while the rest of the floor remains vertical and static.

Step 1 Choose an energetic activity that you could represent using active lines. Ask a classmate to act out the movement of the activity so that you can make several gesture drawings in your sketchbook.

Step 2 Study your sketches. Decide which line directions will best express the movement of the activity. Will you use zigzag, or curved lines? Simplify the figures in your gesture drawings using the lines you have chosen.

Step 3 Decide which objects you will use for the background. Remember that you may use static lines for these objects. Sketch your finished plan on white paper.

Step 4 Go over the lines of your composition with colored pencils or crayons. Press hard to make the colors bright. Vary the lines. Emphasize the action lines by drawing them wide and using bold colors. Make the other lines thinner with softer colors.

Step 5 Color the shapes between the lines and the spaces around the figures with watercolor paints (see Technique Tip 12 on page 432 in the Handbook). Mount or mat the finished work for display.

EVALUATING YOUR WORK

▶ **DESCRIBE** Which energetic action did you choose as the subject of your drawing? Did you make gesture drawings of a real person acting out that movement? How many gesture drawings did you make? How many figures did you put in your finished work? Did you use any objects for the background?

▶ **ANALYZE** Which line directions did you choose to express the action? Which line directions did you choose for the background objects? Which lines did you emphasize and how did you emphasize them?

▶ **INTERPRET** Does your work express the action you were trying to capture? Give your work an expressive title. Do not use the name of the action your figures are doing.

▶ **JUDGE** Have you created a drawing that expresses the movement of people involved in energetic action? Is there anything you would change to make the work more successful? Which aesthetic theory would be best to judge this work?

▲ **FIGURE 4.26A** Student work.

Expressive Line Design

▲ **FIGURE 4.28**

Keith Haring. *Untitled*. 1983. Vinyl ink on vinyl tarp. 213.3 × 213.3 cm (84 × 84"). Tony Shafrazi Gallery, New York, New York. From the collection of Mrs. Rita Cecchi Gorl.

SUPPLIES

- Sketchbook
- Computer
- Paint or Draw application
- Printer

K eith Haring was born in 1958 and raised in Kutztown, Pennsylvania. Even as a high school student, his work exhibited a distinctive and original way of representing people and objects using line. Haring was also fascinated with symbols and signs. This is not surprising because Kutztown, which hosts an art college, is located in a rural area where Amish farmers decorate their barns with hex signs and symbols to bring them good luck, crops, and love.

Look at Haring's *Untitled* (**Figure 4.28**). Lines are everywhere. It is hard to distinguish shapes among the lively lines and bright hues that fill all the spaces. Repeated short, black lines cause your eye to move quickly around the page and eventually focus on a single round shape. You discover a human form with a long neck. Haring was influenced by the break dancers he saw in 1983, when this work was created. He watched dancers contort their bodies by bending and stretching backward to touch the floor with their hands, while other dancers went underneath them in moves called the bridge and the spider. The rhythmic, repetitive lines relate to the rap music Haring heard at the time.

What You Will Learn

You will create an expressive line design in the style of Keith Haring's work. Begin by drawing the shape of a person, animal, or object that fills a page, using a continuous contour line. Add more shapes to fill the page. Emphasize one or more shapes by using thicker lines or increasing their size. Fill the space within and around the shapes with different line types and line variations. Add color, but limit yourself to three colors.

Creating

Explore the tools on your computer application that make different kinds of lines such as Brush, Pencil, and Line. Experiment with them by selecting menus and options that allow you to change line thickness, shape, direction, and texture.

Step 1 Begin by working only in black and white. Select a small Brush or the Pencil tool. Draw a large person, animal, or object that touches three edges of the screen. Draw the contour of the shape using a continuous contour line that has smooth curves, sharp corners, and flat edges. Add more shapes to fill any empty spaces. The shapes may be nonobjective or realistic. Emphasize the large shape by thickening its outline. Save this design with your name and the project title. As you continue to work, use the Save As command and modify the title by adding a number behind the original title to indicate the second, third, or fourth save.

Step 2 Create variety by filling the shapes and the spaces around them with different patterns of line types and line variations. Make perfectly straight vertical, horizontal, or diagonal lines without jagged edges.

Step 3 Unify the design by selecting a limited color scheme of three colors. Use the Bucket tool to add color to enclosed spaces. When your composition looks complete, select the Save As command to retitle your work. Print and display your work. Compare it with the works of your classmates.

EVALUATING YOUR WORK

▶ **DESCRIBE** What shape did you use to start your design? Did you make it touch three edges of your page? Did you use a continuous contour line that had smooth curves, sharp corners, and flat edges? Did you use realistic or nonobjective shapes to fill the rest of the design?

▶ **ANALYZE** Did you emphasize your large shape by using a thick line? What line types and line variations did you use to create patterns to fill the shapes and spaces? What colors did you use?

▶ **INTERPRET** What idea, feeling, or mood does your work convey to the viewer? How did the addition of patterns of lines affect the look of your work? Create a title that expresses the way you feel about your work.

▶ **JUDGE** Did you use a variety of tools to produce shapes and fill all the spaces with many kinds of lines? Would you change anything to make your work more successful? Which aesthetic theory would you use to judge this work?

▲ **FIGURE 4.28A** Student work.

ART CRITICISM IN ACTION

David Malangi. *Abstract (River Mouth Map).* 1983. Ochres on stringy bark. 135 × 78 cm (51⅛ × 30¾"). The Art Gallery of New South Wales, Sydney, Australia.

1 ▶ DESCRIBE What do you see?

- How many dimensions does this work have? List them.
- What media have been used to create this work?
- You know from the title that this is an abstract map of a river mouth. Can you find the river? Try to find the objects in this design that relate to the river. How many familiar objects can you find?

2 ▶ ANALYZE How is this work organized?

- Can you find where Malangi has used line to outline objects? Are all the outlines the same color?
- Can you find implied lines in this work? Where are they? What is unusual in Malangi's use of implied lines?
- Identify all the different kinds of lines (vertical, horizontal, diagonal, curved, and zigzag) in this work. List at least one location for each line type you identify.
- Do you see any line variations such as length, width, and texture in this work? List at least one location for each variation you identify.

3 ▶ INTERPRET What is the artist trying to communicate?

Use the clues you discovered during your analysis to find the secret message the artist is trying to convey to you through this work.

- What does this work say to you?
- Imagine you are the artist. Write a letter to a viewer who may see this artwork. Explain one of your reasons for painting it.

4 ▶ JUDGE What do you think of the work?

- What is your reaction to this work?
- Did it make you think?
- Do you think it is successful? Use one or more of the aesthetic theories of art explained in Chapter 2 to defend your judgment of this work.

MEET THE ARTIST

DAVID MALANGI

Australian, 1934–

David Malangi is an Aboriginal artist in Australia. He was born in Mulanga, near the mouth of the Glyde River, Central Arnheim Land. He is a senior ritual leader and custodian of three tracts of land on either side of the Glyde River.

Malangi has been painting on bark commercially for over 30 years. His works are always created on bark with natural pigments even though other contemporary Aboriginal artists have switched to using acrylics on canvas. The warm brown ochre that he uses is rarely used by other artists in his region. Malangi continues to paint both commercial and ceremonial works.

The History of Ink

◀ **FIGURE 4.30**

Charles White. *Preacher*. 1952. Ink on cardboard. 54 × 75 cm (21⅛ × 29⅜"). Collection of Whitney Museum of American Art, New York, New York. Purchase. (52.25)

Long ago, people made ink from plant dyes and sepia, which is the inky secretion from the cuttlefish, octopus, and squid. The earliest inks were brown in color. By 2500 B.C, the Egyptians and the Chinese were making ink out of carbon or soot suspended in water with a binding ingredient such as gum or mineral oil. Sometimes called india ink, this carbon-based substance is black and permanent. Consequently, many ancient writings and drawings created with india ink are still legible today.

Since the 1940s, inks have evolved rapidly. With the invention of the ball-point pen and the felt-tip marker, new inks were also created. Permanent inks of today usually contain iron sulfate and gallic and tannic acids, which combine to resist both light and water.

Charles White has used the simple technique of ink-drawn lines to create the detailed and vividly expressive drawing in **Figure 4.30.**

Notice how he has built up the dark areas by applying layers of lines that cross each other in different directions. The lines in the gray shadows are clearly visible, while some areas appear totally black. White's use of ink and line adds an interesting sense of texture and consistency to the drawing.

Making the Connection

1. Describe the elements of line and value in Figure 4.30.
2. How do these elements contribute to the meaning of the drawing?
3. Experiment with different inks, pens, and/or brushes. Create as many different effects as you can. How does ink differ as a medium from charcoal, pastel, or paint when it comes to creating shadow and texture?

Building Vocabulary

On a separate sheet of paper, write the term that best matches each definition given below.

1. An element of art that is the path of a moving point through space.
2. The amount of space an object takes up in one direction.
3. A line that shows or creates the outer edges of a shape.
4. A series of points that the viewer's eyes automatically connect.
5. The element of art that describes the darkness or lightness of an object.
6. The technique of using crossed lines for shading.
7. A line that defines the edges and surface ridges of an object.
8. An expressive movement.
9. A term meaning beautiful handwriting.

Reviewing Art Facts

Answer the following questions using complete sentences.

1. Give an example of an implied line.
2. How does a two-dimensional object differ from a three-dimensional object?
3. Name and describe the five basic kinds of lines.
4. Name five major ways in which lines can vary.
5. What are the four factors that affect the value of a group of lines?
6. Name the kind of line that conveys instability, tension, and action.

Thinking Critically About Art

1. **Analyze.** Study Figure 4.1 (page 68) Figure 4.14 (page 75), and Figure 4.19 (page 80). What is the common thread that links the three works?
2. **Synthesize.** Explain why the three related works, Figures 4.1, 4.14, and 4.19, belong in a chapter devoted to the concept of line.
3. **Compare and contrast.** In what ways are Figure 4.20 (page 81) and Figure 4.22 (page 82) similar? In what ways are they different? Consider the element of line and the subject matter in your comparison.

Explore the use of line in dance as shown in the performance of "Danza de la Reata" by Ballet Folklorico de Mexico in the Performing Arts Handbook on page 416. One example of the element of line is the use of the lariat, or lasso, during the performance. Identify other examples.

Explore World Wide Web links related to the contents of each chapter of this book. These preselected links can be found under Hot Links at the Glencoe Fine Arts Site (**www.glencoe.com/sec/art**). Find the chapter you are studying in the Table of Contents and click on one of the "hot links."

▲ **FIGURE 5.1** Tooker's paintings protest the problems of modern technology. He transforms familiar places such as subways, streets, parks, and offices into menacing and alien worlds. The ordinary people in his paintings passively accept his weird world. His works express the powerlessness of people against the bureaucracy of the modern world.

George Tooker. *Highway*. 1953. Tempera on panel. 58 × 45.4 cm (22⅞ × 17⅞″). Courtesy of Terra Museum of American Art, Chicago, Illinois. Terra Foundation for the Arts, Daniel J. Terra Collection.

CHAPTER 5

Shape, Form, and Space

You live in space, in a world full of objects. Each object—whether it be a car, an apple, this book, or you—has a shape or form. Often it is by their shapes or forms that you recognize objects. You identify a stop sign in the distance by its shape long before you can read the word *stop* on it. You may identify a friend in the distance before seeing his or her face.

Shape, form, and space are all closely related to one another. They are elements of art, and artists use their knowledge of how these elements work together to create art. In this chapter you will learn how to "read" the meaning of these elements and how to use them to express your own ideas and feelings.

Notice how George Tooker has arranged very realistic shapes and forms in a natural, yet impossible space in his painting, *Highway* (**Figure 5.1**). What shapes and forms has he used to create the feeling of claustrophobic space? Which forms indicate deep space? Where does he use shape to indicate anger? How? What do you think the white arrows indicate?

OBJECTIVES

After completing this chapter, you will be able to:

- Explain the difference between shapes and forms.
- Create two- and three-dimensional works of art.
- Observe more carefully the shapes and forms in the space around you.
- Use point of view and perspective to create artworks.
- Identify the expressive qualities of shapes, forms, and spaces in artworks.

WORDS TO LEARN

shape
geometric shapes
free-form shapes
forms
space
holograms
chiaroscuro
highlights
perspective

Developing Your
PORTFOLIO

Draw a series of geometric shapes, such as triangles, squares, and circles. Then, alter these shapes by drawing them at odd angles, stacking them on top of each other, or drawing designs inside of them. In your sketchbook, describe how altering the shapes changed their appearance. Next, list several adjectives that come to mind when you look at the first set of geometric shapes. Keep your answers in your portfolio along with the drawings of the shapes.

Shapes and Forms

All objects are either shapes or forms. Rocks, puddles, flowers, shirts, houses, chairs, and paintings are all shapes and forms. The words "shape" and "form" are often used interchangeably in everyday language but, in the language of art, they have very different meanings.

Shape

A **shape** is *a two-dimensional area that is defined in some way.* A shape may have an outline or a boundary around it, or you may recognize it by its area. For instance, if you draw the outline of a square on a sheet of paper, you have created a shape. You could also create the same shape without an outline by painting the area of the square red.

You see many two-dimensional shapes every day. They are found in most designs, which in turn can be seen on many flat surfaces. Look for shapes on such things as floor coverings, fabrics, and wallpapers. Floors and walls are two-dimensional shapes; so are tabletops, book pages, posters, and billboards. The images you create with your computer and the images in the handheld and computer games you play may have the illusion of depth, but they are also two-dimensional shapes.

Geometric Shapes

All shapes can be classified as either *geometric* or *free-form*. **Geometric shapes** are *precise shapes that can be described using mathematical formulas* **(Figure 5.2)**. The basic geometric shapes are the circle, the square, and the triangle. All other geometric shapes are either variations or combinations of these basic shapes. Some of the variations include the oval, rectangle, parallelogram, trapezoid, pentagon, pentagram, hexagon, and octagon.

Geometric shapes are used for decoration, uniformity, and organization. Notice the decorative quality of the geometric shapes in the artwork shown in **Figure 5.3.** How many different simple and complex geometric shapes can you find in Biggers' painting?

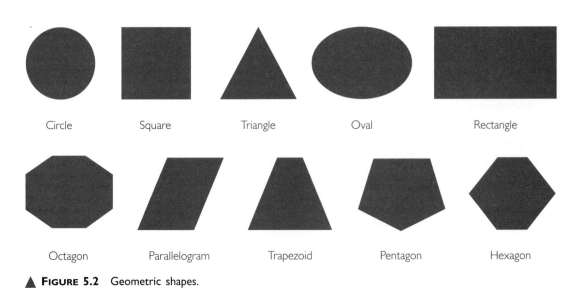

| Circle | Square | Triangle | Oval | Rectangle |

| Octagon | Parallelogram | Trapezoid | Pentagon | Hexagon |

▲ **FIGURE 5.2** Geometric shapes.

Road signs are examples of uniformity. The same kind of sign must always have the same shape. Do you know the shape of a stop sign? Which shape is used for "Yield"? Which shape is used for TV screens? Why do you think ceiling tiles and window panes have geometric shapes?

Free-Form Shapes

Free-form shapes are *irregular and uneven shapes*. Their outlines may be curved, angular, or a combination of both. They often occur in nature. Another word that may be used to describe free-form shapes is "organic." Organic is used when we talk about the shapes that are silhouettes of living things such as animals, people, or trees. Look at the difference between the decorative patterns of geometric shapes in Figure 5.3 and the free-form, organic shapes painted on the vases in **Figure 5.4.** Which looks more organized?

▲ **FIGURE 5.3** Biggers uses the women in this work to represent the African civilizations of Egypt, Benin, and Dogon. The crowns are symbols of these civilizations. The cloth on their laps represents the geometry that has brought order to each culture.

John Thomas Biggers. *Starry Crown.* 1987. Acrylic, mixed media on canvas. 155 × 124.5 cm (61 × 49"). Dallas Museum of Art, Dallas, Texas. Texas Art Fund.

◄ **FIGURE 5.4** Notice the free-form, organic qualities of the dragons and clouds that were painted on this matching pair of vases. Although the forms of the vases are perfectly matched, the paintings are not exactly alike. Look closely to find the differences between the two dragons.

Chinese, *Pair of Vases.* 1426–1435. Ming Dynasty (1368–1644). Porcelain with underglaze blue decoration. 55.2 × 29.2 cm (21¾ × 11½"). The Nelson-Atkins Museum of Art, Kansas City, Missouri. Purchase: Nelson Trust.

Activity	**Geometric and Free-Form Shapes**

Applying Your Skills. Using the printed areas of a newspaper, make two cut-paper designs. Make one design by measuring and cutting precise geometric shapes. Make the second design by tearing free-form shapes. Arrange the shapes and glue them on a sheet of black construction paper. Use a white crayon to print the words *free-form* and *geometric* on the appropriate design. Try to make the letters for *geometric* look geometric, and the letters for *free-form* look free-form.

Computer Option. Use the Shape or Straight Line tools to draw four different geometric shapes. Do not overlap the shapes and space them apart so they can easily be selected and arranged later. Choose a color scheme and make each shape a solid color. Pick the Selection tool and then the Copy and Paste menu to repeat each of the shapes several times on the page. When the page is nearly full, choose a Brush or Pencil tool to draw free-form shapes in between the geometric shapes. Select the Bucket tool to fill these shapes with pattern.

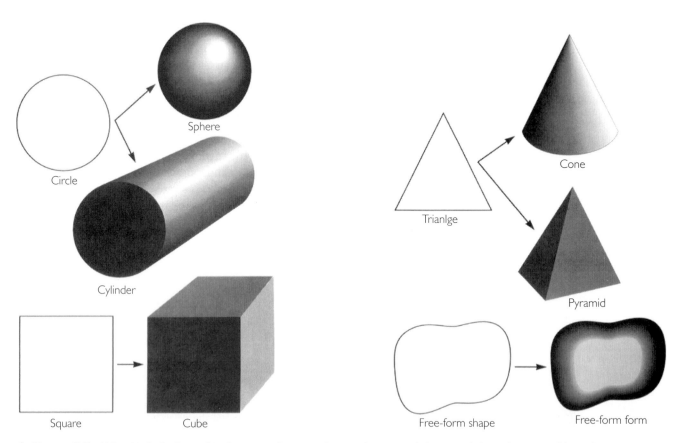

▲ **FIGURE 5.5** What kind of relationship do you see between the two-dimensional shapes and three-dimensional forms?

◀ **FIGURE 5.6** This is one of Smith's earliest stainless steel geometric sculptures. It is made of steel plates joined to form rectangular solids. Smith insisted that his monumental sculptures were made to sit in nature, not in buildings. Because the smooth steel reflected light like chrome on a car, he burnished the surface to diffuse the light so the surface would take on the colors of the natural environment.

David Smith. *Cubi IX*. 1961. Stainless steel. 268 × 149 × 111.4 cm (105¼ × 58⅜ × 43⅞"). Collection, Walker Art Center, Minneapolis, Minnesota. Gift of the T. B. Walker Foundation, 1966. © Estate of David Smith/Licensed by VAGA, New York.

Forms

Although the words *shape* and *form* are often used interchangeably in everyday language, they have different meanings in the language of art. **Forms** are *objects having three dimensions*. Like shapes, they have both length and width, but forms also have depth. *You are a three-dimensional form; so is a tree or a table.*

Two-dimensional shapes and three-dimensional forms are related **(Figure 5.5)**. The end of a cylinder is a circle. One side of a cube is a square. A triangle can "grow" into a cone or a pyramid.

Like shapes, forms may be either geometric **(Figure 5.6)** or free-form **(Figure 5.7** on page 102**)**. Geometric forms are used in construction, for organization, and as parts in machines. Look around you. What forms were used to build your school, your church, your home? Look under the hood of a car. What forms were used to build the motor? Did you know that common table

▲ **FIGURE 5.7** An example of free-form sculpture.

Barbara Hepworth. *Pendour*. 1947–48. Painted plane wood. 30.8 × 74.6 × 23.8 cm (12⅛ × 29⅜ × 9⅜"). Hirshhorn Museum and Sculpture Garden, Smithsonian Institution, Washington, D.C. Gift of Joseph H. Hirshhorn, 1966.

salt is made of a series of interlocking cubes? You can see these cubes when you look at salt through a microscope.

Free-form forms are irregular and uneven three-dimensional objects such as stones, puddles, and clouds. Your own body and the bodies of animals and plants are free-form forms.

☑ Check Your Understanding

1. List three geometric shapes.
2. What is another word for free-form shapes?
3. Is a house a shape or a form? Explain your answer.

Activity	**Creating Forms**

Applying Your Skills. Make a flat sheet of construction paper into a three-dimensional paper sculpture by using cutting and scoring techniques. (See Technique Tip 20 on page 435 in the Handbook.) Give your sculpture a minimum of five different surfaces. Do not cut the paper into separate pieces. Use only slots and tabs if you wish to join any parts. Experiment with scratch paper before you make your final paper sculpture.

Computer Option. Use the Round Shape tool to draw a circle or oval on the screen. Choose the Airbrush to gently add shading around the edges to make the shape appear as a solid form. Draw a free-form shape. Apply shading with the airbrush to represent a form. Consider adding a surface for the three-dimensional forms to sit on and then apply shadows.

Space

Space refers to both outer space and inner space. Rockets move through outer space to explore other planets. People move through the inner space of rooms and buildings. Space can be flat and two-dimensional, such as the space of a window. Space can also be three-dimensional, such as the space filled with water in a swimming pool.

space. You, for example, are a living, breathing form moving through space.

Shapes and forms are defined by the space around and within them. They depend on space for their existence. This is why it is important to understand the relationship of space to shapes and forms.

Space and Its Relationship to Shape and Form

Shapes and forms exist in space. **Space** is *the element of art that refers to the emptiness or area between, around, above, below, or within objects.* All objects take up

Positive and Negative Spaces

In both two- and three-dimensional art, the shapes or forms are called the *positive space* or the *figure.* The empty spaces between the shapes or forms are called *negative spaces* or *ground.* Look at **Figure 5.8** and read the caption for an

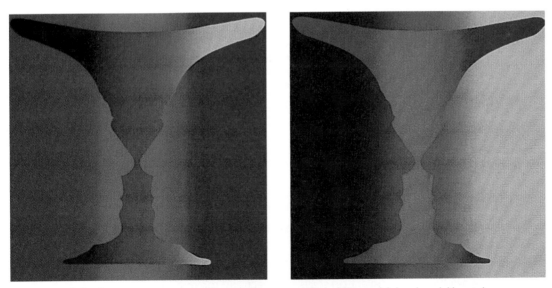

▲ **Figure 5.8**   Do you see a vase or do you see two profiles of Picasso? Johns has deliberately organized this lithograph as a visual puzzle to confuse the viewer. One minute the faces are very clear and they seem to be the figure while the space between the profiles is the ground. The next moment the vase between the profiles becomes the figure and the space around the vase becomes the ground.

Jasper Johns. *Cups 4 Picasso.* 1972. Lithograph. 57 × 82 cm (22½ × 32¼"). The Museum of Modern Art, New York, New York. Gift of Celeste Bartos. © Jasper Johns/ULAE/Licensed by VAGA, New York, NY

example of figure and ground. In a portrait, the image of the person is the positive space; the negative space is the area surrounding the person.

The shape and size of negative spaces affect the way you interpret positive spaces. Large negative spaces around positive spaces may express loneliness or freedom. When the positive spaces are crowded together, you may feel tension or togetherness **(Figure 5.9)**. The full meaning of a work depends on the interaction between the positive and negative spaces. It is not always easy to tell which are the positive spaces and which are the negative spaces in two-dimensional art. Sometimes it is difficult to identify the negative space. This is because some artists give equal emphasis to both the figure and the ground.

Sometimes artists even try to confuse the viewer. They create positive and negative spaces that reverse themselves while you are looking at them. These visual puzzles fascinate some viewers **(Figure 5.10)**.

▲ **FIGURE 5.9** In this sculpture, Brancusi goes beyond the realistic representation of love. He uses the lack of space between the two figures to symbolize the concept of the togetherness, the unity, of a couple in love. The rectangular solid of their combined form reminds us of the solidity of their union.

Constantin Brancusi. *The Kiss.* c. 1908. Stone. Height 50.2 cm (19¾″). Musee National d'Art Moderne, Centre Georges Pompidou, Paris, France.

Activity	**Experimenting with Space**

Applying Your Skills. Select a group of objects to draw. Make an arrangement with a variety of negative spaces between the shapes. Draw the arrangement lightly with pencil or chalk. Finish the work by (a) coloring only the negative spaces with crayons or paint, or (b) filling the negative spaces with closely drawn sets of parallel lines. Leave the positive spaces empty. What shapes did the negative spaces take?

Computer Option. Use the Rectangle shape tool to draw a solid rectangle approximately 3″ x 4″ in the center of the screen. Explore the different shapes of Selection tools to select and move parts of the rectangle away from the original shape. Continue selecting and moving until the rectangle has been broken into many smaller parts with varying spaces in between. Save and Title your work when you have created an interesting composition by adding space within the form.

Born in Leeuwarden, Holland, M. C. Escher (**esh**-ur) studied graphic art at Harlem's School of Architecture and Ornamental Design. He concentrated on illustrating his eccentric inner visions and his fascination with the laws of nature. In his lithographs, he explored a variety of visual jokes and trickery, such as optical illusions and distorted or impossible perspective.

Escher's works achieve their visual puzzles through his clever manipulation of positive and negative space. They skillfully switch forms into places where the viewer would logically expect space, or what appears to be the outer surface of an object reverses into an inner space.

Escher also created designs using positive and negative space to transform one object to another. A flock of birds on the left side of the picture becomes a school of fish on the right side. Each time a change takes place, the negative space becomes dominant and transforms into the new object.

▶ **FIGURE 5.10** At first this print looks normal. Water is falling to turn a water wheel. However, follow the water from the base of the fall. It runs uphill! Escher has created a visual puzzle using the mathematics of perspective.

M.C. Escher. *Waterfall.* 1961. Lithograph. © 1998 Cordon Art–Baarn-Holland. All rights reserved.

Space in Three-Dimensional Art

Over, under, through, behind, and *around* are words that describe three-dimensional space. Architecture, sculpture, weaving, ceramics, and jewelry are three-dimensional art forms. They all take up real space. You can walk around, look through, look behind, peer over, and reach into three-dimensional art.

Architects shape space. They design structures that enclose a variety of spaces for people. They create large spaces for group activities, such as the one you see in **Figure 5.11**. They also create small spaces for privacy. Landscape architects and city planners are also involved in planning spaces for people to use.

Negative areas in three-dimensional art are very real. Most three-dimensional works are meant to be *freestanding*, which means they are surrounded by negative space **(Figure 5.12)**. The viewer must move through this negative space to see all of the different views of a three-dimensional work.

Relief sculpture is not intended to be freestanding. It projects out from a flat surface into negative space. You can find relief sculpture on ceramic pots and plaster ceilings. When the positive areas project slightly from the flat surface, the work is called *bas relief,* or *low relief* **(Figure 5.13)**. When the positive areas project farther out, the work is called *high relief.*

Most jewelry is planned as relief sculpture to decorate human surfaces. The inside of a ring or the back of a pendant is smooth. It is not meant to be seen; it simply rests on the person's surface.

Today many artists are experimenting and changing traditional art forms. Printmakers are creating relief prints. Some printmakers are molding relief designs in handmade paper. Painters are adding a third dimension to the painted surface. Some painters are cutting or tearing real negative spaces in two-dimensional surfaces.

Weaving has also gone in new directions. It started as a practical craft, with weavers making two-dimensional fabrics for clothing, and has evolved into an art form. Today hand weavers are

▲ **FIGURE 5.11** The interior of this cathedral was designed so that the stained glass and the vertical columns would pull your eyes upward toward the heavens.

Reims Cathedral (interior). Reims, France. Begun c. 1225.

creating relief hangings and three-dimensional woven sculptures.

Photographers are creating **holograms**, *images in three dimensions created with a laser beam.* Sculptors are making *kinetic,* or moving, sculpture.

◀ **FIGURE 5.12** This example of folk art from Peru is a freestanding sculpture. Look carefully and you can see forms peeking out from the back. To see them you would have to walk around to the back of the work.

Artist unknown. *Church Quinua,* Ayacucho, Peru. 1958. Painted earthenware. Girard Foundation Collection at the Museum of International Folk Art, a unit of the Museum of New Mexico, Santa Fe, New Mexico.

Activity · Using Three Dimensions

Applying Your Skills. Make a freestanding, three-dimensional design that projects into negative space on all sides. Using pieces of cardboard tubing and small boxes, join the design pieces with glue and tape. Paint the finished work in one color to emphasize its form.

Set up a spotlight on one side of your free-standing sculpture. In your sketchbook draw the contours of the sculpture and the shape of its shadow. Move the spotlight to another angle. Draw the sculpture and its shadow. Notice how the changing light changes the shadow's shape.

Computer Option. Draw a solid cube or rectangular form so the top, side, and front are visible. Add shading by filling each surface with a different value of a color, texture, or gradient. Remove an area within the form by using the Eraser or Selection tool. Explore adding shadows and lines to accurately depict the inner space you see.

 Check Your Understanding

1. Define positive space and negative space.
2. What words specifically describe three-dimensional art?
3. What are the two types of relief sculpture?

▲ **FIGURE 5.13** An example of low relief. Since the design was for the back of a chair, the relief has to be low relief or the chair back would be too uncomfortable to lean against.

Queen Ankhesenamun and King Tutankhamon. Egypt, Eighteenth Dynasty. Wood overlaid with gold, silver, semiprecious stones, and glass paste. Egyptian Museum, Cairo, Egypt. Scala/Art Resource, New York.

How We Perceive Shape, Form, and Space

Look up from this book to an object across the room to see if you can feel the movement of your eye muscles. If you didn't feel anything, try again until you become aware that your eyes are working to refocus.

You have just taken a trip through visual space. Your brain measured the amount of space between you and the object and sent a message to your eye muscles to adjust. The muscles then refocused your eyes so that you could clearly see the object.

Perceiving Depth

Your eyes and brain work together to enable you to see in three dimensions—*height, width,* and *depth.* Each eye sees an object from a slightly different angle. The brain merges these two separate and slightly different views into one, creating a three-dimensional image.

To see how this works try the following experiment. Close your right eye. Point to a specific spot in the room. Without moving your pointing finger, open your right eye and close your left eye. It will appear that you have moved your finger, even though you know you have not.

Point of View

The shapes and forms you see depend on your *point of view.* Your point of view is the angle from which you see an object. Another person at another location will see the same shape or form dif-

ferently. For example, a person looking down on a circle drawn on the sidewalk sees a round shape. If that person lies on the ground beside the circle and looks at it, the circle will appear to have an oblong shape. A person looking at the front end of a car will see a form different from the one seen by a person looking at the side of that same car. **Figure 5.14** shows three different views of a sculpture.

Activity | Shape and Point of View

Applying Your Skills. Look through magazines for three or more different views of one type of object. Look for TV sets, sofas, spoons, toasters, cars, or shoes. Cut out the objects and mount each one on a sheet of white paper. Emphasize the changes in shape by drawing around each outline with a crayon or marker.

Computer Option. Divide the page into three equal sections. Use the Grids and Rulers menu to guide you if available. Choose an interesting but simple object such as a cup, a screw, pliers, a book, or a paint container. Observe and draw three views of the same object using the Pencil, small Brush, Crayon, or Marker tool. After drawing the contour or outer edges of the object, add shading to emphasize the form and surface from different views.

► **FIGURE 5.14** Notice how the feeling expressed by this sculpture changes as your point of view changes. You must view the sculpture from all angles to truly understand it.

Michael Naranjo. *Spirits Soaring*. 1985. Bronze. Height 51 cm (20"). Private collection.

Experiments in Point of View

You can learn about point of view by doing the following experiments. Place your hand flat on the desk and spread your fingers apart. The shape and form you see are the shape and form you would probably draw. They are part of the mental image you have of the object "hand." Now lift your hand and let your fingers relax. Notice how the shape and form of your hand change. Turn your hand and watch what happens. Your hand is still the same hand. Only its shape and form are different.

Next, look at a rectangular table. What shape does the top have when you are sitting at the table? Look at the top through a rectangular viewing frame. Are the edges of the table parallel to the edges of the frame? You know the top is a rectangle, but does it really look rectangular now? What shape does the top seem to take if you are sitting across the room from it? What would the shape look like if you viewed it from the top of a tall ladder? Do you think the shape you see will change if you lie on the floor directly under the table?

▲ **FIGURE 5.15** In this painting the viewer can see all the tabletops easily. All the serving dishes and the food in them are clearly visible. Can you tell what kind of a party this is? Why was this point of view a good one for this painting?

William Kurelek. *Manitoba Party*. 1964. Oil on Masonite. 121.9 × 152.6 cm (48 × 60"). National Gallery of Canada, Ottawa, Canada.

When you looked at your hand, your eyes stayed in the same place, but your hand moved. When you studied the table, it remained in one place, but you moved. In both cases, what you saw changed because your relationship to the object changed. Your point of view depends on where you are and where the object is. Look at **Figure 5.15.** Where is the artist's point of view in relation to the tables in that picture?

Check Your Understanding

1. What three dimensions are we able to see?
2. Define point of view.
3. Why may people who are looking at the same object see different shapes and forms?

How Artists Create Shapes and Forms in Space

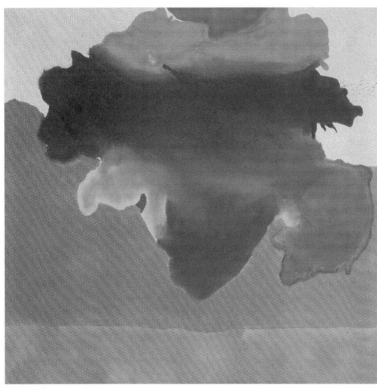

▲ FIGURE 5.16
Frankenthaler is an action painter who creates shapes by pouring thinned acrylic paint onto a canvas that is placed flat on the floor.

Helen Frankenthaler. *The Bay.* 1963. Acrylic on canvas. 201.1 × 207 cm (79³⁄₁₆ × 81½"). The Detroit Institute of Arts, Detroit, Michigan. Founders Society Purchase with funds from Dr. and Mrs. Hilbert H. DeLawter.

Shapes and forms can be classified as *natural* or *manufactured*. Natural shapes and forms are made by the forces of nature. For instance, animals, plants, and stones are natural forms. Manufactured forms are those created by people, whether mass-produced by the thousands in factories or made by hand.

Artists use many materials and techniques to make shapes. They concentrate on both outline and area. Some artists outline shapes in drawings and paintings. Others may paint shapes by placing brushstrokes together without using even a beginning outline. Some may cut shapes and print shapes and some may pour paint to create shapes **(Figure 5.16)**.

Like shapes, three-dimensional forms can be made in many ways. Artists model clay forms, mold metal forms, and carve forms from wood or stone. They use glass, plastic, bricks, and cement to create forms as well as shapes.

The Illusion of Form

Artists can create the illusion of three-dimensional form on a two-dimensional surface. They can give the impression of depth and solidity by using changes in value. **Figure 5.17** is an example of this illusion.

◀ FIGURE 5.17 Artemisia Gentileschi was a Baroque artist who used the arrangement of contrasting light and dark to create a dramatic effect in her work. Notice how the light seems to be coming from a single candle.

Artemisia Gentileschi. *Judith and Maidservant with the Head of Holofernes.* c. 1625. Oil on canvas. 184.2 × 141.6 cm (72½ × 55¼"). The Detroit Institute of Arts, Detroit, Michigan. Gift of Mr. Leslie H. Green.

◀ **FIGURE 5.18** The artist has represented shadows and highlights with photographic reality. Notice how he has made the objects seem to look solid. The seats of the stools look round. The reflections on the metal ceiling indicate rounded form. How does he use light to create the effect of a cool, air-conditioned interior against a hot outdoor scene?

Ralph Goings. *Diner With Red Door.* 1979. Oil on canvas. 112.4 × 153.7 cm (44¼ × 60½″). Courtesy of OK Harris Works of Art, New York, New York.

The arrangement of light and shadow is called **chiaroscuro** (**kyah**-roh-**skoo**-roh). In Italian *chiaro* means "bright," and *oscuro* means "dark." Chiaroscuro was introduced by Italian artists during the Renaissance. Today, chiaroscuro is often called *modeling* or *shading.*

Look, for instance, at an object with angular surfaces, such as a cube. You will see a large jump in value from one surface of the cube to the next. One surface may be very light in value and the next very dark. Now look at an object such as a baseball. The curved surfaces of spheres and cylinders show gradual changes in value.

The area of a curved surface that reflects the most light is, of course, the lightest in a drawing. **Highlights** are *small areas of white used to show the very brightest spots.* Starting at the highlights, the value changes gradually from light values of gray to dark values of gray. The darkest values are used to show areas that receive the least light. An area that is turned completely away from a light source is almost black. Look at **Figure 5.18** to see the different ways an artist has created the illusion of form.

Activity | **Using Shading**

Applying Your Skills. Set up an arrangement of geometric forms. Use boxes, books, balls, and cylindrical containers. Study the way light reflects off the surfaces of the objects. Draw the arrangement. Give the shapes in your drawing the illusion of three dimensions by using the medium and shading technique of your choice. Use values that range from black to white, and employ many value steps in between.

Computer Option. To perfect your shading technique, experiment with the Pencil, Brush, Line, Gradient, and Airbrush tools. Several programs include a Smudge or Blending tool, which softens edges. The Pencil, Line, and small Brush tools can be used with shading techniques you use when working with pen and ink. To explore these options, draw a small square shape. Select, copy, and paste seven more copies of the square in a row across the screen. Then choose from a variety of tools, textures, and settings to create different values from light to dark in the squares.

The Illusion of Depth

In paintings, artists often create the illusion of depth. When you look at these paintings, you see objects and shapes, some of which seem closer to you than others. You seem to be looking through a window into a real place **(Figure 5.19)**. This idea—that a painting should be like a window to the real world—has dominated traditional Western art since the early Renaissance.

There are several terms that will help you as you talk about and create depth in a painting or drawing. The surface of a painting or drawing is sometimes called the *picture plane*. The part of the picture plane that appears nearest to you is the *foreground*. The part that appears farthest away is the *background*. The area in between is called the *middle ground*.

Perspective is *a graphic system that creates the illusion of depth and volume on a two-dimensional surface*. In the following

▲ **FIGURE 5.19** Everything is carefully placed within the frame of this scene. In the foreground, figures dressed in bright robes kneel before the Christ Child. Beyond the human activity there is a background of calm, rolling, green hills. Notice how the artist tries to focus your attention on the child. After reading about perspective, see if you can find examples of each of the six devices used for creating perspective in this painting.

Sandro Botticelli. *The Adoration of the Magi*. Early 1480s. Tempera and oil on panel. 70.1 × 104.1 cm (27⅝ × 41"). National Gallery of Art, Washington, D.C. © 1998 Board of Trustees. Andrew W. Mellon Collection, 1937.

pages you will learn techniques artists use to give their paintings and drawings perspective.

Overlapping. When one object covers part of a second object, the first seems to be closer to the viewer, as in **Figure 5.20**.

▲ **FIGURE 5.20**   Overlapping.

Size. Large objects appear to be closer to the viewer than small objects, as in **Figure 5.21**. The farther an object is from you, the smaller it appears. Cars far down the road seem to be much smaller than the ones close to you. If you stand at the end of a long hallway and raise your hand, you can block your view of a whole crowd of people. You know that each person is about your size, but at a distance the crowd appears to be smaller than your hand.

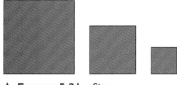

▲ **FIGURE 5.21**   Size.

Placement. Objects placed low on the picture plane seem to be closer to the viewer than objects placed near eye level. The most distant shapes are those that seem to be exactly at eye level **(Figure 5.22)**.

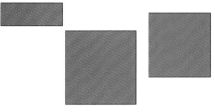

▲ **FIGURE 5.22**   Placement.

Detail. Objects with clear, sharp edges and visible details seem to be close to you **(Figure 5.23)**. Objects that lack detail and have hazy outlines seem to be farther away. Look closely at your own hand. You can see very tiny lines clearly. Now look at someone's hand from across the room. You have trouble seeing the lines between the fingers. All the details seem to melt together because of the distance between you and what you are seeing.

▲ **FIGURE 5.23**   Detail.

Color. Brightly-colored objects seem closer to you, and objects with dull, light colors seem to be farther away **(Figure 5.24)**. This is called *atmospheric* perspective. The air around us is not empty. It is full of moisture and dust that create a haze. The more air there is between you and an object, the more the object seems to fade. Have you ever noticed that trees close to you seem to be a much brighter green than trees farther down the road?

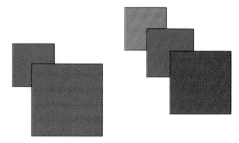

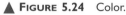

▲ **FIGURE 5.24**   Color.

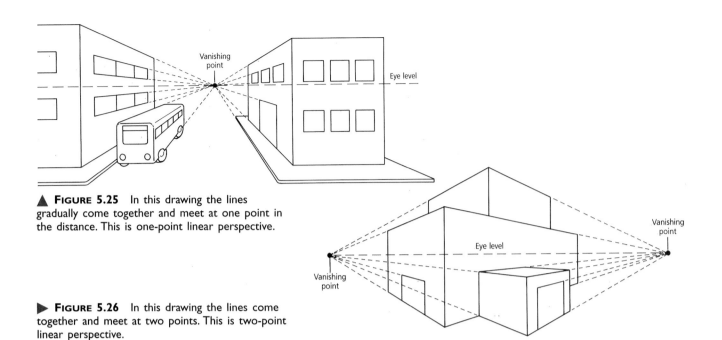

▲ **FIGURE 5.25** In this drawing the lines gradually come together and meet at one point in the distance. This is one-point linear perspective.

▶ **FIGURE 5.26** In this drawing the lines come together and meet at two points. This is two-point linear perspective.

Converging Lines. *Linear* perspective is one way of using lines to show distance and depth. As parallel lines move away from you, they seem to move closer together toward the horizon line **(Figure 5.25)**. When you look at the highway ahead of you, the sides of the road appear to move closer together. You don't worry, though, because you know this is an illusion. The sides of the road ahead of you are actually just as far apart as they are in your present position.

Sometimes lines appear to meet at a point on the horizon line called the *vanishing point.* In two-point linear perspective, different sets of parallel lines meet at different vanishing points **(Figure 5.26)**. Because two-point perspective creates more diagonal lines in a painting,

---

| **Activity** | **Creating Depth** |

Applying Your Skills. Create three different designs on three separate sheets of paper. Each design should contain five shapes. Use the same five shapes in each design as follows:

- Draw all of the items as close to the foreground as possible.
- Draw one item close to the foreground and make the others look as if they are slightly farther back.
- Draw one item close to the foreground, one far in the background, and the other three in the middle ground.

Computer Option. Use the Brush or Pencil tool to draw a landscape that includes a foreground, middle ground, and background. Draw several medium size trees in the middle ground. Draw at least one large tree in the foreground. This tree should touch two or three edges of the paper, and overlap the smaller trees. It should display the most detail. Add other objects and details that might include plants, animals, water, and objects made by hand. Remember the methods for creating the illusion of depth that were discussed earlier in the chapter.

it seems more active. Renaissance artists used strict mathematical formulas to calculate perspective. Most of today's artists rely on visual perception rather than mathematical formulas. Notice the ways in which Doris Lee has used perspective to show depth in her busy kitchen scene **(Figure 5.27)**.

✓ Check Your Understanding

1. How are shapes and forms classified?
2. What effect does chiaroscuro create in artworks?
3. List and describe three techniques artists use to give their works perspective.

LOOKING CLOSELY — Identifying Perspective Techniques

In this painting about the preparations for an old-fashioned Thanksgiving feast, Doris Lee has used all six perspective techniques. The lines in the diagram of the painting indicate one example of each technique. Can you find more examples of the six techniques in the painting?

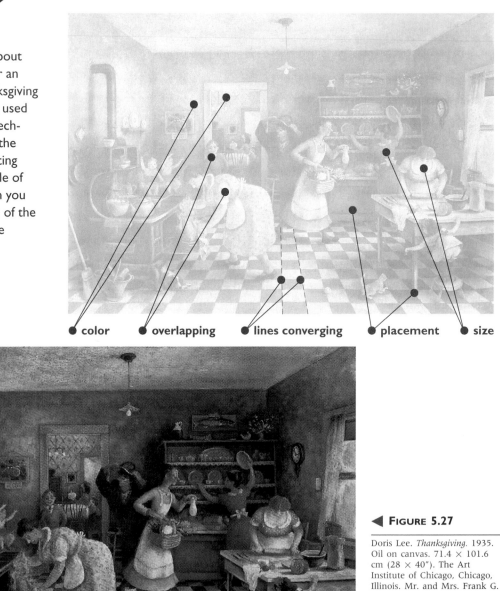

● color ● overlapping ● lines converging ● placement ● size

◀ **FIGURE 5.27**

Doris Lee. *Thanksgiving.* 1935. Oil on canvas. 71.4 × 101.6 cm (28 × 40″). The Art Institute of Chicago, Chicago, Illinois. Mr. and Mrs. Frank G. Logan Prize Fund (1935.313).

What Different Spaces, Shapes, and Forms Express

Shapes, forms, and spaces in art convey certain feelings. This is possible because you associate them with similar shapes, forms, and spaces in real life. When you see a certain shape or form in a work of art, you may think of an object from real life. Any feelings you have about that object will affect your feelings about the artistic work. Artists use this relationship between art and the environment to generate these feelings in the viewer.

Outline and Surface

The outline of a shape and the surface of a form carry messages. Artists often use free-form shapes and forms to symbolize living things. When they want to please and soothe viewers, they use shapes and forms with smooth, curved outlines and surfaces **(Figure 5.28)**. Forms that remind us of well-worn river rocks or curled-up kittens tempt us to touch them. These forms are comfortable. They appeal to us through our memories of pleasant touching experiences.

Angular shapes with zigzag outlines and forms with pointed projections remind us of sharp, jagged things **(Figure 5.29)**. We remember the pain caused by broken glass and sharp knives. We would never carelessly grab a pointed, angular form. If we were to touch it at all, we would do so very carefully.

Geometric shapes suggest mechanical perfection. It is impossible to draw a perfect circle freehand. The special

▲ **FIGURE 5.28** The artist who created this horse used rounded forms to make it appealing to look at and to touch.

Haniwa Horse. Japan, Kofun Period, A.D. 300–550. Earthenware. 66 × 71.8 × 22.9 cm (26 × 28¼ × 9"). The Minneapolis Institute of Arts, Minneapolis, Minnesota. The John R. Van Derlip Fund and Gift of anonymous St. Paul Friends.

◀ **FIGURE 5.29** This painting shows contrast between the static, solid form of the man and the active movement of the stems and thorns. This is a moment of tension. The viewer can imagine the pain that will occur when the blind botanist moves his hands to study the plant.

Ben Shahn. *The Blind Botanist.* 1954. Tempera on Masonite. 132 × 78.8 cm (52 × 31"). Wichita Museum of Art, Wichita, Kansas. The Roland P. Murdock Collection. © Estate of Ben Shahn/Licensed by VAGA, New York.

appeal of geometric shapes and forms has been felt throughout the ages. Their lines, contours, and surfaces are clean and crisp. This appeals to people's sense of order.

As used by modern artists, geometric shapes and forms express less feeling than other types. They are unemotional; in fact, they may express a total lack of feeling. Geometric forms in artworks appeal to viewers' minds rather than to their emotions **(Figure 5.30)**.

Density

The *density* or mass of an object refers to how compact it is. Dense materials are solid and heavy. Granite and lead, for example, are very dense. They are so solid and firm that you cannot make a dent on their surfaces when you press on them. Dense forms seem unyielding. They resist impact. For this reason, you may associate them with the idea of protection. In two-dimensional art, you can depict dense objects using shading techniques and hard-edge contours.

Soft, fluffy forms are less dense. When you press on them, you can make a dent. These forms have air inside them, and they look more comfortable than denser forms. In two-dimensional art, you can depict soft forms by using shading techniques and curved contours.

Openness

An open shape or form appears inviting. It seems to say, "Come in." You can see into or through it. An armchair is an open form that invites you to sit **(Figure 5.31)**. An open door invites you to enter. An empty cup invites you to fill it. Transparent objects, such as a glass wall, invite you to look inside. When you extend your hand to invite someone to join you, the form of your outstretched hand is an open form.

Open spaces in sculpture invite your

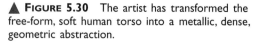

▲ **FIGURE 5.30** The artist has transformed the free-form, soft human torso into a metallic, dense, geometric abstraction.

Constantin Brancusi. *Torso of a Young Man.* 1924. Polished bronze on stone and wood base. 45.7 × 27.9 × 17.8 cm (18 × 11 × 7"). Hirshhorn Museum and Sculpture Garden, Smithsonian Institution, Washington, D.C. Gift of Joseph H. Hirshhorn, 1966.

◀ **FIGURE 5.31**   To Wright, form and function were inseparable, so a chair, which functions for sitting, should be considered along with the whole architectural environment.

Frank Lloyd Wright. *Armchair for the Ray W. Evans House,* made by Niedechen and Walbridge. c. 1908. Oak. 86.9 × 58.5 × 57.1 cm (34¼ × 23 × 22½"). The Art Institute of Chicago, Chicago, Illinois. Gift of Mr. and Mrs. F. M. Fahrenwald, 1970.435.

◀ **FIGURE 5.32**
Notice how the artist has indicated the extreme feeling of isolation one experiences at the loss of a loved one. She has created this effect by using a closed form to represent the grieving person.

Marie Apel. *Grief.* 1940. Bronze. 51 × 17.8 × 15.2 cm (20 × 7 × 6"). National Museum of Women in the Arts, Washington, D.C. Gift of the artist's daughter.

eyes to wander through the work. Weavers leave openings in fabrics and hangings to let you see through them. If you remove an oak table from a room and replace it with a glass table, the room will seem less crowded. Architects use glass walls to open small spaces. Windows open up a building and bring in the outdoors.

Closed shapes and forms look solid and self-contained. Windowless buildings look forbidding. Closed doors keep people out; closed drapes and shades keep light out. When you make a tight fist, your hand is a closed form that seems to say, "Keep away." Folding your arms tightly to your body closes you off from others. Open arms invite people to come closer to you. The woman shown in **Figure 5.32** has wrapped her robes around herself, creating a closed form to repel any contact. She tells you that she wants to be alone without saying a word. Her body language says it all.

Activity and Stability

You have already learned about active and static lines. Shapes and forms, also, can look as if they are about to move or as if they are fixed in one place.

LESSON 5   *What Different Spaces, Shapes, and Forms Express*   **119**

Active shapes and forms seem to defy gravity. They slant diagonally, as if they are falling or running. In **Figure 5.33** notice how the back of the wave and all the horse forms are arranged in diagonal, active positions.

Static shapes and forms are motionless, or stable. Their direction is usually horizontal **(Figure 5.34)**. However, if two diagonal shapes or forms are balanced against each other, a static shape results. For instance, if an equilateral triangle rests on a horizontal base, the two diagonal edges balance each other.

Because static shapes and forms are firmly fixed in position, they evoke quiet and calm feelings. For instance, in landscape paintings the land forms are horizontal and the trees are vertical. They look very peaceful. This is probably why so many landscape paintings are chosen for people's homes.

Activity | Active and Static Shapes

Applying Your Skills. Make a simple design with geometric shapes. Lightly draw it with pencil on a sheet of watercolor paper. Repeat the same design on another sheet of watercolor paper of the same size. Next, paint the first design precisely. Use a pointed brush to make sure that all of the edges are clearly defined. Wet the second sheet of paper by sponging it with water. Using exactly the same colors, paint the second design while the paper is wet so that the edges of the shapes run and look soft. Mount the two designs, side by side, on a sheet of black paper. Label the first "hard-edged" and the second "soft-edged."

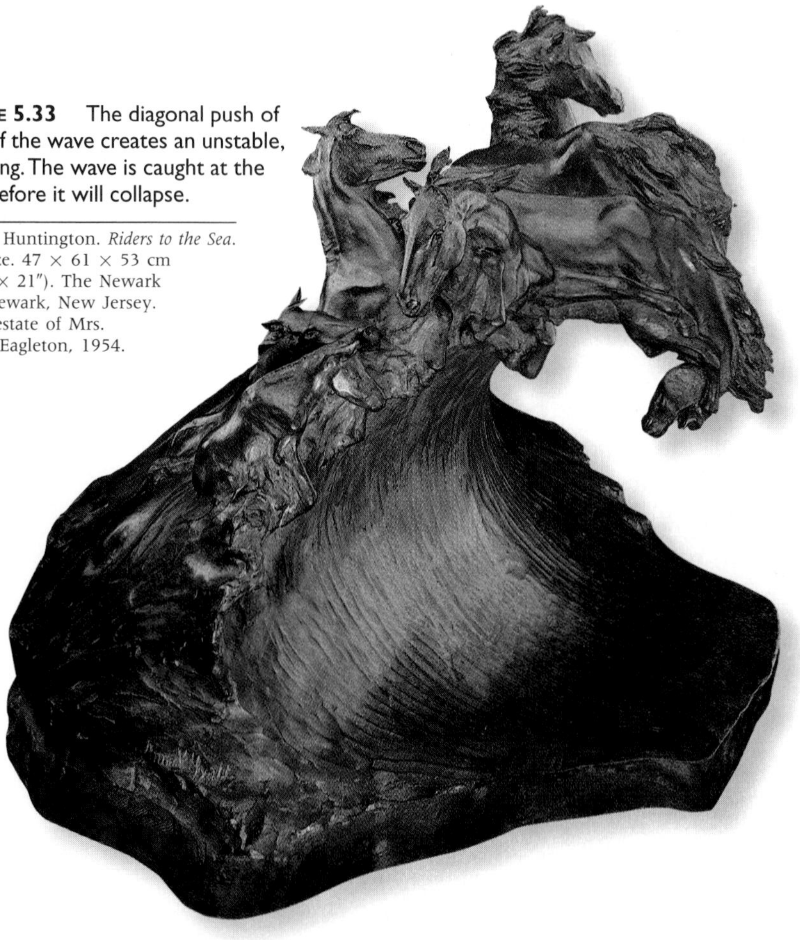

▶ **FIGURE 5.33** The diagonal push of the back of the wave creates an unstable, active feeling. The wave is caught at the moment before it will collapse.

Anna Hyatt Huntington. *Riders to the Sea.* 1912. Bronze. 47 × 61 × 53 cm (18½ × 24 × 21″). The Newark Museum, Newark, New Jersey. Gift of the estate of Mrs. Florence P. Eagleton, 1954.

Computer Option. Choose the Shape and Line tool to make a design that creates a static feeling. The Line tool on most applications can be constrained to draw straight horizontal, vertical, or diagonal lines by holding down the shift key while drawing with the mouse. Title and Save the black line static design. Select a color scheme. Pick the Bucket tool to fill the spaces with solid colors. Use the Save As command to Retitle the work by adding a number or letter after the original title. Open the original line design. Apply the same color scheme but explore the tools and menus, which create active flowing edges. Use the Save As command to retitle the active composition.

Check Your Understanding

1. What do angular shapes suggest?
2. What do geometric shapes suggest?
3. Define density.
4. List one example each of an open shape or form and a closed shape or form.

▲ **FIGURE 5.34** The strong horizontal shape of the orange wheat at the base of the work creates a calm, stable effect.

Jane Wilson. *Winter Wheat*. 1991. Oil on linen. 101.6 × 127 cm (40 × 50″). Photo courtesy of DC Moore Gallery, New York, New York. Private Collection.

Drawing an Outdoor Scene

▲ **FIGURE 5.35**

Larry Smith. *North Georgia Waterfall*. 1993. Pen and ink on paper. 66 × 61 cm (26 × 24″). Collection of the artist.

SUPPLIES

- **Sketchbook**
- **Large sheet of white drawing paper**
- **Drawing board and tape**
- **Pencils and erasers**
- **Viewing frame**

Larry Smith is an artist in love with the land. Born and raised in Georgia, he has committed his professional life to capturing its majestic scenery on paper **(Figure 5.35)**.

Smith uses a realistic style to create his artwork. Regionalists such as Winslow Homer (Figures 3.8 and 3.9 on page 47), and Edward Hopper (Figure 4.16 on page 77) inspired him to preserve the historical significance of a building, a landscape, or an environmental treasure. Smith likes to use pencil, colored pencils, or pen and ink to draw the scenes that represent his local environment. He is concerned with capturing light, and in this landscape he has used stippling for the shadows and has left the white of the paper to represent the white froth of the foaming falls.

Observe the different ways in which Larry Smith has created three-dimensional forms and depth in his landscape. Watch how your drawing springs to life when you use shading to create three-dimensional forms and perspective techniques to show deep space.

What You Will Learn

Make a drawing of an outdoor scene that is interesting to you. This scene should have a foreground, middle ground, and background. Create the illusion of three-dimensional forms in the scene by using a variety of shading techniques. Use values that range from black to various grays to white. Create the illusion of deep, three-dimensional space by using one or more perspective techniques. Mount or mat the finished work for display.

Creating

Larry Smith chooses scenes from his local environment to record for others to enjoy. Find an outdoor scene that is important to you and that you think is important enough to record for the future. Think of the view from your window, a country or park scene, or a view of boats in a harbor. Do not use a photograph or another drawing.

Step 1 Make a viewing frame and use it to help select the exact view you wish to draw. (See Technique Tip 6 on page 430 in the Handbook.) Be sure to include a large shape in the foreground. All parts of the large shape do not have to fit in the picture. Each shape and form will have the same relationship to the edges of the paper as it does to the edges of the frame. Make rough sketches of the scene in your sketchbook.

Step 2 Now look through the frame at the objects in the scene and write notes in your sketchbook about how they are arranged. Pay attention to overlapping, placement, size differences, details, values, and receding parallel lines.

Step 3 Tape your paper to the drawing board and lightly draw in the shapes, paying careful attention to the placement of the major objects on the page. Shade the shapes using a value scale that includes black, white, and all the grays in between. Use a variety of shading techniques to create the illusion of flat and rounded three-dimensional forms.

Step 4 Give your work a title that expresses the mood or meaning of the work. Mount or mat your work for display.

EVALUATING YOUR WORK

▶ **DESCRIBE** What scene did you choose as the subject of your drawing? Tell why you selected this scene. How did the use of the viewing frame affect your work? How did you prepare the work for display?

▶ **ANALYZE** Which shading techniques did you use to create three-dimensional forms? Which perspective techniques did you use to create the illusion of depth?

▶ **INTERPRET** What kind of a feeling does this drawing express? Does the title you chose express the mood or meaning of the work?

▶ **JUDGE** Which aesthetic theory would you use to judge your work? Do you think the work was successful? What would you change to improve it?

▲ **FIGURE 5.35A** Student work.

Clay Plaque with High Relief

▲ **FIGURE 5.36**

Warrior Chief, Warriors, and Attendants. Plaque. Nigeria, Edo. Court of Benin. Sixteenth to seventeenth centuries. Brass. Height 48 cm (18⅞"). The Metropolitan Museum of Art, New York, New York. Gift of Mr. and Mrs. Klaus G. Perls, 1990. (1990.332)

SUPPLIES

- ■ **Sketchbook and pencil**
- ■ **Clay**
- ■ **Clay tools and equipment**
- ■ **Newspaper and scissors**
- ■ **Slip and brush**
- ■ **Large plastic bag**
- ■ **Kiln**
- ■ **Glaze or acrylic paints and brushes (optional)**

The Brass plaque shown in **Figure 5.36** was one of many that decorated the walls of the palace of the Oba, the divine ruler of the Benin kingdom (now the capital of Nigeria's Bendel state). *Warrior Chief, Warriors, and Attendants* depicts ceremonies and rituals that were carried out in the court. In fact, because the plaques so accurately documented the costumes, ornaments, hairstyles, weapons, and musical instruments employed in these ceremonies, they were often used in later centuries to answer questions about court procedures.

The techniques of high and low relief, shown here, indicate a person's rank. Notice how the most important figure, located in the center of the plaque, is larger and in higher relief than the others. People of less importance are placed to the side and are shown smaller and in low relief. Many detailed objects are added to the surface and are used to fill the spaces in between.

What You Will Learn

In this studio project, you will create a clay plaque depicting an event from current events or history that you find interesting. You will use high and low relief to illustrate the scene. In the style of the Benin plaque, the most important person should be the largest and in the highest relief. Your finished work will demonstrate what can be learned about people by their relative sizes and the degrees of relief.

Creating

Do research sketching. Draw examples in your sketchbook of clothing, the setting, and the objects related to the event. Make detail sketches of the most important items. These do not have to be complete drawings. Think of them as visual note taking.

If you have not worked with clay, take time to become familiar with clay and the proper clay-joining techniques. (See Technique Tips on pages 433 and 434 in the Handbook).

Step 1 Make a complete plan for your plaque in your sketchbook. First, sketch the figures using the Benin style of making the most important figure the largest. Then add objects and a natural setting, if necessary. Finally, plan the shape of the plaque.

Step 2 Draw a pattern for the shape of the plaque on a sheet of newspaper and cut it out. Roll out a slab of clay approximately ½ inch thick. Trace the shape of the plaque pattern onto the slab and cut the slab into the shape of the pattern.

Step 3 Model the figures and objects you have designed for the plaque. Add the figures and the objects to the plaque using scoring and slip. Notice how the Benin plaque has details added to the main figures as well as details that are carved and stippled into the work. Use clay tools to add details to your plaque.

Step 4 Punch holes into the slab for hanging the plaque. Make sure they are more than ½ inch from every edge of the slab. When the clay is bone dry, fire it in the kiln following your teacher's instructions.

EVALUATING YOUR WORK

▶ **DESCRIBE** What is the subject matter of your plaque? Describe the event and identify the people you have included. Did you use proper clay-modeling procedures? Did the clay stay joined, and did it come through the firing process successfully? Which option did you choose to finish the work?

▶ **ANALYZE** Did you follow the style of the Benin relief by making the most important figure larger and in higher relief than the others? What kind of a shape did you make the background slab? Did you fill the negative space with patterns?

▶ **INTERPRET** Can the viewer recognize the event by just looking at your work? What is the mood you were trying to convey? Have you caught the mood of the occasion?

▶ **JUDGE** Were the viewers able to understand the event you were illustrating? Which aesthetic theory would you use to judge this work?

▲ **FIGURE 5.36A** Student work.

Landscape Using Surreal Space

▲ **FIGURE 5.37**

René Magritte. *The Blank Signature*. 1965. Oil on canvas. 81 × 65 cm (32 × 25⅝"). National Gallery of Art, Washington, D.C. ©1998 Board of Trustees. Collection of Mr. and Mrs. Paul Mellon.

SUPPLIES

- Sketchbook and pencil
- Sheet of tracing paper
- Two large sheets of white paper
- Yellow chalk and soap eraser
- Oil pastels

René Magritte was a Belgian Surrealist who loved to create visual puzzles. He began his career as a graphic artist, and by the time he was 40, he was able to give up commercial art and work full time as a painter.

While French Surrealists were exploring fantasy, psychology, and the subconscious mind to find subjects for their art, Magritte worked with ordinary images from the real world. His painting style was very realistic, and his ideas were powerful because the images he used were familiar and lifelike.

In the painting *The Blank Signature* **(Figure 5.37)**, Magritte was trying to find a way to express the visible and the invisible. He said, "Visible things can be invisible. When someone rides a horse in the forest, first you see her, then you don't, but you know that she is there . . . the rider hides the trees and the trees hide her."

What You Will Learn

Using oil pastels on white paper, you will create a surreal still life, landscape, or cityscape in which the positive shapes and negative spaces are interwoven into a reversal of the visible and invisible. As in Magritte's painting *The Blank Signature* (Figure 5.37), see if you can turn your painting into a visual puzzle.

Creating

Brainstorm with your classmates about ways that you can create Magritte's visible/invisible effect. Trees, a network of branches, or haystacks might divide the positive and negative in a landscape. Signposts, lampposts, or buildings with big windows can divide the space in a cityscape. Do not limit yourself to vertical and horizontal space divisions. Experiment with large leaves, telephones, a pattern of large and small TV screens, or abstract shapes.

Step 1 Design the realistic scene as a whole first. To make your scene work, choose a subject with which you are familiar. First, make rough sketches in your sketchbook and then organize them into a good composition on a sheet of white paper. Plan to use colors in the realistic scene that are different from and contrast with the color of the dividing scene.

Step 2 Place a sheet of tracing paper over the realistic composition. On the tracing paper, sketch the second drawing into which you will weave your first scene.

Step 3 Using yellow chalk, lightly copy your realistic scene onto the other large sheet of white paper. Then sketch the dividing drawing over the first using another light chalk color. Now decide which scene will be visible in each area. Use the soap eraser to remove the chalk lines that will be invisible.

Step 4 Apply color lightly until you have all the positive and negative areas worked out. Then apply the oil pastel color heavily, blending colors when necessary to build up layers of color.

Step 5 Give your work a title that helps viewers to understand your work. Mount or mat your work for display.

EVALUATING YOUR WORK

▶ **DESCRIBE** Explain how you have created a surreal scene by telling what realistic scene you chose for the subject matter. Then, explain what device you have used to divide the scene so that the visible and invisible are reversed.

▶ **ANALYZE** Explain how you managed to create a reversal of visible and invisible through your arrangement of positive and negative space. Describe how you used contrasting colors to help the viewer see the two different scenes.

▶ **INTERPRET** Describe the emotional effect you have achieved in your work. Does the title you gave your piece help the viewer understand your work?

▶ **JUDGE** Was your attempt to create a surreal space successful? Which aesthetic theory would you use to evaluate this work?

▲ **FIGURE 5.37A** Student work.

One-Point Perspective Drawing

▲ **FIGURE 5.38**

Jan Vermeer. *The Astronomer*. 1668. Oil on canvas. 51.5 × 45.5 cm (20¼ × 18″). The Louvre, Paris, France. Erich Lessing/Art Resource, New York.

SUPPLIES

- Sketchbook
- Computer
- Draw or paint application
- Printer

J an Vermeer was a Dutch painter, best known for his paintings of dramatically lit interior scenes. Vermeer used one-point linear perspective to organize the scene in *The Astronomer* **(Figure 5.38)**. If you trace the lines in and around the window, the lines of the chair, the edges of the books on the cabinet, and even the line at the top right edge of the cabinet, you will find that they all meet at one point—on the man's raised wrist. Vermeer pulls your eyes toward the hand on the globe rather than the man's head to indicate that what the astronomer studies is more important than the man himself.

What You Will Learn

You will create a one-point linear perspective drawing of an interior space. The space may be realistic, or you may create a fantasy interior scene. Incorporate as many other perspective techniques as you need. Begin by drawing guidelines. Then use these guidelines to place rectangular objects in the room using one-point perspective. Complete your drawing by adding details, color, and shading that include value changes from dark to white highlights.

Creating

Decide whether you will draw a vertical or horizontal interior. For a horizontal scene, change the view to Landscape under Page Setup in the File menu.

Step 1 Select a tool, such as Line, from your menu to help you make guidelines. Place the eye level and vanishing point in the middle of the page. Make a dot with the Brush tool to represent this point. Begin by drawing the wall farthest from you. Make an open rectangle around the vanishing point to represent this wall.

Step 2 Draw four thin, straight, diagonal lines that start at the vanishing point and continue through each corner of the rectangle and proceed to the edge of the page. These lines will be the guidelines for the walls of your room and define its edges.

Step 3 Define the space by drawing windows or doorways on these walls. Start with a vertical line to represent the side of the door or window nearest you. From the top of the window or door line, draw a diagonal line that converges with the vanishing point to form the top edge. Form the bottom edge by drawing a second diagonal line that begins at the bottom corner of the window or door line and leads to the vanishing point. Now, determine the width of the opening and draw a second vertical line between the two angled lines.

Step 4 Make the interior space look interesting. Keep size relationships in mind as you place objects within the scene. Continue to use the vanishing point when you draw rectangular objects.

Step 5 When your drawing is complete, erase the vanishing point and any unnecessary lines or marks. Consider techniques to emphasize perspective. Consider the light source and apply color, shading, and shadows to enhance the sense of depth. Explore tools to change value. Print and display your final edition.

EVALUATING YOUR WORK

▶ **DESCRIBE** What kind of an interior view did you draw? Describe the objects you placed in the scene. Where did you place your eye level and vanishing point? Explain how you used the vanishing point to create the walls, windows, and objects in the room.

▶ **ANALYZE** Do all of the receding lines meet at your vanishing point? Do the sizes of the objects fit the room? What other perspective techniques did you use? What other drawing tools did you use to enhance the setting? Did you add color and shading?

▶ **INTERPRET** Describe the mood or feeling of your drawing. Create a descriptive title that sums up your ideas and feelings about the room.

▶ **JUDGE** Did you use perspective correctly? Are the objects in your scene the correct size? Have all the unnecessary marks and lines been erased? What, if anything, would you change to improve this drawing? Which of the three aesthetic theories would you use to judge your work?

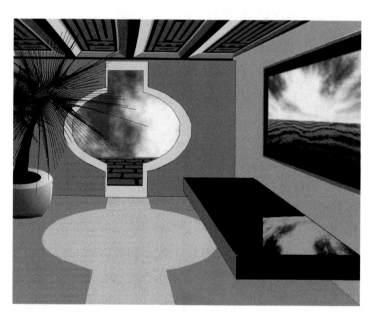

▲ **FIGURE 5.38A** Student work.

ART CRITICISM IN ACTION

Christo and Jeanne-Claude. *Wrapped Reichstag, Berlin, 1971–95.* © Christo 1995. Photograph: Wolfgang Volz.

1 ▶ DESCRIBE What do you see?

This work is probably different from anything you have seen before. It is classified as environmental art. This term refers to work done outdoors in both rural and urban settings.

- How big do you think it is? Look at the people to help you determine the size.
- What materials have been used to create this work?
- Is this work a shape or a form? Does it take up space?
- Is it a freestanding or relief work?

2 ▶ ANALYZE How is this work organized?

Before you study the organization of the shape, form, and space of this work, describe the lines that you see.

- Is the work two- or three-dimensional?
- Does it have any flat shapes? Are the shapes geometric or free-form? Describe them.
- Can you find changes in value? Describe them.
- Are the forms dense or soft? Open or closed? Active or static?
- What have the artists done with space?

3 ▶ INTERPRET What are the artists trying to communicate?

Use the clues you found during your Analysis to help you find a message in this unusual artwork.

- What are the artists communicating to you with this work?
- Why have they wrapped this specific building?
- What has the wrapping done to the forms under the wrapping?

4 ▶ JUDGE What do you think of the work?

- Now that you have evaluated this work of art, what do you think about it?
- Do you feel more comfortable with environmental art than before you saw this work?
- Is it a work of art? Why or why not? Use one or more of the theories of art explained in Chapter 2 to defend your decision.

MEET THE ARTISTS

CHRISTO AND JEANNE-CLAUDE

American, 1935–

Christo was born in Bulgaria in 1935. He studied art at the Fine Arts Academy in Sophia. In 1956, he took advantage of the Hungarian Revolution to escape from Prague. Later, in Paris, he met his future wife, Jeanne-Claude de Guillebon.

Christo's interest in wrapping objects began with such objects as bottles and bicycles wrapped in fabric, plastic, paper, and cord. Before long, he and Jeanne-Claude were wrapping larger objects as well. The planning for *Wrapped Reichstag* (**Figure 5.39**), began in 1971. The actual wrapping was carried out in 1995 by 90 climbers and 120 installation workers. Two weeks from the day of *completion, the Wrapped Reichstag* was unwrapped. All of the materials were recycled.

How Do Artists Use Geometry?

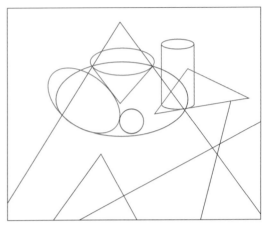

◀ **FIGURE 5.40**

Paul Cezánne. *Apples and Oranges*. Oil
on canvas. 74 × 93 cm (29⅛ × 36⅛″).
Museé d'Orsay, Paris, France.

If you look carefully, you can see geometric shapes all around you. For example, the sun, moon, and planets are spherical in shape. Some evergreen trees are shaped like a cone. A shoe box is a rectangular solid and a soft drink is a cylinder. However, did you know that the first use of geometry was a practical one? The word itself comes from Greek words meaning "earth" and "measure." The concept of geometry was originally used by Egyptian surveyors in the fourteenth century B.C. Every year, the Nile River had severe flooding. People who lived close to the river often lost land when the flooding stopped. Surveyors used geometry to reestablish the boundaries of the fields near the river.

Yet people have also been creating geometrically shaped objects for thousands of years. These shapes appear in ancient pottery, cave paintings, and buildings. The shape of the ancient Egyptian pyramids is an early example of a geometric shape used in architecture.

Over the years, the meaning of geometry has changed and expanded. In art, geometry is often a source of ideas for artists. In *Apples and Oranges* **(Figure 5.40),** Paul Cézanne painted many objects that have natural geometric shapes. In addition to these objects, the overall composition of the painting shows a geometric arrangement. As a result, the painting has a sense of completeness.

Making the Connection

1. Identify the geometric shapes that Cézanne used in this painting.
2. How did Cézanne create a sense of geometry in the overall composition of this work?
3. Why do you think Cézanne called works such as this "constructions after nature"?

Building Vocabulary

On a separate sheet of paper, write the term that best matches each definition given below.

1. A two-dimensional area that is defined in some way.
2. Precise shapes that can be described using mathematical formulas.
3. Irregular and uneven shapes.
4. Objects having three dimensions.
5. The element of art that refers to the emptiness or area between, around, above, below, or within objects.
6. Images in three dimensions created with a laser beam.
7. The arrangement of light and shadow.
8. Small areas of white used to show the very brightest spots.
9. A graphic system that creates the illusion of depth and volume on a two-dimensional surface.

Reviewing Art Facts

Answer the following questions using complete sentences.

1. Name the two basic types of shapes and tell which is more often used in decoration.
2. What is the difference between shapes and forms?
3. Name the two kinds of space found in art.
4. Using a portrait as an example, name the kind of space the subject occupies.
5. Explain how the eyes and brain enable us to see in three dimensions.
6. Explain how an artist creates the illusion of three-dimensional form on a two-dimensional surface.
7. Name the six devices for creating perspective.
8. Name two kinds of perspective.
9. Give an example of an active shape and tell what makes it look active.
10. Give an example of a static shape and tell what makes it look motionless, or stable.

Thinking Critically About Art

1. **Compare and contrast.** Look at *The Adoration of the Magi* by Sandro Botticelli (Figure 5.19, page 113) and *Thanksgiving* by Doris Lee (Figure 5.27, page 116). Evaluate the artists' use of forms and space. In what ways are these two styles similar? In what ways are they different? List your findings.

2. **Synthesize.** *The Kiss* (Figure 5.9, page 104) and *Torso of a Young Man* (Figure 5.30, page 118) are two of Brancusi's abstract works. Make a list of the similarities and differences between them. Do you think his style has changed over the years? Explain and defend the conclusions you reach in a few paragraphs.

Use Performing Arts Handbook page 417 to find out how dancer and choreographer Bella Lewitzky uses the elements of shape and form in dance to express her impressions of Henry Moore's art.

Many choices await you in activities such as virtual field trips, studio tours, collages and crafts, applied arts experiences, and gallery-hopping adventures. Visit us at: **www.glencoe.com/sec/art**

▲ **FIGURE 6.1** Delaunay wanted the subject of his paintings to be the relationship between colors and round shapes. Look closely at the artwork above. Can you find symbols that represent three objects from the beginning of the twentieth century?

Robert Delaunay. *Sun, Tower, Airplane.* 1913. Oil on canvas. 132 x 131 cm (52 × 51⅝"). Collection, Albright-Knox Art Gallery, Buffalo, New York. A. Conger Goodyear Fund, 1964.

Color

olor surrounds us. A blue sky, a lavender sunset, a red brick building—all demand our attention. The expressive qualities of color are so powerful that they can create instant emotional reactions in people. Even the color of a room can affect the way people behave. Blue is thought to have soothing qualities, while red can excite or stimulate people.

In the painting *Sun, Tower, Airplane* **(Figure 6.1),** the artist is moving away from the dull colors of Cubism to a brightly colored style known as Orphism. Orphism is a variation of Cubism named by the French poet and critic, Guillaume Apollinaire. He was referring to the poetic use of pure color and named the style after the legendary Greek poet, Orpheus.

In Figure 6.1, the artist has used bright colors and circular shapes to express the excitement and dynamic movement of the objects represented on the right side of the work. The circular shapes represent the universe and the bright colors express the movement of the light of the universe. Delaunay was interested in exploring the effects of color and light when they were not restricted within the shapes of objects.

Developing Your
PORTFOLIO

Collect a variety of objects that show different combinations of colors. Use magazine pages, fabric swatches, found objects, and the like. Write a paragraph describing what you think of the different color schemes and how you might use them in your own artwork. Keep the sample color schemes and your paragraph in your portfolio.

OBJECTIVES

After completing this chapter, you will be able to:

- Understand how your eyes see color.
- Name the properties of color and the colors of the spectrum.
- Identify different color schemes.
- Use color as the expressive element in creating two- and three-dimensional artworks.
- Recognize the expressive qualities of color that artists use to create meaning.

WORDS TO KNOW

color
color spectrum
hue
color wheel
tint
shade
intensity
complementary colors
monochromatic
analogous colors
pigments
binder
solvent
dyes

The Properties of Color

Color is the most expressive element of art. It shares a powerful connection with emotion. That relationship is why we hear people say, "I'm feeling blue," or "She was green with envy." The connection of color to emotion is also illustrated in a question we often ask friends—"What's your favorite color?" Almost everyone has a favorite color. It might remind us of a favorite childhood toy or a piece of clothing that we love to wear. Our appreciation of color affects many of the choices we make.

In this lesson you will learn what color is and how you see it. You will learn the properties of color. You will also learn how to mix colors to create shades you might use in your artwork.

How We See Color

Color is *an element of art that is derived from reflected light*. You see color because light waves are reflected from objects to your eyes **(Figure 6.2)**. White light from the sun is actually a combination of all colors.

When light passes through a wedge-shaped glass, called a prism, the beam of white light is bent and separated into bands of color, called the **color spectrum.**

▲ **FIGURE 6.2** Chagall has used many different tints and shades of blue. He has also used a few other colors for emphasis. Identify some of the objects he has emphasized this way. As the light outside changes throughout the day, how do you think the artwork changes? What if the day were stormy or rainy? How do you think the artist planned for this?

Marc Chagall. *The American Windows.* 1977. Stained glass. The Art Institute of Chicago, Chicago, Illinois. Gift of the Auxiliary Board of The Art Institute of Chicago in memory of Richard J. Daley, 1977. 938

The colors of the spectrum always appear in the same order: red, orange, yellow, green, blue, and violet.

A rainbow is a natural example of a spectrum. Rainbows occur when sunlight is bent by water, oil, or a glass prism. You can find rainbows in the sky after a storm, in the spray from a garden hose, or in a puddle of oil.

We see color because objects absorb some of these light waves and reflect others. A red apple looks red because it reflects red waves and absorbs the rest of the colors. Special color receptors in your eyes detect the color of the reflected light waves. Another type of receptor detects the lightness or darkness of the color. Colors don't change.

Your ability to distinguish between them does. That is why your eyes have trouble seeing colors in dim light. Not enough light is reflected off of objects for you to see their color.

When you are looking at colors, your eyes can sometimes fool you. For instance, stare at the bright red shape in **Figure 6.3** for 30 seconds; then quickly shift your gaze to the white area below it. Did you see a green shape on the white surface? This is called an *afterimage*. It occurs because the receptors in your eyes retain the visual stimulation even after it has ceased. Your brain creates the afterimage as a reaction to the color you stared at originally.

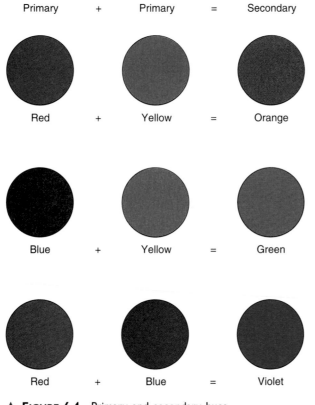

Primary	+	Primary	=	Secondary

Red + Yellow = Orange

Blue + Yellow = Green

Red + Blue = Violet

▲ **FIGURE 6.4** Primary and secondary hues.

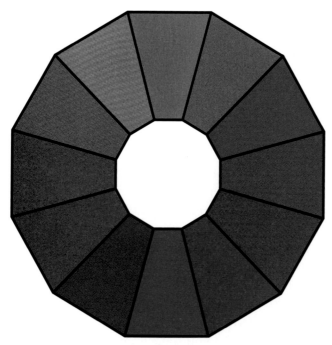

▲ **FIGURE 6.5** The color wheel.

The afterimage of a color is the opposite of that color. Green is the opposite of red. So the afterimage of green is the color red. The afterimage of black is white, and the afterimage of blue is orange. An afterimage isn't a strong color—it is only the ghost of a color. Some artists make use of the way your eyes work when they create optical illusions of color and movement.

Three properties of color work together to make the colors we see. These properties are *hue, value,* and *intensity.*

Hue

Hue is *the name of a color in the color spectrum,* such as red, blue, or yellow. Red, yellow, and blue are the *primary* hues. You cannot make primary hues by mixing other hues together. However, by combining the three primary colors and black and white, you can produce every other color.

The *secondary* hues are made by mixing two primary colors **(Figure 6.4).** Red and yellow make orange; red and blue make violet; and blue and yellow make green. Orange, violet, and green are the secondary hues.

The six *intermediate* colors are made by mixing a primary color with its secondary color. For example, red and orange make red-orange, red and violet make red-violet, blue and violet make blue-violet, and so on. You can make many additional variations by combining the intermediate colors.

A **color wheel** is *the spectrum bent into a circle.* It is a useful tool for organizing colors. The color wheel in **Figure 6.5** is a twelve-color wheel showing the three primary, three secondary, and six intermediate hues.

Value

Value is the art element that describes the darkness or lightness of a color. The amount of light a color reflects determines its color value. Not all hues of the spectrum have the same value. Yellow is the lightest hue because it reflects the most light. Violet is the darkest hue because it reflects the least light.

Black, white, and gray are *neutral colors* **(Figure 6.6).** When white light shines on a white object, the object reflects all of the color waves and does not absorb any. As a result, you see the color of all the light, which is white. A black object absorbs all of the color waves. Black reflects no light; black is the absence of light. Gray is impure white—it reflects an equal part of each color wave. The more light that gray

▲ **FIGURE 6.6** Neutral colors: black, gray, and white.

Tints   Shades

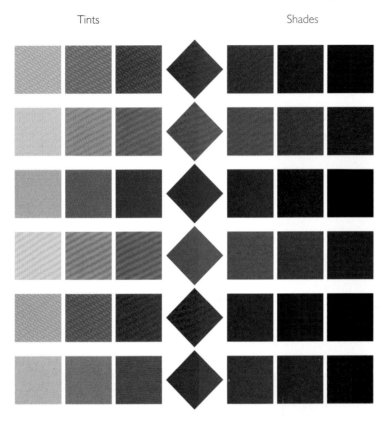

▲ **FIGURE 6.7** Color value scales.

reflects, the lighter it looks; the more it absorbs, the darker it looks.

You can change the value of any hue by adding black or white **(Figure 6.7).** *A light value of a hue* is called a **tint,** and *a dark value of a hue* is called a **shade.** The term *shade* is often used incorrectly to refer to both tints and shades. A tint is created by adding white; a shade is created by adding black.

When artists want to show a bright, sunny day, they use tints **(Figure 6.8).** Paintings having many tints are referred to as *high-key* paintings. Cassatt's *Margot in Blue* is an example of a high-key painting. *Low-key* paintings have shades,

◀ **FIGURE 6.8** Everything except Margot's eyes and hair are painted with tints of color. Even the shadow in the upper left corner of the picture has been softened with gray. The white highlights shimmer and create the effect of a sunny day.

Mary Cassatt. *Margot in Blue.* 1902. Pastel. 61 × 50 cm (24 × 19⅝")
The Walters Art Gallery, Baltimore Maryland.

or dark values, which are used when the artist wants to represent dark, gloomy days, nighttime, and dusk. Dark values can add a feeling of mystery to a work. They can also be used to create a sense of foreboding or danger **(Figure 6.9)**.

If the change in value is gradual, the design produces a calm feeling. If the values take large leaps up and down the scale, from almost white to almost black, the artwork has an active, even nervous, effect.

◀ **FIGURE 6.9** The dark values in this work enhance its ominous mood. Every hue in this work has been darkened with the addition of black except one. Which hue has not been changed? Why?

Rufino Tamayo. *Girl Attacked by a Strange Bird.* 1947. Oil on canvas. 177.8 × 127.3 cm (70 × 50¹/₈″). The Museum of Modern Art, New York, New York. Gift of Mr. and Mrs. Charles Zadok.

Applying Your Skills. Select a hue. Draw a row of three equal shapes. If you are using an opaque paint, such as tempera, add only a small amount of the hue to white. Fill the first shape with the light value. Paint the second shape with the pure hue. Add a small amount of black to the hue to create a dark value, and paint this in the third shape.

If you are using a transparent watercolor paint, make a light value by thinning the paint with water to let more white paper show through. Make a hue darker by adding a small amount of black. Fill the three shapes as in the above directions.

Computer Option. Look at the color palette of your software program. Choose only the tints and shades of one hue to create a computer drawing of a simple cityscape or underwater scene. Colors do not have to be used realistically. Your software program will determine the number of tints and shades that you can use. If your software has the capabilities, mix your own tints and shades for use in this assignment.

Intensity

Intensity is *the brightness or dullness of a hue* **(Figure 6.10).** If a surface reflects only yellow light waves, for example, you see an intensely bright yellow. If a surface reflects other light waves, the color will appear duller. A pure or bright hue is called a *high-intensity color.* Dull hues are called *low-intensity colors.*

Complementary colors are *the colors opposite each other on the color wheel.* The complement, or opposite, of a hue absorbs all of the light waves that the hue reflects **(Figure 6.11).** Red and green are complements. Green absorbs red waves and reflects blue and yellow waves. (Blue and yellow waves combine to appear green.) Red absorbs blue and yellow waves and reflects red waves.

Mixing a hue with its complement dulls the hue, or lowers its intensity. The more complement you add to a hue, the duller the hue looks. Eventually, the hue will lose its own color quality and appear a neutral gray.

The hue used in the greatest amount in a mixture becomes dominant. For this reason, a mixture might look dull

▲ **FIGURE 6.10**   Intensity scale. This scale shows how the intensity of one hue changes as you add its complement to it. The first box is pure, high-intensity green. Each time you add more red, the green becomes duller. Eventually the even mix of green and red creates an interesting, low-intensity gray.

orange or dull blue, depending on the amount of color used. Orange and blue mixtures usually yield brownish results.

Hue, value, and intensity do not operate independently. They rely on one another to create all of the colors that you see around you. When you observe colors, you will see dull tints and bright tints, dull shades and bright shades, light hues and dark hues. Knowing the three properties of color helps you to understand and use color.

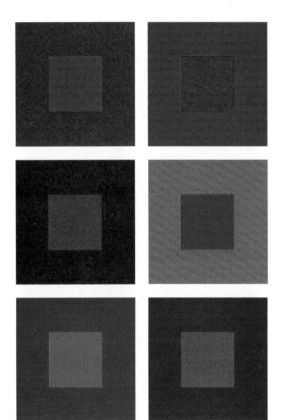

▲ **FIGURE 6.11** Sets of complements. The left column are sets of primary and secondary complements. The right column are sets of intermediate complements.

Activity Working with Intensity

Applying Your Skills. Contrary to what you may have thought, tree trunks are not really brown. They reflect a variety of light and dark low-intensity grays. Draw seven or more bare trees on a large sheet of white paper. Use real trees as models, if possible; if not, find photographs. Combine varying amounts of one primary color and its complement as well as white and black to create a number of different, low-intensity light- and dark-valued colors. Then use these colors to paint each tree a different color.

Computer Option. Design a simple motif using only two solid colors. Use Copy and Paste options to make five copies of the motif. Fill each motif with one primary color or intermediate color and its complement. If your software has the capabilities, mix the two complements together to create a dull or low-intensity version of each. Label each set of complements and mixture sets.

☑ Check Your Understanding

1. What are the three properties of color?
2. Define *color wheel*. What does a color wheel show?
3. Describe the difference between tint and shade.
4. What happens when you mix a hue with its complement?

Color Schemes

Colors are like musical instruments. Each instrument has its own special sound. When you hear an instrument in an orchestra, the sound you hear is affected by the sounds of the other instruments. When the musicians tune up before a performance, you hear confusing, even unpleasant, noises. When they play together in an organized way, they can make beautiful sounds. In the same way, putting colors together without a plan can be confusing and unpleasant to your eyes. Color without organization can look like a visual argument. A plan for organizing colors is called a color scheme.

When two colors come into direct contact, their differences are more obvious. A yellow-green surrounded by a green looks even more yellow. A yellow-green surrounded by yellow, however, appears greener. Grayish-green will seem brighter when it is placed against a gray background. This effect is called simultaneous contrast **(Figure 6.12).**

A color scheme is a plan for organizing colors according to their relationship on the color wheel. By following a color scheme, you can avoid putting together colors in a confusing or unpleasant way. The following are some of the most frequently used color schemes.

Monochromatic Colors

Monochrome means one color. A **monochromatic** color scheme is *a color scheme that uses only one hue and the tints and shades of that hue.* Because this is such a limited scheme, it has a strong, unifying effect on a design **(Figure 6.13).** It is very easy to organize furniture or clothing using monochromatic colors. The drawback to a monochromatic color scheme is that it can be boring.

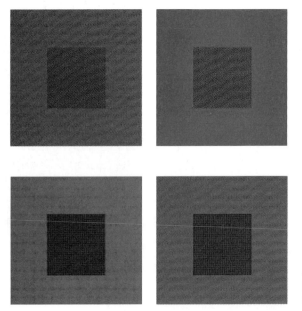

◀ **FIGURE 6.12** Your perception of any color is affected by the colors that surround it. This effect is called simultaneous contrast.

Analogous Colors

Analogous colors are *colors that sit side by side on the color wheel and have a common hue* **(Figure 6.14).** Violet, red-violet, red, red-orange, and orange all have red in common. A narrow color scheme would be limited to only three hues, such as violet, red-violet, and red. An analogous color scheme creates a design that ties one shape to the next through a common color (see Figure 13.34, on page 380).

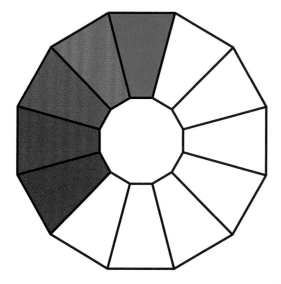

▲ **FIGURE 6.14** Analogous colors are related.

Complementary Colors

The strongest contrast of a hue is produced by complementary colors. When a pair of high-intensity complements are placed side by side, they seem to vibrate. It is difficult to focus on the edge where the complements touch. Some artists use this visual vibration to create special effects. They make designs that sparkle, snap, and sizzle as if charged with electricity **(Figure 6.15)**.

Complementary color schemes are exciting. They are loud, and they demand to be noticed. They are frequently used to catch the viewer's attention. How many ways do people use the red-and-green color scheme? Where else have you seen complementary color schemes used to grab attention?

Not all color schemes based on complements are loud and demanding. If the hues are of low intensity, the contrast is not so harsh. Changing the values of the hues will also soften the effect of the design.

Color Triads

A color triad is composed of three colors spaced an equal distance apart on the color wheel. The contrast between triad colors is not as strong as that between complements. The primary triad is composed of red, yellow, and blue. The secondary triad contains orange, green, and violet **(Figure 6.16)**.

A high-intensity primary triad is very difficult to work with. The contrast between the three hues is so strong that they might make people uncomfortable. A triad can be made more comfortable to the viewer by changing the intensity or values **(Figure 6.17)**. A triad of secondary colors is less disturbing.

▲ **FIGURE 6.16**   Color triads.

▲ **FIGURE 6.15**   This painting is an experiment with the effects of high-intensity, complementary colors. The well-defined squares have been created by precise lines, evenly placed. Notice how the red ground changes color according to the density of the alternating blue and green lines. Stare at this painting. Do the afterimages affect your perception?

Richard Anuszkiewicz. *Iridescence*. 1965. Acrylic on canvas. 152.4 × 152.4 cm (60 × 60″). Albright-Knox Art Gallery, Buffalo, New York. Gift of Seymour H. Knox, 1966. © Richard Anuszkiewicz/Licensed by VAGA, New York, NY

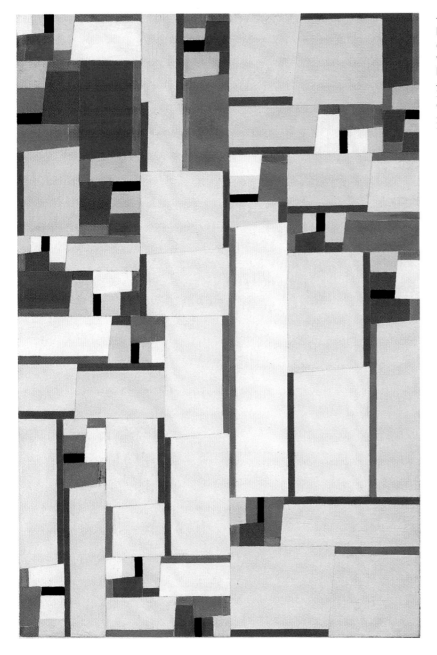

◀ **FIGURE 6.17** Even though this painting is based on the primary triad, it is very comfortable to view. What has the artist done with the colors to make this painting easy to look at?

Fritz Glarner. *Relational Painting #93*. 1962. Oil on canvas. 169.9 × 111.8 cm (66⅞ × 44″). Albright-Knox Art Gallery, Buffalo, New York. Gift of the Seymour H. Knox Foundation, Inc., 1966.

Split Complements

A *split complement* is the combination of one hue plus the hues on each side of its complement **(Figure 6.18).** This is easier to work with than a straight complementary scheme because it offers more variety. For example, start with red-orange. Check the color wheel to find its complement, blue-green. The two hues next to blue-green are blue and green. Red-orange, blue, and green form a split-complementary color scheme.

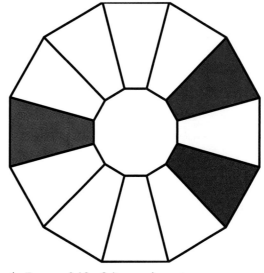

▲ **FIGURE 6.18** Split complement.

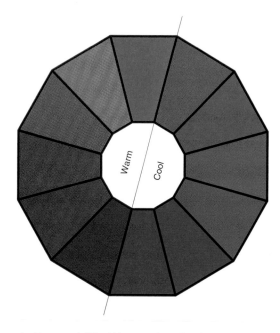

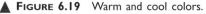

▲ **FIGURE 6.19** Warm and cool colors.

Warm and Cool Colors

Sometimes the colors are divided into two groups, called *warm* and *cool* **(Figure 6.19).** Warm colors are red, orange, and yellow. They are usually associated with warm things, such as sunshine or fire **(Figure 6.20).** Cool colors are blue, green, and violet. They are usually associated with cool things, such as ice, snow, water, or grass **(Figure 6.21).** Warm colors seem to move toward the viewer and cool colors seem to recede, or move away.

The amount of warmth or coolness is relative. Violet on a red background appears much cooler than violet alone. However, the same violet on a blue background seems much warmer than the violet alone.

▲ **FIGURE 6.20** The warm colors in this painting tell us the mood the artist is trying to create.

Rufino Tamayo. *Toast to the Sun.* 1956. Oil on canvas. 80 × 99 cm (31½ × 39″). Wichita Art Museum, Wichita, Kansas. The Roland P. Murdock Collection.

<table></table>

Activity — Using Color Schemes

Applying Your Skills. In your sketch-book, draw several squares. Arrange your initials or the letters of your name in a design in one of the squares. The letters must touch the four edges of the square. Do several different designs using the remaining squares. Play with the letters—turn them upside down, twist them out of shape, make them fat, or overlap them. Consider the letters as shapes. They do not have to be readable.

When you find a design you like, repro-duce it on four squares of white paper. Now paint each design using one of the following color schemes: monochromatic, analogous, complementary, triad, split-complementary, warm, or cool. How do the color arrangements affect the design?

Computer Option. Create a design with the initials or letters of your name. The letters must touch the four edges of the screen. Experiment with the letters—make them different sizes and turn them upside down or twist them out of shape. Try making them thin, fat, wide, or overlapping them. Consider the letters as shapes. They do not have to be readable. Use only solid colors and lines, since you will fill them with new colors as you progress through the assignment. You may use any tools or options available on your computer software.

When you find a design you like, save it. Use various tools to fill in all the shapes, lines, and spaces with each of the following color schemes: monochromatic, analogous, complementary, triad, split-complementary, warm, and cool.

Label and save each color scheme sep-arately as you finish it. When you finish all the color schemes, evaluate their effect on the basic design.

▲ **FIGURE 6.21** The artist has used green in the blue sky and blue in the green foliage. What does this use of color accomplish? How does the color scheme affect the mood of the painting?

Emily Carr. *Above the Trees.* c. 1939. Oil on paper. 91.2 × 61 cm (36 × 24″). Vancouver Art Gallery/Trevor Mills, Vancouver, British Columbia, Canada.

☑ Check Your Understanding

1. Describe a monochromatic color scheme.
2. What types of colors, when placed side by side, seem to vibrate?
3. List two examples of a color triad.

Understanding the Nature and Uses of Color

Artists use color to create special effects in art. Not only do they use color to depict objects the way they actually look, but artists also use color to express ideas and emotions **(Figure 6.22).** As a child, you probably learned that adding too many colors together makes a muddy mess. The more you know about color, the easier it is to avoid making that mistake. By experimenting with color, you will learn what it can do and you will learn how to use it so that you achieve the results you want. Understanding the nature and uses of color allows you to express yourself artistically.

Paint

All paints used in art are made up of three basic ingredients: pigment, binder, and solvent. Artists' **pigments** are *finely ground, colored powders that form paint when mixed with a binder.* Pigment colors cannot match the purity and intensity of the colors of light. The **binder** is *a material that holds together the grains of pigment* in a form that can be spread over some surface. Linseed oil is the binder for oil paints. Wax is used for encaustic paint, gum arabic for watercolor paints, and acrylic polymer for acrylic paints. A chemical emulsion is used to make school tempera paint. Many professional artists use a traditional method of mixing pure pigments with egg yolk for a translucent tempera paint. These binders each give different qualities to the paint.

The **solvent** is *the liquid that controls the thickness or the thinness of the paint.* Turpentine is the solvent for oil paints.

Water is the solvent for watercolors and tempera. Water or acrylic medium is the solvent for wet acrylic paints, but once acrylic paint dries, it is waterproof.

Paint pigments do not dissolve—they remain suspended in the binder. When applied to a surface, the pigments stay on top of the surface and dry there. *Pigments that dissolve in liquid* are called **dyes.** Dyes do not remain on the surface as paints do. Dyes sink into the fabric to which they are applied and color the fabric by staining it.

The pigment, the binder, the solvent, and the surface to which the paint is applied all affect the color you see. Wet colors look brighter and darker than dry ones. Tempera and watercolor paints look lighter and duller after they dry. Oil paints glow even when dry because of their oil binder. If diluted with turpentine, oil paints dry to a dull finish.

The density and color of the surface receiving the paint affects the way the light waves will be reflected back to your eyes. Have you ever applied wax crayon to colored paper? The crayon lets light through to the paper, and the colored paper absorbs some of these light waves and reflects the rest. Only white paper allows the true color of the crayon to show, because it reflects all the light.

Have you ever tried to match colors that are on two different surfaces? A brown leather bag can never truly match a fuzzy brown sweater. A shiny green silk shirt will look brighter than green knit pants even if the same dye is used. Dense surfaces always look brighter because they reflect more light.

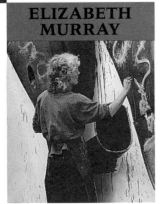
Elizabeth Murray was born in Chicago in 1940. From an early age, she showed an interest in art that her parents encouraged. In elementary school she sold drawings of elephants, cowboys, and stagecoaches to her classmates for 25 cents apiece. This early success kept her interest in art alive.

A high school teacher recognized her talent and created a scholarship for her at the Art Institute of Chicago. Murray took classes in figure drawing, landscape painting, and traditional techniques. She walked through the exhibit halls of the Art Institute museum. Surrounded by masterpieces, she was inspired to become a painter.

In the 1960s, she was told that painting was dead. Everything that could be done had been done. Murray refused to listen and kept painting. Through her perseverance, she developed a style that combines painting with sculpture. Murray is now considered a master of the shaped canvas.

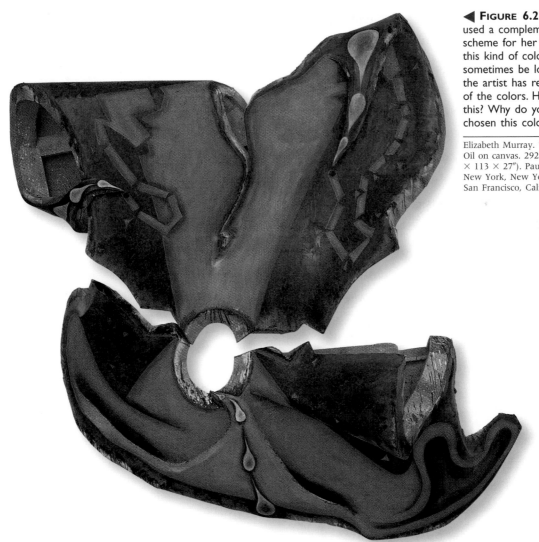

◀ **FIGURE 6.22** Murray has used a complementary color scheme for her artwork. Although this kind of color scheme can sometimes be loud and demanding, the artist has reduced the intensity of the colors. How has she done this? Why do you think she has chosen this color scheme?

Elizabeth Murray. *Things to Come*. 1988. Oil on canvas. 292 × 287 × 71 cm (115 × 113 × 27″). Paula Cooper Gallery, New York, New York. Private Collection, San Francisco, California.

Sources of Pigment

In the past, pigments came from animals, vegetables, and minerals. A kind of beetle and the root of a certain plant were both sources for red pigment. Another plant produced a deep, transparent blue. Ultramarine blue was made by grinding a semiprecious stone. The color ocher was created by using natural clay colored by iron rust.

Today synthetic (artificially made) pigments have been developed by scientists. The synthetics are brighter and more permanent than natural pigments, but some artists still prefer to use natural colors **(Figure 6.23).** Many weavers color their yarns with natural dyes. Some contemporary painters use only natural earth pigments.

The Expressive Effects of Color

Artists use color in the language of art. They use color to express thoughts, ideas, and emotions. There are many ways to use color to convey feelings, and realistic representation is only one of them.

Optical Color

Sometimes artists reproduce colors as they see them. Until the late nineteenth century, this was the way most Western artists painted. Artists would try to capture color as it actually appeared. As we saw earlier in the chapter, colors can change depending on their surroundings. For example, in an automobile dealer's showroom, the color of a blue car is affected by the light, the color of the floor and the walls, and even the colors of the other cars. The car may sparkle as it reflects the showroom lights. Shadows on the car may look dark blue or blue-violet. The red from

▲ **FIGURE 6.23** This Soninke woman is applying a paste of ground natural pigment and water to the mud wall. All the paints are made from materials found in the local environment. The scratch lines on the unpainted wall are the outlines for the paints that will be applied.

Photo from *African Canvas* by Margaret Courtney-Clarke. Rizzoli, 1990.

the car next to it may cause a red-violet reflection on the blue surface.

A painter who is trying to show the car in its setting will use all the colors involved. He or she will make use of *optical color,* the color that results when a true color is affected by unusual lighting or its surroundings. Optical color is the color that people actually perceive. Compare the two paintings by Claude Monet in **Figures 6.24 and 6.25** to see how the time of day affects color.

The Impressionists were deeply involved with optical color and its relationship to light. They tried to express the sensation of light and atmosphere with their unique style of painting. They applied dots and dabs of colors from the spectrum. They did not mix black with any colors. They made gray, low-intensity colors by putting complements together instead of mixing just black and white. These low-intensity grays, such as dull blue and dull green, are much richer and

▲ **FIGURE 6.24** Monet was one of the first artists to take his paints and canvases outdoors. He realized that the colors of the scene changed as the time of day changed, so he carried several canvases. As the light changed, he moved on to another painting. What time of day was this painting done?

Claude Monet. *Poplars.* 1891. Oil on canvas. 100 × 65.2 cm (39½ × 25¹¹/₁₆″). Philadelphia Museum of Art, Philadelphia, Pennsylvania. Bequest of Anne Thomson as a memorial to her father, Frank Thomson, and her mother, Mary Elizabeth Clarke Thomson.

▲ **FIGURE 6.25** What time of day was this painting done? Compare it to Figure 6.24. What are the similarities and differences in the use of color?

Claude Monet. *The Four Trees.* 1891. Oil on canvas. 81.9 × 81.6 cm (32¼ × 32⅛″). The Metropolitan Museum of Art, New York, New York. Bequest of Mrs. H. O. Havemeyer, 1929. The H. O. Havemeyer Collection. (29.100.110)

look more natural in landscapes than do grays made by mixing black and white.

Arbitrary Color

When artists use color to express feelings, they usually ignore the optical colors of objects. They choose the colors *arbitrarily,* that is, by personal preference. They choose arbitrary colors rather than optical colors because they want to use color to express meaning **(Figure 6.26).** In abstract art, color is teamed with the other elements to become the subject as well as the meaning of the work (Figure 6.15 on page 146 and Figure 6.28 on page 156).

Colors affect feelings. Light, bright colors can create happy, upbeat moods.

Cool, dark colors can express mysterious or depressing themes. Warm, low-intensity earth tones seem comfortable and friendly. They are often used to decorate rooms in which people gather. A unique, light value of red-orange has been used to soothe people and has even been successful in calming violent prisoners. Blue is also known for its soothing qualities. Bright yellow is stimulating and pure red excites.

Artists today have put their knowledge of color psychology to work to develop unusual methods for using color. Many of their choices are personal—they make color say what they wish to express.

▲ **FIGURE 6.26** Marc developed his own personal scheme for the symbolic meaning of color. To him, blue represented the spiritual. Red represented matter, and in this work he used it to represent the land. Yellow conveyed comfort, and green served to set off red. The combination of the abstract, curved forms of the horses and the blue, spiritual color reveal Marc's philosophy that animals have a purer relationship with the earth than human beings do.

Franz Marc. *The Large Blue Horses.* 1911. Oil on canvas. 106 × 181 cm (41⅝ × 71¼"). Walker Art Center, Minneapolis, Minnesota. Gift of the T. B. Walker Foundation, Gilbert M. Walker Fund, 1942.

▲ **FIGURE 6.27** Look at the different objects on the table. Identify the number of colors used for each object. Notice how the artist has used dark blue lines to outline the fruit and make each piece stand out. Does this use of color make the objects seem real?

Paul Cézanne. *The Basket of Apples.* c. 1895. Oil on canvas. 65.5 × 81.3 cm (25¾ × 32″). The Art Institute of Chicago, Chicago, Illinois. Helen Birch Bartlett Memorial Collection. (1926.252)

Space

The placement of warm and cool colors can create illusions of depth. Warm colors advance toward the viewer, and cool colors seem to recede and pull away. The French artist Paul Cézanne was the first to use warm and cool colors to create depth. He painted a cool, blue outline around the shape of a warm, round orange. The fruit seemed to be pushed forward by the surrounding blue background **(Figure 6.27).**

Movement

Color can create a sense of movement. When the values in a work jump quickly from very high key to very low key, a feeling of excitement and movement is created **(Figure 6.28**, page 156). When all the values are close together, the work seems much calmer. Today's artists use color to create movement and depth in abstract art.

When you work with color to create movement, remember to use values of pure hues as well as those of tints and shades. You will need to remember, for instance, that the pure hue yellow is much lighter than red or blue.

This is one of Stuart Davis's first abstract works that celebrates his love for New York City. Davis has used strong jumps in value (from bright white, pale blue, and yellow to red, black, and orange) to make your eyes jump around the work. He wants you to feel the excitement and movement of the city. This diagram indicates some of the value jumps. Where can you find others?

Dark ● ● Light ● Light ● Dark

Dark ● Light ● ● Light ● Dark

◀ **FIGURE 6.28**

Stuart Davis. *Hot Still Scape for Six Colors–7th Avenue Style, 1940.* 1940. Oil on canvas. 91.4 × 114.3 cm (36 × 45″). Courtesy, The Museum of Fine Arts, Boston, Massachusetts. Gift of the William H. Lane Foundation and the M. and M. Karolik Collection, by exchange. © Estate of Stuart Davis/Licensed by VAGA, New York, NY

Applying Your Skills. Create four small sketches of trees with leaves. Use a simple color medium such as crayon. Color each sketch to illustrate one of the following: true color; arbitrary color; tonality; optical color; depth through the use of warm and cool colors; or movement through value.

Computer Option. Using the tools of your choice, draw and label six sketches of trees or leaves. Let each sketch illustrate one of the following: true color; optical color; color that expresses personal feelings; depth through the use of warm and cool colors; movement through value; or tonality.

Evaluate the results of your work. Develop your favorite sketch into a finished drawing.

Tonality

Sometimes an artist lets one color, such as blue, dominate a work. In such a case, the work is said to have a blue *tonality* **(Figure 6.29)**. To have a certain tonality, the painting does not have to be monochrome. Other colors may be present. The overall effect of the work, however, will be of one color. Tonality has a unifying effect.

✓ Check Your Understanding

1. All paints are made up of what three basic ingredients?
2. What is the difference between paint pigments and dyes?
3. When might artists use optical color, and when might they use arbitrary color?

◄ **FIGURE 6.29**
The blue tonality of this work conveys the cool impression of the water. The jellyfish are in the inlet and swimming close to the rocks. They are spots of contrast in the blue water. Although blue is the dominant color in this painting, other hues are used. What are they?

Childe Hassam. *Jelly Fish.* 1912. Oil on canvas. 51.4 × 61.6 cm (20¼ × 24¼"). Wichita Art Museum, Wichita, Kansas. The John W. and Mildred L. Graves Collection.

Photo Collage and Mixed Media

SUPPLIES

- **Sketchbook and pencils**
- **Magazines and newspapers**
- **Envelope and scissors**
- **6 × 9″ white paper**
- **White glue, damp sponge, paper towels**
- **Photocopy machine and paper**
- **Crayons**
- **Oil pastels**
- **Colored pencils**
- **Acrylic paints, gloss medium, and brushes**
- **Felt-tip fine-line marker**

▲ **FIGURE 6.30**

Romare Bearden. *Prevalence of Ritual: The Baptism.* 1964. Photomechanical reproductions, synthetic polymer, and pencil on paperboard. 23.2 × 30.5 cm (9⅛ × 12″). Hirshhorn Museum and Sculpture Garden, Smithsonian Institution, Washington, D.C. Gift of Joseph H. Hirshhorn, 1966. © Romare Bearden Foundation/Licensed by VAGA, New York, NY

Romare Bearden's collage **(Figure 6.30)** seems deceptively simple. If you look closely, however, you will see an unusual mixture of media and color. Bearden's art was influenced by his experience as an African-American, but his goal was to create a universal art.

Figure 6.30 is one of Bearden's many collages. In this work, he combined many different pieces to complete the picture. To compose the figures and background, he used photographs of textiles, water, cloth, wood, leaves, grass, metal, and people. He made the faces by cutting details from pictures of African masks, marbles, animal eyes, and mossy vegetation. Then he enlarged his small, original works photographically. Finally, he added paint to complete the colorful collage.

What You Will Learn

In this project, you will create a composition in the style of Bearden. Choose a theme that interests you. Cut out objects and shapes from magazine and newspaper photographs. On a small background approximately 6 × 9 inches, arrange the shapes and recut them as necessary to create a composition similar to Bearden's. Using a photocopy machine, enlarge your work as much as possible. Paint your enlarged work with a color scheme that best expresses the theme of your work. Use any combination of the following: crayons, oil pastels, colored pencils, and school acrylics.

Creating

Study Bearden's collage. Notice how the faces take on a masklike quality because they are made of parts that do not necessarily match. Notice how the entire space is filled. Select a theme related to people to use in your work.

Step 1 Collect magazines and newspapers. Cut small pieces from the photos that you might use. Remember that the first step of the finished product will be small, so keep your pieces small. Put the cut pieces into the envelope for storage. You may combine color with black and white, since the photocopy machine will produce a black-and-white image. However, you must consider how the values of the colors will reproduce in the photocopy.

Step 2 Arrange the cut pieces until you are pleased with your composition. Do not leave any negative space. Every area must be filled. When you are satisfied, glue it down.

Step 3 When your work is dry, enlarge it using the photocopy machine. Make more than one copy so that you can experiment.

Step 4 Choose a color scheme that is appropriate for your theme. Use crayons, oil pastels, colored pencils, school acrylics with gloss medium, and brushes, or any combination of the mentioned color media.

EVALUATING YOUR WORK

▶ **DESCRIBE** Tell the theme you chose and explain how you carried it out. Did you have to create most of the shapes you needed or were you able to find them in photographs?

▶ **ANALYZE** Did the shapes you arranged carry out the effect of your theme? What color scheme did you choose?

▶ **INTERPRET** Did your work express the mood of the theme you selected? Does your title enhance the expressive effect?

▶ **JUDGE** Is your work successful? Does it have the look of the Bearden collage style? Which aesthetic theory would be best to judge this work?

▲ **FIGURE 6.30A** Student work.

STUDIO PROJECT *Photo Collage and Mixed Media* **159**

Photo Enlargement

Pat Steir. *The Bruegel Series (A Vanitas of Style).* 1982–84. Oil on canvas. Sixty-four panels, each 72.4 × 57 cm (28½ × 22½"); total dimensions approximately 5.8 × 4.6 m (19 × 15'). Courtesy of Robert Miller Gallery, New York, New York.

SUPPLIES

- Reproduction of a masterpiece
- Ruler, pencil, soft eraser, and scissors
- Large rectangles of white paper
- Sketchbook
- Acrylic paints and assorted brushes

P at Steir was looking for a unique way to express her vision of the history of painting. She had studied art history, and as a painter she had practiced the styles of the masters. She explored the colors and brushwork of Rembrandt, Bosch, Rubens, and the Bruegels. To practice, she used what she called appropriation: following the themes and styles of the masters. The subject for her painting-about-painting was a reproduction of the sixteenth-century still life by Jan Bruegel (**broi-gul**) the Elder called *Flower Piece in Blue Vase.*

After laying grids over the reproduction to divide it evenly into rectangles, Steir painted each panel as an homage to one of the great artists in history.

What You Will Learn

You will study a work of art by *appropriating* it in the manner of Pat Steir. Working in a group, divide a reproduction of a masterpiece into rectangles using a grid. Distribute the pieces among the group members. Enlarge your individual rectangle using a grid. (See Technique Tip 8 on page 431 in the Handbook for instructions on how to enlarge a work using a grid.) Paint your individual rectangle using colors that are the complements of the original colors.

Creating

Study Steir's *The Bruegel Series (A Vanitas of Style)* **(Figure 6.31).** Notice how each rectangle is painted in a different style.

Step 1 Using a ruler and pencil, divide the back of the reproduction evenly into rectangles. Number them in order and then cut them apart.

Step 2 Follow the directions on page 431 to draw a grid on the face of your rectangle and a matching grid on your large sheet of white paper. Using the grids as a guide, enlarge your section of the reproduction onto the white paper. You do not have to erase the grid lines. They are part of your work.

Step 3 Paint your enlarged composition using complements of the original colors. For example, if one shape was red-orange in the reproduction, you will paint it blue-green. Keep the values the same. If the shape was a light red-orange, paint it a light blue-green.

Step 4 Join all the finished rectangles back together using the numbers as a guide.

▶ **DESCRIBE** What is the name of the artwork your group appropriated? Describe the look of your individual rectangle. Is it realistic or nonobjective? When you join your work with that of the rest of your group, can you recognize the original subject?

▶ **ANALYZE** Describe the lines, shapes, and colors in your individual panel. When you join the group's panels together, do they fit? Do the shapes and lines match? Have you all interpreted the color complements the same way? Do the colors match?

▶ **INTERPRET** Has changing the colors to their complements affected the expressive quality of the whole work? Do the individual styles affect the look of the work?

▶ **JUDGE** Which aesthetic theory would you use to judge your individual panel? Would you use the same theory to judge the whole group's work?

▲ **FIGURE 6.31A** Student work.

Using Color to Create an Expressive Statement

SUPPLIES

- Sketchbook and pencil
- Large sheet of white paper
- Crayons and chalk
- Acrylic paints and assorted brushes
- Scissors and nontoxic rubber cement
- Large sheets of colored poster board

▲ **FIGURE 6.32**

Jaune Quick-To-See Smith. *Spotted Owl.* 1990. Oil and beeswax on canvas, wood panels, and axes. 203 × 294.6 cm (80 × 116"). Courtesy of the Steinbaum-Krauss Gallery, New York, New York. Collection of the artist.

Jaune Quick-To-See Smith was born in St. Ignatius, a small town on the Flathead reservation of the Confederated Salish and Kootenai peoples of southwestern Montana. Her Shoshone grandmother named her *Jaune,* French for "yellow." *Quick-To-See* was an insightful prediction of her life's work.

Drawing came easily to Smith, who wanted to be an artist from childhood. Her hunger for learning took her on a long journey out of the Flathead valley, but the things she learned there are still a part of everything she does. In 1980 she received a master's degree, and in her work she combines her university training with her heritage. She draws deeply from her own life experiences as well as from mainstream modern art to communicate her concern for the vanishing West.

In *Spotted Owl* **(Figure 6.32),** Smith focuses on the new West. This work symbolizes the concern over endangered species, and she uses neutral colors and visual symbols to convey her message that all living things must coexist. Her paintings are a plea to each of us to save the earth.

What You Will Learn

Jaune Quick-to-See Smith expresses her concerns in her paintings. In this project, you will choose an issue that is important to you. Create a shaped painting, without words, that expresses your concern. Use visual symbols and color contrast to emphasize your point.

Creating

Select an issue. Discuss your concerns with your classmates. This may help you think of ways to express your ideas visually. Your subject may be about school issues. It could be a world issue concerning politics or the environment.

Write about your issue in your sketchbook. List words and concepts. Make several small sketches for your painting. Use crayons to plan your color scheme. The shape of your finished work does not have to be rectangular. You may choose a circle, a free-form shape, or the shape of an object that is part of your idea. Objects may protrude from the edges of the shape for emphasis.

Discuss your sketches with a small group of classmates and share composition ideas. For example, you might want to make the people larger, or the negative spaces larger than the positive shape to emphasize loneliness. Try painting everything in warm colors except a calm area. Express the calmness with a cool color.

Step 1 Draw your final idea on a large sheet of white paper with beige or yellow chalk. Paint with acrylics before you cut out the final outline. Remember to use color contrast for emphasis.

Step 2 Cut out your finished piece. Test your work on several different colors of poster board before you choose the final background color. Certain colors could change the message of your painting while others may enhance it. Mount your painting on the poster board. Give your work a title that incorporates a reference to the issue.

EVALUATING YOUR WORK

▶ **DESCRIBE** Name the issue that is the subject of your painting. Tell which visual symbols you selected to illustrate your idea and explain why you chose them.

▶ **ANALYZE** How did you use color contrast to make your point? Which other elements did you emphasize to express your ideas? Explain.

▶ **INTERPRET** Did your work convey your message without words? Were your classmates able to understand your visual symbols?

▶ **JUDGE** Which aesthetic theory would you use to judge this work? Was it successful? If you were to do it over, what would you change?

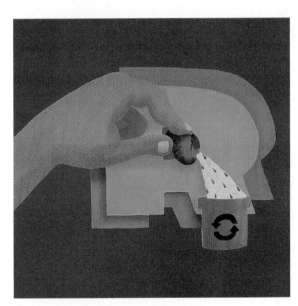

▲ **FIGURE 6.32A** Student work.

Expressive Portrait

▲ **FIGURE 6.33**

Henri Matisse. *Femme au Chapeau (Woman with the Hat)*. 1905. Oil on canvas. 80.6 × 59.7 cm (31¾ × 23½"). San Francisco Museum of Modern Art, San Francisco, California. Bequest of Elise S. Haas.

In 1905, Henri Matisse and a group of his friends presented an exhibit of brightly colored paintings that were more daring than those of van Gogh in their use of color and bolder than Gauguin's in their use of flat shapes. The style enraged one art critic who called the group *Fauves* (wild beasts). Matisse had no complicated theories to explain his artworks. He claimed they had only one purpose: to give pleasure.

In *Femme au Chapeau (Woman with the Hat)* **(Figure 6.33)** you see every loose brushstroke, and the colors used are not related to the shapes they cover. Notice the blue-green line describing the edge of the woman's nose, the green shadow on her forehead, and the red-orange shadow on her neck.

What You Will Learn

You will select a portrait of yourself, a friend, or a celebrity and scan it into your computer. Then, you will alter the image using color and line to create a new mood or emotion that you wish to express. Include text, such as a poem or a phrase, that fits the idea you are trying to express. Arrange the text into a shape that acts as an area of texture in the composition.

Creating

Capture a portrait using a digital camera or scan a color photograph, sketch, or magazine clipping of yourself, a friend, relative, or celebrity. Scan in 256 colors unless your computer has adequate memory for a higher resolution.

SUPPLIES

- **Photograph, sketchbook, magazine, or postcard**
- **Scanner**
- **Computer**
- **Color Editing and/or Paint application**
- **Printer**
- **Sound capacity: computer, tape or CD player**

Step 1 Follow the procedures for your scanner software. Crop, adjust the color, brightness, and size of the image and then scan it. Save and title the image to your hard drive, a disk, or a file. Use a file format that can be read by the software you will use to manipulate the image. If uncertain, pict is a good choice because it is read by most applications. Other common choices include tiff, eps, and jpeg or gif for Web pages. Quit the scanner software application.

Step 2 Launch the paint application to turn your scanned portrait into a work where color is the most important expressive element. Go to the File menu, choose Open, and select the saved scanned file. Begin by further cropping and adjusting the image. Next, explore menus and settings to change color contrast/brightness, lines and edges, hue/saturation, and balance. These options alone can produce intriguing results.

Investigate other options. Use the Undo command immediately after each attempt until you discover an effect you want to keep. Select the Save As command to retitle and save.

Step 3 Decide on a quote, poem, or short verse that corresponds with the mood of the portrait. Pick the Text tool and select a font, style, color, and size. Letters and words can be manipulated to emphasize their meaning. Arrange the text in a shape that acts as an area of colored texture in your total design.

Remember to credit the source for the photograph and text even if they are your own original creations. List these sources on the back of your work.

EVALUATING YOUR WORK

▶ **DESCRIBE** Who is the subject of the portrait? Tell what color changes and effects you have used including the menus, options, and tools that produced these results. Identify the source of the photograph and text.

▶ **ANALYZE** Describe the colors you used. Have these colors created surprising results? Did you arrange the text into a shape that acts as an area of colored texture? How have you altered the lines and edges using different brushstrokes? Did you distort any areas to make the work more expressive?

▶ **INTERPRET** What mood or emotion does your altered portrait express? What special effects support this mood or emotion? Does the text you added enhance the mood you were trying to achieve? Give your work a title that sums up your feelings about it.

▶ **JUDGE** Did you achieve the expressive quality you were trying to convey? Would you make any changes to make your work more successful? Which aesthetic theory would you use to defend your judgment of your work?

▲ **FIGURE 6.33A** Student work.

ART CRITICISM IN ACTION

▲ **Figure 6.34**

Romare Bearden. *Family*. 1988. Collage on wood. 71.1 × 50.8 cm (28 × 20"). National Museum of American Art, Smithsonian Institution, Washington, D.C. © Romare Bearden Foundation/Licensed by VAGA, New York, New York.

1 ▶ DESCRIBE What do you see?

During this step, you will collect facts about the artwork. List all of the information found in the credit line. Use your perception skills to study the objects you see in the work.

- Describe the people you see. Include details about their clothing, their features, and their hair.
- Describe the objects in the work. Remember not to make guesses.

2 ▶ ANALYZE How is this work organized?

This is the step in art criticism that deals with the composition of the work. This is a clue-collecting step. Remember not to make guesses.

- What hues do you see? Where are they? Which are used the most?
- Do you see any neutral colors? Where? Can you find any tints or shades?
- Has the artist used one of the color schemes you studied to organize this work?

3 ▶ INTERPRET What is the artist trying to communicate?

During this step, you will combine the clues you have collected with your personal feelings and experiences to guess what this work is about.

- What family relationship does this artwork express?
- How has the artist organized color to give you hints as to the relationship of the people to each other and to their environment?
- Create a new title for this work based on your personal interpretation.

4 ▶ JUDGE What do you think of the work?

Now it is time to decide if this is a successful work of art. You may make a personal opinion; however, it is important to make an objective judgment based on aesthetic theories.

- Do you find this work interesting? Did it make you think?
- Did the artist use the element of color to convey his message well?
- Do you think this is a successful work of art? Why or why not? Use one or more of the aesthetic theories described in Chapter 2 to defend your judgment.

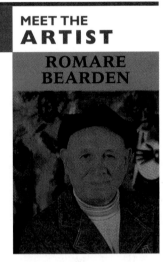

MEET THE
ARTIST
ROMARE BEARDEN

American, 1911–1988

Romare Bearden was born in rural Charlotte, North Carolina. Although he spent his summer vacations with his grandparents in Charlotte, he spent most of his youth in Harlem. Bearden grew up in the 1930s, when many of the talented members of the Harlem Renaissance still lived in Harlem. This influenced his artistic development and his awareness of his heritage. After World War II, Bearden attended the Sorbonne in Paris.

Today his work doesn't fit into any neat category. In his collages he tied together his personal experiences as an African-American, his knowledge of his African heritage, and his understanding of art history and techniques.

Where Do Paint Pigments Come From?

▲ **FIGURE 6.35**

Funerary Stela of Aafenmut. *Aafenmut Offering Before Horus, Above Sun's Barque.* Thebes, Khokha, Third Intermediate Period, Dynasty 22, ca 924–715 B.C. Painted wood. 23 × 18.2 × 3.5 cm (9 × 7¼ × 1⅜"). The Metropolitan Museum of Art, New York, New York. Rogers Fund, 1928. (28.3.35)

About 20,000 years ago, Stone Age people made paint from plant matter and animal parts to decorate their caves, clothing, and bodies. The human desire for variety led to the discovery of minerals that, when ground into powders and mixed with liquids, formed a range of brilliant colors. Ultramarine, crimson, and cerulean blue are just a few of the colors of pigments that derive from minerals.

Different shades of green and blue come from minerals that contain large amounts of copper, such as azurite and malachite. Reddish pigments derive from cinnabar, a mineral containing sulfur and mercury. Yellow pigments can be made from ochre, an iron-rich clay that turns red when heated. Precious minerals such as gold and silver can be pulverized to make glittery pigments.

In addition to mineral-based pigments, many vibrant colors come from plants and animals. For example, saffron yellow comes from the root of the rubia plant. Today, many paint pigments are synthetically produced from coal tars and petrochemicals. The bright and often longer-lasting colors of modern synthetic pigments are achieved through chemical reactions.

Making the Connection

1. What mineral-based pigments do you think were used to decorate the painting in **Figure 6.35**?
2. What are the effects of the artist's use of color in this painting?
3. Look at a good reproduction of one of your favorite older paintings. Make a list of the colors you think the artist used and blended to create the work. Then, approximate as best you can the different minerals that appear on the canvas. Write down your answers.

CHAPTER 6 REVIEW

Building Vocabulary

On a separate sheet of paper, write the term that best matches each definition given below.

1. An element of art that is derived from reflected light.
2. Produced when light passes through a wedge-shaped glass, called a prism, and is bent and separated into bands of color.
3. The name of a color in the color spectrum.
4. A light value of a hue.
5. A dark value of a hue.
6. The brightness or dullness of a hue.
7. The colors opposite each other on the color wheel.
8. A color scheme that uses only one hue and the tints and shades of that hue.
9. Colors that sit side by side on the color wheel and have a common hue.
10. Finely ground, colored powders that form paint when mixed with a binder.
11. A material that holds together the grains of pigment.
12. The liquid that controls the thickness or thinness of the paint.

Reviewing Art Facts

Answer the following questions using complete sentences.

1. Explain how the eye sees color.
2. What is an afterimage? How is it produced?
3. Name the three components of color.
4. What is color value?
5. Name the seven different kinds of color schemes.
6. What are complementary colors? How do complementary colors affect each other?
7. What are synthetic pigments? How do they differ from natural pigments?
8. What is arbitrary color?

Thinking Critically About Art

1. **Synthesize.** Figure 6.20 on page 148 and Figure 6.21 on page 149 use very different color schemes. Compare the two works. List the similarities and differences in their style and use of color.
2. **Interpret.** Look at Figure 6.9 on page 141. The artist has used a color scheme of dark values to create a specific mood. Study the lines and shapes in this work. How do they affect the feeling of the painting? Notice the areas of bright, intense color. How does this add drama? Does the title add to the mood?

 Read how Joanna Featherstone paints a picture with words as a professional storyteller in the Performing Arts Handbook on page 418. Like a painter, Joanna uses tonality, contrast, intensity, and movement to tap into the emotions that each color evokes.

 Explore the use of color in the expressive works of Monet, Morisot, Gauguin, and Kandinsky on the Internet. Find additional information about color theory and the use of color during specific historical periods. Visit us at **www.glencoe.com/sec/art**

▲ **FIGURE 7.1** The artist has used a variety of beads to create different textures. Which area of the throne looks smooth? Which looks rough?

Bamileke. *Throne*. African, nineteenth century. Wood and beads. Height: 47 cm (18½″). The Detroit Institute of Arts, Detroit, Michigan. Founders Society Purchase, Eleanor Clay Ford Fund for African Art.

Texture

Every surface has a texture. **Texture** is *the element of art that refers to how things feel, or look as if they might feel if touched.* Texture includes the slick, smooth surface of ice, the bumpy, rough surface of a brick, and the prickly surface of a scrub brush.

A nineteenth–century African artist created the ceremonial throne shown in **Figure 7.1.** Notice the animal figure that supports the seat. What might be symbolic about the use of an animal as an important part of the throne? Notice how the artist has used different shapes, sizes, and colors of beads to create texture. The areas where he has used many small, white beads look rough. The lines he has created using long blue beads look smooth and slick. Notice the cowry shells around the edges of the seat and the base. What kind of texture do they suggest?

This artwork almost asks to be touched. You can easily imagine what the beads and shells would feel like if you touched them. Do you think the artist meant for the artwork to be inviting in this way? Why or why not? In this chapter, you will learn how artists use texture to convey ideas and feelings through their art.

OBJECTIVES

After completing this chapter, you will be able to:

- Understand how texture is perceived through the senses.
- Describe various textures.
- Reproduce textures by changing values.
- Use texture as the expressive element in creating two- and three-dimensional works of art.
- Understand how artists use texture.

WORDS TO KNOW

texture
visual texture
matte surface
collage
frottage
grattage
decalcomania

Developing Your
PORTFOLIO

Collect small samples of various textures, such as a scrap of sandpaper or a swatch of fabric. You can also use magazine illustrations that show texture. Mount these samples on a piece of posterboard. Under each sample, write two words that describe the texture, such as "slick, smooth" or "bumpy, rough." Then write a short paragraph describing how you could use various textures (or the appearance of texture) in your art. Include your texture board and paragraph in your portfolio.

Texture in Your Life

Textures play a role in decisions you make every day. Think about how fabric textures have influenced your clothing choices. Would you wear a shirt made of rough burlap against your bare skin? Probably not. Clothing manufacturers consider this when they decide what fabrics to use and how to make their clothes. They may use warm, heavy wool for a coat, but then line the coat with silky material so that it feels comfortable.

Think about the textures of food. Imagine the smoothness of ice cream, and consider how different it is from the angular roughness of potato chips. Would grilled steak taste the same if it were ground up in a blender? Textures are important to us in a variety of ways.

How You Perceive Texture

You perceive texture with two of your senses: touch and vision. Infants learn about things by touching them and by putting them into their mouths. Toddlers are attracted to all objects that are within their reach. When you look at surfaces, you are able to guess their textures because you have learned how textures feel. Your eyes tell you what something would feel like if you were to touch it **(Figure 7.2).**

▲ **FIGURE 7.2** What textures are represented in these photographs?

When you actually touch something to determine its texture, you experience real texture. When you look at a photograph of a texture, such as velvet, leather, concrete, or ice, you see surface patterns of light and dark that bring back memories of how those objects actually feel. When this happens, you are experiencing **visual texture,** *the illusion of a three-dimensional surface.* If you touch visual textures, you do not feel what your eyes told you to expect.

There are two kinds of visual texture: *simulated* and *invented.* Simulated textures imitate real textures. Plastic tabletops can be made to look like wood. Vinyl flooring can be made to look like ceramic tile or stone. Manufactured fabrics imitate natural leather and fur.

Artists can do the same. For example, painter Peggy Flora Zalucha simulates textures in her paintings so accurately that you think you might be looking at a photograph **(Figure 7.3).**

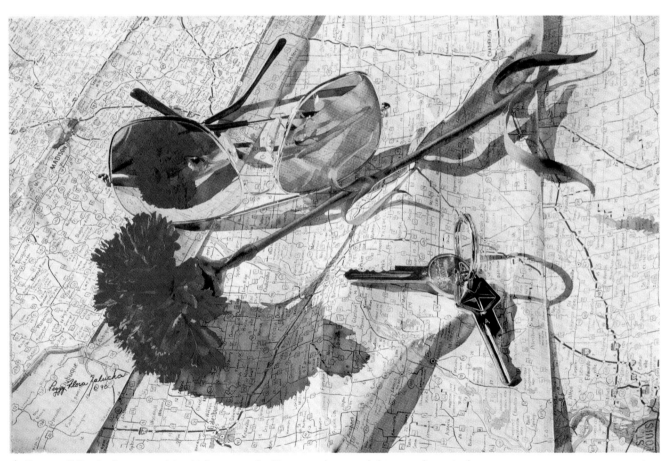

▲ **FIGURE 7.3** At first you might think you are looking at a photograph because the artist has simulated the textures of objects so realistically. This is actually a still-life painting of items associated with taking a road trip. The details of the map are so clear that if you recognized the area of the country, you could read the map. Zalucha has used white highlights to represent the brilliant reflections of light off the shiny surfaces of the glasses and keys, and more subtle changes of value to represent the textures found in non-reflective surfaces, such as the wrinkles on the map.

Peggy Flora Zalucha. *Map Still Life with Carnations, Keys, and Glasses.* 1989. Mixed watermedia. 76 × 111.8 cm (30 × 44″). Private collection.

◄ **FIGURE 7.4** In this painting, the artist has used a number of techniques to suggest texture. A variety of line types and shading techniques have been used. Can you identify the textures? Do they represent real textures or are they invented? The artwork clearly depicts two people and an elephant, but would you call it realistic? Why or why not?

Elephants and Mahouts, circa 1590-95. Ink, color and gold on paper. Brooklyn Museum of Art. Promised gift of Dr. Bertram Schaffner TL 1986.371.4

Invented textures are two-dimensional patterns created by the repetition of lines or shapes. These patterns do not represent real surface qualities, but the patterns of light and dark suggest real texture. The purpose of invented texture is to create decorated surfaces that evoke memories of unusual textures **(Figure 7.4).**

 **Activity** | **Creating Textures**

Applying Your Skills. Make a collection of texture rubbings. To make a rubbing, place a sheet of thin paper against a rough object or surface. Hold the paper in place with one hand. Use the flat side of an unwrapped crayon or the side of a pencil lead to rub over the paper. Rub in one direction—away from the hand holding the paper. Rubbing back and forth can cause the paper or object to slip. Examine the rubbings closely, paying special attention to the lines, dots, shapes, and values.

Computer Option. Explore the textures on your computer application as well as those you can create. Begin with a Pencil, Brush, or Shape tool . Draw objects or shapes. Fill each shape with a different texture from available menus. Make some new textures by editing or adding textures. Use a variety of available tools and paper textures. Experiment with a blending tool to soften surfaces. Identify which objects look rough and which look smooth.

Texture and Value

The appearance of a surface depends on how it reflects light. Every surface displays a pattern of light and dark values. From the pattern of light and dark values, we can make a judgment about the texture of a surface or an object even if we cannot touch it.

Rough and Smooth Textures

The roughness or smoothness of a texture can be determined by looking at its light and dark values. A rough surface reflects light unevenly. It shows irregular patterns of light and shadow. Look at a shag rug, an orange, tree bark, or a patch of bare ground. Notice how the high places catch the light, casting shadows of different sizes and shapes.

A smooth texture reflects light evenly. Look at a sheet of paper, an apple, or a new, unmarked desktop. Your eyes glide across these objects, uninterrupted by shadows, just as your fingers would glide across them, uninterrupted by bumps and dents.

Matte and Shiny Textures

In addition to rough and smooth, textures can be matte or shiny. A **matte surface** is *a surface that reflects a soft, dull light*. It absorbs some light and reflects the rest. Matte surfaces, such as paper, denim, unfinished wood, and your skin, have a soft, dull look.

A shiny surface is the opposite of a matte surface. A shiny surface is a surface that reflects so much bright light that it seems to glow. Shiny surfaces also have highlights. Some surfaces reflect bright sunlight with such intensity that you have to squint your eyes to protect them from the glare. Window glass, a new car, a polished brass candlestick, and the surface of a calm pool of water are all examples of shiny surfaces.

Matte and shiny surfaces can be rough or smooth. Sandpaper is matte rough, and a freshly ironed pillowcase is matte smooth. Aluminum foil is shiny and smooth until it gets crumpled up; then it becomes shiny and rough. In **Figure 7.5** on page 176, Janet Fish has illustrated all of these texture variations.

Activity — Creating Contrasting Textures

Applying Your Skills. Make a series of small drawings and paintings of objects that have different textures. Try to reproduce both smooth and rough textures. You may use a different medium for each drawing, but study the lights and shadows on each object before you choose the medium. For example, you might examine a hairbrush, an old work shoe, weathered wood, a wig, a fuzzy slipper, or a satin slip, then select a medium that would work best for each texture.

Computer Option. Make a series of small drawings and paintings of objects that have different textures, as in the preceding activity. Use the Pencil or Brush tool on the computer. First, sketch your shapes. Then reproduce the texture of each shape using dots, lines, and value blending. Concentrate on the shadows, lights, and highlights of each different texture.

Janet Fish has used pastels to create the visual textures in this work. The diagram points out some areas where she has combined different kinds of visual texture such as shiny-rough, shiny-smooth, and matte-smooth. Can you find more areas where she has created combinations of visual texture?

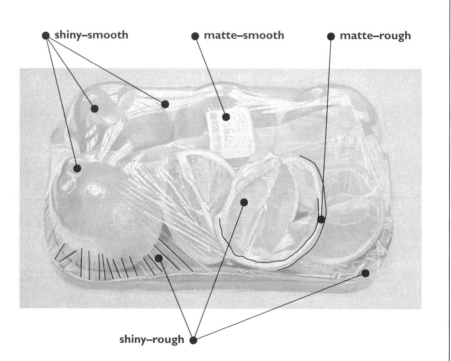

shiny–smooth · matte–smooth · matte–rough

shiny–rough

◀ **FIGURE 7.5**

Janet Fish. *Oranges.* 1973. Pastel on sandpaper. 55.5 × 96.5 cm (21⅞ × 38″). Allen Memorial Art Museum, Oberlin College, Oberlin, Ohio. Fund for Contemporary Art, 1974. © Janet Fish/Licensed by VAGA, New York, NY

✓ Check Your Understanding

1. Define visual texture.
2. Describe, in detail, the two types of visual texture.
3. Compare how rough and smooth textures reflect light.
4. What is the difference between a matte and a shiny surface?

How Artists Use Texture

The texture of surfaces is important in every form of visual art. Our minds are full of texture memories. Artists use both visual and real textures to make you remember those texture experiences.

Ivan Albright was a painter who loved to depict decaying, aging objects with meticulous precision. He painted the skin of the old farm woman in **Figure 7.6** to accent and exaggerate every tiny wrinkle. Look at the painting. How many different kinds of textures can you identify?

In contrast, Pierre Auguste Renoir (ren-**wahr**) painted young people with healthy, glowing complexions **(Figure 7.7).** He preferred to focus on beautiful

◀ **FIGURE 7.6** Albright worked on this painting for two years creating the painstaking details of the surface textures shown in the work.

Ivan Albright. *The Farmer's Kitchen.* 1933–34. Oil on canvas. 91.5 × 76.5 cm (36 × 30"). National Museum of American Art, Smithsonian Insititution, Washington, D.C.

▶ **FIGURE 7.7** Renoir started his career as an artist in a porcelain factory. He copied famous portraits of beautiful women onto the porcelain plates. Renoir spent the rest of his life painting beautiful people. Notice how he uses his brushstrokes to create texture.

Pierre Auguste Renoir. *Madame Henriot.* 1876. Oil on canvas. 66 × 50 cm (26 × 19⅝"). National Gallery of Art, Washington, D.C. Gift of Adele R. Levy Fund, Inc.

▶ **FIGURE 7.8** At times, van Gogh became so impatient with the progress of his work that he squeezed the paint directly from the tube onto the canvas. Then he used anything that was handy, including his fingers, to move and swirl the globs of paint around.

Vincent van Gogh. *Sunflowers*. 1888. Oil on canvas. 92 × 73 cm (36¼ × 28¼"). National Gallery, London, England.

and pleasing subjects. How many different textures can you identify in this painting? Notice that both Albright and Renoir have imitated the texture of human skin. In each case, the artist has used texture to convey a feeling about the subject. In one painting the skin is appealing, in the other it is almost repulsive. Both artists have tried to control your reaction to the subject of the paintings through their use of visual texture.

Many painters use color and value patterns to produce the illusion of textures. Look, for instance, at the painting by Judith Leyster (Figure 10.4, page 257) or Rembrandt van Rijn (ryne) (Fig-

ure 11.5, page 290). These artists were experts at suggesting textures such as soft velvet, shiny satin, delicate lace, and fluffy feathers. When you look closely at their paintings, you discover that these artists do not paint every texture in photographic detail. They use a few brushstrokes to suggest the texture from a certain distance.

Instead of relying only on visual texture, many painters add real textures to their paintings. Vincent van Gogh (vahn **goh**) used such thick paint on his canvas that his swirling brushstrokes created a rough surface **(Figure 7.8).** The surface ridges of the thick paint actually make the paint look brighter. The ridges catch more light and reflect brighter colors to the viewer. If you were to touch a van Gogh painting you would feel the texture you see. Even today, artists feel that such textural qualities enhance their work. Joan Mitchell is one contemporary painter who brushes on paint and does not try to smooth out the brushstrokes **(Figure 7.9).**

Some painters add real textures to their work by attaching various materials to the work's surface. Some artists add sand and other materials to the paint. In some cases, artists create what is called a **collage** (kul-**lahzh**), or *an artwork onto which materials such as textured paper and fabric have been attached.* Although folk artists have used this technique for centuries, fine artists only

▶ **FIGURE 7.9** Joan Mitchell remained an Abstract Expressionist throughout her entire painting career. This work refers to the snow and cold of her Chicago childhood. Notice how she has used the brushstrokes to show the excitement and tension of a snowy day in the city. What kinds of lines do you find in the brushstrokes?

Joan Mitchell. *Dirty Snow.* 1980. Oil on canvas. 220 × 180 cm (86¼ × 70⅞"). The National Museum of Women in the Arts, Washington, D.C. Gift of Wallace and Wilhelmina Holladay.

◀ **FIGURE 7.10** Schapiro invented the word *Femmage* to describe her collages. Rather than scraps of discarded paper, she used pieces of embroidered, appliquéd, and crocheted fabrics that were created by women to add real textures to her work. In this way, she connected her work to the traditional women's arts of the past.

© Miriam Schapiro. *Yard Sale, 1993.* Acrylic & fabric on canvas. 208 × 228 cm (82 × 90"). Courtesy Steinbaum Krauss Gallery, NYC

began using collage in the last century. (The word wasn't even invented until 1919.) Miriam Schapiro, an artist who uses collage, added bits of fabric, lace, and thread to her paintings to enrich the surface and to convey a message **(Figure 7.10).**

Sculptors must also be aware of texture because the texture of each surface must fit the whole. Some sculptors imitate the real texture of skin, hair, and cloth, while others create new textures to fit new forms. In **Figure 7.11,** the artist lets the texture of the cedar wood show through the paint. In contrast, the sculptor of **Figure 7.12,** Edgar Degas, imitated real textures. He even added materials (a cotton skirt and a satin ribbon) to the figure to make it more realistic.

◀ **FIGURE 7.11** John Hoover is an Aleut sculptor. He uses the folklore of his people as subject matter, but he has developed a style that is not traditional. Notice how he lets the texture of the wood show through the paint. He uses only natural pigments. Can you identify the colors?

John Hoover. *Loon Song.* 1990. Cedar and natural pigments. 152 × 61 cm (60 × 24"). Glenn Green Galleries, Scottsdale, Arizona.

Edgar Degas (day-**gah**) was born in Paris in 1834. His family, wealthy bankers, supported his ambition to become an artist. He was educated at the École des Beaux-Arts by a French Classicist who trained him in classical drafting. This expertise in drawing is a main element in Degas' work.

Around 1865, Degas fell under the influence of the Impressionist movement and abandoned academic, classical subject matter and began painting contemporary subjects such as music halls, theatres, and cafés. Unlike the Impressionists with whom he is often associated, however, Degas was not interested in the use of light or in depicting nature on canvas. He worked in a studio and tried to capture his models in natural and spontaneous movements. He preferred women as his subjects and is best known for his studies of ballet dancers, although he also painted milliners (hat makers) and laundresses.

In the 1860s, he began experimenting with unusual methods of composition, such as alternate perspectives, odd visual angles, asymmetrical balance, and accidental cut-offs. These methods of composition would inspire many modern artists. As he grew older, his eyesight began to fail and he turned to a new process: sculpture. In his sculpture, as in his painting, he tried to capture spontaneous movement and realistic poses.

▶ **FIGURE 7.12** What an unusual combination of textures! The figure of the young dancer is cast in bronze. Even the vest and the ballet shoes she wears are bronze. To that Degas added a skirt made of gauzelike fabric and a satin hair ribbon. Why do you think he added real textures to the metal figure?

Edgar Degas. *The Little Fourteen-Year-Old Dancer.* Model ca 1880, cast 1922. Bronze, slightly tinted, with cotton skirt and satin hair ribbon. 104.5 cm (41¼″) high. The Metropolitan Museum of Art, New York, New York. H. O. Havemeyer Collection, bequest of Mrs. H. O. Havemeyer, 1929. (29.100.370)

Architects are also aware of the importance of texture. They use stucco, brick, wood, stone, concrete, metal, and glass to create texture. Frank Lloyd Wright, one of the most influential architects of the twentieth century, believed that a building should develop out of its natural surroundings **(Figure 7.13).** Because of this, he selected textures that seemed natural. Interior designers select textures for rugs, drapes, furniture, and artwork that complement different wall surfaces. This gives a sense of cohesiveness, or unity, to a design.

In crafts, textures are essential. Potters manipulate textures by pressing different objects into wet clay. They can also change surfaces by applying glazes. Some glazes are shiny, while others are matte. Some glazes result in a crackle finish that gives a rough texture to a piece of pottery. Weavers control texture through the use of fibers and weaving techniques. For example, rough wool fibers have a different texture than smooth cotton fibers. In addition, weavers use different techniques to create texture. By twisting fibers as they weave, they can create a rough texture. Other artisans also use texture. Jewelry makers work with different kinds of metal to create various textures. They might emboss or press a raised design into metal or facet a stone to give its surfaces a smooth, shiny appearance. Feathers, river rocks,

▲ **FIGURE 7.13** The colors, forms, and textures of this building were planned so that Taliesin West would blend into the colors, forms, and textures of its desert setting. Wright believed that a building should be in harmony with its environment.

Frank Lloyd Wright. *Taliesin West*. Near Phoenix, Arizona.

seashells, seeds, bones, and teeth have been used to make jewelry and hair ornaments **(Figure 7.14).**

Artists also invent textures to enrich their works. Max Ernst used three unusual techniques—*frottage, grattage,* and *decalcomania*—to create his Surrealist fantasy paintings (Figure 7.16 on page 184). In **frottage** (froh-**tahzh**), *a freshly painted canvas is placed right-side-up over a raised texture and rubbed or scraped across the surface of the paint.* The paint that remains on the canvas creates a pattern that reflects the texture. The texture rubbings you made earlier in this chapter are another form of frottage. To create **grattage** (grah-**tahzh**) effects, *wet paint is scratched with a variety of tools, such as forks, razors, and combs.* In **decalcomania,** *paint is forced into random textured patterns* **(Figure 7.15).** Paint is placed between two canvas surfaces. The canvases are then pulled apart.

▲ **Figure 7.14** The native people of Ecuador used brilliant, tropical bird feathers to create ornaments. The ornaments pictured were created to decorate ears and hair.

Native people of South America. *Featherwork Ornaments.* Collected in 1938 by E. Erskine. National Museum of the American Indian, Smithsonian Institution, Heye Foundation, New York, New York.

 Activity **Inventing Textures**

Applying Your Skills. On a small piece of white paper, draw nine shapes of different sizes with a pencil or felt-tip pen. Some shapes should touch the edges of the paper. Fill each shape with sketches of a different texture. The textures should be invented. For instance, you could put lines of writing close together in one shape, or you could try repeating small shapes in another. Try line patterns, stippling, or smooth shadow.

Computer Option. Explore textures and effects that can be made with the Brush tool or other tools on the computer. Menus provide choices from thick, opaque oils to wet, transparent paint. Experiment. Save your results by applying your discoveries to objects, shapes, or scenes.

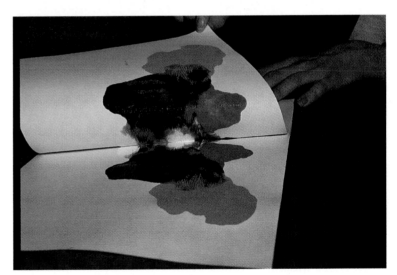

▲ **Figure 7.15** Decalcomania technique.

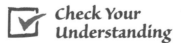 **Check Your Understanding**

1. Define *collage.*
2. Describe a form of frottage.
3. How does an artist create a grattage effect?
4. In what technique is paint forced into random textured patterns?

Fantasy Landscape

▲ **FIGURE 7.16**

Max Ernst. *The Eye of Silence.* 1943–44. Oil on canvas. 108 × 141 cm (42½ × 55½"). Washington University Gallery of Art, St. Louis, Missouri. University purchase, Kende Sale Fund, 1946

SUPPLIES

- Acrylic paints and assorted brushes
- One sheet of heavy paper or canvas
- Scratch paper for practice
- Wax paper
- Scratching and rubbing tools such as combs or rulers
- Magazine clippings
- Scissors and white glue

Max Ernst was among the artists, philosophers, and writers who formed the Surrealist movement in the mid-1920s. Surrealists searched for a new reality—one that rejected the long-established rules of composition and logic. They believed that this reality could be found in the subconscious mind, and they created paintings that took on the look of dreams or nightmares. Salvador Dali (Figure 13.28, page 375) and René Magritte (Figure 5.37, page 126) were members of this movement.

Ernst used three unusual techniques—*frottage, grattage,* and *decalcomania*—to bring his fantasies to life. Ernst then elaborated on the design. Sometimes he cut the textured pieces into forms with which he created collages. Sometimes he painted over areas such as the sky in *The Eye of Silence* **(Figure 7.16).**

What You Will Learn

You will create a fantasy painting using Max Ernst's techniques to produce textured areas. You may cut and rearrange the textured area to make new shapes. Add details and contrasting shapes using paint, oil pastels, markers, and collage. The work should be unified. One object must blend into the next without empty spaces separating them. When you are finished, the work must look like a Surrealist's dream.

Creating

Study Ernst's painting (Figure 7.16). Notice that the woman's face has been cut from another picture and pasted on. Notice also how the realistic sky has been painted up to the edges of the textured areas. Can you guess which shapes have been cut and attached to the surface of the canvas? Can you tell where he has brushed on paint and where he has used decalcomania, frottage, or grattage?

Using scratch paper, experiment with Ernst's three techniques. For decalcomania, try placing translucent wax paper over the blobs of paint so that you can see the way the paint moves as you gently push the colors around. With a little practice you can control the shapes and the blending of colors. Don't let the paint dry before you separate the sheets of paper. You will need a partner to hold the bottom paper down while you quickly pull the top paper off the surface.

Step 1 Apply blobs of color to your large sheet of paper. Place the second painting surface over the first and use gentle pressure to push the paint around. Then pull the surfaces apart quickly. Rub or scratch the wet surfaces if you wish. Allow the paint to dry. Save both surfaces.

Step 2 Study the textured shapes you have made and let them give you ideas for your fantasy picture. Do you see land or animal forms among the shapes and textures? Do you want to cut up one of the surfaces and glue it on the other? Do you need to paint out some parts?

Step 3 Release your imagination. Add details using paint, oil pastels, markers, and collage. If you glue on shapes cut from magazine pictures, you may need to paint over the edges of the added shapes with a color that unifies them with the background.

Step 4 Mount or mat your finished work for display.

EVALUATING YOUR WORK

▶ **DESCRIBE** Identify the subjects of the fantasy scene you created. List and explain the techniques you used to create visual textures in your fantasy scene.

▶ **ANALYZE** How did the visual textures affect the look of your work? Did you attach any textured shapes or magazine cutouts? What color scheme did you use? How did it affect the work? Are the shapes predominantly geometric or free-form? How does that affect the look of the work?

▶ **INTERPRET** What kind of mood does your work express? Give it a title that sums up your feelings about the meaning of this work.

▶ **JUDGE** Which aesthetic theories would be the most important in judging this work? Do you think your work is successful? If you were to do it over, is there anything you would change to improve it?

▲ **FIGURE 7.16A** Student work.

Assemblage

SUPPLIES

- **Sketchbook and pencils**
- **Materials that will serve as a base for the throne**
- **Found objects such as boxes, tubes, lightbulbs, and small spice jars**
- **White glue, nontoxic rubber cement, masking tape, duct tape**
- **String, rope, wire**
- **Scissors and utility knife**
- **Aluminum foil, foil wrapping paper, sequins**

▲ **FIGURE 7.17**

James Hampton. *The Throne of the Third Heaven of the Nations Millennium General Assembly.* c. 1950-64. Gold and silver aluminum foil, colored Kraft paper, and plastic sheets over wood, paperboard, and glass. 180 pieces. 3.2 × 8.2 × 4.4 m (10 ½ × 27 × 14.5′). National Museum of American Art, Smithsonian Institution, Washington, D.C.

James Hampton, a soft-spoken African-American, was born in 1909 in a small South Carolina community. Around 1950, he rented an unheated, poorly lit garage near the boarding house where he lived. By November 4, 1964, the day he died, he had built in that garage an astonishing artwork called *The Throne of the Third Heaven of the Nations Millennium General Assembly,* a collection of 180 glittering objects **(Figure 7.17)**.

Although Hampton never studied art, he had a natural sense of design. Notice how the throne at the rear serves as the heart of the assemblage. Bordering both sides of the throne are matching pairs of objects. Hampton used old furniture and discarded objects, such as cardboard tubes and insulation board, to construct the major pieces. He joined the pieces with strips of cardboard or metal cut from coffee cans. Glass vases, lightbulbs, and jelly glasses completed the tops and

corners of objects. Upholstery tacks, small nails, and straight pins held everything together. Finally, all of the objects were covered with recycled foil of various colors. Some of his foil came from store displays, some from gift wrap, and some was ordinary aluminum foil.

After Hampton's death, the massive construction was moved to the National Museum of American Art in Washington, D.C., where it can be viewed today.

What You Will Learn

You will design and create a small throne with a theme by assembling and joining found materials. Working individually or in small groups, symmetrically join the found materials to make a chairlike structure. Then, as James Hampton did, alter the surface texture by covering the entire structure with foil and foil wrapping paper.

Creating

Brainstorm with classmates for themes for your throne. Think of school subjects such as math, science, or history. Think of activities you do after school. Consider outer-space themes, underwater themes, or time-period themes. Choose a theme.

Step 1 Working in a small group, design a chair-shaped object that will serve as the base for your throne. Collect small discarded objects and pieces of heavy cardboard that can be used to construct and decorate the throne.

Step 2 Each person should look at the collected objects and make sketches of his or her ideas for the throne structure and the decorations that will go on it. Then, as a group, study all the sketches and select the best ideas. Each member of the group should make one final drawing of the combined ideas.

Step 3 Join your found objects, organizing them symmetrically. If necessary, cut shapes out of heavy cardboard. Before you cover the finished work with foil, decorate the surfaces with rope and wire, buttons, and layers of cardboard to create raised surfaces and interesting textures. You may even add words or phrases with raised block letters or rope that imitates cursive writing. Be sure everything is joined securely.

Step 4 Change the surface by covering everything with shiny foil. You may glue paper-backed foil to smooth surfaces, or press aluminum foil tightly to irregular surfaces. Some aluminum foil may be left smooth, and some may be crumpled up. Sequins and other shiny objects can be attached with pins or glue. Give your throne a poetic title.

EVALUATING YOUR WORK

▶ **DESCRIBE** Describe the way you constructed the basic form of the throne. Name the theme. Identify the objects and shapes you attached to the main form and explain how they represented the theme.

▶ **ANALYZE** What kinds of materials did you use to create your throne? Did you use symmetry to organize your decorative objects? How did the addition of shiny foil change the surface quality of the structure?

▶ **INTERPRET** Can your classmates recognize the theme? Did your group find a poetic title that reflects the theme?

▶ **JUDGE** Which aesthetic theories would you use to judge this work? Do you think your throne is successful? If you were going to do it over, what would you change?

▲ **FIGURE 7.17A** Student work.

Paper Sculpture Creature

▲ **FIGURE 7.18**

Artist unknown. Mexico. *Bird*. 1988. Tin and gold paint. 28 × 22 × 17.8 cm (11 × 8½ × 7"). Private collection.

SUPPLIES

- **Sketchbook and pencil**
- **Colored construction paper**
- **Variety of other papers to decorate the surface, such as wallpaper samples, shiny wrapping papers, and paper ribbons**
- **Scissors, ruler, and sharp knife**
- **Pointed tool for piercing, such as a compass point**
- **Transparent tape, white glue, straight pins**
- **Cardboard tubes and containers for internal support**

In Mexico, artists create beautiful traditional tinwork pieces such as frames, candleholders, chandeliers, crosses, and trinket boxes. Using flat sheets of tin, craftspeople cut, score, and pierce the tin to form three-dimensional works of art that are used to decorate their homes and churches.

The bird in **Figure 7.18** was made by a craftsperson in Mexico. The techniques used by the artist have been used in Mexico for more than 200 years. These decorative processes are part of a long tradition of surface decoration developed in Spain and brought to Mexico by the Spaniards.

Such surface decorations, which produce highly textured real and visual effects, are made by cutting, piercing, stamping, scoring, and soldering. Another method of joining, tab-and-slot construction, is also used.

As you study the tin bird in Figure 7.18, you can see how the artist used these processes to create a three-dimensional form. The back has been scored and is bent into a curve. The textural effects of the feathers have been created by layers of fringe that have been curled. Notice the contrast obtained by using fringes of different lengths. The ones on the head and around the eyes are very short. The wing areas have short and long fringes. The longest fringes are shaped into a spiral to create the round tail. The breast of the bird is decorated with oval shapes that have been applied to the form in a repeated, overlapping pattern.

These same techniques can be used to create paper sculpture. Try to use many forms of decoration to give your paper sculpture varied textures. Design a creature that is interesting from every point of view.

What You Will Learn

After studying the Mexican bird and practicing paper sculpture techniques, you will design and create a three-dimensional, freestanding, imaginary paper creature using a variety of strong papers. You will cover the surface with a variety of interesting textures using fringing, cutting, curling, and scoring. This sculpture should look interesting from every point of view.

Creating

Study the paper sculpture techniques on page 435 in the Handbook. Practice them using construction paper. Study the tin bird to see what techniques you think were used to construct it.

Step 1 Make several sketches in your sketchbook to plan your sculpture. Select your best design. Make some sketches showing different views of the sculpture. List the materials and techniques you will use to construct your three-dimensional creature and those you will use to create surface textures.

Step 2 Collect the materials you will need. Construct your sculpture based on the drawings you have made. You may change your plan as you go along. If your creature is too heavy to stand, support it on the inside with cardboard tubes and containers.

Step 3 Place the finished sculpture on a firm base for display. Glue or pin it to the base.

EVALUATING YOUR WORK

▶ **DESCRIBE** List the materials and paper-sculpture techniques you used to create your artwork. Did the practice session with paper-sculpture techniques help you in planning your final project? How did you prepare it for display?

▶ **ANALYZE** What form did you create for your sculpture? Describe the different textures you created. Is the work interesting from every point of view?

▶ **INTERPRET** What kind of mood or idea does your finished sculpture express? Give your work a title that expresses the mood.

▶ **JUDGE** Have you created a freestanding, three-dimensional, fantasy creature? Is your work successful? Is there anything you would change to make the work more successful? Which aesthetic theory would be best to judge this work?

▲ **FIGURE 7.18A** Student work.

Still-Life Collage

Robert Silvers. Based on van Gogh's *Self-Portrait*, 1889, in the collection of Musee d'Orsay, Paris. Photomosaic™. 1997.

SUPPLIES

- **Sketchbook**
- **Computer**
- **Paint or Draw application**
- **Printer**

Optional

- **Scanner**
- **Digital camera**
- **CD–ROM with textures**
- **Real textures and photographs of textures**

R obert Silvers has used an exciting merger of art, photography, and computer graphics to create his unique photomosaics. The inspiration for his high-tech art came from a very low-tech idea. He saw a portrait made of seashells and realized that he could create a similar effect digitally. As a photographer and a student of computer science at the Massachusetts Institute of Technology, he tried to find a way to unite the two. He wrote and refined a computer program that sorted thousands of digitized photographic images by color, density, internal shapes, and light. This program enabled him to create his first photomosaics. The Internet was also important as it gave him access to hundreds of thousands of digitized images he needed for his palette.

When you first look at **Figure 7.19,** you may be tricked because it closely resembles van Gogh's original work. When you look closely, however, you will see that this is a mosaic. Instead of using traditional mosaic materials, such as small cubes of colored marble or glass, Silvers has created a mosaic using individual, rectangular photographs as his "tiles."

What You Will Learn

You will select five or more objects for a still life, arrange them into an interesting composition, and make several sketches from different points of view in your sketchbook. Choose your best idea and draw or scan it into your computer. Then apply different textures and colors to the objects and the background so that the entire image has texture and color. Use color contrast to make one object or area the center of interest.

Creating

Explore the textures your application provides. Locate textures that simulate real surfaces. Discover if your application allows you to edit existing textures or create new textures using the paint tools that you can add to the menu.

Step 1 Use a variety of tools on your palette to create surfaces that represent cloth, wood grain, reflective, and transparent surfaces. For example, the air brush can spray a coarse or fine mist by changing the settings. Other menus allow you to choose colors for a gradient fill as well as selecting the direction and shape of the fill. These can result in reflective textures. Research other sources of textures such as CD–ROMs. If available, use a scanner or digital camera to capture textures from real objects or from photographs.

Step 2 Combine these textures and produce a simple still life with four or five objects, all made from different textures. Look at the textures you have collected and decide what objects you will create. Then make several sketches for your composition. Choose the one you like best.

Step 3 Use your choice of tools to draw these objects and arrange them. Consider a center of interest or focal point that can be emphasized by size, color, shape, or texture.

Step 4 Place the objects in a setting. Are they indoors or outside? What surface are they sitting on? Add details and texture to the background. Include texture on every surface you can—table, cloth, floor, and wall. Remember to save your work. Use the Save As command to retitle and save in editions. Print and display your final textured still life.

EVALUATING YOUR WORK

▶ **DESCRIBE** What objects have you included in your still life? Describe the setting in which you placed the objects.

▶ **ANALYZE** List the textures you selected for each area of your image. Did you repeat any of the textures? What colors did you choose? How did you use color to emphasize one object or area of your work?

▶ **INTERPRET** How has the application of textures to your image affected the mood, feeling, or idea of your still life? Give your work a title that sums up your feelings about it.

▶ **JUDGE** Do you think the textured surfaces create a satisfying still life? Is there anything you would change? What aesthetic theory would you use to evaluate this work?

▲ **FIGURE 7.19A** Student work.

ART CRITICISM IN ACTION

Audrey Flack. *Leonardo's Lady.* 1974. Oil over synthetic polymer paint on canvas. 188 × 203.2 cm (6'2" × 6'8"). The Museum of Modern Art, New York, New York. Purchased with the aid of funds from the National Endowment for the Arts and an anonymous donor.

1 ▸ DESCRIBE What do you see?

List all of the information found in the credit line. Use your perception skills to study the things you see in the work.

- What materials were used to create the artwork? What is the size? Measure it on a wall or the floor to see how big it is.
- This painting has many objects. Organize a system for listing the objects. For example, you may start at one edge and work your way through the painting until you reach the other edge. List reflections of objects wherever you find them.

2 ▸ ANALYZE How is this work organized?

This step deals with the composition of the work. You will collect information about all the elements of art.

- Where do you find lines in this work? Are they static or active?
- Can you find free-form and geometric shapes? Where?
- What hues, values, and intensities of color do you see?
- What kinds of visual texture has the artist used?
- Can you find rough, smooth, matte, and shiny textures in this work? Where?

3 ▸ INTERPRET What is the artist trying to communicate?

Now you will combine the clues you have collected with your personal experiences to decide what the artist is saying.

- How has the artist's unique use of texture affected the look of this work?
- Do you recognize the painting of the lady in the center of the work? Check it to be sure.
- How does this work make you feel?
- Give this work a new title based upon your interpretation.

4 ▸ JUDGE What do you think of the work?

Decide if this is a successful work of art.

- Did the artist use the element of texture successfully?
- Do you think this is a successful work of art? Why or why not? Use one or more of the aesthetic theories described in Chapter 2 to defend your judgment.

MEET THE
ARTIST
AUDREY FLACK

American, 1931–

Audrey Flack. *Self-Portrait.* 1974. Acrylic on linen. 203.2 × 162.6 cm (80 × 64"). Private collection.

Audrey Flack grew up in Manhattan and attended the High School of Music and Art in New York City. Later she won a scholarship to Yale to study art with Josef Albers. He stressed the importance of color relationships and a pared down, minimal use of the other art elements.

Flack is perhaps best known for her Super-realistic paintings. In her art, Flack focuses on the surface qualities of objects. She alerts us through vibrant color, texture, and a unique use of space to the immediate, but often timeless, images of our world.

The Secret of Silk

◄ **FIGURE 7.21**

Central Tibet. Temple Hanging. Detail. 1940. Appliqué with cut silk, brocade, and pearls. 1.2 × 13.1 m (4 × 43′). Los Angeles County Museum of Art, Los Angeles, California. Gift of Mr. and Mrs. James Coburn.

Have you ever heard the expression "as smooth as silk?" Silk is a valuable fiber used to make fine fabrics. It is produced by the silkworm. Silk is also used in decorative textiles, such as the Tibetan Temple Hanging in **Figure 7.21.**

The origin of silk dates back to the twenty-seventh century B.C. The silkworm moth was originally found only in China. For thousands of years, the people of China kept the silk-producing process a secret. Because silk was difficult to obtain, it became a valuable trade item.

Although silk fabric was traded to other countries, it was produced only in China. In about A.D. 300, however, a group of people from Japan smuggled silkworms out of China. They brought the silkworms and four young Chinese women back to Japan to teach them how to produce silk.

About 200 years later, a Roman emperor sent two monks to China to smuggle silkworm eggs. The monks hid the eggs in their hollow walking canes. With the secret revealed, silk production spread throughout Asia and the West.

Making the Connection

1. How do you think silk fabric enhances this textile art?
2. Explain why silk was a valuable trade item.
3. How did the people of Japan learn the Chinese secret of silk production?

Building Vocabulary

On a separate sheet of paper, write the term that best matches each definition given below.

1. The element of art that refers to how things feel, or look as if they might feel if touched.
2. The illusion of a three-dimensional surface.
3. A surface that reflects a soft, dull light.
4. An artwork onto which materials such as textured paper and fabric have been attached.
5. A method of producing textures by placing a freshly painted canvas right side up over a raised texture and rubbing or scraping it across the surface of the paint.
6. The technique of scratching into wet paint with a variety of tools to create texture.
7. A technique of creating random textured patterns by applying thick paint to two surfaces, pressing them together, and then pulling them apart.

Reviewing Art Facts

Answer the following questions using complete sentences.

1. With what senses is texture perceived?
2. What is the difference between real and visual texture?
3. What is the difference between simulated and invented texture?
4. Name the four types of textures.
5. Name two ways in which painters may add real textures to their paintings.
6. In what ways do sculptors create texture in their works?
7. Describe the similarities and differences between frottage, grattage, and decalcomania.

Thinking Critically About Art

1. **Describe.** Look at the photographs in Figure 7.2 on page 172. Describe them without naming any of the objects shown. Describe only the lines, shapes, spaces, values, and textures in the photographs. From your description, have classmates guess which photograph you are describing.
2. **Compare and contrast.** Compare the ways Albright (Figure 7.6, page 177), and Renoir (Figure 7.7, page 177), have used texture in the representation of women's clothes.

Use the Performing Arts Handbook on page 419 to find out how Paul Winter captures the texture of the sounds of nature through his music.

Find out how textures are used in creating two- and three-dimensional works of art. Explore the Glencoe Fine Arts Site at **www.glencoe.com/sec/art** To begin your search, find the chapter you are studying in the Table of Contents and click on one of the "hot links."

THE
PRINCIPLES
OF ART

"The lines employed in Korin's [painting] are very distinctive . . . but actually the manner of brushwork in it contains endless variations matching the different aspects of the motion of water, so that the depiction is very vivid and invigorating."

Teiji Chizawa, *The Art of Korin*

◀

Ogata Korin. Detail from *Waves at Matsushima* (inset). Edo period, eighteenth century. Six-panel folding screen; ink, colors, and gold on paper. 155 × 370 cm (61 × 145⅞"). Fenollosa-Weld Collection. Courtesy, Museum of Fine Arts, Boston, Massachusetts.

▲ **FIGURE 8.1** Shotgun houses are built with a hall in the center that runs from the front door to the back, with all of the rooms lined up on either side of the hall. A "ward" is a district in the city of Houston, Texas. Fourth ward was the oldest African-American community in the city and was originally called Freedmanstown.

John Biggers. *Shotguns, Fourth Ward.* 1987. Acrylic and oil on board. 106 × 81.3 cm (41¼ × 32″). Hampton University Museum, Hampton, Virginia.

CHAPTER 8

Rhythm and Movement

Life is full of rhythmic events. Each year, one season follows the next in a predictable order. Such rhythms are comforting. The rhythmic routines of daily living create a sense of stability and security.

In his painting *Shotguns, Fourth Ward* **(Figure 8.1),** John Biggers recalls the visual rhythms or repetitions in the comforting quilts of his childhood. In the painting, the roofs of the shotgun houses create a quiltlike pattern of diamond shapes. Standing on the front porches of the first row are three women, each holding a miniature shotgun house with a miniature figure standing on the tiny front porch. What other examples of repetition can you find in this work?

Biggers indicates the strength and importance of the women in the painting by placing each one in a spotlight, on the stage of the porch. Each woman holds her miniature house proudly, for she represents the keeper of African-American traditions. These traditions, like the rhythms and repetitions in the painting, are comforting, giving a sense of stability, security, and order.

OBJECTIVES

After completing this chapter, you will be able to:
- Identify rhythms occurring in the world around you.
- Understand how rhythm adds a sense of movement to a work of art.
- Identify and explain motif and pattern.
- Name and identify the types of rhythm.
- Use the principle of rhythm to create your own works.

WORDS TO KNOW

rhythm
visual rhythm
motif
module
pattern
visual movement
kinetic

Developing Your
PORTFOLIO

Rhythm can be comforting and predictable. Make a list of several events and activities that you enjoy that happen in a predictable way. For example, you might list your birthday or track meets each Saturday. Using magazines and newspapers, find images that symbolize the events. A cake could stand for your birthday and a pair of running shoes could stand for the track meet. If you are unable to find appropriate symbols, sketch your own. Then write a brief paragraph about why the rhythm of these events is meaningful. Place the pictures and the paragraph in your portfolio.

Rhythm and Repetition

Rhythm is *the principle of art that indicates movement by the repetition of elements*. The principle of rhythm is found in all the arts: music, dance, poetry, and theatre. In music, rhythm is created by the measure of time between musical sounds. Beats are followed by rests. In poetry, the repetition of words, sounds, and phrases creates rhythm. The visual arts combine repetition and pauses to create rhythm.

Visual Rhythm

Visual rhythm is *rhythm you receive through your eyes rather than through your ears*. Visual rhythm is created by repeated positive shapes separated by negative spaces. Everywhere you look you can see visual rhythms. Books lined up in a bookcase and cars in a parking lot are examples of visual rhythms. A line of people in the cafeteria has visual rhythm. Each person is a positive shape, and the space between each person is a negative space.

In **Figure 8.2,** Chief Black Hawk has used visual rhythm to suggest the rhythms of a dance ceremony. The repeated images of the six Crow men are the major beats, or positive shapes, of the rhythm. The spaces between the men are the rests, or negative spaces, in the rhythm.

▶ **FIGURE 8.2** In the winter of 1880–81, Chief Black Hawk, a Lakota man, supported his family by selling drawings to a trader on the reservation. He was unknown until 1994, when a book of his drawings emerged on the auction market. Chief Black Hawk's book shows natural history drawings, hunting and ceremonial activities of the Lakota, and many pictures of Crow ceremonies.

Chief Black Hawk. *Crow Men in Ceremonial Dress.* 1880–81. Ink and pencil on paper. 26 × 41.9 cm (10¼ × 16½"). Thaw Collection, Fenimore Art Museum, Cooperstown, New York.

ROSA
BONHEUR

French, 1822–1899

Rosa Bonheur (**roh**-zah bah-**nur**) was born in Bordeaux, France in 1822. When she was seven years old, her family moved to Paris. Her father, Raymond Bonheur, was a landscape artist and painting teacher. He trained Rosa and her three siblings. As a member of the religious group called Saint-Simonians, he believed in the equality of women. This attitude allowed Rosa Bonheur to develop unrestrained by traditional women's roles.

When she was ten years old, she refused to be apprenticed to a dressmaker, preferring instead to sketch animals in nearby woods and to draw scenes from the balcony of the family apartment. This lifelong love of animals would inspire her later art. She painted huge compositions in which horses and other animals played a major role. She visited slaughterhouses to learn the anatomy of animals. She also traveled to livestock markets. *The Horse Fair* (**Figure 8.3**) is a painting that depicts one of these scenes. Bonheur became a famous, well-known artist. In 1865, she became the first woman to be awarded the Grand Cross of the Legion of Honor.

▲ **FIGURE 8.3**   Bonheur, a lifelong animal lover, often created large-scale artworks with horses and other animals as the subject matter. In this painting Bonheur has used the horses as a motif. The rhythm the horses create pulls your eyes through the painting. Where does the movement start? From which direction does the viewer get drawn through the art?

Rosa Bonheur. *The Horse Fair*. 1853–55. Oil on canvas. 244.5 × 506.7 cm (96¼ × 199½″). The Metropolitan Museum of Art, New York, New York. Gift of Cornelius Vanderbilt, 1887. (87.25)

▲ **FIGURE 8.4** In this unusual night view of New York City, you can see examples of random rhythms made by the buildings. Each building shows a regular rhythm of windows, but the lit windows create a random rhythm. Notice how the change in value also creates a sense of rhythm.

Berenice Abbott. *The Night View,* 1936. Photograph. Museum of the City of New York, New York. Gift of Mr. Todd Watts.

In visual rhythm, a beat may be one element or a combination of elements. Look at the photograph in **Figure 8.4.** The strongest beats are the big, tall buildings. The lighted windows make a random rhythm. The streets and the spaces between the buildings create negative, empty space—the rest between the beats.

Visual rhythms create a sensation of movement. Rhythms cause the viewer's eyes to follow the visual beats through a work of art. Visual movement is different from real action, which involves a physical change in position. For example, a ball bouncing across a room is real action. Visual movement simply suggests movement. In an artwork, round shapes separated by negative spaces can create the visual sensation of the movement of a ball. Your eyes bounce from one round shape to the next. In **Figure 8.6** on page 203, the artist has used rhythm to pull your eyes through the work. Notice how the curved figures and the slanted hoes give a sensation of visual movement.

Repetition

Rhythm results from repetition. *Motif* and *pattern* are often used to talk about repetition in art. A **motif** is *a unit that is repeated in visual rhythm* **(Figure 8.5).** Sometimes every motif is an exact duplicate of the first unit, and sometimes the repetitions vary from the original.

Look around and you will find examples of motif and repetition. In a marching band, one band member is a motif, even though each band member carries

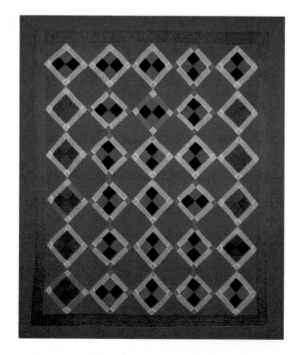

◄ **FIGURE 8.5** There are two major motifs in this design. One is a solid blue square set on its point. The alternating motif is bordered with a light blue band and divided in the center into four smaller squares.

Annie M. Peachey. *Four in Block Work Quilt.* 1925–35. Cotton, rayon, and synthetics. 216 × 184 cm (85 × 72½"). Collection of the Museum of American Folk Art, New York, New York. Gift of Mr. and Mrs. William B. Wigton.

Woodruff has used many random visual rhythms in this work to create the feeling that the workers are singing and working to the rhythm of the song as they hoe the cotton. In the diagram you can see how he has used repeated shapes to move your eyes through the work. How many visual beats can you find in this painting?

◀ **FIGURE 8.6**

Hale Woodruff. *Poor Man's Cotton.* 1944. Watercolor on paper. 77.5 × 57.2 cm (30½ × 22½″). The Newark Museum, Newark, New Jersey.

a different instrument. On a grocery store shelf full of canned goods, one can is a motif. In a herd of cattle, one cow is a motif.

In sculpture and architecture *a three-dimensional motif* is sometimes called a **module.** Modular furniture is composed of standard matching units.

► **FIGURE 8.7**
This elevator grille is a delicate pattern of lines and round forms. It was once part of a large bank of elevators in the 1893 Chicago Stock Exchange. The building was torn down in 1972, but parts of it, such as this grille, have been saved and housed in various museums.

Louis Sullivan. *Elevator Grille.* 1893–94. Bronze-plated cast iron. 185.4 × 78.7 cm (73 × 31″). High Museum of Art, Atlanta, Georgia. Virginia Carroll Crawford Collection, 1982. 291.

Pattern is a word used to describe a decorative surface design. **Pattern** is *a two-dimensional decorative visual repetition.*

A pattern of lines can decorate a piece of fabric or wallpaper. **Figure 8.7** shows a pattern decorating an elevator grille. These are decorative patterns meant to be visually appealing. Other patterns are functional. A bricklayer places bricks in a certain pattern in order to build a sturdy, durable wall. The bricklayer may make the pattern more complex in order to create a finished work that is very decorative, but the main purpose is still functional.

Activity   Motifs and Patterns

Applying Your Skills. Make a collection of decorative patterns. You may use photographs, clippings from magazines, and scraps of fabric. Identify the motif in each pattern by drawing a circle around one. Organize your pattern collection into a poster, a bulletin board, a booklet, or some other type of presentation.

Computer Option. Start with a rectangle and design a simple motif. Use three colors or three original textures in black and white. Create a variety of patterns with that motif. Print your patterns. If your printer is black and white, you can add color with other media such as colored pencil after the design is printed out.

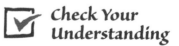

☑ Check Your Understanding

1. Define *rhythm.*
2. What is *visual rhythm?*
3. What is a pattern?

Types of Rhythm

Arranging motifs and space in different ways creates different visual rhythms. There are many ways to combine motifs and space. Each combination gives a different character to the rhythm depicted.

Random

A motif repeated in no apparent order, with no regular spaces in between, creates a random rhythm. One example is autumn leaves that cover the ground. Cracks in mud and splashes of paint are also examples of random rhythm.

Crowds of people often create random rhythms —think of holiday shoppers, rush-hour commuters, and students in the halls between classes. A large group of people pushing onto a bus is full of rhythm. The motif is one person. Every person is different, and the space between and around them is slightly different.

The Sundi woman who created the bowl shown in **Figure 8.8** deliberately splashed the bowl with vegetable juices while it was still hot from the fire. This created the random pattern of round shapes that decorate the surface. If she had dipped the bowl into the liquid, it would have resulted in an even, brown hue. Applying the vegetable liquid to the hot clay allows the bowl to withstand the heat of the cooking fire. The bowl can be used over an open fire without shattering. In some parts of Africa, the marks left by vegetable juices are interpreted as proof of the thermal strength of the vessel.

▲ **FIGURE 8.8** The potter who created this bowl made an aesthetic decision to splash the ware with vegetable juices to create a random pattern of round shapes and lines.

Bowl. Kongo peoples, Congo and Democratic Republic of the Congo. Before 1910. Ceramic, vegetable dye. 11.3 × 15.6 cm (4⁷⁄₁₆ × 6⅛″). National Museum of African Art, Smithsonian Institution, Washington, D.C. Purchased with funds provided by the Smithsonian Collections Acquisition Program, 89-13-31.

Activity | **Using Random Rhythm**

Applying Your Skills. Choose one letter of the alphabet. Look through newspapers and magazines for large examples of that letter. Cut out about 20 letters. Arrange them on a piece of colored paper in a random pattern. If you have trouble finding large letters, draw letters of your own on your design.

Computer Option. Choose one letter of the alphabet. Using different fonts, create about 20 different examples of the letter. You can use Flip, Rotate, Size Change, and Color options if your program has them. Then arrange the letters in a random pattern.

Regular

Regular rhythm has identical motifs and equal amounts of space between them **(Figure 8.9).** Regular rhythm has a steady beat. Regular repetitions are used to organize objects. Parking spaces are laid out with regular rhythm. Stores organize merchandise into regular stacks and rows. This makes it easier for you to find things, and it also makes the displays more attractive than if items were arranged in a random fashion.

A grid is based on regular rhythm. It is a regular arrangement of parallel lines. A football field is laid out in a grid, as is a checkerboard. Windows form a grid pattern on the side of a building. The artist who created the cloth in **Figure 8.10** had a grid pattern in mind when he wove the long, narrow strips of cloth. Later the artist cut and sewed the strips together to make the wide cloth you see. Notice the regular repetition of the various motifs.

Regular rhythm can be boring if it is overdone. It is like playing one note on a piano over and over again. Pop artist Andy Warhol used regular rhythm to make a social-protest statement **(Figure 8.11).** How would you describe the effect of this regular rhythm? What do you suppose Warhol intended to convey with this repeated motif?

▲ **FIGURE 8.9** This building was the first office building to rise above 1,000 feet. Notice how the pairs of windows form a regular beat both vertically and horizontally. The negative spaces between them are the rests between the beats.

William van Alen. *Chrysler Building,* New York, New York. Completed in 1930.

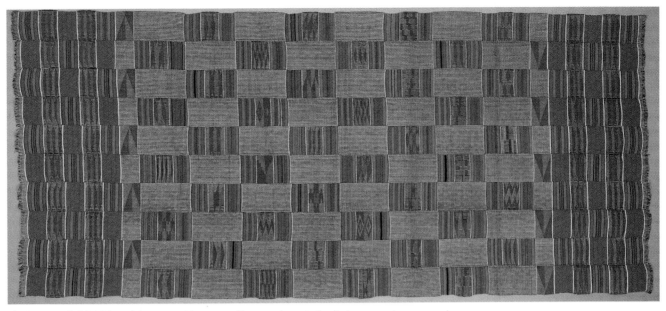

▲ **FIGURE 8.10** This elaborate grid pattern fits together perfectly because the weaver has memorized the whole plan through many years of practice.

Wrapper. Asante peoples, Ghana. Date unknown. Cotton, rayon. 190.2 × 83.2 cm (74⅞ × 32¾″). National Museum of African Art and National Museum of Natural History, Washington, D.C. Purchased with funds provided by the Smithsonian Collections Acquisition Program, 1983–85, Lamb EJ10554.

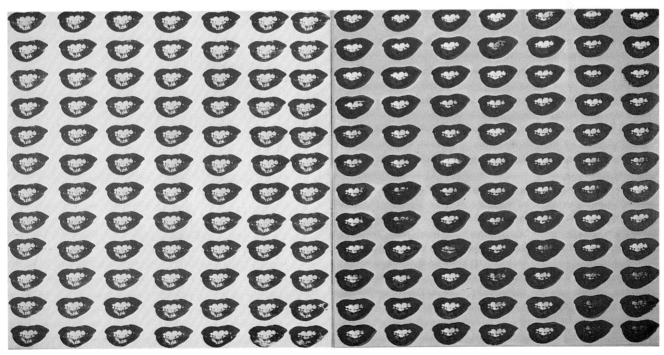

▲ **FIGURE 8.11** One pair of lips on the face of Marilyn Monroe would be beautiful and appealing. What has Andy Warhol done to them by repeating them in a regular rhythm?

Andy Warhol. *Marilyn Monroe's Lips.* 1962. Diptych. Synthetic polymer, enamel, and pencil on canvas. Left: 210.7 × 204.9 cm (82¾ × 80¾″). Right: 210.7 × 209.7 cm (82¾ × 82⅜″). Hirshhorn Museum and Sculpture Garden, Smithsonian Institution, Washington, D.C. Gift of Joseph H. Hirshhorn, 1972.

The artist who painted this dish used an alternating pattern of sets of blue curved lines to symbolize waves of water.

Footed Dish, Japanese. 1700–50. Nabeshima ware (porcelain with underglaze enamel decoration). 5.3 × 20.2 cm (2⅛ × 7⅞"). The Nelson-Atkins Museum of Art, Kansas City, Missouri. Purchase: Nelson Trust.

Alternating

Alternating rhythm can occur in several ways. One way is to introduce a second motif. Another way is to make a change in the placement or content of the original motif. A third way is to change the spaces between the motifs. Sometimes alternation is created simply by changing the position of the motif. For example, the motif may be turned upside down. The Japanese artist who painted the wave design on the bowl shown in **Figure 8.12** created the feeling of movement by alternating the placement of the wave shapes. The Native American who embroidered the shoulder bag in **Figure 8.13** made the design interesting by changing the sets of motifs several times.

Bricks are often laid in an alternating pattern. As a child, did you ever play with interlocking blocks? You had to use an alternating pattern to join the blocks.

An alternating rhythm using two motifs can still be very repetitive. Your eyes keep returning to the first motif even after the second motif joins the design, but the alternation does create interest and relieve monotony.

Flowing

Flowing rhythm is created by repeating wavy lines. Curved shapes, such as rolling hills or ocean waves, create

◄ **FIGURE 8.13** How many sets of motifs can you find embroidered on this Creek shoulder bag? How many different ways has the artist alternated the motifs?

Shoulder Bag. Creek. Georgia or Alabama. 1810–30. Wool fabric, cotton fabric and thread, silk ribbon, glass beads. Strap: 135 × 18.7 cm (53¼ × 7⅜"). Bag: 19.4 × 10 cm (7⅝ × 4"). The Detroit Institute of Arts, Detroit, Michigan. Founders Society Purchase with funds from Flint Ink Corporation.

Activity	Alternating Rhythm

Applying Your Skills. Draw a checkerboard grid on a sheet of white paper. Create an alternating rhythm using one motif. Turn the motif upside down in every other box. Next, draw a checkerboard grid and create an alternating rhythm using two motifs.

Computer Option. Design two motifs using the tools of your choice. Use the Selecttool and the Copy and Paste options to create an alternating rhythm using both motifs. On a new screen, create an alternating rhythm using only one motif. In this design, you can change the placement of the motif. Label and save both designs.

flowing rhythms. In **Figure 8.14,** the artist was able to capture the flowing movement of the waterfall as it rolled over the rocks. Your eyes follow the curving path as it changes direction gradually. There are no sudden breaks in the line. In **Figure 8.15,** the artist has used flowing rhythm to arrange the heads of the singers to create the mood of the flowing melody coming from the harp.

Flowing rhythm is created using upward swells and downward slides. You might think of the upward moves as the beats and the downward moves as the rests. Allan Houser has used flowing rhythms symbolically in his sculpture, *Coming of Age* **(Figure 8.16).** The work expresses the symbolic union of nature and femininity. The thick, rhythmically flowing strands of her hair suggest motion and the act of running. They also suggest the movement of the wind, of water, or even the blazing motion of flames.

◀ **FIGURE 8.14**
Borsky captured the white flow of this waterfall in his photograph by increasing the amount of time he exposed the film to light.

David Borsky. *Waterfall.* Photograph. Courtesy of the artist.

▶ **FIGURE 8.16**
This sculpture, with its upturned head and flowing hair, was created to celebrate feminine youth and beauty. The upturned head symbolizes the girl's desire to run to the four directions of the earth. The small shape above her forehead represents an abalone shell, a fertility symbol. The feather in her hair signifies a long life.

Allan Houser. *Coming of Age.* 1977. Bronze, edition of 12. 19 × 39.4 × 17.8 cm (7½ × 15½ × 7"). Denver Art Museum, Denver, Colorado.

▲ **FIGURE 8.15** This sculpture was inspired by the song *Lift Every Voice and Sing,* which was a popular song among African-Americans in the 1930s. The sculpture was a towering, 16-foot plaster work commissioned for the 1939 World's Fair. There were not enough funds to cast it in metal, so the original was destroyed along with all of the other temporary structures after the Fair ended. All that is left are a few small souvenirs that were sold at the Fair.

Augusta Savage. *Lift Every Voice and Sing.* 1939. Cast iron. 27.6 x 23.5 x 11.4 cm (10⅞ x 9¼ x 4½"). Countee Cullen Collection, Hampton University Museum, Hampton, Virginia.

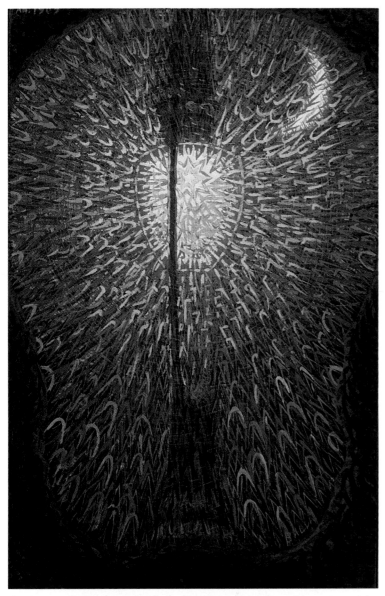

▲ **FIGURE 8.17** The light glowing from the street lamp is represented by a progressive rhythm of both line and color. Notice how the light close to the lamp is white and yellow in color and is created with thin, small V-shaped lines. Why do you think the artist has used the V lines to represent the movement of light from the lamp out into the darkness?

Giacomo Balla. *Street Light* {Lampada—Studio di luce}. 1909. Oil on canvas. 174.7 × 114.7 cm (68¾ × 45¼″). Collection, The Museum of Modern Art, New York, New York. Hillman Periodicals Fund. © Estate of Giacomo Balla/Licensed by VAGA, New York, NY

Progressive

In *progressive* rhythm there is a change in the motif each time the motif is repeated. The change is a steady one. Each time the motif appears, it is slightly different **(Figure 8.17)**. A progressive rhythm may start with a square as its motif. The size of the square may be changed by making it slightly smaller each time it is repeated, or each square may be made a different color of the spectrum or a different step on the value scale each time it is repeated. Shapes can be progressively changed. The sides of a square can be gradually rounded until the square becomes a circle.

| **Activity** | **Progressive Rhythm** |

Applying Your Skills. Start with a simple geometric shape, such as a square, for your motif. Create a progressive rhythm by gradually changing the square into a free-form shape. Next, draw a picture using simple shapes. Change the shapes gradually, using progressive rhythm, to tell a visual story.

Computer Option. Look around the room and select a simple handmade object such as a stapler, a chair, or a faucet. Use the tools of your choice to draw the outline of this shape, adding details. Consider what shapes can be used to simplify and represent the object—circles, squares, rectangles, or triangles. Gradually change the image using a minimum of six or seven steps so that the transition appears smooth. Begin in black and white but later you may explore changes in size, value, or color to enhance the progression. Tip: After completing each step, make a copy of it and place it next to the one you are about to alter, or use the tracing paper option, if available, to guide your changes.

☑ Check Your Understanding

1. Give one example each of random rhythm and regular rhythm.
2. In what ways can an alternating rhythm occur?
3. Describe a progressive rhythm.

How Artists Use Rhythm to Create Movement

Artists use rhythm in a work of art just as they use the elements and other principles of art—to convey feelings and ideas. Rhythm, which can be comforting and predictable, can also be monotonous, symbolic, or graceful, depending on the artist's goals. Rhythm can also create visual movement.

Visual Movement

Visual movement is *the principle of art used to create the look and feeling of action and to guide the viewer's eyes throughout the work of art.* In **Figure 8.18,** the artist has used visual movement to tell her story. Xiong has arranged the figures and objects in her art using visual rhythm to

▲ **FIGURE 8.18** This story cloth tells the story of the artist's flight from Laos, across the Mekong River, to an American refugee camp in Thailand. The story starts in the upper right corner. Can you follow the family as they move toward safety?

Chaing Xiong. *Hmong Story Cloth.* 1987. Pieced and embroidered polyester, cotton blend. 140.3 × 145.4 cm (55¼ × 57¼"). Wadsworth Atheneum, Hartford, Connecticut. Florence Paull Berger Fund.

▲ **FIGURE 8.19** The many repetitions of the legs, feet, tail, and chain in this work give it the appearance of actual movement.

Giacomo Balla. *Dynamism of a Dog on a Leash.* 1912. Oil on canvas. 89.9 × 109.9 cm (35½ × 43″). Albright-Knox Art Gallery, Buffalo, New York. Bequest of A. Conger Goodyear and Gift of George F. Goodyear, 1964. © Estate of Giacomo Balla/Licensed by VAGA, New York, NY

create the sense of movement. The main motif is Xiong's family. Notice how they change slightly from one appearance to the next. Is the rhythm random, alternating, or progressive?

One group of artists tried to do more than control the way in which viewers looked at works of art. This group of artists, called the *Futurists,* used rhythm to capture the idea of movement itself. They used the word *dynamism* to refer to the forces of movement. They believed that nothing was solid or stable. They also believed that art should show such dynamism. They showed forms changing into energy by slanting and overlapping surfaces, which made the surfaces seem to move. In **Figure 8.19,** notice how the dog and its leash practically vibrate off the page. What kind of rhythm did the artist use to suggest this frenetic movement?

When you look at the modern Navajo pottery by Native American artist Lucy McKelvey **(Figure 8.20)**, you will also find rhythmic repetitions of shapes and lines that seem to move across the surface. The designs are inspired by traditional Navajo sandpaintings. McKelvey says that her grandfather, who was a medicine man, told her she could use the designs as long as she didn't reproduce one of the sacred sandpainting figures exactly as it was depicted in a ritual ceremony. She always changes the original and adds something different.

You can also see movement in the visual art of Alexander Calder. He was a

◄ **FIGURE 8.20** McKelvey's repetition of lines and forms that swirl out from the neck of her pot create the illusion of movement. The intricate sandpainting design along the graceful curve of the vessel is the hallmark of a McKelvey pot.

Lucy Leuppe McKelvey. *Whirling Rainbow Goddesses.* Ceramic container. 18 × 30 cm (6¾ × 12″). Keams Canyon Arts and Crafts, Keams Canyon, Arizona.

▲ **FIGURE 8.21** Look closely at the places where the rods are joined by a carefully planned set of loops. Calder's works are so carefully balanced that the slightest movement of air will set the sculpture in motion. Watching a Calder sculpture is like watching a graceful dancer.

Alexander Calder. *Lobster Trap and Fish Tail.* 1939. Hanging mobile. Painted steel wire and sheet aluminum. About 2.6 × 2.9 m (8′6″ × 9′6″). Collection, The Museum of Modern Art, New York, New York. Commissioned by the Advisory Committee for the stairwell of the museum.

mechanical engineer who believed in what the Futurists were doing. In his work he repeated abstract shapes and put them into real motion. He did this using the real forces of air currents and gravity. Calder's creations were dubbed **kinetic** sculpture, because they *actually move in space* **(Figure 8.21).** Artist Marcel Duchamp gave Calder's moving sculptures another name, *mobiles.* Moving sculptures of this kind have been called mobiles ever since.

Check Your Understanding

1. Define *visual movement.*
2. Which group of artists used rhythm to capture the idea of movement itself?
3. Describe a kinetic sculpture. By what other name are these sculptures often referred to?

Painting With a Rhythmic Activity

▲ **FIGURE 8.22**

Antonio M. Ruiz. *School Children on Parade.* 1936. Oil on canvas. 24 × 33.8 cm (9½ × 13¼"). The Metropolitan Museum of Art, New York, New York. © Antonio M. Ruiz/SOMAAP MÉXICO, 1999.

SUPPLIES

- Sketchbook and pencils
- Large white paper
- Yellow chalk
- Acrylic paints and a variety of brushes

A ntonio Ruiz painted *School Children on Parade* **(Figure 8.22)** as a depiction of Independence Day in Mexico. Notice how the artist has used several motifs: the children in their white uniforms and yellow hats is one motif; the tricolor flags they carry is another. Repetition is also shown in the group of adults, dressed in black, who are watching the parade. If you look closely, you will be able to spot other rhythms in the painting.

Ruiz has used repeated colors, sizes, and shapes to create the rhythm of the marching students. The contrast between the light and dark colors adds interest. The painting evokes a serious, dignified mood by its use of repetition.

What You Will Learn

In this project, you will create a painting expressing rhythmic movement. Show one or more groups of people or objects involved in rhythmic activity. Base the figures in your work on your own sketches of people or objects in action. As in Ruiz's *School Children on Parade,* use more than one motif. Strengthen the rhythmic quality of your work by using four of the five kinds of visual rhythm described in this chapter. Use repetition to accent the visual rhythms. Choose a color scheme that will help to express the mood of the rhythms in your work.

Creating

Brainstorm with your classmates for ideas of rhythmic activities. Think of marching bands, sporting events, cheer-leaders, dancers, joggers, or children on a playground.

Select the rhythmic activities you will use in your painting. Do visual research by making gesture sketches in your sketchbook of people or objects involved in the activities.

Step 1 Select your best gesture drawings. In your sketchbook, plan how to organize the figures into a composition. Remember to emphasize rhythmic movement that will pull the viewer's eye through the painting. As in Figure 8.22, you may create several different rhythms by using more than one motif. Be sure to use rhythmic repetition.

Step 2 Choose your best rhythmic composition and sketch it on a large sheet of white paper using yellow chalk. Press lightly with the chalk so that it will not show when you paint over it. Before you start painting, plan how you will repeat the elements of line, shape, space, and color to accent the visual rhythms in your painting. Also plan a color scheme that will express the mood of the rhythms in your work. Make notes with crayons or colored pencils in your sketchbook.

Step 3 Paint your work, covering the entire surface of the paper. Mount or mat your work for display.

EVALUATING YOUR WORK

▶ **DESCRIBE** Tell which rhythmic activities you chose. Describe how you did your visual research. How many motifs did you use?

▶ **ANALYZE** Explain how and where you repeated the elements of line, shape, space, and color. What color scheme did you choose? Which kinds of rhythm did you use? Explain how and where you used them.

▶ **INTERPRET** What is the expressive mood of your work? Which elements helped to create that mood? Give your work a title.

▶ **JUDGE** Which aesthetic theories would you use to judge this work? Were you satisfied with the finished work? If you were to do it over, what, if anything, would you change to improve it?

▲ **FIGURE 8.22A** Student work.

A Pattern Collage

▲ **FIGURE 8.23**

Abd Allah Musawwir. *The Meeting of the Theologians.* c. 1540-50, Uzbek Shaybanid dynasty. Watercolors on paper. 28.9 × 19.1 cm (11⅜ × 7½″). The Nelson-Atkins Museum of Art, Kansas City, Missouri. Purchase: Nelson Trust.

SUPPLIES

- Sketchbook and pencils
- Ruler, scissors, and white glue
- One large sheet of paper or poster board
- A variety of patterned fabrics and papers
- Colored pencils, watercolors, or acrylics
- Assorted brushes
- Small pieces of white paper for figures

Persian miniature paintings such as the one shown in **Figure 8.23** were made to illustrate book manuscripts. The primary purpose of these illustrations is to tell stories about sacred religious events and to depict the exploits of heroes who accomplished superhuman feats.

Persian painters filled every available space with a rhythmic pattern. Notice how each pattern is filled with intense colors. This emphasis on pattern compresses space. Everything seems to lie flat against the picture plane.

The style of Persian art is not like Western Realism. More than one point of view appears in the composition, allowing the artist to portray several events in the same picture.

The Meeting of the Theologians (Figure 8.23) takes place in a religious school, where a young man is seated with a teacher and seven other bearded men. In the doorway a theologian approaches while two beggars hold out their hands begging. This artwork was one page of an illustrated book. Look at it closely and see how the colors, patterns, and calligraphy have been merged to make the story easy to read and visually interesting.

What You Will Learn

You will create a collage in the Persian style by presenting more than one point of view. In this way you can show different aspects of one event in the picture. Organize your work so every shape and space is filled with brightly colored patterns. Create the background shapes using patterned fabrics and papers. People and other objects can be made by drawing and painting them on white paper and cutting them out. The finished composition should look flat. It should not have any feeling of three-dimensional form or space.

Creating

Brainstorm with classmates about complex events that would be appropriate for this project. Think of an event that can be best explained by showing several scenes. For example, a play involves tryouts, rehearsals, costume fittings, and performing.

After the group discussion, choose a situation from your personal experience to illustrate. In your sketchbook, list the different scenes that make up the event. Make some rough sketches. Choose the scenes that you would like to illustrate.

Step 1 Now sketch a plan for dividing your composition into shapes of different sizes and decide where to place your figures. Using the ruler and pencil, lightly draw the dividing lines on a large sheet of paper.

Step 2 Before you add figures, fill all the rectangles with patterns. Measure each shape and cut out patterned fabrics and papers to fit. As you select each pattern for the background, consider how one will look next to another. Use contrasting patterns so you can see the distinction between each shape. If you wish, you may draw and color patterns in some of the spaces. Glue the fabrics and papers to the background.

Step 3 On the small pieces of white paper, draw and paint figures and objects. Consider the pattern you will place each figure against. Make sure the figure will contrast. Cut out the drawn figures and objects and glue them onto the design. Mount or mat your finished work for display.

EVALUATING YOUR WORK

▶ **DESCRIBE** Identify the event you chose to illustrate. Describe the different scenes. What kinds of patterned materials did you use for your background spaces?

▶ **ANALYZE** How did you organize your background spaces? How did you arrange the figures? Did you fill the background with patterns? Is there contrast between patterns and between the figures and the background? Does everything look flat?

▶ **INTERPRET** What mood does your artwork express? Give your work an expressive title.

▶ **JUDGE** Which aesthetic theories would you use to judge this work? Is it successful? If you were going to do it over, what would you change?

▲ **FIGURE 8.23A** Student work.

Coil Baskets

▲ **FIGURE 8.24**

Louisa Keyser (Dat So La Lee). *Basket.* c. 1917–18. Willow, redbud, braken fern. 30 × 41.2 cm (12 × 16¼"). Philbrook Art Center, Tulsa, Oklahoma. Clark Field Collection.

SUPPLIES

- **Core material for the warp**
- **Fibers for the weft: colored yarns, raffia, or natural fibers**
- **Tapestry needle**
- **Sharp scissors**
- **Masking tape**
- **Sketchbook, pencil, and crayons**

The basket shown in **Figure 8.24** was created by Louisa Keyser (Dat So La Lee). She belonged to a small Native American group known as the Washoe. They were hunters and gatherers who ranged through the territory around Lake Tahoe, California. The Washoe women made many types of baskets for carrying possessions as they moved between the lakes, mountains, hills, and valley floors in their yearly gathering circuit. Washoe basketry is woven primarily from willow, which was found in the valleys. The Washoe used the coiling technique to make large storage baskets, watertight cooking baskets, and *degikups,* which were small spherical baskets for ceremonial use.

This basket is one of Keyser's variations of the *degikup* form. It rises gradually from a narrow base until it reaches a maximum width at three-quarters of its height. This design is called the scatter pattern. It consists of a series of stepped triangles arranged vertically. In this basket, the artist has increased the size of the triangles to match the form of the basket. Then she has diminished the design as the form curves inward. She has used the progressive rhythm of the design to emphasize the form of the basket. She created an illusion of perspective in which the exaggerated curve of the design mirrors the form of the basket, unifying the basket with its design.

What You Will Learn

In this project, you will plan your own coil basket. To prepare, study Louisa Keyser's basket to see how she used rhythm in her design. Then practice the coil method of basket making until you have satisfactorily started and completed a simple flat coaster using the "lazy squaw" stitch in a regular rhythm. When you have mastered the technique, design and create a unique coil basket form that has either a functional or decorative purpose. Organize arrangement of the colors of the weft into a random, regular, alternating, or progressive rhythm.

Creating

Study the directions for the coil method of basket making in Technique Tip 24 in the Handbook, on page 439. Following those directions, use about 2 feet of core material to make a small coaster using the "lazy squaw" stitch. If the center of your coaster does not look right the first time, undo it and start over. This is the most difficult part of making the basket. Finish the coaster using the taper method.

Step 1 Draw several plans in your sketchbook and select your best plan. Choose your color scheme and note the materials and colors you will use to make the weft. Decide whether you will use regular, alternating, or progressive rhythm to organize your colors. Note your decision in your sketchbook and color the design to indicate how you will use the colors.

Step 2 Construct the basket based on your design. Control the position of the warp coils by holding them in position as you sew the stitches that connect the coils. You can position them to go up vertically or to slant in or out. Finish your basket using the taper method.

EVALUATING YOUR WORK

▶ **DESCRIBE** Explain the procedures you followed to create your basket, including the practice coaster.

▶ **ANALYZE** Describe the form of your basket. Tell what color scheme you used and explain which type of rhythm you used to organize your colors.

▶ **INTERPRET** Is your basket functional or decorative? Explain. How did your use of color and pattern affect the feeling of your basket?

▶ **JUDGE** Which aesthetic theories would you use to judge this work? If you were to make another basket, what, if anything, would you change? Explain your answer.

▲ **FIGURE 8.24A** Student work.

Progressive Rhythm

▲ **FIGURE 8.25**

M. C. Escher. *Day and Night.* 1938. Woodcut in black and gray, printed from two blocks. 39.1 × 67.7 cm (15⅜ × 26⅝"). © 1996. Cordon Art-Baarn-Holland. All rights reserved.

SUPPLIES

- Sketchbook
- Computer
- Paint or Draw application
- Printer

Mauritius Cornelius Escher (1898–1972) was a Dutch artist and brilliant mathematician. As a child Escher struggled in school, but his tremendous art ability helped him to graduate and later major in graphic arts. Following his studies, Escher traveled through Europe. He was intrigued by the intricate patterns on the Moorish mosaics he saw while in southern Spain. These tiles inspired him to research geometric shapes that could be altered to make recognizable organic forms such as birds, animals, fish, or people. These he used to make mathematical patterns or rhythmic repetitions.

Escher is known for his carefully drawn shapes that undergo a metamorphosis into new shapes. Carefully study *Day and Night* (**Figure 8.25**). Look closely at the white bird on the right and notice all the details. Now notice the negative space between it and the two birds to its left. As you move your eyes from right to left, the white birds lose their details and gradually become the background negative space. The birds in the third column become rectangular fields on the ground as they progress downward. They become open sky as they progress upward. Now notice how the black negative space on the right has changed into sharply defined bird shapes on the left.

What You Will Learn

Create a complex motif of a living creature and use it to create a regular rhythm. You will change the motif gradually three or more times to develop a design illustrating the changes of progressive rhythm in the manner of M. C. Escher. You will also change any negative spaces created in your motif so that they progressively become positive spaces as Escher does in *Day and Night.*

Creating

Choose a favorite mammal, bird, reptile, insect, or sea-life creature. Draw several versions of it in your sketchbook. Give it an irregular outline, including wings, beaks, limbs, feathers, or tails that break out of the main shape into negative space.

Step 1 Choose your best drawing. Using the computer tools of your choice, re-create it on the computer. This is your motif. Title and save your work.

Step 2 Choose the Lasso selection tool and the Copy then Paste option to make several identical copies of the form. Choose the Grids and Rulers option to arrange your motif in a horizontal row of three or more motifs. Explore different placements of the motif so that the negative space between them has interesting possibilities. Retitle this and later editions by adding a different number to the title to indicate the sequence of production.

Step 3 Place an extra copy of the original shape in an area where you can make changes without affecting the original row of motifs. Simplify the shape by eliminating some of the details. Create a second horizontal row of the new motif and place it beneath the row of original motifs. Add some details to the negative spaces between the rows. Continue using the Save As command to retitle and save each new step.

Step 4 Continue modifying the motif, creating new horizontal rows and adding to the negative spaces as often as you can. Print your final work.

EVALUATING YOUR WORK

▶ **DESCRIBE** Tell what creature you used to create your motif. Explain, in detail, how you modified the motif and the negative spaces as you constructed your progressive rhythms. What tools and menu items did you use? How many times did you change the original motif?

▶ **ANALYZE** Did you change your motif, the horizontal rows of motifs, and the negative spaces to create progressive rhythm?

▶ **INTERPRET** What mood or idea does your work express? Give your work a descriptive title that sums up how you feel about it.

▶ **JUDGE** Were you successful in creating a progressive rhythm in the manner of Escher? What, if anything, would you change to improve your work? Which aesthetic theories would you use to judge your work?

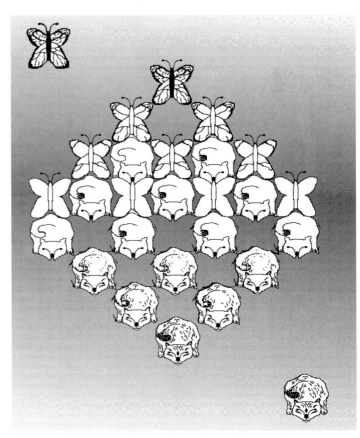

▲ **FIGURE 8.25A** Student work.

Art Criticism in Action

▲ **Figure 8.26**

George Bellows. *Cliff Dwellers.* 1913. Oil on canvas. 102 × 106.8 cm (40³⁄₁₆ × 42¹⁄₁₆"). Los Angeles County Museum of Art, Los Angeles, California. Los Angeles County Fund.

1 ▸ DESCRIBE What do you see?

List all of the information found in the credit line. This will give you an idea about when this was painted, but you really need to study the work carefully to get everything the artist is trying to say.

■ Study the people. Where are they? Describe their activities. What are they wearing?

■ Now look at the objects in this work. What do you see on the ground? Does this give you an indication of the location of this painting? Do not make guesses. Use only what you observe.

2 ▸ ANALYZE How is this work organized?

During this step you will collect information about the way the elements of art are organized using the principle of rhythm. This is still a clue-collecting step, so do not make guesses.

■ List outstanding things you notice about the elements of line, shape, space, color and texture.

■ How does the artist use value to focus your attention? Where are the lightest areas? Where are the darkest areas?

■ Find examples of random, regular, alternating, progressive, and flowing rhythms. Explain the locations of the rhythms you observe.

3 ▸ INTERPRET What is the artist trying to communicate?

Combine the clues that you have collected with your own personal experiences to tell what message the artist is sending to you through this painting.

■ How does the artist's use of elements and different rhythms affect the mood of the work?

■ Were you able to tell the time, place, and season of this work? What do you think about these people and this place?

■ Based on your interpretations, explain what the artist is communicating to you. Give the work a more descriptive title.

4 ▸ JUDGE What do you think of the work?

Now you will decide if this is a successful work of art or not.

■ Is this work interesting? Did it make you think?

■ Did the artist use the elements of art and the principle of rhythm successfully?

■ Do you think this is a successful work of art? Use one or more of the aesthetic theories to defend your judgment.

Rhythm in Design

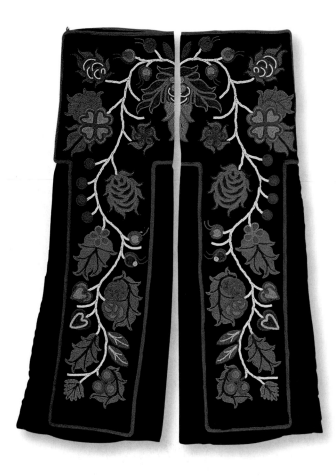

Chippewa Man's Leggings. Minnesota. c. 1890. Cotton velveteen, polished cotton, glass beads, wool twill. 74.6 × 28 cm (29⅜ × 11″). The Detroit Institute of Arts, Detroit, Michigan. Founders Society purchase.

The leggings shown in **Figure 8.27** were designed to be used in Native American dances. For many native peoples, dancing plays an important role in religious, agricultural, hunting, and curing ceremonies. Often the purpose of a dance is to give thanks to the gods, animals, and plants for their generosity. In these ceremonies, dancers represent the harvest or imitate sacred animals. Drumming, chanting, and singing almost always accompany the dancing. Both the music and the movement tend to be highly rhythmic and repetitive.

The most basic element of all dance is design—the organization or pattern of movement in space and over time. In dance, the pattern in time is provided by the rhythm of beats and movements. Similar patterns can also be found in painting, sculpture, and even the intricate beadwork of these leggings. If you look closely at the embroidered design, you will find that, like a dance, it appeals to your sense of rhythm and your awareness of motion. Do these leggings have a rhythm? In fact, they do.

In art, rhythm is produced by the repetition of motifs. Even a static object, such as a painting or a sculpture, can give us a sense of motion. The different arrangements of motif and space allow for variations in rhythm.

Making the Connection

1. How many different motifs can you find embroidered on the leggings in Figure 8.27? How many different ways has the artist alternated the motifs?
2. How would you describe the rhythm of this design?
3. Suppose you wanted to paint a picture of some of your friends in the act of dancing. What techniques would you use in your painting to convey their motion and rhythm?

Building Vocabulary

On a separate sheet of paper, write the term that best matches each definition given below.

1. The principle of art that indicates movement by the repetition of elements.
2. Rhythm you receive through your eyes rather than through your ears.
3. A unit that is repeated in visual rhythm.
4. A three-dimensional motif.
5. A two-dimensional decorative visual repetition.
6. The principle of art used to create the look and feeling of action and to guide the viewer's eyes throughout the work of art.
7. A work of art that actually moves in space.

Reviewing Art Facts

Answer the following questions using complete sentences.

1. In general, how is visual rhythm created?
2. How does rhythm add a sense of movement to a work of art?
3. How are different rhythms created?
4. What is the difference between a module and a pattern?
5. Name and describe four types of rhythm.
6. What is *dynamism* and with what group is it associated?

Thinking Critically About Art

1. **Compare and contrast.** Study the subject matter of the *Hmong Story Cloth* (Figure 8.18 on page 211) and *School Children on Parade* (Figure 8.22 on page 214). List the similarities and differences you find. Are the themes of the two works similar or different? Explain your answer.
2. **Extend.** The *Elevator Grille* in Figure 8.7, page 204, was designed by the architect Louis Sullivan for a building he designed. Find information about Louis Sullivan in the library. Discover what contributions he made to the field of architecture in the late nineteenth and early twentieth centuries. Give a brief report to the class about the importance of Louis Sullivan in the history of American architecture.

A R T
S O U R
R C
ARTSOURCE

Explore rhythm and movement with Chuck Davis and the African American Dance Ensemble in the Performing Arts Handbook on page 420.

*inter*NET
CONNECTION

Explore *Studio Cyberspace* on the Glencoe Fine Arts Site at **www.glencoe.com/sec/art.** You will find links to art museums, artists at work, and other exciting art adventures that will show how artists use the principles of rhythm and movement.

▲ **FIGURE 9.1** Hokusai has used solid white lines to represent falling water. Compare this woodblock print to the photograph of a waterfall in Figure 8.14 on page 209. What similarities and differences can you find in the two depictions of flowing water?

Katsushika Hokusai. *The Kirifuri Waterfall at Mt. Kurokami, Shimozuke Province.* ca. 1831. Color woodblock print. 37.2 × 24.5 cm (14⅝ × 9⅝"). The Nelson-Atkins Museum of Art, Kansas City, Missouri. Purchase: Nelson Trust.

CHAPTER 9

Balance

Balance is a principle of life. Each day we balance work with play. We balance the pros and cons of a decision before we make it. We learn to take conflicting or opposing elements and make them work together. This is the essential purpose of balance. Artists use different kinds of balance to convey information in their work.

The woodblock print, *The Kirifuri Waterfall at Mt. Kurokami, Shimozuke Province* (**Figure 9.1**) by Hokusai shows an inventive, bold use of balance. His work, along with those of other famous Japanese printmakers, had a strong influence on the French Impressionists. His use of balance changed the way many artists organized their compositions, encouraging them to move away from traditional balance and experiment with new kinds of balance. Notice how the waterfall flows from the upper left corner to the water below, but stays primarily on one side of the work. He balanced this strong flowing rhythm of thick white lines with a small area of green grass and busy looking trees and men on the right. In this chapter, you will learn about different types of balance and how artists use them to convey ideas and feelings in their works.

OBJECTIVES

After completing this chapter, you will be able to:

- Understand why balance is important in a work of art.
- Explain how visual weight is created and produce it in your own work.
- Describe the types of balance and use them in your own work.
- Tell what different types of balance can mean in a work of art.

WORDS TO KNOW

balance
central axis
formal balance
symmetry
radial balance
informal balance

Developing Your
PORTFOLIO

Consider how you use balance in everyday life. Make a list of things you do in a normal week, placing them in broad categories. For instance, getting your hair cut, shopping for clothes, and getting dressed in the morning might all be under the heading "Taking Care of Myself." Then list the amount of time you spend on each category. Next, draw a big circle in your sketchbook and divide it into wedges based on how much time you spend on each category. For instance, sleeping probably takes about one-third of your time, so it should take up one-third of your circle. Look at the results. Do your activities seem well-balanced? Draw another circle that represents a better balance. Label each and keep both in your portfolio.

Visual Balance

▲ **FIGURE 9.2** This building is known throughout the world, not because of its beauty or because the architect is well known, but because it leans. The many diagonal lines tell the viewer that this building must either straighten up or fall down. Because it remains off balance, defying gravity, it is famous.

Bell Tower of the Cathedral at Pisa (The Leaning Tower of Pisa). Begun in 1174.

A work of art must contain balance. **Balance** is *the principle of art concerned with equalizing visual forces, or elements, in a work of art.* Visual balance causes you to feel that the elements have been arranged well.

If visual balance creates a feeling that the elements have been arranged just right, visual imbalance creates the opposite feeling. It causes a feeling of uneasiness. It makes you feel that something is not quite right. The Leaning Tower of Pisa **(Figure 9.2)** attracts attention because it is out of balance. It has tilted into a danger zone. The top edge overhangs the base by about 17 feet. This imbalance makes the viewer feel uneasy.

In order to know whether two objects are of equal weight—that is, if they balance—a balance scale can be used. In the visual arts, however, balance must be *seen* rather than weighed. The art elements become the visual forces, or weights, in an art object. A **central axis** is *a dividing line that works like the point of balance in the balance scale.* Many works of art have a central vertical axis **(Figure 9.3)** with

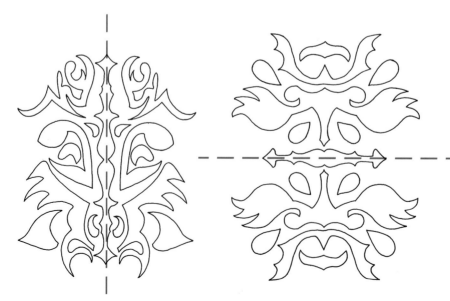

◀ **FIGURE 9.3** *(at left)* With a vertical axis, there is equal visual weight on both sides.

◀ **FIGURE 9.4** *(at right)* With a horizontal axis, there is equal visual weight above and below.

Mexican, 1886–1957

Diego Rivera. *Self-Portrait.* 1941.
Oil on canvas. 61 × 43 cm (24 × 17″). Smith College Museum of Art, Northampton, Massachusetts.

Diego Rivera, the son of two teachers, was born in 1886 in the small town of Guanajuato, Mexico. As a young man, Rivera received a government grant to study art in Spain. He also studied with Picasso in France and traveled to Italy to study the works of Raphael and Michelangelo.

When he returned to Mexico, he decided to paint only Mexican subjects. He used the simplified forms of pre-Columbian art in his work. His concern for the workers, the poor, and the illiterate influenced all of his art. He painted many murals with political themes, considering them a way to teach people who could not read. In his art, he combined the techniques of European painters with the history of Mexico to create a new way to portray his ideas about the people and culture of Mexico.

▶ **FIGURE 9.5** Rivera used his art to show his serious concern for the Mexican working people. Many of his works depicted the labors of the Mexican peasants. His work reflects the style of the solid-looking, pre-Columbian artwork of the Mayans.

Diego Rivera. *Flower Day.* 1925. Oil on canvas. 142.3 × 120.6 cm (58 × 47¹/₂″). Los Angeles County Museum of Art, Los Angeles, California. Los Angeles County Fund. Reproducción autorizada por el Instituto Nacional de Bellas Artes y Literatura.

equal visual weight on both sides of the dividing line. Works of art can also have a horizontal axis. In this case, the visual weight is balanced between top and bottom **(Figure 9.4).**

Formal Balance

One type of balance is called formal balance. **Formal balance** occurs *when equal, or very similar, elements are placed on opposite sides of a central axis.* The axis can be vertical or horizontal. It may be a real part of the design, or it may be an imaginary line, as in Figures 9.3 and 9.4. Formal balance is the easiest type of balance to recognize and to create **(Figure 9.5).** After you find the axis, all you have to do is place similar objects on each side, equally distant from the center.

▶ **FIGURE 9.6** This urn shows a young man wearing a headdress depicting his guardian spirit, the goddess Quetzal, an unforgettably beautiful bird. The artist who created this urn used symmetry to emphasize the seriousness of this work.

Mexican (Monte Alban; Zapotec). *Figural Urn.* A.D. 500–700. Painted earthenware. 63.5 × 63.5 × 31.7 cm (25 × 25 × 12½″). The Nelson-Atkins Museum of Art, Kansas City, Missouri. Purchase: Nelson Trust.

Symmetry

Symmetry is *a special type of formal balance in which two halves of a balanced composition are identical, mirror images of each other.* Another term for this is *bilateral* symmetry **(Figure 9.6).**

Symmetry appeals strongly to us, probably because of the bilateral symmetry of the human body. Objects closely associated with our bodies, such as clothing and furniture, are usually symmetrical. Most traditional architecture, especially public architecture, is symmetrical **(Figure 9.7).**

Symmetry can be very stiff and formal. Artists use it to express dignity, endurance, and stability. Because formal balance is so predictable, however, it can be dull. Many artists avoid boring the viewer by using approximate symmetry, which is *almost* symmetrical.

▲ **FIGURE 9.7** This entrance to the Federal Reserve Building in Washington, D.C. gives the building a dignified, important look. The symmetrical arrangement of vertical and horizontal shapes makes the building appear secure and stable.

Cram, Goodhue, and Ferguson. Federal Reserve Building. 1935. Washington, D.C. Façade. Photography by Sandak, Inc., Stamford, Connecticut.

Approximate symmetry has the stability of formal balance **(Figure 9.8)**. Some small differences make it more interesting than perfect symmetry. If you look carefully in a mirror, you may discover that your face has approximate symmetry. The two sides do not match perfectly.

Activity	Using Symmetry

Applying Your Skills. Arrange a symmetrical still life. Make a pencil drawing of the arrangement on a small sheet of paper. Then rearrange or change the objects slightly to create approximate symmetry. Make a drawing of the second arrangement. Mount the drawings side by side on a sheet of construction paper and label each drawing. Which one do you prefer? Survey your friends to find out their preferences.

Computer Option. If available, use the Symmetry menu and Brush or Pencil tool to create a symmetrical landscape. Vary the Brush shape, thickness, pattern, and color. If the Symmetry menu is not available, determine the central axis or line of symmetry. Draw half of the scene. Use the Select tool and Copy, Paste, and Flip commands to make the matching second half. Title and save the work. Try rearranging the shapes in your scene so that it is not perfectly symmetrical. Compare the two drawings. Which do you prefer?

▲ **FIGURE 9.8** Van Eyck used approximate symmetry to depict this wedding portrait. The halves of the picture are not quite the same. However, the work still has the dignity of perfect symmetry, only the composition is more interesting and less monotonous than if he had used perfect symmetry.

Jan van Eyck. *The Arnolfini Wedding.* 1434. Oil on panel. 83.8 × 57.2 cm (33 × 22.5″). National Gallery, London, England.

▲ **FIGURE 9.9** The use of radial balance adds to the decorative quality of this design. This print is based on the stained-glass dome found in the main synagogue of Szeged, Hungary.

N. Anderson, Israel. *Blue Dome - House Blessing.* 1995. Etching. 43.2 x 43.2 cm (17 × 17″). Private collection.

Radial Balance

Radial balance occurs *when the forces or elements of a design come out (radiate) from a central point.* The axis in a radial design is the center point. In almost all cases, the elements are spaced evenly around the axis to form circular patterns **(Figure 9.9).**

Radial balance is a complex variation of symmetry. While symmetry requires only two matching units, designs with radial balance usually involve four or more matching units. In **Figure 9.10,** notice that the center of the design is a red circle. Flower petals radiate out from that central point. Each flower petal points to the head of a figure, and the body of each figure acts as a continuation of the ray coming from the center point. Each set of matching shapes form a circular ring around the center point.

Radial balance occurs frequently in nature. Most flower petals are arranged around a central axis and radiate out-

▶ **FIGURE 9.10**
This ceremonial cloth from India is an example of radial balance. Even though the pattern repeats itself, the artwork attracts attention because of the kind of balance it uses.

Chamba Rumal. India, Himachal Pradesh. Early nineteenth century. Cotton with colored embroidery (silk). 166 cm (26″) diameter. Philadelphia Museum of Art, Philadelphia, Pennsylvania. Purchased with funds contributed by Ann McPhail and anonymous donors.

ward. Many plants follow radial patterns of growth. For instance, if you cut an apple in half horizontally, you will see a radial star design. Cut an orange the same way and you will notice the radial pattern of segments.

You can find many examples of radial balance in architecture. Domes are designed on the principle of radial balance. Manufactured items such as gears, wheels, tires, dials, and clocks are also radial in structure. Radial designs are used by many potters to decorate the surfaces of their work because they adapt well to the rounded forms of pottery **(Figure 9.11)**.

◀ **FIGURE 9.11** Torivio, a Native American potter, has developed her own style for decorating her pots. She repeats the designs in radial patterns. The motif starts out small at the top rim and then expands to the widest part of the vessel.

Dorothy Torivio. *Vase.* c. 1984. Clay. Height about 20 cm (8″). Heard Museum Collection, Phoenix, Arizona.

Check Your Understanding

1. What is a central axis?
2. What is the easiest type of balance to recognize and create?
3. Which type of balance can be found frequently in nature and in architecture?

Natural Balance

Natural balance gives the viewer the same comfortable feeling as formal balance, but in a much more subtle way. While natural balance can express dignity, endurance, and stability, these qualities are less pronounced. Natural balance seems more realistic because it is closer to what appears in nature. It does not consist of two equal or nearly equal halves or sides. Instead, it relies on the artistic arrangement of objects to *appear* balanced. Natural balance is used in Figure 9.1 on page 226.

Informal Balance

Informal balance, or asymmetry, involves *a balance of unlike objects*. Informal balance creates a casual effect **(Figure 9.12).** Although it seems less planned than formal balance, it is not. What appears to be an accidental arrangement of elements can be quite complicated. Symmetry merely requires that elements be repeated in a mirror image. Informal balance is more complex. Artists must consider all the visual

▲ **FIGURE 9.12** The complex shapes of the wagon and the child are informally balanced by the potted plant and the foliage in this casual scene. Informal balance gives this composition the look of a snapshot.

Thomas Eakins. *Baby at Play.* 1876. Oil on canvas. 81.9 × 122.8 cm (32¼ × 48⅜″). National Gallery of Art, Washington, D.C. © 1998 Board of Trustees. John Hay Whitney Collection.

◀ **FIGURE 9.13** The many small shapes in the lower right corner of this painting balance the large shape of the stage with its closed curtain.

Edward Hopper. *First Row Orchestra.* 1951. Oil on canvas. 79 × 101.9 cm (31⅛ × 40⅛"). Hirshhorn Museum and Sculpture Garden, Smithsonian Institution, Washington, D.C. Gift of the Joseph H. Hirshhorn Foundation, 1966.

weight factors and put them together correctly. Many factors influence the visual weight, or the attraction, that elements in a work of art have to the viewer's eyes.

Size and Contour

A large shape or form appears to be heavier than a small shape. Several small shapes or forms can balance one large shape **(Figure 9.13).**

An object with a complicated contour is more interesting and appears to be heavier than one with a simple contour. A small, complex object can balance a large, simple object.

Color

A high-intensity color has more visual weight than a low-intensity color. The viewer's eyes are drawn to the area of bright color. What does this mean in terms of balance? It means that a small area of bright color is able to balance a larger area of a dull, neutral color **(Figure 9.14).**

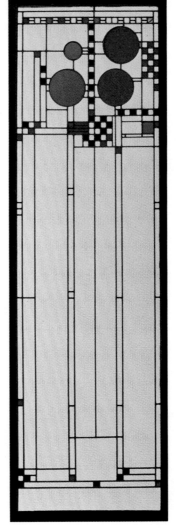

◀ **FIGURE 9.14** In this stained-glass window designed by Frank Lloyd Wright, the bright colors at the top balance the large area of clear glass.

Designed by Frank Lloyd Wright. American stained-glass window, one of a triptych. Twentieth century. Glass, lead, wood. 219 × 71 × 5 cm (86¼ × 28 × 2"). The Metropolitan Museum of Art, New York, New York. Purchase. Edward C. Moore, Jr., gift and Edgar J. Kaufmann Charitable Foundation gift, 1967.

Warm colors carry more visual weight than cool colors. Red appears heavier than blue, and orange appears heavier than green **(Figure 9.15)**.

Value

The stronger the contrast in value between an object and the background, the more visual weight the object has **(Figure 9.16)**. Black against white has more weight than gray against white. Dark values appear heavier than light values. A dark red seems heavier than a light red.

Texture

A rough texture, with its uneven pattern of light highlights and dark, irregular shadows, attracts the viewer's eye more easily than a smooth, even surface does. This means that a small, rough-textured area can balance a large, smooth surface. In a poster or advertisement, a block of printed words has the quality of rough texture because of the irregular pattern of light and dark. Graphic designers must keep this in mind when balancing words with other visual elements.

▶ **FIGURE 9.15** In this Rococo painting, Fragonard balances all the cool, low-intensity colors with the warm, bright red on the dress in the foreground.

Jean-Honoré Fragonard. *A Game of Hot Cockles.* 1767–73. Oil on canvas. 115.5 × 91.4 cm (45½ × 36″). National Gallery of Art, Washington, D.C. © 1998 Board of Trustees. Samuel H. Kress Collection.

▲ **FIGURE 9.16** The face and head scarf of the Virgin are no lighter in value than the infant on his blanket or the shepherd's white skirt. Her face stands out so much more because it is placed against the dark value of the cave's interior, while the infant and the shepherd are placed against the midvalue tan of the ground.

Giorgione. *The Adoration of the Shepherds.* c. 1505–10. Oil on panel. 91 × 111 cm (35¾ × 43½"). National Gallery of Art, Washington, D.C. © 1998 Board of Trustees. Samuel H. Kress Collection.

Position

Children playing on a seesaw quickly discover that two friends of unequal weight can balance the seesaw by adjusting their positions. The heavier child moves toward the center; the lighter child slides toward the end. The board is then in balance **(Figure 9.17).**

In visual art, a large object close to the dominant area of the work can be

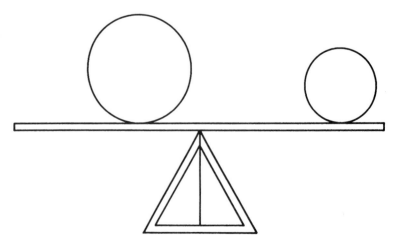

▲ **FIGURE 9.17** Does the seesaw look balanced?

▲ **FIGURE 9.18** Notice the large wave on the left. It is balanced informally by the small triangular shape of Mount Fuji in the distance. Notice the shape of the negative space of the yellow sky. How does it help to balance the positive shape of the wave? How do the three small fishing boats affect the balance of the work?

Katsushika Hokusai. *The Great Wave at Kanagawa* (from the series "The Thirty-Six Views of Mount Fuji"). c. 1823–29. Polychrome woodblock print. 25.7 × 36 cm (10⅛ × 14⁵/₁₆"). The Metropolitan Museum of Art, New York, New York. H. O. Havemeyer, 1929. (JP1847)

 **Using Informal Balance**

Applying Your Skills. Create small designs using cut paper and/or fabric shapes to illustrate five weight arrangements that create informal balance. In each design keep all of the elements as alike as possible. Vary only the weight factors. For example, to illustrate differences in size, a large red circle could be balanced by several small red circles.

Computer Option. Use the drawing tools of your choice to make a series of small compositions that show informal balance. Use both lines and shapes. Explore changes in size, color, texture, value, contour, and position to create these asymmetrical compositions. Make several of each kind. Title, save, and print your best examples. Display them and compare with your classmates.

balanced by a smaller object placed farther away from the dominant area **(Figure 9.18)**. In this way, a large, positive shape and a small, negative space can be balanced against a small, positive shape and a large, negative space.

☑ Check Your Understanding

1. What is the effect of informal balance?
2. Name the six factors that influence the visual weight of an object.
3. Which has a heavier visual weight, an object with a simple contour or one with a complicated contour?

The Expressive Qualities of Balance

The type of balance an artist uses to organize a work of art affects the feeling expressed by that work. Artists choose balance based on the feel- ing they wish to convey. An artist who wants to present a calm arrangement will use formal balance. Formal balance can be used to present a person in a dig- nified portrait **(Figure 9.19).**

LOOKING CLOSELY — Using Formal Balance To Organize A Composition

Frida Kahlo has used formal balance to organize this painting to give it a sense of dignity and impor- tance. In the diagram you can see that if the painting were folded in half along the vertical axis the shapes would match. Notice, however, that there are a few small variations. They would not match perfectly because she has used approximate symmetry. Can you find any matching shapes that were not included in the diagram?

vertical axis

◀ **FIGURE 9.19**

Frida Kahlo. *Self Portrait Dedicated to Leon Trotsky.* 1937. Oil on masonite. 76.2 × 61 cm (30 × 24″). National Museum of Women in the Arts, Washington, D.C. Gift of the Honorable Clare Boothe Luce.

◀ **FIGURE 9.20** Ferdinand Hodler used formal balance to create a stiff, stable portrait of his friend. The line from the sculptor's nose through the line in his shirt divides the portrait vertically into almost perfectly matching halves.

Ferdinand Hodler. *James Vilbert, Sculptor.* 1907. Oil on canvas. 65.4 × 66.4 cm (25¾ × 26⅛"). The Art Institute of Chicago, Chicago, Illinois. Helen Birch Bartlett Memorial Collection, 1926.212

Formal balance can also be used in religious paintings to evoke feelings of dignity and endurance. In the past, paintings used as altarpieces in churches were designed to fit in with the formal balance of the church altar. The artist Ferdinand Hodler developed a personal aesthetic theory called Parallelism that relied on symmetry and repetition to create images that expressed stability **(Figure 9.20).**

Many government buildings, hospitals, and office buildings are designed using formal balance. One purpose of this type of balance is to imply that the business conducted in these buildings is serious and solemn.

With approximate symmetry, artists express the same sense of calm stability, but they avoid the rigid formality of pure symmetry. Georgia O'Keeffe used approximate symmetry in her paintings of large close-ups of flowers. This impresses the viewer with feelings about the importance of the natural world. The use of approximate symmetry lends dignity to the flowing curves and alternating pastel colors of her painting, *White Rose with Larkspur, No. 2* **(Figure 9.21).**

Radial design, on the other hand, is almost purely decorative. It appears in architecture, jewelry, pottery, weaving,

◀ **FIGURE 9.21** How has O'Keeffe arranged the shapes in this painting to create approximate, not absolute, symmetry? Would you like the painting more if it were perfectly symmetrical? Why or why not?

Georgia O'Keeffe. *White Rose With Larkspur, No. 2.* 1927. Oil on canvas. 101.6 × 76.2 cm (40 × 30"). Courtesy, Museum of Fine Arts, Boston, Massachusetts. Henry H. and Zoë Oliver Sherman Fund.

▶ **FIGURE 9.22** Notice how Carr has used informal balance by placing most of the raven to the right of center in this landscape. She made many trips to the Northwest Coast of Alaska to record images of the Native American villages. This work was made in her studio based on sketches she had done on her trip to Queen Charlotte Island. The Haida village had been deserted and the large carving of the raven remained. She has balanced the raven, flowers, and trees near the foreground against the blue mountain in the distance.

Emily Carr. *Cumshewa*. c. 1912. Watercolor over graphite on wove paper. 52 × 75.5 cm (20½ × 29⅝″). National Gallery of Canada, Ottawa, Ontario, Canada.

and textile design. It is not often used by painters in its pure form. You can, however, find loose arrangements of radiating lines in many paintings. Artists use this technique to focus attention on an important part of an artwork.

Informal balance has a more natural look. When you look around your natural environment, you seldom find objects arranged with formal balance. To capture this natural quality in their works, artists use informal balance in arranging landscapes or groups of people **(Figure 9.22)**.

Architects are using informal balance in many modern structures (see Figure 14.21, page 402). Single-family suburban homes have become the symbol of casual living. These houses are often designed using informal balance.

☑ Check Your Understanding

1. What feeling does formal balance convey?
2. What kind of buildings use formal balance? Why?
3. Why might an artist prefer approximate symmetry over pure symmetry?

Activity | Identifying Balance

Applying Your Skills. Look around your neighborhood for buildings that have been constructed using formal or informal balance. Make a rough sketch of one building and describe the feeling it gives you. If you live in a city and the buildings are too tall to sketch, look at the entrances to the buildings and sketch one of them. The entrance includes the door and all the decorative shapes around the doorway.

Computer Option. Use the tools of your choice to create a complex design illustrating one of the following: formal balance, informal balance, symmetry, approximate symmetry, radial balance. Save your work and then print it. If your printer is black and white, use colored pencils to add color. Evaluate your design. Does it meet the criteria for the kind of balance you chose to illustrate?

Formal Portrait

▲ FIGURE 9.23

Artist unknown. *Winxiang, Prince Yi*. Qing dynasty. 1644-1911. Ink and color on silk. 186.7 × 121.9 cm (73½ × 48"). Arthur M. Sackler Gallery, Smithsonian Institution, Washington, D.C. Gift of Richard G. Pritzlaff.

SUPPLIES

- Sketchbook and pencil
- Large sheet of white paper
- Yellow chalk
- Black fine-line marker
- Acrylic paints and brushes

This portrait of a Chinese prince **(Figure 9.23)** is very different from the Chinese landscape paintings that one often sees. The pose is dictated by tradition.

Notice the details in this formal portrait and think about how you can use them in your portrait.

What You Will Learn

You will design and create a formal portrait of a person from history or from current events. Arrange the person in a symmetrical pose in the center of the composition. The figure should fill the page. Use approximate symmetry to place objects that symbolize important events in that person's life on and around the figure. Choose a color scheme that expresses a specific mood you are trying to convey.

Creating

Choose a person you have studied in history or in current events that you admire. Research information about this person. If this person is from past history, you will find information in encyclopedias or in biographies. If your subject is involved in current events, look through newspapers and the *Readers' Guide to Periodicals* for magazines that will provide information about your subject. The Internet may also be a valuable source of information on your subject. Make visual and verbal notes about your subject in your sketchbook.

Step 1 Make rough sketches for your composition. Remember that the figure must be organized in a symmetrical pose and that it must fill most of the paper. Make some accurate sketches of details needed for the portrait such as clothing of the historical period, furniture, symbols that will surround or cover the figure, and an appropriate background setting. Choose your best design and sketch it lightly with yellow chalk on the large white paper.

Step 2 Choose a color scheme that expresses the appropriate mood. Paint your composition. Use large brushes to fill in the largest shapes. Use small brushes to paint the symbols and clothing details. If necessary, use a fine-line black marker to define some of your details and labels.

Step 3 Write a paragraph about your subject. Mount or mat your portrait for display. Integrate the written paragraph into your display.

EVALUATING YOUR WORK

▶ **DESCRIBE** Name the subject of your portrait. What symbols did you select to represent the events in that person's life? How did you do visual and verbal research? Where did you look and what kind of information did you find? How did you prepare your work for display? Did you include a paragraph about the subject? How did you incorporate it into the display?

▶ **ANALYZE** What kinds of balance did you use in your composition? Explain. Describe the color scheme you selected for this work and explain why you chose it.

▶ **INTERPRET** What does your painting express about the subject of your portrait? Did the kinds of balance and the color scheme affect the mood? Give this work a poetic title.

▶ **JUDGE** Which aesthetic theories would you use to judge this work? If you were to do this over, what would you do to improve it?

▲ **FIGURE 9.23A** Student work.

Informal Group Portrait

▲ FIGURE 9.24

Mary Cassatt. *The Tea.* About 1880. Oil on canvas. 64.8 × 92.1 cm (25½ × 36¼"). Courtesy, Museum of Fine Arts, Boston, Massachusetts. M. Theresa B. Hopkins Fund.

SUPPLIES

- Sketchbook and pencil
- Snapshots you have taken
- Large sheet of white paper
- Acrylic paints and an assortment of brushes

Many late-nineteenth-century American artists painted in the Impressionist style, but Mary Cassatt was the only one who actually joined the radical French artists and showed her artwork in their independent exhibitions in Paris. She followed their practice of capturing a moment of everyday life as it would look in a snapshot—one single moment in time. Like snapshots, her compositions were asymmetrical and closely cropped **(Figure 9.24).**

The Japanese woodblock print, which had arrived in Paris in the late 1800s, was one source of inspiration for the Impressionists' asymmetrical compositions. The Japanese printmakers were not afraid to cut off part of a figure. European artists, who had never done this in the past, began to imitate this technique.

The new art of photography also influenced the compositions of the Impressionists. The camera presented them with candid, or unposed, views of people. Snapshots showed familiar subjects from new and unusual points of view. Look at Cassatt's painting. Observe how she used balance, cropped figures, and color.

What You Will Learn

In this project, you will plan and create a painting in the Impressionist style. Use asymmetrical balance, a close-cropped composition, loose brushstrokes that resemble the dabs and dashes of the Impressionists, and the colors of the Impressionists. This painting must be based on an unposed photograph you have taken. It must include at least two people.

Creating

Collect photographs you have taken of your family or friends. Select one that you think will make an interesting painting. Remember that it must show asymmetrical balance, two or more people must be visible, and part of each figure must be cropped off, as in *The Tea*.

Step 1 Make a large, rough sketch in your sketchbook based on the photograph. Work on your first sketch to improve the composition as needed. Do not worry about whether the faces in the sketch and the painting look like the real people.

Step 2 Practice using the colors of the Impressionists in your sketchbook. Use only spectral colors and white. Blues and violets replace grays, browns, and blacks even in the shadows. Make grays by placing complements side by side. Use white side by side with your colors and add white to some of your colors to create light values. Apply the colors using loose brushstrokes and short dabs and dashes of paint.

Step 3 Using a brush and a very light value of yellow, sketch the final composition onto the large sheet of white paper. Use what you have learned during practice in your sketchbook to paint your composition. Create an expressive title for your work.

Step 4 Mount or mat your work for display.

EVALUATING YOUR WORK

▶ **DESCRIBE** What is the subject matter of your work? How many people have you used? What other objects are important in the composition?

▶ **ANALYZE** Did you use asymmetry? Which kind of informal balance did you use? Did you keep the effect of a photograph by cropping off parts of the figures? Did you use Impressionists' colors? How many ways did you use white?

▶ **INTERPRET** Describe the difference between the look of the photograph and the look of your finished painting. How did style affect the look of your work? Give your work a title that expresses the mood of your work.

▶ **JUDGE** Which aesthetic theories would you use to judge this work? If you were to do this over, what, if anything, would you do differently?

▲ **FIGURE 9.24A** Student work.

Linoleum Print Using Radial Balance

▲ **FIGURE 9.25**

Beau Dick. *Sacred Circles.* 1991. Serigraph 98/155. 50 × 50 cm (19³/₄ × 19³/₄″). Private collection.

SUPPLIES

- **Sketchbook and pencil**
- **Ruler, compass, and scissors**
- **Tracing paper and carbon paper**
- **Linoleum and dark marker**
- **Linoleum cutting tools**
- **Bench hook or C clamp**
- **Water-base printing ink**
- **Brayer and inking plate**
- **Printmaking paper**

The making of *serigraphs* (limited-edition silk-screen prints) is a relatively new art form for the Northwest Coast artists. These artists started making serigraphs around 1970. *Sacred Circles* **(Figure 9.25)** was originally designed for a drum. Beau Dick's daughter, who is a teacher in Queen Charlotte, British Columbia, asked him to design something for her students for Rediscovery Week. The Rediscovery program in Canada was begun to teach young Native Americans to rediscover their heritage as a source of self-esteem.

This design shows a group of young people sitting in a circle, holding hands to show unity and friendship. The dark round shapes in the center are stones, inside of which a bonfire is to be built. This symbolizes the artist's belief that children are the ones who will carry on Native American traditions.

What You Will Learn

You will select symbols from your cultural heritage to create one or more motifs for a relief print. Produce an edition of five relief prints. Sign, date, and number your prints.

Creating

Brainstorm with your classmates about well-known symbols for different cultures. Then discuss your cultural heritage with members of your immediate family. Select symbols you prefer and make some rough sketches for arranging them into a radial design.

Step 1 Trace the shape of your piece of linoleum onto a page in your sketchbook. Using the ruler, connect the opposite corners of the rectangle to find the center of the shape. Place the point of the compass on that center and draw the largest circle possible within the shape. Select your best design and draw it in the circle.

Step 2 Trace your finished design onto the tracing paper. Use a piece of carbon paper to transfer the design from the tracing paper to the piece of linoleum.

Step 3 Use a dark marker to color the lines and shapes on the areas of linoleum that will not be cut away.

Step 4 Use a bench hook to hold your linoleum safely in place. You have left the linoleum in the shape of a rectangle so that it can be held in place by the bench hook. Do not cut it into a circle until all your linoleum cuts are finished. Use the narrow V-gouge to outline the shapes. Always move the cutting tool in an outward motion away from your body. Use wider U-gouges to cut away the negative areas. The pattern of your cuts will show in the final print. Plan the direction of the cuts as carefully as you plan the positive shapes in your design. Finally, use the V-gouges to cut the fine lines on the positive shapes.

Step 5 Select your paper to make an edition of five prints. Locate your drying place. Squeeze out an inch of ink onto the inking plate. Roll the brayer in both directions until it is loaded with ink. Ink the linoleum. Make five prints. When they are dry, sign each one in pencil at the bottom of the print. Write the title on the left, the number in the center, and your name and date on the right. The number should include the number of the print and the total number of prints in the edition.

EVALUATING YOUR WORK

▶ **DESCRIBE** List and describe the symbols you used to create the motifs for your radial design.

▶ **ANALYZE** Did you use radial balance to organize the motifs? Did you use size to indicate the dominant motif? Did you use radial lines to help organize the motifs?

▶ **INTERPRET** What is the expressive quality of your personal print? Does it represent your cultural heritage?

▶ **JUDGE** Which aesthetic theories would you use to judge this work? If you were going to do this again, what, if anything, would you change?

▲ **FIGURE 9.25A** Student work.

Invent an Inside View of a Machine

▲ **FIGURE 9.26**

Gerald Murphy. *Watch.* 1925. Oil on canvas. 199.4 × 199.4 cm (78½ × 78½"). Dallas Museum of Art, Dallas, Texas. Foundation for the Arts Collection. Gift of the artist.

SUPPLIES

- **Sketchbook**
- **Computer**
- **Paint or Draw application**
- **Printer**

Optional

- **Scanner or digital camera**

The influences of abstract artists mingled with Gerald Murphy's early training as an architect to create a very precise, hard-edged style. Murphy chose everyday, common objects such as a watch, razor, or pen as the subjects for his compositions.

Notice in **Figure 9.26** how Murphy painted many circular shapes in a variety of sizes. These are carefully arranged to create a composition that not only is formally balanced, but also has a center of interest. All of the watch parts look as if they belong together even though a few of the shapes may have been invented and others appear to be exterior mechanisms. Observe the unusual shapes Murphy has used in the four corners of the painting to quickly lead your eye back to the center.

What You Will Learn

Design an inside view of a machine using one type of formal balance. Use rhythm by repeating similar shapes and related shapes in a variety of sizes. You may repeat the shape using a variety of sizes and use parts of the original shape as Murphy has done. To give your design a strong sense of unity, use overlapping shapes and connect shapes with lines.

Creating

Brainstorm and list different moving, mechanical parts such as cogs, springs, dials, and gears. Consider other modern advances found in today's technology. Decide what kind of formal balance you will use.

Step 1 Choose from the shape tools, such as the Round or Rectangular tool, to begin the inside view of a machine. Be inventive. Make three or four sketches on the computer to help you decide.

Step 2 Select your best idea. Begin with your choice of shape tools to create an interior view. Use the Selection tools and Copy, Paste, and Scale Selection menus to repeat similar, simple shapes in a variety of sizes. Arrange the shapes to match the kind of balance you have chosen.

Step 3 Continue to add interest by representing many different kinds of mechanical parts. Show not only different sizes of similar shapes, but also change line thickness and add details to many of the surfaces. Add a few contrasting shapes.

Step 4 Unify your design. Overlap shapes. If available, use the Arc and Line tools to connect and draw portions of handles, cogs, gears, or dials. Cover every available space with a mechanical part. Title and save your drawing as you work.

Step 5 When your drawing is complete, title, save, and display your work.

EVALUATING YOUR WORK

▶ **DESCRIBE** What kind of machine did you choose for your design? List the different machine parts you drew and the tools you used to create them. How many times have you repeated the same shape? Do the shapes vary?

▶ **ANALYZE** What kind of balance did you use? Did you use repetition to create rhythm? Explain. Have you used overlapping? Do the shapes of the parts of your design look like they belong together? How did you achieve this effect?

▶ **INTERPRET** What mood, feeling, or idea does your machine convey? Identify the elements or principles of art you applied to support this emotion. Does the artwork suggest any other ideas to the viewer? Do you think if you created this design in another medium you could achieve the same effect?

▶ **JUDGE** Were you successful in arranging the parts of your design to create formal balance? Do you think this design would look the same created in another medium? Which aesthetic theory would you use to decide on the success of this work?

▲ **FIGURE 9.26A** Student work.

ART CRITICISM IN ACTION

▲ **FIGURE 9.27**

Alice Neel. *Linda Nochlin and Daisy*. 1973. Oil on canvas. 141.9 × 111.8 cm (55⅞ × 44″). Seth K. Sweetser Fund. Courtesy, Museum of Fine Arts, Boston, Massachusetts.

1 ▶ DESCRIBE What do you see?

Do not be fooled by the limited number of objects in this work. You must use your perceptive skills with care to uncover the message being sent in this painting.

- Find out the size of this oil painting from the credit line and measure it out somewhere so that you can understand how big it is.
- Describe the two people including their features, hair, hands, skin, clothing, positions, and body size.
- List the other objects you see in this work.

2 ▶ ANALYZE How is this work organized?

The elements and principles are very important in this work. The way the artist has used them will give you clues for understanding the work.

- Where can you find rhythmic repetitions? Use your perceptive skills carefully to notice all the repetitions.
- What kind of balance has the artist used to arrange this work? How are things positioned in relation to the vertical axis? Explain.

3 ▶ INTERPRET What is the artist trying to communicate?

Now you will combine the clues you have collected along with your own personal reactions to them to discover the meaning of this work.

- How has the artist's use of balance affected the feeling of this work?
- What is the relationship between these two people? Explain.
- Give this work a new title that sums up your interpretation of it.

4 ▶ JUDGE What do you think of the work?

Decide if this is a successful work of art. You may make a personal opinion, but it is also important to make an objective judgment based on aesthetic theories.

- Is this work interesting? Did it make you think?
- Did the artist use the elements and the principles of rhythm and balance to send a clear message to you, the viewer?
- Do you think this is a successful work of art? Why or why not? Use one or more of the aesthetic theories described in Chapter 2 to defend your judgment.

MEET THE ARTIST
ALICE NEEL

American, 1900–1984

Alice Neel attended the Philadelphia School of Design for Women (now called Moore College of Art), where she was exposed to the ideas of the Expressionists. After graduating she moved to New York City, where she found the inspiration for her work: in people's faces. Her works convey a lively sense of vibrancy and character. She found subjects everywhere, especially in the neighborhoods of Greenwich Village and Spanish Harlem.

Neel "collected" subjects by painting portraits of people and even stopped strangers in the street to ask them to pose for her. Her paintings reflect the personalities of her subjects. Some seem carefully and precisely done, while others are more casual and less formal.

What Is Symbolism?

◀ **FIGURE 9.28**

Rie Muñoz. *Both the Sun and Moon Belong to Women.* 1990. Watercolor. 48.2 × 55.9 cm (19 × 22″). Rie Muñoz Ltd., Juneau, Alaska.

A symbol is something that stands for or represents something else. In this sense, all words are symbols. In literature a symbol is an object, image, event, or even a person that suggests an important meaning beyond itself. For example, in Virginia Woolf's novel *Mrs. Dalloway,* the husband expresses his love for his wife by giving her a bouquet of roses, a conventional symbol for love. Many literary symbols are not so obvious, however.

Artists use symbols in much the same way writers do. In **Figure 9.28,** there are two Inuit women in similar positions. Notice the stylized use of shape and high-intensity color. Smooth curves contrasted with sharp points establish a motif in the work. The painting uses balance for the purpose of visual pleasure; however, it may contribute to the painting's symbolic meaning as well.

The gestures of the women indicate that they are celebrating, but the artist has chosen to express this idea symbolically rather than literally or realistically. The sun, moon, and stars may symbolize the universal nature of artistic expression. However, the painting's title, along with the two women in the painting, suggest something more specific. What symbolic connection do you think the artist is attempting to make between women, the sun, and the moon?

Making the Connection

1. How has the artist symbolized day and night in the painting?
2. What type of balance has the artist achieved in this painting?
3. Interpret the painting as though it were a short story or poem. Describe what you think the women represent. Write your response in the form of a short essay.

Building Vocabulary

On a separate sheet of paper, write the term that best matches each definition given below.

1. The principle of art concerned with equalizing visual forces, or elements, in a work of art.
2. A dividing line that works like the point of balance in the balance scale.
3. The type of balance that results when equal, or very similar, elements are placed on opposite sides of a central axis.
4. A special type of formal balance in which two halves of a balanced composition are identical, mirror images of each other.
5. When the forces or elements of a design come out (*radiate*) from a central point.
6. A balance of unlike objects.

Reviewing Art Facts

Answer the following questions using complete sentences.

1. Why is balance important to a work of art?
2. What are the visual forces, or weights, in art?
3. What is the difference between symmetry and approximate symmetry?
4. What factors in a work of art influence the visual weight of the art elements?
5. Which carry more weight, warm or cool colors?
6. How can value affect visual weight?
7. What does a formally balanced building express?

Thinking Critically About Art

1. **Research.** The Leaning Tower of Pisa (Figure 9.2, page 228) is in serious trouble. It is about to collapse. Search the *Readers' Guide to Periodicals* for recent articles about the tower. Find out what, if anything, is being done to keep it from falling.
2. **Analyze.** Edward Hopper, who painted *First Row Orchestra* (Figure 9.13, page 235), was not considered a member of the Regionalist school of painting. Find a book about him at the library, and look at his paintings. In what way does his subject matter and themes differ from those of the Regionalists? Explain your findings to the class using visual examples to illustrate your conclusions.

Turn to the Performing Arts Handbook on page 421 to learn how Eth-Noh-Tec uses a balance of music, movement, and words to present their unique style of theatre and storytelling.

*inter*NET
CONNECTION

Learn more about why balance is so important in a work of art by exploring the Glencoe Fine Arts Site at **www.glencoe.com/sec/art**. You can also discover your own techniques for creating balance in your art by finding the chapter you are studying in the Table of Contents and clicking on one of the "hot links."

▲ **FIGURE 10.1** This statue represents Guanyin, a Chinese Bodhisattva. In Buddhism, a Bodhisattva is an advanced spiritual being who has chosen to delay nirvana, the state of complete enlightenment, in order to bring salvation to the people. Guanyin, the most popular of the Bodhisattvas, appears to people in 108 different human forms.

Chinese. *The Water and Moon Guanyin Bodhisattva.* Eleventh/twelfth century. Northern Song (960–1127) or Liao Dynasty (907–1125). Wood with paint. 241.3 × 165.1 cm (95 × 65″). The Nelson-Atkins Museum of Art, Kansas City, Missouri. (Purchase: Nelson Trust)

CHAPTER 10

Proportion

"**Y**ou put too much salt in the soup!"

"This desk is too small for me!"

These statements present problems of proportion. **Proportion** is *the principle of art concerned with the size relationship of one part to another.* When you shop for clothes, for example, you look for sizes designed to fit the proportions of your body. The size of a chair for a kindergarten classroom must fit the proportions of small children, while the size of a chair for your classroom must fit your proportions.

The figure of the Bodhisattva, Guanyin **(Figure 10.1),** was created using human proportions. Notice how realistic and lifelike the sculpture appears. Although the Bodhisattva exudes dignity and calm, his proportions make him appear natural and human. In Buddhism, the worshiper is encouraged to feel that this compassionate figure is accessible to ordinary people. Anyone can pray to him for help. If the proportions had been different—for instance, if the statue were monumental, several times the size of a human—the figure would not appear so approachable. The proportions of the figure make the sculpture universally appealing to viewers.

OBJECTIVES

After completing this chapter, you will be able to:

- Explain and recognize the Golden Mean.
- Understand how we perceive proportion and scale.
- Measure and draw human faces and bodies with correct proportions.
- Understand how artists use proportion and distortion to create meaning.

WORDS TO KNOW

proportion
Golden Mean
scale
hierarchical proportion
foreshortening
exaggeration
distortion

Developing Your
PORTFOLIO

Caricatures (**car**-ik-ah-choors) are drawings that use exaggeration and distortion of distinctive physical features for the purpose of comic satire and ridicule. Today caricatures are seen frequently in newspaper and magazine editorial cartoons. Search the editorial pages of newspapers for caricatures of politicians or celebrities. Then look for realistic photographs of the same person. Mount each caricature and photograph of the person side by side. Then, for each set of images, write a brief paragraph about the difference between the photograph and the caricature, explaining what the artist has exaggerated and/or distorted and what expressive effect the artist created.

The Golden Mean

Through the ages, people have sought an ideal of harmony and beauty. One way they have tried to capture this ideal is through correct proportion. Artists and architects have looked for a ratio (a mathematical comparison of sizes) that would produce an ideal form for figures and structures.

The ancient Greek philosopher Pythagoras found that he could apply mathematical equations to both geometric shapes and musical tones. If this was so, he thought, there must also be a way to explain other things—even the universe—in mathematical terms.

Euclid, a Greek mathematician, discovered what he considered a perfect ratio, or relationship of one part to another. He called this ratio the Golden Section, or **Golden Mean,** *a line divided into two parts so that the smaller line has the same proportion, or ratio, to the larger line as the larger line has to the whole line* **(Figure 10.2).** With this ratio, the ancient Greeks felt they had found the ideal proportion. It was used to control the relationship of parts in their sculpture, architecture, and pottery. In math, this ratio is written 1 to 1.6 or 1:1.6.

The Golden Rectangle **(Figure 10.3)** had sides that matched this ratio. The longer sides were a little more than one and a half times as long as the shorter sides. This ratio was thought to be the most pleasing to the eye. If you look closely at Leyster's *The Concert* **(Figure 10.4),** you can see that the wall and the two figures on the right side of the work is a square, while the wall and the single figure on the left is the smaller section of the Golden Rectangle.

One of the many fascinating facts about the Golden Mean is its relationship to the human figure. If you divide the average adult male body horizontally at the navel, the two body measurements that result (head to navel = a and navel to toes = b) have a ratio of 1 to 1.6 **(Figure 10.5).**

The secret of the Golden Mean was forgotten with the fall of Ancient Greece. The ratio was rediscovered, however, during the Renaissance, and a book was written about it. This time the ratio was called the Divine Proportion, and it was thought to have magical qualities.

▲ **FIGURE 10.2** The ratio of the Golden Mean is 1 to 1.6.

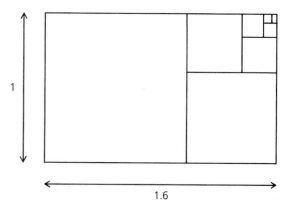

▲ **FIGURE 10.3** The Golden Rectangle is interesting to study. If you divide it into two shapes, one of which is a square, the remaining shape will always be a smaller Golden Rectangle. This new Golden Rectangle can be divided again and again.

▲ **Figure 10.4** Judith Leyster has used the proportions of the Golden Mean to organize this painting. Look at the line dividing the back wall. The section on the right forms a perfect square. The section on the left is a Golden Rectangle. It can be divided just like the smaller section of the diagram in Figure 10.3.

Judith Leyster. *The Concert.* ca 1633. Oil on canvas. 109.2 × 167.6 cm (43 × 66″). The National Museum of Women in the Arts, Washington, D.C. On loan from Wallace and Wilhelmina Holladay.

Since that time, some artists have chosen to use the Golden Mean as the basis for their compositions. Others, unaware of the mathematical ratio, used the Golden Mean just because that arrangement of parts looked good. Most artists now reject the idea that only this one rule can define the "correct" proportions for all works of art. The ratio, however, is found in visual art so often that it is hard to ignore its importance (**Figure 10.6,** on page 258).

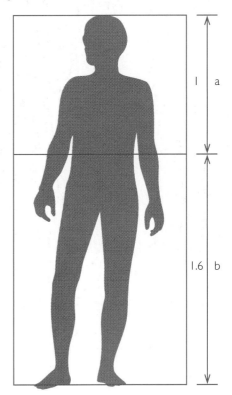

1 a

1.6 b

◀ **Figure 10.5** The relationship of the Golden Mean to the human body. Section a extends from head to navel and section b extends from navel to toes.

Notice how Bellows has used the Golden Rectangle and the diagonal of the square in the rectangle to give this action painting stability. He has used the vertical line for his standing figure and the diagonal line to help him place the leaning figure. Can you find the square in the small rectangle? Can you find any other artworks that use the Golden Mean? Many of them are very subtle and hard to notice.

◀ **FIGURE 10.6**

George Bellows. *Both Members of This Club.* 1909. Oil on canvas. 115 × 160 cm (45¼ × 63⅛″). National Gallery of Art, Washington, D.C. © 1998 Board of Trustees. Chester Dale Collection.

► **Figure 10.7** Le Corbusier has been called the poet of the apartment house. This building has many of the features of a resort, such as a kindergarten and nursery, a roof garden, children's swimming pool, gymnasium, and snack bar. Lead sheets were placed between the walls to soundproof the apartments.

Le Corbusier. *Unite d'Habitation.* Marseille, France. 1947–52.

Many people looked to the human body as a source for perfect proportions. Artists during the Golden Age of Greece believed that the human body was the true expression of order. Statues created during that time were not realistic portraits of real people. The artists of the period showed the ideal form rather than the real form (see Figure 13.3, page 353).

In the first century B.C., Vitruvius, a Roman writer, determined typical ratios for human proportion. These were later used by Leonardo da Vinci and other Renaissance artists. The twentieth-century architect Le Corbusier applied human dimensions to architecture and city planning **(Figure 10.7).**

☑ Check Your Understanding

1. What is the Golden Mean?
2. Describe the Golden Rectangle.
3. What is the ratio of the Golden Mean?
4. How does the Golden Mean apply to the body?

Scale

Scale is much like proportion, but there is a difference. Proportion refers to the relationship of one part to another. **Scale,** on the other hand, refers to *size as measured against a standard reference,* such as the human body. A 7-foot basketball player may not look tall next to other basketball players. The player will look tall, however, when you see him in scale—that is, compared with a crowd of people of average height.

In art there are two kinds of scale to consider. One is the scale of the work itself. The other is the scale of objects or elements within the design.

The pyramids of Egypt are of such large scale that people are overwhelmed by their size. These pyramids were designed to be large to express the eternal strength of Egypt.

Wall paintings inside a pyramid depict important people in a larger scale than less important people. The tomb painting *Nakht and Wife* **(Figure 10.8)** depicts stories about the priest and his wife. They watch their busy servants hunting, fishing, and farming on the priest's land. In the painting, the figures of the priest and his wife are much larger than the servants. *When figures are arranged in a work of art so that scale indicates importance,* the artist is using **hierarchical proportion.** This arrangement disregards the actual size of figures and objects in order to indicate rank in a society. Use of scale to emphasize rank appears in the art of many cultures (Figure 5.36, page 124).

Actual works of art are usually much larger or much smaller than they appear to be when you look at photographs of them. You may have seen photos with a human hand or a human figure added for the purpose of showing the size of the objects in relation to human scale. Without some sort of measure, no illustration in any book can convey the effect of the scale of a work of art.

Some works that seem monumental are really quite small in size. This is why the dimensions are always listed in the credit line of the work. Try to visualize the size of a work in relation to your size. Imagine how it would look if it were in the room with you.

▲ **FIGURE 10.8** The servants in this painting are not all the same size. Two figures are as large as the priest and his wife, some are half their size, and some are even smaller. The painting uses hierarchical proportion. The more important figures are larger than the less important figures.

Nakht and Wife. Copy of a wall painting from the Tomb of Nakht. c. 1425 B.C. 2 × 1.53 m (6.5 × 5′). Egyptian Expedition of The Metropolitan Museum of Art, New York, New York. Rogers Fund, 1915 (15.5.19 e).

▶ **FIGURE 10.9** An ordinary clothespin takes on a whole new meaning when it is 45 feet tall and installed in a plaza in front of the Philadelphia City Hall.

Claes Oldenburg. *Clothespin*. 1976. Cor-Ten Steel. Height: 13.7 m (45'). Centre Square, Philadelphia, Pennsylvania.

Claes Oldenburg often uses scale to make you look at ordinary objects with a new perspective. He created a 45-foot tall pair of binoculars, a soft saxophone that is 69 inches tall, and a 45-foot tall clothespin **(Figure 10.9).** Can you imagine what it would feel like to stand in front of a clothespin that is over eight times taller than you?

Variations in scale within a work can change the work's total impact. For example, interior designers are concerned with the scale of the furniture that is to be placed in a room. The designer considers the scale of the space into which the furniture will be placed. The needs of the people who will use the space must also be considered. An oversized, overstuffed sofa would crowd a small room with a low ceiling. However, the same sofa would fit comfortably in a large hotel lobby with a four-story ceiling. The large scale of the lobby would make the size of the sofa look right.

Activity | Experimenting with Scale

Applying Your Skills. Create a small collage scene using magazine cutouts of people, furniture, and hand-held objects such as books, combs, pencils, hair dryers, and dishes. Arrange the cutouts on a small sheet of paper using realistic, accurate scale. All of the objects in the scene should be in scale with the people, and all of the people should be in correct proportion to each other. Use perspective techniques and arrange things in depth to create an accurate scale. Draw a background environment for the scene using water-base markers, colored pencils, or crayons.

Computer Option. Use digital hardware such as a camera, scanner, or video camera and accompanying software to capture a variety of photographs of people and objects. Use the Selection tool and Copy and Paste commands to assemble a computer collage that shows unrealistic scale. Apply the tools of your choice to manipulate the images. Images can be selected from many other sources such as laser disc, CD–ROM, or the Internet. If you do not have these capabilities, use the drawing and painting tools of your choice to create a surrealistic scene.

▲ **Figure 10.10** In the art of the Benin people, symbolic proportions were used. Notice how large the head of the Oba (in the center of the work) is in proportion to the rest of his body.

Warrior Chief, Warriors, and Attendants. Plaque. Nigeria, Edo. Court of Benin. Sixteenth to seventeenth centuries. Brass. Height: 48 cm (18⅞"). The Metropolitan Museum of Art, New York. Gift of Mr. and Mrs. Klaus G. Peris, 1990. (1990.332)

▲ **Figure 10.11** Wilt Chamberlain, an NBA star, was a seven-time consecutive winner of the NBA scoring title from 1960 to 1966. He retired in 1974. Willie Shoemaker, an American jockey, won 8,833 races in his career and is considered the best rider in thoroughbred racing history. Chamberlain is over seven feet tall, while Shoemaker is approximately five feet tall.

Annie Liebovitz. *Wilt Chamberlain and Willie Shoemaker.* Photograph.

Drawing Human Proportions

In Western art, realistic representation of people has been the dominant style from the Renaissance to this century. However, many artists around the world use symbolic proportions rather than representational accuracy. To the Benin people of West Africa, the head represented life and intelligence. The prosperity of the Benin people depended on the head of the Oba, the divine ruler. In **Figure 10.10** the head of the Oba is one third of the whole body. This demonstrates its symbolic importance.

Figures

People come in a variety of sizes and shapes. Categories for clothes sizes—husky, petite, tall—are just one indication of the many different shapes and sizes of people.

Although they vary in height and width, most people do not vary with regard to proportion. Many basketball players, such as Wilt Chamberlain, are tall. Jockeys, such as Willie Shoemaker, are usually small and light. In **Figure 10.11,** notice that Chamberlain's arms, legs, and torso have the same proportions as those of Shoemaker. Body proportions cannot be defined in inches or centimeters. They can only be defined in ratios of one part of the body to another.

The unit usually used to define the proportions of an individual figure is the length of the head from the chin to the top of the skull. The average adult is seven and one-half heads tall **(Figure 10.12);** a young child is five or six heads tall; and an infant is only three heads long. Many artists use adult proportions when drawing an infant, and the painting looks strange because the head is small in relation to the rest of the body. In Giotto's painting *Madonna and Child* **(Figure 10.13),** the child looks like a miniature adult because of proportion.

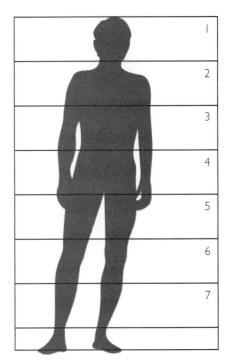

◀ **FIGURE 10.12** Average body proportions.

◀ **FIGURE 10.13** Giotto was the first artist to make a flat surface appear three-dimensional by using shading. He was the first to attempt realism. The child in this painting looks awkward, like a little adult. This is because Giotto used incorrect proportions to depict the child. However, when you compare this work to the *Madonna and Child on Curved Throne* (Figure 13.5, page 354), a work by an earlier artist, you realize how much more lifelike Giotto's work appears.

Giotto. *Madonna and Child.* 1320–30. Paint on wood. 85.5 × 62 cm (33⅝ × 24⅜″). National Gallery of Art, Washington, D.C. © 1998 Board of Trustees. Samuel H. Kress Collection.

◀ **FIGURE 10.14** Siqueiros used foreshortening in this painting to dramatically exaggerate his reach. It is as if the artist wants to grab everything he can. His hand becomes a burst of superhuman energy.

David Alfaro Siqueiros. *Self-Portrait (El Coronelazo).* 1945. Pyroxylin on Masonite. 91 × 121 cm (35⅝ × 47⅛"). Museo de Arte Moderno, Mexico City, Mexico. © Estate of David Alfaro Siqueiros/SOMAAP, Mexico/Licensed by VAGA, New York, NY

Heads and Faces

As you read this section, look in a mirror or at a classmate to check the examples discussed.

The front of the head is approximately oval. No one has a head that is perfectly oval—some people have narrow chins, and some have square jaws.

A face is approximately symmetrical. It has a central vertical axis when viewed from the front **(Figure 10.15).** If the face turns away from you, the axis curves over the surface of the head. You can divide the head into four sections along the central axis. This is done by drawing three horizontal lines that divide the axis into four equal parts, as shown in Figure 10.15.

The top fourth of the head is usually full of hair. The hair may start above the

Sometimes an artist may purposely distort proportion to make a drawing look more realistic. If a person is pointing at you, the arm from the fingertips to the shoulder will look shorter than it actually is. In a painting, an artist will use a technique to visually shorten the arm. **Foreshortening** is *to shorten an object to make it look as if it extends backward into space* **(Figure 10.14).**

Activity	Human Proportions

Applying Your Skills. Use the length of your head (from the top of your skull to the bottom of your chin) as a unit against which to measure the rest of your body. In this way you can calculate the relationship, or ratio, of all parts of your body to your head. You may need a friend to help you obtain accurate measurements. Determine the number of head lengths that each of the following represents: total height, chin to waist, waist to hip, knee to ankle, ankle to bottom of bare heel, underarm to elbow, elbow to wrist, wrist to tip of finger, and shoulder to tip of finger. Record the ratios and create a diagram or chart to show your findings. Compare your find-

ings with those of your classmates. Find averages for the class, because the ratios will not be exactly alike.

Computer Option. Use video digitizing software and a video camera or a scanner to capture a variety of photographs of people and objects. Clip art and videodiscs can also be used. If you do not have these capabilities, use the drawing tools of your choice to create your images. Use the Selection tool and the Copy and Paste options to assemble a computer collage using unrealistic scale. Use the tools of your choice, such as Resize, to manipulate the images. Create a surrealistic scene.

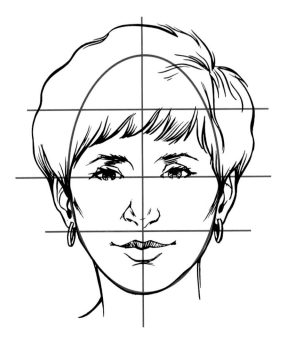

▲ **FIGURE 10.15** Facial proportions.

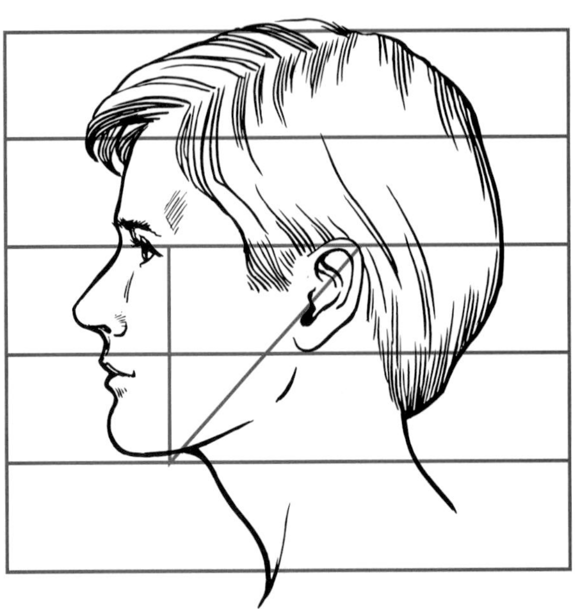

▲ **FIGURE 10.16** Profile proportions.

top horizontal line, or it may fall below it if the person wears bangs.

The eyes usually appear on the central horizontal line. They are at the center of a person's head. Notice the width of the space between the eyes. How does it relate to the width of one eye? The bottom of the nose rests on the lowest horizontal line, and the mouth is closer to the nose than to the chin. Use the sighting technique to determine other relationships, such as nose width, mouth width, and ear placement.

When you view a head in complete profile, or from the side, all of the vertical proportions remain the same as in the front view. However, both shape and contour change. Try to discover the new ratios **(Figure 10.16)**. Notice the relationship between the distance from the chin to the hairline and the distance from the front of the forehead to the back of the head. Can you find a ratio to help you locate the ear in profile? Study the contour of the front of the face. Which part protrudes the most? Notice the jawline from the chin to the ear and the relationship of the neck to the head. In **Figure 10.17,** the artist has drawn

▲ **FIGURE 10.17** The center face in this drawing is a young woman whom Gauguin painted on his first visit to Tahiti. These serene faces with blank eyes look like ancient stone heads sculpted in Egypt or Mexico. The Maori people were the inspiration for many of Gauguin's paintings.

Paul Gauguin. *Tahitians.* c. 1891–93. Charcoal on laid paper. 41 × 31 cm (16⅛ × 12¼"). The Metropolitan Museum of Art, New York, New York. The Annenberg Foundation Gift. 1996, #1996.418.

both the front and two profile views of a woman's head.

Notice that the facial proportions of infants are different, as shown in the print by Bonnard **(Figure 10.18).**

Activity | Drawing the Head

Applying Your Skills. Look through magazines for large photographs of heads. Look for adults, children, and babies. Remember that a head is not flat, and when it is turned, the central axis moves and curves around the shape of the head. You can always find the axis because it goes through the center of the nose, lips, and between the eyes. Draw the central axis and the three horizontal dividing lines on each face you have selected. What are the proportional differences among the faces of adults, children, and infants?

Computer Option. Gather some pictures of the faces of babies, young children, and adults. Notice that facial proportions change with age. Use the drawing tools of your choice to draw a human face using average facial proportions. Save your work. Use the Selection tool and the Copy and Paste options to duplicate the first face you drew. To experiment with the size of facial features, use the Selection tool to select the features of the face but not the outline of the head itself. Use the Resize option to create the correct feature size for a young child. Save your work. Reduce the size even more to create the correct feature size for an infant. The features need to be small and in the lower third of its face. Save your work. If possible, save all three faces on the same screen. Finally, compare the three faces you have created.

▲ **FIGURE 10.18** Even though Bonnard has flattened and simplified this work, the differences in the proportions between the profile of the father and the infant are easily measured. The skull of the infant is very large, and the baby's features seem to be squeezed down into the lower part of the head.

Pierre Bonnard. *Family Scene.* 1893. Color lithograph from "L'Estampe originale." 31 × 17.8 cm (12¼ × 7"). The Metropolitan Museum of Art, New York, New York. Rogers Fund, 1922. (22.82.1-3)

☑ Check Your Understanding

1. What is scale?
2. What are the two kinds of scale present in a work of art?
3. Describe hierarchical proportion.
4. How does the credit line help you understand the scale of an artwork?
5. Explain foreshortening.

How Artists Use Proportion and Distortion

Many artists use correct proportions in their work. They want every viewer to recognize the person, place, or thing being shown. These artists use correct proportion to create illusions of reality. This ability to show objects as though they were real seems magical to many viewers. Other artists choose exaggeration and distortion to create works with unusual expressive qualities.

Realistic Proportion

During the Renaissance in Italy there was a renewed interest in art and literature. Ancient Greek and Roman sculptures were discovered, and artists were inspired to create work with the realistic proportions of the ancient masters. To better understand the human body, the artists Leonardo da Vinci and Michelangelo Buonarroti dissected cadavers in secret because dissection was illegal at that time.

Michelangelo's statue of *David* is an outstanding example of Renaissance proportional accuracy. The artist was asked to create a bigger than life size figure of *David* (**Figure 10.19**) for the façade of the Cathedral in Florence. When it was finished, the people decided that it was too important to be placed high up on the cathedral. Instead, it was placed in the main square and became a symbol of the city of Florence.

Early American artists were hired to paint portraits to record accurate

▲ **Figure 10.19**   One unusual feature of Michelangelo's *David* is the fiery intensity of the young man's facial expression. He is staring at an enemy, the giant Goliath. What do you think David is thinking?

Michelangelo. *David (detail)*. 1501-1504. Marble. Galleria dell' Accademia, Florence, Italy.

▲ **FIGURE 10.20** In this painting, Copley not only tells us what Paul Revere looked like, but he also tells us the man's profession. Revere was a silversmith, and the artist shows Revere holding a finished piece of work. The tools on the table were those used by Revere to engrave designs on the surface of his finished forms.

John Singleton Copley. *Paul Revere.* c. 1768–70. Oil on canvas. 88.9 × 72.3 cm (35 × 28½"). Museum of Fine Arts, Boston, Massachusetts. Gift of Joseph W., William B., and Edward H. R. Revere.

▲ **FIGURE 10.21** This mixed media work is based on a photograph that Marisol found among waste papers near her studio. She uses realistic painting on the flat surfaces of rectangular solids and recycled doors, and combines it with carved wooden forms to create a realistic portrait of the unknown family. Notice the different accurate proportions in this work. Use a ruler and you will see that the head-to-body ratio is appropriate for each figure.

Marisol. *The Family.* 1962. Painted wood and other materials in three sections. 209.8 × 166.3 × 39.3 cm (82½ × 65½ × 15½"). Collection, The Museum of Modern Art, New York, New York. Advisory Committee Fund. © Marisol/Licensed by VAGA, New York, New York.

information about real people **(Figure 10.20).** A contemporary American artist, Marisol, painted in the Pop style in the 1960s. In **Figure 10.21,** she has used an unusual combination of materials, yet she still uses accurate proportions for all of the figures.

Exaggeration and Distortion

Some artists use exaggeration and distortion rather than realistic propor-tion to convey their ideas and feelings. **Exaggeration** and **distortion** are *deviations from expected, normal proportions.* They are powerful means of expression. Artists can lengthen, enlarge, bend, warp, twist, or deform parts or all of the human body. By making these changes, they can show moods and feelings that are easily understood by viewers. The exaggeration used by the artist in

◀ **FIGURE 10.22** The proud anxiety of the mother is expressed through the exaggerated stretch of her arms and body. She encourages her daughter to walk, yet she is ready to catch her if she falls.

Napachie Pootoogook. *My Daughter's First Steps.* 1990. Lithograph. 55.8 × 85.8 cm (22 × 33¾"). Permission courtesy of the West Baffin Eskimo Co-operative Limited.

Figure 10.22 lets us know how the woman feels.

In the past, movie stars of the silent screen had to exaggerate facial expressions and body language to convey meaning without words. If you have ever seen an old silent movie, you have probably laughed at the exaggerated eyelid movements used to express meaning.

It takes study and skill to use exaggeration and distortion effectively. Before an artist can distort a person or an object, he or she must study perception drawing and anatomy of the human figure. It takes knowledge to know what to exaggerate and how to distort images effectively.

In *Single Family Blues* **(Figure 10.23),** Twiggs has used exaggeration to express the feeling of "the blues" that engulf this family. Notice that the hand is twice the size of the child's blue head or the mother's navy blue face. This distortion allows the viewer to see how dominant "the blues" are in this family.

▲ **FIGURE 10.23** Twiggs uses exaggeration to emphasize the hand playing the blues for this family.

Leo Twiggs. *Single Family Blues.* 1996. Batik on cotton. 26.7 × 34.3 cm (10½ × 13½"). Courtesy of the artist.

Spanish 1881–1973

Pablo Picasso (**pah**-blow pee-**cah**-so) was born in Malaga, Spain in 1881. One day his father, a painter and teacher, came home to a surprise. His son had finished a portrait. After examining the work, Pablo's father gave the boy all his art materials. So great was Picasso's work that his father vowed never to paint again. Picasso was just eight years old.

He went to Paris in 1904. There he met other artists and writers. The creative climate encouraged him to develop a new style, which he called Cubism. Combining his appreciation of African art with his interest in geometrical forms, he created a unique and innovative form. His aim was to shock viewers into visual awareness. His intensity drove him to experiment with all media, discovering new forms and new ideas. He painted Cubist works as well as realistic representations of people. He also created prints and collages throughout his long and full life.

▶ **FIGURE 10.24** Picasso exaggerates the thinness of this old man, elongates his limbs, and places him in an impossibly angular position to create a painting that expresses sympathy for his condition. How does the contrast between the thin, angular man painted in blue and the warm brown, rounded guitar affect the meaning of this work?

Pablo Picasso. *The Old Guitarist.* 1903. Oil on panel. 122.9 × 82.6 cm (48¾ × 32½"). The Art Institute of Chicago, Chicago, Illinois. Helen Birch Bartlett Memorial Collection.

Picasso was also a master of distorting proportion to express an idea or feeling. The first years of the twentieth century were called Picasso's "Blue Period." During this time he painted poor and tragic people. Despite the sorrowful condition of the figures, there seems to be a sense of optimism in the works. In *The Old Guitarist* **(Figure 10.24),** the grotesquely thin old man seems unaware of his condition. His head is bent toward the instrument as if nothing matters but the beautiful sound of his music.

▲ **FIGURE 10.25** Chagall's painting shows a childlike belief in love's power to conquer all. He often created distorted fantasies full of bright colors that looked like joyful dreams.

Marc Chagall. *Birthday* {l'Anniversaire}. 1915. Oil on cardboard. 80.6 × 99.7 cm (31¼ × 39¼"). Collection, The Museum of Modern Art, New York, New York. Acquired through the Lillie P. Bliss bequest.

Chagall uses distortion to present a happy theme in his painting *Birthday* **(Figure 10.25).** The subjects of this work are the artist himself and Bella, his fiancée. The birthday is the artist's. Instead of simply showing himself leaning over to kiss Bella, Chagall used distortion. In the painting he appears to leap backward, stretch his neck like a swan, curve it around, and give Bella a kiss as he floats by. It is as if Chagall might have been thinking, "I'm so happy, I'm floating on air," when he created this work.

Artists can create feelings of great stability and calm by placing a small head on a large body. A monumental, or large and imposing, quality results. The monumental quality of Gaston Lachaise's

Walking Woman **(Figure 10.26)** is created through exaggerated proportions and spacing rather than through large scale.

Another use of exaggeration can be seen in the features of a mask. Masks have been used in all societies, from early primitive tribes to our modern computer age **(Figure 10.27).** A mask allows a person to hide his or her real self and become someone, or something, else.

Masks are used in many cultures as part of religious ceremonies and rituals. In many cases the features of the mask are exaggerated for expressive purposes. Each culture has specific traditions and procedures that are followed for making and using masks. Sometimes the mask appears to the person in a dream. Sometimes the mask is part of a cultural tradition. In most cases the mask is intended to aid efforts to communicate with the spirit world.

Cartoons are another way in which exaggeration can be used. Editorial cartoonists use this technique to make caricatures of famous people. The caricatures emphasize unusual facial features. Similarly, characters in comic strips are often made by using proportions that are larger than life. The most distorted comic-strip characters are often the funniest ones.

▲ **FIGURE 10.26** This sculpture is only 19¼ inches (48.8 cm) high and yet it has a monumental quality because Lachaise has made the head small in comparison to the body.

Gaston Lachaise. *Walking Woman.* 1922. Bronze. 48.8 × 26.9 × 18.9 cm (19¼ × 10⅙ × 7½"). Hirshhorn Museum and Sculpture Garden, Smithsonian Institution, Washington, D.C. Gift of Joseph H. Hirshhorn, 1966.

▶ **FIGURE 10.27** Imagine sitting in the dark around a fire when a mysterious figure jumps out of the dark into the dim flickering light wearing one of these masks. How would you feel? How does exaggeration and distortion affect the expressive qualities of these masks?

(bottom right) Mask. New Ireland. c. 1920. Wood, paint, fiber, seashells. Height: 38 cm (15″). Milwaukee Public Museum, Milwaukee, Wisconsin.

(right) George Walkus. Secret Society Mask. (Four Headed Cannibal Spirit) 1938. Wood; cedar bark, shredded; string. 53.34 × 129.54 cm (21 × 51″). Denver Art Museum, Denver, Colorado.

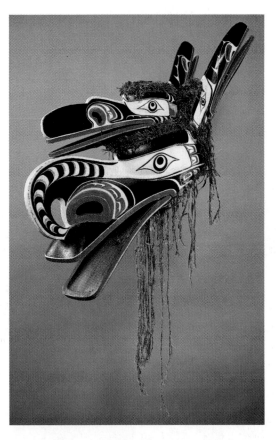

| Activity | **Distorting Proportions** |

Applying Your Skills. Cut two ovals about 9 inches long from any color of construction paper. Using parts cut from magazines, create one face using accurate proportions. On the second oval, create a distorted face.

Computer Option. Use the drawing tools of your choice to draw a human face using average facial proportions. Use the Select tool and the Copy and Paste options to make four or five copies of the head and face on the same screen. Use the Select tool to experiment with the whole head and with individual facial features. Resize, Distort, Rotate, and Bend are some options that may prove useful to you. If your software does not have these options, draw the changes with the drawing tools of your choice. Save your work. Compare the faces you have distorted and changed. How does the distortion affect the way you would use each face in a piece of artwork?

 Check Your Understanding

1. How do exaggeration and distortion affect proportion?
2. What distorting effects can an artist use?
3. Why do artists use distortion?
4. How can artists create monumental qualities without using a large scale?

Storyteller Figure

Annette Romero of the Cochiti Pueblo. *Storyteller Doll.* 1993. Clay and earth pigments. 20 × 10 × 17.7 cm (8 × 4 × 7″). Private collection.

SUPPLIES

- Sketchbook and pencil
- Clay
- Clay modeling tools
- Slip and brush
- Plastic bag
- Tray or board
- Acrylic paints and assorted brushes
- Fine-line black markers

When Helen Cordero of the Cochiti Pueblo shaped the first Storyteller doll in 1964, she brought the Singing Mother, one of the oldest forms of Native American self-portraiture, into the twentieth century. In doing so, she reinvented a dying Cochiti tradition of figurative pottery **(Figure 10.28)**.

The first time Helen exhibited her work, a folk art collector named Girard bought all of her little people. He asked her to make an even larger seated figure with children, and Helen thought about her grandfather, who had been a very good storyteller.

It is impossible to determine how many Storytellers Helen Cordero has shaped since 1964. It is also impossible to measure the influence of her invention, which began a revival of figurative pottery in both her own and other New Mexico pueblos. All sorts of variations have appeared.

What You Will Learn

You will create a clay Storyteller sculpture involving one adult interacting with many children, using proper clay construction techniques. After firing, add color.

Creating

Brainstorm with your classmates to think up variations for the Storyteller project. You may depict a male or female person or an animal as the adult. The children must match the adult; for example, if you choose a bear as the adult, the children must be bear cubs. Use exaggerated scale to illustrate how an adult can enthrall children with storytelling.

Step 1 When you have selected the subject of your sculpture, make several sketches of the adult. Draw different views of your adult. Then make some rough sketches to help you think through how you will arrange the children on the adult.

Step 2 Review clay construction procedures by reading Technique Tips 15–18 on pages 433 and 434 in the Handbook. Decide which process you will use to build the adult figure. Remember that it needs to be hollow, and it needs an opening to allow air to get inside. The Storyteller's mouth would be appropriate for the opening. Decide which process you will use to create the smaller figures. Make notes about your construction plans in your sketchbook.

Step 3 Collect your construction materials. Build the adult first, adding all three-dimensional details. Keep the adult stored tightly in the plastic bag while you construct the children. When you have attached all the children using scoring and slip, cover the sculpture loosely and let it dry. Check it every day to be sure that the little people are not drying too fast. They might shrink faster than the adult and crack off. When the sculpture is bone dry, fire it in the kiln.

Step 4 After firing, paint the sculpture with acrylic paints. Use small brushes or fine-line markers to add linear details. You do not have to cover all of the clay. Use the color of the clay as one of the predominant colors in your sculpture.

Step 5 Write the story that your Storyteller is narrating. Record it on tape. Arrange the Storyteller sculpture in a display. Use a tape player to tell the story to your viewers.

EVALUATING YOUR WORK

▶ **DESCRIBE** Explain the subject of your Storyteller sculpture. How many children did you make? Which clay construction processes did you use?

▶ **ANALYZE** How much did you exaggerate scale in your sculpture? Did you use accurate or distorted proportions? How did you incorporate the color of the fired clay into the color scheme?

▶ **INTERPRET** What is the theme of your story? Does it match the mood of the sculpture?

▶ **JUDGE** Which aesthetic theories would you use to judge this work? If you were to do it one more time, what, if anything, would you change?

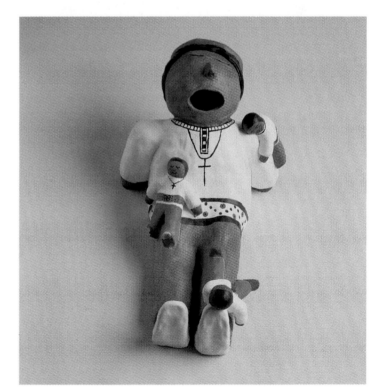

▲ **FIGURE 10.28A** Student work.

Papier Mâché Mask

▲ **FIGURE 10.29**

Henry Hunt, Southern Kwakiutl. *K'umugwe' (Komokwa) Mask.* 1970. Wood, copper, paint. 31.6 × 28.7 × 20.7 cm (12²⁄₅ × 11¹⁄₃ × 8″). Royal British Columbia Museum, Victoria, British Columbia, Canada. #13215.

SUPPLIES

- Sketchbook and pencil
- Newspaper and paper towels
- Nontoxic papier-mâché paste
- Acrylic paints and a variety of brushes
- Scissors and white glue
- Found material for decorations such as yarn and foil

The mask shown in **Figure 10.29** represents the chief of the undersea world, K'umugwe' (Komokwa). The copper teeth, eyes, and eyebrows on this mask are indications of great wealth. This creature, whose dance is part of the Red Cedar Bark dance series, is a monster who causes trouble in the waters. He can stop rivers, create great waves on bodies of water, and swallow or overturn canoes. This mask was designed to be viewed on the head of a costumed figure dancing around a flickering firelight. The movements used in the dance of the K'umugwe' imitate those of a sea mammal in water, including surfacing to breathe. Notice how the wood has been carved into high relief. This is done so that the viewer will see changing shadows alternating with bright light.

Just as the K'umugwe' was used to explain things that happened in the water, you will create a myth that explains something about modern technology. Each member of the team will be an actor in the drama. Each will design and create a high-relief papier-mâché mask using distortion and exaggeration to make the mask expressive. Choose a color scheme that matches the character of the mask. Paint and decorate the mask.

What You Will Learn

Brainstorm with your classmates to list mysteries of modern technology. Make a list of possible themes that could be explained in a storytelling dance drama.

Divide into work teams for a planning conference. Have one group member keep notes from the conference.

Select a specific theme or topic. Choose music. Name and define the character of each participant. Write the story. Decide how you will communicate with the audience. Will you all speak lines, will a narrator tell the story, or will you act it out in pantomime? List the props and setting you will need. Plan body movements to match the music.

Creating

Draw several ideas for your mask. Plan the side view as well as the front view. Use exaggeration and distortion to create the mood you wish your character to express.

Meet with the team to make final decisions about the masks. At this time decide on colors and the extra materials you will need for decorations. Decide if you need costumes.

Step 1 Draw the final plan for your mask in your sketchbook. List the colors and special decorations you plan to add. Collect the extra materials such as yarn, costume jewelry, and fabrics.

Step 2 Construct your mask. See the different directions for papier-mâché construction in Technique Tip 19 on page 434 in the Handbook. Use high relief. Make some ridges rise 2 inches from the surface of the mask. Plan how you will hold the mask on your head. You must be able to see through it when you are wearing it. The holes for your eyes do not have to be the eyes of the mask.

Step 3 When the papier-mâché is dry, paint your mask with acrylic paints. Glue on the additional decorations.

Step 4 Rehearse with your group using all the props you will need for the performance, including special lighting. Perform your dance drama for the class.

EVALUATING YOUR WORK

▶ **DESCRIBE** Explain the theme and story of your dance drama. Describe the music you used and explain why you chose it. List and explain all the characters in your drama. Describe your mask.

▶ **ANALYZE** Did you use high relief? Explain the shadows and highlights that resulted. Explain your color scheme. Which parts of the mask did you exaggerate and distort? Did the body movements you used match the character of the mask and the music?

▶ **INTERPRET** What was the message of your production? Did the audience understand the message?

▶ **JUDGE** Which aesthetic theories would you use to judge the entire production? Are they different from the theories you would use to judge the mask? Why?

▲ **FIGURE 10.29A** Student work.

Soft Sculpture

Faith Ringgold. *Mrs. Jones and Family*. 1973. Mixed media. Mrs. Jones: 152 × 30 × 41 cm (60 × 12 × 16″). Andrew: 122 × 30 × 30 cm (48 × 12 × 12″). Barbara: 58 × 16 × 28 cm (23 × 6½ × 11″). Faye: 63 × 14 × 30 cm (25 × 5½ × 12″). © 1973 Faith Ringgold

SUPPLIES

- Sketchbook and pencil
- Paper for patterns
- Scissors and pins
- Sewing and embroidery threads
- Variety of sewing needles
- Assorted fabrics
- Stuffing material such as fiberfill
- Yarns and other trims
- Sewing machine (optional)

F aith Ringgold, an African-American artist, is a painter and soft sculptor as well as a performance artist. *Mrs. Jones and Family* (**Figure 10.30**) represents Ringgold's family. Mrs. Jones is her mother, and Andrew is her father.

Ringgold started as a traditional painter. Her education, like that of any other art student in the 1950s, was in the European tradition. In the late 1960s, during a period when she was incorporating African designs and motifs into her painted canvases, Ringgold began to experiment first with masks and later with soft sculpture. These projects enabled her to work in the center of her family. The interaction of the people in her family nourished her spirit. Notice in the sculpture *Mrs. Jones and Family* that all the dolls have their mouths open. They are all talking at once!

Look closely at the figures in Ringgold's work to see how she used media, distortion, and exaggeration to create her sculpture. Think about the techniques you can use to create yours.

What You Will Learn

Design and construct a soft sculpture symbolizing a person from history, art history, literature, or current events. Ringgold made the faces large according to African traditions. She made all the mouths open to indicate that her family is very talkative. Use distortion and exaggeration to emphasize the most important attributes of the person you have chosen. Select colors and fabrics to fit the personality of your sculpture, and add details using stitchery and/or appliqué.

Creating

Brainstorm with classmates about subjects to consider for your soft sculpture. Select the person you will symbolize. Do some research about this person. Make visual and written notes in your sketchbook. What is your person famous for? What kind of clothing is appropriate? Which features will you exaggerate? For example, if you are doing a track star, you may make the feet oversized; if you are representing a rock star, you may wish to exaggerate the mouth.

Step 1 Draw a plan for constructing your sculpture in your sketchbook. Draw your sculpture from the front, back, and sides. On a sheet of paper, make a pattern for cutting the body fabric. Cut out fabric and pin the pieces, right sides together. Sew the body together on the inside, leaving a small opening. Then turn it inside out and stuff it. You may shape a three-dimensional face, or you may use stitches and appliqué as Ringgold did. Use yarn or other material to make hair. Make clothes to fit your sculpture, or use doll clothes. Add details with stitchery. See Technique Tip 22 on page 436 of the Handbook.

Step 2 Arrange your soft sculpture for display. You may add props and a setting if desired. Write a few paragraphs about your sculpture and include it in your display.

EVALUATING YOUR WORK

▶ **DESCRIBE** Name the subject of your soft sculpture and explain why you selected that person. Describe the procedures you followed to construct this sculpture. List the attributes of your subject that you chose to emphasize and explain why.

▶ **ANALYZE** Explain how, where, and why you used distortion and exaggeration. Which colors did you select for your sculpture?

▶ **INTERPRET** What kind of a mood does your sculpture express? Give it a title that symbolizes the character of your subject. Do not use the subject's name.

▶ **JUDGE** Which aesthetic theories would you use to judge this work? If you were to do it over, what would you change?

▲ **FIGURE 10.30A** Student work.

Hybrid Creature

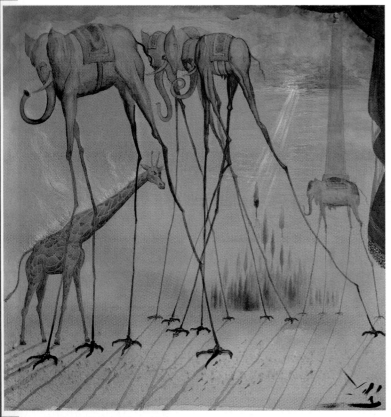

▲ FIGURE 10.31

Salvador Dali. *The Elephants (Design for the Opera La Dama Spagnola e il Cavaliere Romano).* 1961. Pencil, watercolor, gouache. 69.9 × 69.9 cm (27½ × 27½″). Indianapolis Museum of Art, Indianapolis, Indiana. Gift of Mr. and Mrs. Lorenzo Alvary, photograph ©1987 Indianapolis Museum of Art.

SUPPLIES

- **Sketchbook**
- **Computer**
- **Paint or Draw application**
- **Printer**
- *Optional*
- **Scanner or digital camera**

Salvador Dali was a Spanish Surrealist painter and printmaker. Surrealist artists and writers emphasized the role of the subconscious or dreamlike state in their art. Dali's works depict dreamlike images that are painted in a very precise, realistic manner. Commonplace objects, people, and animals are distorted and often changed into bizarre and irrational creations. He placed unrelated objects together in strange, barren landscapes.

In *The Elephants* **(Figure 10.31),** Dali has rendered the bodies of the elephants in a realistic manner and then placed them on thin, birdlike legs with bird claws for feet. You will see that the giraffe is not distorted but some of the trees in the distance seem to be levitating. Also, notice the red curtain in the right corner. It does not seem to belong in this landscape.

What You Will Learn

You will create an imaginary creature using distortion, exaggeration, and illogical combinations of body parts from several animals. After completing the new creature, you will place it in an equally illogical setting using colors that contrast with the creature. Print your final work.

Creating

Begin with a favorite animal. Make several sketches of possible combinations that exchange features such as the head, neck, legs, wings, tail, ears, texture, or animal skin with other animals. Remember that your creature can be based on scientific fact, fiction, or fantasy. Like Dali's *The Elephants,* sometimes pairing the most dissimilar features helps to exaggerate and emphasize an idea or tone. However, different moods from magical to ferocious can be achieved by using unique combinations. Choose the idea and mood you find most appealing.

Step 1 Use your choice of art applications and tools to draw your imaginary creature. If you use photographs or scanned images, make significant changes to include your own drawing and alterations. Choose from the Selection tools to move, delete, or add features. Use the Copy and Paste commands to arrange duplicate parts. While a body part is selected, explore how you might stretch, shrink, or distort proportions. Be adventurous.

Step 2 Use tools, such as Zoom In, or menus to smooth lines, match colors, and clean up leftover pixels. Retitle and save frequently as you work. This records the history of your production so you can return to an earlier point and try another solution.

Step 3 Consider adding duplicates of the creature on the page. While the image is selected, you can arrange it. Try overlapping or choose options to Flip, Rotate, and change sizes or Scale. Consider colors or surface textures to enhance the new creature. These may include scanned textures, menu choices, or invented textures. Apply with a Brush, Bucket, or Selection tool.

Step 4 Select from the tools to add an illogical background with contrasting colors. When you are satisfied, print, view, and make any changes. Display your final copy. Include the source of any photographs or scanned images.

EVALUATING YOUR WORK

▶ **DESCRIBE** What parts have you used to create your imaginary creature? Identify the features you have distorted and exaggerated. Describe the things you have added to create an illogical background. List, in order, the specific software, tools, and menus you used. Name any sources you have used.

▶ **ANALYZE** Explain how you used distortion and exaggeration to create your creature. Describe the colors and textures you used for the creature and the background.

▶ **INTERPRET** Describe the mood, theme, or idea you have created. Explain how combining various body parts, changing proportion, and applying color and texture affect the mood of your work. Give your work a descriptive title that sums up your feelings about it.

▶ **JUDGE** Have you successfully combined, distorted, and exaggerated the features of your animal to emphasize an idea or mood? Is there anything you would change? What aesthetic theory would you use to judge this artwork?

▲ **FIGURE 10.31A** Student work.

ART CRITICISM IN ACTION

▲ **FIGURE 10.32**

Isabel Bishop. *Waiting.* 1938. Oil and tempera on gesso panel. 73.6 × 56.5 cm (29 × 22¼″). Collection of the Newark Museum, Newark, New Jersey. Purchase, 1944. Arthur F. Egner Memorial Fund.

DESCRIBE What do you see?

List all of the information found in the credit line. Next, make a list of all of the objects in the work. Remember not to make guesses.

- Describe the people and their clothing.
- Describe the setting.

ANALYZE How is this work organized?

During this step, you will discover clues that will help you find the message the artist is trying to send.

- What unusual rhythms has the artist created using line?
- Are the proportions of the figures accurate? Are the proportions of the woman the same as those of the child?
- Is there anything in the work to indicate scale?

INTERPRET What is the artist trying to communicate?

During this step, you will express your ideas about the work and decipher the message the artist is sending.

- What is the relationship between these two people? What do you think are they waiting for?
- How has the artist's style affected the mood of the work?
- Create a new title that sums up your interpretation of the work.

JUDGE What do you think of the work?

Now it is time to make a decision about the quality of this work. You may make a personal opinion, but it is also important to make an objective judgment based on aesthetic theories.

- Do you think this is a successful work of art? Use one or more of the aesthetic theories explained in Chapter 2 to defend your decision.

MEET THE ARTIST

ISABEL BISHOP

American, 1902–1988

Isabel Bishop. *Self-Portrait*. 1927. Oil on canvas. 36 × 33 cm (14⅛ × 13"). Wichita Art Museum, Wichita, Kansas. Gift of the Friends of the Wichita Art Museum, Inc.

In 1920, with financial support from an inheritance, Isabel Bishop enrolled at the Art Students' League in New York City. She made the daily trip to Grand Central Station by train and then transferred to the subway, which took her to the studio. During the trips she sketched.

The subjects of her paintings were the working women she saw on the trains and from her studio window. She tried to express the possibility of momentary change. To her, the young women did not belong to a specific class.

Proportion and Scale

▲ **FIGURE 10.33**

Colossal Head, Constantine the Great. Fourth century. Marble. Head about 8¼' (2.5 m) high; original seated figure 30' (9.2 m) high. Palace of the Conservatory, Rome, Italy.

Suppose you wanted to reconstruct the colossal monument of *Constantine the Great.* How would you determine how to accurately re-create his larger-than-life proportions? In art, proportion has to do with the relationship of the size of one part to another. In mathematics, this relationship (proportion) is described in ratios. For example, 4:2 = 6:3 because 4 is twice the amount of 2, just as 6 is twice the amount of 3. This is determined by dividing 4 by 2 and 6 by 3.

Scale refers to size as measured against a standard reference. You have probably seen a scale used on a map. If 1 inch on the scale equals 10 miles, and the distance between two cities is 3 inches, you can multiply to determine that the actual distance is 30 miles. Artists can use scale to create figures with proportions that are larger or smaller than real-life people. If we know the standard height of the average human is 5 feet 6 inches, then we can either multiply the measurements for a larger-than-life artwork or divide them for a smaller depiction.

Making the Connection

1. Using the scale provided in Figure 10.12 on page 263, calculate the total height of the original statue of *Constantine the Great* if Constantine had been standing.
2. Using the calculated height and Euclid's Golden Mean proportions shown in Figure 10.5 on page 257, compute the length of the top of the body (head to navel) and the length of the lower body (navel to feet).
3. What other mathematical processes do you think the original creator(s) of *Constantine the Great* used in building this monument?

Building Vocabulary

On a separate sheet of paper, write the term or terms that best matches each definition given below.

1. The principle of art concerned with the size relationship of one part to another.

2. A line divided into two parts so that the smaller line has the same proportion, or ratio, to the larger line as the larger line has to the whole line.

3. Size as measured against a standard reference.

4. Figures arranged in a work of art so that scale indicates importance.

5. To shorten an object to make it look as if it extends backward into space.

6. Deviations from expected, normal proportions.

Reviewing Art Facts

Answer the following questions using complete sentences.

1. What is the Golden Mean ratio?

2. Explain the difference between scale and proportion.

3. What was the name for the geometric form that had sides matching the ratio of the Golden Mean?

4. What are the two kinds of scale in art?

5. What unit is usually used to define the proportions of any individual figure?

Thinking Critically About Art

1. **Extend.** Do some library research to determine how hierarchical proportions have been used in the art of different cultures. Photocopy examples to show and report your findings to the class.

2. **Compare and contrast.** Siqueiros's painting, *Self-Portrait* (Figure 10.14, page 264) uses a distortion called foreshortening to create a symbolic proportion. The Oba figure (Figure 10.10, page 262) also uses symbolic proportion. Compare the two works. List the similarities and differences. Explain what the distortion conveys in each artwork.

3. **Analyze.** Study the illustration of the Golden Rectangle in Figure 10.3, page 256. Look through this book to find works of art that have been organized using those proportions. Choose at least one to diagram.

Use the Performing Arts Handbook on page 422 to discover how Eugene Friesen explores the elements of exaggeration and distortion of human proportions through the use of masks in his performance of **Cello Man**.

Discover how artists use the elements of art to create different kinds of proportion in their works by visiting the Glencoe Fine Arts Site at **www.glencoe.com/sec/art**. You can also explore the Glencoe *Student Galleria* to see how other students have used proportion and distortion in their two- and three-dimensional art.

▲ **FIGURE 11.1** This building was designed to look like a ship with its sails full in the wind. It sits on Bennelong Point which is named after the first Aborigine born on the site who learned to speak English.

Joern Utzon. Sydney Opera House, Australia. 1959–72. Reinforced concrete. Height of highest shell: 5.1 m (200").

CHAPTER 11

Variety, Emphasis, Harmony, and Unity

The principles of art help artists organize artworks. They use these principles to express their feelings and ideas. You have already learned about the principles of rhythm, balance, and proportion. In this chapter you will learn about three additional principles: *variety, emphasis,* and *harmony.* Finally, you will learn about the most important principle, *unity.* Unity occurs when all the elements and principles of art work together. A unified work is the goal of every artist.

The Sydney Opera House **(Figure 11.1)** is unified with its setting. It looks like it belongs in the harbor because the shells that make up its walls and roof look like the sails of a clipper ship, which you would expect to see in a harbor. Although it is called an "Opera House," the term does not describe the full purpose of the building. It is really a performance arts complex that houses 1,000 rooms including a concert hall, an opera theater, a drama theater, and a playhouse. It also includes a reception hall and four restaurants.

Developing Your PORTFOLIO

Artists usually want their artworks to appear as if everything is in the right place. Sometimes they will deliberately place something unusual or unexpected in an artwork in order to make a statement. Look through magazines and find several pictures or advertisements that show an object that seems to be out of place. Write a sentence or two explaining whether you think this was done on purpose to make a statement, and if so, what the purpose might be. Include the magazine pictures and your explanation in your portfolio.

OBJECTIVES

After completing this chapter, you will be able to:

■ Identify and describe variety, emphasis, harmony, and unity in your environment and in a work of art.

■ Understand how artists use variety and emphasis to express their ideas and feelings.

■ Understand how artists use the elements and principles of art to create unified works of art.

■ Use variety, emphasis, and harmony to create your own unified works of art.

WORDS TO KNOW

variety
emphasis
focal point
harmony
unity

Variety, Emphasis, and Harmony

Variety is a principle of art that adds interest to an artwork. Emphasis is a principle of art that enhances variety because it creates areas that draw your attention. The eye-catching, or dominant, area is usually a focal point that first attracts the attention of the viewer. The viewer then looks at the less dominant, or subordinate, areas. Harmony makes variety and emphasis work together in a piece of art. Variety and harmony complement one another in the same way that positive and negative spaces complement each other. Variety adds interest to an artwork while harmony prevents variety from causing chaos.

Variety

People need variety in all areas of their lives. Imagine how boring it would be if daily routines were exactly the same every day of the week for a whole year. Imagine how visually boring the world would be if everything in it—everything—were the same color.

People put a great deal of time and effort into creating variety in their environment. They may buy new furniture or paint the walls, not because the furniture is old or the paint is peeling, but simply because they need a change. They add variety to other aspects of their lives as well. New clothes, new foods, new friends—people make endless changes to relieve the sameness or boredom in life.

Just as people must add variety to their lives to keep it interesting, so must artists add variety to their works. **Variety** is *the principle of art concerned with difference or contrast.*

◀ **FIGURE 11.2** The artist has used only one shape (an equilateral triangle) and two colors to create this print. How has he used variety to change two elements of art into an interesting design that has the illusion of three dimensions?

Miroslav Sutej. *Ultra AB.* 1966. Color silkscreen. 49.2 × 45 cm (19⅓ × 17¾"). Library of Congress, Washington, D.C. Pennell Fund, 1970.

A work that is too much the same can become dull and monotonous. For example, a work composed of just one shape may be unified, but it will not hold your attention. Variety, or contrast, is achieved by adding something different to a design to provide a break in the repetition **(Figure 11.2)**. When different art elements are placed next to each other in a work of art, they are in contrast **(Figure 11.3)**. This type of contrast, or variety, adds interest to the work of art and gives it a lively quality.

Almost every artist uses contrasting elements to balance unifying elements. Wide, bold lines complement thin, delicate lines. Straight lines contrast with curves. Free-form shapes differ from geometric shapes. Rough textures add interest to a smooth surface. Colors can contrast in limitless ways. The degree of contrast may range from bold to subtle. The amount of difference between the elements depends on the artist's purpose.

▲ **FIGURE 11.3** Which elements of art has Pereira used to create variety in this painting? Which element do you think shows the strongest contrast?

Irene Rice Pereira. *Untitled*. 1951. Oil on board. 101.6 × 61 cm (40 × 24"). The Solomon R. Guggenheim Museum, New York, New York. Gift, Jerome B. Lurie, 1981.

Emphasis

Have you ever underlined an important word or phrase several times in a letter? Have you ever raised the volume of your voice to make sure the person you were talking to understood a key point? These are just two ways that people use emphasis to focus attention on the main points in a message.

LESSON 1 *Variety, Emphasis, and Harmony*   **289**

▶ **FIGURE 11.4** Many different values of red are present in this work. In this way, the artist has created variety and added interest to a painting that might otherwise be boring. Locate areas of the painting that use different values of red.

Robert Rauschenberg. *Red Painting.* 1953. Oil, cloth, and newsprint on canvas with wood. 200.6 × 84.1 cm (79 × 33⅛"). The Solomon R. Guggenheim Museum, New York, New York. Gift, Walter K. Gutman, 1963. © Robert Rauschenberg/Licensed by VAGA, New York, NY

▼ **FIGURE 11.5** The artist has used value contrast to create a focal point in this work. Only the head and the area immediately around it are painted in light values. The background sinks into darkness.

Rembrandt van Rijn (workshop of). *Portrait of Rembrandt.* 1650. Oil on canvas. 92 × 75.5 cm (36¼ × 29¾"). National Gallery of Art, Washington, D.C. © 1998 Board of Trustees. Widener Collection.

In advertisements, music, news stories, your lessons at school, and your day-to-day communications, you see and hear certain ideas and feelings being emphasized over others.

Emphasis is *the principle of art that makes one part of a work dominant over the other parts.* Artists use emphasis to unify a work of art. Emphasis controls the sequence in which the parts are noticed. It also controls the amount of attention a viewer gives to each part.

There are two major types of visual emphasis. In one type, an *element of art* dominates the entire work. In the other type of emphasis, an *area* of the work is dominant over all the other areas.

Emphasizing an Element

If the artist chooses to emphasize one element, all the other elements of the work are made *subordinate,* or less important. The *dominant,* or most important, element affects the viewer's perception of the total work. This element also affects the way in which all the separate items and elements in the work are perceived.

Sometimes the dominant element is so strong that the whole work seems to be drenched in that element. Rauschenberg's *Red Painting* (**Figure 11.4**) is saturated with the color red. Even though he has used a variety of textures to create different areas, the redness takes on a meaning all its own. It affects the viewer's perception of the painting as a whole. It also affects the viewer's perception of the separate parts of the work.

Emphasizing an Area

Sometimes a specific area in a work of art is emphasized. This area, called the **focal point,** is *the first part of a work to attract the attention of the viewer.* The other areas are subordinate to the focal point. Rembrandt used value like a spotlight to emphasize one important area—a focal point—in his paintings (**Figure 11.5**).

It is possible for a work of art to have

◀ **FIGURE 11.6** In this painting the artist used three different greens, three values of brown, and white to make a net of colors. She used thick and thin brushstrokes as well as curves, lines, and dots squeezed straight from the tube. No one color or line advances toward the viewer. All are equal in importance.

Lee Krasner. *The Springs.* 1964. Oil on canvas. 109.2 × 167.6 cm (43 × 66″). The National Museum of Women in the Arts, Washington, D.C. Gift of Wallace and Wilhelmina Holladay.

more than one focal point. Artists must be careful about this, however. Too many focal points cause the eye to jump around and will confuse the viewer. Artists must also determine the degree of emphasis needed to create a focal point. This usually depends on the purpose of the work.

Of course, a focal point is not necessary. Many artists don't create a focal point in their works **(Figure 11.6).** When artists do create focal points, they are usually careful not to over-emphasize it. They make certain that the focal point is unified with the rest of the design.

Artists use several techniques to create a focal point in a work of art. Following are some examples of these techniques.

Contrast. One way to create a focal point is to place an element that contrasts with the rest of the work in that area. One large shape, for example, will stand out among small ones. One angular, geometric shape will be noticed first among rounded, free-form shapes. A bright color will dominate low-intensity colors, while a light area will dominate a dark design **(Figure 11.7).** An object with a smooth texture becomes a focal point in a design filled with rough textures.

◀ **FIGURE 11.7** Rubens has created contrast between the light, smooth skin of Daniel against the dark rocks and the rough fur of the lions. Daniel sits in a closed position while the lions growl and stretch in active poses.

Peter Paul Rubens. *Daniel in the Lions' Den.* c. 1615. Oil on linen. 224.3 × 330.4 cm (88¼ × 130⅛″). National Gallery of Art, Washington, D.C. © 1998 Board of Trustees. Ailsa Mellon Bruce Fund.

Isolation. Artists sometimes use isolation to create a focal point and thereby emphasize one part of their work. They do this by putting one object alone, apart from all the other objects **(Figure 11.8).** This draws the viewer's eye to the isolated object.

Location. Location is another method used to create a focal point for emphasis. A viewer's eye is normally drawn toward the center of a visual area. Thus, something near this center will probably be noticed first. Because the exact center is a predictable location, most artists place the objects they wish to emphasize a bit off center. They select a location a little to the left or right of center and a little above center **(Figure 11.9).**

▲ **FIGURE 11.8** Neel has isolated the red chair to make it the focal point in this painting. How do the elements of color and line create the feeling of isolation?

Alice Neel. *Loneliness.* 1970. Oil on canvas. 203.2 × 96.5 cm (80 × 38″). National Gallery of Art, Washington, D.C. © 1998 Board of Trustees. Gift of Walter M. Bullowa, in honor of the 50th Anniversary of the National Gallery of Art.

▶ **FIGURE 11.9** The young woman appears to be in the center of this painting. If you measure, however, you will see that her head is to the left of the vertical axis and far above the horizontal axis. What devices has Morisot used to make the woman's face the center of interest?

Berthe Morisot. *In the Dining Room.* 1886. Oil on canvas. 61.3 × 50 cm (24⅛ × 19¾″). National Gallery of Art, Washington, D.C. © 1998 Board of Trustees. Chester Dale Collection.

Convergence. When many elements in a work seem to point to one item, that item becomes the focal point. This technique, called convergence, can be created with a very obvious radial arrangement of lines. It can also be achieved through a more subtle arrangement of elements **(Figure 11.10)**.

LOOKING CLOSELY — Creating a Focal Point

Many lines lead your eyes toward the brightly lit, yellow area of the café. Notice the ruts in the cobblestones, the edge of the awning, and the top of the blue door frame all point to the yellow area. How many more objects can you find that point to that area?

◀ **FIGURE 11.10**

Vincent van Gogh. *Café Terrace at Night.* 1888. Oil on canvas. 81 × 65.5 cm (31⅞ × 25¼"). Rijksmuseum Kroller-Muller, Otterlo, the Netherlands.

▲ **FIGURE 11.11** In this painting the artist has chosen a point of view that is at the eye level of the child. We see only the skirt and the hand of Ernesta's nurse. Why is this unusual?

Cecilia Beaux. *Ernesta (Child with Nurse).* 1894. Oil on canvas. 128.3 × 96.8 cm (50½ × 38⅛″). The Metropolitan Museum of Art, New York, New York. Maria DeWitt Jesup Fund, 1965. (65.49)

The Unusual. In a work of art, an object that is out of the ordinary can become the focal point **(Figure 11.11).** In a row of soldiers standing at attention, the one standing on his head will be noticed first. The unexpected will always draw the viewer's attention.

Activity	Using Emphasis

Applying Your Skills. Make a series of small designs with strong focal points, using each of the following: contrast of shape, contrast of color, contrast of value, contrast of texture, isolation, location, convergence, and the unusual.

Computer Option. Use the drawing tools of your choice to create a series of small designs with strong focal points, using each of the following: contrast of shape, contrast of color, contrast of value, contrast of texture, isolation, location, convergence, and the unusual.

One advantage in using computers to create art is the ease with which images can be manipulated. You will be able to transform some designs to others by using the Fill Bucket tool. Others can be changed by using the Selection tool and rearranging the shapes. See if you can create all seven designs by starting with only three designs and making alterations to them. Save your work.

Harmony

Harmony is *the principle of art that creates unity by stressing the similarities of separate but related parts.* In musical harmony, related tones are combined into blended sounds. Harmony is pleasing because the tones complement each other. In visual harmony, related art elements are combined. The result looks pleasing because the elements complement each other.

Used in certain ways, color can produce harmony in a work of art. Repeti-

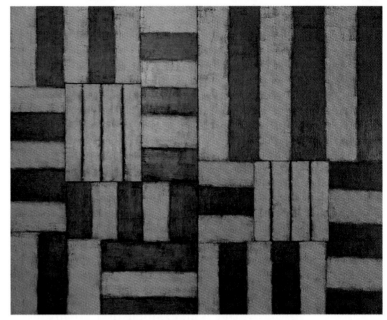

▲ **Figure 11.12** Scully has used related shapes and colors to create harmony in this work. What has he done to introduce variety?

Sean Scully. *White Robe.* 1990. Oil on linen. 243.8 × 304.8 cm (96 × 120″). High Museum of Art, Atlanta, Georgia. Purchase in honor of Richard A. Denny, Jr., President of the Board of Directors, 1991–94, with funds from Alfred Austell Thornton Sr. in memory of Leila Austell Thornton and Albert Edward Thornton Sr. and Sarah Miller Venable and William Hoyt Venable, 1992.5 a-b.

tion of shapes that are related, such as rectangles with different proportions, produces harmony **(Figure 11.12).** A design that uses only geometric shapes appears more harmonious than a design using both geometric and free-form shapes. Even space used in a certain way can produce harmony. If all the parts in a work of art are different sizes, shapes, colors, and textures, the space between the parts can be made uniform to give the work a sense of order.

✓ Check Your Understanding

1. Describe the principle of *variety.*
2. What is a focal point?
3. Name the five ways *emphasis* can be created.
4. What is *harmony?*

Unity

Unity is oneness. It brings order to the world. Without it, the world would be chaotic.

Countries made up of smaller parts are political unities: the United States is such a country. Its 50 states are joined by a single federal government. As a unit, the United States is a world power far stronger than the combined power of the separate states **(Figure 11.13)**.

A tree is an example of unity in nature. It is composed of roots, trunk, bark, branches, twigs, and leaves. Each part has a purpose that contributes to the living, growing tree. An electric lamp is a manufactured unit composed of a base, electric wire, sockets, bulbs, shades, and so on. The parts of the lamp work together as a unified whole to provide light. If any part does not work, the unity of the lamp is impaired.

Creating Visual Unity

In art, **unity** is *the quality of wholeness or oneness that is achieved through the effective use of the elements and principles of art.* Unity is like an invisible glue. It joins all the separate parts so that they look as if they belong together.

Unity is difficult to understand at first because it is not easily defined. It is a quality that you feel as you view a work of art **(Figure 11.14).** As you study an artwork, you may think that you would not change one element or object. You are receiving an impression that the work is a unified whole.

Unity helps you concentrate on a visual image. You cannot realize how important this is until you study a work that lacks unity. Looking at a work that lacks unity is like trying to carry on a serious discussion while your little sister

◀ **FIGURE 11.13** Johns combines the loose brushwork of Abstract Expressionism with the commonplace objects of American Realism. His map of the United States could be pulled apart by the wild action painting, but it is unified by the harmonious, limited color scheme of a primary triad.

Jasper Johns. *Map.* 1961. Oil on canvas. 198.2 × 312.7 cm (78 × 123⅛″). Collection, Museum of Modern Art, New York, New York. Gift of Mr. and Mrs. Robert C. Scull. © Jasper Johns/Licensed by VAGA, New York, NY

▲ **FIGURE 11.14** Rodin created this monument to honor six citizens who gave their lives in 1347 to save the city of Calais, France. Rodin showed the six men getting ready to see the king, who was laying siege to the city. He spent two years modeling faces and bodies to express the men's tension and pain. Each figure would be successful as an individual statue, but Rodin has placed them so that unity results. The work was designed to be placed at street level, not on a pedestal above the heads of the people.

Auguste Rodin. *The Burghers of Calais.* 1886, cast 1930s. Bronze. 2 × 2 × 1.9 m (79⅜ × 80⅞ × 77⅛"). Hirshhorn Museum and Sculpture Garden, Smithsonian Institution, Washington, D.C. Gift of Joseph H. Hirshhorn, 1966.

is practicing the violin, your brother is listening to the stereo, and your mother is running the vacuum cleaner. It would be difficult to concentrate on your conversation with all these distractions. It is the same with a work of art that lacks unity. You can't concentrate on the work as a whole, because all the parts demand separate attention.

To create unity, an artist adjusts the parts of a work so they relate to each other and to the whole work. A potter adjusts decorations on a bowl to complement the bowl's shape, size, and purpose. The artist who decorated the containers in **Figure 11.15** carefully planned where the holes would be

▲ **FIGURE 11.15** The decorations on these containers were created by drilling small holes into which short lengths of wire were inserted to form the various designs. The polished surface is the result of frequent handling and an occasional application of oil.

Used by the Zulu peoples, South Africa; the Tsonga or the Shona peoples, Mozambique and Zimbabwe. *Snuff Containers.* Hard fruit shell with copper, brass, and iron wire. Largest: 6 × 7.6 cm (2⅜ × 3"). National Museum of African Art, Smithsonian Institution, Washington, D.C. Acquisition grant from the James Smithsonian Society. 89-8-27, 28, 29, 30.

Florence Bayless. *Haori Coat.* 1992. Silk peau de soir, Thai silk, and silk lamé. Private collection.

drilled so that the design would complement the shape of the container. Clothing designers choose fabrics that complement the design and purpose of each outfit **(Figure 11.16).** Artists adjust the elements in a work to each other. A "busy" work with a variety of shapes and textures can be unified with a limited color scheme, for example.

Simplicity

Another way to create unity is through *simplicity.* Simplicity is not easy to achieve. An artist must plan carefully to create a good, simple design. This is done by limiting the number of variations of an element. The fewer variations the artist uses, the more unified the design will seem **(Figure 11.17).**

A painting in which the entire surface is covered with a single, even layer of one hue will appear strongly unified. A sculpture of a single person expresses a simple unity **(Figure 11.18).**

◀ **FIGURE 11.17** Carr has used simplification to eliminate the details of bark, grass, and leaves. The foliage seems to be solidified into diagonally flowing living forms.

Emily Carr. *Forest, British Columbia.* 1931–32. Oil on canvas. 130 × 86.8 cm (51⅛ × 34⅛"). Vancouver Art Gallery, Vancouver, British Columbia, Canada. VAG 42.3.9.

Allan Houser created contemporary Apache sculpture. As a child, he listened to his father's stories about the adventures of Chief Geronimo. This gave him a deep attachment to his ancestral background, an attachment that is shown in his artwork. Houser studied at the Indian School in Sante Fe, New Mexico, and then remained in Sante Fe, where he worked as a free-lance artist. During World War II, he traveled to California, where he became interested in the media of sculpture. He created works in a variety of styles and mastered bronze, metal, and stone sculpture. Houser's designs are modern, yet firmly rooted in the special tradition of his Native American forefathers. He drew inspiration from both past and present, but like all successful artists, his sculpture transcends race and language. The sculpture *Reverie* (Figure 11.18) shows a distinct Native American influence, but it can be appreciated by anyone, regardless of his or her background.

▶ **FIGURE 11.18** Notice how the artist has used simple lines and few details to create this artwork. The simplicity serves to emphasize the faces of the mother and child, which become focal points. The unity of the design shows the connection between mother and child. What feeling does this piece evoke?

Allan Houser. *Reverie.* 1981. Bronze, edition of 10. 63.5 × 58.4 × 33 cm (25 × 23 × 13″). Collection of the Duke and Duchess of Bedford. The Glen Green Galleries, Santa Fe, New Mexico. Copyright Allan Houser Inc.

Repetition

The repetition of objects and elements can be an effective way to unify a work of art. Louise Nevelson's assemblages are good examples. She collects objects that are not alike. This presents a problem of unity, which she solves in one or more ways. Often, she places the objects in a series of boxlike containers **(Figure 11.19).** The boxes help to unify the work. She sometimes paints the entire structure the same color. Sometimes she repeats both container shape and color to unify her assemblages.

Most architects are concerned with unity. Their goal is to design structures

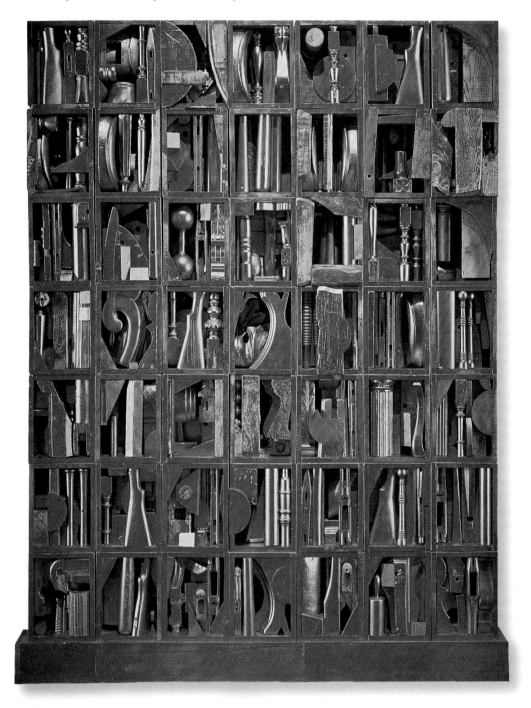

▲ **Figure 11.19** The artist has collected different found objects and assembled them together. What has the artist done to unify this work and make the objects look like they belong together? Can you identify any of the found objects?

Louise Nevelson. *Dawn.* 1962. Wood painted gold. 323 × 240 × 19 cm (127 × 94½ × 7½"). The Pace Gallery, New York, New York.

that blend with the surroundings **(Figure 11.20)**. They may use materials that repeat the colors and textures found in the structure's environment. They may also use materials that reflect the surroundings. For instance, mirrored outside walls have been used on skyscrapers. The mirrors reflect the shapes and colors of the clouds and sky, and the buildings seem to blend with their surroundings and the atmosphere.

Proximity

Proximity, or closeness, is another way of unifying very different shapes in a work **(Figures 11.21** and **11.22,** page 302). This is achieved by limiting the negative space between the shapes. Clustering the shapes in this way suggests unity and coherence. The sense of unity can be made even stronger if the cluster of unlike items is surrounded by an area of negative space.

▲ **FIGURE 11.20** Wright was a genius who dared to be different. In 1936 he was asked to design a house close to this waterfall. Instead, he placed the house right over the falls. Terraces hang suspended over the running water. Even though they are made of reinforced concrete, the terraces repeat the shapes of the natural stone terraces below. The stones that make up the walls come from the building site, which ties the house more closely to its surroundings.

Frank Lloyd Wright. *Fallingwater House. Bear Run, Pennsylvania.* 1936. Photography by Sandak, Inc., Stamford, Connecticut.

◀ **FIGURE 11.21** The artist has used proximity by grouping the children close together. What do the children appear to be doing? What kind of meeting are they having?

Marie Bashkirtseff. *A Meeting.* 1884. Oil on canvas. 190.5 × 172.2 cm (74¹⁵⁄₁₆ × 68¹⁵⁄₁₆″). Musée d'Orsay, Paris, France. Art Resource, New York, New York.

▶ **FIGURE 11.22** Jessup has created a unified composition using many techniques. What has she simplified to unify the work? What has been repeated?

Georgia Mills Jessup. *Rainy Night, Downtown.* 1967. Oil on canvas. 112 × 122 cm (44 × 48″). The National Museum of Women in the Arts, Washington, D.C. Gift of Savanna M. Clark

Activity   Creating Unity

Applying Your Skills. Suppose you have been hired to create a window display for a gift shop that sells many unrelated objects. From magazines, cut out photographs of 15 unrelated objects that represent the merchandise to be displayed. Use as many unifying techniques as you can to create the display. Draw the window and the design for the display and glue the cutouts where the objects would be placed in the design.

Computer Option. Arrange three or four different objects close together on a table. Use the Pencil or small Brush tool to draw the outline of all the objects using a continuous line. Another option is to draw the objects as individual shapes but extend the lines into the background. Select, copy, and repeat a few of the shapes but vary their sizes. Arrange the shapes to emphasize a focal point. Add a simple background. Now, choose and apply a limited color scheme with no more than four or five colors. Title, save, and print your work.

How Artists Use Variety, Emphasis, and Harmony to Enhance Unity

As you know, artists use variety, emphasis, and harmony to make their works more interesting and appealing. If carried to extremes, however, these principles can destroy the unity of a visual work. This means that artists must be careful to balance the contrast-

ing qualities of variety and emphasis with harmonizing and unifying techniques to create a unified work.

Jane Wilson has successfully balanced the harmonizing and varying devices in *Solstice* **(Figure 11.23).** She has divided the work into two contrasting rectangles. The sky in the upper rectangle is painted with both light and dark values. The focal point of the work is the bright yellow glow of sunlight peeking through the dark clouds.

▲ **FIGURE 11.23** Explain how the artist has balanced harmony with variety in this painting.

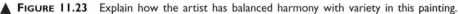

Jane Wilson. *Solstice.* 1991. Oil on linen. 152.4 × 178 cm (60 × 70″). Courtesy DC Moore Gallery, NYC.

You cannot see any specific shapes in the water, shown in the lower rectangle, yet the sky is full of loose triangular shapes. These contrasting factors would pull the work apart if the artist had not used a harmonious color scheme. The entire work is composed of various values of blue, green, and yellow. The artist has simplified this work, showing nothing but clouds, sky, and water. She has tied the work together using repetition. The clear triangle of sky repeats the color of the water. The bright yellow of the sun is reflected along the edge of the clouds and in the water below. The active clouds are repetitions of loose triangular shapes. Without the repetitions and simple color scheme, this work might not be the unified composition that it is.

Check Your Understanding

1. Define *unity.*
2. What is simplicity?
3. How is proximity used to create unity?
4. What can happen if variety, emphasis, or harmony is carried to an extreme?

Assemblage with Handmade Paper

▲ FIGURE 11.24

Lois Dvorak. *Spirit Boxes I.* 1985. Assemblage with handmade paper, construction paper, tree bark, colored pencils, pastels, and embroidery thread. 51 × 76.2 × 5.1 cm (20 × 30 × 2"). Private collection.

SUPPLIES

- Sketchbook and pencils
- Large strong sheet of paper for background
- Your own handmade paper
- Variety of other paper and fabric
- Found materials
- White glue
- Scissors
- Pencils, markers, and/or crayons

Spirit Boxes I is a mixed-media assemblage **(Figure 11.24).** The background is a sheet of paper Lois Dvorak made from cotton pulp. The swirling pattern was drawn with colored pencils and pastels. The dark tree shape was made from construction paper with pastel shading that continues the movement of the design in the background. The boxes were made from bark that was soaked and beaten into a very strong, thin paper, which was then glued and sewn together. Inside the boxes are bits of bark paper embroidered with colored threads. Notice that in some places the details in the boxes are unified with the background. Across the front of the boxes you can see very thin, transparent paper that has bits of homemade and construction paper glued in strategic places to unite the rhythmic repetition of the boxes.

Dvorak is always searching for little treasures in the environment to put in her spirit boxes, such as bits of bird eggshells, locust wings, and dried-out lizards. Begin to think about how you can adapt Dvorak's techniques to your own assemblage.

What You Will Learn

Create a relief assemblage that contains symbols of your life. Each symbol should be protected in a handmade paper container just as Dvorak has protected each symbol in a spirit box. Use the principle of harmony to join the various symbols and containers into a unified composition. Use handmade papers, other papers, fabrics, fibers, and small found objects to construct the relief. Like Dvorak, add details using pencil, crayon, markers, and/or fibers.

Creating

Study Dvorak's assemblage, *Spirit Boxes I.* She has used several different techniques to unify her work. Notice how the forms of the spirit boxes are related. Observe how the paths that weave over and under each other in the background are alike, and most of the shapes between the paths are covered with an invented texture. The boxes are placed close to each other and are held together in the branches of the tree.

Brainstorm with your classmates about objects that can be used to symbolize aspects of your life.

Step 1 Working in groups, make handmade paper to use in this project. See the instructions for making paper in Technique Tip 21 on page 435 in the Handbook. Plan the colors you will use when making the paper, because they will be some of the colors in your final project. Collect other materials and symbolic objects you plan to use.

Step 2 Make plans for your relief assemblage in your sketchbook. List and sketch the symbolic objects you will use and explain what each represents. Design the forms of the containers. Draw each container from two or more views. List the ways that you will use harmony to unify your project.

Step 3 Draw several plans for your mixed-media relief. As you draw, think about the materials you will use for construction and how you will alter them using drawing or stitching materials. Choose the best design.

Step 4 Plan the procedures you need to follow to construct your work and follow your plan. Prepare your finished product for display.

EVALUATING YOUR WORK

▶ **DESCRIBE** Explain the process, step by step, that you used to make paper. Describe the three-dimensional containers you made to hold the symbolic objects and explain how you constructed them.

▶ **ANALYZE** Which elements did you emphasize in this project? List and describe the methods you used to create harmony. Does the work have visual rhythm? Describe.

▶ **INTERPRET** Do the symbols you used represent only one part of your life or all of it? Are the symbols obvious or are they personal?

▶ **JUDGE** Does your work have a strong sense of unity? Which of the aesthetic theories would you use to judge this work? What, if anything, would you change to give it more unity?

▲ **FIGURE 11.24A** Student work.

Clay Sculpture Unifying Two Ideas

▲ FIGURE 11.25

Artist unknown. Folk art from the town of Acallan, State of Puebla, Mexico. *Fiesta Rodeo*. 1975. Ceramic with nichrome wire and acrylic paint. 55.8 × 33 × 33 cm (22 × 13 × 13″). Private collection.

SUPPLIES

- Sketchbook and pencil
- Clay and clay tools
- Slip and brush
- Cloth-covered clay board
- Plastic bags
- Glaze or acrylic paint (optional)

The piece shown in **Figure 11.25** comes from the town of Acallan in the State of Puebla in Mexico. What makes this particular work so unusual is that the artist has taken two themes that are not really related and tied them together by using a balance between harmony and variety. The artist took two different themes of celebration: the secular rodeo and the religious tree of life, and carefully organized the elements of art so that the two themes merged into a unified whole. The rodeo is a worldly event. The tree of life represents the tree in the Garden of Eden from which Adam and Eve gained knowledge.

Notice how the artist has used contrast. The negative spaces in the fence are small rectangles, but when your eyes move up to the tree, the lines explode into active, blossoming curves.

Observe the ways in which the two themes have been related in this sculpture and think about how you will relate two themes.

What You Will Learn

Like the Mexican folk artist who combined two different themes in the sculpture *Fiesta Rodeo*, you will create a clay sculpture that combines two unrelated objects. Create unity in your work by using a balance between variety and harmony. Use some of the following harmonizing techniques: simplification, repetition, and proximity. To help you tie the two parts together, use emphasis of an element and/or emphasis of an area.

Creating

Study *Fiesta Rodeo*. Notice how the artist has unified two different themes. In your sketchbook, describe how the artist has used a balance between variety and harmony to create unity. List the most important elements and explain why they are important. Discuss your findings with your classmates.

Brainstorm with your classmates about different themes or objects that could be unified in a sculpture as the artist has done with *Fiesta Rodeo*. Think of your favorite school subject, your favorite after-school activity, or a hobby. Write the two ideas in your sketchbook. Make verbal and visual notes about how you could create your sculpture. Make some sketches based on your ideas. Choose your best idea. List the harmonizing techniques you want to use and which elements you will use. Then list the way you will use emphasis.

Step 1 Construct your sculpture. For proper clay construction techniques see Technique Tip 16 on page 433. Between work sessions, cover your sculpture tightly with a plastic bag so the clay does not dry. When you are finished with construction, cover your work loosely so the clay does not dry too quickly. Remember that thin clay will dry and shrink more quickly than thick clay, so cover thin areas very carefully.

Step 2 When your work is bone dry, fire it in the kiln. After your sculpture is fired, you may decorate it by glazing and glaze firing the piece or painting it with acrylic paints. Prepare your work for display.

EVALUATING YOUR WORK

▶ **DESCRIBE** List the two different themes or objects you combined in your sculpture. Describe the clay-building techniques you used to construct your work. How did you prepare your work for display?

▶ **ANALYZE** Which harmonizing techniques did you use to unify your work? Describe how you used emphasis to pull the piece together visually. Does your finished product look unified?

▶ **INTERPRET** What is the expressive effect of your sculpture? Give your work an expressive title. Write a poem or a brief paragraph about your sculpture that expresses your feelings toward this work.

▶ **JUDGE** Which aesthetic theories would you use to judge this work? If you were to do this over, what would you change?

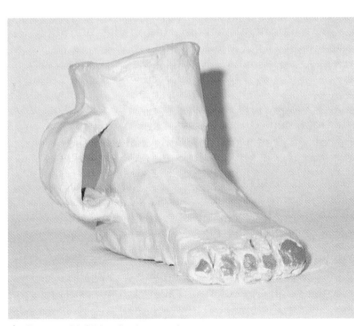

▲ **FIGURE 11.25A** Student work.

Designing a Mural

▲ **FIGURE 11.26**

John Yancy. *Celebration of Arts: Vibrations of Life.* 1991. Permanent exterior mural, acrylic on panels. 2.4 × 9.7 m (8′ × 32′). Located at 1531 West 60th Street, Chicago, Illinois.

SUPPLIES

- Sketchbook, pencil, and ruler
- Photograph of proposed site
- Enlarged photocopy of photograph
- Large sheet of white paper
- Tempera or acrylic paints
- Brushes

John Yancy received his first mural commission during his senior year in high school. He liked murals because of their scale and visibility. During his studies at The Art Institute of Chicago, he began to realize that murals inform, enlighten, and motivate people. His *Celebration of Arts* mural depicts the programs and contributions of the Boulevard Art Center and expresses the excitement and vitality of all the visual and performing arts **(Figure 11.26)**. The patterns on the mural portray textile designs that are seen in the masquerade ceremonies of the Yoruba people of Africa. The dancers in the mural function as dynamic, formal elements to increase movement and drama. The mural was completed with the help of a small crew of 16- to 20-year-old participants who had expressed interest in a career in the arts.

Yancy created the mural to let people know what was going on in the Center. Notice which elements he used to create variety and which ones he used to create harmony in the composition so that the mural became a unified whole.

What You Will Learn

Design and create a presentation painting of a mural for a specific site. Yancy used the events in the building as a theme for his mural. Choose a theme and design a mural using subject matter that is linked to the site. Use a balance between the principles of variety, emphasis, and harmony, to create a unified composition. Make your final painting to scale.

Creating

Brainstorm with classmates about sites and themes for your mural designs. Decide whether you all want to work on the same theme, such as the environment or the history of the community, or whether you all want to use independent themes. Then find an interesting site for your mural and choose your individual idea. Think of the subject matter you will use to express your theme.

Step 1 Photograph your site and enlarge the photograph using a photocopier. Measure the area of the photocopy on which you will place your mural. Make some rough sketches in your sketchbook. Create a unified composition by balancing the varying and unifying techniques. Because this is a plan for a large mural, you may not want to have a single focal point; you may decide to create several centers of interest. Plan your color scheme.

Step 2 Select your best idea and draw it carefully with pencil on the measured area of the photocopy. Enlarge your mural plan, to scale, onto a large sheet of white paper. See Technique Tip 8 on page 431 of the Handbook for directions on using a grid to enlarge a work to scale. Paint the enlarged presentation drawing.

Step 3 Arrange a display that includes the photograph, the enlarged photocopy with the drawing for the mural, the presentation painting, and a written statement that explains your theme, the subject matter, and why you selected them for that specific site.

EVALUATING YOUR WORK

▶ **DESCRIBE** Tell the theme, the subject matter, and the site you selected for your mural.

▶ **ANALYZE** Explain which principles of art you used to create a unified composition. Explain which color scheme you chose and why you chose it.

▶ **INTERPRET** What kind of a mood does your mural express? How do you think the mural would affect the site for which it was planned? Give your work an expressive title.

▶ **JUDGE** Which aesthetic theories would you use to judge this mural? What, if anything, would you change before you painted it on the site?

▲ **FIGURE 11.26A** Student work.

School Web Page Design

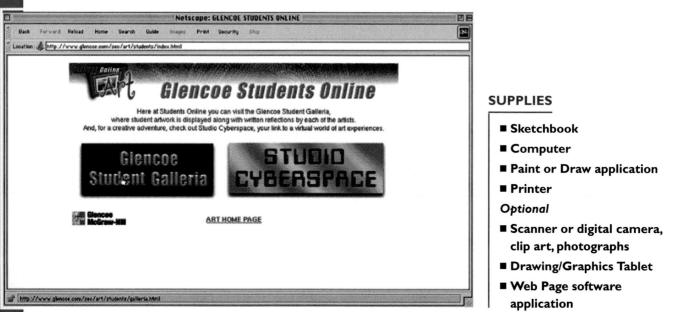

▲ **FIGURE 11.27**

SUPPLIES

- **Sketchbook**
- **Computer**
- **Paint or Draw application**
- **Printer**

Optional

- **Scanner or digital camera, clip art, photographs**
- **Drawing/Graphics Tablet**
- **Web Page software application**

When you view a Web site, you encounter more than words and information. Web sites are designed to catch your eye and hold your attention, as well as to inform you. Web pages and art designed for them are recent developments. General use of the Internet by public schools began around 1993. The technology that artists use to make graphic images for the Internet has improved and changed so rapidly since then that there are literally hundreds of thousands of artists exploring the possibilities of art and Web page design. Artists and Web page designers have learned how to create Web pages that are interesting to view and use. There are as many different ways to design a Web page as there are ways to paint a picture. Like a good art gallery exhibition, good Web page designs keep you coming back to visit.

What You Will Learn

You will design and create a Web page for your school, or for a specific department in your school, using a computer paint program. Use the principles of variety, emphasis, harmony, and unity to organize your design. Include your school name, address, phone number, e-mail address, an introductory paragraph, one or more pieces of artwork and/or photos, and at least four buttons that link to specific information about your school or the department of your choice. Do not forget to credit any sources you use.

Creating

Determine the purpose of your Web page. Consider who the audience will be. Then, research and gather information about your school or the department you are featuring and related topics. What will be emphasized in your layout? How will you use harmony to tie it all together? What size will your artwork or photos be?

Step 1 In your sketchbook, organize your information using diagrams and sketches that show headings, sub-headings, and related information into ideas for your Web page. Create at least three different possibilities. Most computer screens are 9″ high by 12″ wide so your sketches should fit this format.

Step 2 Select your best design. Open your computer paint program and use the outline rectangle tool to map out the size of your Web page on the computer screen.

Step 3 Using the same computer paint tool or the oval outline tool, designate shapes within the Web page for your school name, address, and phone number; four buttons to links about specific school information; the space needed for an introductory paragraph about your school; artwork or photo.

Step 4 Add the details for each of the spaces you designated in your layout. Select a font that is easy to read. Type in the text that you will use to introduce your school. Consider your color scheme. Type in the actual titles that you will use on your buttons.

Step 5 For the artwork or photos, either use the computer paint tools to develop your artwork on your Web page design or open a new file in the computer paint program and work on your

artwork there. Once you have completed your artwork, save it as file. Then copy and paste it into your Web page design. If you have scanned a photo or taken one with a digital camera, import it into your Web page.

Step 6 Print your Web page design to visually check and proofread it. Make any necessary corrections and print out your final copy.

EVALUATING YOUR WORK

▶ **DESCRIBE** Did you include the name of your school and/or the department, the address, phone number, e-mail address, introductory paragraph, artwork and/or photos, and four buttons that lead to specific information? Describe procedures you used to arrange and finish your Web page.

▶ **ANALYZE** Identify the techniques you used to create visual unity. Identify the area of emphasis. How did you create this emphasis? Describe how the components of your design demonstrate variety. How do they also create harmony?

▶ **INTERPRET** What is the feeling or mood of your Web page design? Is it playful or more formal? How do the colors you chose influence the feeling of the design? How does the artwork and/or photos you selected affect the mood?

▶ **JUDGE** Is your design well-planned, informative, and visually satisfying? Are text, graphics, and links logical and easy to view? Have you credited your sources? Would you change anything to make your work more successful?

ART CRITICISM IN ACTION

▲ **FIGURE 11.28**

Henri Rousseau. *Carnival Evening*. 1886. Oil on canvas. 116.8 × 90.2 cm (46 × 35½″). Philadelphia Museum of Art, Philadelphia, Pennsylvania. Louis E. Stearn Collection.

1 ▶ **DESCRIBE What do you see?**
Read the credit line for information about the artwork and then make a list of everything you see in this painting. Remember to be objective. Do not make guesses.

- List the size and media of this work.
- Describe the people and what they are wearing.
- Describe the land, the sky, the trees, and the house.

2 ▶ **ANALYZE How is this work organized?**
Now you will look at the elements of art and how they are organized by the principles of art. You will discover the clues that tell you what the artist is trying to convey.

- Describe the artist's use of the principles of rhythm, balance, and proportion.
- Where is the focal point in this work? Is there a secondary point of interest? How did the artist create these focal points?
- How does the artist use harmony? Explain. How has he unified this work? Which element has he used to create unity?

3 ▶ **INTERPRET What is the artist trying to communicate?**
Now you will combine the clues you have collected and your personal ideas to form a creative interpretation of this work.

- How does the element of color affect the mood? How does the strong focal point affect the way the work looks?
- What are the people doing? Where are they?
- Give this work a new title based on your interpretation.

4 ▶ **JUDGE What do you think of the work?**
Decide if this is a successful work of art. You may have a personal opinion, but it is also important to make an objective judgment based on aesthetic theories.

- Do you think the artist has successfully used the elements and principles of art to create an unusual mood ? Explain.
- Has the artist created an interesting work? Did it make you think?
- Is this a successful work of art? Use one or more of the aesthetic theories you learned in Chapter 2 to defend your decision.

MEET THE
ARTIST
HENRI ROUSSEAU

French, 1844–1910

Henri Rousseau. *Moi-Meme, Portrait-Paysage (I Myself, Portrait-Landscape).* 1890. Oil on canvas. 143 × 110 cm (57⅛ × 44″). Narodni Galerie, Prague, Czech Republic.

Henri Rousseau was born in Laval, France. He lacked formal training and was entirely self-taught. At first he painted mostly street scenes and portraits, but as he gained confidence, he became more adventuresome. He created fantastic landscapes and metaphorical works that used bold colors and flat designs. Rousseau influenced other European painters who attempted to imitate his so-called primitive or naïve style.

He exhibited with artists such as Paul Gauguin, Pablo Picasso, and Georges Seurat, winning their admiration and the acclaim of the art world.

How Does Stage Lighting Create Drama?

◀ **FIGURE 11.29**

Rembrandt. *The Night Watch (Group Portrait of the Amsterdam Watch Under Captain Frans Banning Cocq).* 1642. Oil on canvas. 3.7 × 4.4 m (12'2" × 14'7"). Rijksmuseum, Amsterdam, Holland.

Stage lighting is as essential to the production of a play as characters and dialogue. The way a stage is lit conveys both setting and mood. A lighting director may use downlighting for a shadowy effect or uplighting to distort the features of the characters. General illumination of the stage combines lighting from all sides. Spotlights can also be used to light a specific area. Stage lighting helps us to feel like we are a part of the unfolding drama.

A painting can have a similar impact on viewers. One of Rembrandt's best–known paintings, *The Night Watch* **(Figure 11.29),** achieves an almost theatrical effect. Although there are many figures in this crowded scene, we can spot the main "characters" in part because they are more fully illuminated than the others. The light source emanates from the upper left. Notice how the shadow of the officer's hand falls across the aide's uniform. As the focal point of the painting, the officer's illuminated hand conveys authority. Like theatrical lighting, the painting's use of contrast, light, and shadow helps to convey the activity as well as the emotional intensity of the scene.

Making the Connection

1. Imagine that Rembrandt's painting is actually a moment in a play. What do you think is happening?
2. Study the shadowed figures in this painting. What do they have in common? Why do you think Rembrandt used such dark values to paint them?
3. Experiment with light by using several flashlights in a dark room. Then, pick a scene from a play you have read or seen and design the lighting for it. Write down your directions and explain the effects you desire.

Building Vocabulary

On a separate sheet of paper, write the term that best matches each definition below.

1. The principle of art concerned with difference or contrast.
2. The principle of art that makes one part of a work dominant over the other parts.
3. The first part of a work to attract the attention of the viewer.
4. The principle of art that creates unity by stressing the similarities of separate but related parts.
5. The quality of wholeness or oneness that is achieved through the effective use of the elements and principles of art.

Reviewing Art Facts

Answer the following questions using complete sentences.

1. Why do artists use variety in artworks?
2. Name the two major types of visual emphasis.
3. What is the most important part of an artwork called?
4. Name and describe the five ways in which artists create a focal point.
5. Name and describe three techniques that artists use to create unity in a work of art.

Thinking Critically About Art

1. **Analyze.** Look at Figure 11.1, page 286 and Figure 11.20, page 301. How do these buildings fit into their surroundings? How was the principle of unity achieved?
2. **Compare and contrast.** Notice the variety used in Figure 11.2, page 288. Compare this with the variety used in Figure 11.3, page 289. Explain how each artist used variety and point out the similarities and differences between the two works.
3. **Analyze.** Look through the other chapters of this book to find three examples of works in which the artist has emphasized one element, making all the others subordinate to it. List the works and explain which element has been emphasized.

Read how the "Vocalworks Radio Hour" presents variety and harmony in the re-creation of a live radio broadcast from the 1930s era. Showcasing swing music, comedy, and drama programs, Vocalworks swings us back to the past in the Performing Arts Handbook on page 423.

Learn more about how artists achieve unity through harmony, variety, and emphasis. Visit the Glencoe Fine Arts Site at **www.glencoe.com/sec/art.** To begin your search, find the chapter you are studying in the Table of Contents and click on one of the "hot links."

ART
THROUGH
THE AGES

"Painting is stronger than I am. It makes me do what it wants.**"**

Pablo Picasso
1881–1973

◄

Pablo Picasso. *Still Life*. 1918. Oil on canvas. 97 × 130 cm (38¼ × 51¼"). National Gallery of Art, Washington, D.C. © 1998 Board of Trustees. Chester Dale Collection.

317

▲ **Figure 12.1** This Bella Coola Sun Mask was created by a member of a secret society that staged performance rituals on special occasions. During a ceremony, this mask was raised against the rear wall of the dance house and traveled across the ceiling by means of ropes and pulleys that were not revealed to the viewers. This movement represented the journey of the sun across the sky.

Sun Mask. Bella Coola, nineteenth century. Central British Columbia. Red cedar, alder; carved, painted. 108.5 × 106.9 cm (42¾ × 42⅛"). The Seattle Art Museum, Seattle, Washington. Gift of John Hauberg.

CHAPTER 12

Art Traditions from Around the World

Art from the past shows what the people who created it were like. The art reveals their feelings, their ideas, their actions, and their way of life. This combination of *behaviors and ideas of a group of people* is called **culture**.

The history of visual art is like the history of the world itself—broad and complex. This chapter—and the one that follows—offers just a peek into the world's artistic heritage.

As you look at the Bella Coola mask in **Figure 12.1,** you can see that it was created with great care. Even though you may not know the purpose of this work you can appreciate its colors, shapes, and forms. You can see that formal balance organizes the art elements. Using art criticism, you can try to understand the mask and guess its purpose. If you do art history research, you will learn that this mask represents the sun. By researching, you will learn the symbolic meanings of the objects and shapes painted on the mask.

OBJECTIVES

After completing this chapter, you will be able to:

- Briefly discuss art traditions from many cultures around the world.
- Understand how cultural traditions influence artists' works.

WORDS TO KNOW

culture
Paleolithic period
Neolithic period
megaliths
cuneiform
ziggurats
pharaohs
dynasty
stupas
scroll
pagoda
woodblock printing
mosques
griots
totem poles

Developing Your
PORTFOLIO

Art history is the record of art from past to present. Create a historical time line tracing the development of your own artwork. Consider the work that you have done in the past. Collect a representative sample of artwork you have created, going as far back into your past as you can. Write a brief description of several of these works. Then draw some conclusions about how your art skills have developed as you have grown as an artist. Keep your artwork samples and your written art history in your portfolio.

Art of Earliest Times

The artworks produced many thousands of years ago tell us a great deal about the earliest cultures and civilizations of our world. These ancient people left no written records. What we know of them has been learned from the objects and the art that they left behind.

Prehistoric Art

Prehistoric means before history, or before written records were kept. The objects made by people during this period are all that remain to tell us about the people who lived long ago.

Figure 12.2 is one of many cave paintings left by cave dwellers in Europe during the Paleolithic period. The **Paleolithic** (pay-lee-u-**lith**-ik) **period,** or *Old Stone Age, began about two million years ago, and ended with the close of the last ice age about 13,000 B.C.* It was a time when people began using stone tools. In these cave paintings, the colors are so bright and the animals so realistic that, for a long time, scholars refused to believe they had been created by prehistoric people.

To this day no one knows the purpose of the paintings. Found deep inside caves, far from the entrances and living areas, they probably were not created for decoration. Some scholars believe the paintings were part of a hunting ritual. A shaman, or medicine man, may have created the image of the animal, believing that it would help hunters capture the animal. The paintings may also have been visual prayers for animals to appear during the next hunt. According to another theory, cave dwellers created the paintings to celebrate a successful hunt.

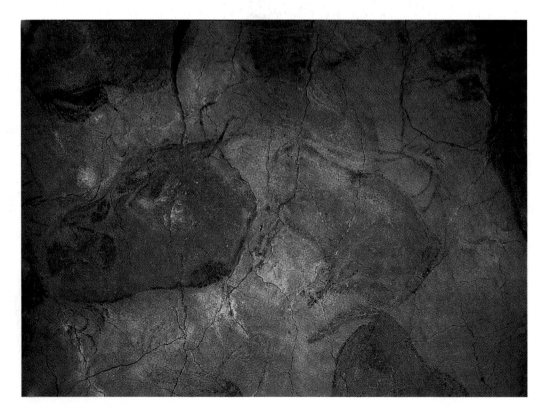

◀ **FIGURE 12.2** An amateur archaeologist excavated in this low-roofed cave for four years before his daughter, who was small enough to stand up straight in the cave and look up, discovered these paintings of sleeping, galloping, and crouching animals.

The Hall of the Bulls. c. 15,000 B.C. Altamira Caves, Spain.

Prehistoric Builders

Eventually prehistoric people moved out of caves and began constructing their own shelters. Small communities developed and some hunters gave up their nomadic life and settled down, becoming farmers. After some time, small tribal groups grew into organized villages surrounded by cultivated fields and domesticated animals.

During the Neolithic period, people built structures of stone. The **Neolithic** (nee-uh-**lith**-ik) **period,** or *New Stone Age, is a prehistoric period stretching roughly from 7000 B.C. to 2000 B.C.* During this time, humans developed agriculture and stone tools were refined. Ancient structures from this period, called megaliths, have been found throughout Europe, Asia, and even North America. **Megaliths** (**meg**-uh-liths) are *large monuments created from huge stone slabs.* As early as 4000 B.C., circular arrangements of huge, rough-hewn stones were created in Western Europe. The most famous of these is Stonehenge in England (see Figure 12.35 on page 348). Built around 2000 B.C., it consists of a series of four concentric rings. Builders used an ancient building method that we now call *post-and-lintel construction.* Upright slabs, called posts, support horizontal slabs, called lintels. If you look at the photograph, you can see how the posts support the lintels. More than half of the original stones still stand. The tallest measures 17 feet and weighs more than 50 tons. Scholars are uncertain how prehistoric people, working with primitive tools, were able to cut these huge stones, transport them many miles, and then raise them into position. The purpose of Stonehenge has also baffled scholars for many centuries. In the past, people believed a great magician created it. Today, Stonehenge is thought to have served as a kind of observatory, enabling people to practice a type of astronomy and serve as an accurate calendar.

As prehistoric peoples learned to herd animals and grow crops, they also learned to live in harmony with their surroundings. This peaceful balance was upset by population growth. Small tribes began to fight over grazing land and soil suitable for growing crops. They were forced to band together into more organized groups for protection and also to be able to produce more food. By around 3000 B.C. four major civilizations had developed at different points on the globe. The ancient civilizations of Mesopotamia, Egypt, India, and China emerged at this time.

Ancient River Valleys

The ancient civilizations of Mesopotamia, Egypt, India, and China, are referred to as river valley civilizations. Each of these civilizations was ruled by a monarchy, practiced a religion based on nature, and achieved great skill in art and architecture.

Mesopotamia

The area of Mesopotamia included the cultures of many people within an extensive region. The region was the fertile crescent of land between the Tigris and Euphrates rivers in the Middle East. The people lived in city-states, and each city was ruled by a monarch. Today, this land is shared by Syria and Iraq.

The Sumerians were the first dominant group in the area. They were the first people to have a system of writing (using symbols to represent spoken language). **Cuneiform** (kyoo-**nee**-uh-form) was *the Sumerian writing system made up of wedge-shaped characters.* These characters stood for concepts and ideas. Because paper was not yet developed, clay tablets were used. Some of these still exist.

▶ **FIGURE 12.3** This figure was placed in the temple to represent the worshiper. The wide eyes, hands folded in prayer, and attention to detail are typical of Sumerian sculpture.

Statua di Donna. c. 2700–2600 B.C. Marble. The Iraq Museum, Baghdad, Iraq.

Sumerian artists depicted figures in a lifelike and realistic way. Look at **Figure 12.3.** This small sculpture shows precise details of dress and facial features. Sumerians also constructed structures known as **ziggurats** (**zig**-uh-rats), or *stepped mountains made of brick-covered earth* **(Figure 12.4)**. These temples had exterior staircases. A temple honoring the god of the city was placed at the top. Does it resemble other buildings that you have seen?

In time, the Sumerian civilization merged with that of Akkad, its northern neighbor, giving rise to the civilization of Babylonia (around 750 B.C.). Babylonian art and architecture resembled Sumerian to a great extent. Another Mesopotamian civilization, called Assyria, emerged after the decline of Babylonia. A distinct Assyrian artistic style began to emerge around 1500 B.C. Assyrian artists created precise, detailed stone reliefs, which they painted using many colors. They depicted royal events, hunts, wars, and animals, especially horses and lions. Human figures were given less emphasis, although they were still depicted in a realistic and detailed way.

◀ **FIGURE 12.4** A temple honoring the god of the city was placed at the top of the ziggurat. This structure was built in 2100 B.C. What other art and architecture was being created throughout the world at that time?

Ziggurat. Ur, Iraq. c. 2100 B.C.

Egypt

The culture of ancient Egypt developed along the banks of the Nile River more than 3,000 years before the birth of Christ. Religion influenced every part of Egyptian life. The **pharaohs,** or *Egyptian rulers, were worshiped as gods and held complete authority over the kingdom.* Egyptians believed in life after death and preserved the bodies of the pharaohs in preparation for the afterlife. The famous pyramids were built as the tombs of the pharaohs.

Egyptian artists decorated temples and tombs according to very strict rules set forth by the priests. The rules required that each part of the body be shown from the most visible angle. Look at **Figure 12.5.** The heads, arms, legs, and feet are shown in profile. The shoulders and eyes, however, are shown from a frontal view.

The paintings found on the walls inside the tombs reveal a great deal about life in Egypt. Scenes from the life of the person buried in the tomb were intended to remind the spirit of life on earth.

India

In the Indus River Valley, the ancient civilization of India arose. Only in recent times have historians realized the age of Indian culture. For many centuries, no one knew that a civilization had flourished on the banks of the Indus River in northwest India. Then in 1865, railroad workers uncovered a hill of crumbling, fired-clay bricks near the city of Harappa (in present-day Pakistan). The bricks were found to be thousands of years old, dating back to 2500 B.C.

In 1922, a second city was discovered in the same area. Called Mohenjo-Daro (moh-hen-joh dahr-oh), meaning "Hill of the Dead" **(Figure 12.6),** the city was

◀ **FIGURE 12.5**
What symbols or features make these figures seem important? Observe the shapes in the boxes along the top border. These are hieroglyphs, an early form of picture writing. They give information about the painted scene.

Egyptian. *The Goddess Hathor Places the Magic Collar on Sethos I.* Thebes, Nineteenth Dynasty. c. 1303–1290 B.C. Painted bas-relief. 226.5 cm (89⅛"). The Louvre, Paris, France.

▲ **FIGURE 12.6** Experts believe the city of Mohenjo-Daro was abandoned because the climate changed. The ancient Indians built with fire-baked bricks, which meant they had ready access to timber. The area is a desert today.

Mohenjo-Daro, India. c. 2500 B.C.

once home to about 35,000 people. Architectural remains indicate that it served as a major commercial center. Wide, open streets divided the city into large blocks. The city featured multi-storied houses made from fired brick and wood, and elaborate, sophisticated drainage systems.

At this archeological site, workers discovered a number of small relief carvings in soapstone **(Figure 12.7)**. These carvings are the earliest known examples of Indian art. As you can see, several unusual lines and shapes are incised above the animals. These are characters from the ancient Harappan system of writing.

Over 70 cities, towns, and villages have been discovered in the Indus valley, as well as evidence of an organized kingdom with a central government that existed about 4,500 years ago.

China

The Yellow River valley became the site of the ancient Chinese civilization, a civilization that retains many of its ancient traditions today. Beginning 4,000 years ago, it is the oldest continuous culture in the history of the world.

As their civilization developed, the Chinese gained skill and knowledge in many different areas. They invented paper, porcelain (a type of ceramic), and

▲ **FIGURE 12.7** The designs on these seals "belonged" to their owners. Seals were pressed into soft clay to secure a container or document.

Soapstone seals from Mohenjo-Daro (Indus Valley culture). Karachi Museum, Karachi, Pakistan.

woodblock printing as well as the compass and gunpowder. Until modern times, emperors ruled China. Its historical periods were divided into dynasties, which were named after ruling families. A **dynasty** is *a period of time during which a single family provided a succession of rulers.* Bronze vessels found in ancient graves reveal that Chinese artisans cast bronze as early as the first imperial Chinese dynasty, the Shang dynasty, which began in 1766 B.C. The ritual wine vessel shown in **Figure 12.8** is an example of the intricate work done at that time. Abstract motifs and spirals cover the vessel. Experts believe the spirals stand for clouds, rain, or water. Such images reveal an ancient Chinese regard for nature. Many early bronze vessels show extraordinary technical mastery—evidence of the centuries of development required before such artworks could be created.

◀ **FIGURE 12.8** This vessel was used in a ceremony to ensure harmony with the spirits of deceased ancestors. Notice the large eyes and beak of an owl on the lower part of the vessel. Can you find other animals in the designs that cover this container?

Ancient China. *Ritual Wine Container.* Shang dynasty. Thirteenth century B.C. Bronze. 30.1 × 12.2 × 12.5 cm (11⅞ × 4¼ × 4⅞″). Arthur M. Sackler Gallery, Smithsonian Institution, Washington, D.C. Gift of Arthur M. Sackler

Activity | Creating a Writing System

Applying Your Skills. Imagine that you are from a past civilization and have been called upon to create a new writing system. As you begin to work on this task, remember that you know nothing of modern alphabets. Think about what ideas you will need to express in your culture and create a shape for each idea. When your system is complete and you have created a key to your language, write a sentence using your symbols and see if anyone in your class can read it.

✓ Check Your Understanding

1. For what purpose might cave paintings have been created?
2. What is a ziggurat?
3. Why and for whom were the pyramids built?
4. Define the word *dynasty.*

Art of Asia and the Middle East

The cultures of India, China, Japan, and the Middle East have all produced exciting art forms, some very different from European art. The art of Asia and the Middle East reflects different philosophies and religious beliefs from those in Western art.

India

The art of India has been strongly influenced by the Hindu and Buddhist religions. Hinduism is one of the world's oldest religions. It began in ancient India around 2000 B.C. It is not one religion but a group of many related sects. Buddhism began as a Hindu reform movement, and had a strong influence over the country from the third century B.C. to the sixth century A.D. Among the earliest, and most important, examples

of modern Indian architecture are **stupas** (**stoop**-uhs), which are *beehive-shaped domed places of worship*. These were built by Buddhist architects to house relics of Buddha, their religion's founder. Each stupa was reached through four gates covered with relief sculptures **(Figure 12.9).**

After the fifth century, Hinduism rose again in popularity because it was encouraged by the monarchs of the period. Hindu temples and sculptures of the Hindu gods were created. Hinduism combined several different beliefs and practices that developed over a long period of time. In Hinduism there are three primary processes in life and in the universe: creation, preservation, and destruction. The three main Hindu gods reflect this belief system. They are Brahma, the Creator; Vishnu, the

▶ **FIGURE 12.9**
Domes such as this were often erected over holy places, burial mounds, and holy relics. What is the purpose of preserving such things?

Great Stupa. Sanchi, Madhya Pradesh, India. c. first century B.C.

Preserver; and Siva, the Destroyer **(Figure 12.10).** In Hinduism, both humans and animals are believed to have souls that undergo reincarnation. Reincarnation is a purification process in which the soul lives in many bodies in many lifetimes until it becomes one with Brahma, the great soul.

India exported its religions to the rest of Asia. In Kampuchea (previously Cambodia) many temples were built of stone in the Indian style. The temple at Angkor Wat **(Figure 12.11)** was originally a Hindu temple built between A.D. 1113 and 1150. Dedicated to Vishnu by its builder, it represents the Hindu view of the universe.

China

China adopted Buddhism during the Han Dynasty, which lasted from 206 B.C. to A.D. 220. Buddhism was easily adopted in China because, like other Chinese religions, it stressed the harmony of human beings with nature. An important part of Buddhism is meditation, focusing one's thoughts on a single object or idea. Chinese artists found that long periods of meditation enabled them to perceive the beauty of an object or a scene with greater clarity. This enabled them to more effectively capture the beauty of the subject in their paintings. Chinese art of the last 2,000 years has been greatly influenced by Buddhism and meditation.

The Chinese were the first people to consider "picture painting" a valuable endeavor. This was because many artists were also scholars who wrote poems in beautiful writing (called calligraphy) using brushes that could make thick and thin lines. They used these same brushes and line techniques to paint pictures.

▶ **FIGURE 12.10** The Hindu god Siva is called the Destroyer. This sculpture is rich in symbolism. Notice what the figure is standing on. The objects he holds are a drum that symbolizes creation and a flame that symbolizes destruction. How is destruction related to creation?

Unknown, India, Tamil Nadu. *Siva as Lord of the Dance.* c. 950. Copper alloy. 76.2 × 57.1 × 17.8 cm (30 × 22½ × 7"). Los Angeles County Museum of Art, Los Angeles, California, given anonymously.

▲ **FIGURE 12.11** The layout of this temple was designed to create a solar calendar by which the summer and winter solstices and the spring and fall equinoxes could be fixed. Why was this important in an agricultural society?

Southeast Asia. Temple at Angkor Wat, Kampuchea (Cambodia). 1113–50.

▲ **Figure 12.12** Notice how small the people are in relation to the landscape. The hut blends in with the natural setting. The calligraphy bordering the drawing is an important part of the picture. Notice how it echoes the shapes of the leaves. How might the calligraphy be part of the "conversation"?

Hua Yen. *Conversation in Autumn.* 1762. Ink and color on paper. 115.3 × 39.7 cm (45⅛ × 15⅝"). The Cleveland Museum of Art, Cleveland, Ohio. The John L. Severance Fund.

They painted fans, pages of books, and scrolls **(Figure 12.12)**. A **scroll** is *a long roll of parchment or silk.* Some were hung on walls, while others were meant to be unrolled a little at a time and read like a book.

The earliest Chinese paintings were filled with images illustrating the beliefs that people should live together peacefully and be respectful of their elders. With the influence of a new religion, Buddhism, the focus of painting began to shift away from humans and toward nature. By around A.D. 1100, the landscape was the main theme of Chinese painting.

The Chinese also produced sculpture for religious purposes and to honor the dead (see Figure 10.1, page 254). During the Sung **(soong)** Dynasty (A.D. 960–1279), artists first produced ceramic objects of porcelain made from a fine-grained white clay called kaolin (**kay**-uh-luhn). Work in porcelain reached its highest point during the Ming Dynasty (A.D. 1368–1644). Today, collectors especially prize porcelain from this dynasty (see Figure 5.4, page 99).

Japan

In A.D. 552 the ruler of a kingdom in nearby Korea sent the Emperor of Japan a gift. The gift was a bronze figure of the Buddha, the founder of Buddhism. Along with the sculpture came priests to spread Buddhist teachings. Eventually many of the people of Japan accepted this new religion. They also learned about different ways of making art. For the next 250 years, Japanese art would show strong traces of Korean, Chinese, and other Asian styles.

The first important Japanese art objects of "modern times" were started in A.D. 594. These were magnificent Buddhist temples that were built throughout the country. Since the islands of Japan are made of volcanic rock, the Japanese could not use stone to build their temples. Instead, they made them from wood. In the process, they elevated the architecture of wooden structures to new levels.

Japanese temples are intricately assembled and richly decorated. They are carefully fitted together with special joints. Because Japan suffers frequent earthquakes and violent storms, the buildings had to be durable. One of the most interesting features of early Japanese temples was the **pagoda** (puh-**gohd**-uh). This is *a tower several stories high with roofs curving slightly upward at the edges* (**Figure 12.13**).

The Japanese also created monumental sculptures, often of the Buddha. Such a sculpture can be seen in **Figure 12.14,** the Great Buddha at Kamakura. It was cast in bronze in A.D. 1252. It is situated outdoors in a grove of trees, which seems an appropriate setting for this contemplative Buddha.

▲ **FIGURE 12.13** This pagoda stands as the oldest wooden structure in the world. Its purpose is to preserve relics.

Pagoda from the Temple Complex at Horyuji, near Nara, Japan. c. A.D. 616.

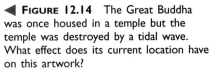

◄ **FIGURE 12.14** The Great Buddha was once housed in a temple but the temple was destroyed by a tidal wave. What effect does its current location have on this artwork?

Great Buddha. Kamakura, Japan. c. A.D. 1252.

Andō Hiroshige (hear-oh-shee-geh), a Japanese painter and printmaker, was born in Edo (now Tokyo) in 1797. Following in his father's footsteps, he became a fire warden. However, inspired by the work of Hokusai, he later decided to apprentice as a painter. He became an apprentice to Utagawa Toyohiro, a renowned artist, and graduated in 1812. At that time he took his teacher's name as a sign of respect and began signing his work "Utagawa Hiroshige."

Hiroshige worked in the Ukiyo-e tradition of printmaking, the last great artist to do so. Eventually he became even more successful than his role model, Hokusai. He depicted the experiences of ordinary people and places, capturing moods and changing times and seasons. For the first 15 years of his career, he created traditional prints of traditional subjects, such as women and the theatre. From 1830 to about 1845, he achieved fame as a landscape artist, creating poetic, lyrical works.

During the last part of his career, the quality of his work suffered as he apparently had difficulty keeping up with demand. A prolific artist, he made more than 5,400 prints. In 1858, he died of cholera in Edo.

▶ **FIGURE 12.15** The Japanese perfected the art of woodblock printing so that all people could afford art. This print depicts a famous pine tree as seen during a rainstorm. How is line used to convey the impression of rain? What is the main color? What effect does this have?

Andō Hiroshige. *Evening Rain on the Karasaki Pine* (from the series Eight Views of Omi Province). Nineteenth century. Woodblock print. 26 × 38.1 cm (10¼ × 15″). The Metropolitan Museum of Art, New York, New York. H. O. Havemeyer Collection. Bequest of Mrs. H. O. Havemeyer, 1929. (JP1874)

In A.D. 784, Japan entered its golden age of art. During this period, Japanese artists developed a painting called *Yamato-e* (yah-**mah**-toh-ay), or "pictures in the Japanese manner." Paintings done in this style were the first examples of pure Japanese art, meaning there was no influence of other Asian cultures in them. Yamato-e screen paintings were often made in sections and were used to brighten the dimly lit interiors of temples and homes as a temporary wall to divide a room.

Another new Japanese style of art was called Ukiyo-e (oo-**kee**-yoh-ay), meaning "pictures of the floating world," which depict different aspects of the pleasures of life. The demand for artworks in this new style was great. To meet this demand, artists turned to a new technique, **woodblock printing.** This is *making prints by carving images in blocks of wood.* Using this technique, artists could produce many inexpensive prints of one image **(Figure 12.15).**

► **FIGURE 12.16** This building was designed to be in harmony with the surrounding garden and pools. Notice the balance and symmetry of all the elements. What feeling does the building evoke?

Taj Mahal, garden and pools. 1632–43. Agra, India.

Art of Islam

In A.D. 570, an event took place that had a major effect on both the religious beliefs and the art of the Middle East and much of Asia. Muhammad was born in Mecca. He grew up and became a merchant, following the tradition of his family. However, he believed he received personal revelations that challenged him to change the religion of his people, the Arabs, who worshiped many idols. Muhammad taught that there was only one god, called Allah. After his death, his teachings were assembled into the Koran, a holy scripture. Islam was the name given to the religious faith of people who followed Muhammad. Worshipers are called Muslims.

Islamic art (art of the Muslim world) was characterized by the use of ornate line, shape, and pattern. The interior of **mosques,** *Muslim places of worship,* were decorated with calligraphy, geometric patterns, and stylized plants and flowers. Art depicting people or animals was not permitted in mosques. Such art was prohibited early in the history of the Islamic religion and was meant to prevent Muslims from worshiping images when they should

instead be worshiping the idea of Allah.

Book illustrators, however, were not limited by the same restrictions. They depicted people and animals in everyday scenes. They filled their illustrations with beautiful decorative patterns. The illustration shown in Figure 12.34, on page 346, depicts such a scene from a book about court life in Iran. The illustration was completed in A.D. 1525, just 25 years after Michelangelo created the *Pietà* (pee-ay-**tah**) (Figure 13.8, page 357).

The religion of Islam, and its influence on art, also spread to the East. Muslims conquered Delhi in India and converted many Indians to Islam. **Figure 12.16** shows a famous building, the Taj Mahal, which was built by an Indian Muslim leader as a memorial to his wife. The building is an outstanding example of Islamic architecture and is considered one of the most beautiful structures in the world. The building emphasizes formal balance and harmony with its surroundings. Its cool marble walls and placid lake evoke a response of serenity and tranquility in those who visit.

☑ *Check Your Understanding*

1. What is a stupa?
2. What medium did the Chinese often paint on that could be hung on walls or read like a book?
3. What material did Japanese architects commonly use and why?

The Art of Africa

Throughout Africa, in both the past and the present—even within the context of modern nation-states—the visual arts are well integrated with other art forms, including music, dance, and drama. The art of Africa was an integral part of the daily lives and religious rituals of the people.

The Role of Art in African Cultures

The huge continent of Africa has a population of millions that is subdivided into about 1,000 cultural groups. The peoples of Africa have long-established, highly developed cultures that have been producing sophisticated art forms for centuries. The arts are as varied as the peoples.

Everything is made with great care, whether for rituals or everyday use (see Figure 11.15, page 297). Art addresses not only the concerns of the living, their ancestors, and those yet to be born, but also those of the spirits of nature. A great deal of African art emphasizes the important events of life and the forces of nature that influence the lives of individuals and communities.

Dominant themes in African art include birth and death; the roles of men, women, and children; coming of age; sickness and healing; the importance of food and water; and the human relationship with nature. Artworks are often linked to celebrations and rituals, both nonreligious and sacred. Westerners are fascinated with objects from these cultures and have put them in museums. It is important to understand the original context in which these objects were made and used.

Ancient Ife

For the Yoruba (**yaw**-ruh-buh)people of Nigeria, the city of Ife (**ee**-feh) is the place where life and civilization began. Yoruba cities developed between the years A.D. 800 and 1000. By A.D. 1100, artists of Ife had developed a highly refined, lifelike sculptural style to create portraits of the first Yoruba kings and queens. The display of royal portraits, with their composed, balanced facial features, added a sense of stability in periods of political transition between rulers, or following the death of a ruler **(Figure 12.17)**.

▶ **FIGURE 12.17** The vertical lines on the face of this figure probably represent ornamental scars made to indicate ancestry and to enhance physical beauty. How did the artist use the principles of art in creating this portrait of a king?

Portrait of a king. Ife, Nigeria. Copper alloy. Eleventh–fifteenth century. H: 36.2 cm (14¼″). Museum of Mankind, London, England.

According to Yoruba beliefs, the world consists of two realms: the real world that can be seen and touched; and the supernatural world of ancestors, gods and goddesses, and spirits. Works of art created for the real, or visible, world tend to be realistic, whereas works of art created for the supernatural, or invisible, world tend to be more abstract.

As memorial portraits of Yoruba royalty, these sculptures celebrate the lives and accomplishments of individuals. Like Yoruba poems, which record family history and personal deeds, these refined works of art encourage living generations to strive for perfection. They encourage the living to match or surpass the cultural accomplishments of previous generations.

The Empire of Mali

Works of art made centuries ago in Ife and elsewhere in West Africa document the rise of city-states throughout the region. The terra-cotta sculptures of cavalrymen and foot soldiers from the Inland Niger Delta, near the ancient city of Jenne, date back to the early thirteenth century, when the empire of Mali was founded by a powerful military leader and king named Sundiata. These figures reveal proud profiles, with jutting chins and heads held high atop sturdy necks. Their bodies appear straight and tall whether shown standing or seated upright on stallions **(Figure 12.18).** The figures represent members of the well-outfitted and well-organized army described in an epic that recounts Sundiata's life history.

The strength of Sundiata's great cavalry and army of foot soldiers enabled him to gain political power. Under his leadership, the empire of Mali became one of the largest and wealthiest kingdoms the world has ever known. The epic story of the rise of Sundiata is passed on by **griots** (**gree**-oh), *oral historians who are also musicians and performers,* throughout West Africa to this day.

The city of Jenne is the oldest city in sub-Saharan Africa. In the art and architecture from this city there is an

▲ **FIGURE 12.18** Because wet clay is soft, artists can easily add texture to the overall forms of clay sculptures. How many different kinds of texture can you identify in this work?

Inland Delta Region, Mali. Equestrian figure. c. thirteenth century. Ceramic. 70.5 cm (27¾"). National Museum of African Art, Smithsonian Institution, Washington, D.C. Museum purchase, 86–12–2.

Bamana peoples, Mali. Bamana iron figure. Iron, string, cowrie shells. Indiana University Art Museum, Bloomington, Indiana. Gift of Ernst Anspach.

▶ **FIGURE 12.20** Notice that the proportions of these figures are expressive rather than realistic.

Seated Man and Woman. Dogon people, Mali. Wood. 76.2 cm (30″). Photograph © 1993 by the Barnes Foundation, Merion Station, Pennsylvania.

emphasis on vertical elements (**Figure 12.19**). This can be seen in the corner pinnacles of house façades, which are made tall and straight.

The sculpture shown in **Figure 12.20,** made by the Dogon (**doh**-gahn) people of Mali, conveys a sense of harmony and balance. As images of the first man and woman described in Dogon myths of creation, this sculpture serves as an inspiration to living generations. These figures are seated on a stool with a circular support that symbolizes the link between the earth below and the spirit world above. Carved from a single piece of wood, the interlocking forms effec-

tively convey Dogon ideas regarding the interdependence of men and women and their complementary social roles.

The Kingdom of Benin

The Benin (**buh**-neen) kingdom, situated in what is now southern Nigeria, was a society of many class levels, with an oral tradition that goes back seven or eight centuries. The kingdom reached the peak of its power in the sixteenth century. Like earlier artists in nearby Ife, Benin artists excelled in creating metal sculptures using a copper alloy possessing many of the same qualities as bronze.

Among the most ambitious of the Benin castings are the high-relief sculptures that once covered the walls and pillars of the royal palace. One of these contains the figure of the *oba* (**oh**-bah), or king, flanked by two chiefs bearing shields, sword bearers, and palace attendants **(Figure 12.21)**.

Here four social ranks are depicted. The king, or *oba* is placed in the center and is the largest figure. The two chiefs are almost as large as the king. Two sword bearers, one a child, are even smaller. Three tiny figures, one supporting the king's foot and two in the top corners, represent the least powerful members of the court.

The *oba* wears a patterned wrapper, or waist cloth, a six-ringed coral necklace, and sits side-saddle on a horse. In Benin culture, horses are symbols of political power.

The Asante Kingdom

The Akan people lived in central and coastal Ghana. In the first half of the eighteenth century, these people joined together to form a powerful confederation of states that included many cultural groups. The largest of these groups was the Asante (ah-**sahn**-tee).

Gold was the measure of wealth for the Asante and their kings, who tightly controlled its use. Items fashioned from the precious metal were made to be worn by these kings as a sign of their divine authority and absolute power.

◀ **FIGURE 12.21** In Benin art the most politically powerful person is represented as the largest figure. This representation reflects the central organization of the kingdom. Less powerful individuals are smaller.

Kingdom of Benin, Edo people, Nigeria. *Mounted King with Attendants.* c. sixteenth–seventeenth century. Bronze. 49.5 × 41.9 × 11.3 cm (19½ × 16½ × 4½″). The Metropolitan Museum of Art, New York, New York. The Michael C. Rockefeller Memorial Collection. Gift of Nelson A. Rockefeller, 1965. (1978.412.309)

▲ **FIGURE 12.22** Works of art made using the lost-wax casting technique often show finely textured details. What elements of art are especially important in this work?

Akan people, Asante Kingom, Ghana. *Necklace*. Nineteenth century. Gold. 2.5 × 40 cm(1 × 15¾"). Virginia Museum of Fine Arts, Richmond, Virginia. The Adolph D. and Wilkins C. Williams Fund.

Asante necklaces, bracelets, and anklets were crafted by stringing cast-gold beads with gold nuggets, glass and stone beads, and other items. In **Figure 12.22,** a pendant in the form of a land crab is used. This necklace was probably designed for a queen mother, because the land crab was widely recognized by the Asante as a symbol for a person of this rank.

The work of goldsmiths in Kumase, the Asante capital, was regulated by the king. He allowed people to commission works of art from these highly skilled craftsmen. Items obtained through the king's court included gold ornaments, staffs, and swords.

The Asante king also controlled the use of special cloth. During the 1600s, weavers created the first *Kente* (**ken**-tee) *cloth*, a brilliantly colored and patterned fabric that became the royal cloth. Kente cloth is woven in narrow strips that are then stitched together to form large pieces with complex patterns (**Figure 12.23**). By the 1720s, Asante

► **FIGURE 12.23** Weavers of Kente cloth have invented many different patterns. These patterns often have names that are immediately recognized by members of Akan societies. What elements of art have been used to create the patterns on this cloth?

Asante people, Ghana. Man's cloth (Kente cloth). Rayon. L: 314 cm (123⅜"), W: 217 cm (85⁷⁄₁₆"). UCLA Fowler Museum of Cultural History, Los Angeles, California. Anonymous gift.

weavers were unraveling imported silk fabrics and reweaving them into cloths featuring their own unique designs. Silk cloths woven with special symbolic patterns were reserved exclusively for kings.

The Bwa People

Although wood is the most common material used to carve face masks and head-resses, African masks were constructed in different ways using a wide variety of materials. For example, the Bwa people of Burkina Faso made masks of leaves, plant fibers, porcupine quills, and feathers. Leaf masks were made at the end of the dry season, before the rains that marked the beginning of the next agricultural cycle. The Bwa people considered leaf masks the most ancient mask form and closely associated them with nature **(Figure 12.24).**

The Bwa people also produced wooden masks that were used during village ceremonies or harvest festivals. The music of flutes, drums, and gongs accompanied the dancers wearing these masks, which took different forms—animal, human, and abstract. All were painted with black, white, and red geometric patterns. Plank masks were among the most abstract of all mask forms made by the Bwa people **(Figure 12.25).**

▲ **FIGURE 12.24** African masks are generally more than just a face covering. Imagine wearing a leaf mask like this one. How would you feel?

Bwa people, Burkina Faso, village of Boni. Detail of a leaf mask. 1985.

▲ **FIGURE 12.25** Though large and cumbersome, plank masks are made of lightweight wood. To help steady the mask, the performer holds a stick between his teeth. This stick projects through rim holes at the back of the mask. How does a person wearing a plank mask see?

Bwa people, Burkina Faso, village of Pa. Plank masks entering performance area, harvest celebration.

| Activity | **Constructing a Mask** |

Applying Your Skills. What happens when you cover your face with a mask? Can you hide your identity from others? Design your own mask using thin cardboard, construction paper, paint, or other materials. In choosing your design and materials, think about what you want your mask to represent.

☑ **Check Your Understanding**

1. What beliefs are reflected in the terra-cotta and bronze sculptures of the Yoruba people?
2. What are griots?
3. How do artists of the Benin kingdom signify the importance of figures in their artworks?
4. What is Kente cloth and what is it used for?

Art of the Americas

Archaeologists believe that the first visitors to North America were groups of Asian hunters who crossed an ancient land bridge across the Bering Strait. They began to arrive in what is now Alaska between 20,000 and 40,000 years ago. Gradually these people spread out to cover all parts of North and South America. In this lesson, you will study the contributions of Native peoples of the Americas.

Art of Mesoamerica and South America

The term *pre-Columbian* refers to the time period before the arrival of Christopher Columbus in the Americas in 1492. Art historians use the term to refer to the art of the Indian civilizations of early Mexico, Central America, and South America. However, archaeologists are discovering that many of these pre-Columbian civilizations were highly sophisticated and created magnificent works of art and architecture.

Olmec Culture

Olmec (**ol**-mek) culture is often called the "mother culture" of Mexico because the artifacts found in the region are the most ancient. The Olmec civilization dates from 1200 B.C. to A.D. 500. The artifacts left by the Olmec had an influence on all the civilizations that were to follow. They carved altars, pillars, sarcophagi (sahr-**kah**-fuh-guy) (stone coffins), and statues. Among the most interesting of the Olmec creations are four huge human heads carved from volcanic rock **(Figure 12.26)**. These were discovered at La Venta, a center for religious ceremonies. These sculptures weigh up to 40 tons and stand 8 feet tall.

Notice the childlike features on this giant face. The full lips, which seem almost to be pouting, are typical of the Olmec style.

Mayan Culture

By around A.D. 800 the Mayan (**my**-uhn) empire covered the Yucatán peninsula, modern Belize, Guatemala, and Honduras. The Maya were gifted mathematicians. They had the most

▲ **Figure 12.26** This monumental sculpture depicts a simple, stylized face. The stone was quarried and transported over many miles of swampland before reaching its destination. What does this indicate about the technology of the Olmec people?

Olmec. Colossal Head. 1200 B.C.–A.D. 500. Basalt. 243.8 cm (8') high. Anthropology Museum, Veracruz, Mexico.

accurate calendar of any people in history and had developed the most advanced hieroglyphic writing in Mesoamerica. They were also great builders. The Maya erected huge temples and cities with tools of wood, stone, and bone. In the late 1800s, scientists discovered an ancient city in northern Guatemala. This Mayan city, Tikal (tih-**kahl**), is known to have covered an area of 50 square miles. The city is thought to have been home to some 55,000 people **(Figure 12.27)**.

The surviving works of Mayan civilization range from the smallest objects to great temples covered with relief carvings. Among the smallest artworks of the Maya are many beautifully designed clay figures only a few inches high. However, most of the Mayan sculpture that has survived consists of relief carvings on buildings and monuments. In the early stages of the Mayan civilization, these carvings were mostly simple and realistic. In some later temples, a more complex, geometric style came to be the rule.

Aztec Culture

The largest of the cultures of ancient Mexico and Central America was the Aztec. This civilization emerged sometime between A.D 1200 and 1325. The Aztecs were a warlike people. Like other pre-Columbian peoples, they were very religious. When their god told them to leave their comfortable homeland and settle where they saw an eagle perched on a cactus, they obeyed. There, they built a magnificent city, which they called Tenochititlán (tay-noch-tee-**tlahn**). A collection of tiny islands, the Aztec city was connected by a network of canals. In the fifteenth century, the Aztecs embarked on an aggressive military campaign to force other groups in Mexico to pay them tribute. They reached the height of their power and domination less than a century before the arrival of the Spanish. By the time Spanish conquerors arrived in 1519, their island city covered over 25 square miles. Today we know the city, which is no longer surrounded by water, as Mexico City.

The Aztecs adopted many of the ways of making art used by the people they conquered. They created a type of painted book called a codex. Such painted books told the stories of mythological or historical events. Like Mayan art, Aztec art was greatly influenced by religion. The Aztecs also built temples

◄ **FIGURE 12.27** The Mayan city Tikal included temples and other stone and stucco structures. The pyramids here are 230 feet high.

Maya. Great Plaza of Tikal, general view. A.D. 150–700. Tikal, Guatemala. Vanni/Art Resource, New York.

◄ **FIGURE 12.28** Machu-Picchu was built on a mountainside to discourage would-be attackers The city has withstood five centuries of earthquakes.

Machu-Picchu, Peru.

and shrines, some carved directly into the mountains. Highly stylized and elaborately ornamented sculptures depicted gods and religious symbols in bold, dramatic style.

Inca Empire

The Inca civilization flourished between the thirteenth and fifteenth centuries, and their empire stretched more than 2,500 miles from north to south. It included present-day Peru plus parts of Ecuador, Chile, Argentina, and Bolivia. In acquiring such a large territory, the Inca Empire absorbed many cultural and religious influences from neighboring groups and from civilizations that had flourished before it. Although governing such an immense territory required a vast administration and bureaucracy, the Incas managed to govern without the benefit of a written language. They made calculations and kept records using pieces of knotted string of different colors, called *quipu* (**kee**-poo). The Incas' ability with numbers is reflected in their art. Inca artifacts were made with great mathematical precision.

The Incas were masters of shaping and fitting stone. They were also highly skilled urban planners. Proof of both talents can be found in the walled city of Machu-Picchu (**mahch**-oo **peek**-choo) (**Figure 12.28**). The stones of its buildings were so carefully matched that a knife blade cannot be slipped between any two.

Native American Art

When Christopher Columbus reached North America in 1492, he thought his ship had landed on the east coast of India. He referred to the natives he found living there as Indians. Today these first settlers are called Native Americans.

Some groups became hunters while others turned to growing crops as a way to survive. Artifacts found in these regions show that all of these people created art of some kind. These works have given us insight into the cultures of these peoples. Native American art and traditions are still being practiced today by these cultural groups.

The Arctic Region

The Inuit (**in**-yuh-wuht) people inhabited present-day Canada and Alaska from the earliest times. Although they are often called Eskimos, they refer to themselves as the Inuit.

Inuit society is loosely organized into family groups that rely on hunting and fishing for survival. The images created by Inuit artists reveal the importance attached to the animals they relied on for food—seal, walrus, fish, whale, and caribou. Other animals such as the fox, wolf, and bear were also represented in their art. The human figure was shown in the masks and dolls that they created.

Figures are also found on the engravings done on walrus ivory. In these engravings, Inuit artists used a kind of pictorial writing that described various activities and events associated with everyday life. In one such engraving on an ivory pipestem, a series of lively drawings record the activities associated with the daily quest for food. Since the surface of this pipestem is less than one inch wide, the engraving takes the form of tiny, decorative circles and miniature figures. Despite their small size, the artist still managed to present an easy-to-read account of the hunt. To accent the engraved lines used in works like this, artists filled them in with color or made them dark with soot.

Frequently, Inuit art was created to serve the religious needs of the people. The mask representing a moon goddess in **Figure 12.29** is an example. An Inuit shaman, or medicine man, wore such a mask during ceremonial dances. While dancing, he would go into a trance and act as a messenger between the world of the living and the mysterious world of spirits.

The Northwest Coast Region

The Northwest Coast Region refers to an area rich in natural resources that runs from southern Alaska to northern California. Native cultural groups in this region, including the Haida (**high**-duh), Tlingit, and the Kwakiutl (kwa-kee-**yoo**-tul), developed a complex culture in which art played a prominent role.

Like other people, the Kwakiutl held annual rituals to initiate new members, reinforce the status of old members, and

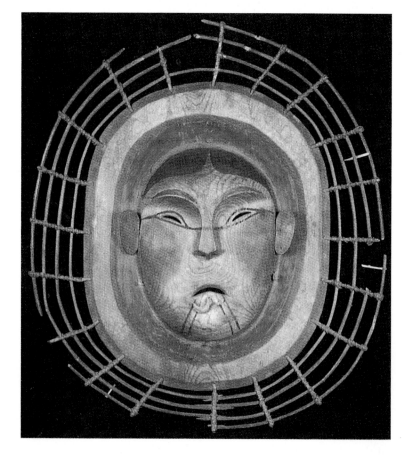

◄ **FIGURE 12.29** A mask of this kind was worn only by a shaman during ceremonial dances. How do you think the purpose of this mask is reflected in its design? What feelings do you think the mask evoked in viewers?

Inuit. Mask of Moon Goddess. Lower Yukon or Northwest Bering Sea. Before 1900. 63.5 cm (25¼") high. Hearst Museum of Anthropology, The University of California at Berkeley, Berkeley, California.

demonstrate their magical powers. Ceremonial masks and dramatic costumes were created for these rituals. Look at the Secret Society Mask pictured in Figure 10.27 on page 273. It is composed of several hinged pieces that moved. This movement was intended to add surprise and drama to the ritual. Often after a Kwakiutl ceremony, or to celebrate another important event, people gathered to enjoy a *potlatch*. This event enabled the members of one clan to honor those of another, while adding to their own prestige.

Native Americans of the Northwest Coast lived in large family groups. Each family group traced descent from a mythological animal or human-animal, from which they took their name. In order to symbolize their association with this mythic ancestor, they carved totem poles. **Totem poles** are *tall posts carved and painted with a series of animal symbols associated with a particular family or clan* **(Figure 12.30).**

The Southwest Region

The Native American groups of the southwestern United States include the Pueblo (**pweb**-loh) and the Navajo (**nav**-uh-hoh). Early Spanish explorers used the term *pueblo*, meaning village, to describe groups of people living in large, highly organized settlements. Ancient Pueblo dwellings were built with adobe, or sun-dried clay, walls.

The Pueblo were especially skillful in creating painted pottery. Each community developed its own distinctive shapes and painted designs. In the Rio Grande Valley of New Mexico, for example, Pueblo potters used black outlines and geometric shapes to create bold designs over a cream-colored base **(Figure 12.31).**

◀ **FIGURE 12.30** Totem poles are similar to a European family's coat of arms and were erected in front of a dwelling as a means of identification and a sign of prestige.

Haida totem pole. Prince of Wales Island. c. 1870. Originally 16.2 m (53') high. Taylor Museum of the Colorado Springs Fine Arts Center, Colorado Springs, Colorado.

▼ **FIGURE 12.31** The materials and techniques used in this water jar identify it as a Pueblo work. What elements of art can you identify in this design?

Water jar. Santo Domingo Pueblo, New Mexico. 1910. Ceramic. 24.13 cm (9½") high × 24.45 cm (9⅝") diameter. Denver Art Museum, Denver, Colorado.

The Navajo, another Southwestern cultural group, learned the art of weaving from the Pueblo. Male Pueblo weavers taught the Navajo weavers, who were women, to make cloth with looms at the beginning of the eighteenth century. As Spanish and Mexican settlers moved into the Southwest, they introduced new designs and patterns which the Navajo adopted. By the first half of the nineteenth century, the Navajo were using European dyes and Spanish wool to create weavings that matched the work produced by the best looms in Europe. A blanket once owned by the Civil War general Philip Sheridan **(Figure 12.32)** exhibits many of the qualities associated with the finest Navajo weavings. These include the closeness of the weave, rich, vibrant colors, and bold design.

Great Plains Region

The Native Americans of the Great Plains followed the huge herds of bison that roamed the broad grasslands of central North America. The different cultural groups of the Plains—including Blackfeet, Crow, Cheyenne (shy-**ann**), and Sioux (soo)—were highly skilled in the preparation of skins used for clothing, footwear, shields, and various kinds of containers. These were then painted or embroidered with porcupine quills and, later, glass beads.

Because they were nomadic hunters, they created the *tepee* (**tee**-pee). This was a portable shelter made of buffalo hide stretched over poles that were lashed together in an upright position. The hides were covered with designs symbolizing the forces of nature and telling stories of heroic events. At its base, a tepee could range anywhere from 12 to 30 feet in diameter. A large tepee contained about as much space as a standard living room of today.

These artisans also created ceremonial headdresses for chieftains, which were worn during ritual dances. The elaborate headdress shown in **Figure 12.33** was created with natural materials found in the surrounding environment.

◀ **FIGURE 12.32** This saddle blanket, created for everyday use, is now on display in a museum. How are the principles of harmony and variety used in this design? How is rhythm suggested?

Saddle blanket. Navajo weaving. c. 1890. Wool. 129.5 × 83.8 cm (51 × 33″). Denver Art Museum, Denver, Colorado.

◀ **Figure 12.33** This feather bonnet was created for a ceremonial dance. Does the use of natural materials seem to fit with the function?

Northwestern Plains people. *Feather Bonnet.* c. 1890. Rooster hackles, wood rods, porcupine hair, ermine skins, horsehair, buckskin, glass beads. 84 × 68.6 cm (33 × 27″). Buffalo Bill Historical Center, Cody, Wyoming. Chandler-Pohrt Collection.

Woodlands Region

The Woodlands made up the largest cultural group of Native Americans east of the Mississippi River. The Woodlands people combined hunting and gathering with simple farming. The Iroquois (**ear-uh-kwoi**), made up of six different Woodlands groups, combined to form the highly organized Iroquois nation.

Expert wood carvers, the Iroquois created wooden masks that were usually painted and decorated with horse hair. The best known masks were created for a society of healers known as the False Faces because of the masks they wore. These False Face masks were thought to be sacred and represented the spirits who gave healers the magic they needed to treat illnesses. Because they were considered to be so powerful, these masks were hidden away when not in use so they would not cause accidental injuries. The masks were considered sacred and were not intended to be seen by nonbelievers.

Activity | **Sketching an Event**

Applying Your Skills. Native Americans of the Great Plains painted tales of their battles on skins. Look through a newspaper or magazine for coverage of an important event in your city or in the world. On a sheet of paper, sketch the story behind the event.

☑ Check Your Understanding

1. What does the term pre-Columbian refer to?
2. Which culture created huge heads carved from volcanic rock?
3. Which culture created the walled city of Machu–Picchu?
4. What were totem poles used for?

ART CRITICISM IN ACTION

▲ FIGURE 12.34

Unknown. *Khamseh: Bahram Gur and the Chinese Princess in the Sandalwood Pavilion on Thursday.* 1524–25. Colors and gilt on paper. 32.4 × 22.2 cm (12¾ × 8¾"). The Metropolitan Museum of Art, New York, New York. Gift of Alexander Smith Cochran, 1913. (13.228.7)

DESCRIBE **What do you see?**
Read the credit line for information about the size and media. List all of the structures, objects, and people you see.

- Start with the architecture. Working from the bottom of the painting up to the top, list all of the structures you find.
- Describe the people, their clothing, and then tell where they are located in the work.

2 **ANALYZE** **How is this work organized?**
During this step, you will study the elements and principles of art to discover clues that will help you discover the message the artist is trying to send. Remember not to make guesses during this step.

- How is this artist's use of space different from that you have found in Western art? Is there any negative space?
- What rhythms do you find? Describe them. What kind of balance has been used to organize this work?
- Are the proportions of the figures accurate?
- Can you find an area of the work that is a focal point? What has the artist done to unify this work?

3 **INTERPRET** **What is the artist trying to communicate?**
Now you will decipher the message the artist is sending to you. Remember to combine the clues you have collected with your personal experiences to form your own interpretation of this work.

- Are all of the people in this work equal in importance? Explain.
- What do you think is happening in this scene? Explain.
- Based on your ideas, give the work a new title.

4 **JUDGE** **What do you think of the work?**
Decide if this is a successful work of art. You may make a personal opinion, but it is also important to make an objective judgment based on aesthetic theories.

- Do you think the artist has used the elements and principles of art effectively?
- Do you think this is a successful work of art? Use one or more of the three aesthetic theories to defend your decision.

Persia is the term often used to refer to the region now known as Iran. The artists who painted the pictures that accompanied ancient Persian books were highly valued, but the most important kind of artist in Persia was the calligrapher. A calligrapher is a person who is skilled in creating the letterforms that make up the alphabet and words of a particular language. Even kings could not resist learning the art themselves, since good calligraphic skills were considered proof of royal virtue.

Even though artists were held in high esteem in Persia, they were usually anonymous until around the late fifteenth and early sixteenth centuries. At that time, the royalty and wealthy merchants who could afford to buy ornamented books became aware of the individual styles and personalities of different artists. Historians began to include short biographies of the artists in their historical records.

The Meaning of Stone Circles

▲ **FIGURE 12.35**

Stonehenge. Wiltshire, Great Britain. c. 2000 B.C.

The English once believed that Merlin, legendary magician of King Arthur's time, created Stonehenge **(Figure 12.35).** Later, scholars thought the structure was the remains of a Druid temple built around the time of the Roman invasion of Britain in A.D. 43. We now know that Stonehenge is even older, and that it was built in three stages by different peoples.

The first stage was built by the Neolithic people of the late Stone Age (c. 2800 B.C.). The second stage was built several centuries later by people of the Bronze age. They erected a double circle of 38 bluestones each. The bluestones (named for their bluish color) came from mountains 135 miles away. The remains of the third stage, built around 2100 B.C., are what we see today. These megaliths, called sarsens, came from about 20 miles away and weigh as much as 56 tons.

What does Stonehenge mean? It may have been a temple for worshiping a sun god or an observatory for studying the movements of the sun and moon. A line that runs through the center aligns with a point on the horizon where the sun rises on the day of the summer solstice (June 21). It is also possible that the circles and holes were used as a calendar. Just how this huge structure was built without the benefit of modern tools is uncertain, however, and its exact meaning remains a mystery.

Making the Connection

1. How do you think the builders of Stonehenge were able to carve and transport stones of such magnitude?

2. Why do you think prehistoric people were interested in seasons and the movements of the sun and moon?

Building Vocabulary

On a separate sheet of paper, write the term that best matches each definition given below.

1. Large monuments created from huge stone slabs.
2. The Sumerian writing system made up of wedge-shaped characters.
3. Stepped mountains made of brick-covered earth.
4. Egyptian rulers who were worshiped as gods and held complete authority over the kingdom.
5. A period of time during which a single family provided a succession of rulers.
6. Beehive-shaped domed places of worship.
7. A tower several stories high with roofs curving slightly upward at the edges.
8. Muslim places of worship.
9. Tall posts carved and painted with a series of animal symbols associated with a particular family or clan.

Reviewing Art Facts

Answer the following questions using complete sentences.

1. During what time period did people begin to build structures of stone?
2. Describe the rules that Egyptian artists were required to follow when painting or sculpting a relief figure.
3. What influenced the style of Chinese "picture painting"?
4. What art technique did Japanese artists perfect to meet the demand for artworks?
5. Describe the differences between the art used in Islamic mosques and the art used in Islamic book illustration.
6. Which culture is often called the "mother culture" and why?
7. What do the images created by Inuit artists reveal about what they valued as a culture?

Thinking Critically about Art

1. **Explain.** For what reasons did people of African and Native American cultures create art? How does this differ from more recent European or American art that you find in a museum?
2. **Compare and contrast.** You can look at visual images from the past to learn what the people who lived before us were like. Compare two of the ceremonial masks in this chapter and explain how they are similar and how they are different.

ART SOURCE Explore ancient folk traditions of music and dance in Asia on page 424 of the Performing Arts Handbook.

*inter*NET CONNECTION Travel through an illustrated art time line that will take you from the beginning of art history up to the twentieth century. Begin your journey on the Glencoe Fine Arts Site at **www.glencoe.com/sec/art**.

▲ **FIGURE 13.1** Cassatt produced this print, one of a series of ten color aquatint prints, in 1891. When she created the series, the artist said she intended to imitate the Japanese printmaking methods. She combined her domestic themes with the decorative quality and grace of a Japanese print. To simulate the look of a color woodblock, she used several etching plates for each print.

Mary Cassatt. *The Letter.* 1891. Drypoint, soft-ground etching and aquatint; printed in color. Third state. From a series of ten. 4.2 × 3 m (13⅝ × 9″). The Metropolitan Museum of Art, New York, New York. Gift of Paul J. Sachs, 1916. (16.2.9)

CHAPTER 13

Western Traditions in Art

This chapter traces the development of Western art. It is called *Western* art because the culture of Western Europe produced it. Later, Western culture—and along with it, Western art—crossed the Atlantic with Europeans who settled in the Americas.

As you read this chapter you will see that developments and changes in Western art were often built on previous works. The print in **Figure 13.1** marks a major turning point in Western art. It is an example of Western art clearly influenced by outside sources. *The Letter* was created at the end of the nineteenth century by Mary Cassatt, the first famous American woman to join the French Impressionists. At this time, the United States and Europe began importing goods from Japan. French collectors acquired Japanese art objects. In 1890, a collection of Japanese woodblock prints was exhibited in Paris. Many Impressionists saw the exhibition and took away new ideas. Cassatt herself was impressed by the Japanese prints. Notice how she has flattened space, and used rhythmic patterns and contours in the manner of the Japanese printmakers (see Figure 12.15 on page 330).

OBJECTIVES

After completing this chapter, you will be able to:
- Identify how historical and cultural events shape art styles.
- Name the major Western art styles and movements.
- Identify major modern artists such as Monet, Cézanne, and Picasso.
- Briefly discuss modern art movements.

WORDS TO KNOW

Byzantine art
Romanesque
Gothic
Renaissance
Mannerism
Baroque
Rococo
Neoclassicism
Romanticism
Impressionism
Post-Impressionism
Expressionism
Cubism
Surrealism
Regionalists
Abstract Expressionism
Minimalism
Super-Realism
Post-Modernism

Developing Your
PORTFOLIO

Take an opinion poll about modern art. Ask family members and friends what they think about modern art and why they feel the way they do. Show them some artworks from this chapter to help them understand what you are referring to. When you have interviewed five to ten people, compile the results of your poll. Write a few paragraphs describing people's responses. Are the responses mostly positive or negative? Do you agree with the responses? Why or why not? Include your poll results and summary in your portfolio.

The Beginnings of Western Art Traditions

Greece was the birthplace of Western civilization. The influence of ancient Greek culture can still be seen today. Almost every city in our country has at least one building with features that resemble the architecture of the classic Greek temple.

The Art of Greece and Rome

The Greeks built temples in honor of their gods. The most outstanding example is the Parthenon in Athens **(Figure 13.2)**. The columns slant slightly inward to prevent a top-heavy look. Inside was a huge statue of the goddess Athena created of ivory and gold. The relief sculpture that covered the area under the roof is missing. Many of the missing pieces are in foreign museums. The Greeks worked to create a logical, harmonious world. They sought perfect proportions in buildings, sculpture, and music by following the guidelines of mathematical proportion. Their artists produced statues that represented the Greek ideal of the perfect body. According to one story, athletes used these

▲ **FIGURE 13.2** Although partially destroyed, you can see that the Parthenon was designed to look harmonious. Architects used mathematical formulas to make the temple look balanced and beautiful.

Parthenon. Temple of Athena. Fifth century B.C. Acropolis, Athens, Greece.

statues, like the one shown in **Figure 13.3,** as inspiration for building up their own muscle structure.

When they were new, Greek temples and statues were not the pure white we see today. The Greeks loved color, and they painted their buildings and sculptures various hues. Time has since worn the paint away.

Even though the Romans conquered Greece in 146 B.C., they did not conquer Greek culture. Instead, the Romans adopted Greek culture, modifying it to suit their own needs. Greek sculptors, painters, architects, philosophers, and teachers exerted a great influence on the culture of the Roman Empire.

Earlier, the Romans had absorbed the culture of the Etruscans in Italy. Two outstanding Etruscan developments that the Romans adopted included a system of drainage and an improved use of the arch in the construction of buildings. What we call Roman art is a blend of the ideal Greek and the practical Etruscan arts.

The Romans added much to what they adopted. They used the arch and concrete to build large-scale structures, including huge vaulted and domed inner spaces. Engineers constructed a network of roads to connect all parts of the Roman Empire. The Romans also developed beautiful interior decoration and created realistic rather than idealized portrait sculpture **(Figure 13.4).**

◀ **FIGURE 13.3** Look at the proportions and detail of this athlete. Notice the idealized muscles and facial features. What does such a sculpture reveal about Greek culture? What features of the human body were admired by them and important to them?

Myron. *Discobolus (Discus Thrower).* c. 450 B.C. Roman copy of a bronze original. Life-size. Italy. Palazzo Vecchio, Florence, Italy.

◀ **FIGURE 13.4** Unlike the Greeks, the Romans did not seek to depict idealized human forms. Notice the attention to detail on this sculpture. The sculpture seems quite lifelike. How would you characterize the man depicted?

Graeco-Roman, from neighborhood of Cumae. *Man of the Republic.* Late first century B.C. Terra–cotta. 35.7 cm (14") high, face 18 cm (7") long. Courtesy of the Museum of Fine Arts, Boston, Massachusetts. Purchased by contribution. Purchase of E. P. Warren Collection.

Activity — Analyzing Architecture

Applying Your Skills. Find a building in your community in the Greek or Roman style. Write the location, the culture from which the style was adopted, the purpose of the building, and anything else you can find out about it. Make a sketch of the building in your sketchbook. Name the ancient culture and describe the features that match the style of the ancient culture.

▲ **FIGURE 13.6** This church was built in the Romanesque style. Identify the rounded arches.

Church of San Clemente. Tahull, Spain.

The Art of the Middle Ages

The Middle Ages began with the conquest of Rome in A.D. 476 by invaders from the north and lasted about 1,000 years. This period of time was also called the *Age of Faith* because the Christian religion exerted such an important influence. Monasteries, or buildings that housed people who had made religious vows, grew in number. The monks who lived in them created finely decorated religious manuscripts. Churches grew in size, number, and political importance, reflecting the prominence of the Christian religion during this period.

Byzantine Art

In the eastern part of the former Roman Empire, a new style of art developed during the Middle Ages. This style thrived around the city of Constantinople (now Istanbul, Turkey) and spread to towns such as Ravenna in Italy. Constantinople, built on the site of the ancient city of Byzantium, served as the capital of the Byzantine Empire. **Byzantine art** featured *very rich colors and heavily outlined figures that appeared flat and stiff* **(Figure 13.5).** Constantinople was close to Asia as well as to Greece, and because of this proximity, Greek, Roman, and Asian art and culture all influenced Byzantine artists.

Romanesque Style

At the beginning of the Middle Ages, many new churches were built in Western Europe in a style of architecture similar to Roman buildings. It was called **Romanesque** and *featured buildings of massive size; solid, heavy walls; wide use of the rounded Roman arch; and many sculptural decorations.*

Churches, castles, and monasteries were all built in the Romanesque style **(Figure 13.6).** Architects building

Romanesque structures could not include many windows because they weakened the structure of the walls and could cause the heavy stone roofs to collapse. As a result, Romanesque buildings were dark and somber inside.

Gothic Style

In Europe in the twelfth century, increasing numbers of people moved from the countryside into towns. Workers such as stone carvers and carpenters organized into craft guilds (or unions), and apprentices learned their crafts from the masters in these guilds. A wealthy new merchant class, pride in their growing cities, and religious faith led to the building of huge cathedrals. Two developments in architecture—the pointed arch and the flying buttress—brought about changes in how buildings were built, and how they looked. The flying buttress removed the weight of the roof from the walls, allowing for higher walls and many more windows than had been possible in Romanesque structures. This new style, called **Gothic,** *featured churches that seemed to soar upward, used pointed arches, and stained-glass windows,* like the cathedral shown in **Figure 13.7.**

By using stained-glass windows, Gothic builders changed the light that entered the churches into rich, glowing color. Gothic sculptors and painters sought more realistic ways to depict subject matter. Religious scenes were painted on church altarpieces with egg tempera paint and gold leaf.

▲ **Figure 13.7** This cathedral was built in the Gothic style. Notice the pointed arches and stained-glass windows. Compare this to Figure 13.6. Describe the similarities and differences between the two churches.

Reims Cathedral. Reims, France. 1225–99.

Check Your Understanding

1. Name the characteristics of Byzantine art.
2. Describe Romanesque buildings.
3. What two developments of the Gothic period allowed builders to place many openings in walls and build churches taller?

Activity | The Gothic Style

Applying Your Skills. Research cathedrals built in the Gothic style. List the names of three of the cathedrals in your sketchbook and tell where and when they were built.

The Beginnings of Modern Art Traditions

At the beginning of the fifteenth century, the Middle Ages began drawing to a close. The invention of the printing press and the European exploration of the Americas and the Pacific Ocean expanded knowledge and contributed to a sense of the dawn of a new era. As the culture changed, so did the art. During the Middle Ages, most art had been made for religious reasons. Even artworks made for wealthy people, such as illuminated books, most often depicted religious subject matter. During the next period, artists continued to paint religious subjects but also expanded their repertoire to include mythological and secular themes.

Renaissance

Renaissance (**ren**-uh-sahns) is a French word for "rebirth." **Renaissance** is *the name given to the period at the end of the Middle Ages when artists, writers, and philosophers were "re-awakened" to art forms and ideas from ancient Greece and Rome*. The Renaissance did not happen all at once, nor did it spread to all parts of Europe at the same time. Rather, it dawned gradually, first in Italy, then spreading through northern Europe, finally reaching France and England. Along with a new appreciation of classical antiquity, social structures also changed. Kings and popes, who had always been extremely powerful, had competition from bankers and merchants, whose wealth also equaled political power. People challenged the authority of the Catholic Church.

Italian Renaissance

An architect named Filippo Brunelleschi (fee-**leep**-poh brew-nell-**less**-key) developed linear perspective, a graphic system that creates the illusion of depth and volume on a flat surface. Linear perspective provided a set of guidelines that allowed artists to depict figures and objects in space on a two-dimensional surface. This system made the placement of objects, and the depiction of their volume or form, measurable and exact, which gave an exciting illusion of reality to works of art. Italian artists sought to create realistic and life-like works. They studied the classical art of Greece and Rome and meticulously observed and recorded the world around them.

Michelangelo Buonarroti (my-kel-**an**-jay-loh bwon-nar-**roh**-tee), an Italian artist, was a master of poetry, painting, sculpture, and architecture. However, he always thought of himself primarily as a sculptor. One of his most famous works is **Figure 13.8,** *Pietà*. A pietà is a work showing Mary mourning over the body of Christ.

Like Michelangelo, Leonardo da Vinci (lay-oh-**nar**-doh da **vin**-chee) studied and mastered a broad range of disciplines, including mathematics, physics, geography, and painting. Although he had many ideas, Leonardo often left paintings and sculptures unfinished because he was not happy with them. One of his famous paintings is Figure 13.41 on page 384.

Italian, 1475–1564

Marcello Venusti. *Portrait of Michelangelo.* Casa Buonarroti, Florence, Italy.

Born in a small village near Florence, Italy in 1475, Michelangelo was apprenticed to a painter when he was 13. While still a teen, he joined the Medici household, a powerful ruling family. There he met many prominent Florentine citizens, artists, and philosophers. In 1494, the Medici family was overthrown and Michelangelo was forced to flee. He traveled to Rome, where many classical statues and buildings were being discovered. He eagerly studied their formal qualities and proportions.

Michelangelo created many masterpieces, mostly on a grand scale. When Pope Julius II asked Michelangelo to design a tomb for him, Michelangelo devised a design calling for 40 sculptures, only a few of which were completed before Pope Julius decided not to spend any more money. Instead, he asked Michelangelo to paint the ceiling of the Sistine Chapel in the Vatican. The chapel had a rounded ceiling high above the floor. Michelangelo was insulted at being asked to paint a ceiling, which was not considered a very prestigious assignment. He also did not know how he could paint a ceiling so far off the ground. However, the pope insisted and Michelangelo gave in. He built a high scaffold and lay on it to paint the wet ceiling plaster. He created nine different sections on the ceiling, each telling a Biblical story, from the creation of the world to the flood.

▶ **FIGURE 13.8** Notice the proportions of the two figures in this sculpture. Mary is much larger than her son. Michelangelo did this on purpose so that she would not seem overwhelmed by her son's body. What feeling does this proportion convey?

Michelangelo. *Pietà.* c. 1500. Marble. 174 cm (5′8½″) high; base 195 cm (6′4⅝″) high. Vatican, St. Peter's Basilica, Rome, Italy.

Women first achieved fame as artists during the Renaissance. They had to overcome political, social, and economic obstacles to achieve artistic success. One of them, Sofonisba Anguissola, was the first Italian woman to gain wide recognition as an artist. The oldest of seven children, her father encouraged her to pursue art and allowed her to study with local artists. He even wrote to Michelangelo to tell him about Sofonisba's skills. Michelangelo responded with kind words of encouragement and a drawing for her to copy and study as part of her training. Much of her early work consisted of portraits of her family and herself **(Figure 13.9).** She also painted religious subjects. As her fame spread, the king of Spain asked her to join his court, where she painted many portraits and enjoyed respect and admiration as a court painter.

Northern Renaissance

The changes that took place during the Renaissance in Italy later filtered into northern European countries such as Flanders (a region in Belgium) and Germany. Flemish artists (those from Flanders) began to use oil rather than egg to bind their pigments. This new medium allowed artists more versatility than ever before.

Northern artists had little interest in recreating the classical art of Greece and Rome. They placed greater emphasis on depicting the accurate and precise details such as an intricate design on clothing or the details of the environment. Symbolism became even more important. Images in art conveyed more than just one meaning.

The art of Jan van Eyck (**yahn** van **eyek**) and his successors made Flanders the center of the Northern art world.

▲ **FIGURE 13.9** Notice the dramatic use of color in this painting. Observe the detail of the dresses the sisters are wearing. What does this tell you about them and their social status?

Sofonisba Anguissola. *A game of chess, involving the painter's three sisters and a servant.* 1555. Oil on canvas. 72 × 97 cm (28½ × 38⅕"). Muzeum Narodove, Poznan, Poland.

Like other Northern painters, Jan van Eyck emphasized precision and accuracy. Look at Figure 9.8 on page 231. Notice the attention to detail, such as the lace on the woman's headcovering and the carpet under the bed. The picture includes many symbols. For example, the wedding couple is shown barefoot to symbolize that they are standing on holy ground. The burning candle indicates the presence of God. The little dog stands for loyalty.

The work of Jan van Eyck influenced another important Northern Renaissance painter, Rogier van der Weyden (roh-**jehr** van duhr **vy**-duhn). Like van Eyck, he paid meticulous attention to detail. Look at **Figure 13.10.** Notice the pins in her veil and the intricate design on her belt buckle.

As is often the case, changes in society brought about changes in artistic expression. In the mid-sixteenth century, religious reformers challenged the authority of the Catholic Church, causing conflict and turmoil. Great artists like Leonardo and Michelangelo had died, leaving behind a vacuum in artistic inspiration

▲ **FIGURE 13.11** Notice the dreamlike quality of the background. It causes the viewer to focus on the two figures in the foreground. What appears to be happening in this painting?

El Greco. *Saint Martin and the Beggar*. 1597/1599. Oil on canvas; wooden strip added at bottom. 193.5 × 103 cm (76⅛ × 40½"). National Gallery of Art, Washington, D.C. © 1998 Board of Trustees. Widener Collection.

and innovation. Artists began showing the tension and struggle they experienced during this period of crisis in their art. The result was an artistic style called **Mannerism,** which *featured highly emotional scenes and elongated figures.* The style was developed by certain artists to be a deliberate shift away from the ideals and perfect forms of Renaissance art. If Renaissance artists preferred balance and harmony, Mannerists preferred imbalance and dynamic movement.

One of the most famous Mannerist artists was El Greco (el **greh**-koh). His name means "the Greek," for his birthplace on the Greek island of Crete. Because of his unusual style, El Greco found it difficult to secure patronage. In 1577, he traveled to Toledo, Spain, where he spent the rest of his life. There he gained a reputation as a superior artist. **Figure 13.11** shows the intense emotionalism and strong sense of movement characteristic of El Greco's work.

The Seventeenth and Eighteenth Centuries

A reform movement known as the Protestant Reformation, which began in the sixteenth century, caused many people to depart from the teachings of the Catholic Church. In order to gain them back, the Church started its own reform movement, known as the Counter-Reformation, in the seventeenth century. Art was an important part of this movement. Catholic Church authorities called upon artists to create works that would inspire renewed religious feeling in viewers.

Baroque Art in Italy

A new art style developed as a result of the Counter-Reformation. **Baroque** (buh-**rohk**) is *an art style emphasizing dramatic lighting, movement, and emotional* *intensity.* The leader of the Baroque style in Italy, a young painter named Michelangelo Merisi da Caravaggio (my-kel-**an**-jay-loh mah-**ree**-see-dah kar-uh-**vah**-jyoh), depicted light in a daring new way. *The Conversion of St. Paul* **(Figure 13.12),** shows only St. Paul, his horse, and an attendant. The figures fill the canvas. Nothing distracts the viewer from the scene. Although the religious meaning may not be apparent at first, Caravaggio's mysterious use of light dramatizes the scene. This dramatic use of light and dark is also evident in the art of one of his followers, Artemisia Gentileschi (see Figure 5.17 on page 111).

Dutch Art

Dutch Protestants did not want religious paintings and sculptures in their churches. Dutch artists had to turn to ordinary people and places for their subject matter. The demand for landscapes, portraits, and still lifes grew as wealthy merchants surrounded themselves with art that depicted scenes of everyday life.

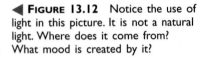
◀ **FIGURE 13.12** Notice the use of light in this picture. It is not a natural light. Where does it come from? What mood is created by it?

Caravaggio. *The Conversion of St. Paul.* c. 1601. Oil on canvas. Approx. 228.6 × 175.3 cm (90 × 69"). Santa Maria del Popolo, Rome, Italy.

The greatest Dutch artist of this period was Rembrandt van Rijn (**rem**-brant van **reyn**). Like other Dutch artists, he painted ordinary people and everyday events. He was somewhat unusual, however, in that he also continued painting religious subjects as well. He was especially interested in the psychological character of the people he portrayed, suggested by his use of light and shadow to create atmosphere. *The Night Watch* (Figure 11.29, page 314), one of Rembrandt's best-known paintings,

shows this use of light. Some figures are clearly illuminated while others remain in shadow, creating a dramatic effect.

Jan Vermeer (yahn vair-**meer**) is another important Dutch artist. For several hundred years, his artwork remained unappreciated, but in the second half of the nineteenth century critics recognized his artistic genius. Vermeer is best known for his use of light and texture. **Figure 13.13** shows his talent in using dark and light values to express a feeling or evoke a mood.

◀ **FIGURE 13.13**
This portrait depicts an ordinary woman engaged in an everyday activity. How does Vermeer add interest to the painting? What mood or feeling does it evoke?

Jan Vermeer. *Girl with the Red Hat.* c. 1665/1666. Oil on panel. 23.1 × 18.1 cm (9⅛ × 7⅛″). National Gallery of Art, Washington, D.C. © 1998 Board of Trustees. Andrew W. Mellon Collection.

Rococo Style

As the seventeenth century ended and the eighteenth century began, France emerged as the strongest, wealthiest nation in Europe. Paris, its capital, became the center of the art world. When pleasure-loving King Louis XIV assumed the throne, a new style of art influenced by his lighthearted personality arose. Called **Rococo** (ruh-**koh**-koh), it is *an art style that expresses free, graceful movement, playful use of line, and delicate colors.*

One of the first painters working in the Rococo style was Antoine Watteau (an-**twahn** wah-**toh**). His paintings depict an idealized world filled with happy, carefree people **(Figure 13.14).**

In England, artists modified the Rococo style. They used its delicate, light-washed techniques but rejected artificial subject matter. One of the most famous English painters of this period, Thomas Gainsborough (**gainz**-bur-roh), began his artistic career as a landscape painter but later became a famous portrait painter for members of English high society.

▲ **FIGURE 13.14** Describe the dress and manners of these people. Notice how the colors and shapes blend together for a dreamlike, misty quality. Is this a happy occasion? How do you know?

Antoine Watteau. *Embarkment for Cythera.* 1717–19. Oil on canvas. 1.3 × 1.9 m (4′ 3″ × 6′ 4½″). The Louvre, Paris, France.

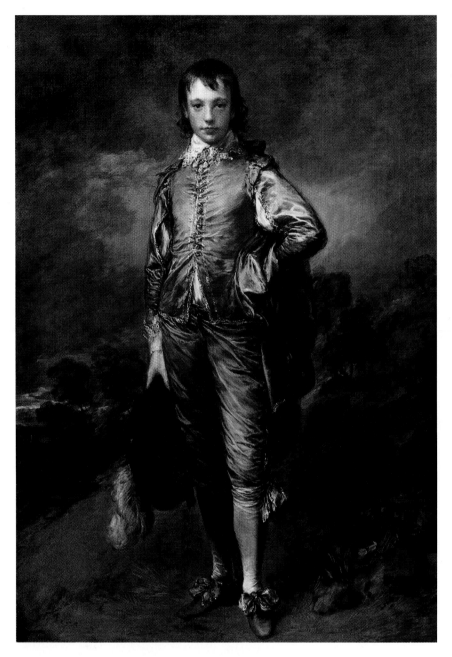

◀ **FIGURE 13.15** The most striking element of this painting is the use of color. What does the background depict? Do you think it is important to the painting?

Thomas Gainsborough. *The Blue Boy*. c. 1770. Oil on canvas. 177.8 × 121.9 cm (70 × 48″). The Huntington Library, Art Collections, and Botanical Gardens, San Marino, California.

Figure 13.15, Gainsborough's most famous painting, resulted from a professional rivalry. A rival painter gave a lecture at the Royal Academy of Art and stated that blue, a cool color, should always be used in the background, never in the main part of a picture. When Gainsborough heard this, he considered it a challenge and painted a portrait of a boy dressed entirely in blue.

In Spain, Francisco Goya (frahn-**seese**-koh **goh**-ya) transformed Rococo art. Early in his career, Goya achieved considerable fame and fortune painting in the Rococo style. However, this changed after he suffered a serious illness and, later, a grave accident. He lost his hearing and endured other physical setbacks. A war in Spain made him aware of the suffering of others. He found he was no longer comfortable painting in the decorative Rococo fashion.

Goya's art reflected his bitterness and disillusionment. One of his most famous paintings shows the ugliness and brutality of war **(Figure 13.16).**

▲ **FIGURE 13.16** The figures are arranged in this painting so that they seem in opposition to each other. Which is the most important figure in this composition? How has the figure been made to stand out? What is the feeling or mood of the piece?

Francisco Goya. *The Third of May, 1808.* 1814. Oil on canvas. Approx. 2.64 × 3.43 m (8'8" × 11'3"). Museo del Prado, Madrid, Spain.

Activity | **Analyzing a Work**

Applying Your Skills. Select one work of art from the Renaissance or Baroque period. Use the four steps of the art history method discussed in Chapter 2 to discuss or write about the work. You may need to research the work of art and the artist in an encyclopedia, a book about the artist, or on the Internet. Write your findings in your sketchbook.

✓ **Check Your Understanding**

1. What is linear perspective?
2. What medium used by Flemish artists revolutionized painting in the Renaissance?
3. Describe Mannerism.
4. What style of painting is characterized by contrast and variety?
5. Name the characteristics of Rococo art.

The Nineteenth Century

In the late eighteenth century, disruption in European society, including the French Revolution, caused artists to abandon the Rococo and Baroque styles, which mirrored the life of the aristocracy. In the nineteenth century, many artists wanted to create art that reflected the world they saw.

Neoclassicism

At the end of the eighteenth century, some European artists developed a new kind of art called **Neoclassicism** ("new classicism"), *an approach to art that borrowed subject matter and formal design qualities from the art of Greece and Rome.* Neoclassicism emphasized realism, minimized emotionalism, and featured epic or heroic events. The French artist Jacques-Louis David (**zjahk** loo-**ee** dah-**veed**) was the major artist working in this style. His work *The Death of Socrates* **(Figure 13.17)** depicts the last moments of the life of the great philosopher, who was tried for religious

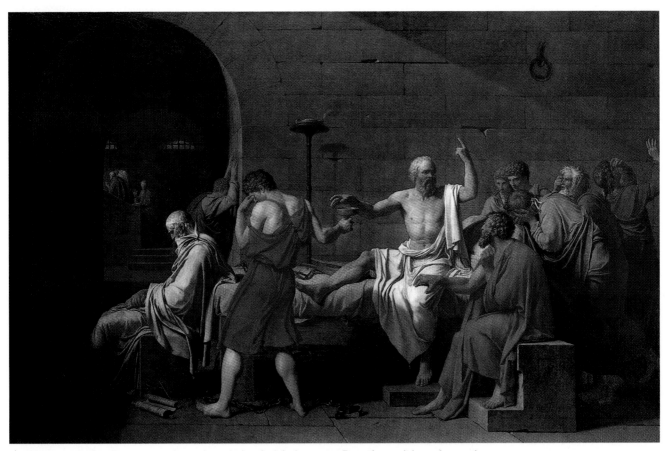

▲ **FIGURE 13.17** This painting has a formal, dignified feeling to it. Even if you did not know the title, you would realize that the artist has depicted a serious and solemn occasion. What in the artwork tells you this? What do the different figures appear to be doing?

Jacques-Louis David. *The Death of Socrates.* 1787. Oil on canvas. 129.5 × 196.2 cm (51 × 77¼"). The Metropolitan Museum of Art, New York, New York. Catharine Lorillard Wolfe Collection, Wolfe Fund, 1931. (31.45)

heresy and sentenced to death. Although his friends and students appealed to the authorities to prevent the sentence from being carried out, Socrates willingly drank the cup of poison hemlock given to him.

Romanticism

At the dawn of the nineteenth century, the struggle to impose a new democratic political and social order continued. People grew anxious in response to ongoing political turmoil and uncertainty. Many did not want to be reminded of the events surrounding them, but instead wanted to be distracted. A new art style evolved as a reaction to contemporary events. **Romanticism,** as it was called, is *a style of art that found its subjects in the world of the dramatic and in cultures foreign to Europe. It emphasized rich color and high emotion.* Romantic artists disliked the cool colors, linearity, and subdued emotion in Neoclassicism.

Eugène Delacroix (oo-**zhen** del-uh-**kwah**) demonstrated a mastery for capturing action in foreign locales. **Figure 13.18** shows one of his famous works.

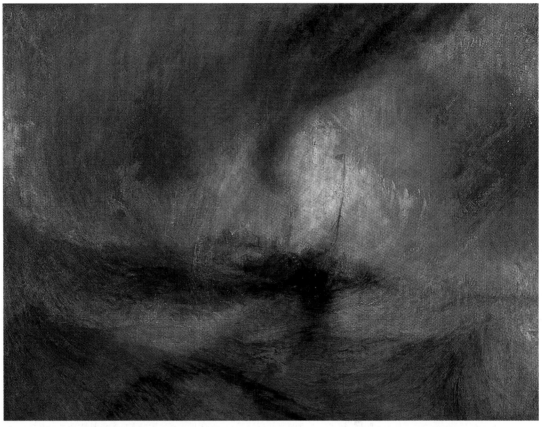

▲ **Figure 13.19** This painting is very different from traditional pictures of ships at sea. Describe the mood created by the swirling colors. What feeling do you experience when viewing this artwork?

Joseph M.W. Turner. *Snowstorm: Steamboat off a Harbours Mouth.* 1842. Oil on canvas. 92 × 122 cm (36 × 48″). Clore Collection, Tate Gallery, London, Great Britain.

Joseph M.W. Turner emerged as England's most dramatic Romantic painter. Turner expected his viewers to use their imaginations. For him, the depiction of light and atmosphere was the most important part of a painting. In **Figure 13.19,** he portrayed nature at its most violent. Instead of using precise detail, he suggests this violence by using loose brushwork to apply bright color and light values in swirling patterns.

Realism

One group of artists grew dissatisfied with both Neoclassicism and Romanticism. They felt that artists should portray political, social, and moral issues, but without glorifying the past or presenting romantic views of the present. Their art movement, called Realism, presented familiar scenes as they actually appeared. Édouard Manet (ay-doo-**ahr** mah-**nay**), an artist who participated in the Realist movement, discovered that the new style of art required new techniques. Therefore, he became more interested in *how* to paint rather than *what* to paint.

In *The Railway* **(Figure 13.20),** Manet painted a simple, common scene. A woman sits with a puppy in her lap. She is reading and has glanced up. A young girl faces away, watching the steam from a train. Manet avoided painting precise detail because he wanted to capture what a person would see with a

quick glance. Rosa Bonheur, a very successful artist of the time, combined the drama of Romanticism with the accuracy of Realism (see Figure 8.3, page 201).

Photography

In the mid-nineteenth century, photography was invented as a method for recording people and events on film. It was exciting for artists interested in realism. Early versions of the photographic process were very expensive and time-consuming, but by the 1850s, several new methods were introduced that made the process easier and less expensive. Because of this, artists could record news events in the second half of the nineteenth century. A famous Civil War photographer, Mathew Brady, documented a battle that took place around 1865 **(Figure 13.21)**. Photography introduced a new kind of realism to art.

▲ **Figure 13.22** Notice the muted colors of this artwork. How does the artist indicate the time of day?

Claude Monet. *Palazzo da Mula, Venice.* 1908. Oil on canvas. 62 × 81.1 cm (24½ × 31⅞"). National Gallery of Art, Washington, D.C. © 1998 Board of Trustees. Chester Dale Collection.

Photographs were more realistic than drawings could be. They preserved a visual record of an event in a single moment in time with more detail and precision than a painter ever could. Photography influenced the development of painting for many years to come.

Impressionism

The Realists had taken a hard look at the real world. This interest in the world outside the studio influenced another group of artists who did much of their painting outdoors. Their style, which came to be known as **Impressionism,** *featured everyday subjects and emphasized the momentary effects of light on color.* Impressionist painters concentrated on the play of light over objects rather than on the shape of objects themselves. These artists broke up solid shapes and blurred the edges of objects by applying paint to the canvas in small dabs of pure color. When viewed from a distance, the dabs blend together visually. If you stand too close to an Impressionist painting, all you will see are colorful brushstrokes of paint. You have to step back to allow your eyes to perform the work of blending the colors.

One of the first artists working in the Impressionist style, Claude Monet (**klohd** moh-**nay**), painted many different series of landscapes, seascapes, and cityscapes that depicted the quality of light at various times of day, and in different seasons of the year (see Figures 6.24 and 6.25 on page 153). In **Figure 13.22,** all the edges and lines of the work have been blurred. The gently moving water distorts the reflection of the building, an effect created by the use of fragmented brushstrokes.

Post-Impressionism

Eventually, some artists felt that Impressionism was not suited to the way they wished to depict the world. These artists began working in a variety of styles that came to be called **Post-Impressionism,** *a more individual approach to painting, unique to each artist working at this time.* The term for this period is Post-Impressionism because these works appeared after Impressionism. The word *post* means *after.* Some of the most outstanding Post-Impressionist artists were Paul Cézanne (say-**zahn**), Paul Gauguin (goh-**gan**) and Vincent van Gogh (van **goh**).

Paul Cézanne, who had originally painted in the Impressionist style, felt that the blurred shapes of Impressionism did not depict the solidity of the world. He wanted to create an art that emphasized form more than light. Cézanne did this by laying down interlocking blocks of color rather than dots and dabs of paint. He joined these patches of color together as if they were pieces of a puzzle. In this way, Cézanne strengthened the underlying structure in his compositions, giving the images a feeling of permanence and solidity. In **Figure 13.23,** he used richly colored patches to create the geometric shapes of the building, trees,

▲ **FIGURE 13.23** Cézanne was interested in the structure of objects. He used small brushstrokes like little building blocks to make forms look like geometric solids. Notice how the foliage looks as solid as the rocks. What does Cézanne's technique do to the appearance of this scene? Does he evoke any particular feeling?

Paul Cézanne. *Le Chateau Noir.* 1900–04. Oil on canvas. 73.7 × 96.6 cm (29 × 38"). National Gallery of Art, Washington, D.C. © 1998 Board of Trustees. Gift of Eugene and Agnes E. Meyer.

and even the sky, which of course, is not a solid object.

Paul Gauguin turned to the use of color and shape to create daring, unconventional works depicting far-off lands and people. Giving up his job as a stockbroker, he traveled around the world to learn about art and experience different artistic traditions. He finally settled in Tahiti, where he produced most of his famous works. Notice the simple shapes and brilliant colors in **Figure 13.24.** Gauguin used arbitrary color in most of his paintings.

Vincent van Gogh, like the other Post-Impressionists, was initially dazzled by Impressionist works but later felt that Impressionism was limited in what it could express. Van Gogh was not interested in achieving visual accuracy. Instead, he explored ways to convey his feelings about a subject. To do so, he used expressive elements in his paintings such as twisting lines, rich colors, and complex textures.

Van Gogh's art was rejected and he only sold one painting during his lifetime. His brother supported him

◀ **FIGURE 13.24**
Notice how color is the dominant element in this painting. Shape and form are also important. How do the elements create a dreamy quality?

Paul Gauguin. *Faaturuma (Melancholic).* 1891. Oil on canvas. 93.9 × 68.2 cm (37 × 26⅞"). Nelson-Atkins Museum of Art, Kansas City, Missouri. Purchase: Nelson Trust.

▲ **Figure 13.25** Notice van Gogh's unusual use of color, texture, and line to depict rhythm and movement. He uses the elements to make the stars swirl and the trees dance as if all of nature was alive.

Vincent van Gogh. *The Starry Night*. 1889. Oil on canvas. 73.7 × 92.1 cm (29 × 36¹/₄″). The Museum of Modern Art, New York, New York. Acquired through the Lillie P. Bliss Bequest.

financially. Toward the end of his life, he painted *The Starry Night* **(Figure 13.25)**. He executed it using quick brushstrokes to create the dark trees that resemble flames. The stars in the sky seem to be alive with movement. He expressed the violent energy and creative force of nature in this painting. Today, we regard this artwork as one of van Gogh's greatest because it reflects his passion and originality in creating an energetic and forceful image.

Activity | **Analyzing a Style**

Applying Your Skills. Find a book about Impressionism in the library or read about it on the Internet. List at least four Impressionist works of art, each one painted by a different artist. Select one of the four works. Use the four steps of art history to write about the work. Include your paper in your portfolio.

✓ Check Your Understanding

1. Describe Neoclassicism.
2. What was Realism a reaction to?
3. What was emphasized in Impressionist painting?

Early Twentieth Century

During the first half of the twentieth century, artists responded to rapid changes in technology, world politics, and culture by creating a variety of approaches in artistic expression. One style replaced another with bewildering speed. With the invention and spread of photography, artists no longer functioned as recorders of the visible world. They launched a quest to redefine the characteristics of art. Soon it became impossible to separate artists into neat categories or to group their works under clear art styles.

Trends in the arts changed rapidly because increased travel and new ways of communication helped artists to compare ideas. One individual or group could easily influence another. It no longer took years for one art movement or style of art to catch on in other areas. In fact, some artists who lived long lives, such as Matisse and Picasso, changed their own styles several times during their careers.

European Art

In general, European artists assumed one of three different directions in artistic expression: self-expression, composition, or imagination. Each direction emphasized a different aspect of art.

In Germany, artists began working in a style later called **Expressionism,** *a style that emphasized the expression of innermost feelings.* The German Expressionists did not think the purpose of art was to make pretty pictures. Instead, because they experienced the terrible economic and social conditions in Germany before and after World War I, they wanted to express their feelings about these conditions. Their emotional subjects ranged from fear and anger to a preoccupation with death. Käthe Kollwitz (**kah**-teh **kohl**-vits), an Expressionist concerned with poverty and war, created many moving images of mothers grieving for dead children. She based her work on personal experience: she lost her eldest son during the first weeks of World War I **(Figure 13.26)**.

In France, a group of artists created works that focused on the qualities of design. Some of these artists created **Cubism,** *a style that emphasizes structure and design.* Three main concepts influenced the Cubists. The first concept was that shapes in nature are based on geometric forms. The second concept, based on a scientific discovery, showed that all

◀ **FIGURE 13.26** Describe the person that you see here. Identify the elements of art that the artist used. How does Kollwitz view herself? Is this a person you would be interested in meeting? Why or why not?

Käthe Kollwitz. *Self-Portrait.* 1921. Etching. 21.6 × 26.7 cm (8½ × 10½″). The National Museum of Women in the Arts, Washington, D.C. Museum Purchase: The Member's Acquisition Fund.

◄ **FIGURE 13.27** Picasso changed the traditional view of the human form. Notice the hints of geometric shapes. How do you think the atomic theory of matter (all matter is made up of atoms that are constantly in motion) influenced Picasso's work?

Pablo Picasso. *Nude Woman*. 1910. Oil on linen. 187.3 × 61 cm (73¾ × 24″). National Gallery of Art, Washington, D.C. © 1998 Board of Trustees. Ailsa Mellon Bruce Fund.

▲ **FIGURE 13.28** Dali has created a strange world in which metal objects that should be firm seem to melt. Realistic details, such as the ants, add to the nightmare quality of the scene. What might the clocks symbolize? Can you recognize the object lying on the ground in the center of the picture?

Salvador Dali. *The Persistence of Memory* (Persistance de la memoire). 1931. Oil on canvas. 24.1 × 33 cm (9½ × 13″). Collection, The Museum of Modern Art, New York, New York. Given anonymously.

matter is made up of atoms that are constantly in motion. The third concept, based on art from other cultures (African sculpture had recently been displayed in Paris), revealed that shape and form could be simplified and rearranged to increase the expressive qualities of an artwork. Pablo Picasso and Georges Braque pioneered the movement. In **Figure 13.27,** you can see how Picasso visually translated the human body into geometric shapes. He tried to paint three-dimensional objects as if they could be seen from many different points of view at the same time.

A third group of artists relied on fantasy to create art that expressed personal feelings. They explored the psychology of the mind as subject matter in their work. **Surrealism** emphasized *art in which dreams, fantasy, and the subconscious served as inspiration for artists.* Surrealists painted very realistic, almost photographic, images but combined objects that didn't belong together. The work of the Surrealists appears strange and dreamlike. Surrealist paintings can be funny or mysterious and frightening. **Figure 13.28** depicts a landscape with a cliff, lake, and tree painted in a realistic manner, but the landscape contains strange objects that don't seem to belong there and don't behave as one might expect.

North American Art

In the United States in the beginning of the twentieth century, a group of young artists turned to the harsh realities of the city for subject matter. They called themselves The Eight and organized an exhibition in 1908. Their original name was soon forgotten when critics immediately labeled them the Ashcan School. Critics expressed displeasure at the subject matter of their work: stark tenement buildings, crowded city streets, poor working people, and ragged children.

Although this realism shocked unwary viewers, the Armory Show of 1913 exerted an even greater impact on the American art world. This show introduced Americans to the work of European artists. Most Americans felt confused by what they saw. The art on display did not fit into their traditional understanding of the nature and purpose of art. However, the show energized many American artists, who responded to the challenge posed by the daring exhibition and took their first steps toward making modern art in the United States.

Alexander Calder, a sculptor, ranks among these twentieth-century innovators. Most sculptors at this time worked with traditional materials and methods. A few experimented with the new materials of modern industry. Calder created a new form of sculpture by arranging wire and sheet metal into balanced arrangements that stayed in motion (Figure 8.21 on page 213). He called these moving sculptures mobiles (**moh**-beels).

As a reaction against the infusion of European styles into American art, some artists decided to focus on strictly American themes. Called **Regionalists,** these artists *painted the farmlands and cities of the United States in an optimistic way.* Each artist had a slightly different style, but all of them portrayed upbeat messages in their work. They focused on the vast expanse, beauty, productivity, and abundance of the United States and depicted happy, hardworking people. **Figure 13.29** is an example of Regionalism. In

▲ **FIGURE 13.29** Notice the curving lines and simple, pure colors in this painting. Benton has used repetition to add interest, variety, and movement to the work. Identify the different figures and objects that are repeated throughout the painting.

Thomas Hart Benton. *The Sources of Country Music.* 1975. Acrylic on canvas. 1.8 × 3 m (6 × 10′). The Country Music Hall of Fame and Museum, Nashville, Tennessee. © T.H. Benton and R. P. Benton, Testamentary Trusts/Licensed by VAGA, New York, NY

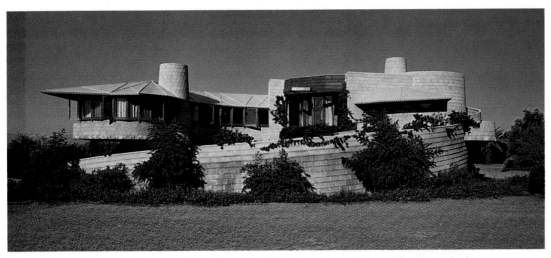

▲ **Figure 13.30** Wright designed this house to be functional as well as to blend in with the environment. What materials did he use to create this natural effect? What elements and principles of art did he use to unify the building with its setting?

Frank Lloyd Wright. *The David Wright House.* Scottsdale, Arizona. 1951.

this mural, Thomas Hart Benton portrayed a group of larger-than-life Americans who display the restlessness of energetic people. He included symbols of industrialization and historical events.

Another American artist working at the same time showed a different side of the American experience. African-American artist Jacob Lawrence used bright, flat areas of color in a geometric style to create his art (see Figure 4.19 on page 80). His series paintings tell the stories of historical African-American figures, as well as describe the struggles of African-Americans moving from the South to the North in the early twentieth century.

The twentieth century also saw vast changes in architecture. New materials and technology and new demands for commercial space led to the development of skyscrapers. Architects designed functional structures with steel frames that emphasized simplicity of form to replace heavy, decorated structures. One famous modern architect, Frank Lloyd Wright, believed that form should follow function, meaning that the look of a building should be based on its use. He designed buildings that blended harmoniously with the landscape around them **(Figure 13.30).**

Like France in the late eighteenth century, Mexico at the beginning of the twentieth century experienced deep social and political unrest. The tension erupted into the Mexican Revolution. Just as European artists groped for a new style of art to depict their response to war and unrest, some Mexican artists also felt the need to develop new approaches to art that would express their feelings about the plight of the people. These Mexican artists were referred to as the Mexican muralists, because they covered walls and ceilings with murals about Mexican history, the suffering of the peasants, and the immoral behavior of the ruling class. Artists such as Diego Rivera (Figure 9.5, page 229) and David Alfaro Siqueiros (Figure 10.14, page 264) combined the solid forms of ancient, pre-Columbian Mexican art with the powerful colors and bold lines of Cubism and Expressionism.

Check Your Understanding

1. Define Expressionism.
2. Name the three main influences on Cubism.
3. Explain Surrealism.
4. What are mobiles?

Art After 1945

After World War II ended in 1945, the European art world was in disarray. Paris was no longer the center of artistic creativity. The war displaced many people. A number of artists who had fled Nazi Germany settled in New York City. They began teaching there and by the 1950s, they and their students established a new center for the

arts. New York City became the new capital of the art world.

In the years since World War II, artists have created many changes in artistic approaches, styles, and techniques. A variety of art forms once considered minor, such as printmaking, weaving, ceramics, and jewelry making, have come to be considered art forms equal to painting and sculpture. New kinds of art, such as computer animation, have also gained prominence.

Abstract Expressionism

Abstract Expressionism, the first new style to arrive on the scene in New York in the years following World War II, *emphasized abstract elements of art rather than recognizable subject matter, and also stressed feelings and emotions.* Following in the tradition of German Expressionism, Abstract Expressionist artists believed that art should function as a spontaneous expression of emotion, and they did not necessarily rely on planned structure to organize the design of their paintings. Look at **Figure 13.31.** It is called *Flowering Swamp,* but you cannot see any realistically depicted flowers or swamps. If you use your imagination, however, you can see how the two rectangles seem to float over a background that suggests water and flowers.

Pop and Op Art

During the early 1960s, artists turned to the mass media, and especially to advertising, for subject matter. Pop art portrayed images of popular culture, such as soda bottles, soup cans, soap

▲ **FIGURE 13.31** Hofmann, who was inspirational to the Abstract Expressionist style that grew in New York, is best known for his use of brilliant colors. What does the artist appear to be expressing here? What is the mood or feeling of this work?

Hans Hofmann. *Flowering Swamp.* 1957. Oil on wood. 122 × 91.5 cm (48⅛ × 36⅛"). Hirshhorn Museum and Sculpture Garden, Smithsonian Institution, Washington, D.C. Gift of the Joseph H. Hirshhorn Foundation, 1966. © Estate of Hans Hofmann/Licensed by VAGA, New York, NY

boxes, giant hamburgers, and comic strips, in a variety of art forms. Pop artists made people take a new look at everyday objects. They often used bright colors and cartoonish graphics to depict their subject matter. **Figure 13.32** is an example of Pop art. Artist Roy Lichtenstein (**lick**-ten-steyn) used a strong sense of design, a limited color scheme, and bold shapes to create a painting that was based on a comic strip.

Another style of art popular in this period took advantage of people's fascination with visual illusions. Op art, or optical art, uses scientific knowledge about vision to create optical illusions of movement. Op art relies on the special arrangement of the art elements such as the precise arrangement of lines, or the placement of complementary colors next to each other to create the illusion of movement. If you look at **Figure 13.33,** you will notice the unusual orange color of the background. The blue-green dots seem to be placed in no

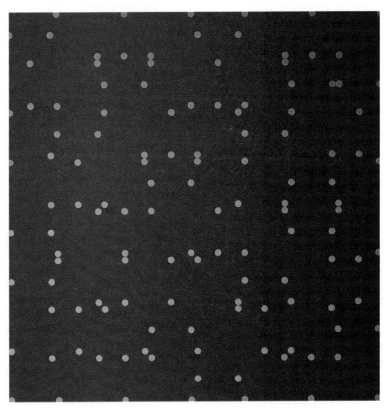

▲ **FIGURE 13.33** This piece of Op art is intended to cause a visual effect. Do you think the artwork has another purpose or meaning? Why or why not?

apparent order, but in fact the artist carefully planned their arrangement. If you look at the dots for a few moments, they appear to vibrate because the after-image causes a visual response that creates the illusion of movement.

Color-Field Painting

As artists experimented with a variety of new styles, they occasionally selected just one element of art to focus on in their work. An example, Color-Field painting, is art created using only flat fields of color. It is created without the precision of Op art and also without its interest in illusion. It is color for the pure sensation of color. Look at the example by Mark Rothko in **Figure 13.34.** His color areas have hazy edges that seem to float in space.

Minimalism

Some artists sought absolute simplicity in their art. This focus came to be known as **Minimalism,** or *art that uses a minimum of art elements.* Minimalists emphasized either color or shape as the dominant element in painting. In sculpture, they used the fewest possible geometric forms. They depicted art at its most austere, arranging only the simplest art elements. Minimalist painters who placed importance on the crisp, precise edges of the shapes in their paintings came to be known as Hard-edge painters. Frank Stella **(Figure 13.35),** used different canvas shapes for his works and created art on a large scale. He relied on thin white lines to set off colors, define shapes, and unify the work.

▲ **FIGURE 13.34** Rothko limited the colors in this painting to an analogous scheme of yellow and orange. He blended the edges to blur the line between the two colors. Standing in front of the painting, which is almost 8 feet (2.4 m) tall, a viewer has an intense visual experience. What might the purpose of creating such an experience be?

Mark Rothko. *Orange and Yellow.* 1956. Oil on canvas. 231.1 × 180.3 cm (91 × 71″). Albright-Knox Art Gallery, Buffalo, New York. Gift of Seymour H. Knox, 1956.

▼ **FIGURE 13.35** Notice the outlines of this painting. It is not a traditional rectangular shape. Observe how the red border ties the work together. How has Stella used repetition and contrast to further unify the painting?

Frank Stella. *Agbatana III.* 1968. Acrylic on canvas. 304.8 × 457.2 cm (120 × 180″). Allen Memorial Art Museum, Oberlin College, Oberlin, Ohio. Ruth C. Roush Fund for Contemporary Art and National Foundation for the Arts and Humanities Grant, 1968.

New Forms of Realism

Although modern American artists have created many abstract and nonobjective artworks, Americans harbor a love for realism. Many American artists continue to portray subjects in a realistic style. Sculpture made by Duane Hanson **(Figure 13.36)** appears so lifelike that it once fooled a gallery security guard. The guard thought that one of Hanson's motionless, seated figures looked ill and called for an ambulance. The painting in **Figure 13.37** looks so accurate in visual detail that a casual observer could easily mistake it for a photograph. This is how the style earned one of its names: Photo-Realism. It is also called Hyper-Realism and Super-Realism. **Super-Realism** is *art that depicts objects as precisely and accurately as they actually appear.*

▲ **FIGURE 13.36** This figure is an example of Super-Realism. If you observed this figure at an airport or in a hotel lobby, could you mistake him for a real person? Why or why not?

Duane Hanson. *Traveler with Sunburn.* 1986. Bronze, oil paint, and mixed media. Life-size. Private collection.

Activity	Applying the Steps

Applying Your Skills. Look through this book to find five paintings that were created after 1950. For each, list the name of the artist, the title of the work, and the style in which the work was painted.

Architecture

After World War II, architects developed the International Style of architecture, a plain, austere building style. Its origins could be traced back to the work of Frank Lloyd Wright and Louis Sullivan, who both designed buildings before World War II. In their Seagram Building, the architects Ludwig Mies van der Rohe (ludd-**vig** meez van der **row**) and Philip Johnson created a simple geometric glass box that exemplifies van der

▲ **FIGURE 13.37** This street scene seems almost like a photograph although it is a painting. How does the artist create this illusion? What is the purpose of painting such an illusion when one could simply take a photograph?

Richard Estes. *Paris Street Scene.* 1972. Oil on canvas. 101.6 × 152.4 cm (40 × 60″). Virginia Museum of Fine Arts, Richmond, Virginia. Gift of Sydney and Frances Lewis. © Richard Estes/Licensed by VAGA, New York, New York/Courtesy Marlborough Gallery, New York.

▶ **FIGURE 13.38**
This simple design, called International Style, appealed to architects as a reaction to the highly ornate Art Deco style that was popular in the 1920s and 1930s. Can you easily identify the purpose of the building? What is its purpose?

Ludwig Mies van der Rohe and Philip Johnson. *Seagram Building.* New York, 1958.

Rohe's favorite saying, "Less is more" **(Figure 13.38).**

Architects of the 1960s looked to the future as well as to the past. **Figure 13.39** shows an apartment complex that looks futuristic in its design but actually echoes the Pueblo apartment complexes built by Native Americans hundreds of years ago. The interlocking apartment units are designed to give occupants a sense of openness and space. Because the units are not lined up next to each other as in traditional apartment complexes, each apartment has plenty of windows that allow sunlight to enter and give the illusion that each apartment is a separate house.

Post-Modern Art

We are currently in a period of art that is rapidly evolving. Some say we are at the end of the modern era. Others insist that we have already entered the postmodern era. The subject is being hotly debated in artistic circles, but the answer is something that only time can judge.

▶ **FIGURE 13.39**
This apartment complex uses space efficiently. Do you find the complex attractive? Why or why not? What are some of the personal touches the residents have added?

Moshe Safdie. *Habitat.* Montreal, 1967.

The term post-modernism first appeared in reference to architecture. **Post-Modernism** is *an approach to art that incorporates traditional elements and techniques while retaining some characteristics of modern art styles or movements.* Post-Modern architecture was a reaction to the plain glass boxes of the International Style. It incorporates decorative elements from the past and takes advantage of the flexibility of new materials.

The Rock-and-Roll Hall of Fame and Museum (Figure 14.21 on page 401), designed by I. M. Pei, is an example of architecture's break from the modern glass box. The museum contains a concert hall, a film and video display center, several sound chambers, and a party area as well as the usual glass display cases for showing off costumes, instruments, sheet music, and the personal belongings of famous musicians. The architect designed a building that reflects the freedom of rock-and-roll, but also functions as a museum to house its memorabilia.

Other Post-Modern artists are breaking traditional restrictions. Painters are creating three-dimensional paintings and sculptors are adding paint to their works. **Figure 13.40** is an example of a Post-Modern work with some identifiable subject matter. Is it a painted sculpture or a three-dimensional painting?

No one knows what will happen next in the art world. The acquisition of images from the past, and the incorporation of them into new works with new meanings, is only one facet of this new era. We have entered a time in art in which the diversity of ideas reflects the diversity of contemporary life.

▲ **FIGURE 13.40** This sculpture represents several musical instruments. Can you identify what these instruments are? Notice how big the sculpture is. Why do you suppose the artist chose to make it so large?

Frank Stella. *St. Michael's Counterguard (Malta Series).* 1984. Mixed media on aluminum and fiberglass honeycomb. 396.2 × 342.9 × 274.3 cm (156 × 135 × 108″). Los Angeles County Museum of Art, Los Angeles, California. Gift of Anna Bing Arnold.

✔ Check Your Understanding

1. What is the subject matter of Pop Art?
2. How is Color-Field painting different from Op art?
3. Why is Super-Realism sometimes called Photo-Realism?
4. Describe Post-Modern architecture.

ART CRITICISM IN ACTION

▲ FIGURE 13.41

Leonardo da Vinci. *Ginevra de' Benci*. c. 1474. Oil on panel, with addition at bottom edge. 42.7 × 37.0 cm (16¹³⁄₁₆ × 14⁹⁄₁₆″). National Gallery of Art, Washington, D.C. © 1998 Board of Trustees. Ailsa Mellon Bruce Fund.

1 DESCRIBE What do you see?

List all of the information found in the credit line. Describe the objects you see in the visual image. Use your perception skills.

- Describe the woman, including her clothing, her hair, and the features of her face.
- Describe the background of the work.

2 ANALYZE How is this work organized?

During this step you will collect information about all the elements and principles of art.

- Did the artist use accurate proportions?
- What kind of rhythm, balance, and proportion has he used to organize the work?
- Which area of the work is emphasized? What techniques did the artist use to create a focal point? What techniques did he use to unify the work?

3 INTERPRET What is the artist trying to communicate?

Now it is time to combine the clues you have collected with your personal experiences to guess what the artist is saying about this woman. You will solve the mystery of the work during this step.

- What is unusual about the woman's eyes and mouth? What feelings does her face express?
- Which elements and principles affect the mood of the work?
- What message do you get from this work? Based on your interpretation, give this work a new title.

4 JUDGE What do you think of the work?

Now you will decide if this is a successful work of art or not. You may make a personal opinion, but the one that is important for now is the objective judgment based on aesthetic theories.

- Did Leonardo da Vinci use the elements and principles successfully?
- Do you think this is a successful work of art? Why or why not? Use one or more of the aesthetic theories described in Chapter 2 to defend your judgment.

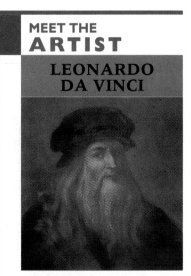
Leonardo da Vinci was proficient in just about everything intellectual and cultural—mathematics, physics, anatomy, geology, botany, geography, music, sculpture, architecture, and, of course, painting.

He was constantly experimenting with new media and although he had many ideas, he did not complete that many works. Perhaps Leonardo da Vinci is most highly regarded today for a mind that was constantly inventing, searching, and trying new ideas. His notebooks fascinate us with ideas for ways to fly, a printing press improvement on Gutenberg's, war machines, plans for domes, anatomical studies, and details of flowers.

Art Criticism in Action **385**

The Harlem Renaissance

◀ **FIGURE 13.42**

Lois Mailou Jones. *The Ascent of Ethiopia.* 1932. Oil on canvas. 59.7 × 43.8 cm (23½ × 17¼"). Milwaukee Art Museum, Milwaukee, Wisconsin. Purchase, African-American Art Acquisition Fund, matching funds from Suzanne and Richard Pieper, with additional support from Arthur and Dorothy Nelle Sanders.

The Harlem Renaissance refers to an explosion of creativity focused in the work of African-American artists and writers during the 1920s. The participants in this movement shared a deep sense of racial pride and a desire to represent faithfully the experiences and feelings of African-Americans. Many artists looked to African cultural traditions for inspiration, while others found their subjects in folk traditions. Topics of interest to both writers and fine artists included: life in the South, as well as the experience of migration to Northern cities; racial prejudice and the desire for social equality; images of Africa; and music, such as the blues and jazz.

Lois Mailou Jones's painting, *The Ascent of Ethiopia* **(Figure 13.42),** captures the essence of the Harlem Renaissance. Behind the foreground figure of an ancient Egyptian royal (possibly King Tut) we see a procession of figures ascending a stairway. Their destination appears to be a modern, urbanized culture of artists represented by musicians, actors, and a painter. Symbolically, the painting depicts the descendants of Ethiopia, or Africa as a whole, rising from adversity and struggle.

Making the Connection

1. What symbols or images can you find in this painting? How would you interpret them in light of the Harlem Renaissance movement?
2. Why do you think artists and writers of the movement wanted to portray African-American history in their works?
3. Read a work of literature by a Harlem Renaissance writer, then write an essay in which you discuss the work's themes and ideas.

Building Vocabulary

On a separate sheet of paper, write the term that best matches each definition given below.

1. A style of architecture in which churches soared upward, used pointed arches, and had stained-glass windows.
2. The period at the end of the Middle Ages when artists, writers, and philosophers were "re-awakened" to art forms and ideas from ancient Greece and Rome.
3. An art style that borrowed subject matter and formal design qualities from the art of Greece and Rome.
4. A style of art that found its subjects in the world of the dramatic and in cultures foreign to Europe. It emphasized rich colors and high emotion.
5. An art style that featured everyday subjects and emphasized the momentary effects of light on color.
6. An art style that emphasized the expression of innermost feelings.
7. A style of art in which dreams, fantasy, and the subconscious served as inspiration for artists.
8. Artists who painted the farmlands and cities of the United States in an optimistic way.

Reviewing Art Facts

Answer the following questions using complete sentences.

1. Why was the Middle Ages also called the *Age of Faith*?
2. What social changes was Mannerism a response to?
3. Identify the characteristics of Romanticism.
4. Name one similarity and one difference between the artworks created by the Realists and the Impressionists.
5. Describe the subject matter chosen by the Mexican muralists.
6. Explain the difference between Expressionism and Cubism.
7. Define Op art.

Thinking Critically About Art

1. **Explain.** In this chapter, you learned how political and social events can shape art movements. You also learned how advances in technology can influence art styles. What social and political events, along with technological advances, paved the way for the Renaissance movement?
2. **Compare and Contrast.** Figure 13.18, page 367, and Figure 13.21, page 369, are both artworks that capture battles, yet they are very different. Compare the two. Explain their differences as well as their similarities, taking into account the media used and the style of art of each work.

Read about one of the most performed dance works created in the twentieth century. The classic *The Green Table*, presented by choreographer Kurt Jooss, is featured on page 425 of the Performing Arts Handbook.

Explore museums and art galleries without leaving your classroom. Visit the Glencoe Fine Arts Site (**www.glencoe.com/sec/art**) and roam through the collections of famous art museums. Or, take a close-up view of folk art and ethnic works at regional galleries.

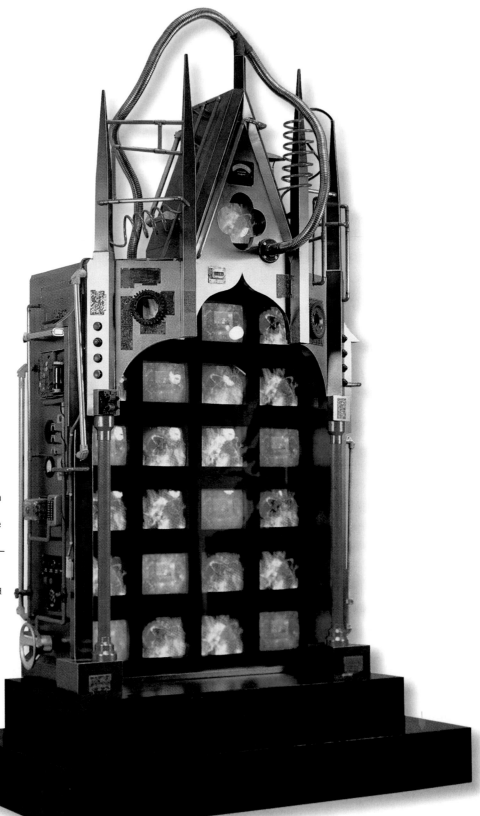

▶ **FIGURE 14.1**
Advances in technology help artists create art in new ways. In this case, technology becomes the artwork itself!

Nam June Paik. *Technology.* 1991. 25 video monitors, 3 laser disc players with unique 3 discs in a steel and plywood cabinet with aluminum sheeting and details of copper, bronze, plastic, and other materials. Approx. 332.6 × 192.1 × 131.7 cm (127 × 75⅝ × 51⅞″). National Museum of American Art, Smithsonian Institution, Washington, D.C. Museum purchase through the Lusita L. and Franz H. Denghausen Endowment.

CHAPTER 14

Careers in Art

In the distant past, a young person who wanted to be an artist would pay a master artist for permission to work as an *apprentice* in the master's studio. These apprentices learned as they observed and assisted the masters. Today students can develop their skills by taking courses in high school and post-secondary schools. Vocational schools and professional art schools provide the education for some art careers. Other careers may require a college degree. However, it's never too early to explore and prepare for a career in the arts.

The artist who created *Technology,* **Figure 14.1,** began his education in the arts at the age of 14 with piano and composition lessons. Nam June Paik's interest in contemporary music led him to performance art, which led him to use video and electronics in his art. He uses the video camera, the TV monitor, and the computer to create installation art and sculpture that has four dimensions: length, width, depth, and time.

OBJECTIVES

After completing this chapter, you will be able to:

- Discuss many fields in which one can pursue a career in art.
- Describe some of the skills artists need for various jobs.
- Determine your own interest in the field of art.

WORDS TO KNOW

graphic designer
logos
illustrator
package designer
photojournalists
animators
storyboards
architect
interior designer
museum curators

Developing Your
PORTFOLIO

Interview a person who is in an art-related career. **Before you interview the person, brainstorm a list of questions to ask. Discover what education and work experience was necessary to obtain the position and find out what the job duties are. Then interview the artist and record the answers. Share the main points of the interview with your classmates and keep your interview notes in your portfolio.**

Careers in Business and Industry

You are probably beginning to consider ideas about your future. If you have art abilities and you enjoy art, this chapter will introduce you to some exciting career possibilities. In addition to the major categories mentioned here, there are many careers within each field. Countless possibilities exist, so plan to explore art careers further. As you read, think about each career and keep those that interest you in mind. You will be surprised at how your skills might fit many different art-related jobs.

Today the business world needs art specialists in many areas. Trained artists design company reports, publications, and advertising. Company employees develop some of this design work. Other, more complex projects are assigned to outside designers or advertising firms with many different kinds of artists on staff. Plenty of opportunities are available for self-employed (or freelance) artists and salaried employees with art ability **(Figure 14.2).**

Technology and Careers in Art

In order to prepare for a career in an art-related field, you should become aware of the role technology plays in art and design. Most positions will require computer skills as well as artistic ability. Using computers, designers can create images that can be moved, changed, erased, duplicated, reduced, enlarged, colored, patterned, textured, and otherwise manipulated. Designers work with hardware tools, such as electric-light pens on electronic tablets, as shown in **Figure 14.3.** Designers also use software programs that enable them to design a page layout and insert artwork. Electronic equipment speeds up the design process. Some systems let the artist see the finished work in a variety of color and size arrangements. There are also computer-aided design programs to be used for other art tasks—

▲ **FIGURE 14.2** If you have art ability, there are many opportunities in art and art-related fields.

such as planning a building (or drafting) or designing the interior of a room. Voice-activated software can be used by the physically challenged to design images. With these tools, designers can create any type of artwork needed.

Once the artwork is completed, computers can also be used to send images by disk or e-mail to customers all over the world. These capabilities also allow collaborations among artists over distances. Technology has changed the way many artists work. In almost any area of art-related employment, artists use computers and other equipment to aid them in their jobs.

In the following pages, you will learn more about the many opportunities available in the art field.

Graphic Design

The early Christian monks who illustrated religious writings were artists **(Figure 14.4).** After the invention of the printing press in the fifteenth century, the craftspeople who arranged type and illustrations were what we now call graphic artists. They had to plan the *layout*, the way items are arranged on the page, before a page could be printed. It was slow work because it all had to be done by hand.

▲ **FIGURE 14.3** This designer uses an electric-light pen and electronic table to create his artwork. Computer technology is essential to many art-related careers.

◀ **FIGURE 14.4** Manuscript illuminators were fine artists. After the introduction of the printing press, craftspeople learned to create and arrange type and illustrations.

Artist unknown. *Missal.* 1389–1404. Tempera colors, gold leaf and gold paint on vellum in a medieval, blind-stamped binding. 33 × 24 cm (13 × 9⁷⁄₁₆″). The J. Paul Getty Museum, Los Angeles, California.

▲ **FIGURE 14.5** Graphic designers plan every detail of a book or magazine page including the selection of the size and kind of typeface or font.

▲ **FIGURE 14.6** Kingslien used a computer drawing program to create these designs. Although the computer is a useful tool, the artist must still use her skill to design and compose a successful work.

Liz Kingslien. *The Seasons.* Macromedia Freehand vector images. Courtesy of the artist.

Graphic Designer

A **graphic designer** *translates ideas into images and arranges them in appealing and memorable ways.* He or she creates plans for visual presentations. Today graphic designers use computers, laser scanners, and other equipment that allows them to work much faster. Still, talented artists are required to use the technology to its greatest potential.

Newspaper, magazine, and book publishers employ graphic designers. A designer, sometimes called a publication or production designer, created the look of this book. The designer carefully planned the size of the type, the length of the lines, the layout of the text and artwork, and the length of the columns **(Figure 14.5).** The designer had to make sure the book was visually appealing while at the same time easy for students to use. Writers typed the manuscript into a computer, and the information was stored on a disk. An editor proofread the manuscript to ensure that the content was clear and concise. The manuscript was then given to the typesetting or printing company. The printer then followed the design plan provided by the book designer. Often the book designer and printer work together very closely.

Advertising Designer

Graphic artists also design promotional material for companies. They may be employed by outdoor advertising agencies to create billboards or by traditional advertising agencies to work on ad campaigns **(Figure 14.6).** When graphic artists apply their skills to promotional work, they are called advertising designers. Advertising designers create **logos,** or *symbols or trademarks that are immediately recognizable.*

Advertising agencies employ many kinds of artists. These artists work together as a team whose efforts are coordinated by an art director. They often work with copywriters and man-

▲ **Figure 14.7** A career as an advertising artist usually requires a college education in art or design.

agers, all of whom may have different ideas and visions, so team-building skills are essential **(Figure 14.7).**

Web Artist

As the Internet continues to grow and expand as a center for information and commerce, businesses need to attract visitors to their Web sites (sometimes called Web pages). Web artists, who are often called Web masters, design Web pages, which may include text, photos, three-dimensional or moving graphics, sound, and interactive devices. The Web artist must make the page visually appealing but easy to use. Because it can take a long time for the viewer's computer to process images, the Web artist must balance beauty with function. A confusing or poorly laid out Web page will cause Internet users to look elsewhere.

Web artists also organize Internet broadcasts of current affairs or events of special interest that television networks do not cover.

Illustration

Many businesses and industries require the work of an **illustrator** who can *create the visual images that complement written words.* Illustrations, or visual images that clarify or decorate a text, can be found in magazines, books, television, film, and elsewhere. Illustrations are used for advertising, editorial, institutional, and educational purposes.

Commercial Illustrator

In addition to the type and the paintings you see in this book, there are drawings by commercial illustrators. Some illustrators specialize in one area, such as fashion, medical, or technical illustration or they may work in several areas **(Figure 14.8).** Some commercial illustrators use computers to help them create maps or charts. They might also create drawings for a children's book by working with an author. Some illustrators work for one company while others prefer to freelance. Freelance artists are self-employed and do many different jobs for many different companies.

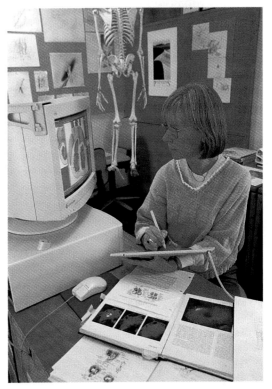

▲ **Figure 14.8** A technical illustrator specializes in drawing diagrams. A medical illustrator must study biology and medicine.

Cartoonist

Cartoonists produce distinctive, entertaining drawings meant to provoke thought and laughter. They submit their work for publication in magazines and newspapers. They may choose to draw single cartoons or comic strips. They usually try to make a humorous point about human nature. Editorial cartoonists, who are interested in politics and current events, present complex ideas in simple, humorous drawings. Editorial cartoonists try to make people think about current issues. They may also try to influence public opinion.

Cartoonists also create comic books and other publications. Several famous cartoonists have created comic books that deal with serious issues such as war and disease. They try to illuminate social problems for people to understand. Some cartoonists work in animation, creating moving cartoons such as those that entertain children (and adults) on Saturday mornings.

▲ **FIGURE 14.9** Industrial designers develop new products. They also make improvements to existing products, such as adding new features or changing the design of an automobile.

Industrial Design

Industrial design is the planning of the products of industry **(Figure 14.9)**. All objects, such as tools, home appliances, furniture, toys, and automobiles, must be carefully designed. These artists work closely with engineers who develop the products. Sometimes industrial designers are asked to work on things as simple as tamper-proof caps for medicines. At other times they are asked to work on projects as complicated as space vehicles. Before they begin work, industrial designers need to know how the product is to be used. Industrial designers plan products based on three requirements. First, it must do the job for which it was designed. Second, it must look like it can do the job. Third, it must be visually pleasing.

Product Designer

Product designers, or artists who plan the products of industry, usually specialize in one industry or product, such as machinery, furniture, medical equipment, or cars. Designers work in teams. For instance, planning a new automobile requires many different types of designers. Special designers plan the outer form or body of the car. Then fabric and plastic specialists create new interiors to go with the body. They must be certain that human needs are met, such as comfortable seats. Designers must make sure that controls are within reach of the driver, without the dash becoming crowded or confusing. Computers help ensure that all the parts fit together correctly. This way, potential problems are identified before the vehicle goes into production.

Raymond Loewy, a famous product designer, is best known for his automotive designs. The 1953 Starlight Coupe was chosen for exhibition at The Museum of Modern Art in New York because of its unique design quality. The Avanti **(Figure 14.10)** is a luxury sports car that was created in 1962. It has such an unusual design that it was produced and sold until 1992. The Smithsonian Institution has one on display as an outstanding example of industrial design.

With recent advances in technology, such as computer-simulated models and three-dimensional animation, designers can see what potential designs look like without having to produce physical models. This helps make product designers better able to meet the requirements of industrial design.

▲ **FIGURE 14.10**   Look closely at this Avanti. Like many of today's aerodynamic cars, it has no grill. How do you think this design might affect the car's performance?

Raymond Loewy. Avanti. 1963.

Package Designer

A **package designer** *produces the containers that attract the attention of consumers.* They make boxes, tubes, bottles, shopping bags, and other kinds of containers. They use shape and color to make packages unique and appealing. Package designers must also consider package function. For example, when pill bottles first came on the market, the caps were so easy to remove that children were able to open them. Designers had to come up with a cap that was childproof but could be easily opened by an adult. It requires imagination and ingenuity to combine the visual, functional, and safety criteria needed to design for consumers.

Fashion Designer

Fashion designers plan and create clothing, hats, handbags, shoes, jewelry, and sportswear **(Figure 14.11).** They must know the appropriate materials to use for the articles being designed. They must also consider comfort and the way the human body moves when creating fashion designs. High-fashion designers create very expensive, one-of-a-kind

◀ **FIGURE 14.11** Fashion designers must come up with fresh, new ideas every season. Anyone considering a career in this area must be able to work under intense pressure to meet deadlines.

originals. Fashion designers also work for manufacturers who make clothes everyone can afford. A team of pattern makers, cutters, tailors, and factory workers who produce the clothes provide the necessary support for a fashion designer.

Photography, Film, and Video

Artists and designers interested in the media of photography, film, and video can find employment in many fields, including publishing and entertainment. Although these fields are not always easy to break into, plenty of aspiring artists eventually achieve success in them. Hard work, persistence, talent, and some special training are all necessary.

Photographer

Photographers work in portrait studios or photograph illustrations for books and magazines. Fashion photography, product and food photography, architectural photography, and fine-art photography are all growing specialties **(Figure 14.12).** Photographers also work for advertising agencies and corporations to create images that help sell products.

Digital cameras, which allow artists to record images digitally and then manipulate them using a computer, are becoming more and more important in the field. Digital cameras do not require special processing labs. The pictures can be viewed and printed immediately. They can also be manipulated and enhanced using computers.

Photographers also work in film and video. Moving picture photography for movies and television is one behind-the-scenes career many photographers find appealing **(Figure 14.13).** Video photographers make documentaries, create visual presentations for companies to distribute to potential investors, and record celebrations, such as birthdays, weddings, and anniversaries, for clients.

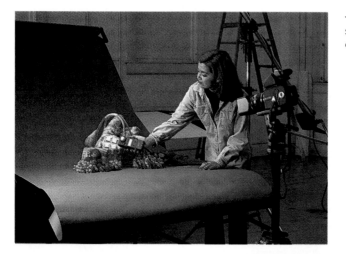

◀ **FIGURE 14.12** Photographers are skilled artists who use their cameras to create artwork.

▶ **FIGURE 14.13** Cinematographers operate movie cameras. They are trained in using light and color.

▲ **FIGURE 14.14** Photojournalists covering a game.

Photojournalist

Photojournalists are *visual reporters.* They work for newspapers and magazines and tell stories through their photographs. Photojournalists must understand design, know how to develop and print their own work, and have an eye for what is interesting to look at **(Figure 14.14).** Other photographers may be able to work in the comfort of a studio, but photojournalists must go where the news is happening.

Animator

Animators, or *artists who create moving cartoons,* use their skills in movies and television. The field of animation requires more visual artists than any other art–related field.

When artists create an animated film, they first select a story. They decide what styles of architecture and dress fit the story. Then they develop the story by drawing **storyboards,** *a series of still drawings that show a story's progress.* They draw approximately 60 sketches for each board. A short film needs three storyboards, and a full-length film may require more than 25. Storyboards look like comic strips. They provide the outline for the development of the film.

Layout artists are responsible for the overall look of the film. Background artists paint the settings from the layout artist's sketches. To create action, animators draw the major poses of each character, then other artists fill in the many drawings required to complete each movement. Each second of film requires 24 drawings to make the movement look smooth. As you can imagine, to create the more than 125,000 drawings required for a 90 minute movie is very expensive and time-consuming **(Figure 14.15).**

This has led to the creation of a new field, computer animation (optical electronic graphic arts), the art of making animated graphics by using the computer to fill in many of the images necessary to create the illusion of movement. An artist creates the main drawings and the important actions and scans these drawings into the computer. The artist may also do the drawings on the computer with the help of a special program. Then, using mathematical models, the computer determines how to make the drawings appear to move. The artist uses the computer to manipulate the images. This is a much less expensive and less time-consuming process than creating all the images by hand.

Special Effects Designer

Special effects designers plan the stunts and illusions in movies in order to make them look real. Training for this field may

require a college degree in art as well as film production and technology courses. Many large universities have cinema departments that offer courses in many aspects of film production.

Special effects artists require the skills of a painter, sculptor, and engineer. These artists have the ability to imagine and create fantasy scenes or imaginary creatures

▶ **FIGURE 14.15** Animator creating characters by hand.

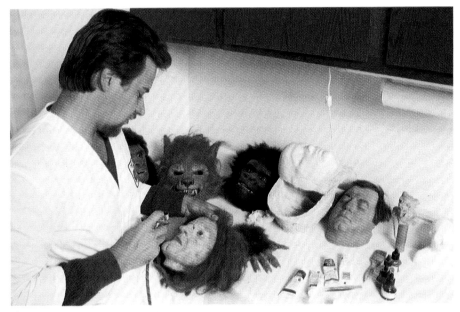

▲ **Figure 14.16** Special effects artist.

that look real **(Figure 14.16).** They can make you believe you are watching a dinosaur driving a car or a battle scene in a galaxy light-years away. In their work they use papier-mâché, plaster, plastic molds, paint, makeup, trick photography, and computers.

Art Director

In film, as well as in theatre, an art director works with set, costume, and lighting directors, as well as makeup artists and hairstylists, to bring all the elements of the show together **(Figure 14.17).** Art directors need to know art history as well as the special techniques of their craft. If a film or play is set in the past, the setting, furniture, costumes, and hairstyles must correctly reflect that time period.

A set or stage designer is an artist who is responsible for planning the backdrops and many of the props for a production. He or she oversees a team of artists who prepare the stage or set itself for the production. The set designer works with the prop master, who supplies everything the actors use during the production. The costume designer is like a fashion designer, but he or she must create clothing that is appropriate to the time and setting of

◀ **Figure 14.17** An art director studies the information that needs to be presented. He or she must decide how that information can be shown in a visually–appealing way.

▲ **FIGURE 14.18** Costume designers must create clothing appropriate to the time and setting of a movie or play.

▲ **FIGURE 14.19** Game designers.

tects, and work with property designers and location planners.

Computer, Arcade, and Video Game Designers

Game designers plan and create all aspects of computer, arcade, and video game design **(Figure 14.19)**. They create the background renderings and the animated figures and objects. They work with computer programmers to design visually appealing and exciting games. Because the game experience is a multi-media experience, the designer must have a special sensitivity to sound, story, and other aspects of game production.

Computer game designers also create virtual reality and three-dimensional worlds that gamers enjoy experiencing. As these technologies become more sophisticated, they will probably be used by more businesses, which means there may be many more opportunities in the field in the future.

Multi-media Designer

Multi-media designers combine text, graphics, sound, and interactive devices into a visually appealing product. They create multi-media presentations using special hardware and software programs. These presentations are used by companies to acquire clients. Multi-media designers also create interactive CD-ROMs and software for business, education, and entertainment. This requires a team approach. One person is usually responsible for the overall concept, while others create the images and text and still others put everything together.

☑ Check Your Understanding

1. What is a graphic designer?
2. What three requirements must a product of industrial design meet?
3. What are storyboards?
4. What types of designers do art directors work with?

the production **(Figure 14.18)**. For productions that travel, the work of the art director and set designer may include considerable technical problems. They may consult with engineers and archi-

Environmental and Education Careers

Environmental Planning and Development

The first environmental designers were prehistoric cave dwellers who eventually moved out of their caves and into the countryside. They learned to build huts for protection and thus became the first architects. Today there are many kinds of designers who plan environmental space. Their jobs involve making homes, workspace, and the surrounding landscape attractive and functional.

Urban Planner

Urban planners are trained architects concerned with the care and improvement of city environments. Every major American city has an urban planner (sometimes called a city planner). This person helps control the growth and development of a city. Some of the responsibilities of the urban planner are land use, urban renewal, and the development of harbors, city parks, and shopping malls. A good urban planner meets the needs of the community while keeping it attractive and appealing **(Figure 14.20).**

Architect

An **architect** must *design buildings that are well-constructed, aesthetically pleasing, and functional.* To function properly, a building must do what it was designed to do. Private houses and apartments must serve as comfortable homes for people. Office buildings, schools, and factories must also be comfortable, safe, efficient, and aesthetically pleasing. The aesthetic

▶ **FIGURE 14.20** Reston, Virginia is a planned community founded in 1962. About 40 percent of the total area is set aside for public use and as open space. Residents can work, shop, live, attend school, and enjoy many activities without leaving the community.

Aerial view of Reston, Virginia, a planned city. Courtesy of the Reston Land Corporation, Reston, Virginia.

If you have ever visited the Rock-and-Roll Hall of Fame in Cleveland, Ohio, or seen a picture of the pyramid entrance to the Louvre in Paris, you will be familiar with the work of the famous architect I.M Pei. Pei was born in Guangzhou (Canton), China, on April 26, 1917. When he was 18, he immigrated to the United States, where he studied architecture at the Massachusetts Institute of Technology and Harvard University. After World War II, he taught at Harvard for several years.

In 1956, he struck out on his own, creating his own company, I. M. Pei & Partners. Soon, he and his company were in great demand, not just in the United States, but all over the world. Pei has designed some of the largest constructions of the twentieth century.

Pei is known for approaching design problems with an innovative flair. Many of the buildings he is asked to design must meet multiple functions, such as the Rock-and-Roll Hall of Fame (Figure 14.21). This structure reflects the spirit of rock-and-roll while housing memorabilia, sound chambers, a concert hall, a film-and-video display center, a party room, and numerous other features.

◀ **FIGURE 14.21**
This building must hold an extensive collection of artifacts while expressing the spirit of rock-and-roll. Do you think it serves its purpose?

I. M. Pei. *Rock-and-Roll Hall of Fame and Museum*, Cleveland, Ohio. 1995.

effect of a building is extremely important. The structure must fit into its environment and enhance or complement the community. Because modern technology is so complex, architects usually specialize in particular types of buildings such as skyscrapers, shopping malls, or homes **(Figure 14.21).**

Architects must be knowledgeable about building materials, ventilation, heating and cooling systems, plumbing, stairways, and elevators. They must know basic engineering concepts so that they do not plan structures that are impossible to build. In addition, architects must be creative, be able to make accurate mechanical drawings, use a computer, have a strong background in mathematics and drafting, and be able to deal with customers.

▲ **Figure 14.22** Landscape architect.

Landscape Architect

Landscape architects design playgrounds, parks, and outdoor areas around buildings and along highways. They work closely with architects and urban planners to use and improve the natural setting so that it is easy to maintain and beautiful to look at. They create designs using flowers, plants, trees, shrubs, rivers, ponds, lakes, walks, benches, and signs, as shown in **Figure 14.22.** Landscape architects work with architectural firms, government agencies, individual homeowners, and facilities such as golf courses.

Interior Designer

An **interior designer** *plans the design and decoration of the interior spaces in homes and offices.* Successful designers use styles and materials that blend with the architecture and that please the client. They must understand decorating styles and materials **(Figure 14.23).** They must be able to look at an empty room and visualize the finished area.

Because interior designers spend as much time with clients as they do at the drawing board or computer, they must have patience and good communication skills. Some designers work for individual homeowners, while others plan and coordinate the interiors of department stores, offices, and hotels.

Exhibit and Display Designers

Exhibit designers plan presentations of collections, temporary exhibits, and traveling shows of all types. They work for trade shows, department stores, showrooms, art galleries, and museums. They decide how objects should be grouped and lit.

Display designers plan merchandise arrangements to attract customers and persuade them to buy products or services. A display designer is an important member of a sales team. The way a designer arranges merchandise in a store window helps draw customers into the store.

Activity	Using Design for Display

Applying Your Skills. Create a display of art objects for a display window in your school or one of flat artwork for a bulletin board display. Invent a title for your display, letter it neatly or use a computer application to print out the title. Include it with your arrangement.

▲ **Figure 14.23** Interior designer.

Art Education

Some art-related careers combine an interest in art with an interest in education. Teachers, art therapists, and museum curators and designers all use their training in different ways. Artistically inclined people who want to help others may find careers in education rewarding and fulfilling.

Art Teacher

Art teachers share their artistic knowledge and skills with students. They work in elementary, middle, or high schools as well as colleges **(Figure 14.24).** Art teachers help students learn to make aesthetic judgments and to develop their artistic skills and talents. In order to be successful, they must have art abilities themselves, but they must also be able to nurture talent in others who might not be self-confident or who might be intimidated by the process of creating art. Some teachers specialize in art history and help students learn about art instead of teaching students to create art. Most art teachers combine both approaches.

▲ **Figure 14.24** Art teacher.

▲ **Figure 14.25** Museum curator.

Art Therapist

Art therapists use art to help people with emotional and physical problems. They help physically challenged children and adults learn to explore the senses of vision and touch through artistic play and creation. Art therapists also help patients with mental and emotional problems change their behavior in a positive way. They show them how to express themselves in a constructive way—through art. Art therapy helps such patients talk about their problems and learn to handle them.

Art therapists may have training in physical therapy or psychology and usually work with members of these fields. They work in medical and psychiatric hospitals, community centers, physical rehabilitation programs, drug and alcohol treatment centers, and prisons.

Museum Curator and Designer

Museums house collections of paintings, sculpture, crafts, costumes, books, jewelry, and artifacts. **Museum curators,** who are usually trained in art history, *oversee the operations of museums.* They organize the collections and are responsible for recommending artworks that fit in with the theme or focus of the museum **(Figure 14.25).** Museum designers assemble and display these museum collections. Other artists might serve as tour guides, leading groups through the displays and providing information to the viewers. Some museums publish books that contain photographs of the objects in their collections, which requires the help of the curator and designers.

Fine Artists

Some artists choose to work independently as painters, sculptors, printmakers, weavers, or jewelers **(Figure 14.26).** They create the art they want to create, not what an employer asks them to make. Such artists are committed to creating art on their own terms. Many need a second job to help pay their living expenses. In the visual arts, as in the performing arts, few opportunities for stardom and large incomes exist. Some fine artists work in commercial art fields to supplement their income. Many teach in schools and colleges. Some, like Jacob Lawrence (Figure 4.19 on page 80), continue teaching even after they have become financially successful, because they feel that the ongoing interaction with art students enhances their creative thinking.

▲ **FIGURE 14.26** The work of artists is usually classified as either fine art or applied art. Fine art, such as a painting, is created to be viewed and appreciated. Applied art, such as ceramics or other craft objects, is created to be used.

Thinking About an Art Career

Are you suited for a career in the art world? It may be too soon for you to make a final decision about your future. However, if you have art ability and art is something you enjoy, then an art career may be right for you.

If you decide you want a career in art, you should begin working toward that goal while in high school. In the meantime, practice your skills. Study the great artists. Learn how to use a computer to enhance your talent. Explore art-related careers. Talk with your art teacher or guidance counselor for advice. You can also write to art schools and college art departments for advice and information on art careers.

☑ Check Your Understanding

1. What is the difference between an architect and a landscape architect?
2. What type of artist or designer plans presentations of collections?
3. What do art therapists do?

Art Criticism in Action

▲ **Figure 14.27**

Sandy Skoglund. *The Green House.* 1990. Cibachrome photograph. 127 × 178 cm (50 × 70″).
Skoglund Art Gallery, New York, New York.

1 ▶ DESCRIBE What do you see?

List all the information found in the credit line. Next, list the objects that you recognize in the photograph. Remember that this is a clue-collecting step. If you are not sure of something, do not guess.

- Describe the people including their poses, clothing, and colors.
- Describe the animals including their poses, breeds, and colors.
- Describe the setting in which these people and animals are placed. Notice the colors and textures.

2 ▶ ANALYZE How is this work organized?

Now you will study how the artist has organized the elements of art using the principles that you have studied.

- How have color, texture, form, and space been used in this work?
- How has the artist used rhythm and proportion?
- Where do you see harmony, emphasis, and variety?

3 ▶ INTERPRET What is the artist trying to communicate?

During this step, you will make guesses about the meaning of the work. You do not need to know what the artist meant. Instead, you will decide what this image says to you.

- How do the poses of the people and the animals affect the look of this work?
- How do color and texture affect the mood of this work? How does the artist's use of the principles of art affect the expressive quality of this work?
- What does this artwork express to you? Give it a creative title that sums up the expressive quality of this work.

4 ▶ JUDGE What do you think of the work?

Now you will decide if this is a successful work of art or not.

- Is this work interesting? Did it make you think?
- Did the artist use the elements of art and the principle of rhythm successfully?
- Do you think this is a successful work of art? Why or why not? Use one or more of the aesthetic theories described in Chapter 2 to defend your judgment.

MEET THE ARTIST
SANDY SKOGLUND

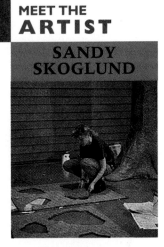

American, 1946 —

Sandy Skoglund is a contemporary American artist who works in an unusual mix of media. She builds installations, working with found materials and strangely colored animal sculptures. Her installations are often intricate reproductions of everyday environments, such as a lawn or a living room being overrun by nature in the form of brightly colored animals. She photographs her works and the prints are considered as much a part of the work as the installation itself.

Each installation Skoglund creates takes an average of six months to complete. She constructs the environment, and hand sculpts the animals that appear in her work. Each work conveys a symbolic message.

How is 3-D Computer Art Created?

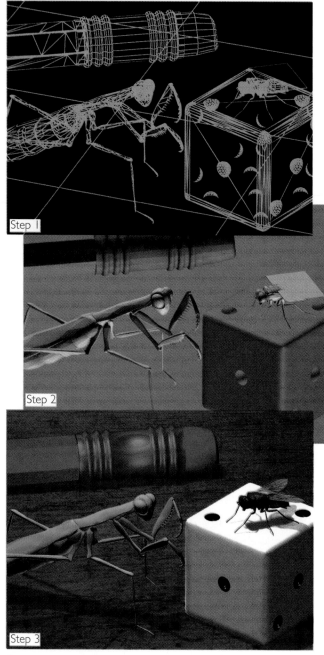

▲ **FIGURE 14.28**

Edward Harvey. *Mantis and Fly.* 1996. Three-dimensional ray-traced image.

Light originates from a source, such as the sun or a light bulb, and bounces off objects. It is the light that is bounced off of objects that allows us to see them as three-dimensional (3-D) objects. Formulas for how light bounces off different types of objects are used by scientists when designing mirrors and lenses.

With the invention of modern computers and software, a tool became available to create images of objects that look three-dimensional. Recreating an image requires tracing many rays of light from their source to their destinations. This process is known as *ray tracing.* Only a computer can make the millions of calculations necessary to trace the path of all the rays of light in a scene.

Today, low-cost desktop computers are powerful enough to do ray tracing. Many artists have begun to use these formulas in their artwork. First, they use 3-D graphics design software to create "wire frames" of objects (see Step 1). Next, they create "skins" for the wire frames, identifying textures and the reflective qualities of the covering material (see Step 2). Then they set up the lights that they will use in the scene. Finally, they "render" the picture by directing the computer to compute the ray tracing. This provides a final picture that is photorealistic (see Step 3).

Making the Connection

1. What does ray tracing mean and how does it help us see objects as three-dimensional?
2. Look at the illustration and use it to explain the steps involved in rendering three-dimensional images.
3. There are other types of animation used by artists, such as clay animation. Find out more about other techniques and how they are used.

Building Vocabulary

On a separate sheet of paper, write the term that best matches the definition given below.

1. One who translates ideas into images and arranges them in appealing and memorable ways.
2. Symbols or trademarks that are immediately recognizable.
3. One who creates visual images that complement written words.
4. Designer who produces the containers that attract the attention of consumers.
5. Visual reporters.
6. Artists who create moving cartoons.
7. A series of still drawings that show a story's progress.
8. Designer of buildings that are well-constructed, aesthetically-pleasing, and functional.
9. One who plans the design and decoration of the interior spaces in homes and offices.
10. Oversee the operations of museums.

Reviewing Art Facts

Answer the following questions using complete sentences.

1. When did the field of graphic design begin? What invention made it possible?
2. What elements of art do package designers use to make packages unique and appealing?
3. How is a costume designer different from a fashion designer?
4. What training do special effects designers need?
5. Why is technology important in art-related fields?
6. For what purposes are illustrations used?
7. What three requirements must industrial designers plan for?
8. How does a photojournalist differ from other photographers?
9. What does an urban planner do?

Thinking Critically About Art

1. **Analyze.** Find a copy of a book you enjoyed reading, preferably one that has an interesting cover design. Look at the design and think about how it relates to the content of the book. Then write a few paragraphs describing the cover design, the meaning of any symbolism the designer used, and your opinion of whether the cover illustrates the story appropriately.

2. **Extend.** With the teacher's permission, show a group of younger students how to make an age–appropriate artwork (such as finger painting or clay modeling). Offer instruction, encouragement, and assistance as they create their own works. If possible, work with a team of other student teachers. Write a few paragraphs describing your experience.

Use the Performing Arts Handbook on page 426 to find out about storyboard artist John Ramirez.

inter NET CONNECTION Learn more about art-related careers, especially those in the growing field of Web design. Visit Glencoe's Fine Arts Site at **www.glencoe.com/sec/art**. Explore the site for information on educational requirements and salary ranges for various careers in art.

HANDBOOKS

"I never plan a drawing, they just happen. In a dream it was shown to me what I have to do, of paintings."

Minnie Evans
1892–1987

◄

Minnie Evans. *Design Made at Airlie Gardens.* 1967. Oil and mixed media on canvas. 50.5 × 60.6 cm (19⅞ × 23⅞"). National Museum of American Art, Smithsonian Institution, Washington, D.C.

Performing Arts Handbook

The following pages were excerpted from Artsource: *The Music Center Study Guide to the Performing Arts,* developed by the Music Center Education Division, an award-winning arts education program of the Music Center of Los Angeles County.

The following artists and groups are featured in the *ARTTALK Performing Arts Handbook.*

■ Faustwork Mask Theater — 413

■ Martha Graham — 414

■ Merce Cunningham Dance Company — 415

■ Ballet Folklorico de Mexico — 416

■ Lewitzky Dance Company — 417

■ Joanna Featherstone — 418

■ Paul Winter — 419

■ African American Dance Ensemble — 420

■ Eth-Noh-Tec — 421

■ Eugene Friesen — 422

■ Vocalworks — 423

■ Korean Classical Music and Dance Company — 424

■ Kurt Jooss — 425

■ John Ramirez — 426

Faustwork Mask Theater

Faustwork Mask Theater.
"The Mask Man." Robert Faust, artistic director. Photo: Craig Schwartz, © 1993.

Robert Faust is an actor, athlete, dancer, choreographer, mask-maker, and the artistic director of his company, Faustwork Mask Theater. Born and raised in New Orleans, he experienced the color and pageantry of the Mardi Gras celebration throughout his youth and college years. Through his studies he came to realize that the carnival characters that annually paraded the streets of his hometown were actually works of art rooted in theatrical traditions. His one-man show, "The Mask Man," provides insights into the artistic, psychological, and historical aspects of masks. In his performance, Faust transforms himself into more than 20 different characters. Some characters speak, wearing *commedia dell'arte* style half-masks. Other characters are created with full masks worn on top of the head or on the back of the head. These masks can transform the performer into creatures on all fours or create distortions that baffle or surprise. Masks, found in many cultures throughout the world, are worn at festivals, celebrations, and rituals. In whatever ways they are used, masks have the power to transform an ordinary person into someone or something else.

■ Discussion Questions

1. The photo on this page shows Robert Faust with masks from "The Mask Man." Study the expression of the masks. What kinds of personalities are being shown? What can you tell about the character's age, culture, and personality traits from the mask alone?
2. The first Greek masks were used in plays to impersonate gods. What Greek gods and goddesses can you name? What were their attributes or symbols?

■ Creative Expression Activities

LANGUAGE ARTS. Read Greek myths such as "Theseus and the Minotaur" or "The Golden Fleece." How might masks be used in these works?

ART. Create a two-sided mask showing contrasting feelings on each side. You might choose happy and sad or good and evil. Think of movements to go with your mask to express each emotion.

Martha Graham

"Lamentation," 1930. Choreography and costume by Martha Graham. Performed by Janet Eilber. Photo: © Max Waldman. Max Waldman Archives.

"No matter what you say, you reveal yourself. Movement does not lie." These words, spoken to Martha Graham by her father when she was just a young girl, would hold great meaning for her later in life. Renowned for her contributions to the art of modern dance, Graham established a new way of communicating through the use of the body. Graham redefined the modern dance form by using movement to express emotion. She developed a vocabulary of movements to describe emotion in physical rather than verbal language. Exploring emotional moves that come from the center of the body, she based her movement system on the "contraction" or folding in of the torso that happens when you sob or laugh, and the "release" that happens when you inhale and unfold. "Lamentation" was created by Graham to represent the essence of grief and became her signature solo piece. Graham continued creating dances until her death, at the age of 96.

■ Discussion Questions

1. What is body language? How might body language be exaggerated and developed into a dance form?

2. Graham said that the movement of the torso called a contraction comes from where you laugh or cry. Think of other emotions that a person might feel. How are these emotions expressed by the body?

3. How do you think the costume in the picture could help in depicting movements that are the essence of grief or sorrow?

■ Creative Expression Activities

SCIENCE. Many of the movements in Graham's technique are based on contraction and release. The action that triggers or generates the contraction and release of muscles is breathing. Graham organized breathing for her stage purposes. Taking in the breath was a "release," pressing it out was a "contraction." Research the muscles involved in breathing and explore the action of your own breathing, trying to match it to the Graham idea of contraction and release.

Art Source / ARTSOURCE

PERFORMING ARTS HANDBOOK

Merce Cunningham Dance Company

Members of the **Merce Cunningham Dance Company** in *CRWDSPCR* (Crowdspacer). Photo: Lois Greenfield.

Merce Cunningham recounts four events that have led to important discoveries in his work: 1) his initial collaboration with composer John Cage in the late 1940s, when they began to separate the music and the dance; 2) his use of chance operations in his choreography; 3) his use of video and film as a meduim to choreograph works specifically for the camera; 4) and his use of dance computer software in the 1990s. With the computer figure, the Sequence Editor, one can create movements, store them in the memory, and eventually have a phrase of movement. It is possible to vary the timing so that you can see the body change from one shape to another in slow motion. Even if the computer produces positions and transitions that are not possible for humans to perform, it opens up new possibilities to explore. The film *CRWDSPCR* (Crowdspacer) documents the choreographic process in which Cunningham and the dancers experiment and adapt the movement sequences derived from the computer.

■ Discussion Questions

1. Study the dancers' positions in the photograph. Discuss similarities or differences from partnering or "lifts" that you have seen in ballet, ice skating, or gymnastics.

2. Look at the group of dancers in the photograph. Can you visually pinpoint a "center of balance" within the group? Is it in the exact center of the group or not? Explain why or why not.

3. Describe how the costumes affect your impression of the dancers and the dance shown in this photograph.

■ Creative Expression Activities

TECHNOLOGY. Learn more about Merce Cunningham's ongoing creative work and the activities of the Merce Cunningham Dance Company on the Internet. Research the company's touring schedules to countries and cities around the world.

SOCIAL STUDIES. Select one particular visual or performing artist from the 1950s and 1960s and find out what events during that period might have influenced their work.

Ballet Folklorico de Mexico

Ballet Folklorico de Mexico, "Danza de la Reata." Amalia Hernández, artistic director. Courtesy of Ballet Folklorico de Mexico.

Amalia Hernández, director of Ballet Folklorico de Mexico, decided at the age of eight to make dance her life's work. Her parents made her dream possible, and her training and experiences inspired her artistic vision. For over 30 years she has researched the roots of Mexican folklore and traditions. Her intention has been to create a contemporary show based on Mexican themes, and to convey the heart and spirit of the Mexican people. From the time of the Olmec Indians to the birth of modern Mexico, more than thirty distinct cultures have influenced Mexican culture. The Spanish brought horses to Mexico and introduced the caballero, or rancher, lifestyle. The dance shown in this photo is called "Danza de la Reata" and celebrates the beauty and harmony of life on the ranchero, or Mexican ranch.

■ Discussion Questions

1. Look closely at the photo of the male and female dancers inside the lariat, or lasso. Describe the costumes and what you think the dance is about.

2. What do you know about Mexican culture and dance? Can you think of any other styles of Mexican dance? Describe the costumes and movements.

3. What dances, songs, or paintings can you think of that refer to the work of a group of people, or to a specific culture?

■ Creative Expression Activities

LANGUAGE ARTS. Look at the photo on this page and use your imagination to write a description about what is taking place. Describe the relationship between the two people and the types of movements that would be done.

SOCIAL STUDIES. The Spanish brought horses and the Catholic religion to the indigenous people of Mexico and taught them a new way of life. The word "Mestizo" is used to refer to the unique blend of European and native cultures and races that make up the majority of the Mexican people of today. Research what other European cultures influenced the people of Mexico.

Lewitzky Dance Company

Lewitzky Dance Company. Bella Lewitzky, director. "Impressions #1 (Henry Moore)." Featured dancers: Jennifer Handel, Nancy Lanier, Laurie McWilliams, Theodora Fredericks, Deborah Collodel, Claudia Schneiderman. Photo: Vic Luke.

Bella Lewitzky has been a modern dance performer, choreographer, and dance educator for over 60 years. During her career, Bella realized that sculpture and other works of art could be used as a source of inspiration for dance movements. In particular, she focused on the work of sculptor Henry Moore. Since it was impossible to bring his sculptures into her studio, she and her dancers worked from photos found in books. They observed that his sculptures have massive physical weight and bulk and they also have two or three balance points, or places where the sculpture touches the ground. There are also holes, or negative spaces, that encourage the viewer to look through the sculptures, which alters the perspective. These observations and movement explorations evolved into a dance work called "Impressions #1 (Henry Moore)."

■ Discussion Questions

1. Look at the photo of the dancers on this page. Use the elements of line, shape, form, and texture to describe what you see.

2. Can you think of other artists who were inspired by an existing work of art and used it as a point of departure for a new work?

3. Use art books to locate a sculpture by Henry Moore. Observe it in terms of size, negative and positive space, form, and the number of balance points. Discuss how these concepts might be communicated through movement.

■ Creative Expression Activities

THEATRE/MOVEMENT. Working with partners, sketch out a few human *sculptures* of your own. Join with other pairs of students and position yourselves in relationship to each other to make more complex forms. Present your forms to the class.

DANCE. Dancers use the movements of their bodies to express action as it relates to weight, flow, space, and time. Explore ways to show the following eight actions using dance movements: press, flick, punch, float, slash, glide, wring, and dab.

SCIENCE. Select an object and answer the following questions: Is it light or heavy? How does it move or balance? How many points are touching the ground? What is the object's shape? Observe it from different perspectives (for example, upside down, and so on).

Joanna Featherstone

Joanna Featherstone. Photo: Craig Schwartz, © 1998.

Theatre artist and storyteller Joanna Featherstone has been "dancing with words" for as long as she can remember. A shy child who taught herself to read by studying cereal boxes, Featherstone read and memorized everything she could get her hands on, including boxes of baking soda, the Bible, and shopping catalogs. She discovered poetry at the age of 10 through a church reading of *Creation,* a work written by African American poet James Weldon Johnson (1871–1938). Featherstone memorized that poem too, although it wasn't until she was in college that she learned that it was the work of a writer of color, a man respected for his work in collecting and preserving much of the early poetry written by African Americans. An accomplished actress, Featherstone has performed on Broadway and off-Broadway stages, as well as for audiences in Europe and in West Africa. She has worked with award-winning string quartets, dancers, jazz musicians, and the New York Philharmonic. However, the performances in which she recites the work of early African American poets such as James Weldon Johnson, Paul Laurence Dunbar (1872–1906), and Phillis Wheatley (1753–1784) is where Featherstone finds her "dance of words" to be most fulfilling and complete.

■ Discussion Questions

1. Do you think it is possible for a solo storyteller or performer to move an audience by just using words? What other "tools" do they need to make an audience feel an emotion?

2. Featherstone taught herself to read by using cereal boxes. How did you learn to read? Have you ever helped someone else improve his or her reading skills? How many times each day do you use your reading skills?

■ Creative Expression Activities

LANGUAGE ARTS. Poetry is normal, everyday speech that has been "heightened" through the use of rhyming words, rhythmic patterns, and strong images. Think of a poem or song lyric that you know well and admire; write it down. Now translate it into normal speech, replacing or moving all rhyming words, changing rhythmic patterns, and turning the word images into less descriptive phrases. How does this "deconstruction" change the impact of the message the original writer tried to convey? Does the altered speech still contain as strong an emotional impact?

Paul Winter

Paul Winter. Photo courtesy of Paul Winter.

The music of Paul Winter includes the voices of animals from all around the world, including whales, wolves, elk, buffalo, eagles, tigers, and elephants. Paul listens to their songs, cries, and howls and adds melodies from his saxophone. In 1968, he heard the songs of the humpback whales, which strongly influenced his music and life. The humpback songs appear on some of his albums, which he considers a highlight in his musical career. The sounds of nature and animals help Paul create what he calls, "living music." Paul has recorded his music in the Grand Canyon, Yellowstone, and Glacier National Parks, and has visited the homes of many creatures throughout the world. These experiences are the foundation of his respect and concern for all living things. Paul views our planet as one big community and has received numerous awards in recognition of his musical efforts for endangered species and the environment, including two Grammy Awards. Paul lives in Connecticut and continues to pursue his love of music, nature, and community.

■ Discussion Questions

1. What is your favorite animal? What does this animal have in common with you?
2. What ecological or environmental issues are important to you, and how can they be reflected in your daily life?

■ Creative Expression Activities

SOCIAL STUDIES. Describe as many communities as you can—cultural, social, intellectual, spiritual, artistic, etc. Which communities are you a part of now or would like to be a part of in the future? How does nature and the environment fit within your definition of community?

LANGUAGE ARTS. Imagine human history with a greater understanding of nature and the environment. How would human progress be changed? What kinds of societies would be created and how would they coexist with nature? How would world relations be affected? Would we have a need for technology?

PERFORMING ARTS HANDBOOK

African American Dance Ensemble

African American Dance Ensemble. Chuck Davis, founder and artistic director. *African Roots in American Soil.*

Chuck Davis, a towering African-American dancer and choreographer, came from a background that was poor financially but rich in love. His first dance break came when he substituted for an injured member of the Richardson Dancers in Washington, D.C. In 1959, he joined the Klara Harrington Dancers and studied and performed with a number of modern, jazz, Afro-Cuban, and African dance companies. With disdain for the way black people were being portrayed in the media, he set out to present the truth about black culture through dance. "I have gone to Africa and I have sat at the feet of elders and I have listened as their words poured like raindrops onto and into my being. I have danced on the dusty earth and the sound of my feet pounding against the earth brought the rhythms of life into my blood," states Davis. After two decades of building his company in New York, he returned to North Carolina to start a second company, the African American Dance Ensemble, which he currently directs. Through dance, he works energetically to bring *all* people his message of "peace, love, and respect for everybody."

■ Discussion Questions

1. Look carefully at the photo on this page and describe the mood, costumes, and actions you observe. What clues do these give you about the style of dance and what is being communicated?

2. What popular dance styles do you think have their roots in traditional African cultural dances?

■ Creative Expression Activities

LANGUAGE ARTS. In many African ethnic groups, it is believed that wise people deliver proverbs. Read the following proverbs, then think of English equivalents: "Rain beats a leopard's skin, but it does not wash out the spots" (Asante); "When spider webs unite, they can tie up a lion" (Ethiopia); "Cross the river in a crowd and the crocodile won't eat you" (Kenya).

Eth-Noh-Tec

Eth-Noh-Tec. Robert Kikuchi-Yngoyo and Nancy Wang, artistic co-directors. Photo: Allen Nomura.

Eth-Noh-Tec, an Asian American Company based in San Francisco, uses a synthesis of music, movement, and words to present their unique style of theatre and storytelling. Their work is characterized by rhythmic dialogue, tightly choreographed poses, comic facial expressions, extensive hand gestures, and body postures with low centers of gravity. The Eth-Noh-Tec performance style reflects ancient Asian theatre styles such as Chinese opera (highly moral stories about the lives of common people) and Japanese Kyogen (comic plays written in everyday language). Company founders Robert Kikuchi-Yngojo and Nancy Wang present stories drawn from centuries-old Asian legends and modern-day experiences of Asian-Americans. The musical sounds of *ditze* (Chinese flute) and *taiko* (Japanese drums) add excitement, color, and punctuation to their performance. The mission of Eth-Noh-Tec is to create a fusion of cultures with a weaving (tec) together of distinctive cultural elements (eth) to create new possibilities (noh).

■ Discussion Questions

1. Look at the photo and discuss the stylized posture, costumes, and facial expressions of these performers. How does this differ from other plays, dances, or films you have seen?

2. One of the stories presented by Eth-Noh-Tec, *The Long Haired Girl,* is about the heroic acts of a young woman who brings water to her village. This ancient story is still being lived out today. Describe some examples of courageous acts done by people who wanted to help others.

■ Creative Expression Activities

HISTORY/SOCIAL STUDIES. There are universal values shared by all cultures in the world. Values such as the importance of family and friendship, respect for bravery, helping others, protecting our homes, and sharing our experiences (storytelling) are common to most cultures. Make a list of other shared values that you think exist in many of our world's cultures.

PERFORMING ARTS HANDBOOK

Eugene Friesen

Eugene Friesen. "Cello Man." Photo: Craig Schwartz, © 1998.

Eugene Friesen has created a unique voice among the cellists of the world. Drawing on a childhood filled with the great masterworks of Western music as well as the influences of hymn, ethnic, and popular music, Eugene uses cello and voice to create new music that is accessible and personal. At age eight Eugene began playing the cello, pulling it in a little red wagon to school for orchestra practice. In high school and college, Eugene played in school and community orchestras and began experimenting in rock and blues styles on an amplified cello. A graduate of the Yale School of Music, Eugene takes the cello out of its traditional classical realm, propelling it forward as an exciting instrument with immense powers of free expression. "Cello Man," featured in the photo, is a solo performance created in collaboration with Faustwork Mask Theater. In the show, Eugene weaves a spellbinding fabric with stories, songs, masks, and inventive techniques on cello and electric cello. The repertoire for "Cello Man" features Friesen's original music in a variety of styles: blues, contemporary, folk, electronic, and pop, and includes a duet with the recorded song of a humpback whale. The use of masks designed and created by director Robert Faust adds a dramatic element to the performance. During segments of the show, Eugene transforms himself with masks and costumes, integrating each character with the music he is playing.

■ Discussion Questions

1. Look at the photo and identify the animal depicted by the mask Eugene is wearing. Can you imagine the characteristics of the music Eugene might play based upon that animal?

2. Do you know how a cello is played? Can you describe the sound a cello makes?

3. Can you name any other instruments in the string family?

■ Creative Expression Activities

LANGUAGE ARTS. Write a story that has a musical instrument as a main character. The instrument's character may be personified, employing human traits and emotions, or it may appear as a key element in the story's plot. Think about the materials used in making the instrument you have selected to write about. Your story could begin with the tree from which a cello was made or the gourd from which a shaker was fashioned.

Vocalworks

Vocalworks. Bruce Cooper, Michael Geiger, Debbie and Tim Reeder, and Dave Eastly perform "Vocalworks Radio Hour." Photo: Richard Hines, © 1998.

Since 1983, Bruce Cooper, Michael Geiger, Tim and Debbie Reeder, and Dave Eastly of Vocalworks have brought the music of the 1930s and 1940s to audiences throughout the United States and abroad. Singing the music of the swing era, they are proud to note that Vocalworks has lasted longer than the swing era itself. In the "Vocalworks Radio Hour," the group re-creates a live radio broadcast from the period when home entertainment meant gathering around the radio in the living room to hear news, music, drama, or comedy programs. The Depression and World War II were very difficult times for the American people. They were concerned about their future and what would become of their country. Swing music was a wonderful escape that allowed people to lift their spirits and forget their troubles for awhile. Vocalworks shows the importance of music in that role and how it can still function in the same way today.

■ Discussion Questions

1. Improvisation is one of the characteristics of swing jazz. Look at the photo on this page. Identify the instruments. Which one is improvised?

2. Swing music was characterized by its positive message during the Depression in the 1930s and during World War II in the 1940s. Swing dance and music has had a resurgence today. How do you account for its renewed popularity?

■ Creative Expression Activities

LANGUAGE ARTS. Read about the Harlem Renaissance and its influence on jazz musicians and poets. Working in groups, present a choral verse reading of one of the following Langston Hughes poems to show how he was influenced by jazz: "The Weary Blues," "The Negro Speaks of Rivers," or "Afro-American Fragment."

SOCIAL STUDIES. Each of three groups will research one of the following periods: 1930–1935, 1936–1940, 1941–1945. Use the group period as a title and divide the paper into three sections: World, United States, and Swing Music. Group members should fill in the significant dates, people, and events during that time period.

Korean Classical Music and Dance Company

Korean Classical Music and Dance Company. Dong Suk Kim, artistic director. Photo: © Craig Schwartz.

Much of Korean folk music can be traced back more than 2,000 years. These rich traditions were passed down from person to person, rather than taught formally, and have remained a part of everyday village life. A childhood interest in Korean folk music developed into a rewarding career for Dong Suk Kim, director of the Korean Classical Music and Dance Company. At the age of twelve he began to study the music and dance of his birthplace, Korea. His studies eventually led him to a membership in a Korean government-sponsored troupe, which performed the music and dances of their country on a world tour. As part of the tour, Mr. Kim visited the United States and decided to make it his new home, eventually settling in southern California. In 1973, he founded a school for the study of Korean music and dance. The Korean Classical Music and Dance Company repertoire includes folk as well as the ancient formal court music and dance.

■ Discussion Questions

1. Look at the photo on this page and describe the details of the costumes the dancers are wearing. How might the costumes enhance the performance?

2. What other cultures can you think of that preserve their history, traditions, and dances by passing the knowledge from one generation to the next?

■ Creative Expression Activities

DANCE. Do some research on a traditional Korean folk dance and an ancient Korean formal court dance. Describe how these two styles of dance are similar or different from one another.

SOCIAL STUDIES. Both China and Japan have dominated Korea throughout its history. Do some research to find out how either China or Japan has contributed to Korean culture and traditions.

Kurt Jooss

The Joffrey Ballet of Chicago performing "The Green Table," Kurt Jooss choreographer. Photo: © Herbert Migdoll, 1998.

The curtain rises on a rectangular green table with ten gentlemen in morning coats and spats. They posture and disagree until pistols emerge, a shot is fired, and war is declared. The scene goes black. Next we see the figure of Death. In the scenes that follow, soldiers are called to fight, battles rage, refugees comfort one another, a profit-maker preys on the miseries of his fellow man, and a lone soldier holds watch. Through every scene, Death stalks the stage, claiming victim after victim, warrior and citizen alike. In the end the scene returns to the table, where the Gentlemen in Black start it up all over again.

"The Green Table," created by choreographer Kurt Jooss in 1932, is a compassionate and humanistic dance drama about the horrors of war. The mysterious figure of Death is a constant companion, simultaneously strong and sensitive, sinister and soothing. Ultimately he comes to each character, slipping into their lives and claiming them. Some victims he takes swiftly and surely, others slowly and gently. Some resist, some welcome him. Through the movement vocabulary, we see each character meeting Death in their own way, just as we all will. Productions of "The Green Table" are given by dance companies almost every year all over the world, making it probably the most performed of all dance works created in the twentieth century.

■ Discussion Questions

1. What do you think a dance theatre or dance drama is? How might it be different from dance pieces you have seen before?

2. Why do you think the gentlemen at the table wear masks?

3. Ballet or dance is, for the most part, made familiar to audiences through the world of myths, fairies, and mechanical dolls. Should dance pieces confront disturbing issues? Can they do so successfully?

■ Creative Expression Activities

LANGUAGE ARTS. There is a theory that dance cannot compete with the complexity offered by the spoken word. Can dance works take on complex intellectual arguments? Discuss these ideas using "The Green Table" as an example. Write a play, a narrative, or a poem based on the characters in "The Green Table." Read or perform it. Compare it with the ballet/dance work you are familiar with.

John Ramirez

John Ramirez, "Every Picture Tells a Story." Photo: © Craig Schwartz, 1998.

Animator John Ramirez likes to mix art with music. Working with professional musicians such as Paul Tracey, he draws storyboards that bring music and words to life. Ramirez has worked as a storyboard artist for both Walt Disney Feature Animation and Warner Brothers Feature Animation. He loved to draw when he was growing up, especially trains, and felt very proud when his mother would make copies of his work. Eventually, he began to create his own comic strips—a form of storyboarding—and later his own animated films. For every animation project a team of highly creative people come together. The process might begin with the storyboard artist listening to the selected music many times, going with the images that come to mind, and then developing them into a rough storyboard sequence. Ramirez then explains the story line and describes the characters to the other members of the creative team. The storyboard artist then goes back to the drawing board and incorporates the new ideas. This process is repeated over and over until the work is refined. Only then does the animation process begin, usually taking about two years to complete a feature film.

■ Discussion Questions

1. Describe in your own words the basic process required in the making of an animated film.
2. Technology has had a great impact on animated films by enabling animators to produce very complex moving images, such as *Toy Story, Babe,* and *Mulan.* What else can you think of that has been enhanced by technology? How has technology affected communication, work, personal relationships?
3. What about animated films do you find the most intriguing? Why?

■ Creative Expression Activities

LANGUAGE ARTS/ART. Think of a specific topic, such as airplanes, cars, animals or people. Look in magazines to identify all the photos you can find that relate to this theme. Create a simple storyboard, then write a simple storyline which describes or sells an idea or product.

ART. Take a pad of unlined paper or make one by stapling 25 to 50 pages together to make a Flip Book. Choose a simple idea like a bouncing ball or a flower growing. Create a series of pictures in the right hand bottom corner that will show action when you flip through the pages.

Table of Contents

Drawing Tips

1	Making Contour Drawings	428
2	Making Gesture Drawings	428
3	Drawing Calligraphic Lines with a Brush	428
4	Using Shading Techniques	429
5	Using Sighting Techniques	429
6	Using a Viewing Frame	430
7	Using a Ruler	430
8	Making a Grid for Enlarging	431
9	Measuring Rectangles	431

Painting Tips

10	Mixing Paint to Change the Value of Color	431
11	Making Natural Earth Pigment Paints	432
12	Working with Watercolors	432
13	Cleaning a Paint Brush	432

Printmaking Tip

14	Making a Stamp Print	433

Sculpting Tips

15	Working with Clay	433
16	Joining Clay	433
17	Making a Pinch Pot	434
18	Using the Coil Technique	434
19	Papier-Mâché	434
20	Making a Paper Sculpture	435

Other Tips

21	Making Paper	435
22	Basic Embroidery Stitches	436
23	Weaving Techniques	437
24	Making a Coiled Basket	439
25	Making a Tissue Paper Collage	440

Display Tips

26	Making a Mat	441
27	Mounting a Two-Dimensional Work	442
28	Working with Glue	442

Safety in the Art Room   443

DRAWING TIPS

1. Making Contour Drawings

When you make a contour drawing, your eye and hand must move at the same time. You must look at the object, not at your drawing. You must imagine that your pencil is touching the edge of the object as your eye follows the edge. Don't let your eye get ahead of your hand. Also, do not lift your pencil from the paper. When you move from one area to the next, let your pencil leave a trail. If you do lift your pencil accidentally, look down, place your pencil where you stopped, and continue.

a. To help you coordinate your eye-hand movement, try this: First, tape your paper to the table so it will not slide around. Then, hold a second pencil in your nondrawing hand and move it around the edges of the object. With your drawing hand, record the movement.

b. If you have trouble keeping your eyes from looking at the paper, ask a friend to hold a piece of stiff paper between your eyes and your drawing hand so the drawing paper is blocked from view. You might also place your drawing paper inside a large paper bag turned sideways. A third method is to put the object on a chair and place the chair on a table. When you are standing, the object should be at your eye level. Then, place your drawing paper on the table directly under the chair. In this way you will be unable to see the paper easily.

c. When you draw without looking at the paper, your first sketches will look strange. Don't be discouraged. The major purpose of blind contour drawing is to teach you to concentrate on directions and curves. The more you practice, the more accurate your drawings will become.

d. As you develop your skills, remember that in addition to edges, contours also define ridges. Notice the wrinkles you see at the joints of fingers and at a bent wrist or bent elbow. Those wrinkles are curved lines. Draw them carefully; the lines you use to show these things will add the look of roundness to your drawing.

e. After you have made a few sketches, add pressure as you draw to vary the thickness and darkness of your lines. Some lines can be emphasized and some can be made less important through the right amount of pressure from your hand.

2. Making Gesture Drawings

Unlike contour drawings, which show an object's outline, gesture drawings show movement. They should have no outlines or details.

a. Using the side of a piece of unwrapped crayon or a pencil, make scribble lines that build up the shape of the object. Do not use single lines that create stick figures.

b. Work very quickly. When drawing people, do the head, then the neck, and then fill in the body. Pay attention to the direction in which the body leans.

c. Next, scribble in the bulk of the legs and the position of the feet.

d. Finally, add the arms.

3. Drawing Calligraphic Lines with a Brush

Mastering the technique of drawing with flowing, calligraphic lines takes practice. You will need a round watercolor brush and either watercolor paint or ink. First, practice making very thin lines.

a. Dip your brush in the ink or paint and wipe the brush slowly on the side of the ink bottle until the bristles form a point.

b. Hold the brush at the metal ferrule so the brush is vertical rather than slanted above the paper. Imagine that the brush is a pencil with a very sharp point—if you press down, you will break the point (Figure T.1).

▲ **Figure T.1**

c. Touch the paper lightly with the tip of the brush and draw a line.

d. When you are able to control a thin line, you are ready to make calligraphic lines. Start with a thin line and gradually press the brush down to make the line thicker. Pull up again to make it thinner (Figure T.2, page 429). Practice making lines that vary in thickness.

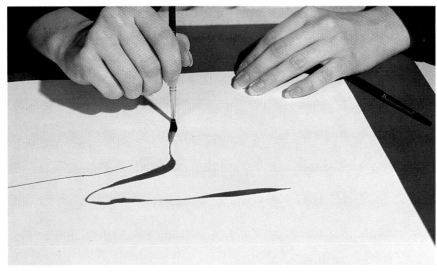

▲ **Figure T.2**

lines or dots far apart and bring them closer together. (Figure T.3.)

5. **Using Sighting Techniques**
   Sighting is a method that will help you determine proportions.

   a. Hold a pencil vertically at arm's length in the direction of the object you are drawing. Close one eye and focus on the object you are going to measure.

   b. Slide your thumb along the pencil until the height of the pencil above your thumb matches the height of the object (Figure T.4).

   c. Now, without moving your thumb or bending your arm,

4. **Using Shading Techniques**
   The following techniques help create shading values.

   - **Hatching:** Use a series of fine parallel lines.
   - **Crosshatching:** Use two or more intersecting sets of parallel lines.
   - **Blending:** Use a smooth, gradual application of an increasingly dark value. Pencil lines may be blended.
   - **Stippling:** Create shading with dots.

   To be effective in forming the shaded areas, your lines and strokes must follow the form of the object. Use lines to show the surface of a flat surface. Let the lines run parallel to one edge of the surface. To show a curved surface, draw a series of parallel curved lines to give the illusion of roundness. The lines should follow the curve of the object.

   Lines or dots placed close together create dark values. Lines or dots spaced farther apart create lighter values. To show a gradual change from light to dark, begin with

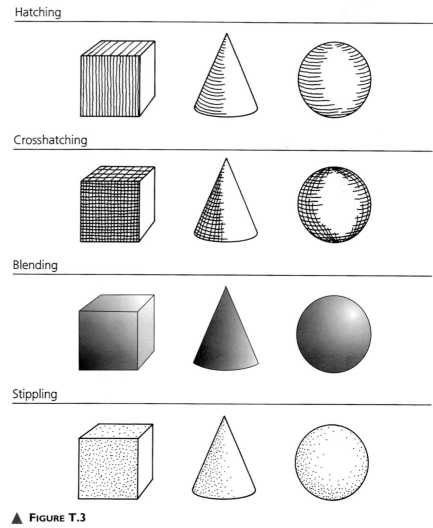

Hatching

Crosshatching

Blending

Stippling

▲ **Figure T.3**

▲ **FIGURE T.4**

subject. Imagine that the opening represents your drawing paper.

c. You can decide how much of the subject you want to include in your drawing by moving the frame up, down, or sideways.

d. You can also move the frame closer or farther away to change the focus of your drawing.

7. Using a Ruler

There are times when you need to draw a crisp, straight line.

a. Hold the ruler with one hand and the pencil with the other.

b. Place the ruler where you wish to draw a straight line.

c. Hold the ruler with your thumb and first two fingers. Be careful that your fingers do not stick out beyond the edge of the ruler.

d. Press heavily on the ruler so it will not slide while you're drawing.

e. Hold the pencil lightly against the ruler.

f. Pull the pencil quickly and lightly along the edge of the ruler. The object is to keep the ruler from moving while the pencil moves along its edge.

hold the pencil parallel to the widest part of the object. Compare the height of the object with its width. You can determine the ratio of height to width by seeing how many times the smaller measure fits into the larger measure. This method can be applied either to different parts of the same object or to two or more different objects. Use one measurement as a base measurement and see how the other measurements relate to it.

6. Using a Viewing Frame

A viewing frame helps you to zero in on an area or object you intend to draw. To make a viewing frame, do the following:

a. Cut a rectangular hole in a heavy sheet of paper (Figure T.5).

b. Hold the frame at arm's length and look through it at your

▲ **FIGURE T.5**

8. Making a Grid for Enlarging

Sometimes you must take a small drawing and enlarge it. To do this, you must first measure the size that the large, finished drawing will be. Then, using proportional ratios, reduce that size to something you can work with.

a. For example: If you want to cover a wall 5 feet high and 10 feet wide, let 1 inch equal 1 foot. Then make a scale drawing that is 5 inches high and 10 inches wide. You may work either in inches or centimeters.

b. After you have completed your small drawing, draw vertical and horizontal grid lines 1 inch apart on the drawing. Number the squares (Figure T.6).

c. On the wall, draw vertical and horizontal grid lines one foot apart.

d. Number the squares on the wall to match the squares on the paper and enlarge the plan by filling one square at a time.

9. Measuring Rectangles

Do you find it hard to create perfectly formed rectangles? Here is a way of getting the job done:

a. Make a light pencil dot near the long edge of a sheet of paper. With a ruler, measure the exact distance between the dot and the edge. Make three more dots the same distance in from the edge. (See Figure T.7.)

b. Line a ruler up along the dots. Make a light pencil line running the length of the paper.

c. Turn the paper so that a short side is facing you. Make four pencil dots equally distant from the short edge. Connect these with a light pencil rule. Stop when you reach the first line you drew.

d. Do the same for the remaining two sides. Erase any lines that

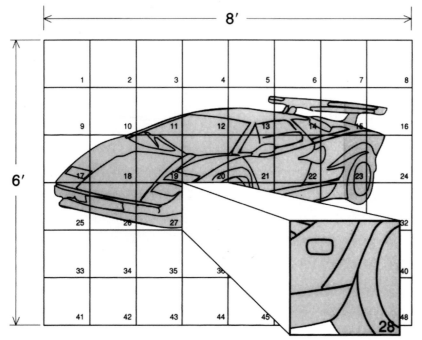

▲ **FIGURE T.7**

may extend beyond the box you have made.

e. Trace over the lines with your ruler and pencil. The box you have created will be a perfectly formed rectangle.

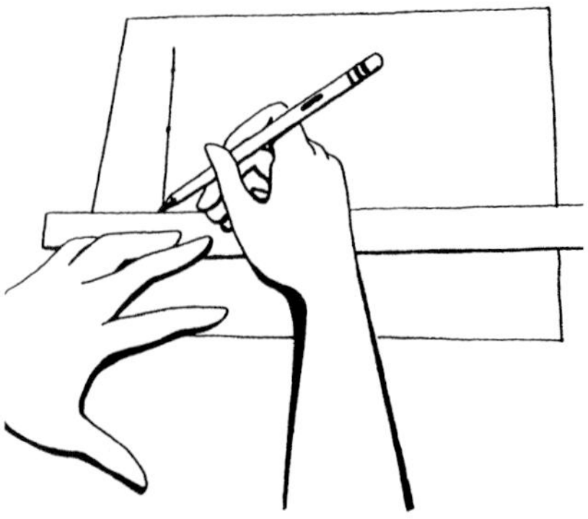

PAINTING TIPS

10. Mixing Paint to Change the Value of Color

You can better control the colors in your work when you mix your own paint. In mixing paints, treat opaque paints (for example, tempera) differently from transparent paints (for example, watercolors).

a. *For light values of opaque paints.* Add only a small amount of the hue to white. The color can always be made stronger by adding more of the hue.

b. *For dark values of opaque paints.* Add a small amount of black to the hue. Never add the hue to black.

c. *For light values of transparent paints.* Thin a shaded area with water. This allows more of the white paper to show through.

d. *For dark values of transparent paints.* Carefully add a small amount of black to the hue.

▲ **FIGURE T.6**

11. Making Natural Earth Pigment Paints

Anywhere there is dirt, clay, and sand, you can find natural earth pigments.

a. Collect as many different kinds of earth colors as you can find (Figure T.8).

▲ **FIGURE T.8**

b. Grind them as finely as possible. If you can, borrow a mortar and pestle from the science lab (Figure T.9). Regardless of the method you use, your finished product will still be a little gritty. It will not have the smooth texture of commercial pigment.

c. For the binder, use one part white glue to one part water. Put a few spoons of pigment into a small container and add some of the binder. Experiment with different proportions of pigment and binder.

d. When you have found the best proportion, apply the mixture to paper with a variety of brushes. Do not allow the brushes you use to dry before you wash them, because the glue will solidify.

e. Keep stirring your paint as you work to keep the pigment from settling. The pigment will keep indefinitely. Mix a fresh batch each time you paint, because the mixed paint is difficult to store for more than a few days.

12. Working with Watercolors

Here are some tips to control watercolor paints.

a. If you apply wet paint to damp paper, you create lines and shapes with soft edges.

b. If you apply wet paint to dry paper, you create lines and shapes with sharp, clear edges.

c. If you dip a dry brush into damp paint and then brush across dry paper, you achieve a fuzzy effect.

d. School watercolors come in semi-moist cakes. Before you use them, place a drop of water on each cake to let the paint soften. Watercolor paints are transparent. You can see the white paper through the paint. If you want a light value of a hue, dilute the paint with a large amount of water. If you want a bright hue, you must dissolve more pigment by swirling your brush around in the cake of paint until you have dissolved a great deal of paint. The paint you apply to the paper can be as bright as the paint in the cake.

13. Cleaning a Paint Brush

Rinsing a paint brush under running water will not clean it completely. Paint will remain inside the bristles and cause the brush to lose its shape. Use the following procedure to help your brushes last a long time.

a. Rinse the thick paint out of the brush under running water.

b. Do not use hot water. Gently "paint" the brush over a cake of mild soap or dip it into a mild liquid detergent (Figure T.10).

c. Gently scrub the brush in the palm of your hand to work the soap into the center of the brush. This will remove paint that you did not realize was still in the brush (Figure T.11).

d. Rinse the brush under running water while you continue to scrub your palm.

e. Repeat steps b, c, and d.

▲ **FIGURE T.10**

▲ **FIGURE T.9**

▲ **FIGURE T.11**

▲ **FIGURE T.12**

f. When your brush is thoroughly rinsed, shape it into a point with your fingers (Figure T.12).

g. Place the brush in a container with the bristles up so it will keep its shape as it dries.

PRINTMAKING TIP

14. Making a Stamp Print

A stamp print is an easy way to make repetitive designs. The following are a few suggestions for making a stamp and printing with it. You may develop some other ideas after reading these hints. Remember, printing reverses your design, so if you use letters, be certain to cut or carve them backward.

- Cut a simple design into the flat surface of a rubber eraser with a knife that has a fine, precision blade.
- Glue yarn to a bottle cap or a jar lid.
- Glue found objects to a piece of corrugated cardboard. Make a design with paperclips, washers, nuts, leaves, feathers, or anything else you can find. Whatever object you use should have a fairly flat surface. Make a handle for the block with masking tape.
- Cut shapes out of a piece of inner tube material. Glue the

shapes to a piece of heavy cardboard.

There are several ways to apply ink or paint to a stamp:

- Roll water-base printing ink on the stamp with a soft brayer.
- Roll water-base printing ink on a plate and press the stamp into the ink.
- Apply tempera paint or school acrylic to the stamp with a bristle brush.

SCULPTING TIPS

15. Working with Clay

To make your work with clay go smoothly, always do the following:

a. Dip one or two fingers in water.

b. Spread the moisture from your fingers over your palms.

Never dip your hands in water. Too much moisture turns clay into mud.

▲ **FIGURE T.13**

▲ **FIGURE T.15**

16. Joining Clay

Use these methods for joining clay.

a. First, gather the materials you will need. These include clay, slip (a creamy mixture of clay and water), brush, a scoring tool (such as a fork), and clay tools.

b. Rough up or scratch the two surfaces to be joined (Figure T.13).

c. Apply slip to one of the two surfaces using a brush or your fingers (Figure T.14).

d. Gently press the two surfaces together so the slip oozes out of the joining seam (Figure T.15).

e. Using clay tools and/or your fingers, smooth away the slip that has oozed out of the seam (Figure T.16). You may wish to smooth out the seam as well,

▲ **FIGURE T.14**

▲ **FIGURE T.16**

or you may wish to leave it for decorative purposes.

17. Making a Pinch Pot

To make a pot using the pinch method, do the following:

a. Make a ball of clay by rolling it between your palms.

b. Set it on the working surface and make a hole in the top by pushing both thumbs into the clay. Stop pushing before your thumbs reach the bottom.

c. Begin to pinch the walls between your thumb and fingers, rotating the pot as you pinch.

d. Continue pinching and shaping the walls of the pot until they are an even thickness and the pot is the desired shape.

18. Using the Coil Technique

Collect all the materials you will need. These include clay, a cloth-covered board, slip and brush, scoring tool, small bowl of water, and pattern for a circular base.

a. Make a base by flattening a piece of clay to about ½ inch thick. Using the pattern, cut the base into a circle.

b. Begin a clay coil by shaping a small ball of clay into a long roll on the cloth-covered board until the roll is about ½ inch thick (Figure T.17). Your hands should be damp so the clay remains damp.

▲ **FIGURE T.17**

c. Make a circle around the edge of the clay base with the roll of clay. Cut the ends on a diagonal and join them so the seam does not show. Using scoring and slip, join this first coil to the base.

d. Make a second coil. If you want the pot to curve outward, place the second coil on the outer edge of the first coil. Place coil on the inner edge for an inward curve. Use proper joining techniques for all coils.

19. Papier-Mâché

Papier-mâché is a French term that means mashed paper. It refers to sculpting methods that use paper and liquid paste. The wet paper and paste material are molded over supporting structures such as a wad of dry paper or crumpled foil. The molded paper dries to a hard finish. Following are three basic methods for working with papier-mâché.

Pulp Method

a. Shred newspaper, paper towels, or tissue paper into tiny pieces and soak them in water overnight. (Do not use slick paper as it will not soften.)

b. Mash the paper in a strainer to remove the water or wring it out in a piece of cloth.

c. Mix the mashed paper with prepared paste or white glue until the material is the consistency of soft clay. Use the mixture to model small shapes.

d. When papier-mâché is dry, it can be sanded, and holes can be drilled through it.

Strip Method

a. Tear paper into strips.

b. Either dip the strips in a thick mixture of paste or rub paste on the strips with your fingers. Decide which method works best for you.

c. Use wide strips to cover wide forms. Very thin strips will lie flat on a small shape.

d. If you do not want the finished work to stick to the support structure, first cover the form with plastic wrap or a layer of wet newspaper strips. If you are going to remove the papier-mâché from the support structure, you need to apply five or six layers of strips. Rub your fingers over the strips so that no rough edges are left sticking up (Figure T.18). Change directions with each layer so that you can keep track of the number. If you are going to leave the papier-mâché over the support structure, then two or three layers may be enough.

Sheet Method

a. Brush or spread paste on a sheet of newspaper or newsprint (Figure T.19). Lay a second

▲ **FIGURE T.18**

▲ **FIGURE T.19**

▲ **Figure T.20**

sheet on top of the first and smooth out the layers. Add another layer of paste and another sheet of paper. Repeat this process until you have four or five layers of paper. This method is good for making drapery on a figure (Figure T.20).

b. If you let the layers dry for a day until they are leathery, they can be cut and molded any way you wish. Newspaper strips dipped in the paste can be used to seal any cracks that may occur.

Support Structures

a. Dry newspaper can be wadded up and wrapped with string or tape (Figure T.21).

b. Wire armatures can be padded with rags before the outside shell of papier-mâché is added.

c. Found materials such as boxes, tubes, and plastic

▲ **Figure T.21**

bowls, can be arranged and taped together to form a base (Figure T.22).

d. For large figures, a wooden frame covered with chicken wire makes a good support. Push and pinch the wire into the shape you want.

▲ **Figure T.22**

20. Making a Paper Sculpture

Another name for paper sculpture is origami. The process originated in Japan and means "folding paper." Paper sculpture begins with a flat piece of paper. The paper is then curved or bent to produce more than a flat surface. Here are some ways to experiment with paper.

• **Scoring.** Place a square sheet of heavy construction paper on a flat surface. Position the ruler on the paper so that it is close to the center and parallel to the sides. Holding the ruler in place, run the point of a knife or a pair of scissors along one of the ruler's edges. Press down firmly but take care not to cut through the paper. Gently crease the paper along the line you made. Hold your paper with the crease facing upward. You can also score curved lines, but you must do this with gradually bending curves or wide arcs. If you try to make a tight curve, such as a semicircle, the

paper will not give. For a tight curve you will have to make cuts to relieve the tension.

• **Pleating.** Take a piece of paper and fold it 1 inch from the edge. Then fold the paper in the other direction. Continue folding back and forth.

• **Curling.** Hold one end of a long strip of paper with the thumb and forefinger of one hand. At a point right below where you are holding the strip, grip it lightly between the side of a pencil and the thumb of your other hand. In a quick motion, run the pencil along the strip. This will cause the strip to curl back on itself. Don't apply too much pressure, or the strip will tear. (See Figure T.23.)

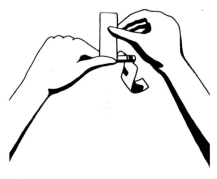

▲ **Figure T.23**

OTHER TIPS

21. Making Paper

Papermaking is a process in which fibers are broken down and reformed as a sheet. In order to make paper, collect all the materials you will need. These include a food blender, two matching stretcher frames approximately 9 x 12 inches each, rustproof window screen slightly larger than the stretchers, staple gun, duct tape, Handi Wipes towels, large pan 5 to 8 inches deep, newspapers, assorted papers, and water.

a. Make the mold by stretching the screen over the frame, stapling it at the edges, and covering the rough edges with duct tape. The second frame is the deckle, the frame that keeps the pulp in place on the mold.

b. Tear paper into 1-inch squares. Put 4 cups water and $1/2$ cup paper scraps into the blender and blend for several minutes until the mixture is the consistency of watery cooked oatmeal.

c. Pour pulp into pan. Continue making pulp until there is about 4 inches of pulp in the pan. Additional water may be added to aid in the papermaking process.

d. Make a pad of newspapers $1/4$ inch thick. Unfold Handi Wipes towels and lay one on the pad; this is the blotter.

e. Align deckle on top of mold. Stir pulp to suspend paper fibers. Scoop mold and deckle under surface of water and shake to align fibers. Lift to drain excess water.

f. Remove the deckle and flip the mold and pulp onto the blotter, pulp side down against the Handi Wipes towel. Blot back of molds with a sponge to remove excess water and to compress the fibers. Remove the mold, using a rocking motion.

g. Lay another Handi Wipes towel on top of the sheet of paper and add more newspapers. Repeat the layering process.

h. Let paper dry slowly for 1–3 days. When dry, peel off the Handi Wipes.

i. To clean up, drain pulp through the mold or a sieve. Squeeze excess water from pulp and save pulp in a plastic bag for one to three days or discard it.

22. Basic Embroidery Stitches

The charts below and on the next page show the most common embroidery stitches.

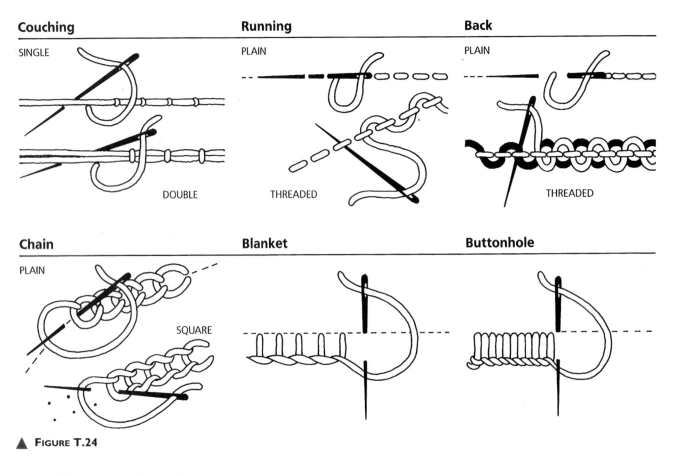

Couching
SINGLE
DOUBLE

Running
PLAIN
THREADED

Back
PLAIN
THREADED

Chain
PLAIN
SQUARE

Blanket

Buttonhole

▲ **FIGURE T.24**

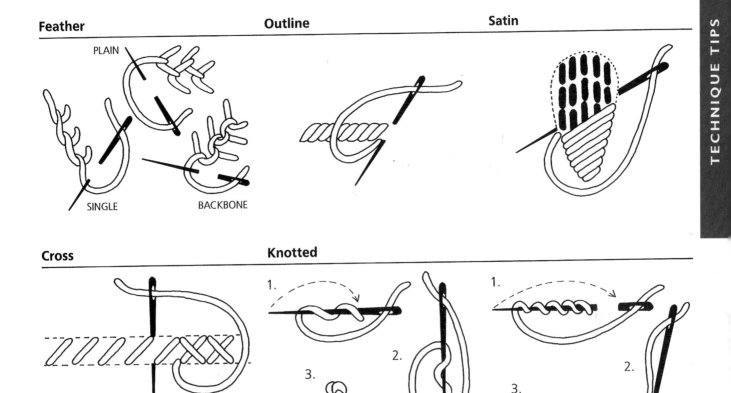

Feather

PLAIN

SINGLE   BACKBONE

Outline

Satin

Cross

Knotted

1.

2.

3.

FRENCH

1.

2.

3.

BULLION

▲ **Figure T.24 (continued)**

23. Weaving Techniques

To make a cardboard loom, gather the materials you will need. They include cardboard, ruler, pencil, scissors, strong, thin yarn for warp, various yarns and fibers for weft, tapestry needle, comb, and dowel.

a. Measure and cut notches ¼ inch apart and ½ inch deep on opposite sides of the cardboard.

b. Tape warp thread to back of loom. Bring it to the front through the top left notch. Pull it down to the bottom of the loom and pass it through the bottom left notch to the back. Move one notch to the right and continue until you reach

the last notch. Then tape the end of the warp thread to the back. (Figure T.25)

c. Start to weave at the bottom of the loom, using a thin yarn. The weft yarns are the horizontal yarns; the easiest way to pull the weft yarn through the warp

threads is to use an over-one-under-one motion. At the end of the row, reverse directions. (Figure T.26)

d. Do not pull the weft threads too tight. Let them balloon, or curve slightly upward (Figure T.27).

▲ **Figure T.25**

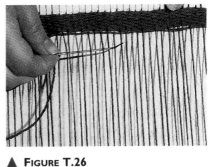

▲ **Figure T.26**

TECHNIQUE TIPS

▲ **Figure T.27**

▲ **Figure T.28**

e. After weaving several rows, pack the weft threads with a comb (Figure T.28). The tighter the weave, the stronger it will be.

f. After there is about 1 inch of tight weave, begin varying weave and materials (Figure T.29). End the process with another inch of thin, tight weave.

g. Before removing the fabric from the loom, weave in the loose ends. Cut the warp threads from the loom carefully and tie two at a time so they will not unravel.

h. Tie or sew the finished fabric to a dowel.

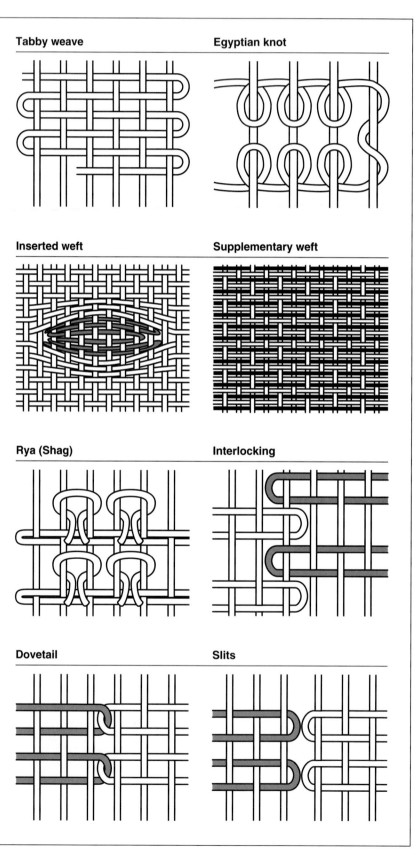

Tabby weave

Egyptian knot

Inserted weft

Supplementary weft

Rya (Shag)

Interlocking

Dovetail

Slits

▶ **Figure T.29**

24. Making a Coiled Basket

Mastering the technique of making a coiled basket takes practice. You will need *core* material (such as heavy cord), weft wrapping materials (such as yarns and fibers), a tapestry needle, scissors, and tape.

Coiling is a stitching technique in which the continuous coils of the *core* material are stitched together with a binding material called the *weft*. The first time you try this your binding and stitches probably will not look neat. Undo the work and begin again. You want to cover the core material completely, and all your weft binding and stitches must be even and tight.

a. Trim the end of the core so it tapers. Thread the tapestry needle with a 3-foot length of weft. Using the loose weft end, begin to wind it around the core starting about 2 inches from the end. Overlap the end as you wind to anchor it. Wind the weft to about 1/2 inch from the tapered end of the core (Figure T.30).

b. Bend the core, catch the tapered end, and make a loop (Figure T.31).

c. Continue winding for about 2 inches, being sure that the tapered core is attached securely to the solid section of core material. Push the tapestry needle through the center of the loop (Figure T.32).

d. Bend the core to form a coil and bring the weft between the core and the coil. (Figure T.33) Begin winding the weft around the core from front to back. You are now ready to begin the Lazy Squaw stitch.

e. Wind the weft around the core from front to back four times.

Then, bringing the weft from behind and over the core, push the needle into the center of the coil (Figure T.34). Pull tightly and hold. Continue to wrap the weft four times around the core and pull the fifth stitch into the center until you complete two coils. Hold them flat between your fingers while you work.

f. As the coiling progresses, you may wrap the weft more than four times between stitches. After the first two coils, you will no longer bring the stitch back to the center; just take it over two coils (Figure T.35). Always insert the needle from the front. This way you can see exactly where you are placing the needle. If you want to create a pattern of long stitches, this is essential.

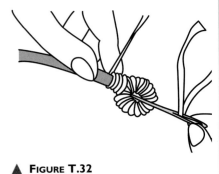

▲ **FIGURE T.32**

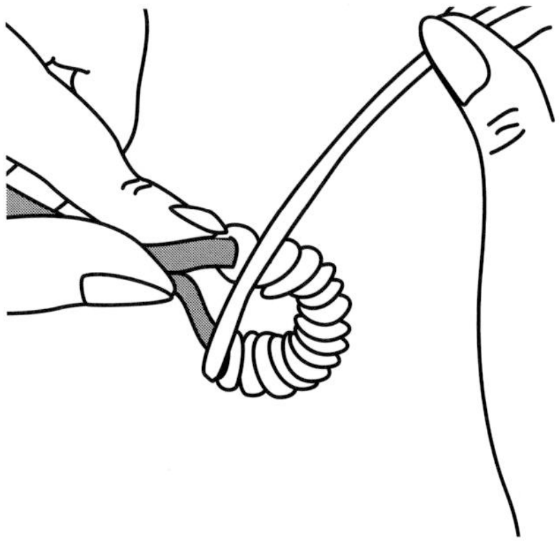

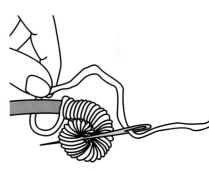

▲ **FIGURE T.33**

▲ **FIGURE T.30**

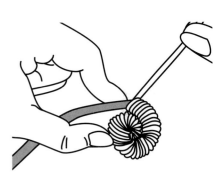

▲ **FIGURE T.34**

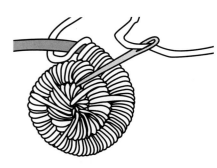

▲ **FIGURE T.31**

▲ **FIGURE T.35**

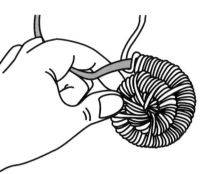

▲ **FIGURE T.36**

g. Hold the coil with your left hand with the core material coming from the left, and wind the weft with your right hand so you do not tangle it with the core (Figure T.36). If you are left-handed, reverse the process. Always pull the weft very tight.

h. You will need to splice, or invisibly join, the ends of separate materials. To splice the core, taper the cut on the old and the new piece. Before working the weft, secure the spliced ends of the core by wrapping them with sewing thread or tape. Always hold the spliced area carefully until it is wrapped with the weft. Splice the weft during the wrapping, not during the stitching. Hold the tail ends of the old and the new weft together against the core as shown in Figure T.37. Wrap the new weft at least once before making a long stitch.

i. When the base is the desired size, it is time to begin making the sides of the basket. If the side is to be perpendicular to the base, lay the first foundation coil directly on top of the last coil. If you want the basket to curve outward, place each new coil on the outer edge of the one below. To make an inward curve, place each coil on the inner edge of the previous coil. Use pressure from the nonstitching hand to keep the coils in place.

j. The best way to finish the basket is to taper the core and make several stitches around the last coil and the tapered coil. Then run the needle back through the wrapping stitches for about an inch and pull the weft thread through. Cut off the excess weft.

k. If you want to make a handle, simply wrap the end of the core until it is as long as you wish.

Then attach it to the other side of the top of the basket following the instructions from Step j.

25. Making a Tissue Paper Collage

For your first experience with tissue, make a free design with the tissue colors. Start with the lightest colors of tissue first and save the darkest for last. It is difficult to change the color of dark tissue by overlapping it with other colors. If one area becomes too dark, you might cut out a piece of white paper, glue it over the dark area carefully, and apply new colors over the white area.

a. Apply a coat of adhesive to the area where you wish to place the tissue.

b. Place the tissue down carefully over the wet area (Figure T.38). Don't let your fingers get wet.

c. Then add another coat of adhesive over the tissue. If your brush picks up any color from the wet tissue, rinse your brush

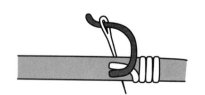

▲ **FIGURE T.37**

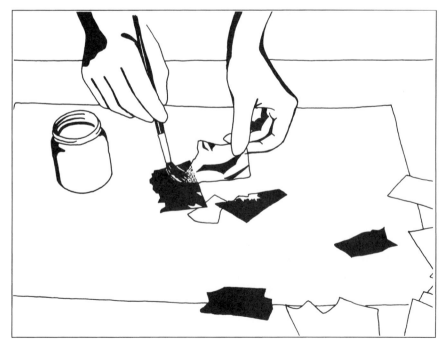

▲ **FIGURE T.38**

in water and let it dry before using it again.

d. Experiment by overlapping colors. Allow the tissue to wrinkle to create textures as you apply it. Be sure that all the loose edges of tissue are glued down.

DISPLAY TIPS

26. Making a Mat

You can add appeal to an artwork by making a mat, using the following steps.

a. Gather the materials you will need. These include a metal rule, a pencil, mat board, cardboard backing, a sheet of heavy cardboard to protect your work surface, a mat knife with a sharp blade, and wide masking tape.

b. Wash your hands. Mat board should be kept very clean.

c. Measure the height and width of the work to be matted. Decide how large a border you want for your work. (A border of approximately $2\frac{1}{2}$ inches on three sides with 3 inches on the bottom is aesthetically pleasing.) Your work will be behind the window you will cut.

d. Plan for the opening, or window, to be $\frac{1}{4}$ inch smaller on all sides than the size of your work. For example, if your work measures 9 by 12 inches, the mat window should measure $8\frac{1}{2}$ inches (9 inches minus $\frac{1}{4}$ inch times two) by $11\frac{1}{2}$ inches (12 inches minus $\frac{1}{4}$ inch times two.) Using your metal rule and pencil, lightly draw your window rectangle on the back of the board $2\frac{1}{2}$ inches from the top and left edge of the mat. (See Figure T.39). Add a $2\frac{1}{2}$-inch

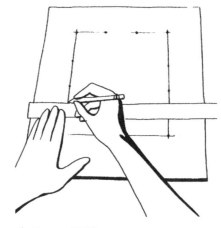

▲ **FIGURE T.39**

border to the right of the window and a 3-inch border to the bottom, lightly drawing cutting guidelines.

Note: If you are working with metric measurements, the window should overlap your work by 0.5 cm (centimeters) on all sides. Therefore, if your work measures 24 by 30 cm, the mat window measures 23 cm $(24-[2 \times 0.5])$ by 29 cm $(30 - [2 \times 0.5])$.

e. Place the sheet of heavy, protective cardboard on your work surface. Place the mat board, pencil marks up, over the cardboard. Holding the metal rule firmly in place, score the first line with your knife. Always place the metal rule so that your blade is on the inside of the frame. (See Figure T.40.) In case you make an error you will cut into the window hole or the extra mat that is not used for the frame. Do not try to cut through the board with one stroke. By the third or fourth stroke, you should be able to cut through the board easily.

f. Working in the same fashion, score and cut through the board along all the window lines. Be careful not to go

beyond the lines. Remove the window.

g. Cut a cardboard backing for your artwork that is slightly smaller than the overall size of your mat. Using a piece of broad masking tape, hinge the back of the mat to the backing. (See Figure T.41.) Position your artwork between the backing and the mat and attach it with tape. Anchor the frame to the cardboard with a few pieces of rolled tape.

▲ **FIGURE T.40**

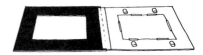

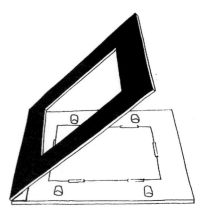

▲ **FIGURE T.41**

27. Mounting a Two-Dimensional Work

Mounting pictures that you make gives them a professional look. To mount a work, do the following:

a. Gather the materials you will need. These include a yard-stick, a pencil, poster board, a knife with a very sharp blade, a sheet of newspaper, and rubber cement.

b. Measure the height and width of the work to be mounted. Decide how large a border you want around the work. Plan your mount size using the work's measurements. To end up with a 3-inch border, for example, make your mount 6 inches wider and higher than your work. Record the measurements for your mount.

c. Using your yardstick and pencil, lightly draw your mount rectangle on the back of the poster board. Measure from the edges of the poster board. If you have a large paper cutter available, you may use it to cut your mount.

d. Place the sheet of heavy cardboard on your work surface. Place the poster board, pencil marks up, over the cardboard. Holding the yardstick firmly in place along one line, score the line with your knife. Do not try to cut through the board with one stroke. By the third try, you should be able to cut through the board.

e. Place the artwork on the mount. Using the yardstick, center the work. Mark each corner with a dot. (See Figure T.42)

▲ **FIGURE T.42**

f. Place the artwork, face down, on a sheet of newspaper. Coat the back of the work with rubber cement. (Safety Note: Always use rubber cement in a room with plenty of ventilation.) If your mount is to be permanent, skip to Step h.

g. Line up the corners of your work with the dots on the mounting board. Smooth the work into place. Skip to Step i.

h. After coating the back of your artwork, coat the poster board with rubber cement. Be careful not to add cement to the border area. Have a partner hold your artwork in the air by the two top corners. Once the two glued surfaces meet, you will not be able to change the position of the work. Grasp the lower two corners. Carefully lower the work to the mounting board. Line up the two corners with the bottom dots. Little by little, lower the work into place (Figure T.43). Press it smooth.

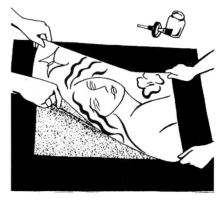

▲ **FIGURE T.43**

i. To remove any excess cement, create a small ball of dry rubber cement. Use the ball of rubber cement to pick up excess cement.

28. Working with Glue

When applying glue, always start at the center of the surface you are coating and work outward.

- When gluing papers together don't use a lot of glue, just a dot will do. Use dots in the corners and along the edges. Press the two surfaces together. Keep dots at least $\frac{1}{2}$ inch in from the edge of your paper.

- Handle a glued surface carefully with only your fingertips. Make sure your hands are clean before pressing the glued surface into place.

- Note: The glue should be as thin as possible. Thick or beaded glue will create ridges on your work.

Many artists, both students and teachers, come into daily contact with dangerous, possibly deadly materials. The unfortunate truth is that many art supplies contain high levels of chemicals, such as hexane, lead, toluene, and asbestos, and many people are unaware of the danger that these substances pose, both to art students and to teachers. In fact, the danger to art teachers, who are often exposed to toxins for several hours a day for many years, is often greater than to the students. Therefore, it is essential that all art teachers and students become aware of the potential hazards in using art materials.

Many art supplies contain materials that can cause acute illness (that is, a severe sudden illness that can be caused by a single exposure to a toxic substance and result in permanent disability or death). Long-term exposure to materials in many other art supplies can cause chronic illness (which develops gradually after repeated exposure) or cancer. Other chemicals in art supplies are sensitizers, causing allergies, particularly in children. Lead, for example, is acutely toxic and can be found in such commonly used supplies as stencil paint, oil paint, some acrylics, gessoes, ceramic glazes, copper enamels, and automotive paint in spray cans. Many highly toxic hydrocarbon-based solvents, including methyl alcohol, are used in school art programs. Other widely used art materials, such as preservatives, formaldehyde, epoxy glues, and dichromates, can contain dangerous chemicals like cadmium, nickel, silica, and pesticides.

There are three ways in which such chemicals can enter the body: absorption, inhalation, and ingestion. They can be absorbed through the skin from cuts or scrapes, resulting in burns or rashes, or into the bloodstream, moving to and damaging other parts of the body. Chemical irritants can be inhaled, causing lung problems like bronchitis and emphysema. Inhaling small particles, like the free silica in clay dust, can cause pulmonary fibrosis or asthma. Chemicals can be ingested through touching the mouth with the hands or fingers while working with supplies or unconsciously placing tools like paint brushes in or near the mouth. Since hazardous substances can easily enter the body, it is extremely important to make sure that the materials used are safe and that they are used safely.

Labeling

Labeling can provide information on any potentially dangerous art supplies, but teachers need to be aware of what various labels mean. The label *nontoxic,* for example, does not guarantee a product's safety. According to federal regulations, toxicity means that a single exposure can be fatal to adults. The effect on young people, who are more likely to be harmed by dangerous substances, is not considered in this definition. Also, the chance of developing chronic or long-term illnesses is not addressed by the legal definition of toxicity. Repeated exposure to nontoxic materials is not always safe. Many dangerous substances, such as asbestos, can legally be defined as nontoxic. Also, some art supplies, particularly those manufactured by small or foreign companies, may be improperly labeled as nontoxic.

Not all products whose labels provide chemical components, but have no warnings or list no information at all, are safe to use. Since manufacturers are not required to disclose ingredients, products without this information or warnings are potentially hazardous.

For more complete information on the presence of hazardous substances in art supplies, teachers may request a Material Safety Data Sheet (OSHA Form 20) from the manufacturer. This sheet provides information on potential heath and fire hazards, a list of chemicals that might react dangerously with the product, and a list of all ingredients for which industrial standards exist. The manufacturer should supply this sheet on request, and a local public health official or poison control center technician can help interpret the information.

Art teachers can also take advantage of voluntary labeling standards developed by the art materials industry. The Art and Craft Materials Institute (ACMI) administers a voluntary testing and labeling program that helps to insure the safety of those who work with art materials. This system uses the labels CP, AP, and HL.

CP (Certified Product) and AP (Approved Product) labels are used mainly on products designed for younger children, while HL (Health Label) is used on products intended for older students and adults. Products labeled CP, AP, or HL (Nontoxic) are certified in a program of toxicological evaluation by a medical expert to contain no materials in sufficient quantities to be toxic or injurious to humans or to cause acute or chronic health problems. Products labeled CP, in addition, meet specific requirements of material, workmanship, working qualities, and color. HL (Cautions Required) means that the product is certified to be properly labeled in a program of toxicological evaluation by a medical expert. The Art and Craft Materials Institute makes available a list of institute-certified products. For a copy, or for more information on the institute's certification program, teachers can write to:

> The Art and Craft Materials Institute
> 715 Boylston St.
> Boston, MA 02116

Safety Rules

There are certain guidelines to be followed in selecting and using art supplies. Perhaps the most important is to know what the materials are made of and what potential hazards exist. If a material is improperly labeled, or if adequate information cannot be obtained about it, don't use it. The following rules are also helpful:

- Be sure that all materials used by younger students (ages 12 and under) have the CP or AP label and that materials used by older students and adults are marked CL.

- Don't use acids, alkalies, bleaches, or any product that will stain skin or clothing.

- Don't use aerosol cans because the spray can injure lungs.

- Use dust-producing materials (such as pastels, clays, plasters, chalks, powdered tempera, pigments, dyes, and instant papier-mâché, except the premixed cellulose type) with care in a well-ventilated area (or better yet, don't use them at all).

- Don't use solvents (including lacquers, paint thinners, turpentines, shellacs, solvent-based inks, rubber cement, and permanent markers) in the art room.

- Don't use found or donated materials unless the ingredients are known.

- Don't use old materials. Many art supplies formerly contained highly dangerous substances, such as arsenic, or raw lead compounds, or high levels of asbestos. Older solvents may contain chloroform or carbon tetrachloride.

Working conditions in the art room also affect safety. A disorderly art room leads to unsafe conditions, particularly when there are many people working close to each other. Controlling the buildup of litter and dust, insuring that tools are in good condition, and keeping workspace reasonably organized not only help prevent common accidents but also make it easier to recognize and eliminate other hazards. An orderly art room is absolutely essential to the students' and teacher's safety.

A

Abbott, Berenice, American, b. 1898, photographer
The Night View, 202

Abrasha, Dutch-American, b. 1948, jewelry designer, goldsmith
Hanukkah Menorah, 72

Albright, Ivan, American, 1897–1983, painter
The Farmer's Kitchen, 177

Andrews, Benny, African-American, b. 1930, painter, printmaker
The Scholar, 81

Anguissola, Sofonisba, Italian, 1527–1625, painter
A game of chess, involving the painter's three sisters and a servant, 358

Anuszkiewicz, Richard, American, b. 1930, painter
Iridescence, 146, 154

Apel, Marie, English, 1880–1970, sculptor
Grief, 119

B

Balla, Giacomo, Italian, 1871–1958, painter
Dynamism of a Dog on a Leash, 212
Street Light, 210

Bashkirtseff, Marie, Russian, 1860–1884, painter
A Meeting, 301

Bayless, Florence, American, b. 1922, craftsperson
Haori Coat, 298

Bearden, Romare, African-American, 1911–1988, painter, printmaker
Family, 166–167
Prevalence of Ritual: The Baptism, 158, 159
Return of Ulysses, 12, 13

Beaux, Cecilia, American, 1863–1942, painter
Ernesta (Child with Nurse), 294

Bellows, George, American, 1882–1925, painter, printmaker
Both Members of This Club, 258
Cliff Dwellers, 222–223

Benton, Thomas Hart, American, 1882–1975, painter
Country Dance, 78, 79
The Sources of Country Music, 376

Berman, Eugene, Russian-American, 1899–1972, painter, stage designer
Vendeur de Chapeaux, 43

Biggers, John, African-American, b. 1924, painter
Shotguns, Fourth Ward, 198, 199
Starry Crown, 98, 99

Bishop, Isabel, American, 1902–1988, painter
Head #5, 44, 45
Self-Portrait, 283
Waiting, 282–283

Black Hawk, Chief, Native American, 19th century, draftsman
Crow Men in Ceremonial Dress, 200

Bonheur, Rosa, French, 1822–1899, painter
The Horse Fair, 201, 369

Bonnard, Pierre, French, 1867–1947, painter, graphic artist
Family Scene, 266

Borsky, David, American, contemporary, photographer
Wall of Machu-Picchu, 55
Waterfall, 209

Botticelli, Sandro, Italian, 1445–1510, painter
The Adoration of the Magi, 113

Brady, Mathew, American, 1823–1896, photographer
Civil War, 369

Brancusi, Constantin, Rumanian, 1876–1957, sculptor
The Kiss, 104
Torso of a Young Man, 118

Brown, Roger, American, 1941–1997, muralist
Hurricane Hugo, 10–11

Bruegel, Pieter, the Elder, Dutch, 1530–1569, painter
Children's Games, 22

C

Calder, Alexander, American, 1898–1976, sculptor
Lobster Trap and Fish Tail, 213
Varese, 84

Canaletto, Italian, 1697–1768, painter
Ascension Day Festival at Venice, 43

Caravaggio, Michelangelo Merisi da, Italian, 1573–1610, painter
The Conversion of St. Paul, 361

Carr, Emily, Canadian, 1871–1945, painter
Above the Trees, 149
Forest, British Columbia, 298

Cassatt, Mary, American, 1845–1926, painter
Margot in Blue, 140
The Letter, 350, 351
The Tea, 244

Catlett, Elizabeth, African-American, b. 1915, printmaker, sculptor, painter
Sharecropper, 48–49

Cézanne, Paul, French, 1839–1906, painter
Apples and Oranges, 132
The Basket of Apples, 155
Le Chateau Noir, 371

Chagall, Marc, Russian, 1887–1985, painter
The American Windows, 136
Birthday, 271
Paris Through the Window, 20–21

Christo, American, b. 1935, sculptor, environmental artist
Wrapped Reichstag (with Jeanne-Claude), 130–131

Clive, Carolyn, American, b. 1931, painter
Amplitude, 86

Copley, John Singleton, American, 1737–1815, painter
Paul Revere, 268

Cram, Ralph Adams, American, 1863–1942, architect
Federal Reserve Building (with Ferguson and Goodhue), 230

D

Dali, Salvador, Spanish, 1904–1989, painter
The Elephants (Design for the Opera La Dama Spagnola e il Cavaliere Romano), 280
The Persistence of Memory, 375

David, Jacques-Louis, French, 1748–1825, painter
The Death of Socrates, 366

da Vinci, Leonardo. See *Leonardo da Vinci*

Davis, Stuart, American, 1894–1964, painter
Hot Still Scape for Six Colors—7th Avenue Style, 1940, 154, 155

Degas, Edgar, French, 1834–1917, painter, sculptor, 0
The Little Fourteen-Year-Old Dancer, 180, 181
Self-Portrait, 181

Delacroix, Eugène, French, 1798–1863, painter
Arabs Skirmishing in the Mountains, 367

Delaunay, Robert, French, 1885–1941, painter
Sun, Tower, Airplane, 134, 135

Dick, Beau, Canadian Native American, b. 1955, printmaker
Sacred Circles, 246

Dillon, Leo and Diane, American, both b. 1933, graphic artists
A Wrinkle in Time (cover illustration), 38

Dunnigan, John, American, 20th century, furniture designer
Slipper Chairs, 33

Dürer, Albrecht, German, 1471–1528, painter, printmaker
An Oriental Ruler Seated on His Throne, 76

Dvorak, Lois, American, 1934–1993, mixed media
Spirit Boxes I, 304, 305

E

Eakins, Thomas, American, 1844–1916, painter
Baby at Play, 234

El Greco, Spanish, 1541–1614, painter
Saint Martin and the Beggar, 360

Ernst, Max, German (in America after 1941), 1891–1976, painter
The Eye of Silence, 183, 184–185

Escher, M. C., Dutch, 1898–1972, printmaker
Day and Night, 220
Portrait of M. C. Escher, 105
Waterfall, 105

Estes, Richard, American, b. 1932, painter
Paris Street Scene, 381

Evans, Minnie, African-American, 1890–1987, painter
Design Made at Airlie Gardens, 410–411

F

Ferguson, American, 20th century, architect
Federal Reserve Building (with Cram and Goodhue), 230

Fish, Janet, American, b. 1939, painter
Oranges, 175, 176
Raspberries and Goldfish, 16–17

Flack, Audrey, American, b. 1931, painter, sculptor
Leonardo's Lady, 192–193
Self-Portrait: The Memory, 82

Fragonard, Jean-Honoré, French, 1732–1806, painter
A Game of Hot Cockles, 236

Frankenthaler, Helen, American, b. 1928, painter
The Bay, 111

G

Gainsborough, Thomas, English, 1727–1788, painter
The Blue Boy, 364

Gauguin, Paul, French, 1848–1903, painter
Faaturuma (Melancholic), 372
Tahitians, 265–266

Gentileschi, Artemisia, Italian, 1593-c. 1652/3, painter
Judith and Maidservant with the Head of Holofernes, 111

Giorgione, Italian, 1477–1511, painter
The Adoration of the Shepherds, 236, 237

Giotto di Bondone, Italian, c. 1266–1337, painter
Madonna and Child, 263

Glarner, Fritz, Swiss-American, 1899–1972 painter
Relational Painting #93, 146, 147

Goings, Ralph, American, b. 1928, painter, sculptor
Diner With Red Door, 112

Goodhue, Betram, American, 1869–1924, architect
Federal Reserve Building (with Cram and Ferguson), 230

Goya, Francisco, Spanish, 1746–1828, painter
The Third of May, 364–365

Graves, Nancy, American, b. 1940, sculptor
Zaga, 51

Grossman, Rhoda, American, b. 1941, digital artist
Self-Portrait After Escher, 59

Gu Mei, Chinese, 17th century, painter
Orchids and Rocks, 83

H

Hampton, James, African–American, 1909–1965, sculptor
The Throne of the Third Heaven of the Nations Millennium General Assembly, 186

Hanson, Duane, American, b. 1925, sculptor
Traveler with Sunburn, 381

Haring, Keith, American, 1958–1990, painter
Untitled, 90

Hassam, Childe, American, 1859–1935, painter, printmaker
Jelly Fish, 157

Hepworth, Barbara, English, 1903–1975, sculptor
Pendour, 101, 102

Hines, Jessica, American, contemporary, photographer
Dream Series, 57, 58

Hiroshige, Andō, Japanese, 1797–1858, printmaker
Evening Rain on the Karasaki Pine, 330

Hodler, Ferdinand, Swiss, 1853–1918, painter
James Vilbert, Sculptor, 240

Hofmann, Hans, German (born in America), 1880–1966, painter
Flowering Swamp, 378

Hokusai, Katsushika, Japanese, 1760–1849, printmaker, painter
The Great Wave at Kanagawa, 237–238
The Kirifuri Waterfall at Mt. Kurokami, Shimozuke Province, 226, 227

Holbein, Hans, German, 1465–1524, painter
Anne of Cleves, 9

Homer, Winslow, American, 1836–1910, painter
  Hound and Hunter, 47
  Sketch for 'Hound and Hunter,' 47
Hoover, John, Native American, Aleut, b. 1919, sculptor
  Loon Song, 180
Hopper, Edward, American, 1882–1967, painter
  Early Sunday Morning, 77
  First Row Orchestra, 235
Houser, Allan, Native American, 1914–1994, sculptor
  Coming of Age, 209
  Reverie, 298, 299
Hua Yen, Chinese, c. 1682–1765
  Conversation in Autumn, 328
Hunt, Henry, Canadian Native American, Kwakiutl, 1923–1985, sculptor
  K'umugwe' (Komokwa) Mask, 276
Huntington, Anna Hyatt, American, 1876–1973, sculptor
  Riders to the Sea, 120

I

Inness, George, American, 1825–1894, painter
  The Lackawanna Valley, 11

J

Jacquette, Yvonne, American, b. 1934, painter
  Town of Skowhegan, Maine V, 70
Jessup, Georgia Mills, American, b. 1926, painter
  Rainy Night, 301–302
Jimenez, Luis, American, b. 1940, sculptor
  Vaquero, 50
Johns, Jasper, American, b. 1930, painter
  Cups 4 Picasso, 103–104
  Map, 296
Johnson, Philip, American, b. 1906, architect
  Seagram Building (with Mies van der Rohe), 382
Johnson, William H., African-American, 1901–1970, painter
  Jitterbugs, 88, 89
Jones, Lois Mailou, African-American, 1905–1998, painter
  The Ascent of Ethiopia, 386

K

Kahlo, Frida, Mexican, 1907–1954, painter
  Self Portrait Dedicated to Leon Trotsky, 239
Keyser, Louisa (Dat So La Lee), Native American, 1850–1925, weaver
  Basket, 218
Kingslien, Liz, American, contemporary, graphic designer
  The Seasons, 15, 392
Kirchner, Ernst Ludwig, German, 1880–1938, painter
  Seated Woman, 35
  Winter Landscape in Moonlight, 34
Kollwitz, Käthe, German, 1867–1945, painter, printmaker, graphic artist
  Self-Portrait, 374

Korin, Ogata, Japanese, Edo period (18th century), silk painter
  Waves at Matsushima, 196–197
Krasner, Lee, American, b. 1908, painter
  The Springs, 291
Kurelek, William, American, b. 1927, painter
  Manitoba Party, 110

L

Lachaise, Gaston, French, 1882–1935, sculptor
  Walking Woman, 271–272
Lange, Dorothea, American, 1895–1965, photojournalist
  Migrant Mother, 57
Larraz, Julio, Cuban, b. 1944, painter
  Papiamento, 32
Lawrence, Jacob, African-American, b. 1917, painter
  Children at Play, 78, 80, 377
Le Corbusier, Swiss, 1887–1965, architect
  Unite d'Habitation, 259
Lee, Doris, American, b. 1905, printmaker, painter
  Thanksgiving, 116
Leonardo da Vinci, Italian, 1452–1519, painter, sculptor
  Ginevra de' Benci, 384–385
  sketchbook page, 42
Leyster, Judith, Dutch, 1609–1660, painter
  The Concert, 178, 256, 257
Lichtenstein, Roy, American, b. 1923, painter
  Blam, 379
Liebovitz, Annie, American, 20th century, photographer
  Wilt Chamberlain and Willie Shoemaker, 262
Loewy, Raymond, French-American, b. 1893, designer
  Avanti, 395

M

McKelvey, Lucy Leuppe, Native American, birthdate unknown, ceramicist
  Whirling Rainbow Goddesses, 212
McKie, Judy Kensley, American, b. 1944, furniture artist
  Monkey Settee, 53
Magritte, René, Belgian, 1898–1967, painter
  The Blank Signature, 126
Malangi, David, Australian, b. 1934, Aboriginal artist
  Abstract (River Mouth Map), 92–93
Manet, Édouard, French, 1832–1883, painter
  The Railway, 368–369
Marc, Franz, German, 1880–1916, painter
  The Large Blue Horses, 154
  Stables, 66–67
Marisol, Venezuelan (in America since 1950), b. 1930, sculptor
  The Family, 268
Matisse, Henri, French, 1869–1954, painter
  Femme au Chapeau (Woman with the Hat), 164
  Purple Robe and Anemones, 24, 25
Michelangelo Buonarroti, Italian, 1475–1564, sculptor, painter
  David, 267
  Pietà, 331, 356, 357

Mies van der Rohe, Ludwig, American, 1886–1969, architect
Seagram Building (with Johnson), 381–382
Mitchell, Joan, American, 1926–1992, painter
Dirty Snow, 179
Monet, Claude, French, 1840–1926, painter
The Four Trees, 153
Palazzo da Mula, Venice, 370
Poplars, 153
Morisot, Berthe, French, 1841–1895, painter
In the Dining Room, 292
Munch, Edvard, Norwegian, 1863–1944, painter, printmaker
The Sick Child, 7
Muñoz, Rie, Dutch-American, b. 1921, painter
Both the Sun and Moon Belong to Women, 252
Münter, Gabriele, German, 1877–1962, painter
Breakfast of the Birds, 18
Murphy, Gerald, American, 1888–1964, painter
Watch, 248
Murray, Elizabeth, American, b. 1940, painter
Painters Progress, 40, 41
Things to Come, 150
Musawwir, Abd Allah, Islamic, 16th century, painter
The Meeting of the Theologians, 216
Myron, Greek, c. 480–440 B.C., sculptor
Discobolus (Discus Thrower), 353

N

Namingha, Dan, Native American, b. 1950, painter
Blessing Rain Chant, 75, 77
Naranjo, Michael, Native American, b. 1944, sculptor
Spirits Soaring, 108, 109
Neel, Alice, American, 1900–1984, painter
Linda Nochlin and Daisy, 250–251
Loneliness, 292
Still Life, Rose of Sharon, 74
Nevelson, Louise, American, 1899–1988, sculptor
Dawn, 300

O

O'Keeffe, Georgia, American, 1887–1986, painter
Cow's Skull: Red, White, and Blue, 30
Oriental Poppies, 2–3
White Rose With Larkspur, No. 2, 240
Oldenburg, Claes, American, b. 1929, painter, sculptor
Clothespin, 261
Orozco, José Clemente, Mexican, 1883–1949, painter
Barricade, 28

P

Paik, Nam June, Korean, b. 1932, kinetic artist
Technology, 388, 389
Paley, Albert Raymond, American, b. 1944, sculptor
Portal Gates, 78
Pei, I. M., Chinese-American, b. 1917, architect
Rock-and-Roll Hall of Fame and Museum, 382–383

Pereira, Irene Rice, American, 1907–1971, painter
Untitled, 289
Picasso, Pablo, Spanish, 1881–1973, painter, sculptor
Las Meninas (after Velásquez), 14–15
Nude Woman, 375
The Old Guitarist, 270
Still Life, 316–317
The Tragedy, 145
Pollock, Jackson, American, 1912–1956, painter
Cathedral, 13–14
Poons, Larry, American, b.1937, painter
Orange Crush, 379–380
Pootoogook, Napachie, Inuit, b. 1938, printmaker
My Daughter's First Steps, 268–269

R

Rauschenberg, Robert, American, b. 1925, painter
Red Painting, 290
Rembrandt van Rijn, Dutch, 1606–1669, painter
The Night Watch, 314, 362
Portrait of Rembrandt, 178, 290
Renoir, Pierre Auguste, French, 1841–1919, painter
Madame Henriot, 177
Ringgold, Faith, African-American, b. 1930, painter, soft sculptor
Bitter Nest Part II: Harlem Renaissance Party, 36–37
Mrs. Jones and Family, 278
Rivera, Diego, Mexican, 1886–1957, painter, muralist
Flower Day, 229
Self-Portrait, 229
Rodin, Auguste, French, 1840–1917, sculptor
The Burghers of Calais, 297
Romero, Annette, Native American, b. 1951, ceramicist
Storyteller Doll, 274
Rothko, Mark, Russian-American, 1903–1970, painter
Orange and Yellow, 380
Roualt, Georges, French, 1871–1958, painter
Christ and the Apostles, 74
Rousseau, Henri, French, 1844–1910, painter
Carnival Evening, 312–313
Moi-Meme, Portrait-Paysage (I Myself, Portrait-Landscape), 313
Rubens, Peter Paul, Flemish, 1577–1640, painter
Daniel in the Lions' Den, 291
Ruiz, Antonio M., Mexican, 1897–1964, painter
School Children on Parade, 214

S

Safdie, Moshe, Israeli, b. 1938, architect
Habitat, 382
Savage, Augusta, African-American, 20th century, sculptor
Lift Every Voice and Sing, 209
Schapiro, Miriam, American, b. 1923, painter, sculptor
Personal Appearance, 62–63
Yard Sale, 180
Scully, Sean, Irish, b. 1945, painter
White Robe, 295

Shahn, Ben, Russian-American, 1898–1959, painter
The Blind Botanist, 117

Silvers, Robert, American, contemporary, digital artist
Vincent van Gogh, 190

Siqueiros, David Alfaro, Mexican, 1896–1974, painter
Self-Portrait (El Coronelazo), 264

Skoglund, Sandy, American, b. 1946, photographer, painter
The Green House, 406–407

Smith, David, American, 1906–1965, painter
Cubi IX, 101

Smith, Jaune Quick-To-See, Native American, b. 1940, painter
Spotted Owl, 162

Smith, Larry, American, b. 1949, painter
North Georgia Waterfall, 122

Steir, Pat, American, b. 1938, painter
The Bruegel Series (A Vanitas of Style), 160–161

Stella, Frank, American, b. 1936, painter, sculptor
Agbatana III, 380
St. Michael's Counterguard (Malta Series), 383

Stella, Joseph, Italian-American, 1877–1946, painter
The Voice of the City of New York Interpreted: The Bridge, 68–69

Straus, Meyer, American, 19th century, painter
Bayou Teche, 6–7

Sullivan, Louis, American, 1856–1924, architect
Elevator Grille, 204
Wainwright Building, 56

Tamayo, Rufino, Mexican, 1899–1991, painter
Girl Attacked by a Strange Bird, 141
Toast to the Sun, 148

Thomas, Alma, American, 1891–1978, painter
Iris, Tulips, Jonquils, and Crocuses, 26

Tintoretto, Jacopo, Italian, c. 1518–1594, painter
Standing Youth with His Arm Raised, Seen from Behind, 82

Tooker, George, American, b. 1920, painter
Highway, 96, 97

Torivio, Dorothy, Native American, b. 1946, ceramicist
Vase, 233

Turner, Joseph M. W., English, 1775–1851, painter
Snowstorm: Steamboat off a Harbours Mouth, 368

Twiggs, Leo, African-American, b. 1934, batik painter
Blue Wall, 28, 29
East Wind Suite: Door, 10, 42
Single Family Blues, 269

Utzon, Joern,
Sydney Opera House, 286, 287

van Alen, William, American, 1882–1954, architect
Chrysler Building, 206

van der Weyden, Rogier, Flemish, 1399–1464, painter
Portrait of a Lady, 359

van Eyck, Jan, Flemish, before 1395–1441, painter
The Arnolfi Wedding, 231, 359

van Gogh, Vincent, Dutch, 1853–1890, painter
Café Terrace at Night, 293
Houses at Auvers, 4, 5
The Starry Night, 372–373
Sunflowers, 178–179

Velázquez, Diego, Spanish, 1599–1660, painter
Las Meninas (The Maids of Honor), 14–15

Vermeer, Jan, Dutch, 1632–1675, painter
The Astronomer, 128
Girl with the Red Hat, 362

Walkus, George, Kwakiutl, 20th century, maskmaker
Secret Society Mask (Four Headed Cannibal Spirit), 272, 273

Warhol, Andy, American, 1928–1987, painter, printmaker
Marilyn Monroe's Lips, 206, 207

Watteau, Antoine, French, 1684–1721, painter
Embarkment for Cythera, 362–363

White, Charles, African-American, 1918–1979, painter
Preacher, 94

Wilson, Jane, American, b. 1924, painter
Solstice, 302–303
Winter Wheat, 120, 121

Wood, Grant, American, 1892–1942, painter
American Gothic, 12

Woodruff, Hale, American, b. 1900, painter
Poor Man's Cotton, 202, 203

Wright, Frank Lloyd, American, 1867–1959, architect
Armchair, 118–119
The David Wright House, 377
Fallingwater House, 300–301
stained-glass window, 235
Taliesin West, 182

X

Xiong, Chaing, Laotian, b. 1953, craftsperson
Hmong Story Cloth, 211–212

Y

Yancy, John, African-American, b. 1956, muralist
Celebration of Arts: Vibrations of Life, 308

CHRONOLOGY OF ARTWORKS

PREHISTORIC–1 B.C.

Artist Unknown, Altamira Caves, Spain
The Hall of the Bulls, 15,000 B.C., 320, Fig. 12.2
Artist Unknown
Statua di Donna, 2700–2600 B.C., 322, Fig. 12.3
Artist Unknown, Indian
Mohenjo-Daro, 2500 B.C., 323, Fig. 12.6
Artist Unknown, Sumerian
Ziggurat, c. 2100 B.C., 322, Fig. 12.4
Artist Unknown
Stonehenge, c. 2000 B.C., 348, Fig. 12.35
Artist Unknown, Egyptian
The Goddess Hathor Places the Magic Collar on Sethos I,
c. 1303–1290 B.C., 323, Fig. 12.5
Artist Unknown, Chinese
Ritual Wine Container, 1200 B.C., 325, Fig. 12.8
Artist Unknown, Mexican, Olmec
Colossal Head, 1200 B.C.–A.D. 500, 339, Fig. 12.26
Artist Unknown, Indian
Great Stupa, c. first century B.C., 326, Fig. 12.9
Artist Unknown, Indian
Siva as Lord of the Dance, c. 950, 327, Fig. 12.10
Myron, Greek, c. 480–440 B.C., sculptor
Discobolus (Discus Thrower), c. 450 B.C., 353, Fig. 13.3
Artist Unknown, Graeco-Roman
Man of the Republic, 50 B.C., Fig. 13.4

A.D. 1–1399

Artist Unknown, Japanese
Pagoda, c. 616, 329, Fig. 12.13
Artist Unknown, African, Yoruba people
Portrait of a King, 11th–15th century, 332, Fig. 12.17
Artist Unknown, African, Mali
Equestrian figure, c. 13th century, 333, Fig. 12.18
Artist Unknown, African, Bamana people
Bamana iron figure, 13th century, 334, Fig. 12.19
Artist Unknown, African, Dogon people
Seated Man and Woman, 13th century, 334, Fig. 12.20
Artist Unknown, Southeast Asian
Temple at Angkor Wat, 1113–50, 327, Fig. 12.11
Artist Unknown, Japanese
Great Buddha, 1252, 329, Fig. 12.14
Giotto di Bondone, Italian, c. 1266–1337, painter
Madonna and Child, 1320–30, 263, Fig. 10.13

1400–1499

van Eyck, Jan, Flemish, before 1395–1441, painter
The Arnolfi Wedding, 1434, 231, Fig. 9.8
van der Weyden, Rogier, Flemish, 1399–1464, painter
Portrait of a Lady, c. 1460, 359, Fig. 13.10
Leonardo da Vinci, Italian, 1452–1519, painter, sculptor
Ginevra de' Benci, c. 1474, 384, Fig. 13.41
Botticelli, Sandro, Italian, 1445–1510, painter
The Adoration of the Magi, early 1480s, 113, Fig. 5.19
Dürer, Albrecht, German, 1471–1528, painter, printmaker
An Oriental Ruler Seated on His Throne, c. 1495, 76, Fig. 4.15

Leonardo da Vinci, Italian, 1452–1519, painter, sculptor
sketchbook page, date unknown, 42, Fig. 3.2

1500–1599

Michelangelo Buonarroti, Italian, 1475–1564, sculptor,
painter
Pietà, c. 1500, 357, Fig. 13.8
Michelangelo Buonarroti, Italian, 1475–1564, sculptor,
painter
David (detail), 1501–1504, 267, Fig. 10.19
Giorgione, Italian, 1477–1511, painter
The Adoration of the Shepherds, c. 1505–10, 237, Fig. 9.16
Artist Unknown, Persian
Khamseh: Barham Gur and the Chinese Princess in the
Sandalwood Pavilion on Thursday, 1524–25, 346, Fig. 12.34
Holbein, Hans, German, 1465–1524, painter
Anne of Cleves, 1539, 9, Fig. 1.6
Musawwir, Abd Allah, Islamic, 16th century, painter
The Meeting of the Theologians, c. 1540–50, 216, Fig. 8.23
Anguissola, Sofonisba, Italian, 1527–1625, painter
A game of chess, involving the painter's three sisters and a
servant, 1555, 358, Fig. 13.9
Bruegel, Pieter, the Elder, Dutch, 1530–1569, painter
Children's Games, 1560, 22, Fig. 1.19
El Greco, Spanish, 1541–1614, painter
Saint Martin and the Beggar, 1597/1599, 360, Fig. 13.11
Tintoretto, Jacopo, Italian, c. 1518–1594, painter
Standing Youth with His Arm Raised, Seen from Behind, date
unknown, 82, Fig. 4.22
Artist Unknown, African, Edo people
Mounted King with Attendants, c. 16th–17th century, 335,
Fig. 12.21
Artist Unknown, African, Edo people
Warrior Chief, Warriors, and Attendants, 16th–17th century,
262, Fig. 10.10

1600–1699

Artist Unknown, African, Asante people
Man's cloth (Kente cloth), 17th century, 336, Fig. 12.23
Caravaggio, Michelangelo Merisi da, Italian, 1573–1610,
painter
The Conversion of St. Paul, c. 1601, 361, Fig. 13.12
Rubens, Peter Paul, Flemish, 1577–1640, painter
Daniel in the Lions' Den, c. 1615, 291, Fig. 11.7
Gentileschi, Artemisia, Italian, c. 1597–after 1651, painter
Judith and Maidservant with the Head of Holofernes, c. 1625,
111, Fig. 5.17
Leyster, Judith, Dutch, 1609–1660, painter
The Concert, c. 1633, 257, Fig. 10.4
Rembrandt van Rijn, Dutch, 1606–1669, painter
The Night Watch, 1642, 314, Fig. 11.29
Gu Mei, Chinese, 17th century, painter
Orchids and Rocks, 1644, 83, Fig. 4.24
Rembrandt van Rijn, Dutch, 1606–1669, painter
Portrait of Rembrandt, 1650, 290, Fig. 11.5
Velázquez, Diego, Spanish, 1599–1660, painter
Las Meninas (The Maids of Honor), 1656, 15, Fig. 1.15

Vermeer, Jan, Dutch, 1632–1675, painter
Girl with the Red Hat, c. 1665/1666, 362, Fig.13.13
Vermeer, Jan, Dutch, 1632–1675, painter
The Astronomer, 1668, 128, Fig. 5.38

1700–1799

Watteau, Antoine, French, 1684–1721, painter
Embarkment for Cythera, 1717–19, 363, Fig. 13.14
Hua Yen, Chinese, c. 1682–1765
Conversation in Autumn, 1762, 328, Fig. 12.12
Canaletto, Italian, 1697–1768, painter
Ascension Day Festival at Venice, 1766, 43, Fig. 3.4
Copley, John Singleton, American, 1737–1815, painter
Paul Revere, c. 1768–70, 268, Fig. 10.20
Fragonard, Jean-Honoré, French, 1732–1806, painter
A Game of Hot Cockles, 1767–73, 236, Fig. 9.15
Gainsborough, Thomas, English, 1727–1788, painter
The Blue Boy, c. 1770, 364, Fig. 13.15
David, Jacques-Louis, French, 1748–1825, painter
The Death of Socrates, 1787, 366, Fig. 13.17
Korin, Ogata, Japanese, Edo period (18th century), silk painter
Waves at Matsushima, date unknown, 196–197
Artist Unknown, African, Akan people
Necklace, 19th century, 336, Fig. 12.22

1800–1899

Artist Unknown, Inuit
Mask of Moon Goddess, before 1900, 342, Fig. 12.29
Goya, Francisco, Spanish, 1746–1828, painter
The Third of May, 1814, 365, Fig. 13.16
Hokusai, Katsushika, Japanese, 1760–1849, printmaker, painter
The Great Wave at Kanagawa, 1823–29, 238, Fig. 9.18
Hokusai, Katsushika, Japanese, 1760–1849, printmaker, painter
The Kirifuri Waterfall at Mt. Kurokami, Shimozuke Province, ca. 1831, 226, Fig. 9.1
Turner, Joseph M. W., English, 1775–1851, painter
Snowstorm: Steamboat off a Harbours Mouth, 1842, 368, Fig. 13.19
Bonheur, Rosa, French, 1822–1899, painter
The Horse Fair, 1853–55, 201, Fig. 8.3
Inness, George, American, 1825–1894, painter
The Lackawanna Valley, c. 1856, 11, Fig. 1.9
Delacroix, Eugène, French, 1798–1863, painter
Arabs Skirmishing in the Mountains, 1863, 367, Fig. 13.18
Brady, Mathew, American, 1823–1896, photographer
Civil War, c. 1865, 369, Fig. 13.21
Artist Unknown, Northwest coast region, Haida
Haida totem pole, c. 1870, 343, Fig. 12.30
Straus, Meyer, American, 19th century, painter
Bayou Teche, 1870, 6, Fig. 1.2
Manet, Édouard, French, 1832–1883, painter
The Railway, 1873, 369, Fig. 13.20
Eakins, Thomas, American, 1844–1916, painter
Baby at Play, 1876, 234, Fig. 9.12

Renoir, Pierre Auguste, French, 1841–1919, painter
Madame Henriot, 1876, 177, Fig. 7.7
Cassatt, Mary, American, 1845–1926, painter
The Tea, about 1880, 244, Fig. 9.24
Degas, Edgar, French, 1834–1917, painter, sculptor
The Little Fourteen-Year-Old Dancer, 1880, 181, Fig. 7.12
Black Hawk, Chief, Native American, 19th century, draftsman
Crow Men in Ceremonial Dress, 1880–81, 200, Fig. 8.2
Bashkirtseff, Marie, Russian, 1860–1884, painter
A Meeting, 1884, 301, Fig. 11.21
Morisot, Berthe, French, 1841–1895, painter
In the Dining Room, 1886, 292, Fig. 11.9
Rodin, Auguste, French, 1840–1917, sculptor
The Burghers of Calais, 1886, 297, Fig. 11.14
Rousseau, Henri, French, 1844–1910, painter
Carnival Evening, 1886, 312, Fig. 11.28
van Gogh, Vincent, Dutch, 1853–1890, painter
Café Terrace at Night, 1888, 293, Fig. 11.10
van Gogh, Vincent, Dutch, 1853–1890, painter
Sunflowers, 1888, 178, Fig. 7.8
van Gogh, Vincent, Dutch, 1853–1890, painter
The Starry Night, 1889, 373, Fig. 13.25
Artist Unknown, Native American
Feather Bonnet, c. 1890, 345, Fig. 12.33
Artist Unknown, Native American, Navajo
Saddle blanket, c. 1890, 344, Fig. 12.32
van Gogh, Vincent, Dutch, 1853–1890, painter
Houses at Auvers, 1890, 4, Fig. 1.1
Sullivan, Louis, American, 1856–1924, architect
Wainwright Building, 1890–91, 56, Fig. 3.17
Cassatt, Mary, American, 1845–1926, painter
The Letter, 1891, 350, Fig. 13.1
Gauguin, Paul, French, 1848–1903, painter
Faaturuma (Melancholic), 1891, 372, Fig. 13.24
Monet, Claude, French, 1840–1926, painter
Poplars, 1891, 153, Fig. 6.24
Monet, Claude, French, 1840–1926, painter
The Four Trees, 1891, 153, Fig. 6.25
Homer, Winslow, American, 1836–1910, painter
Sketch for 'Hound and Hunter,' 1892, 47, Fig. 3.8
Homer, Winslow, American, 1836–1910, painter
Hound and Hunter, 1892, 47, Fig. 3.9
Gauguin, Paul, French, 1848–1903, painter
Tahitians, c. 1891–93, 265, Fig. 10.17
Bonnard, Pierre, French, 1867–1947, painter, graphic artist
Family Scene, 1893, 266, Fig. 10.18
Sullivan, Louis, American, 1856–1924, architect
Elevator Grille, 1893–94, 204, Fig. 8.7
Beaux, Cecilia, American, 1863–1942, painter
Ernesta (Child with Nurse), 1894, 294, Fig. 11.11
Cézanne, Paul, French, 1839–1906, painter
The Basket of Apples, 1895, 155, Fig. 6.27
Cézanne, Paul, French, 1839–1906, painter
Apples and Oranges, date unknown,132, Fig. 5.40
Hiroshige, Andō, Japanese, 1797–1858, printmaker
Evening Rain on the Karasaki Pine, date unknown, 330, Fig. 12.15

1900–1949

Cézanne, Paul, French, 1839–1906, painter
Le Chateau Noir, 1900–04, 371, Fig. 13.23

Cassatt, Mary, American, 1845–1926, painter
Margot in Blue, 1902, 140, Fig. 6.8

Picasso, Pablo, Spanish, 1881–1973, painter, sculptor
The Old Guitarist, 1903, 270, Fig. 10.24

Picasso, Pablo, Spanish, 1881–1973, painter, sculptor
The Tragedy, 1903, 145, Fig. 6.13

Matisse, Henri, French, 1869–1954, painter
Femme au Chapeau (Woman with the Hat), 1905, 164, Fig. 6.33

Hodler, Ferdinand, Swiss, 1853–1918, painter
James Vibert, Sculptor, 1907, 240, Fig. 9.20

Kirchner, Ernst Ludwig, German, 1880–1938, painter
Seated Woman, 1907, 35, Fig. 2.9

Munch, Edvard, Norwegian, 1863–1944, painter, printmaker
The Sick Child, 1907, 7, Fig. 1.3

Monet, Claude, French, 1840–1926, painter
Palazzo da Mula, Venice, 1908, 370, Fig. 13.22

Brancusi, Constantin, Rumanian, 1876–1957, sculptor
The Kiss, c. 1908, 104, Fig. 5.9

Wright, Frank Lloyd, American, 1867–1959, architect
Armchair, 1908, 119, Fig. 5.31

Balla, Giacomo, Italian, 1871–1958, painter
Street Light, 1909, 210, Fig. 8.17

Bellows, George, American, 1882–1925, painter, printmaker
Both Members of This Club, 1909, 258, Fig. 10.6

Artist Unknown, Native American, Pueblo
Water jar, 1910, 343, Fig. 12.31

Picasso, Pablo, Spanish, 1881–1973, painter, sculptor
Nude Woman, 1910, 375, Fig. 13.27

Marc, Franz, German, 1880–1916, painter
The Large Blue Horses, 1911, 154, Fig. 6.26

Balla, Giacomo, Italian, 1871–1958, painter
Dynamism of a Dog on a Leash, 1912, 212, Fig. 8.19

Hassam, Childe, American, 1859–1935, painter, printmaker
Jelly Fish, 1912, 157, Fig. 6.29

Huntington, Anna Hyatt, American, 1876–1973, sculptor
Riders to the Sea, 1912, 120, Fig. 5.33

Bellows, George, American, 1882–1925, painter, printmaker
Cliff Dwellers, 1913, 223, Fig. 8.26

Chagall, Marc, Russian, 1887–1985, painter
Paris Through the Window, 1913, 20, Fig. 1.18

Delaunay, Robert, French, 1885–1941, painter
Sun, Tower, Airplane, 1913, 134, Fig. 6.1

Marc, Franz, German, 1880–1916, painter
Stables, 1913, 66–67

Chagall, Marc, Russian, 1887–1985, painter
Birthday, 1915, 271, Fig. 10.25

Keyser, Louisa (Dat So La Lee), Native American, 1850–1925, weaver
Basket, c. 1917–18, 218, Fig. 8.24

Picasso, Pablo, Spanish, 1881–1973, painter, sculptor
Still Life, 1918, 316–317

Kirchner, Ernst Ludwig, German, 1880–1938, painter
Winter Landscape in Moonlight, 1919, 34, Fig. 2.8

Stella, Joseph, Italian American, 1877–1946, painter
The Voice of the City of New York Interpreted: The Bridge, 1920–22, 68, Fig. 4.1

Kollwitz, Käthe, German, 1867–1945, painter, printmaker, graphic artist
Self-Portrait, 1921, 374, Fig. 13.26

Lachaise, Gaston, French, 1882–1935, sculptor
Walking Woman, 1922, 272, Fig. 10.26

Brancusi, Constantin, Rumanian, 1876–1957, sculptor
Torso of a Young Man, 1924, 118, Fig. 5.30

Murphy, Gerald, American, 1888–1964, painter
Watch, 1925, 248, Fig. 9.26

Rivera, Diego, Mexican, 1886–1957, painter, muralist
Flower Day, 1925, 229, Fig. 9.5

Bishop, Isabel, American, 1902–1988, painter
Self-Portrait, 1927, 283

O'Keeffe, Georgia, American, 1887–1986, painter
Oriental Poppies, 1927, 2–3

O'Keeffe, Georgia, American, 1887–1986, painter
White Rose With Larkspur, No. 2, 1927, 240, Fig. 9.21

Benton, Thomas Hart, American, 1882–1975, painter
Country Dance, 1929, 79, Fig. 4.18

Hopper, Edward, American, 1882–1967, painter
Early Sunday Morning, 1930. 77, Fig. 4.16

van Alen, William, American, 1882–1954, architect
Chrysler Building, 1930, 206, Fig. 8.9

Wood, Grant, American, 1892–1942, painter
American Gothic, 1930, 12, Fig. 1.10

Calder, Alexander, American, 1898–1976, sculptor
Varese, 1931, 84, Fig. 4.25

Dali, Salvador, Spanish, 1904–1989, painter
The Persistence of Memory, 1931, 375, Fig. 13.28

Orozco, José Clemente, Mexican, 1883–1949, painter
Barricade, 1931, 28, Fig. 2.3

Carr, Emily, Canadian, 1871–1945, painter
Forest, British Columbia, 1931–32, 298, Fig. 11.17

Jones, Lois Mailou, African-American, 1905–1998, painter
The Ascent of Ethiopia, 1932, 386, Fig. 13.42

Albright, Ivan, American, 1897–1983, painter
The Farmer's Kitchen, 1933–34, 177, Fig. 7.6

Münter, Gabriele, German, 1877–1962, painter
Breakfast of the Birds, 1934, 18, Fig. 1.17

Cram, Ralph Adams, American, 1863–1942, architect
Federal Reserve Building (with Ferguson and Goodhue), 1935, 230, Fig. 9.7

Ferguson, American, 20th century, architect
Federal Reserve Building (with Cram and Goodhue), 1935, 230, Fig. 9.7

Goodhue, Betram, American, 1869–1924, architect
Federal Reserve Building (with Cram and Ferguson), 1935, 230, Fig. 9.7

Lee, Doris, American, b. 1905, printmaker, painter
Thanksgiving, 1935, 116, Fig. 5.27

Abbott, Berenice, American, b. 1898, photographer
The Night View, 1936, 202, Fig. 8.4

Ruiz, Antonio M., Mexican, 1897–1964, painter
School Children on Parade, 1936, 214, Fig. 8.22

Wright, Frank Lloyd, American, 1867–1959, architect
Fallingwater House, 1936, 301, Fig. 11.20

Kahlo, Frida, Mexican, 1907–1954, painter
Self Portrait Dedicated to Leon Trotsky, 1937, 239, Fig. 9.19

Matisse, Henri, French, 1869–1954, painter
Purple Robe and Anemones, 1937, 24, Fig. 2.1

Roualt, Georges, French, 1871–1958, painter
Christ and the Apostles, 1937–38, 74, Fig. 4.12

Bishop, Isabel, American, 1902–1988, painter
Waiting, 1938, 282, Fig. 10.32

Escher, M. C., Dutch, 1898–1972, printmaker
Day and Night, 1938, 220, Fig. 8.25

Walkus, George, Kwakiutl, 20th century, maskmaker
Secret Society Mask (Four Headed Cannibal Spirit), 1938, 273, Fig. 10.27

Berman, Eugene, Russian-American, 1899–1972, painter, stage designer
Vendeur de Chapeaux, 1939, 43, Fig. 3.3

Calder, Alexander, American, 1898–1976, sculptor
Lobster Trap and Fish Tail, 1939, 213, Fig. 8.21

Carr, Emily, Canadian, 1871–1945, painter
Above the Trees, 1939, 149, Fig. 6.21

Savage, Augusta, African-American, 20th century, sculptor
Lift Every Voice and Sing, 1939, 209, Fig. 8.15

Apel, Marie, English, 1880–1970, sculptor
Grief, 1940, 119, Fig. 5.32

Davis, Stuart, American, 1894–1964, painter
Hot Still Scape for Six Colors—7th Avenue Style, 1940, 156, Fig. 6.28

Johnson, William H., African-American, 1901–1970, painter
Jitterbugs, c. 1941, 88, Fig. 4.27

O'Keeffe, Georgia, American, 1887–1986, painter
Red Hills and Bones, 1941, 30, Fig. 2.5

Rivera, Diego, Mexican, 1886–1957, painter, muralist
Self-Portrait, 1941, 229

Ernst, Max, German (in America after 1941), 1891–1976, painter
The Eye of Silence, 1943–44, 184, Fig. 7.16

Woodruff, Hale, American, b. 1900, painter
Poor Man's Cotton, 1944, 203, Fig. 8.6

Siqueiros, David Alfaro, Mexican, 1896–1974, painter
Self-Portrait (El Coronelazo), 1945, 264, Fig. 10.14

Lawrence, Jacob, African-American, b. 1917, painter
Children at Play, 1947, 80, Fig. 4.19

Pollock, Jackson, American, 1912–1956, painter
Cathedral, 1947, 14, Fig. 1.13

Tamayo, Rufino, Mexican, 1899–1991, painter
Girl Attacked by a Strange Bird, 1947, 141, Fig. 6.9

Hepworth, Barbara, English, 1903–1975, sculptor
Pendour, 1947–48, 102, Fig. 5.7

Hopper, Edward, American, 1882–1967, painter
First Row Orchestra, 1951, 235, Fig. 9.13

Wright, Frank Lloyd, American, 1867–1959, architect
The David Wright House, 1951, 377, Fig. 13.30

1950–1974

Wright, Frank Lloyd, American, 1867–1959, architect
Stained-glass Window, date unknown, 235, Fig. 9.14

Lange, Dorothea, American, 1895–1965, photojournalist
Migrant Mother, date unknown, 57, Fig. 3.18

Wright, Frank Lloyd, American, 1867–1959, architect
Taliesin West, date unknown, 182, Fig. 7.13

Pereira, Irene Rice, American, 1907–1971, painter
Untitled, 1951, 289, Fig. 11.3

Le Corbusier, Swiss, 1887–1965, architect
Unite d'Habitation, 1947–52, 259, Fig. 10.7

White, Charles, African-American, 1918–1979, painter
Preacher, 1952, 94, Fig. 4.30

Rauschenberg, Robert, American, b. 1925, painter
Red Painting, 1953, 290, Fig. 11.4

Tooker, George, American, b. 1920, painter
Highway, 1953, 96, Fig. 5.1

Shahn, Ben, Russian-American, 1898–1959, painter
The Blind Botanist, 1954, 117, Fig. 5.29

Rothko, Mark, Russian-American, 1903–1970, painter
Orange and Yellow, 1956, 380, Fig. 13.24

Tamayo, Rufino, Mexican, 1899–1991, painter
Toast to the Sun, 1956, 148, Fig. 6.20

Hofmann, Hans, German (born in America), 1880–1966, painter
Flowering Swamp, 1957, 378, Fig. 13.31

Picasso, Pablo, Spanish, 1881–1973, painter, sculptor
Las Meninas (after Velásquez), 1957, 14, Fig. 1.14

Flack, Audrey, American, b. 1931, painter, sculptor
Self-Portrait: The Memory, 1958, 82, Fig. 4.23

Johnson, Philip, American, b. 1906, architect
Seagram Building (with Mies van der Rohe), 1958, 382, Fig. 13.38

Mies van der Rohe, Ludwig, American, 1886–1969, architect
Seagram Building (with Johnson), 1958, 382, Fig. 13.38

Smith, David, American, 1906–1965, painter
Cubi IX, 1961, 101, Fig. 5.6

Dali, Salvador, Spanish, 1904–1989, painter
The Elephants (Design for the Opera La Dama Spagnola e il Cavaliere Romano), 1961, 280, Fig. 10.31

Escher, M. C., Dutch, 1898–1972, printmaker
Waterfall, 1961, 105, Fig. 5.10

Johns, Jasper, American, b. 1930, painter
Map, 1961, 296, Fig. 11.13

Glarner, Fritz, Swiss-American, 1899–1972 painter
Relational Painting #93, 1962, 147, Fig. 6.17

Lichtenstein, Roy, American, b. 1923, painter
Blam, 1962, 379, Fig. 13.32

Marisol, Venezuelan (in America since 1950), b. 1930, sculptor
The Family, 1962, 268, Fig. 10.21

Nevelson, Louise, American, 1899–1988, sculptor
Dawn, 1962, 300, Fig. 11.19

Warhol, Andy, American, 1928–1987, painter, printmaker
Marilyn Monroe's Lips, 1962, 207, Fig. 8.11

Frankenthaler, Helen, American, b. 1928, painter
The Bay, 1963, 111, Fig. 5.16
Loewy, Raymond, French-American, b. 1893, designer
Avanti, 1963, 395, Fig. 14.10
Poons, Larry, American, b.1937, painter
Orange Crush, 1963, 379, Fig. 13.33
Hampton, James, African–American, 1909–1965, sculptor
The Throne of the Third Heaven of the Nations Millennium General Assembly, c. 1950–64, 186, Fig. 7.17
Krasner, Lee, American, b. 1908, painter
The Springs, 1964, 291, Fig. 11.6
Kurelek, William, American, b. 1927, painter
Manitoba Party, 1964, 110, Fig. 5.15
Bearden, Romare, American, 1911–1988, painter, printmaker
Prevalence of Ritual: The Baptism, 1964, 158, Fig. 6.30
Anuszkiewicz, Richard, American, b. 1930, painter
Iridescence, 1965, 146, Fig. 6.15
Magritte, René, Belgian, 1898–1967, painter
The Blank Signature, 1965, 126, Fig. 5.37
Sutej, Miroslav, Yugoslavian, b. 1936, lithographer
Ultra AB, 1966, 288, Fig. 11.2
Evans, Minnie, African-American, 1890–1987, painter
Design Made at Airlie Gardens, 1967, 410–411
Jessup, Georgia Mills, American, b. 1926, painter
Rainy Night, 1967, 302, Fig. 11.22
Safdie, Moshe, Israeli, b. 1938, architect
Habitat, 1967, 382, Fig. 13.39
Stella, Frank, American, b. 1936, painter, sculptor
Agbatana III, 1968, 380, Fig. 13.35
Thomas, Alma, American, 1891–1978, painter
Iris, Tulips, Jonquils, and Crocuses, 1969, 26, Fig. 2.2
Twiggs, Leo, African-American, b. 1934, batik painter
The Blue Wall, 1969, 29, Fig. 2.4
Catlett, Elizabeth, African-American, b. 1915, printmaker, sculptor, painter
Sharecropper, 1970, 48, Fig. 3.10
Hunt, Henry, Canadian Native American, Kwakiutl, 1923–1985, sculptor
K'umugwe' (Komokwa) Mask, 1970, 276, Fig. 10.29
Neel, Alice, American, 1900–1984, painter
Loneliness, 1970, 292, Fig. 11.8
Utzon, Joern, Australian, b. 1918, architect
Sydney Opera House, 1959–72, 286, Fig. 11.1
Estes, Richard, American, b. 1932, painter
Paris Street Scene, 1972, 381, Fig. 13.27
Johns, Jasper, American, b. 1930, painter
Cups 4 Picasso, 1972, 103, Fig. 5.8
Fish, Janet, American, b. 1939, painter
Oranges, 1973, 176, Fig. 7.5
Neel, Alice, American, 1900–1984, painter
Linda Nochlin and Daisy, 1973, 250, Fig. 9.27
Neel, Alice, American, 1900–1984, painter
Still Life, Rose of Sharon, 1973, 74, Fig. 4.13
Ringgold, Faith, African-American, b. 1930, painter, soft sculptor
Mrs. Jones and Family, 1973, 278, Fig. 10.30

Andrews, Benny, African-American, b. 1930, painter
The Scholar, 1974, 81, Fig. 4.20
Flack, Audrey, American, b. 1931, painter, sculptor
Leonardo's Lady, 1974, 192, Fig. 7.20
Paley, Albert Raymond, American, b. 1944, sculptor
Portal Gates, 1974, 78, Fig. 4.17
Thomas Hart Benton, American, 1882–1975, painter
The Sources of Country Music, 1975, 376, Fig. 13.29
Bishop, Isabel, American, 1902–1988, painter
Head #5, no date, 45, Fig. 3.7

1975–

Bearden, Romare, American, 1911–1988, painter, printmaker
Return of Ulysses, 1976, 13, Fig. 1.11
Oldenburg, Claes, American, b. 1929, painter, sculptor
Clothespin, 1976, 261, Fig. 10.9
Chagall, Marc, Russian, 1887–1985, painter
The American Windows, 1977, 136, Fig. 6.2
Houser, Allan, Native American, 1914–1994, sculptor
Coming of Age, 1977, 209, Fig. 8.16
Dillon, Leo and Diane, American, both b. 1933, graphic artists
A Wrinkle in Time (cover illustration), 1979, 38, Fig. 2.11
Goings, Ralph, American, b. 1928, painter, sculptor
Diner With Red Door, 1979, 112, Fig. 5.18
Jimenez, Luis, American, b. 1940, sculptor
Vaquero, 1980, 50, Fig. 3.11
Mitchell, Joan, American, 1926–1992, painter
Dirty Snow, 1980, 179, Fig. 7.9
Fish, Janet, American, b. 1939, painter
Raspberries and Goldfish, 1981, 17, Fig. 1.16
Houser, Allan, Native American, 1914–1994, sculptor
Reverie, 1981, 299, Fig. 11.18
Murray, Elizabeth, American, b. 1940, painter
Painters Progress, 1981, 40, Fig. 3.1
Graves, Nancy, American, b. 1940, sculptor
Zaga, 1983, 51, Fig. 3.13
Haring, Keith, American, 1958–1990, painter
Untitled, 1983, 90, Fig. 4.27
Malangi, David, Australian, b. 1934, Aboriginal artist
Abstract (River Mouth Map), 1983, 92, Fig. 4.29
Steir, Pat, American, b. 1938, painter
The Bruegel Series (A Vanitas of Style), 1982–84, 160, Fig. 6.31
Stella, Frank, American, b. 1936, painter, sculptor
St. Michael's Counterguard (Malta Series), 1984, 383, Fig. 13.40
Torivio, Dorothy, Native American, b. 1946, ceramicist
Vase, c. 1984, 233, Fig. 9.11
Dvorak, Lois, American, 1934–1993, mixed media
Spirit Boxes I, 1985, 304, Fig. 11.24
Naranjo, Michael, Native American, b. 1944, sculptor
Spirits Soaring, 1985, 109, Fig. 5.14
Schapiro, Miriam, American, b. 1923, painter, sculptor
Personal Appearance, 1985, 62, Fig. 3.22

Hanson, Duane, American, b. 1925, sculptor
Traveler with Sunburn, 1986, 381, Fig. 13.36
Biggers, John, American, b.1924, painter
Shotguns, Fourth Ward, 1987, 198, Fig. 8.1
Biggers, John, American, b. 1924, painter
Starry Crown, 1987, 99, Fig. 5.3
Clive, Carolyn, American, b. 1931, painter
Amplitude, 1987, 86, Fig. 4.26
Larraz, Julio, Cuban, b. 1944, painter
Papiamento, 1987, 32, Fig. 2.6
Liebovitz, Annie, American, 20th century, photographer
Wilt Chamberlain and Willie Shoemaker, 1987, 262, Fig. 10.11
Xiong, Chaing, Laotian, b. 1953, craftsperson
Hmong Story Cloth, 1987, 211, Fig. 8.18
Bearden, Romare, American, 1911–1988, painter, printmaker
Family, 1988, 166, Fig. 6.34
Jacquette, Yvonne, American, b. 1934, painter
Town of Skowhegan, Maine V, 1988, 70, Fig. 4.2
Murray, Elizabeth, American, b. 1940, painter
Things to Come, 1988, 150, Fig. 6.22
Ringgold, Faith, African-American, b. 1930, painter, soft sculptor
Bitter Nest Part II: Harlem Renaissance Party, 1988, 36, Fig. 2.10
Twiggs, Leo, African-American, b. 1934, batik painter
East Wind Suite: Door, 1989, 10, Fig. 1.7
Brown, Roger, American, 1941–1997, muralist
Hurricane Hugo, 1990, 11, Fig. 1.8
Dunnigan, John, American, 20th century, furniture designer
Slipper Chairs, 1990, 33, Fig. 2.7
Hoover, John, Native American, Aleut, b. 1919, sculptor
Loon Song, 1990, 180, Fig. 7.11
Muñoz, Rie, Dutch-American, b. 1921, painter
Both the Sun and Moon Belong to Women, 1990, 252, Fig. 9.28
Pootoogook, Napachie, Inuit, b. 1938, printmaker
My Daughter's First Steps, 1990, 269, Fig. 10.22
Skoglund, Sandy, American, b. 1946, photographer, painter
The Green House, 1990, 406, Fig. 14.27
Scully, Sean, Irish, b. 1945, painter
White Robe, 1990, 295, Fig. 11.12

Smith, Jaune Quick-To-See, Native American, b. 1940, painter
Spotted Owl, 1990, 162, Fig. 6.32
Dick, Beau, Canadian Native American, b. 1955, printmaker
Sacred Circles, 1991, 246, Fig. 9.25
Paik, Nam June, Korean, b. 1932, kinetic artist
Technology, 1991, 388, Fig. 14.1
Wilson, Jane, American, b. 1924, painter
Solstice, 1991, 303, Fig. 11.23
Wilson, Jane, American, b. 1924, painter
Winter Wheat, 1991, 121, Fig. 5.34
Yancy, John, African-American, b. 1956, muralist
Celebration of Arts: Vibrations of Life, 1991, 308, Fig. 11.26
Bayless, Florence, American, b. 1922, craftsperson
Haori Coat, 1992, 298, Fig. 11.16
Grossman, Rhoda, American, b. 1941, digital artist
Self-Portrait After Escher, 1992, 59, Fig. 3.20
Naminonha, Dan, Native American, b. 1950, painter
Blessing Rain Chant, 1992, 75, Fig. 4.14
Romero, Annette, Native American, b. 1951, ceramicist
Storyteller Doll, 1993, 274, Fig. 10.28
Schapiro, Miriam, American, b. 1923, painter, sculptor
Yard Sale, 1993, 180, Fig. 7.10
Smith, Larry, American, b. 1949, painter
North Georgia Waterfall, 1993, 122, Fig. 5.35
Abrasha, Dutch-American, b. 1948, jewelry designer, goldsmith
Hannukkah Menorah, 1995, 72, Fig. 4.6
Christo, American, b. 1935, sculptor, environmental artist
Wrapped Reichstag (with Jeanne-Claude), 1995, 130, Fig. 5.39
McKie, Judy Kensley, American, b. 1944, furniture designer
Monkey Settee, 1995, 53, Fig. 3.15
Pei, I. M., Chinese-American, b. 1917, architect
Rock-and-Roll Hall of Fame and Museum, 1995, 402, Fig. 14.21
Twiggs, Leo, African-American, b. 1934, batik painter
Single Family Blues, 1996, 269, Fig. 10.23
Silvers, Robert, American, contemporary, digital artist
Vincent van Gogh, 1997, 190, Fig. 7.19

This section contains the important words and phrases used in *ArtTalk* that may be new to you. You may want to refer to this list of terms as you read the chapters, complete the exercises, and prepare to create your own works of art. You can also use the Glossary to review what you have learned in *ArtTalk*.

A

Abstract art Twentieth-century art containing shapes that simplify shapes of real objects to emphasize form instead of subject matter.

Abstract Expressionism Painting style developed after World War II in New York City that emphasized abstract elements of art rather than recognizable subject matter, and also stressed feelings and emotions (13).

Acrylic paint Pigments mixed with an acrylic vehicle. Available in different degrees of quality: school and artists' acrylics. School acrylics are less expensive than the professional acrylics, can be washed out of brushes and clothes, and are nontoxic.

Action Painting See *Abstract Expressionism.*

Active Expressing movement. Diagonal and zigzag lines (4) and diagonally slanting shapes and forms (5) are active. Opposite of static.

Aesthetic experience Your personal interaction with a work of art (2).

Aesthetics The philosophy or study of the nature and value of art (2).

Afterimage Weak image of complementary color created by a viewer's brain as a reaction to prolonged looking at a color. After staring at something red, the viewer sees an afterimage of green.

Age of Faith See *Middle Ages.*

Air brush Atomizer operated by compressed air used for spraying on paint.

Alternating rhythm Visual rhythm set up by repeating motifs but changing position or content of motifs or spaces between them (8).

Analog system A system that uses electromagnetic energy to imprint both sound and pictures on videotape (3).

Analogous colors Colors that sit side by side on the color wheel and have a common hue (6). Violet, red-violet, and red are analogous colors. Analogous colors can be used as a color scheme.

Analysis In art criticism, the step in which you discover how the principles of art are used to organize the art elements of line, color, shape, form, space, and texture. In art history, the step in which you determine the style of the work (2).

Animators Artists who create moving cartoons (14).

Applied art Art made to be functional as well as visually pleasing (3).

Approximate symmetry Balance that is almost symmetrical (9). This type of symmetry produces the effect of stability, as formal balance does, but small differences make the arrangement more interesting.

Arbitrary color Color chosen by an artist to express his or her feelings (6). Opposite of optical color.

Arch Curved stone structure supporting weight of material over an open space. Doorways and bridges use arches.

Architect A person who designs buildings that are well constructed, aesthetically pleasing, and functional (14).

Architecture Art form of designing and planning construction of buildings, cities, and bridges (3).

Art criticism An organized approach for studying a work of art. It has four stages: description, analysis, interpretation, and judgment (2).

Artistic style See *individual style.*

Artists Creative individuals who use imagination and skill to communicate in visual form (1).

Ashcan School Group of American artists working in the early twentieth century who used city people and city scenes for subject matter (6). Originally called "The Eight," they helped to organize the Armory Show.

Assembling A sculpting technique in which the artist gathers and joins together a variety of different materials to make a sculpture. Also called constructing (3).

Asymmetrical balance Another name for informal balance, in which unlike objects have equal visual weight or eye attraction (4).

Atmospheric perspective Effect of air and light on how an object is perceived by the viewer (5). The more air between the viewer and the object, the more the object seems to fade. A bright object seems closer to the viewer than a dull object.

B

Background Part of the picture plane that seems to be farthest from the viewer.

Balance Principle of art concerned with equalizing visual forces, or elements, in a work of art (9). If a work of art has visual balance, the viewer feels that the elements have been arranged in a satisfying way. Visual imbalance makes the viewer feel that the elements need to be rearranged. The two types of balance are formal (also called symmetrical) and informal (also called asymmetrical).

Baroque Artistic style that emphasized dramatic lighting, movement, and emotional intensity. It developed after the Reformation in the seventeenth century. Artists used movement of forms and figures toward the viewer, dramatic lighting effects, contrast between dark and light, ornamentation, and curved lines to express energy and strong emotions (13).

Binder A liquid that holds together the grains of pigment (6).

Blending Technique of shading through smooth, gradual application of dark value (3).

Brayer Roller with a handle used to apply ink to a surface.

Buttress Projecting brick or stone structure that supports an arch or vault. A flying buttress is connected with a wall by an arch. It reaches over the side aisle to support the roof of a cathedral.

Byzantine art Artistic style that developed around the city of Constantinople (now Istanbul, Turkey) in the eastern Roman Empire. It featured very rich colors and heavily outlined figures that appeared flat and stiff (13).

C

Calligraphic lines Flowing lines made with brushstrokes similar to Asian writing (4).

Calligraphy An Asian method of beautiful handwriting (4).

Canvas Rough cloth on which an oil painting is made.

Carving A sculpting technique in which the sculptor cuts, chips, or drills from a solid mass of material to create a sculpture. Material is removed until the sculpture is complete; therefore, carving is referred to as a subtractive process (3).

Casting A sculpting technique in which molten metal or another substance is poured into a mold and allowed to harden. Just as in printmaking, an edition of sculptures can be made from the same mold (3).

Central axis A dividing line that works like the point of balance in the balance scale. The central axis is used to measure visual weight in a work of art. It can be vertical (balance between sides is measured) or horizontal (balance between top and bottom is measured) (9).

Ceramics Art of making objects with clay to produce pottery and sculpture. Pottery is fired in a kiln to make it stronger.

Chiaroscuro The arrangement of light and shadow (5). This technique was introduced by Italian artists during the Renaissance and used widely by Baroque artists. Chiaroscuro is also called modeling or shading.

Classical Referring to the art of ancient Greece and Rome. The Greeks created art based on the ideals of perfect proportion and logic instead of emotion. The Romans adapted Greek art and spread it throughout the civilized world (13).

Clay Stiff, sticky earth that is used in ceramics. It is wet, and it hardens after drying or heating (3).

Clustering Technique for creating a focal point by grouping several different shapes closely together (11).

Coil Long roll joined into a circle or spiral. Clay coils are used to make pottery.

Collage An artwork onto which materials such as textured paper and fabric have been attached (7).

Color An element of art that is derived from reflected light (6). The sensation of color is aroused in the brain by response of the eyes to different wavelengths of light. Color has three properties: hue, value, and intensity.

Color-field painting Twentieth-century art created using only flat fields of color (13).

Color scheme Plan for organizing colors. Types of color schemes include monochromatic, analogous, complementary, triad, split complementary, warm, and cool (6).

Color spectrum The effect that occurs when light passes through a prism; the beam of white light is bent and separated into bands of color. Colors always appear in the same order, by wavelengths, from longest to shortest: red, orange, yellow, green, blue, violet. A rainbow displays the spectrum (6).

Color triad Three colors spaced an equal distance apart on the color wheel (6). The primary color triad is red, yellow, and blue; the secondary color triad is orange, green, and violet. A color triad is a type of color scheme.

Color wheel The spectrum bent into a circle (6).

Compass Instrument used for measuring and drawing arcs and circles.

Complementary colors The colors opposite each other on the color wheel (6). A complement of a color absorbs all the light waves the color reflects and is the strongest contrast to the color. Mixing a hue with its complementary color dulls it. Red and green are complementary colors. Complementary colors can be used as a color scheme.

Composition The way the principles of art are used to organize the elements of art (1).

Content The message the work communicates. The content can relate to the subject matter or be an idea or emotion. Theme is another word for content (1).

Contour drawing Drawing in which only contour lines are used to represent the subject matter (4). Artists keep their eyes on the object they are drawing and concentrate on directions and curves.

Contour line A line that defines the edges and surface ridges of an object (4).

Contrast Technique for creating a focal point by using differences in elements (11).

Convergence Technique for creating a focal point by arranging elements so that many lines or shapes point to one item or area (11).

Cool colors Blue, green, and violet (6). Cool colors suggest coolness and seem to recede from a viewer. Cool colors can be used as a color scheme. Opposite of warm colors.

Crafts Art forms creating works of art that are both beautiful and useful. Crafts include weaving, fabric design, ceramics, and jewelry making (3).

Crayons Pigments held together with wax and molded into sticks.

Credit line A list of important facts about a work of art. A credit line usually includes the artist's name, the title of the work, year completed, medium used, size (height, width, and depth), location (gallery, museum, or collection and city), donors, and date donated (1).

Crewel Loosely twisted yarn used in embroidery.

Criteria Standards of judgment (2).

Crosshatching The technique of using crossed lines for shading (4).

Cubism Twentieth-century art movement that emphasizes structure and design (13). Three-dimensional objects are pictured from many different points of view at the same time.

Culture Behaviors and ideas of a group of people. Studying art objects produced by a group of people is one way to learn about a culture (12).

Cuneiform The Sumerian writing system made up of wedge-shaped characters (12).

Curved lines Lines that are always bending and change direction gradually (4).

D

Dark Ages See *Middle Ages.*

Decalcomania A technique in which paint is forced into random textured patterns by pulling apart canvases between which blobs of paint have been squeezed (7).

Dense Compact; having parts crowded together. Dense materials are solid and heavy. Opposite of soft.

Description A list of all the things you see in the work (2).

Design Plan, organization, or arrangement of elements in a work of art.

Design qualities How well the work is organized (2). This aesthetic quality is favored by Formalism.

Diagonal lines Lines that slant (4).

Digital camera A camera that records images digitally. These images can then be downloaded into computer applications where they can be altered and enhanced (3).

Digital system A system that processes words and images directly as numbers or digits (3).

Dimension The amount of space an object takes up in one direction (4). The three dimensions are height, width, and depth.

Distortion Deviations from expected, normal proportions (10).

Divine Proportion See *Golden Mean.*

Dome Hemispherical vault or ceiling over a circular opening. A dome rises above the center part of a building (13).

Dominant element Element of a work of art noticed first. Elements noticed later are called subordinate (11).

Draw program A computer art application in which images are stored as a series of lines and curves. Objects can be resized without distortion in draw programs (3).

Dyes Pigments that dissolve in liquid. Dye sinks into a material and stains it (6).

Dynamism Term used by the Futurists to refer to the forces of movement.

Dynasty A period of time during which a single family provided a succession of rulers (12).

E

Edition All the prints made from the same plate or set of plates (3).

Elements of art Basic visual symbols in the language of art. The elements of art are line, shape and form, space, color, value, and texture (1).

Embroidery Method of decorating fabric with stitches.

Emotionalism Theory that requires that a work of art must arouse a response of feelings, moods, or emotions in the viewer. One of the three aesthetic theories of art criticism, the others being Formalism and Imitationalism (2).

Emphasis Principle of art that makes one part of a work dominant over the other parts (11). The element noticed first is called dominant; the elements noticed later are called subordinate.

Engraving Method of cutting a design into a material, usually metal, with a sharp tool. A print can be made by inking an engraved surface.

Exaggeration Deviations from expected, normal proportions (10).

Expressionism Twentieth-century art movement. A style that emphasized the expression of innermost feelings (13).

Expressive qualities Those qualities that communicate ideas and moods (2).

F

Fabric Material made from fibers. Cloth and felt are fabrics (3).

Fauves French for "wild beasts." A group of early twentieth-century painters who used brilliant colors and bold distortions in an uncontrolled way. Their leader was Henri Matisse.

Fiber Thin, threadlike linear material that can be woven or spun into fabric (3).

Fiberfill Lightweight, fluffy filling material made of synthetic fibers.

Figure Human form in a work of art.

Fine art Art made to be experienced visually. Opposite of functional art (3).

Fire To apply heat to harden pottery.

Flowing rhythm Visual rhythm created by repeating wavy lines (8).

Focal point The first part of a work to attract the attention of the viewer (11). Focal points are created by contrast, location, isolation, convergence, and use of the unusual.

Foreground Part of the picture plane that appears closest to the viewer. The foreground is usually at the bottom of the picture.

Foreshortening To shorten an object to make it look as if it extends backward into space (10). This method reproduces proportions a viewer actually sees, which depend on the viewer's distance from the object or person.

Forms Objects having three dimensions (5). Like a shape, a form has height and width, but it also has depth. Forms are either geometric or free-form.

Formal balance Way of organizing parts of a design so that equal, or very similar, elements are placed on opposite sides of a central axis (9). Formal balance suggests stability. Symmetry is a type of formal balance. Opposite of informal balance.

Formalism Theory that places emphasis on the design qualities. One of the three aesthetic theories of art criticism, the others being Emotionalism and Imitationalism (2).

Free-form shapes Irregular and uneven shapes (5). Their outlines are curved, or angular, or both. Free-form shapes are often referred to as organic (found in nature). Opposite of geometric shapes.

Freestanding Work of art surrounded on all sides by space. A three-dimensional work of art is freestanding. Opposite of relief (3).

Frottage A freshly painted canvas is placed right-side-up over a raised texture and rubbed or scraped across the surface of the paint (7).

Functional art Works of art made to be used instead of only enjoyed. Objects must be judged by how well they work when used (1).

Futurists Early twentieth-century Italian artists who arranged angular forms to suggest motion (8). They called the forces of movement dynamism.

G

Gallery Place for displaying or selling works of art.

Genre painting Paintings that have scenes from everyday life as their subject matter.

Geometric shapes Precise shapes that can be described using mathematical formulas (5). Basic geometric shapes are the circle, the square, and the triangle. Basic geometric forms are the cylinder, the cube, and the pyramid. Opposite of free-form shapes.

Gesture An expressive movement (4).

Gesture drawing Line drawing done quickly to capture movement of the subject's body (4).

Glaze In ceramics, a thin, glossy coating fired into pottery. In painting, a thin layer of transparent paint.

Golden Mean A line divided into two parts so that the smaller line has the same proportion, or ratio, to the larger line as the larger line has to the whole line (10). Perfect ratio (relationship of parts) discovered by Euclid, a Greek Philosopher. Its mathematical expression is 1 to 1.6. It was also called the Golden Section and the Golden Rectangle. The long sides of the Golden Rectangle are a little more than half again as long as the short sides. This ratio was rediscovered in the early sixteenth century and named the Divine Proportion.

Gothic Artistic style developed in western Europe between the twelfth and sixteenth centuries. Featured churches that seemed to soar upward, pointed arches, and stained-glass windows (13).

Gouache Pigments ground in water and mixed with gum to form opaque watercolor. Gouache resembles school tempera or poster paint.

Graphic designer A person who translates ideas into images and arranges them in appealing and memorable ways (14).

Grattage Wet paint is scratched with a variety of tools, such as forks, razors, and combs for the purpose of creating different textures (7).

Grid Pattern of intersecting vertical and horizontal lines (8).

Griots Oral historians who are also musicians and performers (12).

Hard-edge In two-dimensional art, shapes with clearly defined outlines. Hard-edge shapes look dense. Opposite of soft-edge.

Harmony The principle of art that creates unity by stressing similarities of separate but related parts (11).

Hatching Technique of shading with a series of fine parallel lines (3).

Hierarchical proportion When figures are arranged in a work of art so scale indicates importance (10).

Hieroglyphics Picture writing used by ancient Egyptians (12).

High-key painting Painting using many tints of a color (6). Opposite of low-key painting.

Highlights Small areas of white used to show the very brightest spots (5). Highlights show the surfaces of the subject that reflect the most light. They are used to create the illusion of form. Opposite of shadows.

High relief Sculpture in which areas project far out from a flat surface (3).

High-resolution Producing a sharp image.

Holograms Images in three dimensions created with a laser beam (5).

Horizon Point at which earth and sky seem to meet.

Horizontal line Line parallel to the horizon (4). Horizontal lines lie flat and are parallel to the bottom edge of the paper or canvas.

Hue The name of a color in the color spectrum (6). Hue is related to the wavelength of reflected light. The primary hues are red, yellow, and blue; they are called primary because they cannot be made by mixing other hues together. The secondary hues, made by mixing two primary hues, are orange, violet, and green. Hue is one of the three properties of color.

Illustrator A person who creates the visual images that complement written words (14).

Imitationalism An aesthetic theory focusing on realistic presentation. One of the three aesthetic theories of art criticism, the others being Emotionalism and Formalism (2).

Implied lines A series of points that the viewer's eyes automatically connect. Implied lines are suggested, not real (4).

Impressionism Style of painting started in France in the 1860s. It featured everyday subjects and emphasized the momentary effects of light on color (13).

Individual style The artist's personal way of using the elements and principles of art to express feelings and ideas (2).

Informal balance Way of organizing parts of a design involving a balance of unlike objects (9). Asymmetry is another term for informal balance. Opposite of formal balance.

Intaglio (in-**tal**-yo or in-**tal**-ee-o) A printmaking technique in which ink is forced into lines that have been cut or etched on a hard surface such as metal or wood. The plate's surface is then wiped clean and the prints are made (3).

Intensity The brightness or dullness of a hue. A pure hue is called a high-intensity color. A dulled hue (a color mixed with its complement) is called a low-intensity color. Intensity is one of the three properties of color (6).

Interior designer A person who plans the design and decoration of the interior spaces in homes and offices (14).

Intermediate color A color made by mixing a primary color with a secondary color. Red-orange is an intermediate color (6).

International style A style of architecture developed after World War II that emphasizes a plain, austere building style (13).

Interpretation In art criticism, the step in which you explain or tell the meaning or mood of the work. In art history, the step in which you do research about the artist (2).

Invented texture A kind of visual texture that does not represent a real texture but creates a sensation of one by repeating lines and shapes in a two-dimensional pattern (7). Opposite of simulated texture.

Isolation Technique for creating a focal point by putting one object alone to emphasize it (11).

Judgment In art criticism, the step in which you determine the degree of artistic merit. In art history, the step in which you determine if the work has made an important contribution to the history of art (2).

Kinetic A work of art that actually moves in space (8).

Landscape Painting or drawing in which natural land scenery, such as mountains, trees, rivers, or lakes, is the main feature.

Layout The way items are arranged on the page (14).

Line An element of art that is the path of a moving point through space. Although lines can vary in appearance (they can have different lengths, widths, textures, directions, and degree of curve), they are considered one-dimensional and are measured by length. A line is also used by an artist to control the viewer's eye movement. There are five kinds of lines: vertical, horizontal, diagonal, curved, and zigzag (4).

Linear perspective A graphic system that creates the illusion of depth and volume on a flat surface. In one-point linear perspective, all receding lines meet at a single point. In two-point linear perspective, different sets of lines meet at different points (5, 13).

Literal qualities The realistic qualities that appear in the subject of the work (2).

Lithography A printmaking technique in which the image to be printed is drawn on limestone, zinc, or aluminum with a special greasy pencil or pencil. Ink is attracted to this material (3).

Location The technique of using placement of elements to create a focal point (11). Items near the center of a work of art are usually noticed first.

Logos Symbols or trademarks that are immediately recognizable (14).

Loom Machine or frame for weaving.

Low-key painting Painting using many shades or dark values of a color (6). Opposite of high-key painting.

Low-relief See *bas-relief.*

Mannerism European sixteenth-century artistic style featuring highly emotional scenes and elongated figures (13).

Manufactured shapes/forms Shapes or forms made by people either by hand or by machine. Opposite of organic shapes/forms (5).

Mat To frame a picture or drawing with a cardboard border.

Matte surface Surface that reflects a soft, dull light (7). Paper has a matte surface. Opposite of shiny surface.

Medieval Related to the *Middle Ages.*

Media See *medium.*

Medium Material used to make art. Plural is media (1).

Megaliths Large monuments created from huge stone slabs (12).

Mexican muralists Early twentieth-century artists whose paintings on walls and ceilings used solid forms and powerful colors to express their feelings about the Mexican Revolution. Also called Mexican Expressionists (13).

Middle Ages Period of roughly one thousand years from the destruction of the Roman Empire to the Renaissance. Culture centered around the Catholic Church. The Middle Ages are also called the Dark Ages (because few new ideas developed) and the Age of Faith (because religion was a powerful force) (13).

Middle ground Area in a picture between the foreground and the background.

Minimalism Twentieth-century artistic style that uses a minimum of art elements (13).

Mobile Moving sculpture (8).

Modeling A sculpting technique in which a soft, pliable material is built up and shaped. Because more material is added to build a form, modeling is referred to as an additive process (3).

Module A three-dimensional motif (8).

Monochromatic A color scheme that uses only one hue and the tints and shades of that hue for a unifying effect (6).

Mortar and pestle Ceramic bowl and tool for grinding something into a powder.

Mosaics Pictures made with small cubes of colored marble, glass, or tile and set into cement.

Mosques Muslim places of worship (12).

Motif A unit that is repeated in visual rhythm (8). Units in a motif may or may not be an exact duplicate of the first unit.

Movement See *visual movement.*

Multi-media programs Computer software programs that help users design, organize, and combine text, graphics, video, and sound in one document (3).

Mural Painting on a wall or ceiling.

Museum curator Person who oversees the operations of a museum (14).

Negative spaces Empty spaces surrounding shapes and forms (5). The shape and size of negative spaces affect the interpretation of positive spaces. Negative spaces are also called ground.

Neoclassicism New classicism. French artistic style developed in the nineteenth century after the Rococo style. An approach to art that borrowed subject matter and formal design qualities from the art of Greece and Rome (13).

Neolithic period New Stone Age. A prehistoric period stretching roughly from 7000 B.C. to 2000 B.C. (12).

Neutral colors Black, white, and gray. Black reflects no wavelengths of light, white reflects all wavelengths of light, and gray reflects all wavelengths of light equally but only partially (6).

Nonobjective art Art that has no recognizable subject matter (1).

O

Oil paint Slow-drying paint made by mixing pigments in oil and usually used on canvas (3).

Opaque Quality of a material that does not let any light pass through. Opposite of transparent.

Op Art Optical art. Twentieth-century artistic style in which artists use scientific knowledge about vision to create optical illusions of movement (13).

Optical color Color perceived by the viewer due to the effect of atmosphere or unusual light on the actual color (6). Opposite of arbitrary color.

Organic shapes/forms Shapes or forms made by the forces of nature. Opposite of manufactured shapes/forms (5).

Outline A line that shows or creates the outer edges of a shape (4).

P

Package designer Person who produces the containers that attract the attention of consumers (14).

Pagoda A tower several stories high with roofs curving slightly upward at the edges (12).

Paint Pigments mixed with oil or water. Pigment particles in paint stick to the surface of the material on which the paint is applied (3).

Paint program A computer art application in which images are stored as bitmaps. Paint programs are capable of producing more lifelike pictures than draw programs (3).

Palette Tray for mixing colors of paints.

Papier-mâché French for "mashed paper." Modeling material made of paper and liquid paste and molded over a supporting structure called the armature.

Paleolithic period Old Stone Age. Began about two million years ago and ended with the close of the last ice age about 13,000 B.C. (12).

Parallel lines Lines that move in the same direction and always stay the same distance apart.

Pastels Pigments held together with gum and molded into sticks.

Paste-up Model of a printed page. It is photographed for the purpose of making a plate for the printing process.

Pattern A two-dimensional decorative visual repetition (8). A pattern has no movement and may or may not have rhythm.

Perceive To become deeply aware through the senses of the special nature of a visual object (1).

Perspective A graphic system that creates the illusion of depth and volume on a two-dimensional surface (5). It was developed during the Renaissance by architect Filippo Brunelleschi. Perspective is created by overlapping, size variations, placement, detail, color, and converging lines.

Pharaohs Egyptian rulers who were worshiped as gods and held complete authority over the kingdom (12).

Photogram Image on blueprint paper developed by fumes from liquid ammonia.

Photography The technique of capturing optical images on light-sensitive surfaces (3).

Photojournalists Visual reporters (14).

Photo-Realism See *Super-Realism.*

Picture plane The surface of a painting or drawing.

Pigments Finely ground, colored powders that form paint when mixed with a liquid (6).

Plaster Mixture of lime, sand, and water that hardens on drying.

Point of view Angle from which the viewer sees an object (5). The shapes and forms a viewer sees depend on his or her point of view.

Polymer medium Liquid used in acrylic painting as a thinning or finishing material (3).

Pop art Artistic style used in the early 1960s in the United States that portrayed images of popular culture (mass media, commercial art, comic strips, advertising) (13).

Portrait Image of a person, especially the face and upper body.

Positive spaces Shapes or forms in two- and three-dimensional art (5). Empty spaces surrounding them are called negative spaces or ground.

Post-and-lintel A method of construction in which one long stone is balanced on top of two posts. Currently referred to as post-and-beam construction (3).

Post-Impressionism French painting style of the late nineteenth century that stressed a more individual approach to painting, unique to each artist working at the time (13).

Post-Modernism An approach to art that incorporates traditional elements and techniques while retaining some characteristics of modern art styles or movements (13).

Prehistoric Period before history was written down (12).

Principles of art Rules that govern how artists organize the elements of art. The principles of art are rhythm, movement, balance, proportion, variety, emphasis, harmony, and unity (1).

Print Impression created by an artist made on paper or fabric from a printing plate, stone, or block and repeated many times to produce identical images (3).

Printing plate Surface containing the impression transferred to paper or fabric to make a print (3).

Printmaking A process in which an artist repeatedly transfers an original image from one prepared surface to another (3).

Prism Wedge-shaped piece of glass that bends white light and separates it into spectral hues.

Profile Side view of a face.

Progressive rhythm Visual rhythm that changes a motif each time it is repeated (8).

Proportion Principle of art concerned with the size relationships of one part to another (10).

Protractor Semicircular instrument used to measure and draw angles.

Proximity Technique for creating unity by limiting negative spaces between shapes (11).

R

Radial balance Type of balance in which forces or elements of a design come out (radiate) from a central point (9).

Random rhythm Visual rhythm in which a motif is repeated in no apparent order, with no regular spaces (8).

Rasp File with sharp, rough teeth used for cutting into a surface.

Realism Mid-nineteenth-century artistic style in which presented familiar scenes as they actually appeared (13).

Realists Artists in the nineteenth century who portrayed political, social, and moral issues (13).

Real texture Texture that can be perceived through touch. Opposite of visual texture (7).

Recede To move back or become more distant.

Reformation Religious revolution in western Europe in the sixteenth century. It started as a reform movement in the Catholic Church and led to the beginnings of Protestantism (13).

Regionalists Artists who painted the farmlands and cities of the United States in an optimistic way (13).

Regular rhythm Visual rhythm achieved through repeating identical motifs using the same intervals of space between them (8).

Relief printing A printmaking technique in which the artist cuts away the sections of a surface not meant to hold ink. As a result, the image to be printed is raised from the background (3).

Relief sculpture Type of sculpture in which forms project from a flat background. Opposite of freestanding (3).

Renaissance The name given to the period at the end of the Middle Ages when artists, writers, and philosophers were "re-awakened" to art forms and ideas from ancient Greece and Rome (13).

Repetition Technique for creating rhythm and unity in which a motif or single element appears again and again (11).

Reproduction A copy of a work of art (3).

Rhythm The principle of art that indicates movement by the repetition of elements (8). Visual rhythm is perceived through the eyes and is created by repeating positive spaces separated by negative spaces. There are five types of rhythm: random, regular, alternating, flowing, and progressive.

Rococo Eighteenth-century artistic style that began in the luxurious homes of the French aristocracy and spread to the rest of Europe. It stressed free graceful movement, a playful use of line, and delicate colors (13).

Romanesque Style of architecture and sculpture developed during the Middle Ages in western Europe that featured buildings of massive size; solid, heavy walls; wide use of the rounded Roman arch; and many sculptural decorations (13).

Romanticism Early nineteenth-century artistic style that was a reaction against Neoclassicism. It found its subjects in the world of the dramatic and in cultures foreign to Europe. It emphasized rich color and high emotion (13).

Rough texture Irregular surface that reflects light unevenly (7). Opposite of smooth texture.

Rubbing Technique for transferring textural quality of a surface to paper by placing paper over the surface and rubbing the top of the paper with crayon or pencil (7).

S

Safety labels Labels identifying art products that are safe to use or that must be used with caution.

Scale Size as measured against a standard reference. Scale can refer to an entire work of art or to elements within it (10).

Scanner A device that "reads" a printed image and then translates it into a language the computer can use to make a visual image on the screen (3).

Score To make neat, sharp creases in paper using a cutting tool.

Screen printing A printmaking technique in which a stencil and screen are used as the printing plate. The stencil is placed on a fabric screen stretched across a frame and ink is pressed through the screen where it is not covered by the stencil (3).

Scroll A long roll of parchment or silk (12).

Sculpture Three-dimensional work of art created out of wood, stone, metal, or clay by carving, welding, casting, or modeling (3).

Seascape Painting or drawing in which the sea is the subject.

Shade A dark value of a hue made by adding black to it. Opposite of tint (6).

Shading The use of light and dark lines to give a feeling of depth and texture (3).

Shadows Shaded areas in a drawing or painting. Shadows show the surfaces of the subject that reflect the least light and are used to create the illusion of form. Opposite of highlights.

Shape A two-dimensional area that is defined in some way. While a form has depth, a shape has only height and width. Shapes are either geometric or free-form (5).

Shiny surface Surface that reflects bright light. Window glass has a shiny surface. Opposite of matte surface (7).

Sighting Technique for determining the proportional relationship of one part of an object to another (10).

Silhouette Outline drawing of a shape. Originally a silhouette was a profile portrait, filled in with a solid color.

Simplicity Technique for creating unity by limiting the number of variations of an element of art.

Simulated texture A kind of visual texture that imitates real texture by using a two-dimensional pattern to create the illusion of a three-dimensional surface (7). A plastic tabletop can use a pattern to simulate the texture of wood. Opposite of invented texture.

Sketch Quick, rough drawing without much detail that can be used as a plan or reference for later work.

Slip Creamy mixture of clay and water used to fasten pieces of clay together.

Smooth texture Regular surface that reflects light evenly. Opposite of rough texture (7).

Soft edge In two-dimensional art, shapes with fuzzy, blurred outlines. Soft-edge shapes look soft. Opposite of hard-edge.

Soft sculpture Sculpture made with fabric and stuffed with soft material.

Solvent The liquid that controls the thickness or the thinness of the paint (6).

Space The element of art that refers to the emptiness or area between, around, above, below, or within objects. Shapes and forms are defined by space around and within them (5).

Spectral colors Red, orange, yellow, green, blue, violet (6).

Split complementary colors One hue and the hues on each side of its complement on the color wheel (6). Red-orange, blue, and green are split complementary colors. Split complementary colors can be used as a color scheme.

Stained glass Colored glass cut into pieces, arranged in a design, and joined with strips of lead.

Static Inactive (4). Vertical and horizontal lines and horizontal shapes and forms are static. Opposite of active.

Still life Painting or drawing of inanimate (nonmoving) objects.

Stippling Technique of shading using dots (3).

Stitchery Technique for decorating fabric by stitching fibers onto it.

Stone Age Period of history during which stone tools were used (12).

Storyboards A series of still drawings that show a story's progress (14).

Stupas Beehive-shaped domed places of worship (12).

Style See *individual style.*

Subject The image viewers can easily identify in a work of art (1).

Subordinate element Element of a work of art noticed after the dominant element (11).

Super-Realism Twentieth-century artistic style that depicts objects as precisely and accurately as they actually appear (13).

Surrealism Twentieth-century artistic style in which dreams, fantasy, and the subconscious served as inspiration for artists (13).

Symbol Something that stands for, or represents, something else (1).

Symmetry A special type of formal balance in which two halves of a balanced composition are identical, mirror images of each other (9).

Synthetic Made by chemical processes rather than natural processes.

T

Tapestry Fabric wall hanging that is woven, painted, or embroidered.

Tempera Paint made by mixing pigments with egg yolk (egg tempera) or another liquid. School poster paint is a type of tempera (3).

Texture The element of art that refers to how things feel, or look as if they might feel if touched. Texture is perceived by touch and sight. Objects can have rough or smooth textures and matte or shiny surfaces (7).

Tint A light value of a hue made by mixing the hue with white. Opposite of shade (6).

Tonality Arrangement of colors in a painting so that one color dominates the work of art (6).

Totem poles Tall posts carved and painted with a series of animal symbols associated with a particular family or clan (12).

Transparent Quality of a material that allows light to pass through. Opposite of opaque.

Trompe l'oeil French for "deceive the eye." Style of painting in which painters try to give the viewer the illusion of seeing a three-dimensional object, so that the viewer wonders whether he or she is seeing a picture or something real.

U

Unity The quality of wholeness or oneness that is achieved through the effective use of the elements and principles of art (11). Unity is created by simplicity, repetition, and proximity.

Unusual Technique for creating a focal point by using the unexpected (11).

V

Value The element of art that describes the darkness or lightness of an object (4). Value depends on how much light a surface reflects. Value is also one of the three properties of color.

Vanishing point Point on the horizon where receding parallel lines seem to meet (5).

Variety Principle of art concerned with difference or contrast (11).

Vault Arched roof, ceiling, or covering made of brick, stone, or concrete (3).

Vehicle Liquid, like water or oil, that pigments are mixed with to make paint or dye (3).

Vertical lines Lines that are straight up and down (4). Vertical lines are at right angles to the bottom edge of the paper or canvas and the horizon, and parallel to the side of the paper or canvas.

Viewing frame A piece of paper with an area cut from the middle. By holding the frame at arm's length and looking through it at the subject, the artist can focus on the area of the subject he or she wants to draw or paint.

Visual arts The arts that produce beautiful objects to look at.

Visual movement The principle of art used to create the look and feeling of action and to guide the viewer's eyes throughout the work of art (8).

Visual rhythm Rhythm you receive through your eyes rather than through your ears (8).

Visual texture Illusion of a three-dimensional surface based on the memory of how things feel. There are two types of visual texture: invented and simulated (7). Opposite of real texture.

Visual weight Attraction that elements in a work of art have for the viewer's eyes. Visual weight is affected by size, contour, intensity of colors, warmth and coolness of colors, contrast in value, texture, and position (9).

W

Warm colors Red, orange, and yellow (6). Warm colors suggest warmth and seem to move toward the viewer. Warm colors can be used as a color scheme. Opposite of cool colors.

Warp In weaving, lengthwise threads held in place on the loom and crossed by weft threads.

Watercolor paint Transparent pigments mixed with water (3).

Weaving Making fabric by interlacing two sets of parallel threads, held at right angles to each other on a loom (3).

Weft In weaving, crosswise threads that are carried over and under the warp threads.

Woodblock printing Making prints by carving images in blocks of wood (12).

Y

Yarn Fibers spun into strands for weaving, knitting, or embroidery.

Z

Ziggurats Stepped mountains made of brick-covered earth (12).

Zigzag lines Lines formed by short, sharp turns (4). Zigzag lines are a combination of diagonal lines. They can change direction suddenly.

The following is an annotated listing of books dealing with various areas of art and art education. These books can provide valuable assistance to you as you study and work in the visual arts.

ARCHITECTURE

Baker, John Milnes. *American House Styles: A Concise Guide.* New York: W.W. Norton, 1994. An examination of house styles in the United States from the early colonial period to the 1990s.

Erlande-Brandenburg, Alain. *Cathedrals and Castles: Building in the Middle Ages.* New York: Harry N. Abrams, 1995. The story of architecture in the Middle Ages.

Fletcher, Banister, Sir. *History of Architecture. Edited by Dan Cruickshank.* 20th ed. Boston: Architectural Press, 1996. A comprehensive history of architecture worldwide.

Icher, Francois. *Building the Great Cathedrals.* New York: Harry N. Abrams, 1998. A look at those individuals who studied, designed, and built the cathedrals of Europe.

Lepre, J. P. *The Egyptian Pyramids: A Comprehensive, Illustrated Reference.* Jefferson, N.C.: McFarland, 1990. Study of the pyramids and the pharoahs who built them.

COMPUTER GRAPHICS

Cyber Design: Computer-Manipulated Illustration. Rockport, Mass.: Rockport Publishers, 1996. An overview of the art of design using the latest computer technology.

Ziegler, Kathleen and Nick Greco, eds. *Cyberpalette: A Digital Step-by-Step Guide.* New York: Watson-Guptill, 1998. Ten artists who use computer technology discuss their work from the initial idea to the final image.

DESIGN

Designer Posters. Rockport, Mass.: Rockport Publishers, 1996. This book examines over 300 poster designs.

Hiebert, Kenneth J. *Graphic Design Sources.* New Haven: Yale University Press, 1998. A discussion of design creation including form, technique, and communication.

Landa, Robin. *Thinking Creatively: New Ways to Unlock Your Visual Imagination.* Cincinnati: North Light Books, 1998. A discussion of how to think creatively and how designers apply creative thinking to real projects.

Lauer, David A. *Design Basics.* 4th ed. Fort Worth: Harcourt Brace College Publishers, 1995. Organized by the different principles of design using examples from throughout history.

Martin, Diana. *Graphic Design: Inspirations and Innovations.* Cincinnati: North Light Books, 1995. Discusses sources of inspiration including how graphic artists generate ideas and translate them into designs.

DRAWING

Auvil, Kenneth W. *Perspective Drawing.* Mountain View, Calif.: Mayfield Publishing, 1990. A step-by-step guide to perspective drawing.

Bowen, Ron. *Drawing Masterclass.* Boston: Bulfinch Press, 1992. A drawing technique book, including five different drawing strategies.

Goldfinger, Eliot. *Human Anatomy for Artists: The Elements of Form.* New York: Oxford University Press, 1991. A guide to the anatomy of the human body designed for the beginner to the professional artist.

Hammond, Lee. *Draw Family & Friends!* Cincinnati: North Light Books, 1997. A book about drawing shapes and putting those shapes together to create the human form.

Wilson, Brent, Al Hurwitz, and Marjorie Wilson. *Teaching Drawing from Art.* Worcester, Mass.: Davis Publications, 1987. Presents a unique approach to drawing. Masterworks of art are used to motivate drawing activities.

FIBER ARTS

Batik

Roojen, Pepin Van. *Batik Design.* 2d ed. Amsterdam: Pepin Press, 1994. A history of batik design and patterns.

Needlecraft

Guild, Vera P. *Good Housekeeping New Complete Book of Needlecraft.* NY: Hearst Books, 1971. Directions for a variety of needlecraft techniques.

Silk-Screening

Henning, Roni. *Screenprinting: Water-Based Techniques.* New York: Watson-Guptill, 1994. A how-to book for water-based printing, a new approach to silk-screening.

Weaving

Hecht, Ann. *The Art of the Loom: Weaving, Spinning, and Dyeing Across the World.* New York: Rizzoli, 1990. A worldwide examination of the different techniques, colors, and styles of the art of weaving. Includes an introduction on the basics of weaving, spinning, and dyeing.

Floral Arts

Hillier, Malcolm. *The Book of Fresh Flowers: A Complete Guide to Selecting and Arranging.* New York: Simon and Schuster, 1988. Features hundreds of examples of arrangements with instructions.

Rogers, Barbara Radcliffe. *The Encyclopedia of Everlastings: The Complete Guide to Growing, Preserving, and Arranging Dried Flowers.* New York: Weidenfeld and Nicolson, 1988. A book of plant varieties suitable for preservation. Includes information about each plant and arrangement suggestions.

General Crafts

Sprintzen, Alice. *Crafts: Contemporary Design and Technique.* Worcester, Mass.: Davis Publications, 1987. An introduction to traditional and modern crafts, with instructions for beginners.

Stribling, Mary Lou. *Crafts from North American Indian Arts: Techniques, Designs, and Contemporary Applications.* NY:

Crown Publishers, 1975. Techniques and applications of many different crafts using a variety of materials.

Jewelry

McCreight, Tim. *Jewelry: Fundamentals of Metalsmithing.* Madison, Wis.: Hand Books Press, 1997. Handbook of procedures and tools for making metal jewelry.

Phillips, Clare. *Jewelry: From Antiquity to the Present.* New York: Thames and Hudson, 1996. A history of the art and craft of jewelry.

Sprintzen, Alice. *The Jeweler's Art: A Multimedia Approach.* Worcester, Mass.: Davis Publications, 1995. A guide to making jewelry from various materials.

PAINTING

Akiyama, Terukazu. *Japanese Painting.* New York: Rizzoli, 1990. A history of Japanese painting.

Barnhart, Richard M., et al. *Three Thousand Years of Chinese Painting.* New Haven: Yale University Press, 1997. Overview of Chinese painting and its relationship to the social and cultural developments in China.

Davidson, Abraham. *The Story of American Painting.* New York: Harry N. Abrams, 1974. A history of American painting from the colonial period until the 1960s.

Denvir, Bernard. *Impressionism: The Painters and the Paintings.* London: Studio Editions, 1991. A history of French Impressionism.

Freedberg, Sydney J. *Painting in Italy, 1500–1600.* 3rd ed. New Haven: Yale University Press, 1993. An analysis of High Renaissance painting in Italy and the period of Mannerism that followed.

Gair, Angela. *Acrylics: A Step-by-Step Guide to Acrylics Techniques.* London: Letts, 1994. Introduction to techniques and advantages of painting with acrylics.

Gaunt, William. *The Great Century of British Painting: Hogarth to Turner.* 2d ed. Oxford: Phaidon, 1978. A history of eighteenth-century British painting.

Grabar, André. *Byzantine Painting: Historical and Critical Study.* New York: Rizzoli, 1979. An examination of mural painting, frescoes, and mosaics from the Byzantine period.

Haak, Bob. *The Golden Age: Dutch Painters of the Seventeenth Century.* New York: Stewart, Tabori & Chang, 1996. A history of Dutch painting arranged geographically.

Mayer, Ralph. *The Artist's Handbook of Materials and Techniques.* 5th ed. rev. and updated. New York: Viking-Penguin, Inc.,1991. An up-to-date in-depth look at the varied materials and techniques of painting.

Treman, Judy D. *Building Brilliant Watercolors.* Cincinnati: North Light Books, 1998. A guide to the technique of watercolor painting.

PAPER

Innes, Miranda. *Papier-Mâché.* New York: Dorling Kindersley, 1995. Explains the craft of papier-mâché including construction and decoration.

Johnson, Pauline. *Creating with Paper: Basic Forms and Variations.* Seattle: University of Washington Press, 1981. A variety of approaches to paper sculpture.

Stevenson, Cheryl. *The Art of Handmade Paper and Collage: Transforming the Ordinary into the Extraordinary.* Bothell, Wash.: Martingale & Co., 1998. A how-to book for making paper and collage with inexpensive or free materials.

POTTERY

Peterson, Susan. *The Craft and Art of Clay.* 2d ed. Woodstock, N.Y.: The Overlook Press, 1996. A technical guide to both hand-building and wheel-throwing. Includes works from contemporary ceramic artists.

Speight, Charlotte F. *Hands in Clay: An Introduction to Ceramics.* Mountain View, Calif.: Mayfield Publishing, 1995. A history of pottery-making throughout the world and a technical guide to the art and craft of ceramics.

Triplett, Kathy. *Handbuilt Ceramics: Pinching, Coiling, Extruding, Molding, Slip Casting, Slab Work.* Asheville, N.C.: Lark Books, 1997. A guide to the shaping, decorating, and firing of clay.

PHOTOGRAPHY

Filmmaking

Halas, John. *The Technique of Film Animation.* 4th ed. New York: Hastings House, 1976. A look at the history and techniques of film animation.

Harmon, Renee. *Film Directing—Killer Style and Cutting Edge Techniques: A Step-by-Step Guide to Making Your Film.* Los Angeles: Lone Eagle Publishing, 1997. Advice for the movie director on how make a movie that is appealing to the audience.

Lindenmuth, Kevin J. *Making Movies on Your Own: Practical Talk from Independent Filmmakers.* Jefferson, N.C.: McFarland, 1998. A compilation of advice on making a feature film from 25 successful filmmakers.

Lord, Peter and Brian Sibley. *Cracking Animation.* London: Thames and Hudson, 1998. A guide to 3-D animation from simple techniques to making a film.

Still Photography

Craven, George M. *Object and Image: An Introduction to Photography.* 3rd ed. Englewood Cliffs, N.J.: Prentice-Hall, 1990. An approach to photography as a creative medium.

Eastland, Jonathan. *Essential Darkroom Techniques.* New York: Blandford Press, 1987. A guide to the techniques of film developing and printing.

Feininger, Andreas. *The Complete Photographer.* Rev. ed. Englewood Cliffs, N.J.: Prentice-Hall, 1978. An excellent overview of basic photographic techniques.

Newhall, Beaumont. *The History of Photography: From 1839 to the Present.* 5th ed. New York: Museum of Modern Art, 1997. A history of photography from its invention.

Rosenblum, Naomi. *A World History of Photography.* 3rd ed. New York: Abbeville Press, 1997. A history of photography worldwide.

PRINTMAKING

Illing, Richard. *The Art of Japanese Prints.* London: Octopus, 1980. A history of Japanese wood-block prints from the early eighteenth century through the twentieth century.

Hults, Linda C. *The Print in the Western World: An Introductory History.* Madison: University of Wisconsin Press, 1996. An introduction to the art of printmaking from its European origins.

Johnson, Una E. *American Prints and Printmakers: A Chronicle of Over 400 Artists and Their Prints from 1900 to the Present.* Garden City, N.Y.: Doubleday, 1980. A survey of artists involved in printmaking in the twentieth century.

Toale, Bernard. *Basic Printmaking Techniques.* Worcester, Mass.: Davis Publications, 1992. Focuses on techniques of relief prints, monotypes, and silkscreen prints.

SCULPTURE

Armstrong, Tom, et al. *200 Years of American Sculpture.* Boston: David R. Godine, 1976. An informative look at the evolution of American sculpture.

Davies, Mike. *Woodcarving Techniques and Designs.* Madison, Wis.: Hand Books Press, 1997. An examination of the art of woodcarving.

Hall, Carolyn Vosburg. *Soft Sculpture.* Worcester, Mass.: Davis Publications,1981. Provides useful information for soft sculpture projects.

Hammacher, Abraham Marie. *Modern Sculpture: Tradition and Innovation.* Enl. ed. New York: Harry N. Abrams, 1988. A history of modern sculpture in Europe and America.

Kleiner, Diane E. E. *Roman Sculpture.* New Haven: Yale University Press, 1992. Overview of both public and private sculpture of Rome.

Meilach, Dona Z. *Box Art: Assemblage and Construction.* New York: Crown Publishers, 1975. A guide to the art of box-making.

Morris, John. *Creative Metal Sculpture: A Step-by-Step Approach.* New York: Bruce Publishing, 1971. This book takes the beginning metalworker through the process of creating various types of metal sculpture.

Pope-Hennessy, John. *An Introduction to Italian Sculpture.* 4th ed. London: Phaidon Press, 1996. Covers Gothic, Renaissance, and Baroque sculpture in Italy.

Stewart, Andrew F. *Greek Sculpture: An Exploration.* New Haven: Yale University Press, 1990. A historical presentation of a selection of large-scale Greek sculpture.

ART HISTORY

Ades, Dawn. *Art in Latin America: The Modern Era, 1820-1980.* New Haven: Yale University Press, 1989. An examination art from a wide variety of Latin American countries.

Arnason, H. H. *History of Modern Art: Painting, Sculpture, Architecture, Photography.* 4th ed. New York: Harry N. Abrams, Inc., 1998. History of modern art in Europe and America.

Barnicoat, John. *Posters: A Concise History.* New York: Thames and Hudson, 1985. This book focuses on the importance of the poster, including its role in various artistic movements.

Berlo, Janet. *Native North American Art.* New York: Oxford University Press, 1998. An overview of the history of art of Native North American cultures arranged by region.

Bloom, Jonathan and Sheila Blair. *Islamic Arts.* London: Phaidon, 1997. A history of Islamic arts from all over the Islamic world.

Camille, Michael. *Gothic Art, Visions, and Revelations of the Medieval World.* London: Weidenfeld and Nicolson, 1996. An overview of Gothic art throughout Europe.

Chadwick, Whitney. *Women, Art, and Society.* 2d ed. New York: Thames and Hudson, 1997. Covers the woman artist in Europe and America; from the Middle Ages to the twentieth century.

Feldman, Edmund Burke. *Varieties of Visual Experience.* 4th ed. New York: Harry N. Abrams, 1992. Examines the relationship between art and life.

Gardner, Helen. *Art Through the Ages.* 10th ed. Fort Worth: Harcourt Brace, 1996. A comprehensive survey of art history.

Harle, J. C. *The Art and Architecture of the Indian Subcontinent.* New York: Penguin Books, 1986. A comprehensive look at art of India, Afghanistan, Pakistan, Nepal, and Sri Lanka.

Harbison, Craig. *The Mirror of the Artist: Northern Renaissance Art in its Historical Context.* New York: Harry N. Abrams, 1995. An overview of Northern Renaissance art, including the art of the Netherlands, Germany, and France.

Highwater, Jamake. *Arts of the Indian Americas: Leaves from the Sacred Tree.* New York: Harper & Row, 1983. Provides an overview of the arts of North, South, and Central Native Americans, including culture and history.

Janson, H. W. *A Basic History of Art.* 5th ed. Upper Saddle River, N.J.: Prentice-Hall, 1997. A history of art for the layperson.

Lee, Sherman E. *A History of Far Eastern Art.* 5th ed. Englewood Cliffs, N.J.: Prentice-Hall, 1994. An in-depth look at East Asian art from prehistory to the nineteenth century.

Paoletti, John T. *Art in Renaissance Italy.* New York: Harry N. Abrams, 1997. Covers art in Italy from the mid-thirteenth century to the sixteenth century.

Patton, Sharon F. *African-American Art.* New York: Oxford University Press, 1998. A look at African-American art from colonial America to Postmodernism.

Phillips, Tom, ed. *Africa: The Art of a Continent.* London: Royal Academy of Arts, 1995. Covers art in all media from a variety of African countries.

Sayer, Chloe. *Arts and Crafts of Mexico.* San Francisco: Chronicle Books, 1990. An overview of Mexican crafts including the history and culture. Richly illustrated.

Taylor, Joshua C. *Learning to Look: A Handbook for the Visual Arts.* 2d ed. Chicago: University of Chicago Press, 1981. A guide to the study of art.

Thomas, Nicholas. *Oceanic Art.* London: Thames and Hudson, 1995. Examines the art of the Pacific Islands and New Zealand.

ARTISTS

Ades, Dawn. *Dali.* Rev. ed. London: Thames and Hudson, 1995. A look at the work and life of this Surrealist artist.

Bearor, Karen A. *Irene Rice Pereira: Her Paintings and Philosophy.* Austin: The University of Texas Press, 1993. An examination of the painting and philosophy of this woman artist.

Brookner, Anita. *Jacques-Louis David.* London: Chatto & Windus, 1980. A look at the life and art of David.

Cachin, Francoise. *Cézanne.* New York: Harry N. Abrams, 1996. A major catalog from the exhibition held at the Philadelphia Museum of Art.

Clark, Kenneth. *Leonardo da Vinci.* Rev. ed. London: Penguin Books, 1993. An important work about this artist and scientist of the Italian Renaissance.

Elderfield, John. *Frankenthaler.* New York: Harry N. Abrams, 1989. An examination of the art and life of Helen Frankenthaler.

Flores d'Arcais, Francesca. *Giotto.* New York: Abbeville Press, 1995. An examination of the first artist of the Italian Renaissance.

Hogrefe, Jeffrey. *O'Keeffe: The Life of an American Legend.* New York: Bantam Books, 1992. A biography of Georgia O'Keeffe.

Levin, Gail. *Edward Hopper: The Art and the Artist.* New York: Norton, 1980. A representative collection of Hopper's work, combined with information about the development of the artist's themes.

Locher, J. L., ed. *The World of M. C. Escher.* New York: Harry N. Abrams, 1988. A catalog of the precise and visually intricate artwork of the Dutch mathematician and artist.

Marnham, Patrick. *Dreaming with His Eyes Open: A Life of Diego Rivera.* New York: Knopf, 1998. A biography of Diego Rivera, an artist known for his mural painting.

Mee, Charles L. *Rembrandt's Portrait: A Biography.* New York: Simon and Schuster, 1988. An examination of the life of Rembrandt.

Paz, Octovio and Jacques Lassaigne. *Rufino Tamayo.* New York: Rizzoli, 1982. A book on the life and art of Rufino Tamayo.

Pollock, Griselda. *Mary Cassatt: Painter of Modern Women.* London: Thames and Hudson, 1998. A close examination of this American artist who studied in France.

Powell, Richard J. *Homecoming: The Art and Life of William H. Johnson.* Washington, D.C.: National Museum of American Art, 1991. An overview of the art and life of this important African-American artist.

Prather, Marla. *Alexander Calder: 1898-1976.* Washington, D.C.: National Gallery of Art, 1998. A catalog of an exhibit held at the National Gallery of Art.

Rubin, William, ed. *Pablo Picasso: A Retrospective.* New York: The Museum of Modern Art, 1980. The catalog of the huge Picasso exhibition at The Museum of Modern Art.

Snyder, Robert R. *Buckminster Fuller: An Autobiographical Monologue/Scenario.* New York: St. Martin's Press, 1980. A thorough examination of Fuller's life and work.

Sweetman, David. *Van Gogh: His Life and His Art.* New York: Crown Publishers, 1990. An examination of the life and art of van Gogh.

Varnedoe, Kirk. *Jackson Pollock.* New York: The Museum of Modern Art, 1998. A catalog of a major exhibition organized by The Museum of Modern Art.

Wardlaw, Alvia J. *The Art of John Biggers: View from the Upper Room.* Houston: Museum of Fine Arts, 1995. A major exhibition of Biggers's artwork organized by the Houston Museum of Fine Arts.

A

Aafenmut Offering Before Horus, Above Sun's Barque **(Thebes),** 168
Abbott, Bernice, *The Night View*, 202
Above the Trees **(Carr),** 149
Abrasha, *Hanukkah Menorah*, 71–72
Abstract Expressionism, 378
Abstract (River Mouth Map) **(Malangi),** 92–93
Acrylic paint, 47
Active shapes and forms, 119–120
Activities
    active and static shapes, 120–121
    aesthetic theories, 33
    alternating rhythm, 208
    animation critique, 398
    architecture, 54, 353
    art history, 353, 355, 365, 373, 381
    balance, 231, 233, 238, 241
    calligraphic lines, 83
    careers in art, 398, 403
    color, 139, 142, 143, 149, 152, 157
    color schemes, 149
    color wheel, 139
    contour lines, 81
    contrast, 175, 289
    credit line, 19
    depth, creating, 115
    digital art, 60
    display design, 403
    emphasis, 295
    expressive lines, 78
    forms, 102, 112
    geometric and free-form shapes, 100
    gesture drawing, 82
    Gothic style, 355
    human proportions, 264, 266
    Impressionism, 373
    informal balance, 238
    intensity, 143
    lines, 73, 76, 78, 81, 82, 83
    masks, 338
    mixing colors, 152
    motifs, 204
    patterns, 204
    perceiving, 7
    point of view, 108
    printing plate, 49
    progressive rhythm, 210
    proportion, 261, 264, 266, 273
    radial balance, 233
    random rhythm, 205
    rhythm, 204, 205, 208, 210
    scale, 261, 264, 266
    shading, 112
    shapes, 100, 108, 120–121
    sketchbook, 15
    sketching events, 345
    space, 104, 107, 115
    symbols, 16
    symmetry, 231
    texture, 174, 175, 183
    unity, 302
    value, 76
    values, 142
    variety and contrast, 290
    watercolor, 47
    writing system, 325
Adoration of the Magi, The **(Botticelli),** 113
Adoration of the Shepherds, The **(Giorgione),** 236, 237
Advertising designers, 392
Aesthetic experience, 27

Aestheticians, 31
Aesthetics, 31–33
    activity, 33
    defined, 26
    judging functional objects, 33
    judging your own artwork, 33
    qualities of art, 31
    theories, 31–32
    See also Art criticism; Art Criticism in Action
African American Dance Ensemble, 225, 420
African art, 332–338
    ancient Ife, 332–333
    Asante kingdom, 335–337
    Benin kingdom, 334–335
    Bwa people, 337–338
    Mali empire, 333–334
    role of, 332
African Canvas **(Courtney-Clarke),** 152
Afterimages, 137–138
Agbatana III **(Stella),** 380
Age of Faith, 354
Akan people, 335–336
Albright, Ivan, *The Farmer's Kitchen*, 177
Alternating rhythm, 208
American Gothic **(Wood),** 12
American Windows, The **(Chagall),** 136
Amplitude **(Clive),** 86
Analogous colors, 145
Analog systems, 59
Analysis step
    of art criticism, 27–30
    of art history, 34, 35
Ancient Chinese art, 324–325
Ancient Egyptian civilization, 323
Ancient Greece, 352–353
Ancient Ife, 332–333
Ancient Indian civilization, 323–324
Ancient Rome, 353
Anderson, N., *Blue Dome*, 232
Andrews, Benny, *The Scholar*, 81
Angkor Wat temple, 327
Anguissola, Sofonisba, 358
    A Game of Chess, Involving the Painter's Three Sisters and a Servant, 358
Animators, 397–398
Ankhesenamun, Queen, 107
Anne of Cleves **(Holbein),** 9
Anuszkiewicz, Richard, *Iridescence*, 146, 154
Apel, Marie, *Grief*, 119
Apollinaire, Guillaume, 135
Apples and Oranges **(Cézanne),** 132
Applied art
    crafts, 52–53, 182–183
    defined, 52
    fine art vs., 52
    texture in, 182–183
Applying Your Skills. See Activities
Approximate symmetry, 230–231, 240
Arabs Skirmishing in the Mountains **(Delacroix),** 367
Arbitrary color, 154
Arcade game designers, 400
Architects, 401–402
    landscape architects, 403
Architecture, 54–56
    activities, 54, 353, 355
    ancient Greek, 352, 353
    ancient Indian, 323–324
    ancient Roman, 353
    formal balance in, 240
    Gothic, 355
    Indian, 326, 327
    informal balance in, 241

    International Style, 381–382
    Islamic, 331
    Japanese, 328–329
    media, 57–61
    Mesopotamian, 322
    Post-Modern, 382–383
    pre-Columbian, 340, 341
    prehistoric, 321
    Romanesque, 354–355
    texture in, 182
    twentieth century, 376-377, 381–383
Arctic Region art, 342
Armchair **(Wright),** 118–119
Armory Show of 1913, 376
Arnolfi Wedding, The **(van Eyck),** 231, 359
Art
    as communication, 6–7
    purposes of, 7–9
Art criticism, 26–30
    aesthetics, 31–33
    criteria, 26
    defined, 26
    judging functional objects, 33
    judging your own artwork, 33
    reasons for studying, 26–27
    steps of, 27–30
    See also Aesthetics; Art Criticism in Action
Art Criticism in Action
    Abstract (River Mouth Map) (Malangi), 92–93
    Bitter Nest Part II: Harlem Renaissance Party (Ringgold), 36–37
    Carnival Evening (Rousseau), 312–313
    Cliff Dwellers (Bellows), 222–223
    Family (Bearden), 166–167
    Ginevra de' Benci (Leonardo da Vinci), 384–385
    The Green House (Skoglund), 406–407
    Khamseh: Bahram Gur and the Chinese Princess in the Sandalwood Pavilion on Thursday, 346–347
    Leonardo's Lady (Flack), 192–193
    Linda Nochlin and Daisy (Neel), 250–251
    Paris Through the Window (Chagall), 20–21
    Personal Appearance (Schapiro), 62–63
    Waiting (Bishop), 282–283
    Wrapped Reichstag (Christo and Jeanne-Claude), 130–131
Art directors, 399–400
Art education careers, 404–405
Art history
    Abstract Expressionism, 378
    activities, 353, 355, 365, 373, 381
    African art, 332–338
    after 1945, 378–383
    ancient Chinese art, 324–325
    ancient Egyptian art, 323
    ancient Greece and Rome, 352–353
    ancient Indian art, 323–324
    Baroque art, 360–362
    Byzantine art, 354
    Chinese art, 327–328
    Color-Field painting, 380
    Cubism, 374–375
    early twentieth century art, 374–377
    eighteenth century art, 363–365
    Expressionism, 374
    Futurists, 212
    Gothic art, 355
    Impressionism, 153, 181, 370, 373
    Indian art, 326–327
    International Style architecture, 381–382
    Islamic art, 331, 347
    Japanese art, 328–330
    Mannerism, 360
    Mesopotamian art, 321–322

Middle Ages art, 354–355
Minimalism, 380
Native American art, 341–345
Neoclassicism, 366-367
nineteenth century art, 366–373
Op art, 379–380
Orphism, 135
Pop art, 378–379
Post-Impressionism, 371–373
Post-Modernism, 382–383
pre-Columbian art, 339–341
prehistoric art, 320
Realism, 368–370
Regionalism, 376–377
Renaissance art, 356–360
Rococo art, 363–365
Romanesque art, 354-355
Romanticism, 367–368
seventeenth century art, 360–362
steps of, 34–35
studio project, 160–161
Super-Realism, 381
Surrealism, 184, 375
Artists
defined, 11
reasons for creating, 10
sources of ideas, 11–15
as sources of ideas, 14–15
Art reviews. *See* Aesthetics; Art criticism; Art Criticism in Action
Artsource® Performing Arts Handbook
African American Dance Ensemble, 225, 420
Korean Classical Music and Dance Company, 349, 424
Ballet Folklorico de Mexico, 95, 416
Cello Man, 285, 422
Cunningham, Merce, 65, 415
"Danza de la Reata," 95, 416
Davis, Chuck, 225, 420
Eth-Noh-Tec, 253, 421
Faustwork Mask Theater, 23, 413
Featherstone, Joanna, 169, 418
Friesen, Eugene, 285, 422
Graham, Martha, 39, 414
Green Table, The, 387, 425
Jooss, Kurt, 387, 425
Lewitzky Dance Company, 133, 417
Ramirez, John, 409, 426
Vocalworks, 315, 423
Winter, Paul, 195, 419
Art teachers, 404
Artworks, basic properties of, 18–19
Asante kingdom, 335–337
Asante peoples, Wrapper, 206, 207
Ascension Day Festival at Venice **(Canaletto),** 43
Ascent of Ethiopia, The **(Jones),** 386
Ashcan School, 376
Asian art
ancient Chinese, 324–325
ancient Indian, 323–324
Chinese, 327–328
folk traditions of music and dance, 349, 424
Indian, 326–327
Japanese, 328–330
Assemblage studio projects, 186–187, 304–305
Assembling technique, 51
Assyrian civilization, 322
Astronomer, The **(Vermeer),** 128
Asymmetry (informal balance), 234–238
Atmospheric perspective, 114
Avanti **(Loewy),** 395
Aztec culture, 340–341

B

Baby at Play **(Eakins),** 234
Babylonian civilization, 322
Background, 113
Balance, 226–253
activities, 231, 233, 238, 241
central axis, 228–229
defined, 228
expressive qualities of, 239–241
formal balance, 229, 239–241
informal balance, 234–238, 241
natural balance, 234–238
radial balance, 232–233, 240–241
studio projects
formal portrait, 242–243
informal group portrait, 244–245
inside view of machine, 248–249
linoleum print using radial balance, 246–247
symmetry, 230–231, 240
visual balance, 228–233
Balla, Giacomo
Dynamism of a Dog on a Leash, 212
Street Light, 210
Ballet Folklorico de Mexico, 95, 416
Bamana peoples, 334
Baroque art, 360–362
activity, 365
defined, 360-361
in Holland, 361–362
in Italy, 360–361
Barricade **(Orozco),** 28
Bashkirtseff, Marie, *A Meeting*, 301
Basket **(Keyser),** 218
Basket of Apples, The **(Cézanne),** 155
Bas relief, 106, 107. *See also* Relief sculpture
Bayless, Florence, *Haori Coat*, 298
Bayou Teche **(Straus),** 6–7
Bay, The **(Frankenthaler),** 111
Bearden, Romare, 167
Family, 166–167
Prevalence of Ritual: The Baptism, 158, 159
Return of Ulysses, 12, 13
Beaux, Cecilia, *Ernesta (Child with Nurse)*, 294
Beliefs as sources of ideas, 12–13
Bellows, George, 223
Both Members of This Club, 258
Cliff Dwellers, 222–223
Bell Tower of the Cathedral at Pisa, 228
Benin people, 262, 334–335
Benton, Thomas Hart
Country Dance, 78, 79
The Sources of Country Music, 376
Berman, Eugene, *Vendeur de Chapeaux*, 43
Biggers, John
Shotguns, Fourth Ward, 198, 199
Starry Crown, 98, 99
Binders of paints, 45, 150
Bird Mask **(Yup'ik people),** 13
Bird **(Mexico),** 188
Birthday **(Chagall),** 271
Bishop, Isabel, 283
Head #5, 44, 45
Self-Portrait, 283
Waiting, 282–283
Bitter Nest Part II: Harlem Renaissance Party **(Ringgold),** 36–37
Black as neutral color, 139
Blackfeet people, 344
Black Hawk, Chief, *Crow Men in Ceremonial Dress*, 200
Blam **(Lichtenstein),** 379

Blank Signature, The **(Magritte),** 126
Blanketed Figure Vase **(Qoyawayma),** 50, 51
Blending technique, 44
Blessing Rain Chant **(Namingha),** 75, 77
Blind Botanist, The **(Shahn),** 117
Blue Boy, The **(Gainsborough),** 364
Blue Dome **(Anderson),** 232
Blue Wall **(Twiggs),** 28, 29
Bodhisattva, 254, 255
Bondie, Edith, *Porkypine Basket*, 52
Bonheur, Rosa, 201, 369
The Horse Fair, 201, 369
Bonnard, Pierre, *Family Scene*, 266
Book illustration, Islamic, 331
Borsky, David
Wall of Machu–Picchu, 55
Waterfall, 209
Both Members of This Club **(Bellows),** 258
Both the Sun and Moon Belong to Women **(Muñoz),** 252
Botticelli, Sandro, *The Adoration of the Magi*, 113
Bowl **(Sundi woman),** 205
Brady, Mathew, 369
Civil War, 369
Brahma, 327
Brancusi, Constantin
The Kiss, 104
Torso of a Young Man, 118
Braque, Georges, 375
Breakfast of the Birds **(Münter),** 18
Brown, Roger, *Hurricane Hugo*, 10–11
Bruegel, Pieter, the Elder, *Children's Games*, 22
Bruegel Series, The (A Vanitas of Style) **(Steir),** 160–161
Buddhism, 326, 327
Burkina Faso, 337
Business and industry careers, 390–400. *See also* Careers in art
Bwa people, 337–338
Byzantine art, 354

C

Café Terrace at Night **(van Gogh),** 293
Calder, Alexander, 212–213, 376
Lobster Trap and Fish Tail, 213
Varese, 84
Calligraphic drawing, 83
Calligraphy, 83
Cambodia. *See* Kampuchea
Cameras, digital, 60
Canaletto, *Ascension Day Festival at Venice*, 43
Caravaggio, Michelangelo Merisi da, 361
The Conversion of St. Paul, 361
Careers in art, 388–409
activities, 398, 403
advertising designer, 392-393
animator, 397–398
architect, 401–402
art director, 399–400
art education careers, 404–405
art teacher, 404
in business and industry, 390–400
cartoonist, 394
commercial illustrator, 393
environmental planning and development, 401–403
exhibit and display designers, 403
fashion designer, 395
fine artists, 405
game designers, 400
graphic design, 391–393

graphic designer, 392
illustration, 393–394
industrial design, 394–395
interior designer, 403
landscape architect, 403
multimedia designer, 400
museum curator and designer, 404
package designer, 395
photographer, 396
photography, film, and video, 396–400
photojournalist, 397
product designer, 394–395
special effects designer, 398–399
technology and, 390–393
urban planner, 401
Web artist, 393
Caricatures, 255
Carnival Evening **(Rousseau),** 312–313
Carr, Emily
  Above the Trees, 148, 149
  Cumshewa, 241
  Forest, British Columbia, 298
Cartoonists, 394
Carving technique, 51
Cassatt, Mary, 244
  Margot in Blue, 140
  The Letter, 350, 351
  The Tea, 244
Casting technique, 51
Cathedral **(Pollock),** 13–14
Cathedrals
  Gothic, 355
  at Pisa, Bell Tower, 228
  Reims, 106, 355
Catlett, Elizabeth, *Sharecropper,* 48–49
Cave painting, 320
Celebration of Arts: Vibrations of Life
  (Yancy), 308
Cello Man, 285, 422
Central axis, 228–229
Ceramics
  Chinese, 328
  pottery clay, 64
  texture in, 182
  See also Clay
Cézanne, Paul, 371
  Apples and Oranges, 132
  The Basket of Apples, 155
  Le Chateau Noir, 371
Chagall, Marc, 21
  The American Windows, 136
  Birthday, 271
  Paris Through the Window, 20–21
Chamba Rumal, 232
Chamberlain, Wilt, 262
Cheyenne people, 344
Chiaroscuro, 112
Children
  games and social skills, 22
  proportions, 263
Children at Play **(Lawrence),** 78, 80, 377
Children's Games **(Bruegel),** 22
Chinese art, 327–328
  ancient, 324–325
Chinese pair of vases (Ming Dynasty), 99
Chippewa Man's Leggings **(Native**
  American), 224
Christ and the Apostles **(Roualt),** 74
Christo, 131
  Wrapped Reichstag (with Jeanne-Claude),
  130–131
Chrysler Building **(van Alen),** 206
Church Quinua **(Peru),** 107
Cinematographers, 58
Civil War **(Brady),** 369

Clay
  crafts processes, 53
  pottery clay, 64
  science connections, 64
  studio projects, 124–125, 274–275, 306–307
  texture using, 182
  See also Ceramics
Clay soldiers from tomb of Qin
  Shihuangdi, 64
Cliff Dwellers **(Bellows),** 222–223
Clive, Carolyn, *Amplitude,* 86
Clothespin **(Oldenburg),** 261
Coil baskets studio project, 218–219
Collage, 179–180
  activity, 261
  defined, 179
  studio projects, 158–159, 190–191, 216–217
Color, 134–169
  activities, 139, 142, 143, 149, 152, 157
  afterimages, 137–138
  analogous colors, 145
  arbitrary color, 154
  color schemes, 144–149
  color spectrum, 136–137, 138
  color triads, 146–147
  color wheel, 138–139
  complementary colors, 142–143, 146, 150
  defined, 136
  expressive qualities, 135, 136, 144–148,
    152–157
  hue, 138–139
  informal balance using, 235–236
  intensity, 142–143
  mixing colors, 140, 143, 152, 153–154
  monochromatic colors, 144–145
  movement and, 155–156
  nature and uses of, 150–157
  optical color, 152–154
  paint, 150–152
  perception of, 136–138, 144
  perspective technique, 114, 116
  pigments, 44–45, 150, 151–152, 168
  properties of, 136–143
  shades, 140–141
  simultaneous contrast, 144
  space and, 155
  split complements, 147
  studio projects
    expressive portrait, 164–165
    expressive statement, 162–163
    photo collage and mixed media, 158–159
    photo enlargement, 160–161
  texture and, 178–179
  tints, 140
  tonality, 157
  value, 139–142, 155–156
  warm and cool colors, 148–149, 155
Color-Field painting, 380
Color schemes, 144–149
  activity, 149
  analogous colors, 145
  color triads, 146–147
  complementary colors, 146, 150
  defined, 144
  monochromatic colors, 144–145
  split complements, 147
  warm and cool colors, 148–149, 155
Color spectrum, 136–137
  color wheel and, 138
Color triads, 146–147
Color wheel, 138–139. *See also* Color
  schemes
Colossal Head, Constantine the Great
  (Roman), 284
Columbus, Christopher, 341

Coming of Age **(Houser),** 209
Commercial illustrators, 393
Commissions as sources of ideas, 15
Communication, art as, 6–7
Complementary colors, 142–143
  in color schemes, 146
  defined, 142
  intensity and, 143, 150
  split complements, 147
Composition of artworks, 18–19
Content of artworks, 19
Computer Options. *See* Activities
Computers, 59–61
  activity, 60
  animators, 398
  art tools, 60–61
  careers in art and, 390–393
  creating art with, 59–60
  game designers, 400
  3-D computer art, 408
  See also Technology Studio Projects
Concert, The **(Leyster),** 178, 256, 257
Connections features
  dance, 224
  history, 194
  language arts, 38, 252, 386
  math, 132, 284
  science, 64, 168
  social studies, 22, 94, 348
  technology, 408
  theatre, 314
Constantine the Great, 284
Constantinople, 354
Constructing technique, 51
Content of artworks, 19
Contour, informal balance using, 234–235
Contour drawing, 81, 84–85
Contour lines, 81
Contour wire sculpture, 84–85
Contrast
  activities, 175, 289
  for focal point, 291
  simultaneous contrast, 144
Convergence for focal point, 293
Converging lines (perspective technique),
  115, 116
Conversation in Autumn **(Yen),** 328
Conversion of St. Paul, The **(Caravaggio),**
  361
Cool colors, 148–149, 155
Copley, John Singleton, *Paul Revere,* 268
Cordero, Helen, 274
Country Dance **(Benton),** 78, 79
Courtney-Clarke, Margaret, *African*
  Canvas, 152
Cow's Skull: Red, White, and Blue
  (O'Keeffe), 30
Crafts, 52–53, 182–183
Cram, Federal Reserve Building (with
  Ferguson and Goodhue), 230
Creating
  reasons for, 10
  sources of ideas, 11–15
Creative techniques as sources of ideas,
  13–14
Credit line, 19
Criteria, 26
Critiquing artworks. *See* Aesthetics; Art
  Criticism; Art Criticism in Action
Crosshatching, 44, 76
Crow Men in Ceremonial Dress **(Chief Black**
  Hawk), 200
Crow people, 344
Cubi IX **(Smith),** 101
Cubism, 374–375
Cuneiform writing, 321

Cunningham, Merce Dance Company, 65, 415
Cups 4 Picasso (Johns), 103–104
Curved lines, 73, 77–78. *See also* Line

D

Daguerre, L. J. M., 57–58
Daguerreotype, 58
Dali, Salvador, 280
    The Elephants (Design for the Opera La Dama Spagnola e il Cavaliere Romano), 280
    The Persistence of Memory, 375
Dance connections, 224
Daniel in the Lions' Den (Rubens), 291
"Danza de la Reata", 95, 416
Dat So La Lee (Louisa Keyser), *Basket*, 218
David, Jacques-Louis, *The Death of Socrates*, 366
David (Michelangelo), 267
David Wright House, The (Wright), 377
da Vinci, Leonardo. *See* Leonardo da Vinci
Davis, Chuck, 225, 420
Davis, Stuart, *Hot Still Scape for Six Colors—7th Avenue Style, 1940*, 154, 155, 156
Dawn (Nevelson), 300
Day and Night (Escher), 220
Death of Socrates, The (David), 366
Decalcomania, 183, 184–185
Degas, Edgar, 180, 181
    The Little Fourteen-Year-Old Dancer, 180, 181
    Self-Portrait, 181
Delacroix, Eugène, 367
    Arabs Skirmishing in the Mountains, 367
Delaunay, Robert, *Sun, Tower, Airplane*, 134, 135
Density, 118
Depth, illusion of, 113–116
Depth perception, 108
Description step
    of art criticism, 27–30
    of art history, 34–35
Design Made at Airlie Gardens (Evans), 410–411
Design principles. *See* Principles of art
Design qualities, 31
Detail, illusion of depth and, 114
Developing Your Portfolio
    art criticism, 25
    art-related career interview, 389
    balance, 227
    caricatures, 255
    color schemes, 135
    favorite artworks, 5
    geometric shapes, 97
    historical development, 319
    identifying entries, 69
    illustrating text, 41
    opinion poll, 351
    out-of-place objects, 287
    rhythm, 199
    textures, 171
Diagonal lines, 72, 78. *See also* Line
Dick, Beau, *Sacred Circles*, 246
Digital cameras, 60
Digital systems, 59
Dillon, Leo and Diane, *A Wrinkle in Time* (cover illustration), 38
Dimension, 70
Diner With Red Door (Goings), 112, 113
Direction of lines, 73
Dirty Snow (Mitchell), 179
Discobolus (Discus Thrower) (Myron), 353

Display and exhibit designers, 403
Distortion and exaggeration, 268–273
Dogon people, 334
Dominant element, 290
Drawing
    activities, 15, 104, 112, 115, 231, 241, 264, 266, 345
    calligraphic drawing, 83
    caricatures, 255
    contour drawing, 81
    gesture drawing, 82
    heads and faces, 264–266
    human figures, 262–264
    media, 43–44
    overview, 42–43
    shading techniques, 44
    sketchbook, 15
    studio projects
        expressive movement, 88–89
        hybrid creature, 280–281
        invent an inside view of a machine, 248–249
        landscape using surreal space, 126–127
        one-point perspective, 128–129
        outdoor scene, 122–123
        progressive rhythm, 220–221
Draw programs, 60
Dream Series (Hines), 57, 58
Duchamp, Marcel, 213
Dunnigan, John, *Slipper Chair*, 33
Dürer, Albrecht, *An Oriental Ruler Seated on His Throne*, 76
Dutch Baroque art, 361–362
Dvorak, Lois, *Spirit Boxes I*, 304, 305
Dyes, 151–152
Dynamism, 212
Dynamism of a Dog on a Leash (Balla), 212
Dynasties, 324–325

E

Eakins, Thomas, *Baby at Play*, 234
Early Sunday Morning (Hopper), 77
East Wind Suite: Door (Twiggs), 10, 42
Editions, 48
Edo people, 335
Educational functions of art, 8–9
Education careers, 404–405
Egyptian art, ancient, 323
Eighteenth century art, 362–365
Eight, The, 376
El Coronelazo (Self-Portrait) (Siqueiros), 264
Elements of art
    color, 134–169
    composition and, 18–19
    defined, 16
    form, 100, 101–102, 111–121
    line, 68–95
    in nonobjective art, 18
    overview, 16–17
    shape, 98–100, 101, 108–121
    space, 103–107, 111–121
    texture, 170–195
    See also specific elements
Elephants, The (Design for the Opera La Dama Spagnola e il Cavaliere Romano) (Dali), 280
Elevator Grille (Sullivan), 204
El Greco, 360
    Saint Martin and the Beggar, 360
Embarkment for Cythera (Watteau), 363
Emotionalism, 31–32
Emphasis, 289–295
    activity, 295
    of areas, 290–295

    defined, 290
    of elements, 290
    focal point, 290–295
    unity enhanced by, 302–303
England, Rococo style in, 363–364
Environmental planning and development careers, 401–403. *See also* Careers in art
Equestrian figure (Mali), 333
Ernesta (Child with Nurse) (Beaux), 294
Ernst, Max, 183, 184
    The Eye of Silence, 183, 184–185
Escher, M. C., 105
    Day and Night, 220
    Portrait of M. C. Escher, 105
    Waterfall, 105
Estes, Richard, *Paris Street Scene*, 381
Eth-Noh-Tec, 253, 421
Evans, Minnie, *Design Made at Airlie Gardens*, 410–411
Evening Rain on the Karasaki Pine (Hiroshige), 330
Events as sources of ideas, 12
Exaggeration and distortion, 268–273
Exhibit and display designers, 403
Expressionism, 374
Expressive qualities
    activity, 157
    of balance, 239–241
    of color, 135, 136, 152–157
    of color schemes, 144–149
    defined, 31
    Emotionalism and, 31–32
    exaggeration and distortion, 268–273
    of line, 77–83
    of shapes and forms, 117–121
    studio projects, 88–91, 162–165
    of value, 140–141, 155–156
Eye of Silence, The (Ernst), 183, 184–185

F

Faaturuma (Melancholic) (Gauguin), 372
Faces, 264–266, 272
Fallingwater House (Wright), 300–301
False Faces, 345
Family (Bearden), 166–167
Family Scene (Bonnard), 266
Family, The (Marisol), 268
Fantasy landscape studio project, 184–185
Farmer's Kitchen, The (Albright), 177
Fashion designers, 395
Faustwork Mask Theater, 23, 413
Feather Bonnet (Northwestern Plains people), 345
Featherstone, Joanna, 169, 418
Featherwork Ornaments (South America), 183
Federal Reserve Building (Cram, Ferguson, and Goodhue), 230
Femme au Chapeau (Woman with the Hat) (Matisse), 164
Ferguson, Federal Reserve Building (with Cram and Goodhue), 230
Fiber processes, 53. *See also* Weavings
Fiesta Rodeo (Mexican folk art), 306, 307
Figure, 103. *See also* Positive space
Film, 58, 397–400
Fine art, 52
Fine artists, 405
First Row Orchestra (Hopper), 235
Fish, Janet
    Oranges, 175, 176
    Raspberries and Goldfish, 16–17

Flack, Audrey, 193
  Leonardo's Lady, 192–193
  Self-Portrait: The Memory, 82
Flower Day (Rivera), 229
Flowering Swamp (Hofmann), 378
Flowing rhythm, 208–209
Focal point, 290–295
Footed Dish (Japan), 208
Foreground, 113
Forest, British Columbia (Carr), 298
Formal balance, 229, 239–241
Formalism, 31
Formal portrait studio project, 242–243
Forms
  active vs. static, 119–121
  activities, 102, 112
  creation in space, 111–116
  defined, 101
  density, 118
  depth perception, 108
  expression with, 117–121
  illusion of form, 111–112
  natural vs. manufactured, 111
  openness, 118–119
  overview, 101–102
  point of view and, 108–110
  relationship to shapes, 100, 101
  relationship to space, 103
  surfaces, 117–118
Four in Block Work Quilt (Peachey), 202
Four Trees, The (Monet), 153
Fragonard, Jean-Honoré, *A Game of Hot Cockles*, 236
Frankenthaler, Helen, 111
  The Bay, 111
Free-form forms, 102
Free-form shapes, 99–100
Freestanding works, 50, 106, 107
French Revolution, 366
Friesen, Eugene, 285, 422
Frottage, 183, 184–185
Futurists, 212

G

Gainsborough, Thomas, 363–364
  The Blue Boy, 364
Game designers, 400
Game of Chess, A, Involving The Painter's Three Sisters and a Servant (Anguissola), 358
Game of Hot Cockles, A (Fragonard), 236
Games, social skills and, 22
Gauguin, Paul, 371–372
  Faaturuma (Melancholic), 372
  Tahitians, 265–266
Gentileschi, Artemisia, 111
  Judith and Maidservant with the Head of Holofernes, 111
Geometric shapes
  activity, 100
  defined, 98
  expressiveness, 117–118
  overview, 98–99, 100
  portfolio ideas, 97
Geometry, artists' use of, 132
Gesture drawing, 82
Gestures, 82
Ginevra de' Benci (Leonardo da Vinci), 384–385
Giorgione, *The Adoration of the Shepherds*, 236, 237
Giotto, *Madonna and Child*, 263
Girl Attacked by a Strange Bird (Tamayo), 141
Girl with the Red Hat (Vermeer), 362

Glarner, Fritz, *Relational Painting #93*, 146, 147
Glass processes, 53
Goddess Hathor Places the Magic Collar on Sethos I, The (Egyptian), 323
Goings, Ralph, *Diner With Red Door*, 112
Golden Mean, 256–259
Golden Rectangle, 256
Golden Section. *See* Golden Mean
Goodhue, Federal Reserve Building (with Cram and Ferguson), 230
Gothic art, 355
Goya, Francisco, 364
  The Third of May, 364–365
Graham, Martha, 39, 414
Graphic design, 391–393
Graphic designers, 392
Graphics tablets, 61
Grattage, 183, 184–185
Graves, Nancy, *Zaga*, 51
Gray as neutral color, 139–140
Great Buddha at Kamakura (Japan), 329
Great Plains Region art, 344
Great Plaza of Tikal, 340
Great Stupa (Sanchi, India), 326
Great Wave at Kanagawa, The (Hokusai), 237–238
Greece, ancient, 352–353
Green House, The (Skoglund), 406–407
Green Table, The, 387, 425
Grief (Apel), 119
Griots, 333
Grossman, Rhoda, *Self-Portrait After Escher*, 59
Ground, 103. *See also* Negative space
Guanyin, 254, 255

H

Habitat (Safdie), 382
Haida people, 342–343
Haida totem pole, 343
Hall of the Bulls, The (cave painting), 320
Hampton, James, 186
  The Throne of the Third Heaven of the Nations Millennium General Assembly, 186
Haniwa Horse, 117
Hanson, Duane, 381
  Traveler with Sunburn, 381
Hanukkah Menorah (Abrasha), 71–72
Haori Coat (Bayless), 298
Haring, Keith, *Untitled*, 90
Harlem Renaissance, 386
Harmony, 295
  defined, 295
  studio project, 304–305
  unity enhanced by, 302–303
Harvey, Edward, *Mantis and Fly*, 408
Hassam, Childe, *Jelly Fish*, 157
Hatching technique, 44
Head #5 (Bishop), 44, 45
Heads, 264–266, 272
Hepworth, Barbara, *Pendour*, 101, 102
Hierarchical proportion, 260
High-intensity colors, 142
High-key paintings, 140
Highlights, 112–113
High relief
  African, 335
  defined, 106
  studio project, 124–125
  See also Relief sculpture
Highway (Tooker), 96, 97
Hinduism, 326–327
Hines, Jessica, *Dream Series*, 57, 58

Hiroshige, Andō, 330
  Evening Rain on the Karasaki Pine, 330
History connections, 194
History of art. *See* Art history
Hmong Story Cloth (Xiong), 211–212
Hodler, Ferdinand, 240
  James Vilbert, Sculptor, 240
Hofmann, Hans, *Flowering Swamp*, 378
Hokusai, Katsushika
  The Great Wave at Kanagawa, 237–238
  The Kirifuri Waterfall at Mt. Kurokami, Shimozuke Province, 226, 227
Holbein, Hans, *Anne of Cleves*, 9
Holograms, 107
Homer, Winslow, 46
  Hound and Hunter, 47
  Sketch for Hound and Hunter, 47
Hoover, John, *Loon Song*, 180
Hopper, Edward
  Early Sunday Morning, 77
  First Row Orchestra, 235
Horizontal lines, 72, 77. *See also* Line
Horse Fair, The (Bonheur), 201, 369
Hot Still Scape for Six Colors—7th Avenue Style, 1940 (Davis), 154, 155, 156
Hound and Hunter (Homer), 47
Houser, Allan, 299
  Coming of Age, 209
  Reverie, 298, 299
Houses at Auvers (van Gogh), 4, 5
Hue, 138–139
  defined, 138
  intermediate colors, 138
  primary hues, 138
  secondary hues, 138
  shades, 140–141
  tints, 140
  value and intensity and, 143
Human figure
  activities, 264, 266
  drawing human proportions, 262–266
  Golden Mean and, 256, 257, 259
  heads and faces, 264–266
Hunt, Henry, *K'umugwe' (Komokwa) Mask*, 276
Huntington, Anna Hyatt, *Riders to the Sea*, 120
Hurricane Hugo (Brown), 10–11
Hybrid creature studio project, 280–281
Hyper-Realism, 381

I

Ife, ancient, 332–333
Illusion
  of depth, 113–117
  of form, 111–112
  from positive and negative spaces, 103, 105
Imagery and story interpretation, 38
Imagination landscape studio project, 86–87
Imitationalism, 31
Implied lines, 71
Impressionism, 153, 181, 370, 373
Inca empire, 341
Indian art, 326–327
  ancient, 323–324
Individual style, 35
Indus River Valley, 323
Industrial design, 394–395
Industry and business careers, 390–400. *See also* Careers in art
Infant proportions, 263
Informal balance, 234–238, 241. *See also* Balance

Informal group portrait studio project, 244–245
Ink, history of, 94
Inness, George, *The Lackawanna Valley,* 11
Inspiration, sources of, 11–15
Intaglio, 49
Intensity, 142–143
  activity, 143
  complementary colors, 142–143, 150
  defined, 142
  hue and value and, 143
  mixing colors, 143, 152–154
  scale, 142
Interior designers, 403
Intermediate colors, 138
  complements, 142
International Style architecture, 381–382
Interpretation step
  of art criticism, 27, 28–29
  of art history, 34, 35
In the Dining Room **(Morisot),** 292
Inuit people, 342
Invent an inside view of a machine studio project, 248–249
Invented textures, 174, 183
Iridescence **(Anuszkiewicz),** 146, 154
Iris, Tulips, Jonquils, and Crocuses **(Thomas),** 26
Iron figure (Mali), 334
Islamic art, 331, 347
Isolation for focal point, 292
Italian Renaissance, 356–358

J

Jacquette, Yvonne, *Town of Skowhegan, Maine V,* 70
James Vilbert, Sculptor **(Hodler),** 240
Japanese art, 328–330
  influence on Western art, 351
Jeanne-Claude, *Wrapped Reichstag* **(with Christo),** 130–131
Jelly Fish **(Hassam),** 157
Jenne, 333–334
Jessup, Georgia Mills, *Rainy Night,* 301–302
Jewelry
  Asante people (Africa), 336
  as relief sculpture, 106
  texture in, 182–183
Jimenez, Luis, *Vaquero,* 50
Jitterbugs **(Johnson),** 88, 89
Johns, Jasper
  Cups 4 Picasso, 103–104
  Map, 296
Johnson, Philip, *Seagram Building* **(with Mies van der Rohe),** 382
Johnson, William H., *Jitterbugs,* 88, 89
Jones, Lois Mailou, *The Ascent of Ethiopia,* 386
Jooss, Kurt, 387, 425
Judgment step
  of art criticism, 27, 29–30
  of art history, 34, 35
Judith and Maidservant with the Head of Holofernes **(Gentileschi),** 111

K

Kahlo, Frida, *Self Portrait Dedicated to Leon Trotsky,* 239
Kampuchea, 327
Kaolin clay, 328
Kente cloth, 336, 337
Keyser, Louisa (Dat So La Lee), *Basket,* 218

Khamseh: Bahram Gur and the Chinese Princess in the Sandalwood Pavilion on Thursday **(Persian),** 346–347
Kinetic sculpture, 107, 213
Kingslien, Liz, *The Seasons,* 15, 392
Kirchner, Ernst Ludwig
  Seated Woman, 35
  Winter Landscape in Moonlight, 34
Kirifuri Waterfall at Mt. Kurokami, Shimozuke Province, The **(Hokusai),** 226, 227
Kiss, The **(Brancusi),** 104
Kollwitz, Käthe, *Self-Portrait,* 374
Kongo peoples, *Bowl,* 205
Koran, 331
Korean Classical Music and Dance Company, 349, 424
Korin, Ogata, *Waves at Matsushima,* 196–197
Krasner, Lee, *The Springs,* 291
K'umugwe' (Komokwa) Mask **(Hunt),** 276
Kurelek, William, *Manitoba Party,* 110
Kwakiutl art, 342–343

L

Lachaise, Gaston, *Walking Woman,* 271–272
Lackawanna Valley, The **(Inness),** 11
Landscape architects, 403
Landscape studio projects, 86–87, 122–123, 126–127, 184–185
Lange, Dorothea, *Migrant Mother,* 57
Language arts connections, 38, 252, 386
Language of art
  composition of artworks, 18–19
  content of artworks, 19
  credit line, 19
  elements of art, 16–17
  principles of art, 17–18
  subject of artworks, 18
  See also Elements of art; Principles of art
Large Blue Horses, The **(Marc),** 154
Larraz, Julio, *Papiamento,* 32
Las Meninas (after Velásquez) **(Picasso),** 14–15
Las Meninas (The Maids of Honor) **(Velásquez),** 14–15
Lawrence, Jacob, 80, 377
  Children at Play, 78, 80, 377
Leaf masks (Bwa people), 337–338
Leaning Tower of Pisa, 228
Le Chateau Noir **(Cézanne),** 371
Le Corbusier, *Unite d'Habitation,* 259
Lee, Doris, *Thanksgiving,* 116
Legends as sources of ideas, 12
L'Engle, Madeleine, 38
Length of lines, 73, 75. *See also* Line
Leonardo da Vinci, 42, 259, 356, 385
  Ginevra de' Benci, 384–385
  sketchbook page, 42
Leonardo's Lady **(Flack),** 192–193
Letter, The **(Cassatt),** 350, 351
Lewitzky Dance Company, 133, 417
Leyster, Judith, 178
  The Concert, 178, 256, 257
Lichtenstein, Roy, 379
  Blam, 379
Liebovitz, Annie, *Wilt Chamberlain and Willie Shoemaker,* 262
Lift Every Voice and Sing **(Savage),** 209
Lighting, stage, 314
Linda Nochlin and Daisy **(Neel),** 250–251
Line, 68–95
  activities, 73, 76, 78, 81, 82, 83
  basic kinds, 72–73, 75

  calligraphic drawing, 83
  contour lines, 81
  defined, 70
  expressive qualities, 77–83
  gesture drawing, 82
  implied lines, 71, 75
  meaning of, 70–71
  movement, 77–80
  outlines, 71
  perspective technique, 115, 116
  studio projects
    contour wire sculpture, 84–85
    drawing expressive movement, 88–89
    expressive line design, 90–91
    imagination landscape, 86–87
  value and, 75–76
  variations in appearance, 72–73, 75
Linear perspective
  defined, 115, 356
  in Italian Renaissance, 356
  studio project, 128–129
Linoleum print studio project, 246–247
Lintels, 321
Literal qualities, 31
Lithography, 49
Little Fourteen-Year-Old Dancer, The **(Degas),** 180, 181
Lobster Trap and Fish Tail **(Calder),** 213
Location
  in credit line, 19
  for focal point, 292
  placement (perspective technique), 114, 116
  See also Position
Loewy, Raymond, *Avanti,* 395
Logos, 392
Loneliness **(Neel),** 292
Looking Closely
  focal point, 293
  formal balance, 239
  Golden Mean, 258
  line types and variations, 75
  perspective techniques, 116
  visual movement using value, 156
  visual rhythm and movement, 203
  visual texture, 176
Loon Song **(Hoover),** 180
Low-intensity colors, 142, 143
Low-key paintings, 140–141
Low relief, 106, 107. *See also* Relief sculpture

M

Machine view studio project, 248–249
Machu-Picchu (Peru), 55, 341
McKelvey, Lucy Leuppe, *Whirling Rainbow Goddesses,* 212
McKie, Judy Kensley, *Monkey Settee,* 53
Madame Henriot **(Renoir),** 177
Madonna and Child **(Giotto),** 263
Madonna and Child on Curved Throne **(Byzantine),** 354
Magritte, René, *The Blank Signature,* 126
Maids of Honor, The (Las Meninas) **(Velásquez),** 14–15
Malangi, David, 93
  Abstract (River Mouth Map), 92–93
Mali empire, 333–334
Manet, Édouard, 368
  The Railway, 368–369
Manitoba Party **(Kurelek),** 110
Mannerism, 360
Man of the Republic **(Graeco-Roman),** 353
Mantis and Fly **(Harvey),** 408

Manufactured vs. natural shapes and forms, 111
Manuscript illuminators, 391
Map **(Johns),** 296
Map Still Life with Carnation, Keys, and Glasses **(Zalucha),** 173
Marc, Franz
  The Large Blue Horses, 154
  Stables, 66–67
Margot in Blue **(Cassatt),** 140
Marilyn Monroe's Lips **(Warhol),** 206, 207
Marisol, *The Family,* 268
Mask **(New Ireland),** 272, 273
Mask of Moon Goddess **(Inuit),** 342
Masks
  activity, 338
  Bella Coola, 318–319
  Bwa people, 337–338
  exaggeration and distortion in, 272–273
  False Faces, 345
  Inuit people, 342
  Kwakiutl people, 276
  papier mâché mask, 276–277
  Yup'ik people, 13
Math connections, 132, 284
Matisse, Henri, 374
  Femme au Chapeau (Woman with the Hat), 164
  Purple Robe and Anemones, 24, 25
Matte surfaces, 175
Mayan culture, 339–340
Media, 40–65
  architecture, 54–56
  computers, 59–61
  crafts, 52–53
  defined, 41
  drawing, 42–44
  film, 58
  multimedia art, 61
  painting, 44–47
  photography, 57–58
  printmaking, 48–49
  sculpture, 50–51
  technological, 57–61
  three-dimensional, 50–56
  two-dimensional, 42–49
  video, 59
Medium, in credit line, 19
Meeting, A **(Bashkirtseff),** 301
Meeting of the Theologians, The **(Musawwir),** 216
Meet the Artist
  Bearden, Romare, 167
  Bellows, George, 223
  Bishop, Isabel, 283
  Bonheur, Rosa, 201
  Chagall, Marc, 21
  Christo, 131
  Degas, Edgar, 181
  Escher, M. C., 105
  Flack, Audrey, 193
  Hiroshige, Andō, 330
  Homer, Winslow, 46
  Houser, Allan, 299
  Lawrence, Jacob, 80
  Leonardo da Vinci, 385
  Malangi, David, 93
  Michelangelo Buonarroti, 357
  Murray, Elizabeth, 151
  Neel, Alice, 251
  O'Keeffe, Georgia, 30
  Pei, I. M., 402
  Persian artists of Islam, 347
  Picasso, Pablo, 270
  Ringgold, Faith, 37
  Rivera, Diego, 229

  Rousseau, Henri, 313
  Schapiro, Miriam, 63
  Skoglund, Sandy, 407
  Wood, Grant, 12
Megaliths, 321
Mei, Gu, *Orchids and Rocks,* 83
Melancholic (Faaturuma) **(Gauguin),** 372
Mesopotamian civilization, 321–322
Message of artworks, 19
Metal processes, 53
Mexican muralists, 377
Mexican Revolution, 377
Mexican tinwork, 188
Michelangelo Buonarroti, 356, 357
  David, 267
  Pietà, 331, 356, 357
Microprocessors, 59
Middle Ages, 354–355
Middle Eastern art
  ancient Egyptian, 323
  Islamic art, 331
  Mesopotamian, 321–322
  Persian miniature paintings, 216
Mies van der Rohe, Ludwig, *Seagram Building* (with Johnson), 381–382
Migrant Mother **(Lange),** 57
Ming dynasty, 328
  vases, 99
Minimalism, 380
Missal illuminated manuscript, 391
Mitchell, Joan, 179
  Dirty Snow, 179
Mixed media studio project, 158–159
Mixing colors
  activity, 152
  changing intensity, 143, 153–154
  changing value, 140
Mobiles, 213, 376
Modeling, 51, 112
Modules, 204
Mohenjo-Daro, 323–324
Moi-Meme, Portrait-Paysage (I Myself, Portrait-Landscape) **(Rousseau),** 313
Monet, Claude
  The Four Trees, 153
  Palazzo da Mula, Venice, 370
  Poplars, 153
Monkey Settee **(McKie),** 53
Monochromatic colors, 144–145
  tonality versus, 157
Morisot, Berthe, *In the Dining Room,* 292
Mosques, 331
Motifs, 202, 204
Motion pictures (film), 58, 397–400
Mounted King with Attendants **(Edo people, Nigeria),** 335
Movement
  color and, 155–156
  of lines, 77–80
  rhythm creating, 211–213
  studio project, 88–89
  visual movement, 211–213
Movies (film), 58, 397–400
Mrs. Dalloway, 252
Mrs. Jones and Family **(Ringgold),** 278
Muhammad, 331
Multimedia art, 61
Multimedia designers, 400
Multimedia programs, 61
Munch, Edvard, *The Sick Child,* 7
Muñoz, Rie, *Both the Sun and Moon Belong to Women,* 252
Münter, Gabriele, *Breakfast of the Birds,* 18
Murals
  Mexican muralists, 377

  studio project, 308–309
Murphy, Gerald, 248
  Watch, 248
Murray, Elizabeth, 151
  Painters Progress, 40, 41
  Things to Come, 150–151
Musawwir, Abd Allah, *The Meeting of the Theologians,* 216
Museum curators and designers, 404
My Daughter's First Steps **(Pootoogook),** 269
Myron, *Discobolus (Discus Thrower),* 353
Myths as sources of ideas, 12

N

Nakht and Wife **(Egyptian),** 260
Namingha, Dan, *Blessing Rain Chant,* 75, 77
Naranjo, Michael, *Spirits Soaring,* 108, 109
Native American art, 341–345
Natural balance, 234–238. *See also* Balance
Natural vs. manufactured shapes and forms, 111
Nature as source of ideas, 11
Navajo people, 343–344
Necklace, 8, 9
Necklace **(Akan people, Ghana),** 336
Neel, Alice, 251
  Linda Nochlin and Daisy, 250–251
  Loneliness, 292
  Still Life, Rose of Sharon, 74
Negatives, 58
Negative space
  activity, 107
  artists' manipulation of, 103, 105
  defined, 103
  overview, 103–104
  in three-dimensional art, 106–107
Neoclassicism, 366-367
Neolithic period, 321
Neutral colors, 139–140
Nevelson, Louise, *Dawn,* 300
New Stone Age, 321
Night View, The **(Abbott),** 202
Night Watch, The **(Rembrandt),** 314, 362
Nineteenth century art, 366–373
  Impressionism, 153, 181, 370, 373
  Neoclassicism, 366–367
  Post-Impressionism, 371–373
  Realism, 368–370
  Romanticism, 367–368
Nonobjective art, 18
Northern Renaissance, 358–360
North Georgia Waterfall **(Smith),** 122
Northwest Coast Region art, 342–343
Nude Woman **(Picasso),** 375

O

Oba, 262, 335
Odyssey, The, 12
Oil-based paints, 46–47, 150
O'Keeffe, Georgia, 30
  Cow's Skull: Red, White, and Blue, 30
  Oriental Poppies, 2–3
  White Rose With Larkspur, No. 2, 240
Oldenburg, Claes
  Clothespin, 261
Old Guitarist, The **(Picasso),** 270
Old Stone Age, 320
Olmec culture, 339–340
One-point linear perspective, 128–129
On-screen tools, 61
Op art, 379–380
Openness, 118–119

Optical color, 152–154
Orange and Yellow (Rothko), 380
Orange Crush (Poons), 379–380
Oranges (Fish), 175, 176
Orchids and Rocks (Mei), 83
Oriental Poppies (O'Keeffe), 2–3
Oriental Ruler Seated on His Throne, An (Dürer), 76
Orozco, José Clemente, *Barricade,* 28
Orphism, 135
Outdoor scene studio project, 122–123
Outlines, 71, 117–118
Overlapping (perspective technique), 114, 116

P

Package designers, 395
Pagoda from the Temple Complex at Horyuji (Japan), 329
Paik, Nam June, *Technology,* 388, 389
Paint, 150–152
    basic ingredients, 44–45, 150–151
    oil-based, 46–47, 150
    pigment sources, 151–152, 168
    water-soluble, 47, 150
Painters Progress (Murray), 40, 41
Painting
    Chinese, 327–328
    Golden Mean in, 258
    Japanese, 330
    media, 44–47
    studio projects
        fantasy landscape, 184–185
        formal portrait, 242–243
        imagination landscape, 86–87
        informal group portrait, 244–245
        mural design, 308–309
        painting with a rhythmic activity, 214–215
    texture in, 177–180
Paint programs, 60
Palazzo da Mula, Venice (Monet), 370
Paleolithic period, 320
Paley, Albert Raymond, *Portal Gates,* 78
Paper studio projects, 188–189, 276–277, 304–305
Papiamento (Larraz), 32
Papier mâché mask, 276–277
Paris Street Scene (Estes), 381
Paris Through the Window (Chagall), 20–21
Parthenon (Greece), 352
Pastels studio project, 126–127
Pattern collage studio project, 216–217
Patterns, 204
Paul Revere (Copley), 268
Peachey, Annie M., *Four in Block Work Quilt,* 202
Pei, I. M., 402
    Rock-and-Roll Hall of Fame and Museum, 402
Pendour (Hepworth), 101, 102
People as sources of ideas, 12
Perceiving
    activity, 7
    color, 136–138, 144
    defined, 6
    optical color, 152–154
    texture, 172–174
Pereira, Irene Rice, *Untitled,* 289
Performing Arts Handbook. *See* Artsource® Performing Arts Handbook
Persian artists of Islam, 347
Persian miniature paintings, 216
Persistence of Memory, The (Dali), 375

Personal Appearance (Schapiro), 62–63
Personal functions of art, 7
Perspective, 113–116
    atmospheric, 114
    defined, 113
    in Italian Renaissance, 356
    linear, 115, 356
    studio project, 128–129
    techniques, 114–116
Pharaohs, 323
Photo collage studio project, 158–159
Photo enlargement studio project, 160–161
Photographers, 396
Photography, 57–58, 396–397
Photojournalists, 397
Photomosaics, 190
Photo-Realism, 381
Physical functions of art, 8
Picasso, Pablo, 270, 374
    Las Meninas (after Velásquez), 14–15
    Nude Woman, 375
    The Old Guitarist, 270
    Still Life, 316–317
    The Tragedy, 145
Picture plane, 113
Pietà (Michelangelo), 331, 356, 357
Pigments
    defined, 150
    natural versus synthetic, 152
    in paints, 44–45, 150, 151–152
    sources of, 151–152, 168
Pisa, Bell Tower of Cathedral at, 228
Placement (perspective technique), 114, 116. *See also* Location; Position
Plank masks (Bwa people), 338
Plaque: Oba or Chief (Nigeria), 262
Plaque studio project, 124–125
Point of view, 108–110
Pollock, Jackson, 13–14
    Cathedral, 13–14
Poons, Larry, *Orange Crush,* 379–380
Poor Man's Cotton (Woodruff), 202, 203
Pootoogook, Napachie, *My Daughter's First Steps,* 268–269
Pop art, 378–379
Poplars (Monet), 153
Porcelain, Chinese, 328
Porkypine Basket (Bondie), 52
Portal Gates (Paley), 78
Portfolio development. *See* Developing Your Portfolio
Portrait of a king (Ife, Nigeria), 332
Portrait of a Lady (van der Weyden), 359
Portrait of M. C. Escher (Escher), 105
Portrait of Rembrandt (Workshop of Rembrandt), 290
Portrait studio projects, 164–165, 242–245
Position
    informal balance using, 237–238
    proximity and unity, 301–302
    See also Location
Positive space, 103–104, 105
Post-and-lintel construction, 321
Post-Impressionism, 371–373
Post-Modernism, 382–383
Potlatch, 343
Pottery clay, 64
Preacher (White), 94
Pre-Columbian art, 339–341
Prehistoric art, 320
Prevalence of Ritual: The Baptism (Bearden), 158, 159
Primary hues, 138
    complements, 142

Principles of art, 287
    balance, 226–253
    composition and, 18–19
    defined, 18
    emphasis, 289–295, 302–303
    harmony, 295, 302–303
    movement, 211–213
    overview, 17–18
    proportion, 254–285
    rhythm, 199–225
    studio projects, 304–311
    unity, 296–302
    variety, 288–289, 302–303
    See also specific principles
Printing plates, 48, 49
Printmaking, 48–49
    basic steps, 48
    defined, 48
    editions, 48
    Japanese woodblock printing, 330
    prints vs. reproductions, 48
    studio project, 246–247
    techniques, 48–49
Prints, 48
Product designers, 394–395
Profile proportions, 265
Programs, computer, 60–61
Progressive rhythm, 210, 220–221
Proportion, 254–285
    artists' use of, 267–273
    defined, 255
    exaggeration and distortion, 268–273
    Golden Mean, 256–259
    human proportions, 262–266
    math connections, 284
    realistic, 267–268
    scale, 260–266
    studio projects
        hybrid creature, 280–281
        papier mâché mask, 276–277
        soft sculpture, 278–279
        storyteller figure, 274–275
Proximity, unity from, 301–302
Pueblo people, 343
Pueblo Scene: Corn Dancers and Church (Vigil Family, Tesuque Pueblo), 8
Purple Robe and Anemones (Matisse), 24, 25
Purposes of art, 7–9
Pythagoras, 256

Q

Qoyawayma, Al, *Blanketed Figure Vase,* 50, 51
quipu, 341

R

Radial balance
    activity, 233
    defined, 232
    expressive qualities, 240–241
    overview, 232–233
    studio project, 246–247
Railway, The (Manet), 368–369
Rainbows, 137
Rainy Night (Jessup), 301–302
Ramirez, John, 409, 426
Random rhythm, 205
Raspberries and Goldfish (Fish), 16–17
Rauschenberg, Robert, *Red Painting,* 290
Realism, 368–370
Red Painting (Rauschenberg), 290
Regionalists, 376–377
Regular rhythm, 206–207
Reims Cathedral, 106, 355

Relational Painting #93 (**Glarner**), 146, 147
Relief printing, 48–49
Relief sculpture
  high relief, 106
  jewelry as, 106
  low relief or bas relief, 106, 107
  overview, 50
  space in, 106
  studio project, 124–125
Religious beliefs as sources of ideas, 12–13
Rembrandt van Rijn, 178, 290, 362
  The Night Watch, 314, 362
  Portrait of Rembrandt, 290
Renaissance, 356
Renaissance art, 356–360
  activity, 365
  Italian Renaissance, 356–358
  Northern Renaissance, 358–360
Renoir, Pierre Auguste, 177–178
  Madame Henriot, 177
Repetition
  rhythm from, 202, 204
  unity from, 300–301
Reproductions, 48
Reston, Virginia, 401
Return of Ulysses (**Bearden**), 12, 13
Reverie (**Houser**), 298, 299
Reviewing artworks. *See* Aesthetics; Art criticism; Art Criticism in Action
Rhythm, 198–225
  activities, 204, 205, 208, 210
  alternating, 208
  defined, 200
  in design, 224
  flowing, 208–209
  modules, 204
  motifs, 202, 204
  movement created by, 211–213
  patterns, 204
  progressive, 210
  random, 205
  regular, 206–207
  repetition and, 200–204
  studio projects
    coil baskets, 218–219
  painting with a rhythmic activity, 214–215
  pattern collage, 216–217
  progressive rhythm, 220–221
    types of, 205–210
  visual rhythm, 200–202
Riders to the Sea (**Huntington**), 120
Ringgold, Faith, 37, 278
  Bitter Nest Part II: Harlem Renaissance Party, 36–37
  Mrs. Jones and Family, 278
Ritual Wine Container (**Chinese, Shang dynasty**), 325
Rivera, Diego, 229
  Flower Day, 229
  Self-Portrait, 229
Rock-and-Roll Hall of Fame and Museum (**Pei**), 402
Rococo art, 363–365
Romanesque architecture, 354-355
Romanticism, 367–368
Rome, ancient, 353
Romero, Annette, *Storyteller Doll,* 274
Rothko, Mark, 380
  Orange and Yellow, 380
Roualt, Georges, *Christ and the Apostles,* 74
Rough texture, 175
Rousseau, Henri, 313
  Carnival Evening, 312–313

Moi-Meme, Portrait-Paysage (I Myself, Portrait-Landscape), 313
Rubens, Peter Paul, *Daniel in the Lions' Den,* 291
Ruiz, Antonio M., *School Children on Parade,* 214

S

Sacred Circles (**Dick**), 246
Saddle blanket (**Navajo**), 344
Safdie, Moshe, *Habitat,* 382
Saint Martin and the Beggar (**El Greco**), 360
St. Michael's Counterguard (Malta Series) (**Stella**), 393
Savage, Augusta, *Lift Every Voice and Sing,* 209
Scale, 260–266
  activities, 261, 264, 266
  defined, 260
  hierarchical proportion, 260
  human proportions, 262–266
  math connections, 284
  photographs of art and, 260
Scanners, 61
Schapiro, Miriam, 63, 180
  Personal Appearance, 62–63
  Yard Sale, 180
Scholar, The (**Andrews**), 81
School Children on Parade (**Ruiz**), 214
School Web page design, 310–311
Science connections, 64, 168
Screen paintings, Japanese, 330
Screen printing, 49, 246
Scrolls, 328
Scully, Sean, *White Robe,* 295
Sculpture, 50–51
  African, 334–335
  ancient Greek and Roman, 352–353
  Chinese, 328
  defined, 50
  Indian, 326, 327
  Japanese, 328
  kinetic, 107, 213
  media, 50
  mobiles, 213, 376
  Post-Modern, 383
  pre-Columbian, 339–340
  relief sculpture, 50, 106–107
  sculpture in the round, 50
  studio projects
    assemblage, 186–187
    assemblage with handmade paper, 304–305
    clay plaque with high relief, 124–125
    clay sculpture unifying two ideas, 306–307
    contour wire sculpture, 84–85
    paper sculpture creature, 188–189
    soft sculpture, 278–279
    storyteller doll, 274–275
  techniques, 50–51
  texture in, 180, 182
Seagram Building (**Mies van der Rohe and Johnson**), 381–382
Seals (**ancient Indian**), 324
Seasons, The (**Kingslien**), 15, 392
Seated Man and Woman (**Dogon people, Mali**), 334
Seated Woman (**Kirchner**), 35
Secondary hues, 138
  complements, 142
Secret Society Mask (Four Headed Cannibal Spirit) (**Walkus**), 272, 273
Self-Portrait After Escher (**Grossman**), 59

Self-Portrait (**Bishop**), 283
Self-Portrait (**Degas**), 181
Self Portrait Dedicated to Leon Trotsky (**Kahlo**), 239
Self-Portrait (El Coronelazo) (**Siqueiros**), 264
Self-Portrait (**Kollwitz**), 374
Self-Portrait (**Rivera**), 229
Self-Portrait: The Memory (**Flack**), 82
Serigraphs, 246
Serigraphy (screen printing), 49, 246
Seventeenth century art, 360–362. *See also* Baroque art
Shades, 140–141
Shading, 44, 112
Shahn, Ben, *The Blind Botanist,* 117
Shang dynasty wine vessel, 325
Shapes
  active vs. static, 119–121
  activities, 100, 108, 120–121
  creation in space, 111–116
  defined, 98
  depth perception, 108
  expression with, 117–121
  free-form, 99–100
  geometric, 97, 98–99, 100, 117–118
  natural vs. manufactured, 111
  openness, 118–119
  outlines, 117–118
  overview, 98–100
  point of view and, 108–110
  relationship to forms, 100, 101–102
  relationship to space, 103
Sharecropper (**Catlett**), 48–49
Sheridan, Philip, 344
Shihuangdi, Qin, clay soldiers from tomb of, 64
Shiny surfaces, 175, 176
Shoemaker, Willie, 262
Shotguns, Fourth Ward (**Biggers**), 198, 199
Shoulder Bag (**Native American**), 208
Sick Child, The (**Munch**), 7
Silk, 194
Silvers, Robert, 190
  Vincent van Gogh, 190
Simplicity, unity from, 298–299
Simultaneous contrast, 144
Single *Family Blues* (**Twiggs**), 269
Sioux people, 344
Siqueiros, David Alfaro, *Self-Portrait (El Coronelazo),* 264
Siva, 327
Siva as Lord of the Dance (**Tamil Nadu**), 327
Size
  in credit line, 19
  informal balance using, 235
  perspective technique, 113–116
Sketchbooks, 15, 42
Sketch for Hound and Hunter (**Homer**), 47
Skoglund, Sandy, 407
  The Green House, 406–407
Slipper Chair (**Dunnigan**), 33
Smith, David, 101
  Cubi IX, 101
Smith, Jaune Quick-To-See, *Spotted Owl,* 162
Smith, Larry, 122, 123
  North Georgia Waterfall, 122
Smooth texture, 175
Snowstorm: Steamboat off a Harbours Mouth (**Turner**), 368
Snuff Containers (**Zulu, South Africa**), 297
Soapstone seals (**ancient Indian**), 324
Social functions of art, 7
Social studies connections, 22, 94, 348

Soft sculpture studio project, 278–279
Software, 60–61
Solstice **(Wilson),** 302–303
Solvents of paints, 45, 150–151
Sources of Country Music, The **(Benton),** 376
Sources of ideas, 11–15
Southwest Region art, 343–344
Space
   activities, 104, 107, 115
   color and, 15
   defined, 103
   depth perception, 108
   expression with, 117–121
   illusion of depth, 113–116
   overview, 103–107
   perspective techniques, 113–116
   positive and negative, 103–105
   relationship to shape and form, 103
   shapes and forms in, 111–116
   in three-dimensional art, 106–107
Special effects designers, 398–399
Spectrum of colors, 136–137
   color wheel and, 138
Spirit Boxes I **(Dvorak),** 304, 305
Spirits Soaring **(Naranjo),** 108, 109
Spiritual beliefs as sources of ideas, 12–13
Spiritual functions of art, 7–8
Spotted Owl **(Smith),** 162
Springs, The **(Krasner),** 291
Stables **(Marc),** 66–67
Stage lighting, 314
Stained-glass window (Wright), 235
Stalling Elephant With Two Riders **(India),** 174
Standing Youth with His Arm Raised, Seen from Behind **(Tintoretto),** 82
Starry Crown **(Biggers),** 98, 99
Starry Night, The **(van Gogh),** 372–373
Static lines, 77
Static shapes and forms, 120–121
Statua di Donna **(Sumerian),** 322
Steir, Pat, *The Bruegel Series (A Vanitas of Style),* 160–161
Stella, Frank
   Abgatana III, 380
   St. Michael's Counterguard (Malta Series), 393
Stella, Joseph, 69
   The Voice of the City of New York Interpreted: The Bridge, 68–69
Still-life collage studio project, 190–191
Still Life **(Picasso),** 316–317
Still Life, Rose of Sharon **(Neel),** 74
Stippling technique, 44
Stonehenge, 321, 348
Storyboards, 397
Storyteller Doll **(Romero),** 274
Storyteller figure studio project, 274–275
Straus, Meyer, 6
   Bayou Teche, 6–7
Street Light **(Balla),** 210
Studio Projects
   assemblage, 186–187
   assemblage with handmade paper, 304–305
   clay plaque with high relief, 124–125
   clay sculpture unifying two ideas, 306–307
   coil baskets, 218–219
   color for expressive statement, 162–163
   contour wire sculpture, 84–85
   drawing expressive movement, 88–89
   expressive line design, 90–91
   expressive portrait, 164–165
   fantasy landscape, 184–185
   formal portrait, 242–243
   hybrid creature, 280–281
   imagination landscape, 86–87

   informal group portrait, 244–245
   invent an inside view of a machine, 248–249
   landscape using surreal space, 126–127
   linoleum print using radial balance, 246–247
   mural design, 308–309
   one-point perspective drawing, 128–129
   outdoor scene, 122–123
   painting with a rhythmic activity, 214–215
   paper sculpture creature, 188–189
   papier mâché mask, 276–277
   pattern collage, 216–217
   photo collage and mixed media, 158–159
   photo enlargement, 160–161
   progressive rhythm, 220–221
   soft sculpture, 278–279
   still-life collage, 190–191
   storyteller figure, 274–275
   Web page design, 310–311
Stupas, 326
Style, individual, 35
Stylus and graphics tablet, 61
Subject of artworks, 18
Subordinate elements, 290
Sullivan, Louis
   Elevator Grille, 204
   Wainwright Building, 56
Sumerian civilization, 321–322
Sundiata, king, 333
Sunflowers **(van Gogh),** 178–179
Sung dynasty, 328
Sun Mask **(Bella Coola),** 318–319
Sun, Tower, Airplane **(Delaunay),** 134, 135
Super-Realism, 381
Surfaces, expressiveness of, 117–118
Surrealism, 184, 375
Surreal space studio project, 126–127
Sydney Opera House (Utzon), 286, 287
Symbolism, 252
Symbols, 16
Symmetry, 230–231, 240

T

Tahitians **(Gauguin),** 265–266
Taj Mahal **(India),** 331
Taliesin West **(Wright),** 182
Tamayo, Rufino,
   Girl Attacked by a Strange Bird, 141
   Toast to the Sun, 148
Teachers of art, 404
Tea, The **(Cassatt),** 244
Techniques
   printmaking, 48–49
   sculpting, 50–51
   shading, 44
   as sources of ideas, 13–14
Technological media, 57–61
   computers, 59–61
   film, 58
   multimedia art, 61
   photography, 57–58
   video, 59
Technology and careers in art, 390–393
Technology connections, 408
Technology **(Paik),** 388, 389
Technology Studio Projects
   expressive line design, 90–91
   expressive portrait, 164–165
   hybrid creature, 280–281
   inside view of machine, 248–249
   one-point perspective drawing, 128–129
   progressive rhythm, 220–221
   still-life collage, 190–191

Web page design, 310–311
Tempera, 47
Temple at Angkor Wat, 327
Temple Hanging (Central Tibet), 194
Tenochititlán, 340
Tepees, 344
Texture, 170–195
   activities, 174, 175, 183
   artists' use of, 177–183
   color and, 178–179
   defined, 171
   informal balance using, 236
   invented textures, 174, 183
   of lines, 73, 75
   matte or shiny, 175
   perception of, 172–174
   rough or smooth, 175
   studio projects
      assemblage, 186–187
      fantasy landscape, 184–185
      paper sculpture creature, 188–189
      still-life collage, 190–191
   value and, 175–176
   visual texture, 173–174, 176
Thanksgiving **(Lee),** 116
Theatre connections, 314
Things to Come **(Murray),** 150
Third of May, The **(Goya),** 364–365
Thomas, Alma, *Iris, Tulips, Jonquils, and Crocuses,* 26
Three-dimensional art
   computer art, 408
   space in, 106–107
Three-dimensional media, 50–56
   architecture, 54–56
   crafts, 52–53
   sculpture, 50–51
Throne **(Bamileke),** 170, 171
Throne of the Third Heaven of the Nations Millennium General Assembly, The **(Hampton),** 186
Tibetan Temple Hanging, 194
Tikal, 340
Tintoretto, Jacopo, *Standing Youth with His Arm Raised, Seen from Behind,* 82
Tints, 140–141
Tinwork, Mexican, 188
Toast to the Sun **(Tamayo),** 148
Tonality, 157
Tooker, George, 96
   Highway, 96, 97
Torivio, Dorothy, 233
   Vase, 233
Torso of a Young Man **(Brancusi),** 118
Totem poles, 343
Town of Skowhegan, Maine V **(Jacquette),** 70
Tragedy, The **(Picasso),** 145
Traveler with Sunburn **(Hanson),** 381
Triads of colors, 146–147
Turner, Joseph M. W., 368
   Snowstorm: Steamboat off a Harbours Mouth, 368
Tutankhamen, throne of, 107
Twentieth century art
   Abstract Expressionism, 378
   after 1945, 378–383
   architecture, 377, 381–383
   Color-Field painting, 380
   Cubism, 374–375
   early twentieth century, 374–377
   in Europe, 374–375
   Expressionism, 374
   International Style architecture, 381–382
   Minimalism, 380

in North America, 376–377
Op art, 379–380
Pop art, 378–379
Post-Modernism, 382–383
Regionalism, 376–377
Super-Realism, 381
Surrealism, 184, 375
Twiggs, Leo, 10
Blue Wall, 28, 29
East Wind Suite: Door, 10, 42
Single Family Blues, 269
Two-dimensional media, 42–49
drawing, 43–44
painting, 44–47
printmaking, 48–49

U

Ukiyo-e, 330
Unite d'Habitation **(Le Corbusier),** 259
Unity, 296–302
activity, 302
creating, 296–302
defined, 296
enhancing, 302–303
studio projects
clay sculpture, 306–307
mural design, 308–309
Untitled **(Haring),** 90
Untitled **(Pereira),** 289
Unusual objects for focal point, 295
Urban planners, 401
Urn, Mexican (Monte Alban; Zapotec),
230
Utzon, Joern, *Sydney Opera House,* 286,
287

V

Value, 139–142
activity, 142
defined, 75, 139
expressive qualities, 140–141, 155–156
focal point using, 290
hue and intensity and, 142–143
informal balance using, 236, 237
line and, 75–76
movement and, 155–156
neutral colors, 139–140
scales, 140
texture and, 175–176
Van Alen, William, *Chrysler Building,* 206
Van der Weyden, Rogier, 359
Portrait of a Lady, 359
Van Eyck, Jan, 358
The Arnolfi Wedding, 231, 359
Van Gogh, Vincent, 372-373
Café Terrace at Night, 293
Houses at Auvers, 4, 5
The Starry Night, 373
Sunflowers, 178–179
Vanishing point, 115
Vaquero **(Jimenez),** 50
Varese **(Calder),** 84
Variety, 288–289, 302–303
Vases (Chinese, Ming dynasty), 99
Vase **(Torivio),** 233
Velázquez, Diego, *Las Meninas (The Maids
of Honor),* 14–15
Vendeur de Chapeaux **(Berman),** 43
Vermeer, Jan, 362
The Astronomer, 128
Girl with the Red Hat, 362
Vertical lines, 72. *See also* Line

Video
game designers, 400
media, 59
Vigil Family, Tesuque Pueblo, *Pueblo
Scene: Corn Dancers and Church,* 8
Vincent van Gogh **(Silvers),** 190
Vishnu, 326, 327
Visual balance, 228–233. *See also* Balance
Visual movement, 211–213
Visual rhythm, 200–202
Visual texture, 173–174, 176
Vitruvius, 259
Vocalworks, 315, 423
"Vocalworks Radio Hour", 315, 423
*Voice of the City of New York Interpreted,
The: The Bridge* **(Stella),** 68–69

W

Wainwright Building (Sullivan), 56
Waiting **(Bishop),** 282–283
Walking Woman **(Lachaise),** 271–272
Walkus, George, *Secret Society Mask (Four
Headed Cannibal Spirit),* 272, 273
Wall of Machu-Picchu **(Borsky),** 55
Wall paintings, 260
Warhol, Andy, 206
Marilyn Monroe's Lips, 206, 207
Warm colors, 148, 155
Warrior Chief, Warriors, and Attendants
(Nigeria), 124
Watch **(Murphy),** 248
Water and Moon Guanyin Bodhisattva, The
(Chinese), 254, 255
Watercolor, 46
Waterfall **(Borsky),** 209
Waterfall **(Escher),** 105
Water jar (Santo Domingo Pueblo), 343
Water-soluble paints, 47, 150
Watteau, Antoine, 363
Embarkment for Cythera, 363
Waves at Matsushima **(Korin),** 196–197
Weavings
Asante people (Africa), 336
Navajo, 343–344
space in, 106–107
texture in, 182
Web artists, 393
Web page design studio project, 310–311
Western traditions in art, 350–387
Abstract Expressionism, 378
after 1945, 378–383
ancient Greece and Rome, 352–353
Baroque art, 360–362
Byzantine art, 354
Color-Field painting, 380
Cubism, 374–375
early twentieth century art, 374–377
eighteenth century art, 363–365
Expressionism, 374
Futurists, 212
Gothic art, 355
Impressionism, 153, 181, 370, 373
International Style architecture, 381–382
Mannerism, 360
Middle Ages art, 354–355
Minimalism, 380
Neoclassicism, 366–367
nineteenth century art, 366–373
Op art, 379–380
Orphism, 135
Pop art, 378–379
Post-Impressionism, 371–373
Post-Modernism, 382–383

Realism, 368–370
Regionalism, 376–377
Renaissance art, 356–360
Rococo art, 363–365
Romanesque art, 354-355
Romanticism, 367–368
seventeenth century art, 360–362
Super-Realism, 381
Surrealism, 184, 375
Whirling Rainbow Goddesses **(McKelvey),** *212*
White as neutral color, 139
White, Charles, *Preacher,* 94
White Robe **(Scully),** *295*
White Rose With Larkspur **(O'Keeffe),** *240*
Width of lines, 73, 75. *See also* **Line**
Wilson, Jane
Solstice, 302–303
Winter Wheat, 120, 121
Wilt Chamberlain and Willie Shoemaker
(Liebovitz), *262*
Wine vessel **(Shang dynasty),** 324
Winter Landscape in Mooonlight
(Kirchner), *34*
Winter, Paul, 195, 419
Winter Wheat **(Wilson),** *120, 121*
Winxiang, Prince Yi **(Chinese, Qing
Dynasty),** *242*
Woman with the Hat (Femme au Chapeau)
(Matisse), *164*
Woodblock printing, Japanese, 330
Wood, Grant, 12
American Gothic, 12
Woodlands Region art, 345
Wood processes, 53
Woodruff, Hale, *Poor Man's Cotton,* 202,
203
Woolf, Virginia, 252
Works of art, basic properties, 18–19
Wrapped Reichstag **(Christo and Jeanne-
Claude),** *130–131*
Wrapper **(Ghana),** 206, 207
Wright, Frank Lloyd, 182
Armchair, 118–119
The David Wright House, 377
Fallingwater House, 300–301
stained-glass window, 235
Taliesin West, 182
Wrinkle in Time, A **(cover illustration)
(Dillon),** *38*

X

Xiong, Chaing, *Hmong Story Cloth,* 211–212

Y

Yamato-e, 330
Yancy, John, *Celebration of Arts: Vibrations
of Life,* 308
Yard Sale **(Schapiro),** *180*
Year, in credit line, 19
Yellow River valley, 324
Yen, Hua, *Conversation in Autumn,* 328
Yoruba people, 332–333
Yup'ik people, *Bird Mask,* 13

Z

Zaga **(Graves),** **51**
Zalucha, Peggy Flora
*Map Still Life with Carnation, Keys, and
Glasses,* 173
Ziggurats, 322
Zigzag lines, 73, 78. *See also* **Line**

CREDITS